Preface

" ... To serve as a center for the cultural enrichment and education of the community and the general public and to disseminate knowledge, understanding and appreciation of such materials, data and information relating to the culture and history of Kent County, the State of Maryland."

The Historical Society of Kent County, Inc.
Articles of Amendment, May 12, 1969

ALTHOUGH KENT IS THE SMALLEST COUNTY IN MARYLAND BOTH IN AREA AND POPULATION, IT IS ONE OF THE richest in colonial history and surviving early architecture. Much of the fascination with Kent County lies in its unbelievably beautiful scenery and in its historic small towns and pleasing rural structures.

The vernacular architecture of early Kent County reflected the form and style England had to offer at the time. In order for the colonist to build his dream house, he had to rely heavily on his memory and had to work with tools and materials that were available locally. He was more than likely the architect, contractor, builder, and the financier. Kent County is very fortunate that many of these buildings, regardless of age, have survived and provide important records of the county's development since 1642.

Unknowingly, these builders left many elegantly embellished houses throughout the county. One of the finest collections of early stately buildings in the entire country remains today in what was the colonial Port of Chester.

One by one these historic structures are slowly disappearing. Many have gone by the wayside leaving little or no evidence of having ever been built. It is a heritage that is vanishing very rapidly and that a permanent record of these architectural treasures is essential to preserve this heritage not only for our generation, but for generations to come.

To achieve this goal, the Society appointed a Publication Chairman in 1991 with a mandate to publish an architectural history of Kent County. A committee was selected for this ambitious undertaking. A task of such complexity required detailed planning and extensive research. The publication had to be financially sound before any format could be decided. The stunning success of a designer showcase at River House in May and June of 1992 provided the necessary funds to start the project. With the full support of the officers, directors, and the membership of the Society, the Committee was able to secure grants from the Maryland Historical Trust. The seed money from the River House Designer Showcase and the grant assistance from the Maryland Historical Trust made this publication possible. They deserve particular recognition.

The citizens of Kent County have been most generous with their time and in sharing their knowledge of local history. The property owners have opened their doors and have been extremely cooperative and gracious by allowing their homes to be invaded, photographed, and listed in this very important history.

Yes, the past is very much alive in Kent County!

Eugene ̄
T ̄

Geddes-Piper House, Headquarters for
The Historical Society of Kent County.
Michael C. Wootton photograph, 1996

Introduction

OCUMENTS AND ARTIFACTS, FURNITURE AND OTHER everyday objects have their place in our understanding of the past, but none of these provides a more tangible facet of history than the buildings which remain from years gone by. Often historic buildings influence our lives in ways we are not aware. For some the experience of living in an old house has resulted in a deep appreciation for the materials and spaces which were created years ago. For others, the experience of living in "other people's houses" has been one which the occupants simply endured until they could remodel or build anew. Unfortunately, over the years, many of the buildings of Kent County have been owned by people of the latter category; consequently, history has been lost. This, combined with a veritable dearth of published history on Kent County has created a challenge for all who wish to understand the past. Often only vignettes have survived and frequently they have been embellished by storytellers to such a degree that it is now difficult to determine fact from fiction. While it would be impossible to write about the history of Kent County without resurrecting some of these stories, it is the intention of the author to present pertinent information which has been determined through physical examination or can be verified by historical records.

The project was originally conceived as a study of forty buildings representing typical and atypical residential plans and forms from the seventeenth century to the Civil War. As the original objective was later broadened to include as many of the buildings of the period as possible, the depth and breadth of the necessary research grew and the time originally allotted to the project lengthened. Research generally was begun with the examination of a given building followed by a search of the property's chain of title. The latter was undertaken in order to ascertain both the name of the builder as well as the historic name of the land on which the building had been constructed. In many instances the historic rather than common name has been used in the text.

This study has revealed that Kent County has only a few buildings that can be classified as stylistically up-to-date; such as Widehall and Brampton. The remainder mostly fall into the category of vernacular architecture, i.e. buildings whose construction was not driven by style alone, but are instead products of the period and region, the inhabitants' needs, the builders of the area and availability of materials. While Kent's vernacular buildings often differ from those of neighboring Cecil, Queen Anne's and New Castle Counties, similarities can also be found. For example, the dated gable buildings found in the lower part of the county and pent eaves found in houses along the Sassafras River are both features which appear in nearby Cecil and New Castle counties, while they are rarely found in Queen Anne's County

Godlington Manor, including the house and dairy, is one of four frame buildings standing on the 1000 acre tract in 1783. It is the only one to remain standing and it is located on part of the Manor that has remained in the same family from 1686 to the present. Historic American Buildings Survey, 1972.

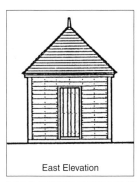

East Elevation

South Elevation

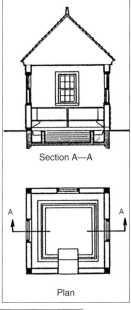

Section A—A

Plan

Before: The dairy at Godlington Manor before restoration. Late eighteenth century. Historic American Buildings Survey, 1972.

After: Godlington Manor dairy after restoration. Late eighteenth century, Gene Johnstone photograph, 1995.

Godlington Manor. Drawings made for the restoration of the dairy (milk house) for the Historic American Buildings Survey. Measured by M. Bourne and R. Bunney; drawn by Peter Newlin and Chinh Hoang, 1976.

Plans and forms of houses differ slightly during the period of study. Both the original plan of Carvill Hall, with its inner room, outer room, back-to-back fireplaces and porch tower, and the hall-parlor plan were direct imports from England. The former is not known to occur again in Kent, but the hall-parlor plan continued throughout the period, becoming the plan of the less well-off by the mid-nineteenth century. For a short period of time, a compact four room plan was used in the 1770s, only to be replaced in the next decade by the side passage, double parlor plan. The plan which appears to have gained the most popularity is the central stair passage with two flanking rooms. It remained the plan of choice in Kent County farmhouses well into the twentieth century.

The study does not go deeply into materials, but for the most part, building in Kent County was confined to brick and wood construction, with some stone used for basement or foundation walls. In most cases floors and interior woodwork were of long leaf yellow pine, although poplar, oak and white pine were sometimes encountered. Walnut, oak, and poplar were used in addition to yellow pine for window and door frames, with varying degrees of success, poplar being less resistant to the elements than the others. The use of nails, hinges and other hardware follow the pattern seen elsewhere in the Chesapeake area.

Descriptions of the buildings in this volume frequently include the way in which the building was first constructed as well as the way in which they appear today. Historic Site Surveys have provided the impetus for much of the work. This book fills a gap in the series of Eastern Shore architectural publications that was initially conceived by the Maryland Historical Trust. Arranged chronologically, it begins with a brief introduction into the area between the Sassafras and Chester rivers prior to the arrival of English settlers written by Dennis Curry. Chapter II through V discuss the beginnings of the county and its surviving structures. The final chapter, by Davy McCall, discusses the buildings either owned or occupied by free blacks before the Civil War.

The book is not intended to be a history of the county, but a record of its architectural resources. Some inaccuracies have most likely occurred and the author would be most appreciative if they were brought to his attention in the event there is a future edition. It is hoped that this book will be a stepping stone for future studies into the political and socioeconomic history of the county. It is also hoped that this work will become an educational tool that will create a greater understanding and appreciation of Kent County's architectural heritage and to help encourage a desire to preserve it for generations to come.

Michael Owen Bourne
Highfield May 1998

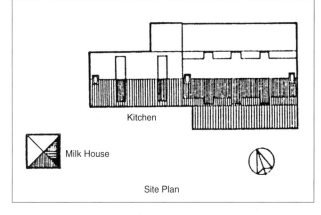

Kitchen

Milk House

Site Plan

Acknowledgements

UNDER THE NATIONAL HISTORIC PRESERVATION ACT of 1966, each state was directed to prepare a statewide survey and inventory of its historic sites. The Maryland Historical Trust which had been created in 1961 took over the task of conducting and preparing the *Historic Sites Inventory* for the State of Maryland. The site survey consists of architectural and historical data, and photographs made on the premises of each building and location. The early surveys of Kent County's inventory were undertaken by Bob Neill, Kathleen White, Marsha Fritz, Marge Fallaw and Chuck Engstrom from 1979 to 1984. The surveys were planned and financed by the Maryland Historical Trust along with the Kent County Planning Commission, the Historical Society of Kent County, and the Town of Chestertown.

In 1991, the Historical Society of Kent County realized that this wealth of information needed to be brought to the attention of the public in a more permanent form, thus the Publication Committee was appointed and given the task of raising funds, to research, write, compile, and print this book. The River House Designer Showcase in 1992 (see Appendix C, page 530) provided the necessary funds to start the project. Darlene Moulds Housley became the Chairman of this ambitious undertaking and it is due to her hard work in raising funds, her legal background and her organizational skills that made this book financially sound. Thank you, Darlene.

Since the surveys were to provide the basis for this publication, it was determined that some thirty-three structures of the period covered in this book (1642-1860) had never been surveyed. In 1994 the Publication Committee applied for and received a grant from the Maryland Historical Trust to complete the survey of these sites as well as several African-American sites that had never been recorded. Michael Bourne and Davy McCall researched and compiled the site surveys. At the same time a study of the housing in the Black Community was undertaken and written by Davy McCall.

Contributions by the Kent County Commissioners, the Town of Chestertown, and the Kent County Arts Council were gladly received and appreciated.

THE PUBLICATION COMMITTEE

Chairman:
Eugene Hall Johnstone

Members:
Michael Owen Bourne,
Karen E. Ashley,
Darlene Moulds Housley,
Donald George Rypka,
Marian Metcalfe Fry,
Robert Titus Hollett,
Philip Wilmer Hoon,
David Wade Singer
Jane G. Eliason.

Chestertown, a river view.
Skip Willits photograph, 1993

From the Author

A book covering three-hundred buildings involves so many people that it is difficult to know where to begin to acknowledge their contributions. Without the guidance of the Committee and the encouragement and advice from those who had undertaken similar publications, this would not have been possible. My thanks to Rick Rivoire, Paul Touart, Lyl Wray, Orlando Ridout, Gail Yerges, Jayne Foard, Marcia Miller, Michael Day, Becky Hutchinson, Cary Carson and Elizabeth Hughes.

For providing the records to research, thanks first to Mark Mumford and Janet Ashley who shepherd the land and probate records of Kent County, and to those in charge of special collections at the Maryland State Archives, the Maryland Historical Society, the Pennsylvania Historical Society and the Winterthur Library. Thanks to the following people who shared their own research with me: Carolyn Cooper, Mildred and Robert Strong, John Wilson and Rick Kanaski, Joanne and Dick Revie, Jim Berna, M. P. White, Gregory Straub, Alen Hollomon, Dean Burt, Patsy Hornaday, Ellie and Tom Noble, Kathryn Pinder, Alex and Paula Gish, Jeff and Alyse Colen, Mary and Calvin Welch, the late Miss Harriett Welch, Honey and the late Cordrey Wood, Stanley Quick, Davy McCall and Francis Lamb.

Special thanks are extended to Mame Warren, formerly of the Hall of Records, to Averil Kadis, Laura Rice and Jeff Goldman, Elizabeth Alley, H. Hurtt Deringer, Trish McGee, M. L. deSarran, Barbara Shepherd, and Margaret Wright Ingersoll.

My thanks to Edna Ross and Ann Bourne for typing the first draft, to Kelly Rae for typing the final draft and to Colleen Blenkstone, Martie Chidsey and Bob Hollett for proofreading the text.

Dennis Curry deserves special recognition for contributing the text for Chapter I, about the area between the Chester and Sassafras Rivers before the arrival of the white man. And thanks to Davy McCall for contributing the text for Chapter VI, on housing for the black population of Kent County before the Civil War.

Gene Johnstone has taken piles of typed pages, photos and drawings, edited them, organized the immense task of photographing anew, and with the help of Karen Ashley, has edited and compiled the chaos into a work of art. Very special thanks!

Last and never least, my thanks to Mark and Sarah who suffered the loss of their father over six years and nevertheless made contributions to this publication. And to Ann, my unsung heroine, who was my constant confidant and encouragement and who made sense of my original long hand, my thanks and love.

—*Michael Owen Bourne*

From the Editor

It is a big undertaking to publish any book, but to lift it out of the ordinary so it will excite the mind and delight the eye, one must excel. The research for the text must be thorough and the writing creative. The content must be well organized, planned, and have an editorial objective. The appearance must be attractive with layout and design that show skill and imagination. I believe we have accomplished all this criteria in *Historic Houses of Kent County*.

The author, Michael Bourne, has long been an advocate of historic preservation and his interest in restoration is well known. His love of Kent County is always present. Working with him over the past six years, through what at times seemed like an endless tunnel, has been a most rewarding experience for me.

I would like to express my appreciation to H. Russell Morrison, Jr. and Owen Henderson for allowing the use of their priceless edition of *A Relation of Maryland*. My sincere thanks go to Audrey Johnson and Charles W. Carter for letting us photograph their rare collections of Indian artifacts.

Throughout this book every effort has been made to give each contributor credit for his work where presented. To the homeowners, thank you for opening your doors and allowing us to photograph your historic houses. Over one-thousand such entries enhance this volume. Your generosity is appreciated.

My very special thanks go to Constance Stuart Larrabee, Jane Sprinkle, Robert Ramsey, Bill Seitzer, Robert J. H. Janson-La Palme, Tyler Campbell, Michael Wootton, Bob Hollett, Dan Hunt, and Martie Chidsey. Thanks to Edna Ross for all her patience. She has seen these pages many times.

And to you extra special folks (and you know who you are), Darlene Housley, Business Manager; Donald Rypka, Treasurer; Marian Fry, Index Editor; Kelly Rae, Production Assistant, this is your book—remember! And I must add that if it were not for the talent and design skills of Karen Ashley this would be just another book.

I am very grateful to all my friends who contributed toward this publication and played a part in putting it in final form.

My dear wife Peggy, my seven children and my sixteen grandchildren, I promise to clean up my mess and get back into the family.

—*Eugene Hall Johnstone*

"*The sommer is hot as in Spaine; the winter cold as in France and England ... The windes here are variable, but the like thunder and lightning to purifie the ayre I have seldome seene or heard in Europe ... Sometimes there are great droughts, other times much raine, yet great necessitie of neither, by reason we see not but that all the raritie of needful fruits in Europe, may be there in great plentie ... within is a country that may have the prerogative over the most places knowne, for large and pleasant navigable rivers, heaven and earth never agreed better to frame a place for man's habitation; ... Here are mountaines, hils, plaines, valleyes, rivers, and brookes, all running more pleasantly into a fiare bay, compassed but for the mouth, with fruitful and delightsome land.*"

—*Captain John Smith,*
July, 1608

*A description of the Chesapeake Bay
as seen by Captain John Smith on the second trip
of the Bay and recorded in his *General History*.

To:
The builders of these Historic Houses
And to:
Those who have restored and maintained them
And to:
Ann Bourne, Peggy Johnstone and Allan D. Housley
for their patience and support.

Tyler Campbell, photograph, 1992

Chapter 1
Prehistoric Kent County

Dennis C. Curry

By the end of the seventeenth century, the 11,000 year-long occupation of Kent County by Native Americans had ended, and only their accumulated debris remained.

THE FIRST IMMIGRANTS TO WHAT IS NOW KENT County, Maryland arrived some 11,000 years ago. These people, or perhaps more accurately their immediate ancestors, had entered the North American continent from Siberia generations earlier during an era in which glacially induced lower sea levels created a land bridge in the Bering Straits, thereby connecting the two continents. From their initial entrance into North America, these first immigrants (termed Paleoindians by archeologists) eventually spread south to the tip of South America and east to the Atlantic shores. While little direct evidence of these people is known from Kent County, their presence is certain based on finds from elsewhere in the state. It is from this nearby evidence that our picture of Paleoindians in Kent County emerges.

Kent County 11,000 years past differed markedly from that of Kent County today. At the end of the glacial period, which saw the nearest glacial ice sheets in what is now Pennsylvania, the lower sea levels which created the Bering land bridge also changed the look of Kent County. With lower sea levels, the Chesapeake Bay had not yet formed. Instead, Kent County was bounded by the ancestral Susquehanna River on the west and the Sassafras and Chester rivers to the north and south respectively. All of these rivers were more deeply entrenched versions of their modern-day embayed forms. This difference affected both the resources contained within the rivers (for instance, shellfish had yet to establish themselves in the area) and the settlement patterns of the Paleoindians. In fact, the latter may be one explanation for the current absence of evidence of Paleoindian occupation in Kent County. Since the glacial rivers bordering Kent County were more deeply entrenched than today's broad embayments, more land area (that is, the ancient riverbank areas) was exposed in the past. These shoreline areas were undoubtedly prime settlement areas, just as they are today. However, subsequent inundation and embayment after millennia of sea level rise during the post-glacial period has flooded whatever evidence of Paleoindian occupation that may have been in these areas. As a result, locating this evidence today is largely a fortuitous occurrence (the waterman tonging for oysters is more likely to uncover this evidence than archeologists). The evidence may still be there, it is just hidden from view.

At the end of the glacial period, just prior to the Paleoindian arrival, Kent County was largely covered with grasslands mixed with spruce and pine forests containing minor deciduous elements. The fauna included mammoth, mastodon, musk ox, moose, elk, caribou, peccaries, and giant beaver. At about the time people first arrived in Kent County, most of these species were on their way to extinction, already extinct, or had migrated northward out of the region. In fact, what the Paleoindians first witnessed were the initial stages of the transformation from a glacial to a modern environment (geologically, the transition from Pleistocene to Holocene). Pine began to replace spruce, and closed boreal forests replaced grasslands. This loss of grasslands and their associated edge environments led to the extinction of browsing and grazing megafauna and saw a rise in species such as deer, elk, and moose.

Paleoindians subsisted within these environments using a hunting and gathering technology which relied largely on hunting. The cultural remains left by Paleoindians, including the diagnostic artifacts known as fluted points, reflect this hunting emphasis. Fluted points are lanceolate spear tips chipped from often high quality, and sometimes exotic, cherts and jaspers. The spears were thrusting spears which required close proximity to prey

Fluted spearpoints from the Paleoindian period (10,000 to 8,000 B. C.). Rock Hall vicinity. Charles W. Carter Collection; Michael Wootton photograph.

Facing Page: Cornfields, Broad Neck. Constance Stuart Larrabee photograph.

POWHATAN

Held this state & fashion when Capt. Smith was deliuered to him prisoner 1607

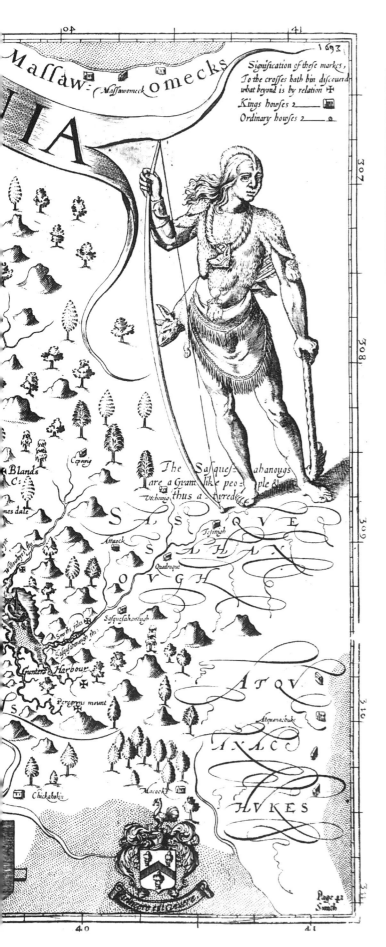

during the kill. Other stone implements including choppers, scrapers, and drills were part of the Paleoindian tool kit used for butchering and modification of animal carcasses and hides. This activity provided both food and raw materials for clothing and shelter. In addition, smaller game was likely trapped, fish were exploited (according to evidence from the Shawnee Minisink[1] site along the Delaware River in Pennsylvania), and other supplementary foods, including roots, nuts, and berries, were gathered.

Paleoindian society seems to have been based on territorial semi-nomadic bands. Within a territory, each band exploited a variety of resources necessary for subsistence. This involved movement across the landscape in response to various factors, including animal herd movement, seasonal availability of resources, and the need for stone tool kit replenishment. This latter aspect has been shown in Virginia's Shenandoah Valley to constitute a major focal point of the Paleoindian settlement pattern.[2] There, a series of satellite sites (including hunting/kill sites, butchering sites, quarries, and other limited activity areas) surrounded a larger base camp. The base camp was located near a ready source of high quality stone, and also served as a congregating point where various parts of the band would coalesce (especially

Left: Virginia, a map drawn by Captain John Smith in 1608. The main focus of this map is the Chesapeake Bay. It was the first printed map of the Bay area and is remarkably correct in its topography. It provides almost the only record of the location of the Indian tribes of the area in the early seventeenth century. Its depiction of the coastline, waterways and landmarks is superb in view of the tools and time available to Smith for surveying.

Detail Above: Much enlarged section of the John Smith map showing the villages of the Tockwogh and Ozinies Indian Tribes. This is the general area of present day Kent County. Courtesy of the Maryland State Archives; Huntingfield Maps of Maryland Collection.

Ground stone tools, including three-quarter and full-grooved axes, celt, sinew stone, plummets (possibly used as netsinkers), stone ball, possible amulet or bar gorget, and stone pipe. Rock Hall vicinity.

Ground stone axes. Rock Hall vicinity.

Ground stone tools including axes, spuds, celts, and a gouge. Rock Hall vicinity. Charles W. Carter Collection; Michael Wootton photographs.

when seasonally available resources, such as nuts, could be best exploited through the efforts of a larger group). Within the base camps, the different groups within the band, most likely defined by kinship, probably also arranged their structures according to family units. Evidence for Paleoindian structures is scant, although a wooden sapling framework presumably covered with bark or animal hides is inferred from the Thunderbird site in Virginia's Shenandoah Valley. At the Adkins site[3] in Maine, archeologists found evidence of a Paleoindian stone slab-supported lean-to, again presumably covered with animal skins. Perhaps it can best be said that Paleoindians were innovative in their house designs, and constructed them with available local materials sufficient to provide adequate shelter.

Closer to Kent County, several Paleoindian sites on the Eastern Shore have been found in areas that would have been inland, well removed from the ancestral Susquehanna River channel. In two instances, one in Talbot County and one in Dorchester, the variable that determined site location seems to have been an inland swamp.[4] Such areas would have served as game attractants, as well as affording a diverse array of plant resources. In fact, researchers have proposed a cyclical movement of Paleoindians on the Eastern Shore focused on known lithic resource outcrops (such as the Delaware Chalcedony Complex in the Newark area or extensive cobble sources along the Chesapeake Bay) and interior swamps.[5] It is during such movement that Paleoindians likely visited Kent County.

The Early Archaic period (8000 to 6500 B. C.) continued many of the trends established during the Paleoindian period. Hunting and gathering remained the subsistence focus, again with a strong emphasis on hunting. Likewise, technologically, the Early Archaic resembled the Paleoindian period. Two of the most notable changes were a shift from exotic high quality cherts to local sources of quartz and quartzite for tool production, and a shift from lanceolate fluted spear points to notched and stemmed point types. The de-emphasis of the need for high quality cherts and jaspers may have affected Early Archaic settlement patterns. No longer was it necessary to travel long distances to obtain stone for tool kit replenishment. The shift to quartz and quartzite meant that readily available local cobble sources could be used, and that tool curation (reworking or resharpening overused tools to extend their serviceable life) was less of a concern given abundant replacement material close at hand. This in turn may have led to a somewhat more sedentary lifestyle during the Early Archaic. For instance, while inland swamps and riverine areas remained settlement foci,[6] the general wandering pattern during the Early Archaic could have been restricted to more discrete territories since it was no longer necessary to schedule distant quarry visits in the seasonal itinerary. The other notable change during the Early Archaic, the adoption of notched and stemmed projectile point styles, very likely marked a technological breakthrough which would have affected hunting strategies. Several archeologists have proposed that the appearance of notched and stemmed points in the Early Archaic period signals the invention of the spearthrower (or atlatl).[7] The spearthrower was a device that in essence lengthened the thrower's arm, thereby extending the fulcrum and allowing greater force to be exerted in the throwing action. The use of notched and stemmed spear points with the atlatl was needed to strengthen the point-to-shaft hafting mechanism sufficient to withstand the greater velocities and torque created. This innovation changed hunting from an in-close encounter with a thrusting spear to a more removed activity relying on skills such as stealth and accuracy. With the spearthrower, the spear could be propelled farther, harder, faster, and more accurately than a simple hand-thrown spear. This increased efficiency greatly aided the Early Archaic hunter's pursuit of smaller, more solitary animals such as deer.

The Middle Archaic period (6500 to 3000 B. C.) saw continued environmental change which ultimately reached modern conditions, although the distribution of resources may have been different from today. Climate included a general warming trend with wetter conditions. Sea level continued to rise, but shellfish had probably not yet established themselves.[8] Dense mesic forests supported large populations of deer and turkey. Diagnostic projectile points from the Middle Archaic include bifurcated base forms which have been found in far greater numbers than points from the Paleoindian and Early Archaic periods. This increase in point production, their distribution over the landscape, and the occurrence of larger occupation sites indicate that the Middle Archaic was a time of substantial population growth. Settlement patterns expanded into more and more environmental settings, especially emerging swamps and marshes newly created by continuing sea level rise. Site types included both large (macroband) and smaller (microband) base camps as well as procurement sites,[9] and the location and timing of established sites appears to have been more seasonally influenced than in earlier periods. On the Eastern Shore, the Chance site in Somerset County

Ground stone tools found in Kent County. Celts (top row, left and center) and grooved Axes. Audrey Johnson Collection.

Bottom left: Mortar and three pestles used for grinding and processing plant foods and materials. Still Pond vicinity. Charles W. Carter Collection. Michael Wootton photographs.

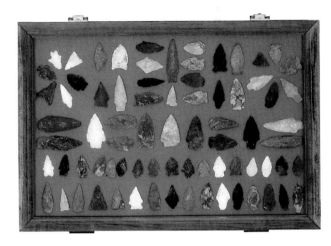

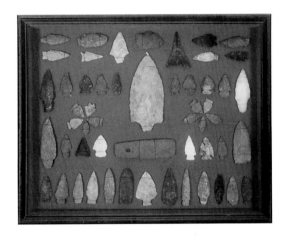

Spearpoints and arrowheads from the Archaic and Woodland periods (6,500 B.C. to A.D. 1600). Object in lower center is a one-holed gorget. Artifacts all from Kent County. Charles W. Carter Collection.

Spearpoints and arrowheads from the Archaic and Woodland periods (6500 B.C. to A.D. 1600). The earliest types include the LeCroy point (white, with an indented base, upper left), while the latest are the triangular arrowpoints (upper left and near lower left) dating to between A.D. 800 and 1600. Rock Hall vicinity. Charles W. Carter Collection.

Archaic (4000 to 1000 B.C.) spearpoints (top) found at Shellpoint. Audrey Johnson Collection. Michael Wootton photographs.

represents one of the best examples of a Middle Archaic macroband base camp. There, dozens of bifurcate base projectile points (as well as earlier Early Archaic forms) have been found on Deal Island.[10] The focus of the site appears to have been an interior swamp created by sea level rise. From the Chance site, resources associated with the swamp as well as riverine resources of the ancestral Susquehanna and nearby cobble quarries could have all been exploited by a macroband group[11] as part of the group's seasonal rounds.

Technologically, the most important innovation of the Middle Archaic was the adoption of ground stone tools, including axes, adzes, gouges, and grinding stones. The appearance of these tools in the prehistoric inventory indicates a much heavier exploitation of wood and plant products. For instance, it can be inferred from the appearance of axes and adzes that wooden artifacts such as mortars, bowls, and other utilitarian objects (which have not survived in the archeological record) were being manufactured. Also, the addition of formal grinding stones to the tool kit indicates an emphasis on plant food processing, such as the grinding of nuts. House construction (presumed to still be wigwams of sapling frameworks covered by bark or thatch) would have also been facilitated by the addition of woodworking tools, and would have helped meet the needs of growing populations.

The Late Archaic period (3000 to 1000 B.C.) marks perhaps the time of greatest change in the prehistory of Kent County. In some areas, such as interior Kent County along the upper Chester River, the greatest number of sites are represented by Late Archaic components,[12] giving us a broader view of this period than any earlier times.

Climatically, the Late Archaic first saw warmer and drier conditions, followed by a longer period of wetter and cooler, more modern conditions. During the warm/dry period, macroband base camps tended to be located near reliable water sources. Later, as the climate ameliorated, sites were scattered across the landscape. These later sites included a mixture of seasonal and possibly semi-permanent

Bannerstones were weights used on atlatls (or spearthrowers) during the Archaic period (circa 6000 to 1000 B. C.). Rock Hall vicinity. Charles W. Carter Collection; Michael Wootton photograph.

The atlatl (spearthrower) which preceded the bow and arrow as a weapon was probably developed during the Early Archaic period (8000 to 6500 B. C.) The bannerstone's use remains problematical, however recent research indicates they were used as balancing weights on atlatls. Drawing by Marcy Dunn Ramsey.

base camps—occupied from fall to early spring—located on well-drained soils near water sources; sites on well-drained soils removed from major water sources that would have served as fall procurement sites during which nut crops and deer were exploited; and transient camps on poorly drained soils from which roots could be collected or deer harvested.[13]

Sea level continued to rise, but at a lower rate, which caused the embayment of local streams and rivers (including formation of the Chesapeake Bay). The creation of estuaries allowed shellfish populations to become established and saw a proliferation of other plant and animal species (including, significantly, anadromous fish by around 2000 B. C.[14]).

The tool kit, technologically, became even more varied than during previous periods. Hunting was still undertaken primarily with spear and spearthrower. Projectile point styles were extremely varied, and included notched, stemmed, and broadspear types. The spearthrower was enhanced with the addition of a stone counterweight (called a bannerstone). Stone bowls, carved from dense, soft soapstone or steatite, also appeared during the Late Archaic. Ground stone tools again included mortars and pestles, axes, adzes, and gouges, but these tools appear in both greater numbers and variety. Also the woodworking tools appear fashioned for heavier use, and it is inferred that single-log dugout canoes were being constructed at this time. The appearance of the dugout canoe is significant in terms of both transportation (easing the burdens of travel as well as allowing efficient transport of heavy

loads, such as soapstone bowls) and exploitation of riverine (e. g., anadromous and other fish) and estuarine (e. g., oysters) resources.

Settlement patterns shifted somewhat as well, largely due to intensification. The reliable, seasonal availability of certain resources (such as abundant fall nut crops in the oak/hickory dominant forests, extensive oyster beds in the Chesapeake Bay and its embayed tributaries, and spawning anadromous fish runs in the upstream sections of the Bay's many tributaries) allowed Late Archaic peoples to establish more sedentary, and larger, base camps. Within these base camps, houses may have taken the more permanent form of semi-subterranean pit structures, based on evidence from Delaware.[15] The sedentary nature of these sites was enhanced with the introduction of storage technologies (including storage pits, smoking of oysters, drying of fish, etc.) that allowed surplus harvests to be stockpiled for use during

Cold-hammered copper spearpoint shown actual size. Still Pond vicinity. Clifford Lefferts photograph.

Late Woodland (A. D. 800 to 1600) pottery sherds. Ceramic vessels were used for both cooking and storage purposes. Rock Hall vicinity. Charles W. Carter Collection; Michael Wootton photograph.

lean times. The ability to accumulate surpluses also allowed additional population growth at this time.

Social systems became more complex during the Late Archaic, both as a response to the increased availability of food resources, the need to schedule and coordinate cooperative collection of these resources, and as a means to regulate the territoriality which concomitantly increased. Also evident during the Late Archaic period were far reaching trade and exchange systems.[16] These probably resulted from greater social complexity (i. e., the shift from simple band society to a Big Man-influenced society), greater resource availability, and improved transportation modes (especially the dugout canoe). Indications of trade and exchange in the artifact inventories of Late Archaic Kent County sites included the presence of soapstone bowls and ornaments (soapstone occurs in the Piedmont regions of Maryland's western shore) and the presence of rhyolite (from the Blue Ridge Moun-

tains of Maryland and Pennsylvania) and argillite (from the Piedmont uplands of Delaware, Pennsylvania, and New Jersey). This incipient trade and exchange network culminated in the well-known Early Woodland Delmarva Adena ceremonialism discussed below, but hints of Late Archaic ceremonialism are also known from the Kent County archeological record. A photograph in the Maryland Historical Trust's archeological slide collection depicts a six-and-a-half-inch copper blade reported to have come from the Arrowhead Farm site along Still Pond Creek in Kent County. This blade is reminiscent of similar Late Archaic Old Copper Culture artifacts generally restricted to sites in Wisconsin and occasionally found in Michigan, Minnesota, Illinois, and Ontario.[17] The occurrence of such an artifact in Maryland is remarkable and, given the meager evidence of only a color slide of a reported artifact find, could easily be dismissed with a number of plausible arguments (e. g., error on the part of the recorder, an artifact obtained from elsewhere and later attributed to Maryland, etc.). However, the Kent County find is not so easily dismissed. An obscure early twentieth century reference[18] to *"villages on the Eastern Shore of Maryland"* illustrates a twelve-inch copper blade virtually identical to Old Copper finds in Wisconsin, and lists as its provenience *"Still Pond Creek."* This specimen

is described as a copper spear head twelve inches long, one and one quarter inches at its greatest width, with a shank marked with deep clear-cut notches for securing it to a shaft. The spear head was reportedly plowed out of an Indian grave and was also associated with a very heavy copper *"hoe blade"* measuring seven inches in length, with a semicircular edge six inches wide. That these characteristic Old Copper artifacts were recovered in a typical burial context, in the same reported Still Pond location as a find recorded in the 1970s, and were published decades before archeologists had defined the distinctive traits of the Old Copper Culture is truly remarkable and argues that the finds are bona fide. What is more remarkable is that the finds were made in Maryland—hundreds of miles from the Old Copper heartland. Indeed, this chapter in Kent County prehistory remains a true archeological enigma.

The possible connection to the Old Copper Culture aside, definite far-reaching links can be demonstrated for the people of the Early Woodland period (1000 B. C. to A. D. 200). The Early Woodland built on the complex social systems established during the Late Archaic, and some of the most apparent furtherances are seen in terms of ceremonialism and trade and exchange, culminating in the Delmarva Adena complex. In its most visible archeological form, Delmarva Adena is characterized by large mortuary sites containing elaborate grave goods. Only a few of these spectacular

cemetery sites are known in the region (the closest being at Sandy Hill on the Choptank in Dorchester County and at St. Jones River near Delaware Bay in Delaware), but their artifact assemblages and attendant ceremonialism attest to the social complexity achieved during this time. The artifacts include large and extremely well-made points and blades of Flint Ridge (Ohio) chalcedony, tubular blocked-end pipes made from Indiana limestone and Ohio fireclay, stone effigy pipes, highly polished gorgets fashioned from shales and slates originating in Ohio and Pennsylvania, birdstones, finely made and highly polished paint cups carved from steatite and hematite or made from copper, and rolled copper beads.[19] Perhaps most striking, beyond even the spectacular nature of these artifacts, is the origins of the material from which they were made. Virtually all of these raw materials derive from the Ohio Valley and Great Lakes region, some 500 miles distant. The extensive trade networks which must have been operative to allow this influx of exotic materials to Maryland, and the communal organization necessary to establish such exchange systems, bespeak of a new level of social complexity—that of an incipient ranked society. No longer was one's status earned solely through deed, but now status could be ascribed. Portions

Ralph Hall Map of Virginia, with Maryland and the Chesapeake Bay in one main focus, drawn by Ralph Hall in 1636. It is a derivative of John Smith's earlier map. Numerous pictures of Indians with bows and arrows, in log canoes, and a bird's eye view of a stockaded village are displayed here. Many fur bearing animals that attracted traders such as William Claiborne to this area are shown, along with boats, monsters, houses, huts, and castles. Maryland State Archives, Huntingfield Corporation Maps of Maryland Collection

Indians cooking fish over an open fire. From a drawing by John White in 1586 and engraved by Theodore DeBry.

Theodore DeBry engraving from a 1585 drawing by John White of Indians making a dugout canoe. Courtesy of The British Museum and Dover Publications.

more common. The latter may be related to an increased intensification of plant food production with the advent of horticulture at this time. Also noted is an increase in shellfish exploitation, to the point that procurement sites can be seen shifting locations following the brackish/freshwater interface as sea level continued to rise.

Technologically, the marked advancement of the Early Woodland period is the development of pottery. Fired-clay cooking vessels replace carved soapstone bowls (in fact, the first pottery types used crushed soapstone—presumably salvaged from newly obsolete stone bowls—as a tempering agent), allowing more portability and greater cooking efficiency.

The cultural patterns established during the Early Woodland period continued throughout the Middle Woodland period (A. D. 200 to 800), with the exception of the Adena mortuary patterns. Larger macroband base camps continued to be situated along major waterways, while the smaller microband base camps were located along more minor drainages and inland swampy areas where the variety and abundance of resources served as the main attractants. Shellfish usage remained a subsistence focus, although late in the Middle Woodland period an intensification in plant use is noted. Ceramics continued to be refined, and dominant ware types were commonly tempered with crushed oyster shell or finely crushed quartz.

Towards the end of the Middle Woodland, a mortuary ceremonial complex—similar to, though unrelated and less extensive than Adena—developed in the Delmarva region. Known as the Webb Complex, it incorporates cemetery sites once again characterized by elaborate associated grave goods. These distinctive artifacts include Jacks Reef pentagonal and corner-notched projectile points, large pentagonal bifaces made from non-local jaspers and argillites, bone and antler tools, and steatite platform pipes. As with the Adena mortuary sites, no Webb Complex cemeteries are known in Kent County (the nearest examples are at Oxford in Talbot County and at Island Field on Delaware Bay), although supporting base camps are likely present. An example of this may be the Fairlee Neck shell midden site on Chesapeake Bay. Here, evidence of continued seasonal exploitation of shellfish resources, as well as hickory, butternut, and acorn or chestnut mast resources, is clearly evident, and demonstrates either long-term site re-use, support of a large population, or a combination of both.[22] Interestingly, large habitation/base camps do not appear to be associated with the Webb Complex cemeteries. In fact, large base camps of any kind seem to be rare during this latter portion of the Middle Woodland, while smaller microband base camps proliferate, leading to speculation that traditional social networks were collapsing in the face of continued population growth.[23] At any rate, the

of society could be born into the elite class, and thus be accorded positions of power during life and appropriate commemoration in death.

Certainly, though, this reverence paid to the elite class did not occur in a vacuum. Such elaborate ceremonialism required more numerous, though less archaeologically visible, commoners. And while no Adena mortuary centers have been found in Kent County, sites attributed to the supporting population are indicated in the archeological record. An example of this is site 18KE214,[20] a typical habitation site situated on the banks of Jacobs Creek near the confluence with the Sassafras River from which a single side-notched projectile point fashioned from Flint Ridge chalcedony hints at Adena ties.[21] Certainly dozens of such habitation sites and procurement sites were needed to sustain even a few large mortuary sites, and these support sites are likely pervasive (but difficult to identify as evidenced by 18KE214). By A. D. 0, the Adena influence on the Delmarva Peninsula had all but disappeared.

Sites dating to the Early Woodland period continued the Late Archaic trend of increasing sedentariness, with sites becoming larger and the use of storage features

This remarkable drawing by John White in 1590 of an Indian village shows the two main money crops, corn (H. G.) and tobacco (E), that later made Kent County an important exporter from Colonial times until now. The corn was planted in staggered rows (H) in order not to choke its growth (G). A scaffolded seat (F) was built above the ripe corn for a watchman to keep "fowles and beasts" from devouring their crop. *A Briefe and True Report of the New Found Land of Virginia* by Thomas Harriot, 1590; engraved by Theodor de Bry. Courtesy of the British Museum and Dover Publications.

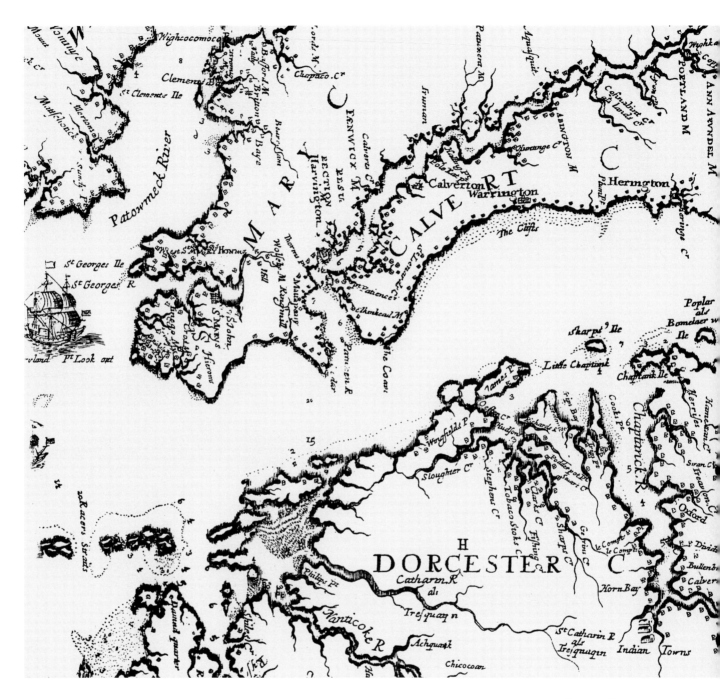

resurgence of cemeteries containing specialized grave goods and the extensive trade and exchange networks involving exotic raw materials witnessed during the Webb Complex had collapsed by A. D. 1000.

The Late Woodland period (A. D. 800 to 1600) in the Middle Atlantic region is characterized by significant social and technological change. In general terms, social organization became much more complex, culminating in several chiefdoms on the Western Shore of Maryland and Virginia. Full-blown agriculture became the main subsistence focus for a number of groups at this time. Settlement patterns shifted to accommodate agricultural

pursuits and, late in the period, to effect defensive strategies necessitated by intertribal hostilities.

On the Eastern Shore, and in Kent County in particular, though, these broad changes seemed to have occurred on a lesser scale. Late Woodland peoples here had certainly adopted agricultural pursuits (based on corn, beans, and squash), but domesticated plant cultivation never seems to have been full-time; rather, gathering of wild plant foods, collection of the ubiquitous oyster, and hunting remained important subsistence quests. While Late Woodland groups on the Western Shore made dramatic shifts to floodplain settings (even to the point of

abandoning productive estuarine settings) in response to the need for arable lands, this does not appear to have been the case in Kent County, where settlement patterns continued virtually unmodified from those established during the Middle Woodland. And while Eastern Shore Late Woodland sites may have evolved from macroband base camps to larger, semi-sedentary villages, archeological evidence is lacking that they developed into the very large, defensively palisaded villages known in areas like the lower Potomac River. On the technology front, the introduction of the bow and arrow at around A. D. 800 marked a significant advancement over the spearthrower used for the past 7000-8000 years. The rapid adoption and spread of this new hunting device is documented in the archeological record by the appearance and widespread distribution of the characteristic small triangular arrowpoint. Advancement in ceramics manufacture continued to occur, with vessels generally becoming better made and more durable. Of note from an archeological perspective is the occurrence of more complex decorative designs on ceramic vessels of this time. The use of incised lines and cord-wrapped stick impressions to achieve design motifs has allowed

Excavations carried out at a prehistoric shell midden site on Fairlee Neck by the University of Delaware in 1988. Dennis C. Curry photograph.

archeologists to define two Late Woodland wares associated with two distinct archeological complexes.

The Slaughter Creek Complex, associated with shell-tempered Townsend ware pottery, is widespread on the Eastern Shore, generally to the south of Kent County. Site types are characterized by large macroband base camps or possibly sedentary villages which have high densities of storage features, and seasonal microband base camps. Structures at the village sites are likely to have been semi-subterranean pit houses, based on initial data from Delaware.[24] Site 18KE228 on Fairlee Creek is a likely example of a Slaughter Creek macroband base camp,[25] while a series of sites on Eastern Neck Island[26] represent corresponding microband base camps which served as shellfish exploitation sites.

The other major Late Woodland complex on the Eastern Shore is referred to as Minguannan. Sites from this complex largely occur to the north of Kent County, and are characterized by sand, grit, and crushed quartz-tempered Minguannan ceramics with complex incised and impressed decorative designs. Macroband base camps from the Minguannan Complex differ little from those of the previous Middle Woodland period. Few of these sites have been found in Kent County, although the Arrowhead Farm site near Still Pond represents one of the Minguannan Complex's better known examples.[27] At Arrowhead Farm, a series of overlapping, revisited macroband base camps is indicated as

An Indian Canoe made out of a Tree with their Battles or Oares with the manner of Rowing over the Rivers

opposed to a single semi-sedentary village. Minguannan Complex microband base camps and procurement sites in Kent County are even less well-represented. In fact, the overall few numbers of Late Woodland sites, especially in northern Kent County, has led to speculation that the county may have represented an area of sparse Late Woodland populations, effectively creating an *"empty"* area between the Slaughter Creek and Minguannan core areas.[28]

When Captain John Smith sailed up the Chesapeake in 1608, he noted two native groups of people in or near what is now Kent County—the Tockwoghs to the north [along the Sassafras River?] and the Ozinies (also known as the Wicomiss) to the south [on the Chester River?].[29] He describes these as such:

"On the East side of the Bay is the river of Tockwogh, and vpon it a people that can make 100 men, seated some 7 miles within the river: where they haue a Fort very wel pallisadoed and mantelled with the barke of trees. Next to them is Ozinies with 60 men."[30]

Smith goes on to relate a visit to the well-fortified village of Tockwogh, recounting evidence of the Tockwogh's recent animosities with the Massawomecks, and observing *"[m]any hatchets, kniues, and peeces of yron and brasse"* which the Tockwoghs had received from the Susquehannocks.[31] Smith's narratives are noteworthy on several accounts. First, that only two settlements are noted in 1608 attests to the sparse native population at the dawn of the seventeenth century. Using Smith's counts of warriors (100 and 60, respectively), the entire native population in Kent County has been estimated to be as low as 500 persons.[32] Second, his graphic description of a heavily defended, palisaded village at Tockwogh provides evidence of Eastern Shore fortifications that is currently missing from the archeological record. And third, the inventory of European trade items already in the possession of the Tockwoghs shows the extent to which the white man's presence was already being felt by native peoples.

Archeological evidence of the Contact period in Kent County is scant, but hints of early seventeenth century occupation have been found at the Arrowhead Farm site on Still Pond Creek. There, two native-made, pillow-shaped gunflints manufactured from local pebble chert, several fragments of rouletted clay pipes, several scraps of brass, and a single sherd of North Devon gravel-tempered pottery indicate a possible Contact component at the site.[33]

Largely, the effects of European contact on native populations included decimation resulting from newly introduced diseases, increased intertribal warfare (due in large part to competition induced by the fur trade), and an increased reliance on European goods at the expense of traditional technologies and lifeways.[34]

In any event, native groups had been pushed south out of the Kent County area probably by the 1650s (Augustine Herrman's 1673 map of Virginia and Maryland shows a total absence of Indian settlements). The surviving groups who had been pushed south were nearly obliterated by colonial forces during the Wicomiss War of 1669, with their remnants deported to Barbados.[35] By the end of the seventeenth century, the 11,000 year-long occupation of Kent County by Native Americans had ended, and only their accumulated debris remained.

DENNIS C. CURRY is Senior Archeologist in the Archeological Research Unit of the Maryland Historical Trust's Office of Archeology. He resides with his wife and four children in Columbia, Maryland.

1. Charles W. McNett, Jr., *Shawnee Minisink: A Stratified Paleoindian-Archaic Site in the Upper Delaware Valley of Pennsylvania* (Academic Press, Inc., Orlando, 1985), pp. 73, 322.

2. William M. Gardner, *The Flint Run Paleo-Indian Complex: A Preliminary Report, 1971-73 Seasons* (The Catholic University of America, Washington, D. C., 1974).

3. Richard Michael Gramly, *The Adkins Site: A Paleo-Indian Habitation and Associated Stone Structure* (Persimmon Press, Buffalo, 1988).

4. Darrin Lowery, "The Paw Paw Cove Paleoindian Site Complex, Talbot County, Maryland," *Archaeology of Eastern North America* 17:143-163 (1989); Darrin Lowery and Thomas Phillips, "The Meekins Neck Paleoindian Site Complex, Dorchester County, Maryland: A Development of a Paleoindian Settlement Model for the Lower Delmarva Peninsula," *Maryland Archeology* 30(2):29-36 (1994).

5. Lowery; Jay F. Custer "Analysis of Early Holocene Projectile Points and Site Locations for the Delmarva Peninsula," *Archaeology of Eastern North America* 14:45-64 (1986).

6. Custer (1986).

7. Gardner p. 24.

8. Steve Wilke and Gail Thompson, *Prehistoric Resources of Portions of Coastal Kent County* (Report prepared for the Division of Archeology, Maryland Geological Survey, 1977) and *Archeological Survey of Western Kent County* (Report prepared for the Maryland Historical Trust, 1977). Wilke and Thompson report a number of radiocarbon assays run on oyster shells from Kent County shell middens. Some of these assays returned dates in the late Middle Archaic range (ca. 3100 B. C.). Custer has questioned the reliability of these dates on the basis of archeological associations [Jay F. Custer, *A Management Plan for the Archaeological Resources of the Upper Delmarva Region of Maryland* (Maryland Historical Trust Manuscript Series No. 31, 1983), p. 41] and the reliability of radiocarbon dates run on oyster shell [Jay F. Custer, "Accelerator Radiocarbon Dates from 18KE17," *ASM Ink* 10(6):3-4 (1984)]. Most archeologists are more comfortable with Late Archaic or later dates for Kent County shell middens.

9. Jay F. Custer, *Delaware Prehistoric Archaeology: An Ecological Approach* (University of Delaware Press, Newark, 1984), Fig. 9.

10. Paul Cresthull, "Chance (18So5): A Major Early Archaic Site," *Maryland Archeology* 7(2):31-52 (1971) and 8(2):40-53 (1972).

11. Jay F. Custer, *Prehistoric Cultures of the Delmarva Peninsula: An Archaeological Study* (University of Delaware Press, Newark, 1989), pp. 135-136.

12. Maureen Kavanagh, *Archeological Reconnaissance of Proposed Channel Improvements in the upper Chester Watershed, Kent and Queen Annes Counties, Maryland* (Maryland Geological Survey, Division of Archeology, File Report No. 147, 1979).

13. Kavanagh.

14. Timothy A. Thompson and William M. Gardner, *A Cultural Resources and Impact Area Assessment, Eastern Neck National Wildlife Refuge, Kent County, Maryland* (Report prepared for the U. S. Department of the Interior, Interagency Archeological Services, 1978).

15. Custer (1989) pp. 196-198.

16. R. Michael Stewart, "Late Archaic through Late Woodland Exchange in the Middle Atlantic Region" (in *Prehistoric Exchange Systems in North America*, edited by Timothy G. Baugh and Jonathan E. Ericson, Plenum Press, New York, 1994).

17. James B. Stoltman, "The Archaic Tradition," *The Wisconsin Archeologist* 67(3-4); 207-238 (1986).

18. Francis Jordan, Jr., *Aboriginal Fishing Stations on the Coast of the Middle Atlantic States* (Philadelphia, 1906), pp. 34-38.

19. T. Latimer Ford, Jr., "Adena Sites on Chesapeake Bay," *Archaeology of Eastern North America* 4:63-89 (1976).

20. Archeological sites are formally designated using a trinomial system. The first number indicates the state (Maryland is the 18th state alphabetically); the second unit is a two-letter county abbreviation; and the third unit is the inventory number of the particular site within the county. Thus, 18KE214 refers to the 214th site recorded in Kent County, Maryland.

21. Custer (1983), p. 71.

22. Jay F. Custer, *Survey and Test Excavations at Fairlee Neck Shell Midden (18KE17), Kent County, Maryland* (Center for Archaeological Research, University of Delaware, 1987).

23. Custer (1989), p. 295.

24. Custer (1989), p. 319.

25. Custer (1989), p. 322.

26. Thompson and Gardner.

27. Jay F. Custer, Patricia A. Jehle, H. Henry Ward, Scott C. Watson, and Claire Mensack, "Archeological Investigations of the Arrowhead Farm Site Complex, Kent County, Maryland," *Maryland Archeology* 22(2):20-35 (1986).

28. Custer (1983), p. 82.

29. Captain John Smith, [Map of] Virginia (1608, originally published in 1612).

30. Edward Arber (editor), *Travels and Works of Captain John Smith, President of Virginia, and Admiral of New England, 1580-1631* (Two volumes. John Grant, Edinburgh, 1910), p. 55.

31. Arber, pp. 117-118.

32. Christian F. Feest, "Nanticoke and Neighboring Tribes" (in *Handbook of North American Indians, Volume 15: Northeast*, edited by Bruce G. Trigger, pp. 240-252, Smithsonian Institution, 1978), p. 242, Table

33. Custer et al.

34. Custer (1989), pp. 335-338.

35. Feest, p. 243.

Chapter 2
The Seventeenth Century

The beginnings of Kent County in Tidewater Maryland were partially brought about by the desire of the Colonists for private lands. They were anxious to satisfy the increasing market for tobacco in England.

THE BOUNDARIES OF A COUNTY, LIKE THE FENCES around one's yard, give a land geographical definition. Interestingly, however, they often help to characterize their inhabitants as well. The first charter in America, the original Virginia Charter encompassed four-fifths of the present entire continental United States, beginning at the 45th parallel and running south to the 34th parallel (the southern border of present day Virginia) and extending from the Atlantic coast as far west as could be imagined. This Charter, however, was annulled in 1626 as a result of settlement in New England in the 1620s and the colony was made considerably smaller.

In 1632, after having unsuccessfully attempted to establish *Avalon* in Newfoundland in the late 1620s, George Calvert, Lord Baltimore was granted part of the lands lying north of the Potomac River. These lands were largely unexplored and the lack of maps resulted in an ambiguity of the boundaries of the Maryland Charter. While it was specified that Maryland was to encompass those lands bordered by the Atlantic Ocean on the east and lying between the 38th and 40th parallels, its western border, like Virginia's was simply to extend as far as could be imagined, providing the land had not previously been settled or cultivated. In only two years time, the first settlers of Maryland would arrive and their vessels would sail northward from the mouth of the Chesapeake Bay.

Just one year prior to the Maryland Charter, in 1631, William Claiborne had received permission from the Virginia authorities to explore, trade and settle on the largest island on the east side of the Bay. He did so with about 100 other individuals. Located approximately midway between the mouth of the Potomac River and the head of the Bay, Claiborne named this island *Kent* in honor of his home county in England. Despite these original ties to Virginia, the Isle of Kent was considered by Lord Baltimore to be part of his territory. And thus the struggle began. As the story of Claiborne's dispute with Lord Baltimore has been discussed in detail elsewhere, it is not necessary to dwell on this dispute which lasted for years.[1] Suffice it to say, that Claiborne left his mark on the area and that mark consisted not only of the very people he brought with him, but the name of Kent as well.

A Relation of Maryland, September 8, 1635, title page.

The Charter of Maryland, June 20, 1632, page one. Maryland State Archives, Huntingfield Corporation Collection. Courtesy of H. Russell Morrison, Jr.

Opposite: This mighty oak was demolished during hurricane Hazel in 1955. There is only one tree left in a grove that once stood in St. Paul's Churchyard. It is believed to be over four-hundred years old. Constance Stuart Larrabee photograph.

Even before the controversy between Claiborne and Baltimore was settled, inhabitants of the Island who had agreed to acknowledge the authority of Lord Baltimore looked to St. Mary's for direction and government. By 1638, Kent Island had grown in population to such an extent that it was made a hundred of St. Mary's County, (the sixth to be made so) by a special Act of the General Assembly.

"An Act for the Government of the Isle of Kent

Be it enacted by the Lord Proprietary of this Province of and with the advice and approbation of the same that the Island commonly called the Isle of Kent shall be erected into a hundred and shall be within the County of St. Maries (until another County shall be erected of the Eastern shore and no longer) and shall be called by the name of Kent hundred and the commander of the said Island from time to time appointed by the Lord Proprietary or his Lieutenant Generall shall be a Justice of the Peace within the said hundred durring such time as he is commander with all power and authority to a Justice of Peace belonging by the laws of this Province and the said commander shall appoint some one to be Clerk or Register for the Recording of all matters pertaining to that office and the said commander and Register for the time being shall be a Court of Record and shall be called the hundred court of Kent ... ."[2]

As the Island had a sort of *head start,* it was only natural that it would be a prime area of development during the first ten years of the Maryland adventure. In the act cited above, three points were clearly made: 1) the name of Kent, as given it by Claiborne, was unequivocal, 2) the boundaries of the hundred were limited to the Island itself, and 3) provisions had been made for a future county. The last of these would come to be in only four short years.

In September of 1642, following the passage of the Act for the Establishment of Judges, a judge was appointed over the area previously known as Kent Hundred. It is this date which has become accepted as the date for the founding of Kent County. Since the original Decree of Establishment has been lost or perhaps was never recorded, there is no way of knowing the actual extent of the boundaries in 1642. It has been proposed that the new county may have included the entire Eastern Shore, as well as other islands of the Chesapeake.

Oswald Tilghman in his History of Talbot County suggested that prior to the establishment of Baltimore and Talbot Counties, those inhabitants scattered along the waterways of the Eastern Shore would have transacted their business on either Kent Island or in St. Mary's. Rich Neck Manor, located across Eastern Bay from the southern end of Kent Island and in present day Talbot County, was part of Kent County when originally patented in 1651. It shared this distinction with several of the earliest patents on the mainland Eastern Shore. For settlers such as those at Rich Neck, the proximity of the lower end of Kent Island made it a logical

Continued on page 20

Kiplin Hall, Yorkshire, England. Built by George Calvert, First Lord Baltimore and birthplace of Cecilius Calvert (1605-1675), founder of the colony of Maryland. Photograph courtesy School of Architecture, University of Maryland, Mr. David Fogle.

The shield of Lord Baltimore

A Description of the Countrey.

"The predecents discourse gives you to understand, how the first Colony (Saint Maries, March 27, 1634) sate downe in Maryland, what progresse they made, and in what estate it is at the present: Now my purpose is to speake of the Countrey in generall, that who so looks that way, may beforehand know something thereof. It is seated betweene the degrees of 38 and 40 of North Latitude, Virginia bounds it on the South, New-England on the North, and the Ocean on the East, but the Western parts are not yet discovered."

" … The Timber of these parts is very good, and in aboundance, it is usefull for building of houses, and shippes; the white Oake is good for Pipe-staves, the red Oake for wainescot. There is also Walnut, Cedar, Pine, & Cipresse, Chestnut, Elme, Ashe, and Popler, all which are for Building, and Husbandry. Also there are diverse sorts of Fruit-trees, as Mulberries, Persimons, with severall other kind of Plummes, and Vines, in great aboundance. The Mast and the Chestnuts, and what rootes they find in the woods, doe feede the Swine very fat, and will breede great store, both for their owne provision, or for merchandise, and such as is not inferior to the Bacon of Westphalia.

Of Strawberries, there is plenty, which are ripe in Aprill; Mulberries in May; and Raspices in June; Maracocks which is somewhat like a Limon, are ripe in August.

In the Spring, there are severall sorts of herbes, as Corn-sallet, Violets, Sorrell, Purslaine, all which are very good and wholesome, and by the English, used for sallets, and in broth.

In the upper parts of the Countrey, there are Bufeloes, Elkes, Lions, Beares, Wolues, and Deare there are great store, in all places that are not too much frequented, as also Beavers, Foxes, Otters, and many other sorts of Beasts.

Of Birds, there is the Eagle, Goshawke, Falcon, Lanner, Sparrow-hawke, and Merlin, also wild Turkeys in great aboundance, whereof many weigh 50 pounds, and upwards; and of Partridge plenty: There are likewise sundry sorts of Birds which sing, whereof some are red, some blew, others blacke and yellow, some like our Black-birds, others like Thrushes, but not of the same kind, with many more, for which wee know no names.

In Winter there is great plenty of Swannes, Cranes, Geese, Herons, Ducke, Teale, Widgeon, Brants, and Pidgeons, with other sorts, whereof there are none in England.

The Sea, the Bayes of Chesopeack, and Delaware, and generally all the Rivers, doe abound with Fish of severll sorts, for many of them we have no English names: There are Whales, Sturgeons uery large and good, and in great aboundance, Grampuses, Porpuses, Mullets, Trouts, Soules, Place, Mackerell, Perch, Crabs, Oysters, Cockles, and Mussles. But above all these, the fish that have no English names, are the best except the Sturgeons: There is also a fish like the Thornebacke in England, which hath a taile a yard long, wherein are sharpe prickles, with which if it strike a man, it will put him to much paine and torment, but it is very good meate: also the Tode-fish, which will swell till it be ready to burst, if it be taken out of the water … " Cecilius Calvert, Second Lord Baltimore

Excerpts from: *A Relation of Maryland,* A tract published by Lord Baltimore, September 8, 1635, Chapter II, page 13 and Chapter III, pages 18 and 19. Maryland State Archives, Huntingfield Corporation Collection

Constance Stuart Larrabee photograph.

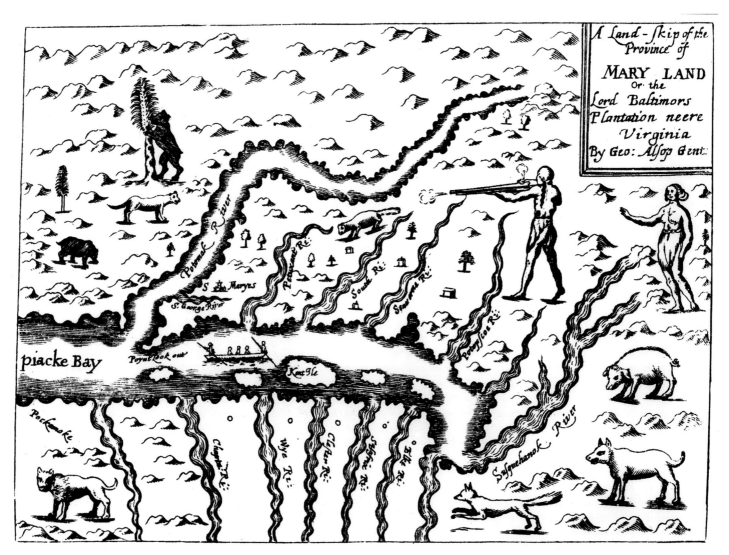

base for economic and political activity. For those inhabitants south of the Choptank, crossing the Bay to St. Mary's for governmental needs made better sense.

The years 1658 and 1659 produced events which would mark the next milestone in the development of Kent County. In these years, the first land patents were granted along the Bay and the boundaries of Kent County were changed again with the establishment of Baltimore County. It was to include all of the area north of Kent Island, on both sides of the Bay, with the small exception of Eastern Neck and Eastern Neck Island. These exceptions were laid out for several individuals who had been and continued to be influential in the Kent County (Kent Island) government. They included Joseph Wickes, Thomas Smith, Nathaniel Hynson and others.

Two years later, in 1661, Talbot County was established and encompassed a large land mass, lying between borders of the Chester River on the north and the Nanticoke to the south (most of present day Dorchester, Talbot, Caroline and Queen Annes Counties). Once again the boundaries of Kent remained ambiguous. Few references are available to help shed light on Kent's exact boundaries at this time. One in 1664, however, described a ferry at Head of Chester (Millington) as being the dividing line between Talbot and Baltimore Counties. Another described Thornton, a tract on the northeast side of Morgan Creek, as being in Talbot County.

When Cecil County was created in 1674, the boundaries given in the Act of the Assembly stated that it would extend from the Susquehanna River down to the Chester, around Hail Point on Eastern Neck Island, and back up to the head of the Chester. However, before these boundary changes were actually put in place, the southern boundary was altered to run from the head waters of Fairlee Creek to an undetermined eastern boundary, in a line which ran approximately through the center of the County. Talbot County lay to the southeast of Cecil borders and Kent to the south. County locations, as included in land grants of these years, are often contradictory. In 1695, the boundaries of Kent County were altered yet again.

During all of these changes, Kent Island remained the one stable part of Kent County. For 38 years, from 1642 to 1680, the Isle of Kent was the seat of county government and its boundaries were never in dispute with Baltimore, Talbot, or Cecil counties.

The final rearrangement of Kent's borders occurred in 1706, as a result of the petitions of some inhabitants of Cecil and Talbot Counties. The act that resulted, however, was the final one in the establishment of not only present day Kent, but also Cecil County.

Kent's boundaries were finally defined in the following manner:

"... And that from and after the said first Day of May one thousand seven hundred & seven Kent County shall begin at the South Point of the easterne Neck and from thence run up Chesapeake bay to Sarsafrax river and up the said river to the South end of the Long horse bridge lying over the head of the said River and from thence with a line Drawn East and by south to the Exteriour bounds of this Province and with the Exteriour bounds of this province untill it intersect the line of Queen Anns County and with the said County down Chester river to Eastern Neck where it first begun and shall containe all the land within the said bounds."[3]

The eastern boundary described here as the "Exteriour bounds of this province" remained unsettled for decades to come, causing a disagreement between Lord Baltimore and William Penn.

In the final rearrangement, another new county was created. Formed from parts of Talbot and Kent County, Queen Annes, as it would be called, included all of the area lying to the south of the Chester River and north of the Wye, and Kent Island itself.

Early Courthouses

In 1680, the center of county government was moved from Kent Island to the port town of New Yarmouth on Greys Inn Creek at the southern end of the County. Located on Eastern Neck, New Yarmouth was created out of the northeast corner of a 1200 acre parcel of land called Huntingfield which had been granted to Thomas Ringgold in 1661. This central location was thought to be more convenient to its inhabitants, who were gradually moving further north as they continued to settle the hinterlands.

In 1695, responding to the petitions of several of the County's landholders residing along the Chester River, the General Assembly acted once again to alter the boundaries of the County in 1695.

"... Whereas Diverse of the Inhabitants of the Countys of St Marys and Kent have by theire Petitions Complained That through the irregularitys of their Countys being so ill scituated that theire Court houses or Chief places of Judicature within their Countys canot be Seated for the Conveniency of the Inhabitants and Suitors to the Same ... And be it further Enacted by the Authority aforesaid by and with the advice and Consent aforesaid That from and after the Twenty third day of Aprill next after the end of this present Sessions of Assembly the Island of Kent shall be Added to and made part of Talbott County and Deemed reputed and Taken as part thereof And That part of Talbott County lying on the North side of Corsecia Creek running up the main Eastern Branch to the head thereof and then with a Course drawn East to the out side of this Province shall be the Southerly Bounds of the County of Kent and on the North by the County of Cecill any Law Statute or usage heretofore to the County notwithstanding ... ."[4]

As this shift caused the then 16 year old courthouse at New Yarmouth to become inconvenient to many of the County's inhabitants, a new location for the courthouse was established near Quaker Neck Landing.

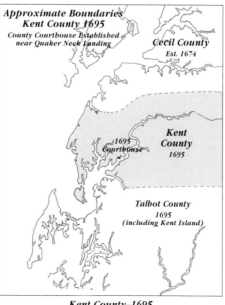

Approximate Boundaries Kent County c. 1675
County Seat Established at New Yarmouth on Greys Inn Creek.

Cecil County Est. 1674 (From part of Baltimore County)

New Yarmouth Courthouse

Kent County Est. 1642

Talbot County Est. 1661

Kent County–1675

Approximate Boundaries Kent County 1695
County Courthouse Established near Quaker Neck Landing

Cecil County Est. 1674

1695 Courthouse

Kent County 1695

Talbot County 1695 (including Kent Island)

Kent County–1695

By January 1696, the courthouse had been built on its new site on the banks of the Chester River. The location adjoined the lands of Isaac Caulk and Edward Fry. A report at the March session of the following year described the courthouse as built with a wooden chimney and states that the county records were kept within the building, and that there was no ordinary at the site.[5]

Just ten years later, the final boundary changes of 1706/07 resulted once again in an inconveniently located courthouse. In the April 19th session of the General Assembly of that year, an *"Act for the Advancement of Trade and Erecting Ports and Towns in the Province of Maryland"* was passed which proposed the establishment of a new town in Kent County.

"In Chester river on a plantation of Mr. Joce's between Mr. Willmores and Edward Walvins Plantation ... ."[6]

The site which was laid out in the same year, a bit to the south of Mr. Joce's land, was to become Chestertown. The centrality of this location made it an ideal choice for the site of the new courthouse.

LAND GRANTS AND MANORS

In the tedious process of acquiring the Charter for the establishment of a colony in the new world, Lord Baltimore had become indebted to certain individuals and had promised land to others. In the *Conditions of Plantation* the initial scheme was to set up large grants of land to be modeled after the manor system of England. It was a simple system which allowed the landlord to be the judge of all that transpired on his lands. The system was passing from use in England, however, and ultimately had little impact on settlement in Kent County. Assuredly, manors were laid out in Kent, but by the time those lands had been populated, the system had been abolished and all disputes were handled by the developing system of county government.

Tracts within the present borders of Kent County which were granted with true manor privileges include Great Oak Manor, Worton Manor, and the Manor of Stephen Heath. All of these were surveyed in 1658 and patented in 1659, the year in which Baltimore County was established.

In order to encourage the development of land not previously promised to the friends of Lord Baltimore, parcels were granted to people who transported themselves and others to the colony. Settlers who brought with them less than five men between the ages of 16 and 50 were granted 100 acres per head (an amount much less than those settlers of greater wealth). At one point, in 1641, the allowances had dropped as low as 50 acres per head for the same, but rose again to 100 in 1649. The first land grants were of this type and continued until 1683 when no more free lands were available. It then became necessary for those who wanted land to purchase it at a ratio of 100 pounds of tobacco for each 50 acres. In the following year the price rose to 120 pounds of tobacco. While this was a twenty percent increase in cost, it remained such a bargain that people continued to pour into Kent County. Between the years 1705 and 1712, the population of the county increased from 1800 to 2800 inhabitants.

From 1642 to 1658, the Isle of Kent (then Kent County) was the location of the majority of residential and business development in the County. The signing of a treaty by the proprietary government with the Susquehannock Indians in 1652, however, freed up the lands in the upper bay. By 1658, as the threat of Indian attack passed, settlers began to file claims along the upper Bay and up the rivers.

The first of these surveys were prepared for influential individuals associated with the proprietary government, such as Josiah Fendall, Edward Packer, John Langford and others. Their grants included Great Oak Manor, a 2000 acre parcel located between Fairlee and Worton Creeks; Packerton, 800 acres adjoining Great Oak; and Langford Neck, 1500 acres between Greys Inn Creek and the west branch of Langford Creek. They were followed by the burgesses of Kent County who received large grants of land on Eastern Neck, Eastern Neck Island and between the Bay and Swan Creek. A large number of mariners received grants of free land in return for bringing new inhabitants to Maryland. Most of them, however, never lived on the land themselves. Instead the land grants were a means to future profit either by populating their holdings with indentured servants (generally not well documented) or by selling off their land in smaller parcels to individuals unable to afford the whole. The

property of George Garnett illustrates such an arrangement. As County Surveyor, he purchased the entire 1000 acres of Stradford Manor only to resurvey it and sell off smaller farms. Garnett's endeavor is one of the most obvious early efforts to turn a profit by means of land sales in Kent County.

By the 1680s, the majority of the river frontage along the Sassafras and Chester Rivers had been patented. Thereafter, the interior lands were surveyed and patented. Frequently, after one generation, the boundaries of the original tract were lost and it became necessary to petition the County or the Assembly to rectify the situation with a subsequent survey. At these times, additional land which had been left vacant or unsurveyed would be added by purchase and would be included in the new survey and/or patent. These vacant tracts were often given names such as *Discovery, Chance,* or *Addition.*

DEVELOPMENT OF TOWNS & COMMERCE

Throughout the seventeenth century, in an attempt to promote commerce in Maryland, various acts were passed in the General Assembly for the establishment of inspection stations along the waterways, the erection of ports and towns, and the encouragement of mills and ordinaries. While the first boundaries of the counties usually had been based solely upon the physical features of the

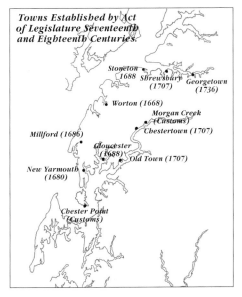

Towns Established by Act of Legislature Seventeenth and Eighteenth Centuries.

Stoneton 1688
Shrewsbury (1707)
Georgetown (1736)
Worton (1668)
Morgan Creek (Customs)
Chestertown (1707)
Millford (1686)
Gloucester (1688)
Old Town (1707)
New Yarmouth (1680)
Chester Point (Customs)

Continued on page 26

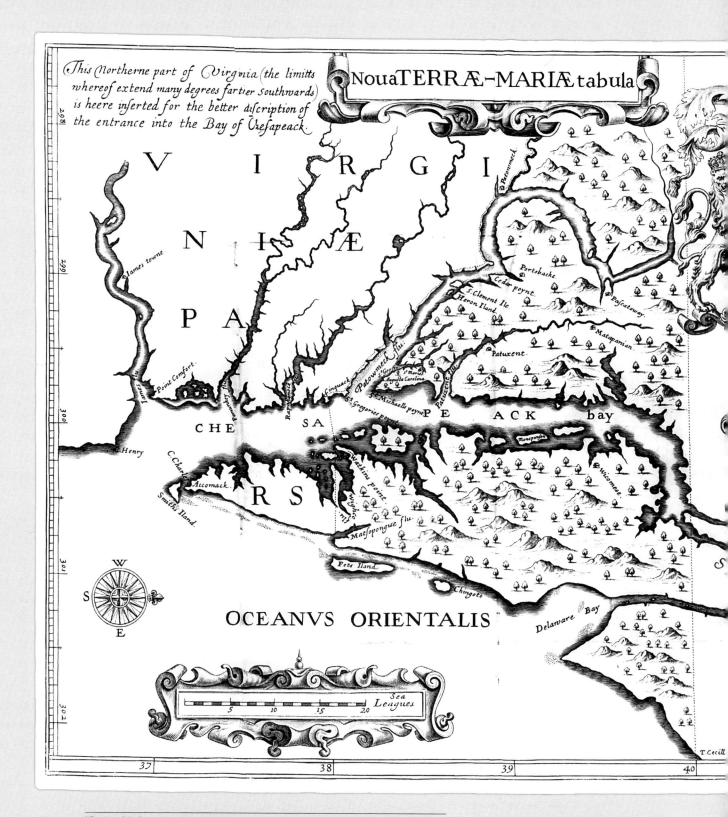

This Northerne part of Virginia (the limitts whereof extend many degrees farther southwards) is heere inserted for the better discription of the entrance into the Bay of Chesapeack.

NouaTERRÆ-MARIÆ tabula

VIRGINIÆ

PA

James towne

Point Comfort

C. Henry

C. Charts

Accomack

Smiths Iland.

CHE   SA   RS

Watkins point

Matsopongue flu.

Fets Iland

Chingoto

OCEANVS ORIENTALIS

Patowmeck.

Portobacke

Cedar poynt.

S. Clement Ile

Heron Iland.

Pascatoway.

Matapanian

Patuxent

S. Georg. S. Maries

Augusta Carolina

S. Michaells poynt

S. Gregories poynt.

PE   ACK   bay

Monoponson

Wicomese

Delaware Bay

Sea Leagues.

5   10   15   20

T. Cecill.

The Lord Baltimore Map, Maryland's first, taken from A Relation of Maryland, dated September the 8, Anno. Dom. 1635. The northern border extends across present day Delaware and New Jersey to the Atlantic Ocean. It is the first map to show Maryland boundaries, to name the Delaware Bay, and to print the Baltimore Coat of Arms. The island in the Chesapeake Bay named Monoponson is redrawn and named Kent County in the later 1671 Ogilby edition. Maryland State Archives, Huntingfield Maps of Maryland Collection.

The Lord Baltimore Map 1635

A Relation of Maryland, a tract issued by Cecilius (Cecil) Calvert, the Second Lord Baltimore on September 8, 1635 was a promotional booklet. Its main purpose was to interest potential colonists and investors in coming to the new colony or to help finance its development. Actually, it was a prospectus not unlike the ones used by investors today.

The following paragraph, taken from this tract shows clearly that Lord Baltimore was aware of William Clairborne's trading post on Kent Island; however, he does not mention the problems he was having with this Virginia trader.

" … It happened the last yeere, that some of the Sasquehanocks and the Wiscomesses (who are enemies) met at the Island of Monoponson, where Captain Cleyburne liveth, they all came to trade, and one of the Sasquehanocks did an Injury to a Wiscomesse, whereat some of Cleyburnes people that saw it, did laugh. The Wicomesses seeing themseleves thus injured and despised (as they thought) went away, and lay in ambush for the returne of the Sasquehanocks, and killed five of them, onely two escaped; and then they returned againe, and killed three of Cleyburnes People, and some of his Cattle; about two months after this was done, the Wicomesses sent a messenger unto his Lordships Governor, to excuse the fact, and to offer satisfaction for the harme that was done to the English … ."

Taken from Lord Baltimore's pamphlet: A Relation of Maryland, September, 8, 1635, Chapter V, pages 33 and 34. Maryland State Archives, Huntingfield Corporation Collection, Courtesy: H. Russell Morrison, Jr.

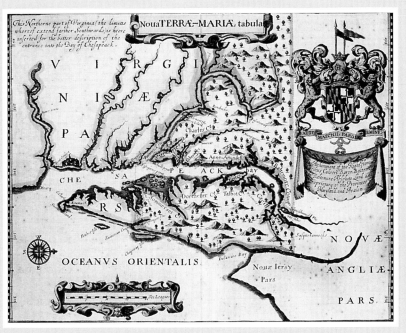

In 1671, a second edition of the Lord Baltimore map was done by John Ogilby (1600-1676). It identifies nine of Maryland counties then in existence as well as one, Cecil, which was actually established in 1674. In this map there is a clearer delineation of the small islands in the Chesapeake Bay, naming Kent as one of the counties. Ogilby has attempted to correct Maryland's northern border by adding two more rows of trees and pushing the line further north. Maryland State Archives, William T. Snyder Collection.

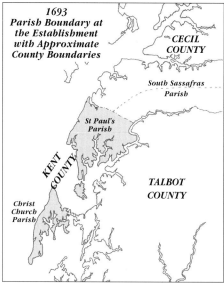

1693
Parish Boundary at
the Establishment
with Approximate
County Boundaries

The Church of England–1693

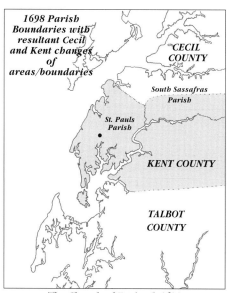

1698 Parish
Boundaries with
resultant Cecil
and Kent changes
of
areas/boundaries

The Church of England–1698

land, their subsequent changes, more often than not, reflected the needs of the local economies as they developed.

In 1668, seaports for the Chester River were recommended at Chester Point, at the bottom of Eastern Neck Island, and at Morgans Creek.[7] In the 1686 Act for the Establishment of Towns two of the towns mentioned essentially had been established already—New Yarmouth on Greys Inn Creek, Eastern Neck and Worton (Buck Neck) described as being in *"Caecil County."* Other towns to be erected were Canterbury (possibly located at the upper reaches of the Chester River) and Milford on Swan Creek.[8] The year before, another town is mentioned at the *"Forke in Chester River"* (probably Cacaway Point at the end of Broad Neck which is mentioned again later as *"Gloucester"* in the Acts of the Assembly).[9] Two other early towns are recorded on the Sassafras River at Shrewsbury Towne and at William Price's Plantation (probably Stoneton). Several other tracts on the Sassafras River were given the name *town*, but it is unlikely that they were ever more than plantations.

The earliest recorded encouragement of water mills occurs in an act of the Assembly in 1669.[10] It is likely, however, that windmills had preceded them in the low lying southern section of the County. Water mills generally require a higher elevation of ground, such as was evident in the 1694 water mill that John Biddle built for Simon Wilmer on Radcliffe Creek. Others were to follow soon thereafter and the practice would continue as mills were built and rebuilt into the twen-

tieth century. Nearly every large creek in the County boasted at least one water mill. Some, such as Morgan Creek and Prickly Pear Creek had two. Mills are mentioned frequently in the land records and often they are owned in partnership.

Another facet of the seventeenth century development of Maryland included the establishment and regulation of ordinaries. As the population was frequently on the move, inns and ordinaries were necessary for the accommodation and refreshment of travelers. Normally, an ordinary was set up near the county courthouse in order to serve the needs of the judges and others attending court. Such an establishment had existed at New Yarmouth when the courthouse was located

schools for many years. In actuality, the first settlers were Catholic, but it is frivolous to think that Baltimore believed his colony could survive with Catholic settlers alone. The goal of the Calvert Colony was to separate the authority of Church and State and create a place of religious tolerance. To a certain extent, the Calverts were successful in their efforts, even through the Puritan Revolt of the mid-seventeenth century. By the fourth quarter of the same century, however, the Anglican Bishop of London, who had been nominally in charge of religion in the colonies, began to make waves about the lack of organized religion in the Province of Maryland.

The accession of protestants William and Mary to the throne of England and their revocation of the Charter to the Lords Baltimore, brought a Royal Governor to Maryland to oversee and organize the State into something more akin to an English shire. In addition to moving the capital from St. Mary's to Annapolis in the 1690s, Governor Francis Nicholson, in 1692, instituted the first of several acts to establish the Church of England in Maryland with the formation of thirty parishes. At that time, the seat of government for Kent County was located at New Yarmouth and the County still included Kent Island. As divided, there were two parishes in Kent—Christ Church Parish on Kent Island and St. Paul's Parish in lower Kent County. While the number of parishes remained constant even after the county boundaries were changed in 1707, South Sassafras Parish (originally in Cecil County) replaced Christ Church as the second parish in Kent County. St. Paul's is the sole parish to have survived from Kent's earliest days.

A Map of Virginia, 1652, cartographed by Domina Virginia Farrer. This map shows how easily an Englishman could be misled about the Atlantic region and the country as a whole. It states that the South Sea is a ten days march from the head of the James River. The Hudson River is connected by a lake to the Sea of China. There are plenty of wild life, rabbits, bear, and even a nest of heron in a tree top. Kent Isle has been named and the Chester River, not named, is partially hidden behind a tree. Maryland State Archives, Johns Hopkins University, John Work Garrett Library.

Below: The first St. Paul's Parish Church. This conjectural floor plan with a brick tile floor is based on specifications in the vestry records of April 15, 1695. Drawing by Michael Bourne.

there, but as mentioned before, none was recorded for the 1697 Courthouse on Quaker Neck. Others were established at ferry crossings and along well traveled routes. In 1695, Daniel Toas petitioned the Assembly to be relieved of the cost of licensing for the ferry at Head of Chester (Millington) because he also had to pay for the license to operate an ordinary. The same petition mentioned that Isaac Caulk ran another ferry across the Chester, but he did not operate an ordinary (this would have been at the site of the 1697 Courthouse).

CHURCHES

The founding of Maryland as a Catholic refuge by Lord Baltimore is a myth which has been taught in Maryland

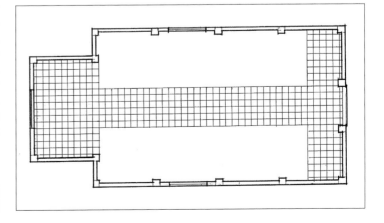

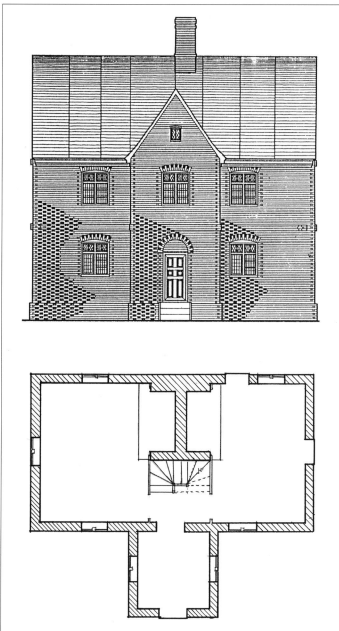

The Act of Establishment required all inhabitants of the Province to support the Church with yearly taxes. From that revenue, the clergy and buildings were maintained. In addition, more revenue was demanded each time there was a major building project or renewal. From an architectural standpoint, it was the Act of Establishment which created the groundwork for the erection of some of the most enduring buildings in the Colony.

St. Paul's Parish set about building their church on part of Arcadia, which had been sold to the vestry by one of its own, Michael Miller. The first church proposed was to be a large edifice of brick. However, this was abandoned in favor of a smaller frame building

with a brick tile floor. It is described in the vestry records of April 15, 1695:

"At a meeting of the Vestry at the House of Mr. Thos Joce at New Yarmouth for the Parish of St. Paul's on the north side Chester ... The Vestry have agreed with Mr Daniel Norris to build a Church according to the following Dimensions Viz. Forty foot long, and Twenty and four foot wide from outSide to outSide. The foundation to be raised with Brick three foot above the Ground, and upon the Brick to be Framed with good Substantial Timber Ten foot pitch above the Brick, the posts to stand Ten foot Asunder With fine Girders & five Principal Rafters, and other Timber proportionable & with following. Doors to the same, a pair of folding Doors in the Front, a Ten foot Chanal to be pav'd with tile, and a six foot Ile the length of the church to be pav'd with Tile, and from the Door to the Ile Six foot. In Consideration of Twenty one Thousand pounds of Tobacco—whereof he is paid the sum of Fifteen Thousand p.ds Five Hundred and Ninety nine."[11]

In July of 1697, the vestry again contracted with Norris to ...

"arch the Church of said Parish fit for Plastering according to Dimentions given ... To wainscot the Church round about six foot high with a Good Molding, or Balexion on top."[12]

Charles Tilden and Simon Wilmer, acting on behalf of the Vestry, continued to contract with Norris to build seats in the chancel, a black walnut communion table with drawer for the books and further specify that the wainscoting was to be of good seasoned white oak.

EARLIEST HOUSES

Simon Wilmer was one of the most prominent men in late seventeenth century Kent County. He was the County Surveyor, laid out the land for the courthouse in 1695 and recorded the plat. After marrying Rebecca Tilghman, the daughter of Dr. Richard Tilghman of the Hermitage, Wilmer received land from his in-laws and patented several tracts amounting to more than 2000 acres around present day Chestertown. He was a vestryman of St. Paul's Parish and involved in the church's construction.

Wilmer was probably responsible for the construction of what is now the back

Conjectural restoration of southwest facade, including porch tower, central chimney, casement windows and clapboard roof. Historic American Buildings Survey; 1976 drawing by Cary Carson and Chinh Hoang.

Conjectural first floor plan, c. 1695.

Opposite: Carvill Hall c. 1695 facing Fairlee Creek. All four walls were constructed in Flemish bond with glazed headers. The chimneys, windows and dormers date from the Phase II remodeling, c. 1820. Library of Congress, Historic American Buildings Survey. R. Langenbach photograph

wing of Stepney, at one point called White House. It is depicted in a late eighteenth century over mantel painting which was formerly located in the house and is now on display at Washington College.[13] (A photograph of the painting is found on the dust cover of this book.) Stepney was a four-bay, one-and-a-half-story, brick house, laid in Flemish bond with glazed headers, over a full basement. It measured 19' x 38' and had a chimney inside each gable end. The basement entrance was beneath the arch of the eastern-most chimney prior to the construction of an attached kitchen on that gable.

Wilmer's inventory, taken after his death in 1699, included two *"setts of Surveyor's Instruments"* valued at £3, *"two pair Millstones"* valued at £10, twelve slaves and *"Negro James"* who, according to the records regarding the construction of the second courthouse, had supplied the hair for the plastering of the same. James also ran Wilmer's Mill. The value of Wilmer's personal property was £584.5.10, a surprisingly modest amount for such a prominent gentleman. Wilmer was, however, the first of his generation in America and as a settler it was more important to acquire land than furnishings and other material goods. At the time of his death, he held about 4600 acres in Kent and Cecil Counties.[14]

One of the most important houses of Kent County actually was located in Cecil County at the time it was built in 1695. John Carvill, the High Sheriff of Cecil County in 1694-96 and 1699-1700, patented 26 acres of his father's land, Salters Load, in 1694. On this tract, located on the east side of Fairlee Creek, he built Carvill Hall. The name of his 26 acre patent, Carvill's Prevention, may indicate that the larger patent was going to revert to Lord Baltimore and that Carvill's settling on the tract would guarantee its retention by his family.

Carvill Hall is a two-story, three-bay house, which was constructed above a half basement. Unusual for its time, the house was built completely of brick, laid in Flemish bond with glazed headers. Its principal three-bay facade faces southwest toward the Creek and was originally distinguished by a porch tower in the central bay. The tower was tall enough to provide a room on each of the three levels. The plan of the house consisted of a hall and parlor, with porch, stair passage, and back-to-back fireplaces in the center bay. The floor systems are constructed of two girts and summer beam and the roof system of four major trusses with purlins connecting them and minor rafters laid flat wise over the purlins. At each end upbraces extend from the trusses to the purlins. The attic and supra-attic were originally lighted by windows in the gables only. Initially, the entire roof was covered with riven oak clapboard, a common roofing material of the period, but rarely seen today. The original layer of clapboards was covered with a second generation of clapboards and later by wood shingle. Both periods of clapboards survive in place and are visible from the attic.

When John Carvill died in 1709 at the age of 39 years, he left a widow, Mary, and five small children. The inventory taken of his personal belongings after his death, revealed a remarkably well-furnished house and kitchen. In the margins of the original document the appraisers included the names of the rooms: *"the inner room," "the outter room"* on the first floor with chambers on the second story and in the garret, plus *"the porch chamber"* and *"the porch garret,"* above an unfinished porch, which could either have been an open affair or a closed room with built-in benches. In addition to his personal property (valued over £1000), he owned 1600 acres.[15] His home, Carvill Hall is the most substantial and unique house to survive from the last years of the seventeenth century in Kent County.

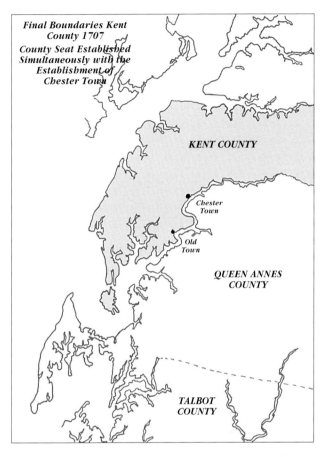

Final Boundaries Kent County 1707
County Seat Established Simultaneously with the Establishment of Chester Town

KENT COUNTY

Chester Town

Old Town

QUEEN ANNES COUNTY

TALBOT COUNTY

Similar to Carvill Hall, but one story shorter, was Wickcliffe, the Eastern Neck Island home of Joseph Wickes. Wickes was one of the first to cross the Chester River from Kent Island and settle on what would later become the southern tip of Kent County. He is another example of a first generation Kent County gentleman who acquired significant land holdings during his lifetime. Wickes was a burgess, justice, and sheriff, as well as a merchant. The last of these professions is evident from his inventory, recorded by Hans Hanson and Thomas Smyth in February of 1692/93. Like John Carvill's inventory, taken after his death in 1709, the items were listed room-by-room,

providing some clues to the size and plan of his house. These room designations, *"Inner Room, Little Chamber, Great Chamber, Outer Room and Store House"* indicate Wickcliffe was a hall-parlor house, most likely one-and-a-half or two stories in height. The sixteen-page inventory of Wickes' personal property included such luxuries as curtains and a lengthy list of books. All in all, his belongings totaled nearly £1100.[16] It is uncertain as to how long Wickcliffe survived.

1. For a concise history of the Claiborne/Lord Baltimore conflict, read R. C. Hammett's History of St. Mary's County, Maryland.
2. Maryland Archives, Vol. I, January 1637/38 (Act for Government of Isle of Kent)
3. Maryland Archives, Vol. XXVI, p. 621.
4. Maryland Archives, Vol. XIX, pp. 212, 214.
5. Maryland Archives, Vol. XXII, p. 102.
6. Maryland Archives, Vol. XXVI, p. 636.
7. Maryland Archives, Vol. II, p. 31.
8. Maryland Archives, Vol. VIII, pp. 500-502.
9. Maryland Archives, Vol. VII, p. 609.
10. Maryland Archives, Vol. II, p. 199.
11. Vestry Records of St. Paul's Parish, Kent County.
12. Ibid.
13. For further details regarding the overmantel, see "A View of Chestertown from the White House Farm," by Robert Jansen La-Palme, Maryland Historical Magazine, Vol. 88, pp. 38-511, 1993.
14. Inventories: Lib. 21, fol. 76.
15. Inventories: Box 2, folder 66 (original).
16. Inventories: Box 1, folder 30 (original).

WICKLIFFE

MAJ. JOSEPH WICKES, WHO SETTLED ON EASTERN NECK ISLAND C. 1658, WAS CHIEF JUSTICE OF KENT COUNTY. BEFORE 1674 THE COURT MET AT WICKLIFFE, HIS HOME HERE (NO LONGER STANDING.) BY 1680 HE HAD ACQUIRED 864 ACRES. THE SOUTHERN HALF OF THE ISLAND, WHICH HE HELD UNTIL HIS DEATH IN 1692. HIS GREAT-GRANDSON CAPT. LAMBERT WICKES, WHO SPENT HIS EARLY YEARS HERE, SERVED WITH DISTINCTION IN THE CONTINENTAL NAVY, WAS LOST AT SEA WITH HIS SLOOP-OF-WAR REPRISAL OCT. 1, 1777.

CAPTAIN LAMBERT WICKES FOUNDATION
AND
MARYLAND HISTORICAL SOCIETY

Stepney

Chestertown
c. 1690

IN 1659 PETER BOVERY, MARINER, WAS granted 500 acres on the west side of the Chester River adjoining the lands of Mark Pensax (Radcliffe Cross).[1] The grant extended from Radcliffe Creek to beyond Barroll Bight along the river and included lands later taken up by both Chestertown and the Kent Free School. The land escheated to the Proprietor and was later (1666) re-patented to Mary Bateman.[2]

In the 1728 deed for the Kent Free School land there is reference that Mary Bateman sold her land to Richard Perry who later sold it to Mary Tilghman, widow of Dr. Richard Tilghman (d. c. 1675).[3] Mary Tilghman sold the 500 acre tract to Simon Wilmer, who had married her daughter Rebecca. This deed, however, was not recorded. In 1688 Mary Tilghman also transferred her adjoining 1000 acres called Tilghman and Foxley Grove (Patented 1675), to Simon and Rebecca Wilmer.[4]

Simon Wilmer originally came to the Patuxent area of Maryland in 1678 or 1679. By 1680 he was in the area which was to become Kent County where 500 acres, located adjacent to Tilghmans & Foxley Grove, was patented to him under the name Wilmer's Farm. He continued acquiring and selling land for the next fifteen years and became involved in many aspects of seventeenth century colonial life. He was burgess from Kent County between 1689-1699, served as surveyor of Kent County in 1694 and assisted in laying out the boundary between the newly established parishes of the county. Wilmer also served as one of the first vestrymen for St. Paul's Parish. He died in Kent County in September of 1699 and was buried at the Hermitage the home of his brother-in-law in Queen Anne's County.[5]

Simon and Rebecca Wilmer (d. 1725) may have built the one-and-a-half-story brick house (19' x 38') now forming the back section of the present house. From the remaining evidence, it can be conjectured that the walls were laid originally in Flemish bond with glazed headers above an English bond basement. Due to the lack of original fabric, the initial kitchen situation is uncertain. It was either located in the basement or in a detached structure. Eventually a new kitchen was built on

the east gable of the house. The unusual feature about the later kitchen is that it had a full basement at a period when most kitchens were built with a dirt or brick floor close to grade. From additional information in the basement it appears that the space was divided into two nearly equal spaces with chimneys at both ends. The arch support on the east end continued through the wall in such a way as to suggest there was a bulkhead predating the kitchen, just as was done at the Adventure near Sassafras.

The first alteration to the building appears to be the addition of the aforementioned kitchen on the east, a 19' x 19' structure which appears in the 1783 Tax Assess-

Three periods of building are represented in this view. The oldest being the Flemish bond area around the third window from the right and just right of the screened porch. The family cemetery was formerly located south of the house. Tyler Campbell photograph, 1996

A 1720 resurvey of Stepney for Simon Wilmer II, including 200 acres more than the original 1659 patent. Survey by Charles Hynson, Deputy Surveyor for Kent County.

Opposite: Detail of Flemish bond with glazed headers of the first Phase of the buildings history. C. Engstrom, photograph, 1977.

Stepney. The east facade showing the results of the c. 1928 remodeling of the third floor. C. Engstrom photograph, 1977.

Stepney. First floor plan with periods of construction clearly marked. Only dendrochronology could pinpoint the construction of Phase I. Drawing by Michael Bourne.

Opposite: The stair in the newer part of the house, extending to the third floor. An unusually wide hall. C. Engstrom photograph, 1977

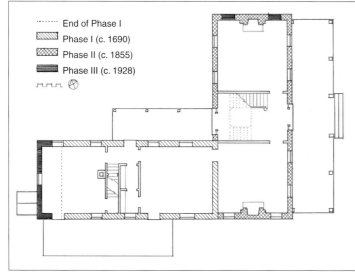

-------- End of Phase I

Phase I (c. 1690)

Phase II (c. 1855)

Phase III (c. 1928)

ment and on an overmantel painting originally painted of the house in the 1790s and now at Washington College.[6]

Simon Wilmer II acquired most of Stepney after his father's death. When the county was resurveyed in 1706, he was responsible for the laying out of *Chester Town*, the new county seat, which was situated on his own land. Soon after, he began to sell lots. Simon Wilmer II also continued to operate the grist mill which he had inherited from his father and near the grist mill established a saw mill.[7] He is most likely responsible for the construction of the brick Miller's House mentioned in his will and which will be discussed later. In 1737, Simon II left specific farms to his sons William, Lambert and Charles and lots in town to his daughters Dorcas, Mary and Mar-

garet, but to Simon III, he left *"all the rest & residue of my lands, houses and improvements,"* ie. Stepney.[8]

Apparently, Simon III moved to the Sassafras River on a farm now called Shorewood. Lambert, his brother, owned Stepney in 1750, when his will was written. Lambert bequeathed Stepney to his son Simon IV,[9] who is recorded as owner of the farm and mill in 1783, when the Tax Assessment was recorded. Simon IV, son of Lambert owned 123 acres of Tilghman and Foxley Grove and 127 acres of Stepney in that assessment. There were eight whites and two blacks living on the farms. The buildings are briefly described as *"two brick dwelling houses and kitchens, one grist mill, 7 out Houses, two orchards—joining Chestertown."*[10]

Simon IV was a contributor to the founding of Washington College and holder of Pew No. 19 at the Chapel of Ease of Chester Parish in Chestertown. His first wife was Ann Ringgold and his second, Mary Dunn. When Simon IV wrote his will in 1794, he bequeathed *"the land on which I now dwell with the houses and improvements ... ."* to his son James. To his second son Simon V, be bequeathed land extending from the *"lot sold to the trustees of the poor at the foot of Stoney Hill"* (opposite Chester Cemetery) to and including the Grist Mill. His son William H. Wilmer received the land bordering the Grist Mill on the opposite side of the road from Simon's bequest. John Ringgold Wilmer's bequest adjoined that of William and the College lands. Peregrine, his seven year old son, received a parcel of land between those of James and William and daughter Ann received a *"lot adjoining the Methodist meeting House, now in occupation of Thomas Worrell ... ."* (at the end

James F. Gordon and his wife Sarah Marie were responsible for constructing the three story, five-bay long brick structure on the east side of the old house. Its exterior was severely simple with a full length porch on its east facade. When constructed, the house had a low-pitched hip roof, with monitor in the center similar to Middle Plantation. In form it was also like Fairfield. Judging from the photograph taken around the turn-of-the-century, the old rear wing was raised to two full stories, but built of frame. On the west end of the old building a three-bay, one-and-a-half story, frame wing was constructed, probably housing a kitchen and pantry.

The interior of the *new* house was quite simple, with large proportions. The stairhall was nearly twelve feet wide having a continuous railing from the carved newel post to the third floor. Its painted, tapered balusters were identical to those at Radcliffe Cross, but the latter are of natural tiger maple. When constructed, the north parlor had six windows, but two flanking the fireplace were later bricked up.

James F. Gordon had, like his father, been Clerk of the Court (1851-56) for Kent County. Before selling the property in 1862 to his brother-in-law, he and his family had moved to Howard County.[17] James B. Ricaud, his brother-in-law, was Judge of the Circuit Court of this district and intimately involved with affairs of the area, including Washington College. He and his family lived at the *White House Farm* until his death in 1866, after which time it descended to his second wife, Cornelia, and later to his daughter Mary Rebecca Walker, wife of William S. Walker.[18]

William Walker was the son of John W. and Elizabeth Constable Walker, born in 1832. He attended Washington College and Princeton and returned to farm. In 1884 he was elected judge of the Orphans Court. He was very active in the Episcopal Church and was on the board of Visitors and Governors of Washington College.

In fulfillment of James B. Ricaud's will, after the death of Mary R. Walker, his farm Stepney was to go to his granddaughter Anna Walker, who was later to marry Walter H. Beck of St. Louis, MO. Both mother and daughter, however, joined in a deed in 1909, transferring Stepney to Walter Wright for nearly $5,000 less than Judge Ricaud had paid for it in 1862.[19]

Walter and Joanna Wright lived at Stepney until 1924 when they sold the farm to Frank H. Worrell of Swarthmore, Pennsylvania,[20] who subsequently sold it to Thomas W. Spranklin in 1928.[21] In 1928 and 1936, the Spranklins sold off several parcels along the water for an oil company, the National Guard Armory, and the sewage treatment plant.

Perhaps it was the income from the sale of the waterfront that enabled the Spranklins to undertake the most ambitious remodeling of Stepney since that of James F. Gordon in the 1850s. Their remodeling included remov-

of Princess St.). He even made provisions for an unborn child, which as it turned out, was Lemuel.[11]

When Simon's inventory was listed in 1798 the appraisers were the same as for the estate of Emory Sudler, his neighbor at Radcliffe Cross: John Rowles and Joseph Garnett. The estate inventory included eleven slaves and eighteen horses and the total value was over £1525. Simon V and James were the executors of his estate.[12]

In 1801 James Wilmer and his wife Ann, who had moved to Queen Anne's County, sold the home place to Thomas Worrell. It is not known by the author whether Thomas Worrell's wife, Ann, was a Wilmer. If not, their seven year ownership of Stepney would be the only break in family ownership for many years.[13]

The Rev. Simon Wilmer V purchased Stepney from Thomas Worrell in 1808, then sold it in 1818 to his youngest brother Lemuel.[14] Lemuel sold the home as well as the lot left him by his father in 1822 to his second cousin Mary Frisby Gordon, the wife of Joseph N. Gordon (daughter of James and Ann Frisby of the Violet Farm; her great grandfather was Simon II).[15]

Joseph Nicholson Gordon is referred to as *"Dr. Gordon"* in the account of the Battle of Caulk's Field. He was the Clerk of the Court between 1822-1845. In the Tax Assessment for 1841, Gordon is listed as residing at the Nicholson House on Queen Street. In that same year, he and his wife Mary sold Stepney to their son, James Frisby Gordon, who had resided there as early as 1841. In this deed Stepney is referred to as *"commonly called White House."*[16] The Tax Assessment mistakenly records James' personal property in the town instead of in the Second Election District.

ing the third story and replacing the whole with a bold gambrel roof giving more headroom to the third floor rooms. On the back section, the one-and-a-half story frame wing, which appears in the early photograph, was removed. The west gable of the old house was demolished and a six foot extension was added. At the same time, its second story was reconstructed of old brick, producing a more typical antebellum appearance than had been produced seventy-five years earlier. A porch was built across part of the south facade. Its new plan then consisted of a kitchen and dining room, with pantry and back stair between.

Sarah Spranklin, in 1936, sold the farm three years after the death of her husband Thomas.[22] Margaret R. Massey, a nurse for the County Health Department, owned the farm for ten years, during the same period she owned the Harris House on High Street. Between 1946 and 1953, Stepney was owned by John and Lois Jones, from New York and later Detroit.[23] In 1953 Arthur and Esther Lusby purchased the farm and established a trotting track, which remains in use today.[24]   K-85

1. Patents, Lib. 4, fol. 472.
2. Patents, Lib. 10, fol. 198.
3. Land Records, Lib. JS 10, fol. 267.
4. Land Records, Lib. C, fol. 125.
5. Skirven, Percy, Seven Pioneers of the Colonial Eastern Shore, Maryland Historical Magazine Vol. Page 414, 19 .
6. Janson-LaPalme, Robert J. H., A View of Chestertown from the White House Farm, Maryland historical Magazine, Vol. 88, 1993, P. 38-51. Mr. Janson-LaPalme's article illustrates and documents the house and the painting which originally was an overmantel in one of the rooms. The painting depicts not only the house and its smaller kitchen wing, but also a bee-hive oven on the kitchen gable covered by a shed.
7. When Rebecca Wilmer died in 1725 it was stipulated in her will that her "Negro man James" 'keep' the mill for two years for Simon II's use, as well as the use of her brother Richard Tilghman. Tilghman had bought a half interest in the mill in 1709. James was to be set free after his two years of service at the mill. Simon II was executor of his mother's will.
8. Wills, Lib. 2, fol. 58.
9. Wills, Lib. 3, fol. 137.
10. 1783 Tax Assessment, Worton and Chester Hundred.
11. Wills, Lib. 7, fol. 608.
12. Inventories, Lib. 11, fol. 50.
13. Land Records, Lib. TW 1, fol. 514.
14. Land Records, Lib. BC 5, fol. 293; Land Records, Lib. WS 2, fol. 268.
15. Land Records, Lib. TW 4, fol. 166.
16. Land Records, Lib. JNG 12, fol. 252. Joseph N. Gordon was buried in the family graveyard south of the house. None of the markers remain, but three stones were retrieved from the creek in recent years, one being that of Joseph N. Gordon who died at age 73 years in 1848.
17. Land Records, Lib. JKH 3, fol. 215.
18. Wills, Lib. JB 1, fol. 334; Lib. JF 1, fol. 354.
19. Land Records, Lib. JTD 19, fol. 575.
20. Land Records, Lib. RRA 2, fol. 640.
21. Land Records, Lib. RAS 3, fol. 346.
22. Land Records, Lib. RAS 15, fol. 512.
23. Land Records, Lib. RAS 40, fol. 205.
24. Land Records, Lib. WHG 29, fol. 162.

Wickcliffe Site

Eastern Neck Island
1659

O NCE THE LAND ON KENT ISLAND WAS ALLOCATED TO THE new population, early English settlers had to find land on the mainland or smaller islands in the Bay to inhabit. Closest in proximity, Eastern Neck Island was a likely choice, as it lay just to the north. Wickcliffe was the first tract patented there in 1659. It was held jointly by Joseph Wickes and Thomas Hynson, who together continued to acquire more land until they owned the island in it's entirety. In 1680, after Hynson's death, Eastern Neck Island was divided between the two families, with the southern half remaining in possession of Joseph Wickes. There he built his home and while the house is gone today, the site of Wickliffe is one of the most valuable historical archeological sites in the county.

Within a year of arriving in Maryland in 1650, Major Joseph Wickes was appointed Judge of the County Court, a position which he held for the next five years. Chosen as a burgess for Kent County in 1658, he continued to hold public office in various positions throughout the

The "New Frame House" mentioned in the 1852 Tax Assessment. Horace Loller Collection, c. 1930.

Conjectural floor plan based upon inventory of Joseph Wickes (d. 1692). Rooms mentioned include "Inner Room, Outter Room, Little Chamber, Great Chamber." The kitchen was not named, but its presence is assumed from the concentration of contents after the "Outter Room." Drawing by Michael Bourne.

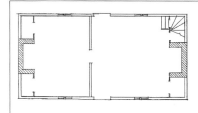
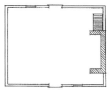

next thirty years.[1] From the southeastern tip of his farm there was a custom check point for all vessels entering or leaving the Chester River.

The house which Joseph Wickes first built was probably a one-and-a-half-story dwelling. From the inventory of his estate taken after his death, the picture becomes a bit clearer, as the items are listed by room. Those rooms included:

"Inner Room, Little Chamber, Great Chamber, Outer Room and Store House"

Apparently the scribe who recorded the inventory in the county records omitted *kitchen* from his notation. It is obvious, however, from the list of contents that a kitchen would have existed.

The curious entry *"Chest stands on the stairs"* may indicate either a wide corner stair or the presence of a stair tower or some other atypical arrangement. Other items of interest in the inventory include many tools and guns which were listed, as in the *storehouse*. Also, two entire pages of the inventory listed books, mostly pertaining to religion. All four of the first floor windows were listed as fitted with curtains, a rare commodity in the new settlement. On Wickcliffe, nine slaves and a *"man to serve four years"* were listed as well. The inventory, as appraised by Thomas Smyth and Hans Hanson, totaled £1092.16.10.[2]

Joseph Wickes was an extraordinary person who amassed a fortune while aiding in the development of the Eastern Shore. He began a dynasty of men eager and able to serve their colony and state.

Upon his death, Wickcliffe was divided between his two sons, Joseph and Samuel. Samuel took the western half of the farm on which his father had built the house mentioned in the will. This farm remained in Samuel's possession, then passed to Samuel, Jr., Samuel III and then eventually to William. By 1852, it was listed in the estate of Col. William Wickes from which it passed to James Page Wickes and his wife, Charlotte A. Spencer. In the 1852 Tax Assessment there were 375 acres remaining in the farm and a *"New Frame House & other Buildings in good repair."*[3]

The farm remained in the Wickes family until 1902, after which it was purchased by James W. Stevens. During the latter's ownership the house was occupied by the Loller family. Mr. Horace Loller recalls that there was a wing behind the left half of the house in the photograph, which might have been earlier than the front. The house was demolished in 1935 to make way for a caretaker's residence for J. Edward Johnston, who built a large gunning lodge to the south.   K-274

1. Papenfuse, p. 887.
2. Inventories, Original; Box 1, fldr. 30.
3. Kent County Tax Assessment, 1st District, 1852.

Cedar Point Farm Site

Eastern Neck Island
1693

CEDAR POINT FARM IS LOCATED ON THE SOUTHERN POINT OF land which extends into the Chester River from Eastern Neck Island. Part of the original Wickcliffe grant which was first patented in 1659 and resurveyed for Joseph Wickes in 1680, the farm descended first to his son, Joseph Wickes, Jr. and remained in the family for roughly another one hundred years.

In 1804, Richard B. Mitchell, a Wickes descendant, acquired the farm. In the Tax Assessment of 1852, a *"Brick House & other Buildings in Tolerable repair"* is mentioned. Mitchell did not live here, but resided at Bowlingly in Queenstown, Queen Annes County, where he was a prominent businessman.

In 1879, Cedar Point Farm was purchased by Benjamin Sappington, whose wife, Frances, was a Wickes. It remained in that family until 1928 when it became known as Cedar Point, Inc.

The house mentioned in the 1852 Tax Assessment was replaced by a large frame building which was demolished in 1933 by the owner of the Cedar Point Gunning Club. It remained a private gunning club until the early 1960s, when it, along with the remainder of the island was acquired by the United States Government as a nature preserve.   K-509

Cedar Point House, west elevation. This c. 1880 house replaced the brick house mentioned in the 1852 Tax Assessment. Probably built by Benjamin and Frances Wickes Sappington. This is the site of the Historical marker honoring members of the Wickes family.

Cedar Point is located on that part of Wickliffe which was devised to Joseph Wickes II in 1692. This c. 1880 frame house replaces an earlier building which stood on the property. Annette Sappington Spencer Collection.

Cecil Quaker Meeting House Site

Near Lynch
1694

THE SITE OF CECIL QUAKER MEETING HOUSE IS LOCATED about one half mile west of Lynch on Route 298. The original graveyard remains and is surrounded by a white wooden fence, but there are no traces of the building which once shared the site.

According to Kenneth Carroll in his book entitled Quakerism on the Eastern Shore, construction of the original brick meeting house was begun in 1694 and the first meeting held there in 1698. Its form has been thought to have been a plain rectangular structure approximately 20' x 40' with a relatively steep pitched roof. From the old photo in the collection of the Kent News, it was built on a brick foundation with a water table and the facade was laid in Flemish bond. The visible gable in the photograph is laid in common bond. The photograph also indicates that the Flemish bond facade was undisturbed only to the left of the first window. The remainder of the facade appears to have been laid in common bond with a row of headers every seventh course. Moreover, the windows and door have exposed

Cecil Friends Meeting House stood near the village of Lynch. Its name is derived from the fact that it was constructed in 1694 when this part of Kent was still part of Cecil County. Kent County News photograph from a glass negative, c. 1910.

wood lintels; a feature not consistent with seventeenth or eighteenth century building practices.

The photograph also suggests some building history that has not yet been recorded. The facade appears to have been reconstructed between the two bays, since a large patch is laid in common bond rather than the undisturbed Flemish bond between the windows and the corners of the structure. Wood lintels over the windows and door suggest a second quarter of the nineteenth century date for the remodeling.

Quaker meeting houses of the Eastern Shore have had their times of prosperity and times of neglect. Cecil Meeting is perhaps similar to Third Haven in that they both were periodically neglected due to lack of attendance. This caused the buildings to deteriorate, and then to be rebuilt. The lack of care at Third Haven caused so much deterioration to the original back wing that it was rebuilt in 1797. At Cecil Meeting the damage from neglect appears to have been confined to the center of the building. The exact date of rebuilding will be left to Quaker historians.

In the photograph there is a window in the gable indicating there was a space on the second floor. At Third Haven, that space was finished with plaster and had built-in benches around the room. It is said that traveling Quakers often stayed over in that area and the benches were used as beds. Perhaps the same accommodations were available at Cecil Meeting.

Cecil Monthly Meeting was the principal place of worship for Quakers of Kent County, although other meeting houses were built at Quaker Neck in 1700, Head of Swantown Creek (east of Galena) in the 1760s and Head of Chester (Millington) in 1784, none of which remains.

If the deed to the property was recorded, it would be in the Cecil County records; however, there must have been questioning officials in mid-eighteenth century Kent County because Joseph Warner entered into a deed of gift of three and one half acres to George Rasin and Thomas Bowers, two people of the Cecil Quaker Meeting, stating:

"Whereas my Grandfather George Warner gave and laid out a parcel of ground for the people called Quakers ... and the title to the said land may be precarious ... ."

The deed was dated 26 May 1755.[1]   K-135

---

1. Land Records, Lib. 7, fol. 556.

Carvill Hall

Near Fairlee
c. 1695

WITHIN THE DEVELOPMENT OF GREAT OAK ESTATES on the shores of Fairlee Creek stands the oldest documented surviving residence in Kent County. Carvill Hall was built on a tract called Carvill's Prevention soon after it was patented to John Carvill in 1694.[1]

The original land grant was an 800 acre tract called Packerton laid out in 1658 for Edward Packer.[2] After his death, the property escheated to the Proprietor, who gave it to William Boarman in 1681 in recognition of his services to the Province. Boarman assigned it to Thomas Carvill, a planter of St. Mary's County who had it re-

patented in 1682 under the new name of Salter's Load, the name of his home town in Norfolk.[3]

In 1694 twenty six acres of the tract were re-patented for John Carvill, the son of Thomas, five years after he had married Mary Phillips of Harford County.

John Carvill was a very prominent citizen of the area serving initially as a burgess from St. Mary's County (1692) and later in the same capacity from Cecil County (1698-99).[4] Between 1694-96 and again 1699-1700 he was High Sheriff of Cecil County,[5]

Carvill Hall, constructed c. 1695 on Carvill's Prevention by John Carvill I (d. 1709), with later alterations and additions. Tyler Campbell photograph, 1996.

one of the most lucrative and powerful local appointments. He refused the position in 1702.[6] He was elected to the General Assembly in 1708, a year after his home plantation became part of Kent County.[7] In the same year he was also appointed to a commission to *"erect a port and town in Kent County at Chester Ferry at or near the place where the old Courthouse stood."*[8] He was to serve on the vestry of St. Paul's Church prior to his death in 1709. After his death, an inventory of his personal estate was appraised for £932, a considerable sum when added to the nearly two-thousand acres of land in his possession.[9] One of the most revealing notations in his inventory was room names written in the margins of the document. These names have enabled the building to be dated prior to 1709 as they nearly correspond to the existing building.

As constructed, the house consisted of the main two-and-a-half-story block of the existing structure plus a porch tower in the center of the creek facade and a detached kitchen, located about twenty feet to the south east. The entire structure was constructed of Flemish bond brick with glazed headers above the stepped water table. There were string courses at second and third floor levels, and only one chimney located in the center of the building, indicating the division of the interior spaces. All windows were fit with casements. The floor plan consisted of an *inner room,* an *outer room* heated by large back-to-back fireplaces, and an entry porch and stair passage. The second and third floor plans included the *porch chamber* and *porch garrett*[10] in addition to the inner and outer chambers and garretts. Noteworthy too, is the use of summer beams and girts in the construction of the floor systems as well as the roof structure. It is composed of four major rafters with purlins at third floor ceiling level which are braced at the outer walls, all of which are expressed in the garrett rooms. Minor rafters were attached to the outer surfaces of the purlins and riven oak clapboard was nailed thereto. Apparently, there were two coverings of clapboards before shingles were installed later. The roof construction techniques are similar to the original Holly Hill roof in southern Anne Arundel County, which dates from about 1689.

At some time during the eighteenth century, a one-and-a-half-story addition was built to connect the main house and kitchen. The outline of the steeply pitched roof is still visible in the attic over the present kitchen. This was probably undertaken by John Carvill II, who was a minor when his father died.

After the death of John Carvill I, his widow married Richard Smithers (d. 1730). Together they handled the Carvill estate, including maintaining Thomas Carvill un-

Carvill Hall, central stairhall, occupying the space of the original back-to-back fireplaces, stair and cross passage. Historic American Buildings Survey photograph, 1972.

Carvill Hall's creek side (southwest). The porch tower was located in the central bay, between the ends of the belt course. Library of Congress, Historic American Buildings Survey, 1972

Carvill Hall. Floor plan, 1972, with indications of former tower and central chimney (Phase I) and clear indications of early nineteenth century chimneys and partitions flanking the contemporary stair (Phase II). Historic American Buildings Survey; 1976 drawing by Cynthia Hamilton and Chinh Hoang.

Carvill Hall. Northeast elevation with clear indications of original window and door positions. Historic American Buildings Survey, 1976.

Ground Plan

East Elevation

til his death in 1719. After Mary Carvill Smithers died in 1738, John Carvill II became sole owner of Salters Load. He established a grist and saw mill at the headwaters of Fairlee Creek and patented Carvill's Adventure in 1750, a tract between Salters Load and Howell's. This acquisition joined the tracts his father had acquired before his death in 1709. John Carvill II is referred to as Captain in the settlement of his estate in 1773. The title may refer to a position in the local militia or to the command of a ship. Part of his estate included a schooner called Swallow. Ann Carvill administratrix, advertised it for sale in the Maryland Gazette stating that *" … she was built under the eye of the late Mr. Carvill … ."*[11]

Unhappily for John Carvill II, his son, John III, predeceased him by two years, but after he and his wife, Ann Ringgold had children of their own. John Carvill IV inherited Carvill Hall after he came of age, which was after 1783. In that year the property was still listed in the name of Ann (Ringgold Carvill), his mother.[12]

John Carvill IV married Sarah Ward and had three children to survive childhood. He died in 1806 after living at the Smith Ringgold House in Chestertown. His property was divided in 1825 between his children, John W., Henry Ward and Caroline M. Carvill.[13] John

Roof structure which indicates location of original chimney, between ends of riven oak clapboard. Historic American Buildings Survey photograph, 1972.

Carvill Hall. Section through building indicating existing conditions (1972) and original framing, roof covering and place of central chimney, basement and roof. Note diagonal bracing. Historic American Buildings Survey; 1976 drawing by Cynthia Hamilton and Chinh Hoang.

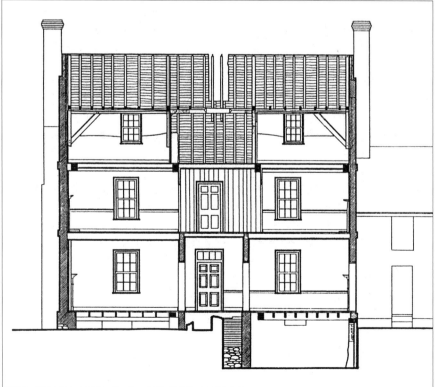

Carvill V inherited 518 acres of Salters Load, including the old house, where he lived. He died in 1828, a bachelor and bequeathed it to his brother Henry Ward Carvill,[14] who had been given the Mill and the property between it and the village of Fairlee (Belaire).

Between the death of John Carvill IV in 1806 and the division of the land between his heirs in 1825, the house underwent major remodeling by his widow Sarah. The one hundred year old house needed repair. The remodeling consisted of the demolition of the porch tower and chimney, enlargement of the windows and changing the plan to the quintessential Kent County farmhouse: a central stair hall with one room on each side. Without the central chimney it was necessary to construct end chimneys on the outside of both gables. But, this placement took away the light from the attic rooms which had windows on the gables. Consequently, dormers were added to both sides of the roof to supply light and air.

Henry Ward Carvill inherited the house as it had been altered, but it is unlikely that he lived there. He retained the farm until 1860, when he sold it and built a new house closer to Chestertown now known as Brampton.[15]

Carvill sold the farm to a non-family member, Edward Comegys, the elderly bachelor who resided at Comegys Bight. Comegys also owned Big Fairlee on the southern side of Fairlee Creek, along with several other farms. When he died in 1866, Carvill Hall was purchased by his niece and heir, Ann Rebecca Curry.[16] It later belonged to J. Ford Dorrance, who sold it in 1922 to Hynson Rogers, a Chestertown attorney.[17] Rogers sold the farm in 1938 to Russell Grace D'Oench, heir of the Grace Line, who built Great Oak Manor house on the adjoining property the year before.[18] Ten years later D'Oench sold his entire property to Frank Russell, the founder of Rusco Windows.[19] Russell created Great Oak Club overlooking the mouth of Fairlee Creek and the Bay and subdivided the waterfront into building lots.

Carvill Hall was included on Lot No. 5 of the subdivision and was sold in 1961 to Ward and Virginia Tanzer who made it their weekend home.[20] Since the Tanzer ownership there have been three owners of Carvill Hall, each owner making alterations and additions to the old house. During the ownership of Mr. and Mrs. Braden Kane, the house was thoroughly documented and placed on the National Register of Historic Places.[21] K-241

1. Patents, Lib. B 23, fol. 149-50.
2. Rent Rolls, Lib. I No. 5, fol. 5.
3. Patents, Lib. CB 3, fol. 90, 91. Salters Load included the same acreage that originally had been patented to Edward Packerton in 1659, named Packerton. The first bounded tree of the survey was a "Great Oake" that stood in the ravine near the present Great Oak Landing. This tree was also the beginning point of Great Oak Manor and that from whence the name was derived.
4. Papenfuse, p. 202.
5. Archives of Maryland, Vol. XX, p. 77, 111, 488; and Papenfuse, Ibid.
6. Archives of Maryland, Vol. XXV, p. 125.
7. Archives of Maryland, Vol. XXVII, p. 209.
8. Ibid., p. 347. This location has been identified as near Quaker Neck Landing.
9. Inventories, Lib. 1, fol. 27.
10. Ibid.
11. Maryland Gazette, 13 May 1773.
12. 1783 Tax Assessment, Lower Langford Bay Hundred. The tax assessment does not mention whites living on Salters Load possibly indicating that Ann Carvill was living in Chestertown (Lot No. 98 was owned by the Carvills between 1737 and 1794) or at the Plains, the farm she inherited from her father in 1780.
13. Land Records, Lib. TW 4, fol. 619.
14. Wills, Lib. 11, fol. 80.
15. Land Records, Lib. JKH 1, fol. 733.
16. Inventories and Sales, Lib. BFH, fol. 29. On the 1877 Atlas, the farm appears in the ownership of A. R. Denny.
17. Land Records, Lib. RRA 1, fol. 167.
18. Land Records, Lib. RAS 19, fol. 276.
19. Land Records, Lib. WHG 2, fol. 594, 597.
20. Land Records, Lib. WHG 70, fol. 37.
21. National Register Nomination Form.

Chapter 3
Colonial Kent County 1706-1783

The Eighteenth Century was a period of great development throughout the county. By 1750, Chestertown, a port of entry, had become the largest and most important town on Maryland's Eastern Shore.

THE EIGHTEENTH CENTURY IN KENT COUNTY WAS A time of continual development. Starting in the early part of the century, port towns were established usually as a result of Acts of Establishment by the General Assembly. As the century moved on and development continued, smaller towns sprang up sometimes merely as a result of two major roads intersecting. By the end of the century, Kent's population had risen from 2753 settlers in 1710 to 11,187 inhabitants in 1800. [1]

CHESTERTOWN

Spawned by an act of the Maryland General Assembly in 1706, Chestertown was actually not established until the following year. The act, entitled *"An Act for the Advancement of Trade Erecting Ports and Towns in the Province of Maryland,"* first designated its location as follows:

"In Chester river, on a plantation of Mr. Joce's between Mr. Willmore's [Wilmer's] and Edward Walvins Plantation." [2]

However, the General Assembly passed a subsequent act in April of the following year which stated:

"The place for the Town and Port by the said Act [see above] Erected upon Chester River. To be deserted. And in lieu thereof, the said Port and Town, with the Courthouse of the said County, shall be built where the commissioners have purchased land for the same ... " [3]

While this has been interpreted for many years as an actual change in location for the proposed town, it seems rather to be a more specific definition of the site, as the first description was vague at best. It is interesting to note that earlier in 1690, Thomas Joce has purchased 100 acres of Stepney which was described in the deed as *" ... in the occupation of Mr. Wilmer."* [4]

As with most Maryland counties, the histories of Kent's earliest public buildings are incomplete. Whether this is the result of fire or loss, or simply a lack of original documentation, gaps in the records exist. Such is the case with both the second and third courthouses in Kent.

The first reference to an established courthouse in Chestertown is found in the records of the court proceedings of August 1707. *"Court held at Courthouse at ye Town and Port of Chester."* [5] While this helps to pinpoint the date of its construction (between April and August of that year) and indicates the commissioners must have acted swiftly to construct the building without the usual petition to the General Assembly, it lacks any specifications for construction. The appearance of the courthouse in Chestertown in 1707 therefore can be but pure conjecture. It may have been similar to its predecessor

Kent County Courthouse prior to 1860. This sketch on the Martenet Map of Kent County probably indicates the 1720 round ended courtroom with the 1750 and/or 1798 additions. Jane Brooks Sprinkle Collection.

Queen Anne's County Courthouse, 1708. This one-room building located in Queenstown was constructed at the same time as the first courthouse in Chestertown. Maryland Historical Trust, Michael Bourne photograph, 1997.

Opposite: The past comes alive at the annual reenactment of the Chestertown Tea Party. Constance Stuart Larrabee photograph.

Kent County Jail. Sketch from Martenet Map of Kent County, 1860.

Kent County Jail, before 1883. The county petitioned the General Assembly for funds to build a jail in 1792. This is the result of that initial petition. Robert Wright Calder, Sheriff, with family, (L to R) Wright Ringgold Calder, Mollie Calder, Mrs. Calder, the Sheriff, Matilda Calder. Margaret S. Payne Collection.

at Quaker Neck Landing, with a wooden chimney. However, brick chimneys had been recommended before this time by the General Assembly. Most likely, the building resembled its contemporary in Queenstown, a plain, three-bay, one-story structure built over a full basement with one brick chimney.

The 1707 courthouse burned at the hands of an arsonist in 1719 and substantial funds were raised to erect a replacement constructed in 1720. While descriptive records are sparse, this building must have been rather substantial. It cost 55,000 pounds of tobacco, exceeding that of its predecessor at Quaker Neck Landing (1696) by nearly 47,000 pounds of tobacco, but falling short of the 70,000 pound cost of building St. Paul's Church in 1711. This suggests a building of substantial brick construction, but somewhat smaller in scale than St. Paul's.

By 1750, the 30 year old courthouse was in need of repair and another 50,000 pounds of tobacco were expended at that time. It was after this renovation that Phillip Fithian described the Kent County Courthouse as both *"elegant"* and *"grand."*

At the close of the century, the courthouse was again in need of repair and the commissioners obtained authorization from the General Assembly to spend £400. In their petition for the same, it was stated that they were in need of a place that was *"secure for records."*

Looking at the Martenet Map of 1860, the sketch shows a small building located between the Courthouse and Emmanuel Church labeled *"Registrar's Office."*

This may have been what resulted. The main courthouse as depicted in the sketch resembles St. Paul's Church with its one rounded side. This is not surprising as similarities between court, church, and residential structures were common in this period. The drawing, however, indicates a hip roof on the courthouse rather than an *A* roof as on the church.

In 1732, a bill was passed by the General Assembly which authorized various counties, including Kent, to construct jails on credit. While there are no references to the date of construction, location or appearance of a jail, a number of interesting references indicate that a

jailing facility had existed as early as the first quarter of the eighteenth century. [6] By 1773, it must have been in poor condition as a petition was read by the General Assembly to *"build a new prison and wall in a yard to the same."* [7] However, due to the poor economy and the intervening revolution, it was not until the 1790s that a replacement structure was actually built.

Another building to be erected at public expense in Chestertown was the market house in the town square (west of the courthouse square). The actual date of construction for the first market house here is unknown. However, in the Maryland Gazette of December 2, 1773 there was an advertisement for a *"Scheme of a Lottery"* which was to enable the town of Chestertown to build a market house, ferry stairs and improve the town wharf: *"The necessity of repairing the town wharf, and building ferry stairs for the convenience of the public, will be readily acknowledge ... and the ruinous condition of the Market-House, must induce every friend to the prosperity of the town or country, not only to wish, but to assist, in having it removed and a near and convenient edifice erected in its room."* [8]

Due to inclement weather and the subsequent inability to distribute tickets in a timely fashion, the lottery was delayed. It is unlikely that the market house was actually constructed before the Revolution, as the General

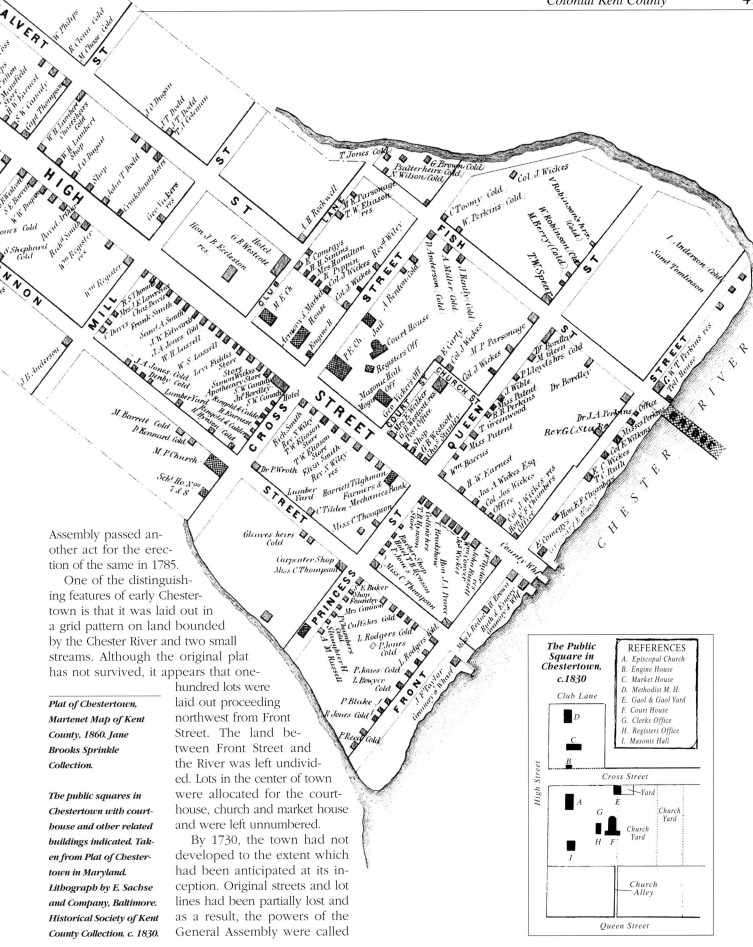

The map labels include (reading across the map):

CALVERT ST · HIGH · MILL · CANNON · CROSS STREET · COURT ST · CHURCH ST · QUEEN ST · FISH STREET · ST · STREET · PRINCESS · FRONT · CHESTER RIVER

Assembly passed another act for the erection of the same in 1785.

One of the distinguishing features of early Chestertown is that it was laid out in a grid pattern on land bounded by the Chester River and two small streams. Although the original plat has not survived, it appears that one-hundred lots were laid out proceeding northwest from Front Street. The land between Front Street and the River was left undivided. Lots in the center of town were allocated for the courthouse, church and market house and were left unnumbered.

By 1730, the town had not developed to the extent which had been anticipated at its inception. Original streets and lot lines had been partially lost and as a result, the powers of the General Assembly were called

Plat of Chestertown, Martenet Map of Kent County, 1860. Jane Brooks Sprinkle Collection.

The public squares in Chestertown with courthouse and other related buildings indicated. Taken from Plat of Chestertown in Maryland. Lithograph by E. Sachse and Company, Baltimore. Historical Society of Kent County Collection. c. 1830.

The Public Square in Chestertown, c.1830

Club Lane

High Street

Cross Street

Church Yard

Church Yard

Church Alley

Queen Street

REFERENCES

A. Episcopal Church
B. Engine House
C. Market House
D. Methodist M. H.
E. Gaol & Gaol Yard
F. Court House
G. Clerks Office
H. Registers Office
I. Masonis Hall

upon to rectify the situation. What ensued was entitled *"An Act, for laying out the Town a-new, commonly called Chester Town, in Kent County; and for ascertaining the Bounds thereof."*

And Whereas, it is represented to this General Assembly, That the said Town is very commodious for Trade, and several People desirous to settle in the same, could they but be well secured in their Lots; And there being no Provision made by any Act in Force, for the taking up, and building on Lots in the same Place, within a certain Time … That James Harris, Esq; Mr. Philip Kennard, Mr. George Wilson, Capt. Ebenezer Blackistone, Mr. James Caulder, Mr. John Gresham, and Mr. William Frisby, or the major Part of them, be and are hereby appointed Commissioners; and are by Virtue of this Act, authorized and empowered to survey and lay

out the One Hundred Acres of Land formerly laid out for a Town, on Chester River, in Kent County, by the name of Chester Town, and commonly called New Town, as agreeable as conveniently may be the original Plat and Survey thereof, when first laid out for a Town … "[9]

Due to a lack of original record in some of the earliest property transfers in Chestertown, in conjunction with the above sited act, subsequent transfers required not only the signature of the seller, but also that of Simon Wilmer II (original owner of the town lots) in order for the purchaser to gain clear title to his land. This was the case with the White Swan Tavern when John Lovegrove joined with Simon Wilmer to transfer Lot No. 76 to Joseph Nicholson in 1733.

In 1732, an act passed by the General Assembly required swine, sheep and geese to be penned in or kept beyond the limits of town. While this paints a rather dim picture of living conditions in Chestertown prior to this time, it also implies an effort to make the town

A PLOT OF CHESTER TOWN, IN MARYLAND.

REFERENCES

A Episcopal Church
B Engine House
C Market House
D Methodist M.H.
E Gaol & Gaol Yard
F Court House
G Clerks Office
H Registers Office
I Masonic Hall

AREA OF TOWN PLOT—100 ACRES.

BY A SCALE OF 10 PERCHES TO AN INCH.

Latitude, 39° 13' North.
Longitude, 0° 57' West of Philadelphia.
Longitude, 0° 61' East of Washington City.
Longitude, 76° 6' West of Greenwich.

A CERTIFICATE OF CHESTER TOWN PLOT.

Beginning at a bounded Locust Post, standing at the Westernmost corner of the beginning of the North-East line of Front street, and running thence for the Town Lots, as follows:—

NUMBERS OF THE LOTS.	COURSE.	DISTANCE.			PERCHES.
		Perches.	Feet.	Inches.	
1 { From Station No. 1,	S. E.	6			Station 1, S. E. & W. 6 Perches to the Post.
Station No. 3,	West	13			Station 4, N. E. 14 Perches.
Station No. 5,	S. E.	2			to the beginning of Front line from thence.
2 { From Station No. 1,	N. W.	2			Station 2, S. W., 14.
Station No. 3,	N. W.	11			Station 4, N. E., 12.
Station No. 5,	S. E.	11			Station 6, N. W. 4, to the post at the entrance
3 { From Station No. 1,	N. W.	12			No. 2, N. E. 6, W. 14.
Station No. 3,	N. E.	4			No. 4, S. E. 11, to beginning.

THE CHILD LOTS.	LENGTH.			BREADTH.		
	Perches.	Feet.	Inches.	Perches.	Feet.	Inches.
4, 5, 6, 7, 8, 9, 10, 11,	11			9		
12, 13,	11			10		
14, 15, 16, 17, 18,	22	8		at each end 14	4	at N.W. end end
19,	11	4		10		
20, 21, 22, 23, 24,	11			10		
25,	15	14	6	6		
26,	12			7	14	6
27, 28, 29,	12			8		
30, 31, 32,	12			at one end 8, at the other.		
33,	12			10		
34,	15	14		6		
35,	18			7		
36, 37,	17	8	6	6		
38,	17	8	6	at one end 6, at the other.		
39,				Perpendicular.		
40, a Triangle,	15			8		
41, 42, 43,	15	8		at top, and 15 at other end.		
44,	16			7	10	6
45, 46, 47,	at top.			7	10	6
48,	17			7	10	6
49, 50,	17			8		
51, 53, 56, 57, 59, 60, 61, 62,	16			8		
52, 54, 56, 58,	17			8		
63,	16			5		
64,	17			5		
65, 66, 67, 68,	17			5		
69,	11 on top, 9 at bottom.			5		
70,	9 at bottom, 11 at top.			5		
71,	12 top, 9at bottom.			6		
72, 73, 74,	14	8	3	6		11
75, 76, 77, 78, 79,	18			6		
80, 81, 82, 83, 84, 85, 86, 87, 88, 89, 90, 91,	18			8		
92,	19 at top, and 14 at bottom.			8		
93, 94, 95, 96, 97, 98,	8	3		10		
99,	11 on top, 9 at bottom.			8		
100, Triangle,	9	12		base	Afragon decular.	
The Market Place Land,	15			13		
The Court House Land,	18			17		
The Church Land,	18			9		

ALPHABETICAL LIST OF STREETS & ALLEYS.

	Perches.	Feet.	Breadth Feet.
Calvert Street, in length	98	6	66
Cannon Street,	160		52
Church Alley,	12		8
Club Lane,	39		25
Crab Alley,	30		8
Cross Street,	87	10	66
Fish Street,	57	10	53
Front Street,	68½		60
High Street,	177		90
Kent Street,	73		50
Mill Street,	77	11	50
Princess Street,	43		60
Queen Street,	37½		52

WATER LOTS.

NUMBERS.	BREADTH.
1,	6 Perches.
2, 3, 4, 5, 6, 7,	3 "
8,	7 "
9, 10, 11, 12,	3 "
13,	4½ "
14, 15, 16,	3 "
17,	6½ "
18,	3 "
19,	3 "
20, 21, 22, 23, 24, 25,	4½ "
26,	4 "

KENT STREET   50 Feet Wide

MILL STREET   50 Feet Wide

CLUB LANE   25 Feet Wide

CROSS STREET   66 Feet Wide

PRINCESS STREET   50 Feet Wide

QUEEN STREET

FRONT STREET   60 Feet Wide

FRONT STREET   52 Feet Wide

CANNON STREET

HIGH STREET

CALVERT STREET

FISH STREET

Old Club House

Market House

Church Yard

CHESTER BRIDGE

CHESTER RIVER.

View of Chestertown waterfront from Queen Anne's County, c. 1910. Nine eighteenth century residences are shown from this angle. University of Maryland School of Architecture. Bullock Collection (formerly property of Miss Marian Weeks).

Map to Georgetown, from Martenet's Map of Kent County,

A view of Georgetown from Fredericktown, Cecil County. c. 1880 photograph.

more desirable and promote its further development. Indeed, after the 1730s, Chestertown experienced a bit of a rebirth as lots began to sell with more regularity. Water lots originally intended for commercial purposes were purchased for residential use with the wharves and warehouses basically confined to the area adjoining High Street and to the south. The growth of Chestertown continued throughout the eighteenth century, with the last known lot being purchased from Simon Wilmer IV in 1777. That lot was located at the northwest end of High Street.

NEW YARMOUTH

In its heyday, New Yarmouth was not only the center of local government (Kent's first courthouse being located there), but also an area known for ship building. A small number of references to this now vanished town remain. From 1680, a deed recording the transfer of the lot on the corner of East Street from James Ringgold to the Lord Proprietor survives. Fifteen years later, in the vestry records for St. Paul's Church a meeting of the vestry is recorded as having been held *"at the House of Mr. Thos. Joce at New Yarmouth."* Given its location on Greys Inn Creek, it is possible that when the Commissioners provided for public tobacco warehouses in 1748, the listing of Samuel Tovey's warehouses actually referred to a situation in New Yarmouth too.

SHREWSBURY TOWN

A contemporary to *Chester Town, Shrewsbury Town on the Sassafrax River* was authorized by the General Assembly in 1706 and 1707. The land for the town was purchased in 1707 from Mr. Richard Bennett.[10] Very few deeds referring to Shrewsbury Town remain. A description in a deed of 1710 places the town's location at the tip of Shrewsbury Neck (the site of present

day Kentmore Park), where the land faces west and down river.[11] The latest deed to be found which refers to Shrewsbury Towne is dated 1721 and coincides with its demise.

GEORGETOWN

As the settlement of Shrewsbury Town had not endured, the General Assembly was petitioned by inhabitants of the Sassafras area to have a town and port laid out about five miles up river at Ferry Point. The first lots sold in this area had actually been transferred three years prior to the act which authorized the creation of the town. These were sold by Gideon Pearce.

"An Act for Erecting a Town in Kent County on the South Side of Sassafras River on a Tract of Land

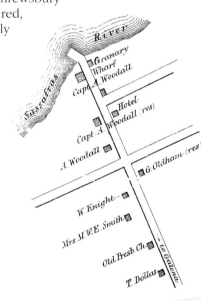

Called Tolchester at the place where the Ferry is now kept … Be it therefore Enacted by the Right Honourable the Lord Proprietary by and with the Advice and Consent of his Lordships Govenour and the upper and Lower Houses of Assembly and the Authority of the same that Captain George Wilson, Master Philip Kennard, Master Christopher Hall, Master Jervis Spencer & Master Thomas Hynson or any three of them shall be and are hereby Appointed Commissioners for Kent county aforesaid & are hereby authorized and Empowered as well to Agree for the buying and purchasing sixty Acres of Land out of a Tract aforesaid most Convenient to the said Ferry Landing not included in the Lots to be Erected with the Lots aforesaid thereto adjoining into a Town … [12]

As with Chestertown, the original plat for Georgetown has been lost. The one extant plat from the eighteenth century is dated 1787 and the number of lots differ from the original one-hundred specified in the Act of 1737. Instead there are 141 lots, with no land allocated for a church, market place or public square. Laid out in a strict grid pattern, there was no regard for the steepness of the terrain which resulted in some lots being unuseable for residential purposes. The lack of a church lot was undoubtedly due to the nearby location of Shrewsbury Parish Church. However, as a number of Georgetown's inhabitants were of Scottish origin, it is not surprising that a lot was purchased by the Presbyterian Church in the first year of Georgetown's existence. As more and more merchants established their businesses in Georgetown, it became a mercantile center for much of the surrounding area. A number of the merchants had businesses in Chestertown as well.

NEW MARKET

Mentioned in a 1728 deed for part of a tract named Vianna, New Market was located at the crossroads today designated as Chesterville. In the 1720s a market had been set up there for the provision of the northeastern section of the county. Gradually, over the next 60 years, New Market developed into a small village. There were several residences, a tiny school and two brick stores in the 1780s. New Market was never actually recognized as a town by the General Assembly and only one building survives from this eighteenth century settlement today.

MILLINGTON

Originally called Head of Chester, Millington was recognized by the General Assembly when the community applied for the right to establish and regulate a market at Bridgetown in 1798. This actually occurred long after the crossroads on the tract of London Bridge was first settled. London Bridge had been patented in the late seventeenth century for Daniel Toas, who had run the ordinary and ferry there in 1695. In 1707, Richard Bennett (mentioned earlier in regard to Shrewsbury Towne)

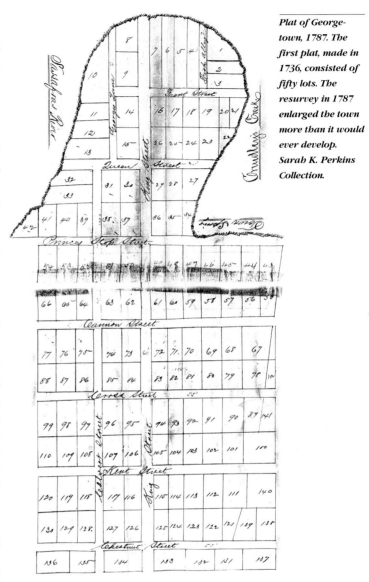

Plat of Georgetown, 1787. The first plat, made in 1736, consisted of fifty lots. The resurvey in 1787 enlarged the town more than it would ever develop. Sarah K. Perkins Collection.

purchased 1650 acres from the heirs of Daniel Toas, only to sell the same to Gilbert Falconer in 1724. It was Falconer who divided the land into 50 acre parcels and constructed the bridge there in 1748. At this point the settlement gained the name of Bridgetown. The crossroads area, however, does not appear to have been subdivided until the late 1760s when parcels ranging from one-half to three acres were sold off.

GEORGETOWN CROSSROADS

Like Head of Chester and New Market, Georgetown Crossroads essentially grew out of two roads intersecting. As early as 1745, a dwelling on the southwest corner of the town owned by Cuthbert Hall, provided space for a tailor's shop which was run by Benjamin Vansant. In lieu of the rent (£3/year), Vansant was to provide tailoring for the entire Hall family in exchange for the space.

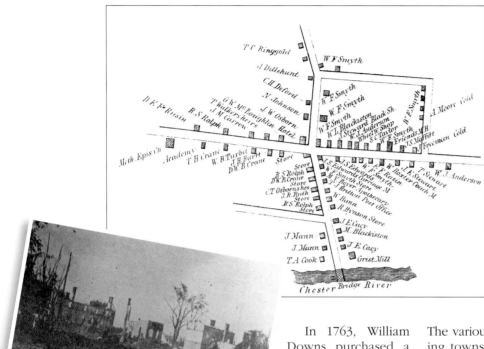

Map of Millington, formerly Bridgetown and Head of Chester, from Martenet's Map of Kent County, 1860. G. W. McLaughin owned the Hotel at this time.

Millington, after the fire of 1904 destroyed most of the 'downtown' area. The large structure in the background was an important tavern and stage coach stop. Historical Society of Kent County. Usilton Collection.

eighteenth century. The ferry was advertised in 1769 in the Maryland Gazette by James Hodges as *"Rock Hall-Whitehouse to Annapolis, Baltimore-town or elsewhere."* The development of Rock Hall as a town occurred in a somewhat haphazard manner. By as late as 1860, the present downtown section of Rock Hall had not yet developed.

OTHER TOWNS

Like Galena and Rock Hall, a number of other towns located throughout the county find their roots in the eighteenth century as crossroad settlements. Massey, Stillpond, Fairlee (Bel Aire) and others began this way, but did not develop into villages until later in the nineteenth century.

TRADE AND TOBACCO

The various acts of the General Assembly for establishing towns were prompted by the desire to facilitate trade in the counties. By creating ports and towns, the crops and products of the inhabitants could be shipped elsewhere, while products from afar could be received. More than a simple agricultural product, tobacco was the medium of exchange in early eighteenth century America. Its processing required considerable labor, as it had to be grown, dried and safely stored before shipment. This final step in the process required warehouses. In the early part of the century many warehouses were privately owned, but with time, regulations imposed by the provincial government eventually led to the authorization of the construction of tobacco warehouses at public expense.

In 1748, the Proceedings of the Justice for Inspection of Tobacco describe both warehouse locations and appearances. In the records of 20 August 1748, the following names were listed as Justices for Kent County. Many of these men resided not far from the warehouses themselves.

Bedingfield Hands	Samuel Tovey
Richard Lloyd	Daniel Cheston
Jervis Spencer	Hugh Wallis
John Williamson	Paul Whichcote
Simon Wilmer	William Hynson

The major location authorized for the county was at Chestertown, where the largest of the warehouses was to be constructed on one-half-acre of John Page's Lot No. 12. The building was to be 60' long by 30' wide by 10' high to the eaves. It was to be fitted with two doors at each end *"to answer two allies that goes between hogsheads."* [13] This warehouse has an interesting, although short history. On April 24, 1760, the fate of the warehouse was recorded in the Maryland Gazette:

"The Beginning of This Month, some People in Kent

In 1763, William Downs purchased a one-acre parcel on the northwest corner of the crossroads for £25 (part of McCay's Purchase). Downs built an inn on the property and for years thereafter, the area became known as *Downs Crossroads*. The next major subdivision of this area did not occur until after the Revolution when a number of tradesmen established their businesses there.

SASSAFRAS

At the head of the Sassafras River two streams had been dammed for mills. This created a place for a roadway which enabled travelers to cross the Sassafras without making use of the ferry at Georgetown. Following construction of the mills, dwellings were built. While little information is available regarding the area in the eighteenth century, there are frequent references to *Head of Sassafras* in the records. In 1756, William Boyer bequeathed 35 acres to Shrewsbury Parish for the establishment of a school. The exact extent of the school's useful life is not known, however, it was in operation between at least 1758 and 1768. By 1822, seventeen lots were listed in the tax assessment, fourteen of which were listed as improved.

ROCK HALL

Lying at the southern end of the county, Rock Hall consisted essentially of a ferry terminus and tavern in the

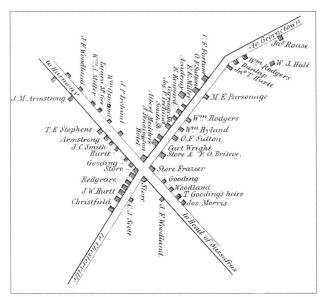

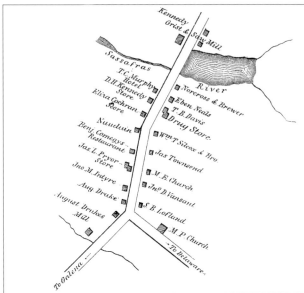

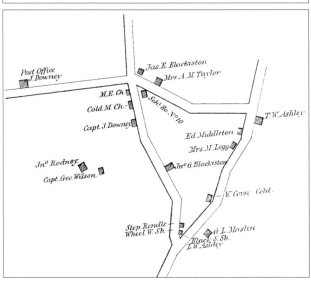

County, having carelessly made a Fire in a Tobacco House, under some Tobacco which was hanging up on the Joists, and leaving it to go to Breakfasts, the Tobacco catch'd Fire, and communicated itself to the House. On their return, one Michael Hodgeson, got upon the Roof in order to extinguish it, but was so much suffocated with the Smoke, that he fell in and was burnt to Death. About 7000 Weight of Tobacco was destroy'd with the House."

Other warehouse locations are mentioned at Samuel Tovey's on Greys Inn Creek, at William Graves' on Buck Neck, at Abram Falconer's at Head of Chester and at Georgetown. At Greys Inn, the house to be constructed was to measure 40' x 22' x 8 ½" and have two 5' wide doors and a shed large enough to cover six prizes. The Graves and Falconer properties had previously constructed wharves and Falconer had in fact had his own warehouse, but now, however, it was to be repaired at public expense. The buildings planned for Buck Neck and Georgetown were to be only half the size of the warehouse at Chestertown. At Georgetown, the warehouse was to be constructed by two merchants, John Tilden and William Rasin, *"guardians to Samuel Whetherhead"* and was to be located one lot back from the water on Lot No. 9.

Specifications for the warehouse on Miles Mason Shehaun's property at Walnut Point on Langford Bay is typical of the entire group of six structures which were intended for the use of the county for the remainder of the colonial period.

" … will build a good substantial well framed timber House of the length of thirty feet in the clear and the bredth of twenty eight feet in the clear and the height of ten feet between the sill and the plate and two doors of five feet wide at each end and to provide the prized compleatly and substantially fitted up the poles to be thirty three feet in length and a gallows for raising said prized with a shade at one side of the said to cover the said prizes where the said hogsheads shall stand to be prized of ten feet in width with followers and blocks and a good substantiall warff to reach five feet water in depth at a midling tide with a well fitted and substantial crane at the end thereof sufficient to hoyst hogsheads tobacco out and in craft that shall or may bring and carry of Tobacco for to be inspected … " [14]

How quickly these buildings were constructed was not recorded, but by November 1754, the Kent County Court was informed that the warehouses were *"much out of repair."* The Court instructed the various justices to meet at the warehouses to determine the extent of the repairs needed and contract with a person to undertake the work.

Map of Galena, formerly Georgetown Crossroads, from Martenet's Map of Kent County, 1860.

Map of Sassafras, formerly Head of Sassafras from Martenet's Map of Kent County, 1860.

Map of Rock Hall from Martenet's Map of Kent County, 1860

Gilpin Mill, Millington, c. 1763. Brick mill covered with ivy with nineteenth century frame addition. C. Engstrom photograph, 1977.

Water Mill Sites in Kent County, 17th & 18th Century
Other wind mills formerly along bay side

Wind Mill ▲

Daniel Perkins built his first mill on the upper reaches of Morgan Creek in 1710. In the following years, others followed his example and mills were built on Prickle Pear Branch near Crumpton, Mill Branch and Andover Branch near Head of Chester, at Head of Sassafras (two), and on Swan, Quidley's and Woodland Creeks, tributaries of the Sassafras River. Grist, saw, and fulling mills were also constructed at the heads of Stillpond, Churn, Worton, Fairlee and Langford Creeks.

In those areas lacking sufficient elevation for an adequate head of water, wind mills were constructed. This occurred especially along the Bay Side. In the Maryland Gazette of February 14, 1764, Richard Bennett Lloyd advertised:

"Flour Manufactured in the neatest Manner, either for family use, or Shipping off, by the Subscriber at his Wind-Mill opposite Pool's Island"

Another advertisement was placed in the Gazette by Richard Gresham:

"Notice ... Baking Business ... by William Ossen, Baker at the Subscribers Plantation on Grasing Creek, near the mouth of Chester River ... " [16]

Given the lack of height at Greys Inn Creek, such an operation may have required a wind mill which could have been located either nearby or on the subscriber's home plantation on the Bay.

Tanneries

Two known tanning operations in eighteenth century Chestertown may have been the result of another act of the General Assembly (1692) whose specific intent was to encourage the establishment of such businesses.[17] Between 1707 and 1733, John Lovegrove purchased Lot No. 76 in Chestertown where upon he built a small dwelling for himself and subsequently set up a tanning operation in his back yard. The will of Thomas Garnett, a Quaker who died in 1730, clearly indicates that he planned a profession in the leather trade for his sons George, Bartholomew, Joseph and Jonathan, as he bequeathed to them *"all the shoemakers tools of what kind soever"* and a lot in Chestertown *"where a place is digged and designed for a Tan House with the frame, boards, etc,"* as well as a *"corner lot ... adjoining the lot of John Lovegrove"* (Lot No. 75).[18] Joseph and Jonathan did go into the tanning and saddle making business. While their house and operation have not survived the years, Lovegrove's modest dwelling has, as the kitchen of The White Swan Tavern.

At the December session of the Assembly in 1773, warehouses were mentioned again. This time inspection days were established and annual fees for inspections set. In these proceedings only four warehouses were mentioned, Georgetown and Falconer's were not included. This is possibly an indication of the decline of tobacco's importance in the late eighteenth century.

Mills

The construction of water mills in Kent County was also prompted by an act of the General Assembly. Enacted in 1669, the legislation pertaining to the construction of mills provided anyone willing to set up a mill with an eighty year lease.[15] One of the first mills in Kent County was a water powered grist mill built by Simon Wilmer in the 1690s at the head waters of Radcliffe Creek.

As the population of the county increased, more mills were constructed, generally in areas of higher elevation where a good head of water could be dammed.

Kent's Eighteenth Century Dwellings

The 1720s and 1730s

THE JOHN LOVEGROVE HOUSE

Originally, this was a one-story, frame, hall-parlor plan house which measured a modest 16' x 23' ½". It possessed only one chimney in the hall with the parlor and unfinished loft left unheated. The interior walls, including a partition which served to divide the structure into two rooms were plastered. The ceiling was exposed. The Lovegrove House possessed the unusual feature of gunstock corner posts which provided a more substantial member into which the end beams were mortised. Sometime after 1733, the house was converted into a

kitchen for the residence of Joseph Nicholson, a dwelling which would eventually be known as the White Swan Tavern.

MARSHY POINT

Like John Lovegrove's house, Marshy Point dates from the first quarter of the eighteenth century. It too had a hall-parlor plan with oak

John Lovegrove House, Chestertown. This c. 1720 house was incorporated into Joseph Nicholson's brick residence after he acquired the property in 1733. Drawn by Michael Bourne.

Marshy Point, detail of gunstock corner post, one of three Kent County buildings to have this construction technique. Michael Bourne photograph, 1978.

Marshy Point, detail of eave construction. The rafter is tenoned into the end of the joist without the need for a false plate. Michael Bourne photograph, 1978.

gunstock corner posts. This small farmhouse is located on the Sassafras River, and was built for either William Pearce or his son, Daniel. In its original form, the house measured 18' x 30'. The roof at Marshy Point was constructed without a false plate, but with the ends of the rafters being mortised into the overhanging ends of the joists.

WHITE HOUSE FARM

White House Farm or Ridgely, was built in 1721 by Daniel Perkins, a miller and inn holder who had established a grist mill on the upper reaches of Morgan Creek in 1710. Built of brick, the date of its construction is indicated in numerals made of glazed headers on the west gable. This is the first recorded use of a glazed date in Kent County. The principal facade is laid in Flemish bond and is three bays long with two dormers above. Interestingly, White House Farm was fitted with two stairs, one in each of the principal rooms which afforded greater privacy to the chambers above.

MARROWBONE

Built by Jervis Spencer around 1728 when his land was patented, Marrowbone had both a hall-parlor section and a shed addition which was located to the rear of the parlor. There were large fireplaces in both the hall and parlor, the latter of which had small recesses in each cheek. The firebacks were laid in a herringbone pattern to ease in their replacement once burned through. The stair at Marrowbone was located in the corner of the hall behind a two-panel door adjacent the bolection molded fireplace wall. Surrounding the fireplace, the paneling left no exposed masonry, similar to two contemporary houses, Bounds Lott and Pemberton Hall, both located in Wicomico County. The rafters, like those at Marshy Point, were spaced to

Presbury, the home of William Comegys (d. 1735) across the river from Crumpton. This steeply pitched roof house had a tilted false plate at the end of the joists to which the rafters were nailed. Michael Bourne photograph, 1979

Marrowbone, c. 1720s. This was the residence of weaver/planter, Jervis Spencer. Michael Bourne photograph, 1968.

White House Farm, 1721. The oldest part is to the right of the chimney. James Wilfong photograph, 1979.

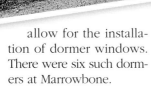

allow for the installation of dormer windows. There were six such dormers at Marrowbone.

Originally, the house was constructed without a basement, but late in the eighteenth century, a bulkhead was built on the glazed headed south facade and soil was removed from beneath each room. Curiously, the area dug out was about 2½ feet smaller on all sides than the rooms above. These earthen walls were repeatedly whitewashed so that the result was like a thin coat of plaster. Before Marrowbone was disassembled in 1976, the building was recorded for HABS. During the recording process, traces of original hardware were found which included foliated H hinges on the interior doors and shutters.

PRESBURY

A short distance down river from Marrowbone, Presbury was the residence of William Comegys (father-in-law to Jervis Spencer). Laid in Flemish bond, this brick building which measured 18' x 25' 5", had a full basement with kitchen therein and a commodious finished garret as well. The walls above the basement were only one brick thick and the ceiling heights were low, 7' in the basement and 7' 3" on the first story respectively. Like Marrowbone and White House, the fireplaces at Presbury were large. Its roof structure was similar to Carvill Hall, with oak sawn members laid horizontally. They lapped half over the 4½" x 6½" tilted false plate. The roof pitch was approximately 14½" in 12".

GODLINGTON MANOR

The development of Godlington Manor was similar to that of Presbury. When its construction was begun in the second quarter of the eighteenth century, it was a

one-and-a-half-story, one-room dwelling in which the corner posts, door posts and plate were exposed, as they were all of greater thickness than the stud walls. There was a large fireplace on the east side of the room which had an adjoining stair.

The exterior of the house was covered with sawn flush shiplap which was painted dark red. Even after the house was lengthened in the third quarter of the eighteenth century (an alteration which converted it into a hall-parlor plan), the original *A* roof line remained. It was not until the last decade of the century that the roof was changed to its gambrel form and three dormers were added on either side in order to provide light to the bed chambers. At this time, the original hall was remodeled. When the house was restored in the 1970s, ox skulls were found in the ceiling above each of the front doors—most likely a talisman to ward off evil spirits.

LAMB'S MEADOW, LAMB'S RANGE AND REDMORE'S SUPPLY

Throughout the eighteenth century, houses with hall-parlor plans were constructed in Kent County, just as they had been in the seventeenth century. The chief difference lay in that they were built of better materials, such as brick or set upon brick foundations over basements. Some of the plans included variations on placement of a stair or fireplace, some included variations of house form.

Lamb's Meadow, Lamb's Range and Redmore's Supply, all located near Stillpond and dating from around the 1730s were built with the same plan (including basement kitchen) and gambrel roof form. It was not

until 1753 that a grade level kitchen was constructed at Lamb's Meadow with the date spelled out in glazed headers. These buildings were distinguished by molded water tables, glazed Flemish bond, paneled fireplace walls and feather edge vertical board partitions. At Lamb's Meadow, the hall had cabinets built into the overmantel, a feature seen in the next decade at The Reward on Quaker Neck.

BUCK-BACCHUS STORE AND THE BUCK CHAMBERS HOUSE

John Buck, a merchant living in Bideford, Devonshire, England, constructed two buildings in the 1730s which have

Godlington Manor prior to restoration. The house began with one room on the right to which two subsequent additions were built within the eighteenth century. Historic American Buildings Survey, 1973.

Lamb's Meadow, c. 1733, had its kitchen built into the basement. The at-grade kitchen was added in 1753. C. Engstrom photograph, 1977.

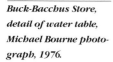

Buck-Bacchus Store, detail of water table, Michael Bourne photograph, 1976.

Buck-Bacchus Store, detail of belt course, Michael Bourne photograph, 1976.

Buck-Bacchus Store, c.1735. It was built for a Devonshire merchant who had plantations in Virginia and saw mills in Maine. Drawn by Jack R. Schroeder, 1986.

two-room plans in their main sections. Both were distinguished in their use of glazed Flemish bond, but the Buck-Bachus Store on the corner of High and Queen Streets was built with a molded water table which rises above its arched basement windows, a feature which was later used on several other houses in and around Chestertown. It was also built with a belt course that jogs down on the side. This feature has been found on only one other Kent County house, Scotch Folly.

The four-bay, Buck Chambers House was laid out like a typical hall-parlor house with end chimney, but its kitchen was located to the rear. At the Buck-Bacchus Store however, the plan included an unheated store space with its own entrance along the High Street facade. The back room with fireplace and adjoining stair had its own entrance from Queen Street. Unknown until this study was begun, there had also been a stone, one-story, two-room wing which extended down High Street and which was intended to be part of the back room accommodations.

Both of the Buck buildings had vertical beaded board partitions with double beads at the tongue and groove joints. Their walls and window jambs were plastered with only a sill to relieve the simplicity. For some unexplained reason, the ceiling of the store room at the Buck-Bacchus Store was about 14 inches lower than the back room, which in turn created higher ceilings in the two chambers above. The Buck-Bacchus Store is the first instance of a hip roof with plaster cove cornice being constructed in Kent County.

ESAU WATKINS HOUSE AND THE THOMAS GARNETT HOUSE

Similar to the Buck-Bacchus Store, the Esau Watkins House has a hip roof and plaster cove cornice and its narrow side faces the street. It was constructed sometime after 1737 on Water Lot No. 11 for blacksmith, Esau Watkins and his wife. The house appears to have had a hall-parlor plan with central chimney which served back-to-back fireplaces. Constructed on the river bank, the building was built with a basement kitchen, an unfortunate design as extremely high tides have proven.

In 1730, Thomas Garnett was planning a house for Water Lot No. 13, which he bequeathed to his son, George. There is no description of the house other than that included in his will:

"To my loving son George ... the water lot in Chestertown ... whereon the frame of my designed Dwelling House Stands with all the Plank, bricks, oyster shell, nails, and other materials that is now ready for the Dwelling house with all the finishes and appurtenances belonging to said lot ... " [18]

This and at least one other house on Water Lot No. 14 or 15 were replaced by post-Revolutionary buildings.

Joseph Nicholson House

During the decade of the 1730s, Joseph Nicholson, mentioned above, purchased Lot No. 76 from John Lovegrove. He constructed a still larger house facing High Street and the courthouse opposite. It was a large, five-bay, gambrel roof brick house, 20' x 48' that included the first recorded central stair hall with two flanking rooms. Like others of the period, the principal facade was dressed with Flemish bond brickwork with glazed headers, above a molded water table. Inside, the 11' high walls were finished with a bold, five-part, classical cornice and the fireplace walls were paneled. Like the Buck houses, the walls and window jambs were finished in plaster only, without trim.

The 1740s

Stanley's Hope and Caulk's Field

During the next decade, continued prosperity was evident in the buildings constructed in Kent County. Two buildings in the outlying countryside continued the tradition begun by Daniel Perkins at White House Farm, by including the date in glazed headers on the gable. Both constructed in 1743, Stanley's Hope and Caulk's Field incorporated the common use of Flemish bond with glazed headers on their principal facades and possess hall-parlor plans. Caulk's Field however, was one story taller providing its inhabitants with two additional chambers. It also retains many original features. Especially noteworthy is the wall of paneling with its bolection molding around the fireplace and the doors which

enclose the stair and closet. The latter is lighted by a small four-pane casement. The practice of lighting closets and stairs with a small gable window was prevalent in both the second and third quarter of the eighteenth century.

Dougherty's Tavern

Around the same time, in Chestertown, Walter Dougherty, innkeeper, built his house on half of Lot No. 34. It was well-sited on the first block of High Street and combined a plan similar to Nicholson's house with the height of Caulk's Field. Dougherty's was a two-and-a-half-story, brick building, five bays long, with glazed Flemish bond, molded water table which jogged above the basement windows and a central entry wide enough for double doors. The principal room was fully paneled with seats at the windows and a sophisticated cornice which *breaks out* above the windows. The King of Prussia marble hearth and surround may have been added 20 or so years later.

The Custom House
and the Dr. William Murray House

Two other houses built in the 1740s embarked on a variation of the central hall plan. The Custom House, begun by another innkeeper, Samuel Massey, and completed by Thomas Ringgold IV, was built on a corner lot at the edge of an embankment. Its position on both High and Front Streets, adjoining the slope to the town dock, gave the builder the opportunity to have an extra story on its High Street side. This lower story was originally used for kitchen facilities with access to a storage vault which is located beneath the Front Street terrace above. This is the earliest example of such a vault.

The Front Street facade is five bays long and the High Street facade four. Both have glazed Flemish bond, jogging water tables and plaster cove cornices beneath a partially hipped roof. Like Dougherty's

Esau Watkins House, c. 1739, like several other neighboring houses had a basement kitchen. It is one of the three Water Street houses to have a plaster cove cornice. Tyler Campbell photograph, 1978.

Joseph Nicholson House, c. 1733. Conjectural restoration of High Street elevation. This is known as the White Swan Tavern. Drawn by Michael Bourne.

house, the central entrance was provided with a double door with transom.

Inside, the plan consists of a central stair hall with room on either side. The best room of the house is located behind the corner room and both are served by a central chimney which adjoins an entry from High Street. With the kitchen on the ground floor, access from above was provided by a separate stair in the corner room. This adjoined an access corridor to the stair hall and best room.

The best room has paneling across the fireplace wall with four flanking doors leading to the entry, side passage, closet and a stair to the upstairs corner room. The splayed jamb window trim is tied into the cornice, similar to Dougherty's main room. The southwest room is paneled on all four walls, but here the paneling is of vertical beaded boards. The fire box of this room was built with widely splayed jambs with a herringbone brick back.

Across Front Street from the Custom House, on the corner of Cannon Street, Dr. William Murray built a large brick house soon after purchasing the lot in 1743. The form included a fully hipped roof on a two-story, rectangular box. The plan consisted of a central stair/entry flanked by a large, fully-paneled room on the southwest, and two rooms on the northeast. In the southwest room the fireplace is positioned on the rear wall. The two northeast rooms are served by back-to-back corner fireplaces. The principal facade was laid in all-header bond above a jogged water table, features which were to be repeated in several other large houses built thereafter.

During the 1740s, classical Georgian design was just beginning to be employed on the Eastern Shore, and in a somewhat naive manner. Pilasters of the first period could be ill-proportioned and lack either a base or capital. The pilasters flanking the fireplace in Murray's large corner room were narrow and terminated beneath the cornice, producing a *tacked on* appearance. The flank-

Custom House.

*The High Street facade.
Michael C. Wootton
photograph, 1996.*

*Begun in the mid-1740s
and enlarged before
1772, was the center of
Thomas Ringgold's mer-
cantile establishment as
well as his residence.
Maryland Historical
Trust. Michael Bourne
photograph, 1969.*

*First floor plan as built
in 1745-49. Drawn by
M. L. Fritz.*

*Detail of cornice over
window in original river
side room, the best
room in the house.
Maryland Historical
Trust, c. 1976.*

Murray House (Hynson-Ringgold House) paneled south parlor, with fluted pilasters lacking capitals. Tyler Campbell photograph, 1995.

Murray House, first (and second) floor plan(s) before the Ringgold addition. Michael Bourne.

Opposite: Dr. William Murray's house was the front section of the Hynson-Ringgold House. Constance Stuat Larrabee photograph.

ing cabinets, although they possessed shell tops, were also naively designed and executed.

THE REWARD

On Quaker Neck during the same decade, Charles Tilden, a third generation gentleman farmer, came into his majority and took possession of his inherited plantation, The Reward. He constructed a house which incorporated several details which were standard to the construction of Kent County houses: Flemish bond with glazed headers, molded water table jogging over basement windows, wide front door, and, like the Custom House, windows on the second floor which were half the size of those on the first.

Tilden's plan and form, however, were unique. He created a four-room-square plan by using a hall-parlor plan in the front half and central passage plan in the back. An open stair was placed in the hall between the two paneled rooms. Diagonal fireplaces on the outside rear corners also service the rooms behind. The west back room was accessible from the hall, but the parlor was accessible to the passage, creating a separate space for the kitchen in the north room. There was an enclosed stair in the kitchen to a separate room above for the servants.

The form of The Reward is unique in that the house is two stories in the front and only one story in the back. Because these were covered by one roof, the end result was that of a cat slide or saltbox effect.

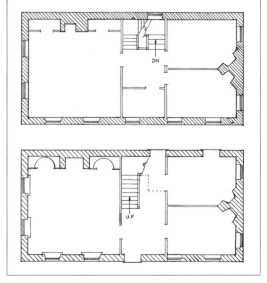

The two large chimneys at the apex of the roof are reduced in depth by a sloped weathering and then divided into two by a vertical withe. This is the earliest example of this detail, and possibly a signature of Tilden's mason, as it was found on other houses built later.

The 1750s

STERLING CASTLE
AND THE JOHN BOLTON HOUSE

During the 1750s, earlier styles persisted as houses continued to be constructed of frame and brick. Sterling Castle, a small, frame, one-and-a-half-story dwelling on Mill Street in Chestertown is framed like the original part of Godlington Manor. It has a hall-parlor plan with tall ceilings and 9/9 sash windows. The exterior is covered with beaded weatherboard.

John Bolton's first house was similar to Sterling Castle in its size, shape and even in its framing, as the major posts were on the long facade. The parlor was actually the entry and contained an enclosed stair to the second story. Soon after he added a leanto and brought the original rear wall forward to make two nearly equal rooms served by a new chimney with corner fireplaces. Like the less sophisticated rooms at The Reward, Bolton's front room was sheathed with vertical feather edge boards.

THE HANDS HOUSE
AND WORRELL'S TAVERN

Two other frame houses built in mid-eighteenth century Chestertown include the Hands House and Worrell's Tavern. Both were substantial two-and-a-half-story buildings. Hands House was four bays across its facade, but had a central stair hall plan, the stair having bold handrail and turned balusters. The Tavern plan was not recorded prior to its early twentieth century demise, but one photograph captured the unique pent eave which extended across one gable at cornice level.

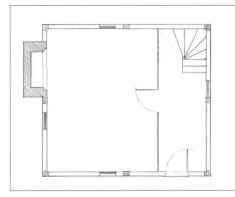

WHICHCOTE CASTLE,
CLARK'S CONVENIENCY
AND BUNGAY

Farmhouses of the 1750s include Whichcote Castle, reputed to have a glazed date 1750 on its gable. Its one-and-a-half-story, hall-parlor plan was like Boxley, built around 1757, but the former had a basement and the latter none. Boxley also has a less steeply pitched *A* roof.

Clark's Conveniency, built for Thomas Wilkins, was more finished with paneled fireplace walls, and paneled wainscot around the rest of the room. Paneling in both rooms was stepped out, flanking the fireplace for inclusion of the enclosed stair on one side and closet on the other. The rusticated wood lintels of the exterior three-bay facade are later remodelings of typical segmental arches. Clark's Conveniency, for its size, has a

Chestertown Tea Party

*O*n May 23, 1774 after hearing the news that the Port of Boston had been closed by the British, a group of undisguised townsmen in Chestertown ventured aboard the brigantine "Geddes," and angrily threw the tea that had arrived a few days before into the Chester River. History comes to life each year with a dramatic reenactment of the colorful event. Chestertown Tea Party, reproduced from a painting by Howard M. Burns.

Clark's Conveniency, c. 1750. It was built by Thomas Wilkins, and has a well executed interior.

Clark's Conveniency. Detail of window and cornice.

The Violet Farm. James and Rebecca Frisby recorded their initials and date of construction on the west gable.

The Violet Farm. Detail of roof and dormer framing.

C. Engstrom photographs, 1977.

well developed service wing with kitchen and pantry or dining room in a nearly equal addition. The chimney detailing above the roof resembles that at the nearby Reward.

Bungay built in 1757 for Charles and Phoebe Carvill Hynson, has similar chimney detailing, as well as the initials of the owners and the date of its construction documented in glazed headers. This two-story, brick house has the only example of semi-circular arched double doors in the county. It's tempting to believe that the design was copied from the porch door of Phoebe's childhood home, Carvill Hall. Bungay is the first of four central hall houses to possess a secondary stair enclosed behind the paneling of the less important room. Like Clark's Conveniency, the principal room has paneled dado in addition to the fireplace wall.

The 1760s

During the 1760s, houses continued to be built with the same plan and form as originated in the seventeenth century. Maslin's Possession and St. Paul's Vestry were of the one-and-a-half-story form, while Depford, Comegys House and the Plains were constructed with the same plan but with a gambrel roof.

The Violet Farm

At the Violet Farm, like Bungay, the date of construction, 1762, and the initials of the owners are recorded in glazed headers on the west gable. James and Rebecca Ringgold Frisby must have employed the same mason as the Hynsons, at Bungay. Glazed header Flemish bond was used on both long facades above the jogged and molded water table. The plan of the Violet Farm and its exterior plaster cove cornice were the same as those used at Dr. Murray's house in Chestertown, but here the roof was a standard *A* roof with three original dormers on each side which provided light for the attic rooms (these rooms were never finished). Its north facade is distinguished by a second door which gave access to the basement stair, a phenomenon seen again on Comegys Bight. Both houses had the same chimney de-

sign, but the latter was only three bays long in comparison to the five bays at Frisby's house and was dated 1769.

THE ADVENTURE

With an interior that was equal to the Violet Farm, The Adventure was built during the same decade, a time which produced a unique fireplace design. The firebox was actually narrower than the outside opening. At The Adventure this difference was finished with a beaded plaster cove, but others of the same decade were plastered to conform to the set-backs in the brickwork.

The Adventure, like Bungay, includes a secondary stair enclosed behind the dining room paneling. It has a most attractive closed string main stair, with bold square newel posts and turned balusters. The period of its construction is the last in which bolection molding is used for chair rails and around fireplace openings.

DULLAM'S FOLLY

Dullam's Folly, built nearby was a simple hall-parlor plan house, originally one-and-a-half stories tall. Like

most houses with this plan, the stair was enclosed behind paneling, but here it is the principal

stair. On the opposite side of the fireplace wall was a double door, semi-circular headed closet that possessed a shell cupboard. Beneath the rectangular bolection molding around the fireplace, the paneling continued beneath the molding to conform to the arch of the fireplace. In that space there were small panels carved into the paneling. The Adventure, Violet Farm, Rose Hill and Clark's Conveniency all have this feature in conjunction with the fireplace type mentioned above. Another peculiarity of this decade was the introduction of a parlor fireplace that was flush with the exterior wall, requiring that the chimney stack protrude from the gable. This was found at Dullam's Folly and Duncan's Folly, both simple brick farmhouses with well-executed details.

PARTNER'S ADDITION AND THE RYLEY FARM

Both Partner's Addition and the Ryley Farm have interior detailing that looks as though it could have come from the same hand. While both have hall-parlor plans they are quite different. The parlor fireplaces at Partner's Addition were located in the northwest corner of the house, where the mason spanned a diagonal arch in the basement. This plan is encountered again at the Brice-Johnson Farm and the Knock Farm in the same Hundred.

Like Widehall and the Smith-Ringgold House, Partner's Addition had window and door frames made of walnut, a very durable wood. Most exterior doors throughout the eighteenth century were composed of panels on the exterior with an interior surface made of thin beaded boards applied as either chevrons, or on diagonal, vertical, or horizontal axes. The houses which digress from this basic design are more sophisticated, such as Widehall and Rose Hill.

Both the Ryley Farm and Partner's Addition had pent eaves, a roof which projected about 4 feet from the wall between the first and second stories. There are six houses in the county which had pent eaves originally, but none have completely survived. At Shepherd's Delight, a part of one can still be seen in an attic. The others were found on Locust Hill, Scotch Folly and Tibbalds.

TIBBALDS

Tibbalds, a house built by Isaac Freeman in the late 1750s or early 1760s had the same plan as The Adventure and similarly did not employ the use of glazed headers on its principal facade. Here, the pent eave extended around three sides of the building. Other examples had them only on the front and rear. The balustrade at Tibbalds is the best surviving stair of the period, with three walnut balusters per step and bold newels and handrail. In its three flights, it resembles The Adventure. Tibbalds is the only farmhouse of the decade to have had a basement kitchen until a later one was built at grade.

THE SMITH-RINGGOLD HOUSE

The biggest change during this period was the wider use of a two room depth. The Smith-Ringgold House began as a central hall plan to which a nearly equal size addition was added on the river side. The addition included two rooms and central passage. Both sections of this house were built with full size windows flanking the fireplace on the southwest gable wall, a phenomenon which was to continue into the early nineteenth century, then vanish until it was reintroduced in the mid-century.

The Smith-Ringgold House was one

Ryley Farm, recently called Heritage Farm, originally had a pent eave below the second story windows. M. Q. Fallaw photograph, 1985.

Tibbalds. Detail of stair from the second floor. Michael C. Wootton photograph, 1995.

Tibbalds, the home of Revolutionary War hero Isaac Freeman, Jr. had the same plan and same details as the Adventure. The kitchen wing was rebuilt in the 1950s. M. Q. Fallaw photograph, 1985

Smith-Ringgold House c. 1913. Note the falles between the house and river. Historical Society of Kent County, Usilton Collection.

Smith-Ringgold House, Chestertown. Two of the three phases of construction are clearly visible from the street. Maryland Historical Trust, James M. Kilvington photograph, 1975.

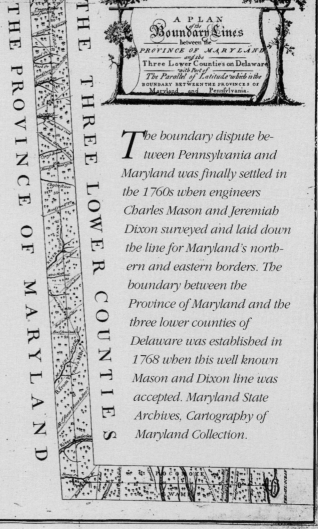

Mason & Dixon Line

A PLAN
of the
Boundary Lines
between the
PROVINCE OF MARYLAND
and the
Three Lower Counties on Delaware
with Part of
The Parallel of Latitude which is the
BOUNDARY BETWEEN THE PROVINCES OF
Maryland and Pennsylvania.

THE PROVINCE OF MARYLAND

THE THREE LOWER COUNTIES

THE PROVINCE OF MARYLAND

The boundary dispute between Pennsylvania and Maryland was finally settled in the 1760s when engineers Charles Mason and Jeremiah Dixon surveyed and laid down the line for Maryland's northern and eastern borders. The boundary between the Province of Maryland and the three lower counties of Delaware was established in 1768 when this well known Mason and Dixon line was accepted. Maryland State Archives, Cartography of Maryland Collection.

of the few houses to have falls or terraces and the only one of the period in Chestertown. Here, there are three modest falls to the River, in contrast to a single terrace in front of the Violet Farm. Rose Hill also had a series of terraces on the front and road side, probably installed when the house was finished.

ROSE HILL

Rose Hill was probably built in the decade of the 1760s and epitomizes the common practice of this period of building within a specific set of geometric proportions. In the Historic Structure Report for Rose Hill, Marsha Fritz noted: *"The geometrical construction is set upon a 40' square plan. The base line is assumed to be the bottom of the basement window frame. Upon the base is constructed an equilateral triangle, its apex being the*

roof peak. The unusual central position of the chimneys is established by drawing a circle, the radius of which is formed by the distance (31½ feet) from the center of the baseline to the edge of the cornice. The outside edges of the chimneys are located where this arc intersects the roof slope."

Rose Hill is unique in other ways too. The walls are constructed of Flemish bond on the south and all header bond on the east. Both of these facades have double belt courses between the first and second story windows. Originally, both doors had large two-pane high transoms. Neither the windows nor the doors had arches, but support was produced by the frames themselves which were unfortunately made of poplar, a wood which does not possess the enduring qualities of yellow pine, oak or walnut. The interior of the building was laid out with two rooms and stairhall in the rear and one room along the front. Only the rear rooms were finished and they had fireplaces and paneling common to this decade. The front half of the house was not finished until 1788-90.

WIDEHALL

The zenith of late Georgian ideals in Kent County was exemplified in the house built in 1769 for the prominent merchant, Thomas Smyth. Like Rose Hill, Widehall's two street facades were intended to be viewed,

Rose Hill, c. 1760. The main entrance before restoration. Michael Bourne photograph, 1975.

Rose Hill, after restoration. Michael C. Wootton photograph, 1995..

The main entrance at Rose Hill after restoration by present owners. Mr. and Mrs. Edwin R. Fry Collection.

Widehall. Thomas Smyth, merchant, built his house near the town dock in 1769. Drawing by Jack Schroeder.

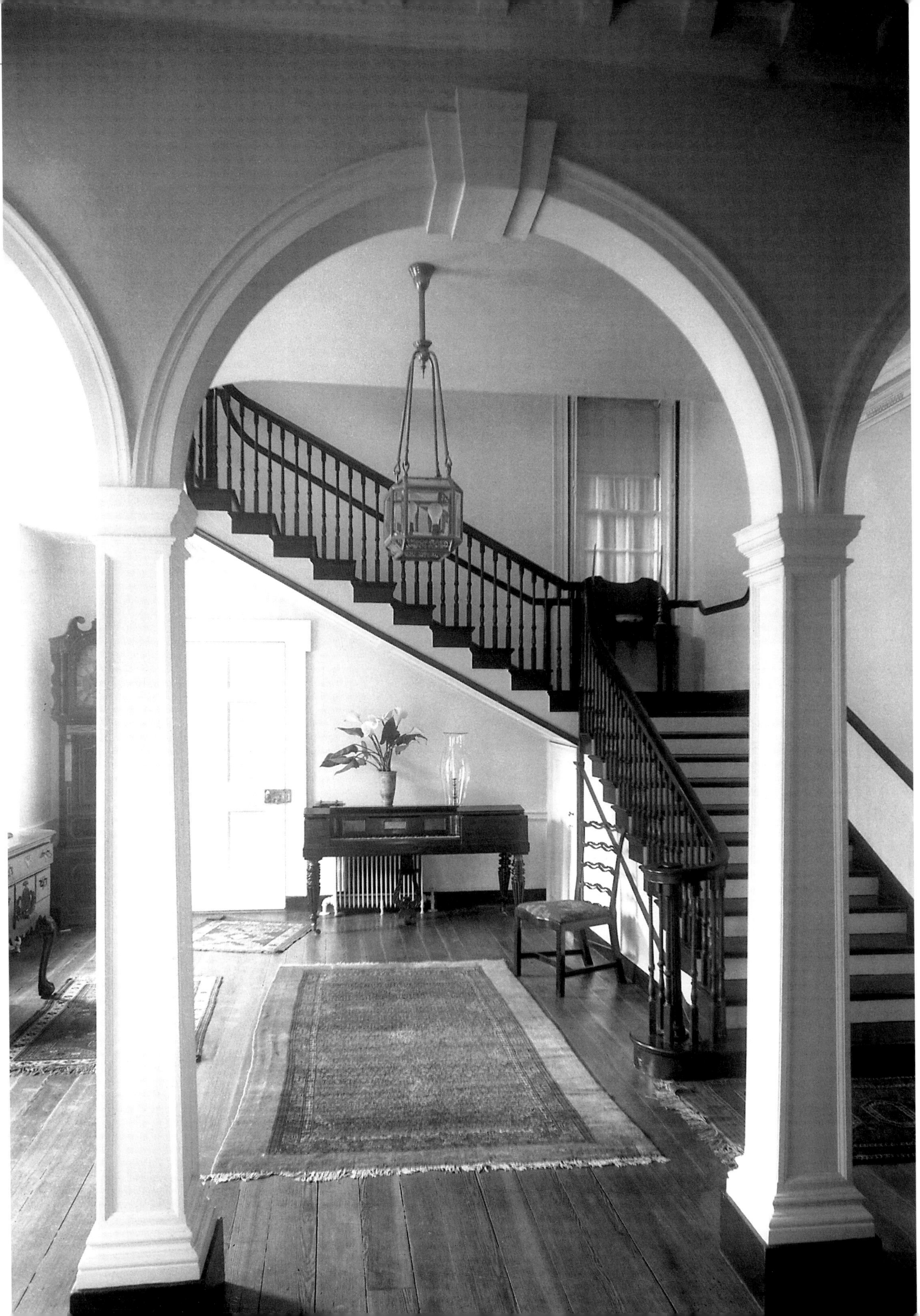

the principal elevation facing Front Street and the side view facing High Street. Both facades were laid in all header bond above a stone basement and molded brick water table. The main door was framed by an extraordinary Doric architrave with engaged fluted columns and the windows were dressed with rusticated wooden jack arches with superimposed keystones. When constructed, it had a hip roof with two central chimneys and some dormers, and a two-story service wing attached to the rear of the building.

The interior plan consisted of a central passage with four nearly equal size rooms, one being the stairhall which was separated from the passage by a series of three arches. The stair itself was wide with low risers and ascended to the second story in three unequal flights. Its balustrade was made of mahogany with three turned balusters per step and a volute at the bottom thereof. Here and in other late Georgian houses there is plain wood wainscoting with pilasters beneath the crossetted window trim. All three rooms had pedimented tabernacle overmantels and cornices, each with different motif. The plan and many of the details are identical to a house built for Henry Pratt, a Queen Annes County merchant and farmer, a few years before. The chief difference was the use of two rooms in the service wing rather than the three found at Pratt Mansion.

The 1770s

HYNSON-RINGGOLD HOUSE

Only one other house in the county that was to approach the grandeur of Thomas Smyth's house was probably begun in the late 1760s with its construction continuing into the early 1770s. Smyth's cousin, Thomas Ringgold, purchased William Murray's house located just one block away. To that existing building, Ringgold added an 'L' out the back which doubled the size of the house and then added to that a three-room service wing. The addition produced the same number of rooms as Smyth's house, but the facade was not changed from its early Georgian simplicity. The stair, with many details

similar to Smyth's house, differed in layout. Ringgold had a pair of stairs ascend in two flights to a central landing and from there in one flight to the second floor. In 1771, the original two rooms with corner fireplaces were reduced to one with a new fireplace built into the back wall. The whole room was then paneled and a new tabernacle overmantel added with carved garlands. The stair from the stairhall was removed and the whole space turned into an entry/passage. In the chamber above, the walls were paneled in plaster, the same treatment that can be seen in the Ridout and Brice Houses in Annapolis and at Cloverfield in Queen Annes County.

The great Georgian houses of Kent County are few, but those that remain

Hynson-Ringgold House. Thomas Ringgold added the entire rear wing onto the original Murray House. Michael Bourne photograph, 1985.

Hynson-Ringgold House c. 1910, with a glimpse of the steps and door to the stair hall on the left. Kent County News Collection.

Opposite: Wideball. The central passage is separated from the stair hall by a series of three arches. Historic American Buildings Survey, 1940.

possess a plethora of detail that cannot be included in this brief outline. Suffice it to say that the ideals that are part of the period can be seen in some ways repeated in what would be considered Federal architecture. What can be gathered from the decade of the 1770s in Kent County is a full development of late Georgian building details along with vernacular tradition.

WALLIS-WICKES HOUSE AND THE ARCHIBALD WRIGHT HOUSE

Two Kent County merchants built Georgian houses, but they were of a plainer style than those mentioned above. Samuel Wallis inherited his father's property on the corner of High and Front Streets in 1769. Whether the house had been started by his father, Hugh, or Samuel built it himself will be proven with additional research. The large scale brick building has a central stair hall and four adjoining rooms heated with diagonal fireplaces. The house was equipped with basement kitchens that were accessible from grade on the Front Street gable. It was plainly exe-

Lambert Wickes

The action between the Continental ship REPRISAL and His Majesty's packet SWALLOW, February, 1777. From a painting by Maryland artist Peter Egeli, 1976. Courtesy of the artist.

Captain Lambert Wickes was born in Kent County around 1742. His great-grandfather, Major Joseph Wickes settled on Eastern Neck Island about 1650 and by 1660 had built Wickcliffe where Lambert was probably born. Lambert grew up near the shipyard close to his home on Shipyard Creek and the one nearby on Gray's Inn Creek. No doubt their proximity and family connections, especially his older brother Samuel, influenced his love of the sea. By 1776 he had begun his naval career and was well on his way to become a true Revolutionary War hero. On October 1, 1777, Captain Lambert Wickes, and his gallant ship the *Reprisal* went down in a storm off the banks of Newfoundland. All hands, except the cook, were lost. For more on Captain Wickes read: *Lambert Wickes, Pirate or Patriot?* by Norman H. Plummer, Chesapeake Bay Maritime Museum, St. Michaels, Maryland, 1991.

cuted with Flemish bond on the facade and common bond elsewhere. No belt course was installed and the degree of finish is not known. For the period it is distinguished by the fact that it had seventeen rooms, beside four hallways, and fifteen fireplaces.

The same plan house, on a smaller scale, can be seen in the Archibald Wright House (the rear of the Kitty Knight House Inn). Wright did use a belt course on his Flemish bond facade, but it is composed of three courses, the top protruding farther than the two below. This detail can be seen on contemporary houses in Cecil County. The principal room in the house has a tabernacle overmantel and the window and door trim have crossettes.

SPRINGFIELD FARM AND PINEY GROVE

A plan which developed in this decade is the four room plan, consisting of a stairhall and small room behind the stair, sometimes heated, sometimes not, plus two larger rooms which were heated. The first appears to be Springfield, a one-and-a-half-story, brick structure with a glazed date and the initials of the owners in its west gable:

1770
BR

In Benjamin Ricaud's house, the plan includes a very small unheated room beyond the stair and both large rooms are served by diagonal fireplaces that have fielded panel chimney breasts. It has two details in common with The Reward, the chimney stack and cupboards in the paneling of the back room.

The next house to be built with this plan was Piney Grove or Tilghman's Farm on Quaker Neck, after 1773. There the stair ascended in the room on the river side. The placement of the fireplaces in two principal rooms differed; the river side being on the party wall and the land side being diagonal. The reason for this difference was the location of a cooking fireplace in the basement in the river side room. The fourth room was heated with its own chimney.

Springfield Farm from the back.

Piney Grove. The 1770s section is the three-bays on the right.Constance Stuart Larrabee photographs.

BORDLEY-USILTON HOUSE, HEPBRON'S CHOICE AND HOPEFUL UNITY

Three other houses were built on the same plan: the Bordley-Usilton House, Hepbron's Choice and Hopeful Unity, all original owners being members of the Chester Parish Vestry. Each of these three has been changed in some way, but Hepbron's Choice has one original room that is paneled with featheredge boards and has a fine glazed corner cupboard. This type paneling was used in Kent County from the 1740s to the 1780s, so in this location it does not help in dating the building.

Dr. William Bordley House, Chestertown, had the same plan as the original part of Piney Grove. Michael C. Wootton photograph, 1996.

Photo of the back yards east of the Bordley Usilton House taken from its back porch. Kent News Collection, c. 1910.

HOPEWELL, TOWN RELIEF, THE HOUSTON HOUSE, RADCLIFFE CROSS AND FAIRY MEADOW

A unique example of the four room plan is found at Hopewell, in the large addition built adjacent to the original one-room-and-loft-house. The difficulty in dating this structure lies in the fact that the gunstock corner posts used in its construction would usually point to a construction date in the early eighteenth century.

Both Town Relief (the Wroth homestead) and the Houston House in Chestertown possess a variation on the four room plan (a side hall with double parlors and kitchen opposite to the parlor) which would become very common after the Revolution. Again, the dating of these two buildings has not been as precise as with other four room plan dwellings.

Yet another variation on the 1770s plan is the house with essentially a hall-parlor plan where the stair hall is taken out of one or the other. At Radcliffe Cross, this original floor plan is evident from the first floor framing. Now gone, Fairy Meadow, the Worrell farm, had a stair hall across three of its five bays.

CENTRAL HALL PLANS OF THE 1770S

As the 1770s progressed, more houses were constructed with a central stairhall plan. In Chestertown, toward the upper end of High Street, the Hopkins House has a central hall. The McHard House was another such example. Its facade was laid in all header bond and the water table jogged up and over the kitchen basement windows. Neither of these houses had glazed headers in regular bonding.

In the country, central hall plans occurred at Hebron, the John Williams House and Hinchingham on the Bay. At Hebron the stairhall is very narrow and the woodwork throughout is confined to baseboards, chair rails and mantels, with very little paneling used.

The John Williams House had the date of 1770 installed in glazed brick on its east gable in a somewhat haphazard manner across the projecting chimney. The chimney is located in the hall or larger room end of the house. Here, there is an enclosed secondary stair similar to those found in houses of the previous decade.

Hinchingham on the Bay has the date of 1774 displayed in glazed brick on its south gable. James Frisby had come into possession of this tract through his marriage to his first wife. He built the house after he had married his third wife, and after he had recorded his second marriage with initials at the Violet Farm. The interior of Hinchingham is one that could be classified early Georgian and is more like his previous home, the Violet Farm, than those with tabernacle overmantels that were being introduced in Kent County in the 1770s. Here, the principal room has well-proportioned pilasters flanking the fireplace and arched, glazed, shell cabinets flanking the pilasters. The dining room has a wall of plain fielded paneling that can be seen on houses of the previous decade.

The 1780s

BROAD NECK

One house that is difficult to classify is Broad Neck on Morgan Creek. It appears, however, to have been built before the 1783 Tax Assessment, since a *"large brick*

house" is mentioned in that document. Its plan is similar to Violet Farm in that there is a large room on one side of the stairhall and two on the other. The difference is that the second room protrudes several feet from the back wall and is covered with a cat slide roof. The latter protrusion has a corner chimney serving two fireplaces within. This is the only house where rubbed brick jack arches and belt course are used in combination with a semi-circular headed fanlight above the main entrance. The latter feature usually is found on houses of 1800 or later in Kent County. This may be an instance where the house was begun in the mid 1770s, like Reed's Creek, Queen Anne County, and not finished until after the Revolution.

WORTH'S FOLLY, SALUTATION, FRIENDSHIP, AND PROVIDENCE

Four houses built before the 1783 Tax Assessment include Worth's Folly, Salutation, Friendship, and Providence, all the product of Quaker owners. Of the four, Providence is neatly dated and initialed in glazed headers, 1781, for William and Mary Trew. Although appearing to be a hall-parlor house, it has a protruding third room that resembles Broad Neck. The Providence interior is almost entirely intact from the original period and possesses features that have become part of the vernacular tradition of Kent. The paneled fireplace wall contains an enclosed stair and a glazed cabinet with butterfly shelves. The fireplace surround has crossettes

Houston House, Chestertown. This house was built by William Houston or his son James. Michael C. Wootton photograph, 1996

Worth's Folly, c. 1780 lacks a center window on the second story rear facade because of the position of the attic stair. C. Engstrom photograph, 1977.

Broad Neck, c. 1780, has an off-set on its rear facade indicating two rooms in depth on the east side of the house. C. Engstrom photograph, 1977.

Hinchingham on the Bay. James Frisby built his second house on the Bay with a central hall plan. This was to become the most popular house plan for the next hundred years. Constance Stuart Larrabee photograph.

and the rest of the room has paneled wainscoting. The parlor is all sheathed in vertical featheredge boards, except the diagonal overmantel which has fielded panels and a glazed corner cupboard. The back room has a paneled overmantel and wainscoting beside an enclosed stair to the second story. Its interior finish resembles the Reward that was built nearly forty years before.

Worth's Folly is a two-story, three-bay, hall-parlor house with a wall of paneling enclosing the stair and a closet flanking the fireplace. For a house that is relatively standard, the reason for installing a first floor framing system with center girder is obscure, just as was done at Tibbalds and

the second story of Muddy Branch. Worth's Folly and its near twin, Duncan's Folly, have the same placement of attic stair, in the center of the house and not above the main stair.

Friendship or Warner's Addition was unfinished when the Tax Assessor arrived in 1783, but what was in the process of being constructed was a two-room building which consisted of a kitchen and hall. Both rooms had exposed beaded joists and enclosed stairs to separate chambers, similar to Salutation Farm, another house in the vicinity of Cecil Quaker Meeting. The latter plan consists of a stairhall and one room beside the kitchen. It was an arrangement similar to Robert Reed's

"Washington and His Generals at Yorktown" by Charles Willson Peale, c. 1781

*S*hortly after General Charles Cornwallis' surrender at Yorktown, on October 19, 1781, Charles Willson Peale captured the aftermath of Washington's victory in this painting. General George Washington is in the foreground, third from the left, and on the far right is Lieutenant Colonel Tench Tilghman. He was Washington's Senior Aide-de-Camp and a friend of Peales. He holds in his left hand the Articles of Capitulation which he delivered to the Continental Congress in Philadelphia. After leaving Yorktown, Tilghman landed at Rock Hall, then he rode on horseback following the old post road through Kent County passing Edesville, St. Paul's Church, then to Chestertown, and on to Georgetown. After four days he arrived in Philadelphia. Tench's father, James Tilghman lived on High Street and is buried in Old St. Paul's Cemetery. Maryland Historical Society, Baltimore

house, which abutted his brother's house on High Street in Chestertown.

JOHN PALMER HOUSE, SIMON WICKES HOUSE & FANCY FARM

In 1782, John Palmer built his house just up the street from Robert Reed. It was a standard one-and-a-half-story, hall-parlor house that was built not of brick, but of stone. Often portrayed as predating the town, Palmer's house was one of several stone or partially stone buildings in Kent County. Camelsworthmore falls into the latter category, being a brick, hall-parlor house with stone kitchen wing. Several stone outbuildings are extant from Camelsworthmore to Town's Relief, an indication of a modest run of fieldstone in that area.

Simon Wickes, a merchant, bought a water lot on Front Street in the early 1780s and built his house to match the McHard House down the street. Its facade is all header bond with usual jogged water table and the southwest gable was fitted with full size windows to take advantage of the sun, but its northwest gable was laid in Flemish bond with glazed headers, nearly a decade after the pattern had lost favor. Another late example of a glazed Flemish bond gable was William's Venture, a story-and-a-half building on Swan Creek which possessed a hall-parlor plan, with a full blown two flight mahogany stair.

The last house of this group which was mentioned in vague terms in the 1783 Tax Assessment is the frame part of Fancy Farm, a four-bay, two-story, building with central stairhall plan. It was a plain building which had leanto porches built around three sides and the interior was finished simply.

Providence Plantation, 1781, showing the two original sections of the house.
C. Engstrom photograph, 1977.

The Palmer House on the right, with the Hopkins House on the left. The Palmer house is the only stone house remaining in Chestertown.
James M. Kilvington photograph, 1975.

Footnotes:
1. Archives, Lib. XXV, fol. 258; United States Census, 1800.
2. Archives, Lib. XXVI, fol. 636.
3. Archives, Lib. XXVII, fol. 160.
4. The acts of both 1706 and 1707 refer to part of Stepney, the Wilmer family farm, parts of which had been purchased by Mr. Walvin and Mr. Joce. The initial site intended may have been located on 100 acres adjoining present day Chestertown. This property was later purchased for the Kent Free School.
5. Court Proceedings, 1707-1709, Accession No. 8568, Hall of Records.
6. Between 1717 and 1720, several petitions were made to the General Assembly by Philip Eilbeck and Christopher Bateman, debtors, and others in which they asked to be released from jail by the Sheriff of Kent County. Archives, XXXIII, fol. 131, 361.
7. Maryland Gazette, September 8, 1773.
8. Maryland Gazette, December 2, 1773.
9. Archives, Lib. XXXVII, fol. 172.
10. Archives, Lib. XXVII, fol. 71.
11. Land Records, Lib. 2, fol. 109.
12. Archives, Vol. XXXIX, fol. 493.
13. Proceedings of the Justices for the Inspection of Tobacco, 20 August 1748, Hall of Records.
14. Ibid.
15. Archives, Vol. II, fol. 211.
16. Maryland Gazette, February 14, 1764.
17. Archives, Vol. XIII, fol. 496.
18. Wills, Lib. 1, fol. 407.

Eighteenth Century Church Architecture in Kent County

SOME OF THE MOST NOTABLE EARLY BUILDINGS TO HAVE ENdured in Maryland are the churches which were built between the 1692 Act of Establishment and the Revolution. Initially, Kent County was divided into two parishes, St. Paul's and South Sassafras. At the time of the Act of Establishment each taxable inhabitant of Maryland was obligated to contribute to the maintenance of their parish. These funds were used to hire the services of a minister, construct and maintain the buildings and care for those who were in need. With such allocation of funds, it is not surprising that each of Kent's parishes was able to construct a church soon after 1692.

The minutes of 1694 for St. Paul's Parish record the first construction project as consisting of a 19' x 20' frame structure, presumably intended for the rector. The following year the vestry entered into an agreement to build a 24' x 40' frame church which was finished over a number of years as funds became available to pay for the work. At Shrewsbury by 1704, the original 24' x 30' frame structure was in need of a 20' extension. Originally, both churches were covered with riven oak clapboards, a drafty covering, prone to leaking which would require frequent repairs over their short lives. Both early churches also included a gallery as well as box pews on the ground floor.

By 1711, less than fifteen years after their first church, the vestry of St. Paul's determined to build anew. This time, they built of brick, a material which they had only considered in 1695. The new 30' x 40' structure had a semicircular apse and was to receive box pews, a gallery, and plaster finish over the next four years. The brickwork was of the finest quality of the day, well fired and laid in Flemish bond with an excellent quality

Shrewsbury Church. Rendering of first church including the 1705 addition by James T. Wollon, Jr. A.I.A. and Michael Booz. First illustrated in Katherine M. DeProspo's: A History of Shrewsbury Parish Church, 1988.

St. Paul's Church with vestry house on the left, c 1875. Note the short window in the loft. St. Paul's Parish Collection.

St. Peter's Church, I.U. The south elevation based upon the Articles of Agreement made between the vestry, Chester Parish, and Charles Tilden, House Joiner, in 1766. Michael Bourne.

Shrewsbury Church, including the 1722-29 structure with the addition of 1750-52, by James T. Wollon Jr., A.I.A. and Michael Booz. Illustrated in Katherine M. De-Prospo's history.

mortar joint. Only the apse was laid in glazed header Flemish bond.

About the same time as the construction of the new church at the headwaters of the west branch of Langford Creek, a chapel of ease was built in Chestertown. Specifications for that chapel have been lost, so little is known of its appearance until the need for repairs was recorded in the 1760s. By this time it had become part of the newly formed Chester Parish.

Shrewsbury Parish continued to repair and enlarge their original church building until 1721 when the vestry agreed to construct a new church. They also chose brick and constructed a 40' x 60' structure (twice the size of St. Paul's Church) with twenty-six pews and a gallery.

The first mention of a chapel of ease for Shrewsbury occurs in the vestry minutes of 1739. Located east of Massey's Crossroads the frame structure was 26' x 42'. Its construction continued over a period of six years.

At about the same time (1745 and 1750), both parishes had grown to the point of needing additional space. Extending perpendicularly to their original buildings, *T* plans were created which required the relocation of the pulpit and several pews. Throughout the county larger and better quality dwelling houses were also being constructed at this time, but it is obvious that the best building going on was being done by the Church, undoubtedly due to the availability of funds through taxation.

In 1765 an Act of the General Assembly created Kent's third parish by taking parts of Shrewsbury and St. Paul's. Even though Chester Parish was to include the existing chapel of ease at Chestertown, the vestry decided to build a new parish church at I. U. near the former glebe of Shrewsbury Parish. The new 40' x 60' church was built of brick and may have looked similar to Shrewsbury's earlier church. Unlike both previous churches, the new parish church had its altar on the west end of the building as opposed to the east.

During the same period, St. Paul's Parish entered into a contract with Charles Tilden, contractor for I. U. Church, to erect a brick vestry house, on which Tilden would leave the date, 1766, and the initials IOT. Shrewsbury had built its vestry house in 1745 and I. U.

St. Paul's Vestry House, built in 1766 by Charles Tilden, has the form of many small houses that existed in Kent County. Chimneys on both gables possess sloped weatherings. Library of Congress, Historic American Buildings Survey.

Chapel of Ease of Chester Parish. This 1860 sketch on Martenet's Map of Kent County illustrates the superior detail the church possessed before being remodeled in the 1880s.

had commissioned its vestry house a year before the church.

During the same period, an extension was planned for the chapel of ease in Chestertown; however, townspeople convinced the vestry that they were instead willing to fund the construction of a new building. The decision was made to create the most ambitious church structure in Kent County to that date. Under the guidance of William Ringgold, the new church took the form of a two-story rectangular building, similar in form and plan to Old Drawyers near Odessa, Delaware. Its interior was fitted with a pulpit and communion table in the center of the long northeast wall surrounded by box pews and a gallery on the three remaining walls. The exterior included the latest Georgian de-

tails: a central pavilion with classical architrave and Palladian windows facing High Street, corner pilasters, modillion cornice, and a full pediment on the northwest gable, on which there was also a classical entrance, facing Cross Street. This building, finished in 1772, would remain the best public building in town until the construction of Washington College in 1784.

Thus, in the eighteenth century, as all of the parishes of Kent County were in good financial shape, their buildings were also in very good condition. And while it seemed as though things would continue in this way, both the Revolution and the rise of Methodism left their impressions on Kent County and the colony of Maryland as a whole. Of the earliest houses of worship, only two have survived, St. Paul's and part of the chapel of ease of Chester Parish, now enveloped in the much altered Emmanuel Church.

Kent County Courthouse

High Street, Chestertown
1707

TWO OF THE MOST CONTROVERSIAL ISSUES CONCERNING the history of Kent County involve the locations of its first two courthouses. New Yarmouth, the seventeenth century settlement which was the seat of Kent County government between 1680 and 1696, vanished many years ago. Its location (and subsequently the location of its courthouse) was the subject of an article written in 1940 by Robert L. Swain, Jr. A second courthouse is reported to have existed between the years 1696 and 1707 and likewise its location is disputed.

Morris Radoff in his work on Maryland courthouses states that while there are no records which describe the courthouse at New Yarmouth, there is a small amount of information regarding the courthouse which followed. Reasoning for the change in location of the courthouse in 1696 stems from the fact that the county boundaries were altered and New Yarmouth no longer remained central to the majority of the county's popula-

tion. It was in 1696 that the Maryland Assembly authorized

" ... the Commissioners of the County of Kent to purchase three acres of land whereon to build a Courthouse ... ." [1]

" ... on the north side of the Chester River between the Plantations of Edward Fry and Isaac Caulk beginning at a bounded Persimon tree standing by the river side and running from thence North northwest seventeen perches then west southwest twenty six perches unto a small cove and down with the said cove and up the River until it intersects a line drawn south southeast from said Persimon tree and with the said line North northwest to the first bounded tree containing and laid out for three acres ... ." [2]

This location appears to have been on *Utrick*, part of a parcel which was given to Elizabeth Fry in 1692 by her father, Cornelius Comegys. (Its present location

1860 Kent County Courthouse, c. 1915, before enlargement of 1937. Kent County News collection of glass negatives.

Plaques erected by Historical Society of Kent County on Kent County Courthouse. Tyler Campbell photograph.

Kent County Courthouse, c. 1915. Same photograph used in Usilton's History of Kent County. Kent County News Collection of glass negatives.

would be west of the village of Quaker Neck Landing.)

The Commissioners contracted with John Sutton to build the courthouse, which was ready for use by March of 1697/98. In a report to the Assembly, it is stated:

"… that in Kent Conty there is no Ordinary near the Court House, it is built with a wooden chimney and the Records are Generally kept att the Clerks house unless in Court times."[3]

This basic courthouse was most likely similar to other buildings of the period, with walls and roof covered with riven oak clapboard. The wooden chimney is a feature it had in common with the Baltimore County Courthouse of the same period.

In 1706, after at least two years of petitions to the Legislature by residents of Cecil, Kent and Talbot Counties for a more equitable division of land, the Legislature authorized the formation of a new county called Queen Anne's. In the process of this Act, their boundaries were of course altered. Certainly the culmination of their wishes would be a large impetus to build a new courthouse in a location that was even more centrally located in the *new* County of Kent. The other three counties were to establish new *"seats of Judicature"* within a very short period of time.

There was a great controversy centered around the establishment of the *port of entry* which would be authorized in the Act for Advancement of Trade and Erection of Ports (1706). In 1707 its location was changed from Mr. Joce's plantation to that of Simon Wilmer (both were located within the original Stepney tract). According to the Kent County Court Proceedings, [6] Aug. 1707, court was *"… held at Courthouse at ye Town and Port of Chester … ."*

The controversy as to exact locations of these first two courthouses will most likely continue, but the fact is that there was a courthouse at Chestertown by 1707 and it existed for only twelve years before it was set afire by one Charles Hill. Apparently the fire took its toll, for it took 55,000 pounds of tobacco and over a year for the courthouse to be reconstructed. Radoff suggests that it was built anew. It is probable that a portion of that 1721 building remained until the time of the Martenet Map (1860).

From the crude sketch on that map the building appears to have had a plan similar to the courtroom at the Capital in Williamsburg, with a curved end. In form it

might have been similar to St. Paul's Church, built ten years earlier, with the apse being wider. Its roof looks as though it was hipped over the rectangular portion of the building, with a conical roof over the *apse* tapering into the hip. How the building was used has not been recorded, but parallels could be drawn to the one room at Williamsburg and the simple one room building constructed for Queen Annes County at Queenstown.

In 1750 the County officials petitioned the Legislature for 50,000 pounds of tobacco for repair and enlargement of the courthouse.[4] No county records have survived from this period. It is not until 1774 that the appearance of the courthouse is briefly described by Philip Fithian on his journey home to New Jersey from tutoring in Virginia. In his journal he writes:

"Rode home from Rock Hall over a delightful part of the country to Chester-Town 13 Miles—this is a beautiful small Town on a River out of the Bay navigable for Ships. The situation is low and I apprehend it is subject to summer Fevers—It has an elegant I may say grand Court-House, in which is the town clock ... ."[5]

By the 1790s, the courthouse was in need of repair and enlargement. In 1798, as recorded in both the Archives of Maryland and the Maryland Gazette, the Legislature authorized building a record office in Kent County. It is perhaps the record office that is represented in the Martenet map sketch to the right of the old courthouse. On the map itself, it seems that this other building faced south rather than southwest to the street.

On the same map (1860) a separate building is indicated and called the *Registrar's Office*. This is perhaps the result of the State Legislature authorizing the County $700 to repair the offices of the Clerk of the Court and Register of Wills in the early 1830s.

In 1860, the old courthouse and Register's Office were torn down and replaced by a new building to house all of the County offices under one roof. It was designed in the current Italianate style and looked similar to the Frederick County Courthouse on a smaller scale. The walls were finished with smooth cut brick with narrow mortar joint. At the corners were butress like pilasters. Between the pilasters and central pavilion, beneath a bracketed cornice, were a series of brick corbels. Gauged jack arches were used above the shuttered first floor windows, while gauged segmental arches were used over the unshuttered window above. Its central entrance had double doors, sidelights and transom in a pedimented architrave. The pediment echoed the lines of the pavilion roof. A date plaque was installed above the double windows, *1860*. The

Kent County Courthouse, 1996. Michael Wootton photograph.

building had a *T* plan with offices flanking the grand double stair to the second floor on the High Street side. A minor passage through the back with flanking vaults and storage rooms were located beneath the second floor courtroom.

In 1912 and 1937 the building was enlarged in the same style as the original building, but in 1969, the new addition which nearly doubled its size was designed in the *Colonial* style that was in vogue then. Since 1969 there have been no major additions or deletions. Only the removal of the 1883 jail and landscaping of the Cross Street yard have been done in an effort to create a new entrance.   K-50

1. Archives of MD, Vol. XIX, 30 April 1696.
2. Land Records, Lib. C, fol. 119.
3. Archives of MD, Vol. XXII, p. 102.
4. Radoff, Morris K., The County Courthouses and Records of Maryland, Vol. 1. Annapolis: Hall of Records, 1960.
5. Diary of Philip Vickers Fithian - April 1774.

Presbury

Near Crumpton

c. 1710

ATENTED IN 1675 FOR THOMAS NORRIS AS A 150 ACRE parcel, Presbury was located on the north side of the Chester River across from present-day Crumpton.[1] Later acquired by Cornelius Comegys, he in turn deeded it to his son, William, in 1690. William Comegys is the probable builder of the first part of the one-and-a-half-story, brick house which once stood on the tract. It is difficult to say when exactly William took up residency on Presbury, as prior to his father's death, he had owned property at the tip of Broad Neck, then called Gloucester. Also, he inherited an additional 300 acres, described in his father's will as *"… in Piney Neck over against him (William) in Chester River … ."* [2] However, it is certain that he lived there at the time of his own death in 1735, as his will states this. To his youngest son, Edward, William Comegys bequeathed his *"… now dwelling plantation with all the lands thereunto belonging, Viz. Presbury, Little Worth & Chance and one-third of an Island Marsh in Queen Annes County called Sandy Hurst."* [3]

Presbury. The original early eighteenth century house of William Comegys with a nineteenth century frame wing. Michael Bourne photograph, 1979.

The earliest part of the house measured 18' 0" wide by 25' 5" long. Its one brick thick walls were laid in a random Flemish garden wall bond above a stepped water table. The south facade had two windows to the east of the entrance door. The north facade had a centered entrance. Evidence found in the basement indicated that there was a wide chimney base or fireplace slightly off-center on the east gable, which allowed enough room for a newel stair in the northeast corner.

The room arrangement from the first period was either a hall-parlor or simply one room. The ceiling height was 7' 3", 3" taller than that in the basement. A small casement in the east gable shed light into the stair well. Light for the attic room was probably provided from the west gable. All ceilings were plastered, including that in the basement. One of the unique features of the construction of the roof was use of tilted false plates and rafters laid on the wide side, indication of its early construction, c. 1710

William Comegys' son, Edward, had a 14 acre part of his farm resurveyed as the Landing in 1742.[4] It was located on the southeast corner of the property, near the beginning of Presbury. He may have been responsible for constructing the 20' extension to the west gable of his father's house. With the extension, the house measured 45' 9" long. The addition had a door and window on both facades. The wing was built without a basement and the floor level was about one foot lower than the original, even though the exterior cornices line up. It is probable that the dormers were installed across both sides of the steeply pitched *A* roof at this time. The new room had a newel stair in the southwest corner and a cabinet in the northwest corner flanking the fireplace.

Edward Comegys also owned one of the mills at Prickle Pear Branch which he had acquired from the heirs of the builders, John Earle and William Butcher.[5] He died intestate in 1751 with a personal estate valued in excess of £1000. One of his creditors was John Hamner, an agent for the Liverpool firm of Foster Cunliffe who operated a mercantile business at Townside on the adjoining farm.[6] His widow, Ann, and her second husband, Jesse Cosden, continued to administer his estate until 1756 when the proceeds were finally distributed between Ann and her son William.[7]

William Comegys married Mary Forrester and, before his death in 1764, they had one child whom they named Mary. Mary Comegys became heir to Presbury, etc., but the deeds between 1767 and 1783 have not been located.[8]

In the Tax Assessment of 1783, the property appears under the ownership of Joseph Williams who later in that decade was bankrupt. In a deed from the debtor to his trustees, it states that he came into possession of Presbury, etc. by his wife, Avarilla. Her daughter, Mary Freeman, spinster, purchased the farm from the trustees in order to pay her stepfather's debts.[9] Avarilla Williams' name appears again in the 1822 Tax Assessment. The farm appears to have remained in the family of Avarilla Williams until 1856 when it was sold to Henry B. Slaughter, who also owned the Comegys House on Buck Hill and Billy's Lott.[10]

The lands were sold at public auction in 1874 due to Slaughter's default. In the court ordered sale, all of Slaughter's lands were resurveyed and each section sold separately.[11] The part of his properties which contained the Presbury house was sold to Thomas and Eliza Jane Massey, who appear in the 1877 Atlas. The following year, the Masseys sold the 139 acre farm to

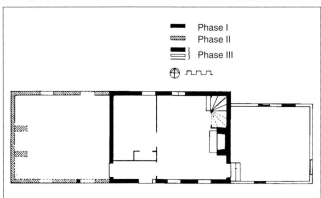

	Phase I
	Phase II
	Phase III
⊕	

Presbury. The earliest section is in the center of the photograph. The left side collapsed soon after this 1963 photograph. Michael Bourne Collection.

Presbury, c. 1710. First floor plan. Michael Bourne, 1997.

Dr. and Mrs. F. N. Sheppherd who had acquired Buck Hill and Billy's Lott at auction four years before.[12] Since that time the two farms have been in the same ownership and the old house, before its disintegration was occupied by tenants.[13]   K-200

1. Patents, Lib. 15, fol. 478.
2. Wills, Lib. 1, fol. 92.
3. Wills, Lib. 2, fol. 33. William Comegys is reputed to have built his house in 1708 on property called Buck Hill and Billy's Lot.
4. Patents, Lib. LG No. E, fol. 51.
5. Land Records, Lib. JS 23, fol. 56; Lib. JS 25, fol. 81.
6. Inventories, Lib. 4, fol. 88, 178.
7. Accounts, Lib. 4, fol. 66.
8. Land Records, Lib. DD 2, fol. 519.
9. Land Records, EF 7, fol. 413.
10. Land Records, JFG 3, fol. 391. This house is referred to as Townside.
11. Chancery, Lib. JKH 6, fol. 26.
12. Land Records, Lib. DCB 3, fol. 469.
13. The physical description of Presbury is the result of an investigative visit to the house by the author in 1979. At that time the house was but a ruin. Surprisingly the remaining walls stood until 1994 when the house finally collapsed.

St. Paul's Church and Vestry House

Near Fairlee
1711

S T. PAUL'S CHURCH IS THE EARLIEST RELIGIOUS STRUCTURE to survive in Kent County. With the possible exception of Old Trinity in Dorchester County, it may be the earliest surviving religious structure built on the Eastern Shore of Maryland after the Act of Establishment in 1692. The church with its accompanying vestry house also stands in the most picturesque churchyard of the area.

An earlier church, St. Peters, had existed on Eastern Neck, but due to the geographical shift in population, the present site of St. Paul's on Arcadia was chosen for its more convenient location. The existing church is actually the second structure to have been built here.

St. Paul's Church, 1711, with nineteenth and twentieth century embellishments. Tyler Campbell photograph, 1995

From the Vestry Minutes of 1692 and 1693, it is apparent that the first vestry was desirous of building a brick church from the beginning, but their contractor, Daniel Norris, failed to begin making bricks in time, which in turn caused them to cancel their contract with him. After Norris had completed a 20' x 19' frame building to be used as the rectory, he presented a proposal to the vestry to erect a frame church, 50' x 26', but it was rejected. They decided instead to wait and collect the levies before moving forward. In 1695, the vestry finally contracted with Norris to build a frame church, 40' x 24'. Two years later, another contract was made to *"arch the Church ... fit for plastering,"* but due to the lack of plasterers in the area, it was entirely wainscoted with boards, including the arched ceiling. The aisles and chancel were paved with tiles. Apparently the execution of the interior dragged on. By 1700, however, there is mention that the brickwork was already beginning to show signs of wear and tear.

By 1711, the church had begun to deteriorate to such a degree that the vestry contracted with James Harris, William Potts and James Smith to:

"Build or Cause to be Built one Brick Church in

same Convenient Place near the sd Church in our said Parish of St Paul's, which sd Church is to be forty feet in Length in the Clear & Thirty foot broad in the Clear & the Brick for sd House to be good Well Burnt Bricks & the Water Table of sd House to be two Brick & one half thick, thence two Brick Thick to the Plate & the sd Wall to be Sixteen feet High from the Ground to the Plate, & an Arch to be at the East End of sd Church for the Communion Table, Answering to such a Building, The Making of the Windows & the Doors for sd house at the Discretion of the Carpenter that doth the Work of sd house & the Vestry of the Parish how they shall be made & also the Cornish for sd house to be left as Afsd, The Afsd house to be well shingled wth Good Cypress Shingles & to be Good Shutters for all the sd House & the Arch in the roof of sd House to be Finish'd Workmanlike, & the Afsd House to be Finished Workmanlike according to the Above sd Dimensions at or before the Tenth Day of October in the Year of our Lord Christ one Thous'd Seven Hund'd

*S*t. Paul's Church, 1711. During recent remodeling of the balcony it was discovered that some structural members were found to have been "used" materials. The vestry minutes of May 16, 1715 reaffirms that supposition: "This day this Vestry hath agreed with Wm Mackey to Build a Gallery in the Church and what work is necessary to be done that will not hinder the Plaisterer is to be done by the first Day of August And the sd Mackey is to make use of any of the old stuff in the Old Church that he hath need, or can make use of And the sd Gallery to be fully finished by the twentieth Day of Sept next … ."

& Thirteen. And when so Built the Afsd house to be Delivered to Mr. Alexr Williamson, Col. Thos Smyth, Mr Wm Frisby, Mr Wm Harris, Mr Wm Scott, Edwd Scott, to them or Either of Them … for the only use & Benefit of our Sd Parish of St Paul's in our Sd County … ."[1]

When the contract was fulfilled, the church was not actually complete. Through a series of subsequent contracts, the 34 pews, pulpit and reading desk were installed, the windows were glazed, herringbone brick was laid in aisle floors, the interior was plastered and a balcony was constructed. The same sequence of contracts can be found in the vestry minutes in regard to the construction of the vestry house, as well as the construction of Chester Parish Church at I. U., both of which were constructed in 1766. It is of interest to note that both of the aforementioned projects were partially undertaken by Charles Tilden, the grandson of one of the vestryman who contracted with

The old White Oak Tree which formerly stood in St. Paul's Churchyard. L. Dudley Reed photograph.

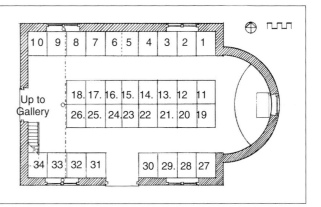

The gallery at St. Paul's during recent renovation. Shown here is one of the three columns supporting the girder that runs across the width of the church.

This joint, a piece of the "old stuff," is mortised into the girder. Tyler Campbell photographs, 1997.

St. Paul's Vestry House, 1766. Contracted by Charles Tilden, grandson of one of the first vestrymen and contractors for the 1696 Church. C. Engstrom photograph, 1977.

Robert Norris for installing the arched ceiling in the frame church in 1697.

In the 1740s, during the time which the Rev. James Sterling was rector at St. Paul's, the congregation grew to such an extent that an addition was built onto the north side of the church, including enough space for 23 new pews. The pulpit and reading desk were relocated to serve both sections of the church. This addition was pulled down in 1824, when the congregation dwindled. The patched brickwork can still be discerned on the north side of the building.

In 1841, the church saw a second remodeling. The box pews were replaced with congregational seating on a new wood floor, as opposed to the original brick, and a sacristy was built on the east end of the north wall. Even later in the nineteenth century the balcony and communion rails were replaced with a country gothic design, which has the same trim as the renewed doors and windows. In the early twentieth century a small organ room was constructed adjacent the sacristy. The building was again refurbished in the mid-twentieth century through the generosity of Mr. Glen L. Martin, who owned the adjoining Poplar Neck Farm.[2]

The distinctive features of St. Paul's Church are its uniform Flemish bond brickwork with both plain and glazed heads, neatly-struck mortar joints (where they have not been replaced with Portland cement) and the rubbed brick semicircular arches above the windows and doors. Modillion cornices are exceedingly rare on the Eastern Shore. At St. Paul's such a cornice exists on the south side of the building and is original to its 1711 construction. Also, only three other churches on the Shore possess apses (referred to in the contract for St. Paul's as the *" ... arch at the east end ... ."*). They are St. Luke's in Church Hill, Trinity Church at Church Creek, and St. Andrew's in Princess Anne.   K-123 & K-124

St. Paul's Church was contracted to be built in 1711. In 1713 the vestry authorized Wᵐ Salsbury to "set up 34 pews ... pulpit & reading desk according to model by the Sᵒ Vestry drawn ... ." Possibly pews 5 and 6 were taken up by the pulpit and reading desk. The position of the center block of pews is entirely conjectural, as is the communion rail and table. In 1715 the vestry contracted with Wᵐ Mackey to construct the "gallery," just after making arrangements to have Thoˢ Cook to plaster the Church and lay the altar and aisles in herringbone brick. In 1717, Wᵐ Mackey was again contracted to "make a window shutter at the East end of Church, new & framed work ... ." Michael Bourne, 1997.

1. Vestry Minutes, St. Paul's Parish, Kent. Hall of Records, Annapolis, MD.
2. In 1993, a history of St. Paul's was published by the Church. Entitled "St. Paul's Church, Kent," it was edited by Davy H. McCall and is recognized here as a source for much of the history sited above.

Hopewell

Near Chestertown
c. 1720

Hopewell is the name given to a 1000 acre tract of land patented in 1686 to Richard and Joseph Hopewell and located north of the Chester River and west of Morgan Creek. On a part of the tract, an early eighteenth century owner, possibly Richard Hopewell, built a small, one-room house which measured 16' 6" x 20' 6" and had a loft beneath its *A* roof. The house was constructed over a field stone foundation and basement but had a chimney constructed of brick. Laid in Flemish bond, the back of the fireplace was exposed to the outside.

After a period of time, a two-room-deep addition was constructed on the east end. This was also covered with an 'A' roof, with its apex no taller than that of the earlier section. The unusual features of the newer section included the use of gunstock corner posts in its framing and a unique room arrangement (see plan). There also appears to have been a third addition off

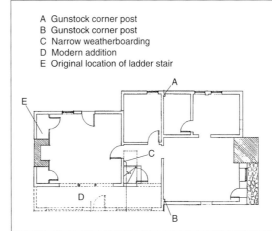

A Gunstock corner post
B Gunstock corner post
C Narrow weatherboarding
D Modern addition
E Original location of ladder stair

Hopewell Farm, first floor plan. Note position of corner posts in newer section. M. L. Fritz. 1980.

Hopewell Farm c. 1720, with later addition. The addition is built with gunstock corner posts. Maryland Historical Trust, M. L. Fritz photograph, 1980.

this section's east gable, its fireplace back-to-back with that of the middle section. This was possibly a kitchen.

From the time Hopewell was acquired by Thomas Ringgold in the 1760s, the farm appears to have been owned primarily by absentee landlords. They included Richard Snowden Thomas, John Constable, G. W. T. Perkins, and William Jarrell. In the 1783 Tax Assessment it was assigned to William Ringgold who was the trustee of Thomas Ringgold.   K-205

Marshy Point

Near Locust Grove
c. 1720

MARSHY POINT IS LOCATED ON THE Sassafras River between Island and Freeman Creeks. It was originally known, in the seventeenth century, as Harmon's Point, but a resurvey was undertaken during the ownership of William Pearce and the name was changed at that time. Pearce owned the parcel from the late seventeenth century until he deeded it to his son, Daniel, in 1720.[1, 2]

The house on Marshy Point was situated near the middle of the farm, but at the head of a small gut which empties into Island Creek. Built either by Daniel or by his son and heir, Andrew Pearce, both had lived on the plantation. The house, in its original form, was a one-and-a-half-story structure, three bays long, with central doors on each facade which were flanked by two 6/6 sash windows. There were two similar sized dormers built on each side of the *A* roof. Its framing members were distinguished in the use of gunstock corner posts. (Only a few examples of these remain in Kent County.) The ceiling joists were exposed and beaded in both the hall and parlor. The two rooms were divided by a vertical beaded board partition. The fireplace wall was covered by paneling which incorporated two closets and an enclosed stair. The second floor was originally divided into two small rooms.

Andrew Pearce remained on Marshy Point until he sold it in 1747 to Isaac and Hannah Freeman, who had lived on the west side of Freeman Creek.[3] Isaac gave that portion of Marshy Point which contained the house to his oldest son, Abraham, in 1756.[4]

By 1783, Marshy Point was in the possession of James Woodland. Roughly 75 years later the farm is identified as in the ownership of J. L. Woodland. It has remained in the same family to the present day.

Marshy Point. Plat of farm indicating approximate location of house. Kent County Chancery, Lib. JKH, fol. 237.

Marshy Point, c. 1720. This small hallparlor house was remodeled in the late nineteenth century to a central stair plan. It is one of three Kent County houses with gunstock corner posts. M. Bourne photograph, 1978.

In the latter part of the nineteenth century, the house had fallen into disrepair, so a major remodeling was undertaken. The kitchen, which was originally located on the east side of the house, was reconstructed reusing some of its hewn members. The main section was gutted and the plan changed from a hall-parlor to a central stair with two flanking rooms. The fireplace was dismantled and replaced with stove flues. The north door was eliminated and the south door was made into a double door. Wide eaves with decorative pierced-work gingerbread were added to both sections of the house.

In 1985, the house was in the process of being remodeled when it was decided that it should be moved closer to the river. During the move, the building was reoriented by 180 degrees and placed over a full basement. Two additions to the kitchen were constructed and the original section of the house was converted into a single room with a large fireplace having paneling across the enclosed stair and closets.

Marshy Point has been a tenant house since the late eighteenth century, with short periods of occupancy by Woodland family members.   K-207

1. Wills, Lib. 1, fol. 207 (1720).
2. William Pearce was an important figure in early Cecil (later Kent) County, holding offices of importance in the legislature and as Sheriff, Justice, vestryman of Shrewsbury Parish and in the local militia. By the time of his death, he held 1450 acres and his personal estate was valued at £1153. Likewise, his son Daniel held positions in the Lower House, was a surveyor for Cecil County and later Clerk. He was also a vestryman at Shrewsbury Church and served as a captain in the militia. Daniel held over 1000 acres and his personal estate was worth nearly £800. (Papenfuse).
3. Land Records, Lib. JS 26, fol. 98, 134, 217, 274.
4. Wills, Lib. 4, fol. 6.

White House Farm

Near Kennedyville
1721

WHITE HOUSE FARM IS ONE OF THE BEST document-ed early eighteenth century houses remaining in Kent County. It is associated with four generations of the Perkins family, beginning with Daniel Perkins (1685-1744) and ending with his great-grand-daughter, Mary Stuart Corse, wife of Unit Corse, who owned Locust Grove, an adjoining farm.

Daniel Perkins acquired the milling rights at the head of Morgan Creek in 1710. In 1719, he acquired Ridgely, an adjoining tract upon which he built his dwelling in 1721. That first house remains as part of White House Farm today. In its original form, it was a one-and-a-half story, hall-parlor plan, brick house which was distinguished by the use of the date 1721 in glazed header numerals on the north gable. This house was similar to Marrowbone located to the southeast on the Chester River and built in the same decade, except that White House had a stair in both rooms and only two chambers above. How soon after 1721 the 33', two-room extension was constructed has not been determined, but in 1778 it is mentioned in a description of the house prepared for Perkins' orphaned granddaughter, Mary Perkins. In that document, there is mention of the 72' house, plus a 10' x 12' brick shed addition and a log kitchen.

In the earliest deeds Daniel Perkins is called *"Stone-cutter."* He owned Lot No. 12 in Chestertown which he sold to Jonathan Page, and which was later purchased by Hugh Wallis. Elsewhere, Perkins is called *"mill-wright."* He acquired several tracts in the area, a clear sign of the prosperous nature of his mill. In 1742, Perkins took out a license to operate a tavern, but its location remains a mystery. There is also the question of whether or not Perkins actually had been running a tavern prior to the application.

Upon Daniel Perkins' death in 1744, White House Farm, including the mill, were bequeathed to his son, Thomas

White House Farm, 1721. Built by Daniel Perkins eleven years after establishing a grist mill at the upper reaches of Morgan Creek. Michael Wootton photograph, 1996.

White House Farm. The glazed date, 1721, is the earliest of Kent County's dated houses. Glazed dates were used between 1721 and 1784 in Kent. Michael Wootton photograph, 1996.

White House Farm. 1830s remodeling of second story bedroom. C. Engstrom photograph 1977.

White House Farm, 1721. First floor plan. Michael Bourne, 1997.

Perkins (1720-1768). Thomas remained at White House and continued to operate the farms and mills. In 1751, he married Ann Hanson and together they had four children. Only Mary, the youngest, survived to maturity and was subsequently the sole beneficiary of her parents' estate. It was for Mary that the inventory of the property was recorded by the Orphans Court in 1778. Besides the house and kitchen mentioned above, there were four frame houses, three barns, three mills, and corn, bake, milk and meat houses on the plantation, which was at that time occupied by John Turner.

In 1779, Mary Perkins married John Wilson and settled at White House Farm where they raised five children. After Wilson's death, Mary married Dr. Alexander Stuart and moved to Delaware where she had another four children. After her death in 1808, the estate was unsettled until the children reached maturity in 1822. White House Farm was acquired by Mary's namesake, Mary Stuart Corse. It was probably during this last ownership that the house was allowed to deteriorate.

Robert Constable purchased the house and 216 acres from Mary Corse's estate in 1831 and remodeled the house, partially rebuilding some of the south wall, reducing the size of the fireplace and retrimming the house throughout. The present interior is mostly the re-

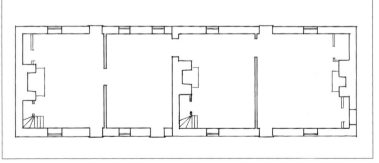

sult of the Constable remodeling/renewal which occurred in the late Federal period.

Since that time there have been seven other owners, the last of whom purchased the farm in 1947 and set about making it an attractive home. It has been opened to the public on occasion.[1]   K-203

1. Lutz, Thomas, Chronology of White House Farm, Research paper presented to owner, Mrs Arthur Pinder, 1989.

Huntingfield Site

Eastern Neck
1722

ONE OF THE LARGEST TRACTS IN THE LOWER COUNTY was Huntingfield, a 1200 acre tract patented to the first Thomas Ringgold in 1659.[1] Ellendale is one of the several farms into which it was divided as the Ringgold family grew. The early house on the property is described by Mary Camp in a missive to Mary Ringgold Willson:

"The original house, which was long looked upon as one of the oldest in the county, had the date of its erection, 1722, in glazed black brick in the east gable, large figures. This home was destroyed by fire winter of 1851 and rebuilt on old foundation the following summer. The old house was one-and-a-half stories high and the brick walls, including inside partitions, started from cellar foundations. On the first floor was a large central hall with two rooms on either side. The windows in the two front rooms were placed between broad fluted columns which extended from floor to ceiling. The window seats were deep and window panes quite small.

The parlor mantel was broad at either end yet narrow in the center and rested on fluted columns like those at the windows. Above the mantel, fixed in the wall, was a large oil painting (pastoral scene). The newel post in the hall was large and square and beautifully carved and paneled to match wainscoting. There was little plaster in the house, four bedrooms on the second floor, sloping walls, dormer windows and queer little end windows. In lower hall two outside doors were double paneled on inside and arranged in diamonds on outside. Front door had huge brass knocker on a heavy plate.

Main building was brick, kitchen at east end was frame." [2]

From Mary Camp's description, the old house sounds as though it was similar to White House Farm, the one and a

"Huntingfield, Surveyed for Messrs Thomas Ringgold, Josias Larkin, Elias Ringgold & Wm Ringgold Guardians to James Ringgold a minor," 1720.

Huntingfield or Ellendale, reputedly had a race track between the house and Bay. In 1954 Hurricane Hazel began to consume the house.
Louisa Kelly Collection

Marrowbone

Near Crumpton
c. 1728

Located on the upper reaches of the Chester River, Marrowbone was one of the truly early eighteenth century dwellings in Kent County to survive into the last quarter of the twentieth century. In 1972, it was included in a joint recording venture between the Maryland Historical Trust and the St. Mary's City Commission. In 1976, it was dismantled and to this day, awaits reconstruction.

In 1728, Jervis Spencer, a weaver by trade had acquired 74 acres of The Conclusion and 90 acres of Darby. He had these lands, as well as, 236 adjacent vacant acres resurveyed into a 400 acre parcel which he called Marrowbone.[1]

On this tract, Spencer built his dwelling. It consisted of a one-and-a-half-story, brick structure with a hall-parlor plan with a leanto or shed addition on the east end of the north facade. The walls were laid in English bond, except for the south facade which received the decorative treatment of Flemish bond with glazed headers. A plain, stepped water table surrounded the building one course above the floor level. The only other decorative feature was a segmental arch with alternating glazed headers located above the central entrance. On the north facade there were three-centered arches over the doors, and flat arches above the window—all were composed of vertical headers in a single row.

The hall was originally well-finished with a 6' 2½" wide fireplace and an enclosed winder stair adjacent in the southwest corner. This fireplace had a large bolection-molded panel above the mantel shelf and two-panel closet doors on either side. These doors, as well as the stair door, were all hung on foliated *H* hinges. The fireplace itself was surrounded by a wide bolection molding. Although the door and window trim were very plain, with only a bead on the outer edge of the jamb, there was a chair rail and a two piece cornice as well. The two exterior doors had been hung on heart-ended strap hinges.

A 9" brick wall separated the hall and parlor. The parlor had chair rail and cornice and a closet north of the fireplace which was lighted by a small window. South of the huge fireplace there was an original door in the gable. This may have led to a detached kitchen originally, but later a kitchen was attached to the east gable. The fireplace in the parlor differed from that in the hall in that its cheeks were one brick thicker. This enabled the builder to install two recesses inside. The back of the fireplace had been laid in herringbone brick. Lighting was accomplished by only one window on the

---

half story brick house built by Daniel Perkins bearing the glazed date of 1721 in its gable. But, the interior here sounds more sophisticated and in that way similar to the Violet Farm, a 1762 residence built by James Frisby and his Ringgold wife, Rebecca.

After the original house burned, the remodeled house was reworked in a very simple Greek Revival style. It had a partially submerged basement with four rooms and central hall which was devoted to kitchens and pantries. The first floor had a similar arrangement with two additional rooms in a frame shed-roof addition. The second floor also had four rooms and a central hall. It was similar in plan to other mid-nineteenth century farmhouses, except that the second floor was frame on the old patched brick walls of the first floor. Along the south front of the house there was a porch with brick floor on grade and brick columns supporting a porch with Greek architrave having dentil molding.

The farm had been purchased in the 1830s by Captain George H. Willson and it was he who rebuilt the house after the fire.[3] In the 1852 Tax Assessment, Willson was assessed on *"398 acres of Huntingfield with a New House & other Buildings in good repair."* Amongst his taxed property was the schooner *Pearle*—a 24 ton sailing vessel.[4]

The house and some of the farm was purchased in the 1880s by Mr. Louis E. Smith in whose family it remains to this day.[5] Sadly, years of erosion brought the shores of the Chesapeake closer and closer until the house was eventually consumed by the power of the Bay.   K-269

Huntingfield or Ellendale, rebuilt in 1852 on the foundations of James Ringgold's 1722 house. Maryland Room, Enoch Pratt Free Library, c. 1930.

Huntingfield or Ellendale, the 1852 front porch showing brick floor and columns. 1930 Louisa Kelly Collection.

1. Patents, Lib. 4, fol. 300.
2. Letter in possession of Mary Louisa E. Kelley.
3. Land Records, Lib. JNG 7, fol. 313.
4. 1852 Tax Assessment.
5. Land Records, Lib. SB 3, fol. 272.

south, as there was a door on the north side leading to the frame shed addition.

The second floor was divided by board partitions into a corridor on the south with a heated bed chamber over the parlor and an unheated chamber over the rest of the hall. Again, the doors had two panels and were hung on foliated *H* hinges. The parlor chamber fireplace was 3' 3" wide with a segmental arch. This wall probably had paneling with closets flanking the fireplace. Flooring was very wide on the second floor, the boards being 11"–13" wide. Three dormer windows on each side of the roof lite the second floor rooms.

Marrowbone was home to Jervis Spencer and his wife, Ann Comegys (daughter of Spencer's neighbor, William Comegys). Together they had six children, Isaac being the eldest, it was to him that Jervis left *"my Plantation whereupon I live called 'Marrowbone,' being about 400 acres ... also my plantation near Prickle Pare Mill, called Darby ... about 400 acres."* Jervis Spencer also left 110 acres and grist Mill on Unicorn Branch Queen Annes County to his grandson, Christopher Williams, son of daughter Mary, deceased, and directs that he be under the care of Isaac until he reaches 21, and that Isaac shall rebuild the Mill before that time.[2]

Jervis Spencer's personal estate was valued at the time of his death to be £1368.12.5. It included 21 slaves,

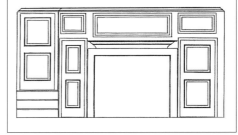

Marrowbone, c. 1728. The north side of the house with an early twentieth century frame addition, c. 1930. Maryland State Archives, Patty Moffet Seitzer Collection.

Marrowbone c. 1728. The parlor fireplace shown with original herringbone removable brick fireback. Michael Bourne photograph, 1977.

Marrowbone, c. 1720, Hall paneling drawn from fragments found during disassembly in 1976. Michael Bourne.

17 horses, 42 cows, 91 sheep and 48 pigs, along with much household furniture and furnishings.[3] Two additional inventories made, when the crops were in and the debts assembled, amounted to an additional £187.12.7 and £536.13.8,[4] respectively. Jervis Spencer was one of the wealthiest citizens of Kent County. He had risen from the stature of weaver to that of Gentleman in a relatively short time.

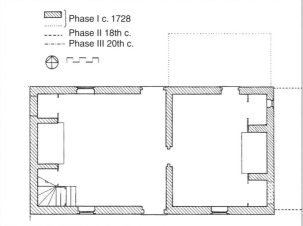

Phase I c. 1728
Phase II 18th c.
Phase III 20th c.

Marrowbone, c. 1728.
Conjectural Restoration
of south facade. Michael
Bourne.

Marrowbone, c. 1728.
Floor plan, Michael
Bourne.

Isaac Spencer, continued to live on the home plantation and to buy and sell real estate. He apparently built the Store House in New Market after purchasing the Northwest Corner lot in 1773. From here he had an outlet for his mercantile interests. Not only did he rebuild the Unicorn Mill for his nephew, he also joined with his brother-in-law, John Comegys in constructing a second mill on nearby Prickle Pare Branch. He later bought out the other half.

Isaac appears to have *jumped the gun* on producing a family, for he was brought before the Vestry of Shrewsbury Church for co-habitating with Hannah (probably Comegys, his cousin).

Nothing is specifically documented about Isaac and Hannah's use of the house. It is known that the house was lengthened to the east sometime in the eighteenth century and that there was a log or plank meathouse northeast of the house. There obviously would have been barns for the crops, sheds for the livestock and quarters for the slaves, but there is no record of them.   K-179

1. Patents, Lib. PL 7, fol. 494.
2. Wills, Lib. 4, fol. 128.
3. Inventories, Lib. 5, fol. 54.
4. Inventories, Lib. 5, fol. 164; Lib. 5, fol. 269

Lamb's Meadow

Near Still Pond
c. 1730, 1753

Lamb's Meadow has been a favorite subject of many authors. Certainly its gambrel roof form, superior brickwork and workmanship are features which have attracted the attentions of generations on their way to and from the northern part of Kent County. But perhaps most uniquely, Lamb's Meadow has remained in the same family since 1694.

Pearce Lamb had Lamb's Meadow surveyed on the nineteenth day of March in 1694. It contained 215 acres. Upon his death in 1709, Pearce left Lamb's Meadow to his wife Mary Howe, stipulating that after her death it was to be divided between their two sons, Francis and Pearce. As the will states: *"that they may set in any place of the tract which is above mentioned."*[1] This stipulation infers that their father's own dwelling may have been located elsewhere, perhaps on Lamb's Range adjoining[2], which was patented about ten years before.

Francis Lamb (b. 1689) lived a long and prosperous life. On April 3, 1714, he married Rosamund Beck, at St. Paul's Church. While the records of all of his children's births and deaths are found in the Quaker records of the county, it remains difficult to ascertain when Francis took over the property as the date of his mother's death is unrecorded.

Family tradition holds that Francis' brother Pearce died shortly after their father, leaving Francis sole heir of the tract. But according to a resurvey conducted for Francis in 1743, there were only 103 acres of the original grant in his possession.[3]

When Francis Lamb began the construction of his house is not easy to determine. Again according to family tradition, the house was built by Pearce and Mary Lamb, but that is improbable, as there are no other gambrel roof structures dating from before the 1730s on the Eastern Shore.

The original house measured about 20' x 40' and had a full basement with kitchen fireplace on the south end wall, adjacent a bulkhead. Both long facades had two windows with 12/12 sash flanking a central door, and each of those had segmental arches. There were windows lighting the basement as well. Three sides of the building were laid in Flemish bond, but only the west facade and north gable had glazed headers. Within each gable was a bold chimney rising above the apex of the roof. Two shed roof dormers with 6/6 sash were placed above the first floor windows on each side of the gambrel roof.

The plan was laid out in a predictable hall-parlor arrangement, with exterior doors opening into the hall.

Both rooms had paneling installed across the fireplace wall, enclosing closets and stairs. Over the fireplace in both are double door cabinets fitted with shelves, similar to those at the Reward. The hall was further embellished with raised panel dado and window seats, but the jewel of the room was the close string turned balustrade with square newel and ball finial. It ascends only four steps to the door before disappearing behind the paneling. A basement stair was located beneath this stair for access to the original kitchen.

As mentioned elsewhere, the plan and form of this house was similar to adjoining Lamb's Range and Redmore's Supply, but Lamb's Meadow is the best of the three and the only one to have remained with few alterations. All three were built in the second quarter of the eighteenth century and each initially had a kitchen in the basement.

One of the first alterations to the house was the addition of the kitchen wing. It is a two-bay, one-and-a-half-story brick structure built on the south gable and

Lamb's Meadow, c. 1733. The kitchen gable bore the date 1753 until reconstructed c. 1976. The first kitchen was located in the basement. Maryland Historical Trust, M. Bourne photograph, 1968.

Opposite: Lamb's Meadow, c. 1733. One of the best examples of Flemish bond with glazed headers. Former closet windows blocked in nineteenth century. C. Engstrom photograph, 1977.

Lamb's Meadow, c. 1733, built for Francis and Rosamund Beck Lamb, was typical of three gambrel roof houses built in the same decade near Stillpond. Historical Society of Kent County Collection.

Lamb's Meadow, c. 1733. Balustrade of hall stair. C. Engstrom photograph, 1977.

encompassing the original basement bulkhead. It had a dirt or brick floor originally, a large fireplace with wooden lintel and exposed champhered ceiling joists. In the south gable end the builder installed the date in glazed headers—1753.

At one time, a leanto room was installed on the south third of the east facade, lengthening the original window to the floor for access. How long this was used has not been documented. It was gone in the early twentieth century. When the owners returned the building to its rectangular plan, they bricked up the opening to a window again. Included in the bricking project was the elimination of two small closet windows in the north gable, which had segmental arches of alternating glazed header.

In the early twentieth century, the kitchen was moved into the parlor and a porch was installed across two thirds of the west facade. In order to have easy access to the kitchen, another door was added south of the window. Its placement necessitated relocating the paneled face of the closet inside. It was set back far enough to clear the door. A small bathroom pod was constructed in 1975 on the center of the east

facade. The glazed date which had been thought to have been 1733 was found to be 1753, a very subtle difference found in the placement of one of the glazed headers at the top of the numeral. The date was one of two in Kent County from the 1750s—the other being Bungay Hill.

In his will of 1765, Francis Lamb left the land on the north side of the road leading to GeorgeTown to his sons, Joshua and Thomas. But that on the south side (where the house is located) he left to John. He also gave to his wife, Susannah, *"one half of his now dwelling house."*[4] Francis' death occurred in 1774, a year after his son John had the farm resurveyed.[5] John was listed as owner of 193 acres of *"Lamb's Meadow Re-Surveyed"* in the 1783 Tax Assessment, even though it had been resurveyed for 222 acres. He acquired 25⅜ acres of vacancy in 1796 which he called *"Lamb's Discovery."*[6]

John Lamb was married to Mary Smith in 1764 and they had five children. John died in 1800 and his oldest son, David, inherited the home farm. David was married to Ann Meirs Stavely, but apparently they had no children, for he willed the farm in 1811 to his sister Rebecca. Rebecca resided on the farm and remained single. In her will in 1840, she bequeathed most of her estate to her niece, Ann Elizabeth Allen, wife of Dr. Robert T. Allen of Harford County, and daughter of William and Sarah Bowers. Mrs. Allen's brother, John Lamb Bowers, occupied the dwelling for eight years after his sister's death, the last descendant to live on the farm.[7] In 1879, Mrs. Allen left the farm to her daughter, Robertine Raymond, the wife of James Hazlett Raymond.[8]

The Raymonds were world travelers, living in Philadelphia, New York and Paris and spending summers at Willowfields on Swarthmore Farm adjoining Lamb's Meadow to the east. The Raymond's only daughter, Ann Terese Fell Raymond, was born in Paris and became owner of the farm upon the death of her mother in 1910. It is now owned by her grandsons, the ninth generation to own Lamb's Meadow.[9]   K-113

1. Wills, Lib. 1, fol. 123.
2. Lamb's Range was patented in 1683 to Pearce Lamb.
3. Unpatented Certificate No. 124, Hall of Records.
4. Wills, Lib. 5, fol. 149.
5. Patented Certificate No. 323, Hall of Records.
6. Patented Certificate No. 321, Hall of Records.
7. Wills, Lib. JFB 1, fol. 241.
8. Wills, Lib. JF 1, fol. 458.
9. Some information gleaned from notes written by Francis Lamb.

Hynson's Division Site

Eastern Neck Island
c. 1730

THE ONLY DOCUMENTATION OF THE APPEARANCE OF Spencer Hall was undertaken in 1957-58 by H. C. Forman and recorded in Old Buildings and Furniture of Maryland. In his book, he indicated that the gambrel roof structure with brick ends was built in two stages (similar to Godlington Manor and Presbury). Like Godlington, the first section of the house had exposed major framing members and a large fireplace with winder stair in the corner. There was one door and one window on each side and a basement with bulkhead on its south gable. On the east side of the first section, there was one dormer, but on the west side there were two—one to light each chamber. The first building measured 24' 1½" x 20' 8".

Later in the eighteenth century, an extension was built on the north side nearly doubling the building's size. (The extension measured 21' 3".) It too had a single room with enclosed stair in one corner, similar again to Godlington Manor and to Presbury. Further to the north there was a kitchen wing, which by the time it was recorded in 1957, had been replaced with a board and batten structure.

The building appears to have been altered periodically, with new windows or doors. Even the weatherboard may have been replaced in the nineteenth century when the building was probably a tenant house.

From the land records, it appears that the majority of Eastern Neck Island was owned by Thomas Hynson and Joseph Wickes from 1658 to 1680 when it was divided between them. John Hynson (d. 1705) devised " *... the plantation where I now dwell and all the land I have in the eastern neck ... .*" to his son, John. During the eighteenth century it is difficult to determine how Hynson's Division was subdivided amongst the descendants. By 1783, parts of Hynson's Division were owned by Charles Chambers (320 acres), Nathaniel Hynson (300 acres), Benjamin Hynson and Benjamin Hynson, Jr. (200 acres between them), and Mary Wickes (100 acres).[1]

In 1817, Nathaniel Hynson (probably the fourth) sold 350 acres of Hynson's Division on Eastern Neck Island, which he had inherited from his father, to Thomas Worrell.[2] After Thomas Worrell died (intestate), the farm was sold to Richard Spencer, Jr., but the deed was unrecorded. Richard may not have lived on Eastern Neck Island, as he refers to his dwelling plantation on Davis Creek, the same dwelling plantation as his father (Richard Spencer, d. 1825). When Richard II wrote his will in 1836, he bequeathed his Eastern Neck Farm to his daughters, Martha and Maria.[3]

By 1852, the property was listed under the name of Alexander Harris, (husband of Maria Spencer). The buildings were described as *"Frame House & other Buildings in Tolerable repair, Formerly to Martha Spencer."*[4] The farm remained in the family until 1940.

In 1966, the entire property was acquired by the U. S. Fish and Wildlife Service and combined with other properties for the Eastern Neck National Wildlife Refuge.   K-273

Hynson's Division. Early eighteenth century house as recorded and conjectured by H. Chandlee Forman in his book: **Old Buildings, Gardens, and Furniture in Tidewater Maryland***, 1967. Drawing by Michael Bourne.*

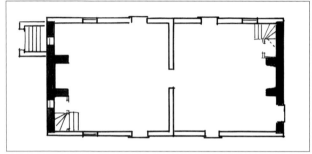

1. Kent County Tax Assessment, Lower Langford Bay and Eastern Neck Hundreds, 1783.
2. Land Records, Lib. WS 1, fol. 277.
3. Wills, Lib. JFB 1, fol. 18.
4. Kent County Tax Assessment, 1st District, 1852.

Redmore's Supply

Still Pond
c. 1730

Redmore's Supply was patented in 1678 to John Hodgeson. The tract encompassed part of the present village of Still Pond and the old house stood southwest of the crossroads. Two-hundred fifty acres of Redmore's Supply was purchased in 1721 by John Gale, Sr., planter[1] who subsequently first deeded 50 acres to his son John, Jr. in 1724[2] and then the remainder in 1732.[3] The house which John Gale, Jr. built at this juncture was very similar to two other eighteenth century houses in the general vicinity— Lamb's Meadow and Lamb's Range.

All three dwellings were brick, gambrel roof structures built originally with their kitchens in the basement. Each had Flemish bond brick work with glazed headers and English bond below the water table. Redmore's Supply differed from the others in the use of English Garden Wall bond (one course of headers; two courses of stretchers) in the second story gable. The upper roof pitch differed also in that it was less steep than those at Lamb's Meadow and Lamb's Range.

Prior to its collapse and disassembly in 1978, measurements and notes were taken. From these conjectural drawings (plans and elevations) were made to illustrate this type period house and its corresponding neighbors.

Redmore's Supply was a hall-parlor plan house with paneled fireplace walls and vertical board partitions. Fragments of the second floor partitions found during the disassembly evidenced a featheredge design in that location. There was an exterior door in the parlor adjacent the fireplace which gave outside access to the kitchen, until a ground level kitchen was built later. The outline of an early addition was evident in its east gable. This one story wing might have been the same one which appears in twentieth century photographs and which had been raised to two stories by that time.

Access to the basement kitchen was also available from a winder stair in the southwest corner of the hall. The kitchen fireplace was located beneath the parlor and the entire floor was paved with brick. Notes were not taken on the division of the basement, but if it were to follow the usual design in the area, part of the space beneath the hall would have been for storage.

Redmore's Supply stayed in the Gale family until 1811 when it was sold to John Hepbron, blacksmith.[4] When the house was disassembled a board with the inscription *Lewis Hepbron 1857* was found which documents a major remodeling which consisted of changing the position of the stair to the northeast corner and making the original hall fireplace smaller. The location of the partitions was also changed. The enlargement of the frame kitchen may have taken place at this time as well.

John Hepbron built a blacksmith shop on the north side of the road leading to Still Pond and gave several parcels along the road to his children. Thus, the hamlet of Still Pond developed. In his will, Redmore's Supply is referred to as the *"Home Farm."*[5] After 1891 it appears to have ceased being the home farm to its owners and became a tenant house.   K-235

Redmore's Supply. The house was built for John Gale, Jr. c. 1730. It was similar in plan and form to Lamb's Meadow and Lamb's Range nearby. M. Bourne photograph, 1966.

Redmore's Supply c. 1730. Conjectural restoration of south elevation. Drawing by M. Bourne.

Redmore's Supply c. 1730. Conjectural first floor plan. Drawing by M. Bourne.

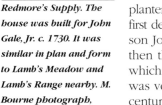

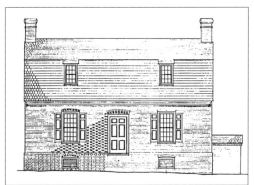

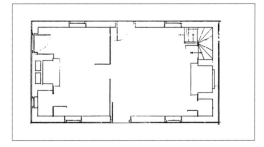

1. Land Records, Lib. JS 8, fol. 170.
2. Land Records, Lib. 8, fol. 398.
3. Land Records, Lib. JS 16, fol. 203.
4. Land Records, Lib. BC 6, fol. 404.
5. Wills, Lib. 11, fol. 331.

Lamb's Range

Near Stillpond
c. 1730

O N THE FARM ADJOINING LAMB'S MEADOW, THIS TWO-AND-a-half-story, brick house has been called Lamb's Range in recent years. If it is indeed located on the Lamb's Range tract, the land was patented to Pearce Lamb in 1683 and remained in his family until the late eighteenth century.

The house was a near replica of Lamb's Meadow and Redmore's Supply. In its original configuration, it had a hall-parlor plan, a basement kitchen and a gambrel roof. The walls were constructed of Flemish bond with glazed headers above a champhered water table with English bond below. Segmental arches above the openings resemble the work at Redmore's Supply, which stood less than a mile away.

In the nineteenth century, the house underwent a transformation similar to Depford, with the gambrel roof being removed and the walls being heightened to two full stories with an attic. At the same time, the plan was changed. A central stairhall was added and the trim was updated. The kitchen wing was rebuilt three times throughout the building's evolution, the last of which was removed in the mid-1960s.

This building is an important eighteenth century vernacular structure to survive into the late twentieth century. It and the adjoining farm should be thoroughly researched to further determine the extent of the Lamb family's influence on eighteenth century Kent County. K-224

Lamb's Range c. 1730. Originally constructed as a gambrel roof structure similar to neighboring Lamb's Meadow. During the later remodeling the hall-parlor plan was changed to a central hall plan. Maryland Historical Trust, M. L. Fritz photograph, 1980.

Wilmer's Mill House

High Street, Chestertown
c. 1733

S IMON WILMER (D. 1699) ACQUIRED STEPNEY AND ESTAB-lished a mill on the upper reaches of Radcliffe Creek in the late seventeenth century. Rebecca Tilghman Wilmer (d. 1725), Simon's widow, stipulated in her will that the *"negro man James"* was to keep the mill for two years for the use of her son Simon and brother Tilghman (Richard), after which he was to be free.[1] Simon Wilmer II (d.1737) bequeathed in his will *"part of my lands on which the grist and saw mills stand ... with mills and Miller's House"* to his sons Lambert and Charles.[2]

In its original configuration the mill house was a three bay long, gambrel roof dwelling with its Flemish bond facade facing *"the road leading from my mill to Chestertown."*[3] Its first kitchen was located on the east gable and was probably a single room, one-and-a-half-story brick structure. The plan of the house was unique in the area. Double doors opened into the hall which had a large fireplace with flanking closets, paneling stretching across the entire composition. On the opposite side of the room there were two doors, one close to the back door which opened onto a stair that ascended against the north wall with winder at the top, the other door opening into an unheated room lighted by the south window. On the west gable a date had been laid in glazed headers. The numerals *17_3* were still discernible before the house fell into ruin in the 1970s.

Lambert Wilmer died in 1750, leaving the majority of Stepney, including the mill, to his son Simon. In the 1783 Tax Assessment, Wilmer's lands are described as having *"two brick dwelling Houses and Kitchens, one Grist Mill, seven out Houses, two Orchards joining Chestertown."*[4]

To his son, Simon V, Simon Wilmer left that part of Stepney which was *"located on the southwest side of the road leading from my Mill to Chestertown up along the same as to the northwest corner of a lot of ground sold*

Wilmer's Mill House, c. 1733. Home for the miller for Simon Wilmer II's Mill. Paneling from this house was removed to Long Island by H. F. duPont in the late 1920s. M. Bourne photograph, 1963

Wilmer's Mill House. The brick gable originally had a large glazed date, 1733. It was later covered by the frame catslide roof addition. M. Bourne photograph, c. 1968.

Wilmer's Mill House, the Topping House and the Mill c. 1910, with Washington College and Chestertown in the background. Tyler Campbell Glass Negative Collection.

feature was the location of an exterior batten door next to the back corner post on the west wall with a 3/6 window immediately adjacent. Also interesting, the room had been constructed on brick piers with clapboard infill whereas the front room and the main house were constructed on a stone and brick basement respectively.

At the same time as the construction of this addition, a third part was built to house a kitchen. Most likely the brick kitchen mentioned in 1783 was removed at the same time that the new west extensions were made.

The year before Simon V sold his inheritance, including the mill, mill house and land, he purchased his boyhood home, the White House Farm or Stepney.[6] By the time he sold the old farm to his younger brother, Lemuel, in 1818, he was no longer residing in Kent County, but in New Jersey.[7]

John Whaland purchased the mill in 1809 [8] and the mill and mill house remained in the Whaland family until 1880 when it was sold to Hiram and Mary Elizabeth Brown.[9] The Whalands in the meantime had built a house on the opposite side of the road which remained until the 1940s.

The Chestertown Strawboard and Manufacturing Company purchased Whaland's Mill in 1882 [10] which it held until 1898 when it was sold to Thomas Topping.[11] The Toppings built another house between the old miller's house and the mill. They sold the Mill Farm in 1924. In 1927, the interior of the old brick house was sold to Henry Francis duPont, who transported it to Long Island and incorporated it into his summer house called *Chestertown House*.

From that point to the early 1970s, the house remained vacant and deteriorated until it was finally torn down. Some of the bricks from the old house were used in a new wing at Hodges Bar Farm.   K-78

by me to the Trustees for the Poor of Kent County, just below the hill called Stoney Hill—then to the Creek and up the Creek ... and the Mill and Mill Seat ... ." [5] From 1798 to 1809 Simon V retained ownership of the mill and miller's house.

It was probably during this period, or perhaps in the last years of his father's (Simon IV) life that the millhouse underwent a major remodeling. A new frame wing was built on the west gable, two rooms deep, covered by an asymmetrical roof. The principal room had its fireplace built back-to-back to the old fireplace. The front room was finished with paneled wainscoting and a corner cupboard. A built-in bench adjacent the second floor fireplace served as a balustrade for the stair. A window seat was built into the single dormer on the south. Access between this and the main part of the second floor was achieved via a break in the brick wall. This change resulted in the obliteration of the decade numeral in the gable. The *3* remained behind the plaster and slightly above the roof. The *17* was concealed by the chimney.

On the first floor, the back room of the addition had chair rail and other period trim, but the most curious

1. Wills, Lib. 1, fol. 275.
2. Wills, Lib. 2, fol. 58.
3. Wills, Lib. 3, fol. 137.
4. Kent Co. Tax Assessment, 1783.
5. Wills, Lib. 7, fol. 608.
6. Land Records, Lib. BC 5, fol. 293.
7. Land Records, Lib. WS 2, fol. 268.
8. Land Records, Lib. BC 5, fol. 523.
9. Land Records, Lib. SB 1, fol. 298.
10. Land Records, Lib. SB 2, fol. 635.
11. Land Records, Lib. JTD 1, fol. 327.

James Anderson House

Cannon Street, Chestertown c. 1733

THE LOT ON WHICH THE ANDERSON HOUSE IS LOCATED IS designated No. 97 on the plat of Chestertown and was first sold in 1733 to Elias Ringgold.[1] Upon his death in 1737, it was sold to James Anderson for the sum of £200. It is likely that a frame house was located on the property at that time as the deed states *"messuage tenement lott and parcell of land ... ."* indicating that the lot had been improved.[2]

Before his death in 1783, James Anderson enlarged his dwelling by building a large brick house, incorporating into it the old frame structure which was the original tenement of Elias Ringgold. The floor plan that resulted was quite unusual. There was a central stair passage with two flanking rooms, and a kitchen in a separate frame wing near Cannon Street. Behind the brick section were additional spaces, including a long narrow room and a porch. These were covered by a leanto roof originating at attic level which, with the floor level a few steps lower, allowed the same amount of space on the second story. While the plan possessed similarities to those at Broad Neck and Shepherd's Delight, the two story porch made it exceptional.

The room on the northwest originally had a wall of paneling which contained a secondary stair leading to the second floor corridor. The room behind had a diagonal fireplace in the west corner with a simple period mantel, chair rail and baseboard. The stairhall was relatively narrow, with open-string staircase having turned balusters ascending on the southeast side. At the top of the first flight, the stair was divided and ascended the last few steps in both directions to a corridor extending across the back of the main block. On the southeast end of the house, the chimney was located on the exterior of the building, creating a fireplace flush with the interior wall.

On the second floor there were two rooms in the front with corridor behind and two rooms behind the northwest room, one with diagonal fireplace. The last two rooms were at a lower level, as was the room below. The northwest room had a wall of paneling, while the other front room had a fine strapwork mantel. From the southeast end of the corridor, an enclosed stair ascended to the attic. Close thereto was a door which opened into the second story porch.

When James Anderson wrote his will in 1783, he left 584 acres in Anne Arundel County and a farm in Kent County called *Anne Arundel Grove*. In addition he bequeathed to his son James Mouat Anderson the *"house and lot whereon I now dwell ... lot No. 97 ... half of lot No. 85 fronting the house where I live"* and *"all medicines, drugs, chirurgical instruments and also all debts due upon medical books of James Anderson and Son."*[3] Before his death Anderson had purchased ¾ acre from Simon Wilmer which he left to his son as well.

Wilmer owned all of the land to the southwest of Anderson's residence and was a witness to his will. The gate to his farm, adjoining Anderson's residence, is mentioned as a landmark and a division line between bequests.

James Mouat Anderson had five children who were all raised in the house: James, Harriett, Edward, Emily and Maria. Maria died before her father's death in 1821. Harriet married William McClean

James Anderson House, Chestertown. A two-story back porch was enclosed and a one-story kitchen was moved to the rear when the house was converted to a duplex. Michael Wootton photograph, 1996.

and lived at Sterling Castle across the street. The use of Anderson's house was left to his third daughter, Emily, for one year and it was designated that after that time everything was to be sold at public auction and distributed equally between his children.[4] The house and lot were purchased by Mary Smith, mother-in-law to his eldest son.[5] It then passed to her daughter and eventually to her grandson, John B. H. Anderson (1819).[6] After 1866 the property was sold out of the family.

In the Lake, Griffing, Stevenson Atlas (1877) the owner is listed as J. M. Vandyke, whose wife Olivia had acquired it the year before (1876).[7] After the Vandyke ownership, the house was turned into a duplex. The back porch was then enclosed and the old kitchen moved to the rear of the house. A second kitchen was built next thereto. With the porch being enclosed, it became necessary to get more light into the front room, so one window on the southeast gable was introduced at that time. Other than a few minor changes, the house has remained in the same form since then. It has, however, been reconverted into a single family dwelling.   K-71

1. Land Records, Lib. 4, fol. 282.
2. Land Records, Lib. 6, fol. 146.
3. Wills, Lib. 7, fol. 99.
4. Wills, Lib. 10, fol. 217.
5. Land Records, Lib. TW 3, fol. 478.
6. Land Records, Lib. WS 2, fol. 336.
7. Land Records, Lib. DCB 2, fol. 140

Rebecca Lloyd Anderson House

High Street, Chestertown
c. 1733

T HE HOUSE AT 411 HIGH STREET IS A TWO-AND-A-half-story, three-bay brick house which stands out because of the presence of glazed headed Flemish bond brickwork on the first floor facade and gables. On close examination of the brickwork of the gables, the outlines of a gambrel roof can be traced. The uniform unglazed brickwork of the second story appears to originate between the two first floor windows, suggesting that a major remodeling took place in the late eighteenth century.

The chain of title suggests that the original house was constructed for Rebecca Lloyd Anderson, wife of William Anderson, merchant, and daughter of Edward Lloyd of Wye House. The construction occurred some time be-

Rebecca Lloyd Anderson House, Chestertown, c. 1733. The original gambrel roof can be traced in the gables. A late eighteenth century owner enlarged and remodeled the building. Tyler Campbell photograph, 1996.

tween when she acquired the lot in 1733 and 1789 when it was sold by her heirs.[1] Possibly Samuel Wallis, merchant and owner of the Wallis-Wickes House undertook the remodeling after his acquisition in that year.

Its original plan is not easily discernible. The basement is divided nearly in two, each side with a cooking fireplace of its own. The plan above, however, does not line up with that below. The first floor plan is composed of a central stairhall with two flanking rooms. Both the stair and the strapwork mantel in the southeast room are typical of late eighteenth century work in and around Chestertown.

Samuel Wallis left all of his real estate to his son, Philip, stipulating that he sell none of it until he was 30 years of age. In 1829 Philip sold the house to John Turner who sold it the following year to David Arthur.[2] In the 1841 Tax Assessment, David Arthur is listed as owner and occupant of the building *"in tolerable repair."* It was appraised for $800.

David Arthur first sold the part of the lot he had purchased in 1830. He later sold the part with the *"brick house"* to William Bacchus in 1866.[3] Bacchus who had previously bought the Buck-Bacchus Store, possibly moved to this location with his family, leasing the living quarters at the store, as had been done by previous owners.

The Bacchus family continued to own this building until 1959, even after moving to the Smith-Ringgold House next to the bridge.[4] The house was a rental property, until being purchased recently as a residence.   K-60

1. Land Records, Lib. 4, fol. 296; Lib. EF, fol. 517.
2. Land Records, Lib. JNG 2, fol. 177; Lib. JNG, fol. 391.
3. Land Records, Lib. JNG 6, fol. 260.
4. Land Records, Lib. WHG 58, fol. 216.

White Swan Tavern

High Street, Chestertown
c. 1733

THE WHITE SWAN TAVERN IS SITUATED ON LOT NO. 76 of the original plat of Chestertown. the first recorded deed of the property occurred on August 22, 1733, between John Lovegrove, *"Shoemaker of Chestertown"* and Joseph Nicholson. Sometime before 1733, Simon Wilmer had sold the lot to John Lovegrove, but had not recorded the deed. Since Wilmer was the original owner of all of Chestertown when it was laid out, it was necessary for him to enter in the deed of 1733 in order to establish clear title for Joseph Nicholson.[1]

Lovegrove operated a tanning business on the premises before 1733. He had constructed the small frame dwelling on the lot which was later used as the kitchen of the tavern.[2]

Nicholson built a vernacular gambrel roof brick building with glazed Flemish bond on its five-bay facade. Its plan consisted of a central stair hall with room on each side thereof, each having interior fireplaces with flanking closets. The first floor rooms had eleven foot ceilings crowned with a very bold five-part cornice. The window jambs were splayed and plastered, like the windows of the Buck House on the corner of Queen Street, built in the same decade.

White Swan Tavern, Chestertown. After restoration.

Austin Walmsley photograph, 1981

White Swan Tavern, Chestertown. The Nicholson Room restored, based upon fragments found in the investigation. "Japaned clock" was listed in Joseph Nicholson's inventory (1787). Joan Norton-Taylor photograph, 1981.

White Swan Tavern, Chestertown. The Bordley Room retained more original woodwork than any other second story room. Joan Norton-Taylor photograph, 1980.

Structural evidence in the frame kitchen indicated it was a small-scale hall-parlor plan dwelling with unfinished loft. Originally, its walls were plastered, even the partitions separating the two small rooms. The joists, however, were never ceiled. The small house was moved back on the lot, perpendicular to the street, and attached to Nicholson's house by a narrow hyphen. In the third quarter of the eighteenth century, the hyphen was replaced by a room with fireplace.

Joseph Nicholson's first wife was Hannah Smith, sister of the long time Clerk of the Court, James Smith, and Katherine, the wife of Dr. William Murray. Three of their sons became very important figures in the founding of the United States Navy, along with their Murray cousins.

In 1775, Col. Joseph Nicholson was a member of the Committee of Correspondence. In 1775 and in 1777, he was an advocate of a bill introduced into the Upper House to prevent the growth of Toryism. It may be assumed that his title *Colonel* was bestowed on him for his role in Revolutionary activities. He was Register of Wills of Kent County, Sheriff in 1768 and a visitor to the Kent County Free School. He was also influential in the founding of Washington College to which he was a subscriber and first Board Member. In 1783, Joseph Nicholson, Sr.'s town property was assessed the value of £500.

It was not until his death that there is any indication that he was anything other than an active revolutionary period gentleman. The inventory of his personal estate, which exceeded £1900, included many items that

would have been superfluous for a typical house of the period. As part of the estate there were lists of debts, three of which include the notation: *"for eleven days in 1787."* These notations reveal that Joseph and Mary, his second wife (whom he married in the early 1770s), also ran a tavern at the house.[3]

Mary Hopper Nicholson, Joseph's widow, then living in Queen Anne's County, sold the property, in 1793, to John Bordley of Kent County for £350.[4]

John Bordley, the youngest son of John Beale Bordley of Wye Island, may have lived on the large estate which his father owned west of town. In the 1790 Census he had a sizable household, with five family members, five other free people and twelve slaves. His name appears in the Chestertown Apollo in 1793 as a member of the Jockey Club, which met at Worrell's Tavern. He does not appear in the Census of 1800, but is listed as a resident of Kent County when he sold the town property in 1801.

During the time that Bordley owned the property, across the street from the courthouse, the building was transformed from a gambrel roof residence, into its present form. Similar transformations had occurred at the Smith-Ringgold House and the Buck-Chambers house in

town. Bordley's remodeling was more drastic, perhaps due to the deteriorated condition of the Nicholson house. Here the gambrel roof was partly removed (the upper members are still in place) and the facade was raised to two full stories. The rear wall was also raised, but it became an interior wall. The connector between the house and kitchen was demolished and a series of three rooms on each floor was added to the rear, covered by a continuation of the rear roof pitch. The roof of the kitchen was then continued to the new roof. The old interior chimneys were demolished and replaced with new chimneys that were located mostly outside the gable walls. The new chimneys were flanked by full size windows on both stories. This created more light and more space in all four of the principal rooms.

The entire interior was renewed, but one element was reused from the first installation; the interior cornice members were reinstalled with reduced facias and soffit. All of the street side window openings were lengthened inside to accommodate paneled window seats. Both chimney breasts protruded from the face of the wall and were also paneled. According to the tradition stated in Usilton's history of Chestertown (1898), the bar was located in the principal room. The rear rooms and the second story rooms were finished with simpler trim. The old kitchen was stripped of its plaster and siding. A new door was installed close to the back door, both covered by a leanto porch, and a window was installed in the center bay of the kitchen. Its interior was then whitewashed. Both the kitchen floor and a large area outside were paved, the kitchen with brick and the patio with a combination of 18" square Pennsylvania flagstone, square paving brick and regular brick.[5]

Isaac Cannell purchased the property from Bordley in 1801 for the sum of £1000, a £650 increase over Bordley's purchase.[6] Cannell appears in the records of Kent County owning

White Swan Tavern Sign. Michael Wootton photograph, 1996.

White Swan Tavern, Chestertown. First floor plan as it existed in 1978, with phases of building construction indicated by key.

White Swan Tavern, Chestertown, before restoration. Historic American Buildings Survey; 1978 drawing by Michael Bourne and Christina A. Eger.

▨	·c. 1733
▧	·c. 1770
▨	·c. 1795
▨	·c. 1855

- - - - Overhead ceiling variation
.... Former partition
-··-··- Patch in flooring

White Swan Tavern, Chestertown. Stenciled border from the period when T. W. Eliason used the front rooms for a store (between 1855-1895). Michael Bourne photograph, 1979.

White Swan Tavern, Chestertown. The office of Thomas W. Eliason c. 1895, with son Wilbur leaning on desk. John Eliason Collection.

White Swan Tavern, Chestertown. The Wilmer Room with simple plastered fireplace, typical of eighteenth century Kent. Tyler Campbell photograph, 1981.

750 acres on Stillpond Creek in 1783. His first wife was Sarah Wilmer. He sold a farm near Millington just before purchasing the Bordley property. He appears in both the 1790 and 1800 census records. In 1808 he was appointed Justice of the Peace by the Governor. In the inventory of his personal property after his death in 1812, there are many items that would be necessary for running a first rate tavern, most of which were sold at public auction. Three items in the sale were unsold, with the notation, *"... Abram, one stove, a billiard table leased with the tavern."*[7] This was the first instance in the records that the property was actually referred to as a tavern.

Isaac Cannell, Jr., after inheriting one half of his father's real estate, sold his half interest in the lot and building in 1814 to the The Rev. Mr. and Mrs. William H. Wilmer, all of whom were residing in Alexandria. He made an arrangement with the Wilmers that if his brother died and he inherited the other half, he would sell it to them. This agreement was exercised in 1832, after the death of The Rev. Mr. Wilmer.[8]

While he lived in Kent County, The Rev. Mr. Wilmer ministered to Shrewsbury Parish before being called to St. Paul's Church, Alexandria. While in Alexandria, he was instrumental in forming a Theological class which eventually became the Theological Seminary of Virginia. He was later called to Bruton Parish, Williamsburg, where he served as rector as well as head of the College of William and Mary. There he died in August of 1827. His remains were buried under the aisle of the parish church.

Their interest in the White Swan Tavern was administered by the Chestertown lawyer, John B. Eccleston. He advertised in the Chestertown Telegraph in November and December of 1825 *"... that long established and well-known Tavern in Chestertown now occupied by Thomas Peacock ... Any person wishing to rent can be accommodated with sundry articles of the tavern furniture of Mr. Peacock."*[9]

Late in January and into February of 1826, another advertisement appears in the *Telegraph:*

"Public House in Chestertown
Wm Sims
Respectfully informs the public that he has taken that commodious house, in the center of town, opposite the Courthouse, and formerly occupied by Mr. Thomas Peacock. This house is admirably adapted for the accommodation of travelers and permanent boarders, being situated in the center of the business and having good stabling and experienced ostlers. His bar and table are constantly supplied with the choicest liquors and provisions, and every attention given to render comfort and pleasure to such as favour him with their patronage. His charges, either by the meal, day, week or year, will be found not only reasonable but very low."[10]

There is no mention of the tavern being called by the name The White Swan in either land records or newspaper advertisements, but only by the names of the proprietors. The name is first encountered in print in the History of Chestertown (1898). Between 1825-1853 ads in the local papers announce the sale of properties to be held at the tavern door of Misters Peacock, Sims, and Lusby. Its proximity to the courthouse was undoubtedly one reason for its popularity as a place to meet. It was also very convenient for Thomas Lusby, the last proprietor, as he was Sheriff of Kent County during the last years of its operation.

Finally, in 1853, the following advertisement appears:

"Tavern property in Chestertown FOR SALE the undersigned as agent, offers at private sale the desirable Tavern Property now occupied by Mr. Thomas Lusby. This is considered the best Tavern Stand in town. Its situated in the most business part of the town, nearly opposite the Court House.

Apply to Jos. Wickes."[11]

The ad continues in the Kent News until the beginning of November, but the actual deed for the property was not recorded in the land records until September of the following year, 1854.

Thomas W. Eliason of Chestertown purchased the property from Ann Brice Wilmer, the third wife and widow of The Rev. Mr. Wilmer, then residing in Bedford County, Virginia. Eliason had made an agreement to purchase the property from George T. Wilmer, one of the sons, in July, but due to a technical defect in the deed, it was not executed until September.[12]

Thomas W. Eliason had come to Chestertown in 1842 from Smyrna, Delaware, via Centreville, and established a general store in the Masonic Building, across the street from Lusby's Tavern. When he began advertising in the Kent News in October of 1842, his ads were larger than any other merchant of the day. Moreover, on occasions, there were several ads in the same paper, advertising general merchandise, clothing, fabrics, stationery, and plaster lath. In 1851, he began to sell lumber.

He evidently moved his business into the old tavern soon after the purchase. In the 1867 tax assessment, he is listed occupying the store building with his son. In his own records at this period, there is mention of funds being expended on porch posts and roof and decoration of the interior of the store. His remodeling was nearly as extensive as John Bordley's rehabilitation in the 1790s. In the front half of the building all partitions were removed and the entire space was converted into a single room. A new front double door replaced the old door that had been moved to the rear of the building. With the removal of the main stair, it became necessary to install a short flight from the rear second floor to the large single room on the second floor. Since it was used primarily as a store and warehouse, removal of architectural trim was confined to the large front room.

Soon after the death of Thomas Wilson Eliason in 1893, his son Thomas Walker Eliason changed their emphasis from general merchandise to lumber and fertilizer, as well as managing the farms which had been purchased with the profits of the business. It was then that the big store room was altered again, this time being divided into two rooms, one extending from the central door to the northwest, the other, with new door in the former window to the southeast. The latter became the office for the business and the former was rented out. In 1895 a two story brick store was constructed on the northwest side of the old building and connected thereto on the second story. The stair however was built in the old building and was accessible from a third door added to the facade. Many other minor alterations occurred to the building during the twentieth century, but the essential elements of the building remained until 1977, when the property was sold to Mr. and Mrs. Horace Havemeyer, Jr.[13]

White Swan Tavern, Chestertown. The Love-grove kitchen, was the residence of John Love-grove, tanner c. 1720s. Joan Norton-Taylor photograph, 1981.

Soon thereafter, an archeological dig and historical and architectural research were undertaken to determine the most appropriate period to which the building should be restored. The period chosen was when the building was enlarged by John Bordley and used as a Tavern. It was decided that it would again function as a public facility, offering rest to the traveler, but with a great deal more comfort than it did originally. The White Swan Tavern Bed and Breakfast was opened to the public in 1981 and has served the community in that capacity since.   K-49

1. Land Records, Lib. 4, fol. 285
2. Information about the Love-grove occupation was gleaned from an archeological dig at the site in 1978, as well as the will of George Garnett, who bequeathed Lot No. 77 to his sons, mentioning that it was next to Lovegrove. The Garnetts were all involved in leather businesses.
3. Inventories, Lib. 8, fol. 530; Original Inventories, Hall of Records, Box 40, folder 5.
4. Land Records, Lib. BC 3, fol. 346, 427.
5. Prior to the restoration of the tavern, an Historic Structures Report was compiled by the author in which the architectural sequence of building and its history was researched and ascertained. A copy is on file at the White Swan Tavern as well as at the Maryland Historical Trust.
6. Land Records, Lib. TW 1, fol. 660.
7. Inventories, Lib. 12, fol. 469.
8. Land Records, Lib. BC 8, fol. 81; Lib. JNG 3, fol. 14.
9. The Telegraph, December 2, 9, 23, 1825.
10. The Telegraph, Jan. 27, Feb. 3, 10, 1826.
11. Kent News, June 18, 1853.
12. Land Records, Lib. JFG 2, fol. 248.
13. Land Records, Lib. EHP 77, fol. 556.

The Buck-Chambers House

Queen Street, Chestertown
c. 1735, 1786

Lot No. 34 in Chestertown contains two of the earliest surviving houses in the town, both built in the mid-1730s for an absentee owner, John Buck. When Jonathan Page, mariner, sold the northwest half of lot 34 in 1735, the deed stated that it *" ... is now marked out for building ... opposite a dwelling house lately built by one James Moore (bricklayer) ... ."* [1] (Moore's house was probably located on the north corner of High and Queen Streets). John Buck, Esquire, of Bideford, Devonshire, Great Brittain, soon improved his lot with the construction of not one, but two houses, built of a combination of brick and stone. The larger building is located on the High Street end of the lot while the other is constructed at the opposite end, facing Queen Street. The former is discussed under the name of Buck-Bacchus Store and the latter is the subject of this study.

The Buck family was one of the most prosperous merchant families of Bideford in the late seventeenth and eighteenth centuries. Besides a large estate at home, they owned properties in Maryland, Virginia and Maine. A hatchment bearing the family Coat of Arms remains in the church of St. Mary's, Bideford to this day. Even though Bideford was their home, the names of John and his sons, William and George, appear frequently in the county court records of the second and third quarter of the eighteenth century. Most of those entries involve collecting debts from numerous clients.[2]

The smaller of the two houses built on lot No. 34 was constructed without a basement under the main section, and consequently closer to grade. Its two story facade was laid in Flemish bond brick with glazed headers on a stone foundation. The side walls were built of stone up to the second floor level, then brick to

the roof. It had a unique four bay facade with entry in the second bay from the northeast end. The two central bays had segmental arches while the two end bays had Jack arches. The second story had only three bays, symmetrically arranged above the four below. The steeply pitched roof was probably without dormers when first constructed, the attic rooms being lighted by gable windows.

The floor plan consisted of hall and parlor with a kitchen off the rear. In the hall was a winder stair to the second story located east of the fireplace. Separating the two rooms was a board wall with double beaded seams, a feature which it has in common with the Buck-Bacchus Store. Originally there was no stair in the parlor, but only a fireplace. The sec-

ond story was divided into a stair hall with two large rooms facing the street and a smaller room at the end of the hall lighted by a window in the southwest gable.

After the death of John Buck in 1745, his sons William and George inherited the Chestertown property, which they held until 1771, when their attorney advertised them for sale. *"On the same Lot is a large Brick House, which, with a little Expence, might be converted into a good Store-Room and Compting-House. For Terms of Sale, apply to Joseph Earle."* [3] In their deed, the fact that there were two houses was again confirmed by the statement: *"all and singular their two brick messuages or tenements and Lott ... late in the possession of Dr. John Scott and now in the possession of the said Emory Sudler ... ."* [4]

Emory Sudler owned the property between 1771-1785 and is known to have been a successful merchant. At one time he was in partnership with Thomas Smyth under the name of *Smyth & Sudler.* Emory Sudler was married to Martha, Smyth's half sister.[5] Sudler acquired part of lot No. 25 adjoining lot No. 34 on the northeast. He sold his entire holdings on Queen Street in 1785 for the large sum of £2998.6 to Smyth[6], after which he removed to Radcliffe Cross.

Within a month of the purchase, Thomas Smyth advertised the property for sale in the Maryland

Gazette. He divided it into two separate parcels, one being the corner and *"the other lot is 92 feet in front of Queen St., running back 180 feet, has on the said Street a brick House, two stories high, 2 rooms in the lower and three in the upper, with a good framed kitchen, under which is a good dry cellar. There are also on the premises a carriage house and stable ... ."* [7]

The advertisement for the house in 1785 clearly corresponds to part of the existing building, even though it states simply that it is a brick house, when in fact the first story walls of all but the facade were stone. The *"dry basement"* in the rear, which had to be built at the same time as the front, since there is a common wall, presents questions about the form of the *"framed kitchen."* Possibly it a was a very long *"lean-to with shed roof having a chimney at one or both ends."* Whatever its form, it was not to last long.

In 1786 Smyth sold one quarter of Lot No. 34 and part of Lot No. 25 to Benjamin Chambers, attorney and one time Clerk of the Court.[8] Chambers paid £650 for the house and property but soon began to enlarge his

Opposite: Buck-Chambers House, Chestertown, c. 1735. John Buck, a Bideford, Devonshire, merchant built this house which was enlarged by attorney, Benjamin Chambers.

Buck-Chambers House, Chestertown. The dining room was built by Benjamin Chambers after 1786. Tyler Campbell photographs, 1995.

new home. First he pulled down the frame kitchen and built a two story brick structure on the existing basement, nearly doubling the size of the front section. Its floor plan appears to have been two rooms with central passage leading to a new frame kitchen. The second story had two rooms without passage. The 'third room', mentioned in the advertisement was turned into part of the corridor for access to the new south bedroom, which created a four room plan with corridor between. In form and plan it was similar to 201 Water Street, the house built by William Smith and enlarged by William Ringgold on the corner of Maple Avenue and Water Street.

Chambers retained the original interior board partitions with double beaded joint. In the new wing the first floor window jambs were plastered, like the existing house, but the second floor window trim appears to have been designed for interior shutters. Fireplace design was more up-to-date with paneled overmantel and cabinet adjoining in the east room. A simple dentil-molded mantel and corresponding dentil cornice were installed in the west room.

Benjamin Chambers resided in this house until he and his wife Elizabeth (Forman) were able to purchase Widehall from Robert Wright in 1810. The following year they deeded part of their home property to their daughter Augusta, wife of Judge James Houston.[9] The same year, 1811, the other portion of their lot, with house they had built, was deeded to their son, Ezekiel.

Augusta and James Houston lived at 113 Queen Street, three doors away, and at Airy Hill after 1814. During Augusta's ownership 103 Queen Street was rented. After Judge Houston's death, Airy Hill was sold, but not the Queen Street houses.

Before her death in 1833, Augusta Houston had married John Bowers, probably brother-in-law to her brother Ezekiel. They raised the two Houston girls, but had no children of their own. In her estate, executed by her brother-in-law John Bowers Eccleston, one of the accounts receivable states *"balance of rent due by Joseph Redue (one of the appraisers of the estate) to the deceased for her house in Queen Street for 1831 ... ."*[10] This entry confirms that the house was rented after General and Mrs. Chambers moved to Widehall.

Buck-Chambers House, Chestertow. First floor plan, indicating the Buck and Chambers sections with outline of twentieth century kitchen. Michael Bourne.

By the time of the Tax Assessment of 1841, the property is listed belonging to Elizabeth F. Patton, Augusta and James Houston's second daughter, who had married Thomas Patton of Philadelphia. The house was assessed for $1,200, is in good repair and is occupied by The Reverend William Kesley.[11] After her husband's death, Elizabeth Patton moved from Philadelphia to Baltimore and in 1862 she transferred the Queen Street property to her nephew James Houston Eccleston, son of her sister Augusta.[12]

In 1868 Eccleston transferred the house to William Vannort,[13] a well-to-do landowner and businessman of Chestertown. He resided on Water Street, so the house continued to be rented. The house remained in the Vannort and related Simpers family until it was sold to John and Anna Allspach in 1957.[14]

During this long period of ownership, the Vannorts had a frame house built between the two brick Chambers Houses which incorporated an early brick smoke house that had belonged to the Chambers.

In 1914 the Chambers house was divided into two apartments. Its facade was altered by placing entrances in the two end bays and making a window out of the original entrance. It was divided by existing partitions. A new stair was installed in the south corner of the southwest room, mirroring the placement of the original stair. In 1942 the old frame kitchen in the back was torn down and a new two story frame kitchen was built on old foundations. It housed double kitchens and baths.

In 1963 the duplex was purchased by Norman and Alice James and subsequently re-converted back to a single family residence.[15] It was the first time since the Chambers occupancy that the house was occupied by its owners.   K-27

1. Land Records, Lib. 4, fol. 542.
2. Civil Docket, 1728-39 (c. 1037-1).
3. Maryland Gazette, 1 Dec. 1768.
4. Land Records, Lib. DD3, fol. 513.
5. Papenfuss, E., Biographical Dictionary of Maryland Legislature.
6. Land Records, Lib. EF 6, fol. 487.
7. Maryland Gazette, 26 Aug. 1785.
8. Land Records, Lib. EF 7, fol. 77.
9. Land Records, Lib. BC 7, fol. 49.
10. Accounts, Lib. 15, fol. 373.
11. Kent County Tax Assessment for 1841, Chestertown.
12. Land Records, Lib. JKH 3, fol. 161.
13. Land Records, Lib. JKH 7, fol. 341.
14. Land Records, Lib. WHG 62, fol. 447.
15. Land Records, Lib. EHP 1, fol. 312.

Redue House Site

Water Street, Chestertown
c. 1735

T HE EARLIEST DEED FOUND FOR THE REDUE HOUSE was recorded in 1759, when Thomas Ringgold purchased the property described by the executors as *"the Water Lot which Daniel Dulaney made over to Hugh Campbell in 1743 for £600 ... together with the Mansion House or Messuage thereon erected lately in the possession of Nathaniel Palmer ... ."*[1] It is curious that Ringgold paid only a third of the 1743 price, as it is likely that the house was standing on the property at the time.

From the one extant photograph of the house, it is not possible to determine the brick bond used in its construction, but the existing southwest and southeast foundation walls are laid in common bond. The structure was three bays long. The central entrance was flanked by two windows with 9/6 sash. Two dormers on either side of the roof had 9/6 sash also—an uncommon, if not unique length of dormer in Kent County. Like the Custom House, the dormers were constructed with a full pediment. Connecting it to the adjoining one-story store building there was a small, one-story filler, probably built in the third quarter of the eighteenth century, after both properties were in Ringgold's possession.

The building remained the property of the Ringgold family through most of the eighteenth century and is possibly *"the Counting House," "Bath House,"* or *"Dry Goods Store"* mentioned in the 1776 will of Thomas Ringgold V.[2] In 1796 it was acquired by William Slubey, a local merchant.[3] How it was later transferred to Elizabeth Comegys is unknown, but the property is listed as her residence and in her possession in her will of 1819 when she bequeathed it to her daughter, Emeline.[4]

Emeline Comegys later married Joseph Redue, a person who was to distinguish himself in the community, first as merchant in the 300 block of High Street,[5] and later becoming the Post Master, Sheriff and Tax Collector. In 1831, he purchased the Wharf property between his residence and the river.[6] In the 1841 Tax Assessment, Joseph Redue's real property was assessed for $900.00 with the following remarks:

"House and Water Lot No. 19 by Self
In good Repair"
His personal property included:
"Stock in Trade Merchandise $2500
Private Securities 500
Live Stock 45
House Hold Furniture 400
Plate 37 oz. 37
Watch Silver 10" [7]

Redue House c. 1735, formerly stood adjacent to the Custom House on Front Street. Joseph Redue was a nineteenth century merchant, Post Master, Sheriff and Tax Collector. Maryland State Archives, Miss Harriet Welsh post card collection.

By 1860, the property was in the possession of the Redue's daughter, Miss Josephine Redue, who ran a school and taught privately from her residence.[8] She mortgaged the property in 1878 to Mary S. Hynson[9] and in 1886, advertised the property for sale:

"PUBLIC SALE OF
DESIRABLE PROPERTY
The Improvements consist of a
STORY AND A-HALF
BRICK DWELLING HOUSE
in ordinary repair
This is one of the most desirable
properties in Chestertown having
numerous shade trees and a full view
of Chester River" [10]

Apparently, however, Miss Redue did not sell the property. It instead descended to her niece, Maria Waters. Maria and her husband, William sold the property in 1905.[11] In 1910 the property was purchased by Wilbur W. Hubbard who demolished its upper story, as well as the buildings next door.[12] He then built four tenements on the old foundations, which remain to this day.   K-503

1. Land Records, Lib. JS 29, fol. 93.
2. Wills, Lib. 5, fol. 230.
3. Land Records, Lib. BC 4, fol. 475.
4. Wills, Lib. 10, fol. 290.
5. Telegraph, 13 April 1827.
6. Land Records, Lib. JNG 2, fol. 357.
7. Kent County Tax Assessment, Chestertown, District 4, 1841.
8. Martenet Map, 1860, Insert of Chestertown.
9. Land Records, Lib. DCB 4, fol. 442.
10. Kent News, 3 July 1886.
11. Land Records, Lib. JTD 11, fol. 50.
12. Land Records, Lib. JTD 21, fol. 151

Buck-Bacchus Store

High Street, Chestertown
c. 1735

ON THE NORTH CORNER OF HIGH AND QUEEN STREETS there stands one of the earliest brick houses remaining in Chestertown (c. 1735). The building, currently known as the Buck-Bacchus Store, was restored in 1977. During the process, information about its former appearance and layout was discovered, recorded and the building restored accordingly. The single most important feature of the building discovered was its original floor plan. This consisted of two rooms on the first floor, each having its own exterior entrance, with only one of these rooms having a fireplace. Of the two, the unheated room faced High Street and appears to have been intended for use as a store or commercial space.

John Buck who purchased the northwest half of lot No. 34 in 1735 from Jonathan Page, was a merchant from Bideford, Devonshire, England. Buck was a third generation merchant whose family had helped to put

Bideford on the map in the seventeenth century by exporting local pottery and woolen cloth to the colonies and bringing back to England tobacco and timber for reexport. He is known to have had plantations in Maryland, Virginia and a sawmill in Maine.

Soon after he acquired the lot, Buck set about building two tenements; one on the corner, now numbered 101 Queen Street, and the other a little way down Queen Street. It is possible that he employed his neighbor, James Moore, a bricklayer, who had just built a house on the opposite corner of Queen and High Streets to work on these tenements as well.

The house Buck built on the corner was originally two and a half stories tall with a hip roof on the three bay High Street facade and a gable at the back. This created an asymmetrical roof on the three bay Queen Street facade. Stone was used in the basement foundation with brick in an English bond pattern above the basement windows. The molded water table was designed to jog up and over the basement windows on Queen Street but remain straight on the High Street facade, where the original basement bulkhead entrance was located to the right of the High Street door. Glazed headed Flemish bond was used above the water table on the two principal facades. A two-brick belt course was designed to jog down on the Queen Street facade, similar to that at Scotch Folly in the upper county and at Cloverfields in Queen Anne's County. Windows on both floors were of the same size with 9/9 sash—the lower windows were fitted with shutters.

How the building was used in the eighteenth century is only hinted at in the available documents. Ownership, however, by merchants, a doctor and an innkeeper certainly support its worth as a commercial building.

When John Buck's sons and heirs decided to sell the property, they asked Fredericktown attorney Joseph Earle to take care of the details. In 1768 Earle advertised the property for sale in the Maryland Gazette:

"Frederick-Town, Caecil County, Oct 24, 1768

To be Sold, by virtue of a Power of Attorney from George and William Buck, Efqrs., Merchants of Biddeford, a Dwelling-Houfe in Chefter-Town, compeatly finifhed, with Eight Rooms, Six of which are richly papered. There is an excellent Kitchen adjoining, in which are Two good Fire-Places, and every Thing Compleat. On the Lot is a commodious Stable, with Nine Stalls, Two of which are clofe; a large Yard, with a good Well and new Pump in it, and every other Conveniency fit for a Gentleman's Family in private Life, or public Bufinefs. On the fame Lot is a Brick Houfe, which, with a little Expense, might be converted into a good Store-Room and Compting-Houfe. For Terms of Sale, Apply to

(tf) JOSEPH EARLE" [1]

In the deed to the next owner it is stated that the building was at one time in the possession of Dr. John Scott. Possibly he used one of the rooms as his office.

"All and Singular their two Brick messuages or tenements and Lott with the appurtenances thereunto belonging situate lying and being in Chester Town afs late in the possession of Doctor John Scott and now in the possession of the said Emory Sudler ... purchased by John Buck of Jonathan Page ... ." [2]

In 1785, Thomas Smyth purchased the lot and Sudler's part of the lot No. 25 adjoining. Smyth, like his brother-in-law Sudler, was a merchant. They were, in fact,

Frederick-Town, Cæcil County, Oɛ̃. 24, 1768.

TO be Sold, by virtue of a Power of Attorney from *George* and *William Buck*, Efqrs., Merchants of *Biddeford*, a Dwelling-Houfe in *Chefter-Town*, compleatly finifhed, with Eight Rooms, Six of which are richly papered. There is an excellent Kitchen adjoining, in which are Two good Fire-Places, and every Thing compleat. On the Lot is a commodious Stable, with Nine Stalls, Two of which are clofe; a large Yard, with a good Well and new Pump in it, and every other Conveniency fit for a Gentleman's Family in private Life, or public Bufinefs. On the fame Lot is a large Brick Houfe, which, with a little Expence, might be converted into a good Store-Room and Compting-Houfe. For Terms of Sale, apply to
(tf)   JOSEPH EARLE

in business together during the period in which Sudler owned the buildings. Within a month of buying the property from Sudler, Smyth placed another advertisement in the Maryland Gazette which lists many of the features that did not survive into the twentieth century.

"To be sold by subscriber on 30 Sept.

Two house + lots in C'tn situated in the most public part of town viz one a corner brick house, two stories high, with three rooms in lower story and four in upper, a good dry cellar under the whole house, bounded by Main or High St. on one side, and Queen's St. on the other, with a stone house adjoining which forms the kitchen and a convenient family dining room, composing all together a building on High St of 65 feet long and running on Queen's St. with the ground belonging thereto. 92 feet and back 90 feet. There are also a good framed stable and carriage house, and stone smokehouse on the said lot, all in good repair. The other lot is 92 feet in front of Queen's St, running back 180 feet, has on the said street a brick house, two stories high, 2 rooms in the lower and three in the upper, with a good framed kitchen, under which is a good dry cellar there are also on the premises a carriage-house and stable. These houses + lots ... 1/6 purchas 1

Buck-Bacchus Store, Chestertown c. 1735. Before restoration. The flat roof was installed after a mid-nineteenth century fire destroyed the original. Maryland Historical Trust, Michael Bourne photograph, 1976.

Opposite: Buck-Bacchus Store, Chestertown, c. 1735. After restoration by Preservation, Inc. Michael Bourne photograph, 1995.

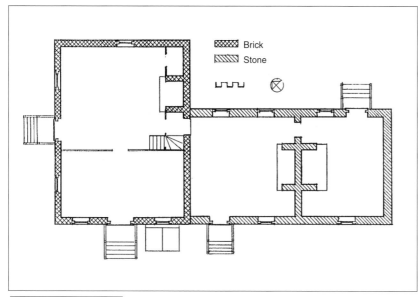

Brick

Stone

Buck-Bacchus Store,
Chestertown. Conjectural
first floor plan based
upon 1768 advertisement
in Maryland Gazette.
Michael Bourne.

Jan.

Thomas Smyth
(Jas Ringgold)" [3]

During the restoration, when plaster was removed from the southeast wall of the present bathroom, an outline of a low pitched *A* roof was discovered, indicating the presence of an earlier wing. At the time, it was a mystery, but the advertisement clearly gives form and size to a fact which had been covered since the 1820s.

Thomas Smyth was successful in disposing of his properties but only in several parcels over a two year period. When the deed was finally recorded in 1787 for the corner house and lot to one *"Harriett Buchanan, gentlewoman,"* the house was then occupied by John Rolph, an innkeeper.[4] It is not stated whether Buchanan lived in the building or rented it out, but when she sold it twenty years later, she was residing in New Castle County, Delaware.[5]

In 1818 Thomas and Christianna Walker became owners. Thomas Walker, also a merchant, advertised in the local papers as well. It was during the Walker's long ownership (1818-1854) that the store was altered twice. First, the stone kitchen wing was demolished and replaced by a narrow entry/stair hall, the full depth of the building. Then the old chimney was also demolished and a new one installed in the northeast wall. Without the stone kitchen, it was necessary to build a new one. This was done along the Queen Street side. With a formal entrance on High Street, the original Queen Street entrance was superfluous, so it was carefully bricked up and converted into a window. Also during this period, the storeroom was fitted with shelves. This new addition was constructed in brick using the common bond pattern in contrast to the Flemish bond of the original structure.

An interesting aside is the paint treatment which was employed on the exterior of the brick building after the stone kitchen had been demolished and before the plaster was applied inside the new stair hall. The entire building was painted with thick brick-red paint and then each of the mortar joints was painstakingly painted white with an equally thick paint, forming a contrast even more garish than the original glazed brickwork. Another feature uncovered from the 1820s was a blue and gray damask type wallpaper applied over the original beaded board partitions in the principal bed chamber. In the process of being removed, the manufacturer's name appeared on one of the 18" x 22" blocked sheets:

"Manufactured by
H. P. Borrekens
151 Chestnut St., Philada"

Borrekens is known to have been in the paper hanging business at this address in 1823-24, which helps to narrow the date range of remodeling to within a short time.[6]

The other alteration which may have occurred during the Walker ownership is hinted at in his will.

"I give and devise unto Thomas McLoughlin, son of George ... in consideration of essential service done me by his father during my fire on Jany 8th 1844 ... ." [7]

Prior to the restoration, the roof of the Buck-Bacchus Store was a near flat hip roof, covered with raised seam tin. Traces of fire damage were visible in the attic flooring and joists and also in the board partition between the two front bedchambers. The fire appears to have originated where a stove pipe penetrated the roof. The flat roof was undoubtedly installed after the fire, as was much of the interior plasterwork over the board partitions.

By the time the house was sold in 1854 to William Bacchus, the lot had been reduced to a fraction of its 1735 bounds. Bacchus and his wife and family not only carried on the store, but made the house their residence as well. After William's death in 1874, the building was transferred to his daughter Harriett. The store was maintained, although the floor was dropped to near street level and the windows and doors were lengthened. A canvas awning was installed on High Street. This change eliminated interior access between the store and residential parts. According to the memories of two Chestertown residents, the residence was rented to Dr. and Mrs. Charles Whaland while Harriett Bacchus' brother continued to operate the store in the remainder of the building.

After 1922, when Eva Topping became the owner, the store was incorporated into the residence. The High Street openings that had been lengthened during the Bacchus period were reconverted into windows. The back wing, which had previously incorporated a dining room and kitchen was removed, and the tiny lot on which it stood, sold. A porch was built along the back and the kitchen brought into the brick part of the house—a plan better suited to twentieth century living.

Between 1939–1971 the house was the home of the W. Burgess Schreiber family. Finally, in 1975 the building was purchased by Preservation, Inc., a Chestertown preservation group who, with the financial assistance of many, restored it as a store/residence. Today it is a private residence, open to the public at special times during the year.   K-331

1. Maryland Gazette, Dec. 1, 1768.
2. Land Records, Lib. DD 3, fol. 513.
3. Maryland Gazette, Aug. 26, 1785.
4. Land Records, Lib. EF 7, fol. 142.
5. Land Records, Lib WS 1, fol. 432. (Harriett Buchanan was the daughter of Robert Buchanan of Drayton Manor.)
6. Research supplied by Dr. Roger W. Moss, Dir. Athenaeum, Phila, PA. Samples of this wallpaper were donated to the Cooper-Hewitt Museum, NY, NY. The kitchen built in this period was later moved down the street where it is the back wing of 103 Queen Street.
7. Wills, Lib. IF 1, fol.4.

Valley Cottage

Georgetown
c. 1737

Valley Cottage is one of the most picturesque houses in the upper part of Kent County, as well as being one of the few properties which has remained in the same family for eight generations. It is situated on Lot No. 51 of the original town plat of Georgetown (1737), on the south side of Princess Stop Street.

Thomas Atkinson, Brick Maker, purchased the lot in 1737 from the town founder, Gideon Pearce.[1] It is presumed that Atkinson built at least part of the house in fulfillment of the terms of ownership established by the Legislature. When Atkinson died in 1746, he bequeathed *" ... the two houses where I lived"* to his widow, Elizabeth.[2]

Valley Cottage was built in two sections, the first being a one room log or plank building, the second section being a framed section. Both have their own doors and are entered into from the north porch. In the log

sections, the door opens into a stairhall which was possibly installed when the two houses were joined. Here, a vertical beaded board partition separates it from the east room (dining room) which appears to have been a kitchen with a relatively modest size fireplace with wooden lintel. The present kitchen is located in a leanto on the south wall.

The stair has a delicate balustrade with fluted newels and rectangular balusters. Clearly however, the most impressive feature of the eighteenth century, forty-two foot, gambrel-roof house is the paneling on the west walls of the frame section. In both the living room and chamber above, well-executed raised paneling embellishes the fireplace walls. Each fireplace is flanked by two closets.

By tradition, in 1762, the house was occupied by Archibald Wright, a Scotsman, who had settled in Georgetown and had developed a mercantile busi-

Valley Cottage, c. 1737. North facade with 1950 extension on west end. Michael Bourne photograph, 1979.

Valley Cottage, c. 1737. Late eighteenth century living room paneling. Library of Congress, Historic American Buildings Survey, E. H. Pickering photograph, 1936.

Valley Cottage. Prior to 1950 a two-story wing was located on the west gable. Sarah K. Perkins Collection, c. 1900.

Valley Cottage, c. 1737. East gable in 1936.

Valley Cottage, c. 1737. West bedroom paneling. Library of Congress, Historic American Buildings Survey, E. H. Pickering photographs.

ness in conjunction with his usual profession as cordwainer and tanner. By 1773, he purchased the adjoining Lot No. 37 and erected the brick house[3] which still stands as the southern end of the Kitty Knight House Inn. When Wright died, his real estate was bequeathed to his widow and after her death to his two sons, John and William.[4] It is difficult to trace the ownership of Valley Cottage after Wright's death, but it appears to have been owned by Archibald Wright's daughter and son-in-law, Ann and John Rumsey, of Delaware. In 1832, Valley Cottage was acquired by the Reverend Purnell Fletcher Smith at a tax sale in which it is simply referred to as the *"Rumsey Property."*[5] The Rev. Mr. Smith was Ann Rumsey's nephew by marriage.

In both The Reverend Mr. and Mrs. Smith's wills (1842 and 1855 respectively),[6] the property is bequeathed to their son, Benjamin E. Smith. After his death, Valley Cottage was acquired by his nephew, John P. Wallis, a Master in the U. S. Navy.[7] He transferred the property in 1875 to his mother, the widow of Arthur I. Wallis. In that deed, the property is referred to as the *"Rumsey Property"* or *"Valley Cottage."*

In 1899, Mrs. Wallis bequeathed Valley Cottage to her seven remaining children in equal parts.[8] Over the years they all occupied Valley Cottage, but the two unmarried daughters, Anna and Mary, remained there until it was acquired in 1950 by their niece, Sarah Karsner Wallis, daughter of Richard Sappington Wallis, and wife of Dennis J. Perkins.[9] Mrs. Perkins died in 1997. She was the eighth generation to own the property.   K-148

1. Land Records, Lib. 4, fol. 444.
2. Wills, Lib. 3, fol. 27.
3. Archibald Wright's house is listed elsewhere in this book.
4. Wills, Lib. 7, fol. 24.
5. Land Records, Lib. JNG 2, fol. 641.
6. Wills, Lib. JFB 1, fol. 124; Wills, Lib. JF 1, fol. 387.
7. Land Records, Lib. DCB 2, fol. 137.
8. Wills, Lib. JTD 1, fol. 214.
9. Land Records, Lib. WHG 18, fol. 371.

Esau Watkins House

*Water Street, Chestertown
c. 1739*

Esau Watkins House, c. 1739. Built originally with a central chimney, the building was enlarged c. 1880 and covered with stucco. The Flemish bond with glazed header brick with its many irregularities resurfaced in the 1946 remodeling. Michael Wootton photograph, 1996.

The earliest remaining dwelling on the Chester River in Chestertown is 109 Water Street. Built by Esau and Sarah Watkins, it stands on Water Lot No. 11, which was deeded to them on August 24, 1739 by Sarah's father, William Ringgold. In that deed, as well in other deeds, and in his own will, Esau is listed as a blacksmith by trade.

In general form and material the house is similar to the Buck-Bacchus Store, a building constructed a few years earlier on the corner of High and Queen Streets. Like the store, the principal facade of the Watkins house was the narrower dimension of the house. Its front door, however, was located not in the center of the three bays, but to the left. This facade and its southwest counterpart are laid in flemish bond with glazed headers. Again like the store, the water table jogs above the basement windows, which have segmental arches of alternating stretchers and double headers. The roof is hipped and has a plain plaster cove cornice. There is one dormer on the facade and two on the flanking sides.

The plan of the Watkins House appears to have had two rooms per floor with a central chimney stack adjacent its southwest wall and the stair on the opposite side of the chimney with passage between the two rooms. Its plan would have been similar to a typical New England house, except for the placement of the entrance. Being constructed at grade on the river side, the kitchen was located in the basement, like other houses on the street. The presence of soot on the cellar beams in the room closest to the river points to its original use as a kitchen. In the attic or third floor, original feather edge board partitions separate the hall from the bedrooms. There is one original four-panel door and one five-panel door dating from late in the century.

In his will, Esau Watkins left his dwelling to his son, John and for whom he stipulated Dr. William Murray as guardian until he reached 21 years of age. In 1776, John was planning to leave the area. He was heavily indebted to the firm of Morgan and Sluby, and the house was mortgaged to them to secure the debt.[1] Interestingly, three years later he was still living in Kent County.[2]

109 Water Street passed through many hands until it was purchased in 1820 by Samuel Merritt of Godlington Manor. It remained in the Merritt family until 1880 when it was sold to Benjamin Fleming for $1,000. It was probably during the Fleming period that the house was lengthened by 6' 10" toward the river. A fate similar to 103 Water Street befell this house: the belt course was chopped off, windows were altered and the difference in brickwork was concealed by the addition of a coat of stucco. The old central chimney was removed and a new one installed in the new addition. The floor plan was altered to suit the owners. It remained in the Fleming ownership until 1944 when Miss Francis Denton, of River House, purchased it and built the block and brick wall separating the two properties.

Louis and Ellen Perry Skinner acquired the property in 1946 and remodeled it into the existing plan, with a side stairhall, kitchen and pantry in the front, dining room in the center with bay window overlooking the River House garden and a living room. A screened porch was built on the river side which was later enclosed.

K-13

1. Lib. DD 5, fol. 140.

2. Lib. DD 5, fol. 374.

Godlington Manor

Quaker Neck
c. 1740

WITHIN THE CONFINES OF PRESENT DAY KENT COUNTY, Godlington Manor is one of seven such named manors to have been patented in the seventeenth century. Originally a land grant to Thomas Godlington in 1659, Godlington in its original form amounted to 1,000 acres.[1] In 1685, the property was purchased by Thomas Claggett.[2] However, the following year it was acquired by Michael Miller, a major figure in early Kent County. Miller lived in the lower part of the county, where he owned Miller's Purchase (part of Hinchingham) and Arcadia. (In 1693, he sold a small part of Arcadia to St. Paul's Parish where he served as a founding vestryman.)

After Miller's death in 1698,[3] Godlington Manor descended to his son, Arthur. When Arthur Miller died in 1739,[4] it again passed from father to son, this time to Arthur Miller, Jr. Although the property was not improved during the ownership of Michael Miller, it is uncertain as to whether or not Arthur or his son actually constructed the first structure which is known today as Godlington Manor.

This first house consisted of a 17' 6" x 22' 0", three-bay, one-story, frame house with its large fireplace located on the east wall. The framing was assembled in three bays with large posts and plate which protruded from the face of the interior plaster walls. It served as a one-room dwelling until the 1760s, when a 16' addition was constructed on the west gable. The addition adjoined the old exterior shiplap wall and was built with a full basement and a paneled wall across the stair, fireplace and closet on the west end.

Godlington Manor, c. 1740. The river side prior to restoration. The house had seen years of vacancy and neglect. Library of Congress, Historic American Buildings Survey, R. Langenbach photograph, 1973.

Godlington Manor, after restoration. The earliest part (left) was incorporated into a fully developed late eighteenth century farmhouse. The smokehouse is early nineteenth century. Tyler Campbell photograph, 1995.

Godlington Manor, living room before restoration. The late eighteenth century interior occupies the earliest part of the building. Library of Congress, Historic American Buildings Survey, R. Langenbach photograph, 1973.

Godlington Manor, living room after restoration. Stenciling on walls and ceiling was discovered under layers of whitewash and paint. Tyler Campbell photograph, 1995.

Godlington is one of four frame houses listed under the name of Arthur Miller, Jr. in the Tax Assessment of 1783. He owned a total of 1,100 acres, although eight years earlier he had deeded a part of Godlington Manor and East Huntington to his daughter, Sarah. In 1799, her son, Samuel Merritt, inherited Godlington Manor from his grandfather.[5] Upon the death of Sarah Miller Merritt, those parts of Godlington deeded to her in 1775 were bequeathed to her two children. Finally, after trading amongst themselves, Samuel became the sole owner of both Godlington Manor and East Huntington in 1799.[6]

In regard to the house itself, Samuel Merritt was responsible for its next enlargement and for several of the refinements which brought the *Manor House*, more or less, to the form it exhibits today. The *A* roof was removed and a taller, more commodious gambrel roof was installed. The original one-room structure was remodeled with the installation of a smaller fireplace within a wall of paneling which included glazed cabinets and a concealed, winding stair.

It is apparent that the *new* west gable was exposed to the elements for a short time before a 30', *A* roof kitchen wing was added. Constructed with wrought nails, it would have been built only a few years after the other. The new wing consisted of a pantry and kitchen with large pyramidal fireplace and a ladder to the space above intended as quarters for kitchen help. Both downstairs rooms were lighted by only one small window in each. The last addition to the house was a leanto constructed off the pantry which was fitted with storage shelves and a window which had been reused from its predecessor.

Samuel Merritt built a fine homeplace at Godlington Manor. It included several outbuildings, a brick stable, a frame hen house and such. Today, only the brick smokehouse and pyramidal roof frame dairy remain. These have been restored in their original locations, west of the house.

Merritt died without a will in 1827. Commissioners were appointed to divide his holdings into four portions of equal value and allow his heirs to have their choice of farms.[7] It was Arthur Miller Merritt who chose the homeplace on 443 acres and it is he who was probably responsible for the decorative treatment on the interior walls with vivid colors and stenciled patterns. Arthur Miller Merritt also most likely constructed the porches which run the full length of the gambrel section on both sides of the house. Merritt died in 1848 and left five heirs.[8] Seventeen years later, in 1865, Merritt's two sons purchased the farm from their three sisters.[9] However, the brothers did not fare well in the fifteen years to follow and eventually sold it back to

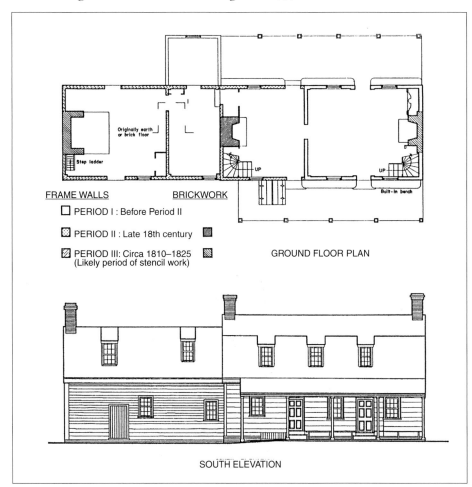

FRAME WALLS   BRICKWORK

☐ PERIOD I : Before Period II

▦ PERIOD II : Late 18th century ▨

▨ PERIOD III: Circa 1810–1825 ▧
(Likely period of stencil work)

GROUND FLOOR PLAN

SOUTH ELEVATION

Godlington Manor ground floor plans, South elevation and West elevation. Library of Congress, Historic American Buildings Survey, Drawing by Peter Newlin and Chinh Hoang, 1976

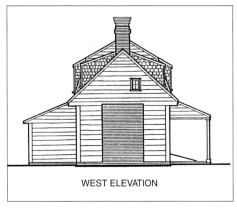

WEST ELEVATION

Godlington Manor, fireplace in left wing with step ladder to second floor. Library of Congress, Historic American Buildings Survey,. 1973.

Godlington Manor, hasp on basement bulkhead.

Godlington Manor, detail of original open face "wishbone" latch. Tyler Campbell photograph, 1995.

Godlington Manor, second floor west chamber showing wall stenciling. Tyler Campbell photograph, 1995.

their sister, Mary Elizabeth Merritt Brown, widow of Hiram Brown, in 1880.[10]

In 1882, Mary E. Brown sold the farm to her three children.[11] By 1910, Henry Clay Brown had become the sole owner of Godlington Manor after a series of transactions amongst his siblings.[12,13] Hard times again returned and in 1930 the farm was sold to the son of Henry's double first cousin, Hiram Staunton Brown.[14,15]

Godlington Manor was restored in the early 1980s. The house and lands are now held by granddaughters of Hiram Staunton Brown, the eleventh generation of the family which has owned the manor since the seventeenth century. It is one of only two properties in the county to have descended within a single family over a 300 year period.   K-88

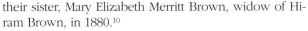

1. Patents, Lib. 4, fol. 274.
2. Patents, Lib. NS No. B, fol. 261.
3. Wills, Lib. 1, fol. 57.
4. Wills, Lib. 2, fol. 122.
5. Wills, Lib. 7, fol. 256.
6. Land Records, Lib. TW 1, fol. 289.
7. Land Records, Lib. JNG 8, fol. 128.
8. Wills, Lib. JFB 1, fol. 256.
9. Land Records, Lib. JKH 4, fol. 576.
10. Land Records, Lib. DCB 5, fol. 600.
11. Land Records, Lib. SB 5, fol. 586.
12. Land Records, Lib. JTD 13, fol. 516.
13. Land Records, Lib. JTD 20, fol. 292.
14. Land Records, Lib. RAS 5, fol. 99.
15. Hiram Staunton Brown (1882-1950)—son of Hiram Brown (1853-1914) & Mary Elizabeth "Nanny" Hazzard (1861-1942), grandson of William Henry Brown (1819-1861) & Margaret Ann Merritt (1828-1894) bought the farm from Henry Clay Brown—son of Hiram Brown (1814-1864) {also William Henry Brown's brother} & Mary E. Merritt {also Margaret Ann Merritt's sister}.

Levi Rodgers House

Water Street, Chestertown
c. 1740

T HE LEVI RODGERS HOUSE IS LOCATED AT 202 FRONT STREET on Lot No. 5 of the plat of Chestertown. While it appears to have been remodeled around 1830-40 and enlarged around the turn of the century, its original eighteenth century form remains evident. Its origins were confirmed when whitewashed shiplap siding secured with rosehead wrought nails was revealed when a portion of the back wall was exposed. Also, the roof structure had been found to be constructed of common rafters laid on the flat sides, similar to Carvill Hall (c. 1695) and the Reward (c. 1740). Its current plan with addition consists primarily of four rooms on each floor with an enclosed stair between the two front rooms and a vestibule directly beneath. The front portion of the Levi Rodgers House may indeed be the tenement which was bequeathed by Dr. William Murray to his daughter Ann in 1768 and which was described as the house *"wherein Charles Brunningin now lives."*[1]

Perhaps most interestingly, the house or a building nearby was used as a gathering place for nineteenth century oyster lovers. As owner and occupant in the second quarter of the nineteenth century, Levi Rodgers, a free black man, advertised his business in the Kent News several times.

After Rodgers' death, his widow and daughter continued to advertise in the Kent News at the same location.

K-6

---

1. Wills, Lib. 4, fol. 352.

OYSTERS!!!

THE subscriber respectfully informs the public generally that he has the **CAPE MAY SALOON** neatly fitted up, and is prepared to serve up OYSTERS in all the various ways.— Also Terrapins; in season; oysters by the gallon, &c; Gentlemen wishing to partake of these delicacies, will have every attention paid them by the public's ob't serv't
LEVI RODGERS.

Sept 8, '49—tf

Advertisement for Oysters for Sale by Levi Rodgers, Kent News, September 8, 1849 and following.

Levi Rodgers House, c. 1740. The front portion may be the tenement which was bequeathed to Ann Murray by her father in 1768, "... wherein Charles Brunningin now lives." Levi Rodgers, a free black and his family lived in this house in the 1840s. Chestertown Town Office, R. Neil photograph, 1976.

Piner's Grove Site

Near Chestertown
c. 1740

The old house that stood on Piner's Grove was constructed in the mid-eighteenth century by one of the Piners, for whose family the patent had been named in the late seventeenth century.

When initially constructed, the house measured approximately 18' 6" x 36' with a 31' kitchen wing. Both parts were one-and-a-half stories with steep *A* roofs and dormer windows—the most common form in Kent County at the time. The facade of the main section had two windows west of the entry and one to the east. There were probably two dormers on the roof. The north facade was nearly symmetrical, with one window on each side of its door.

This hall-parlor house contained two very good walls of paneling and other well-executed interior details. Enclosed within the west wall of paneling of the hall was a winder stair to the room above. There were two large panels flanked by paneled pilasters, with triglyph and frieze capital, centered above the fireplace. The pilasters actually terminated above the fireplace trim. To the south there was a narrow, three-panel closet door with panel above. On the north side of the fireplace there was a six-panel closet door with two panels above, the whole flanked by two narrow sections of paneling. The cornice broke out above the pilasters, doors, and windows. The latter feature is similar to the original riverside room at the Custom House. Pieces of

Piner's Grove paneling, re-installed in a new Kent County residence. Inset: detail of pilaster. Michael Wootton photographs, 1997

Silhouette of Joseph Wickes III (1759-1822) who married Mary Piner (1764-1823). Their tombs are located on the property along with their descendants. Mrs. Daniel Wickes Dietrich Collection.

Piner's Grove, c. 1740. South elevation based upon evidence found inside when the house was being dismanteled.

Piner's Grove, c. 1740. first floor plan. Michael Bourne.

Piner's Grove, c. 1740. this frame house was originally one and one-half stories with superior interior. It burned in the 1980s. It remained in the Piner and Wickes family until 1922. Maryland Historical Trust, M. L. Fritz photograph, 1981..

bolection type chair rail remained on the paneling.

In the parlor, the paneling was similar and included a second stair. This would have resulted in a two-room plan above and made a corridor on the second story unnecessary.

The service wing can only be conjectured, but it probably had a kitchen and pantry with two chambers above for use by the house servants. There were probably separate stairs.

The farm is known to have come into the possession of Colonel Joseph Wickes through his mother, Mary Piner Wickes.[1] In 1852, he is listed as the owner of the farm composed of 392 acres of *"Stepney, Piners Grove and Tilghman's Choice."* The *"Frame House and other Buildings in tolerable repair."* [2]

Upon Col. Wickes' death, his body was interred at Piner's Grove, later to be joined by his wife and son Benjamin. The farm then passed to Judge Joseph A. Wickes.[3] It was sold out of the family in 1922.[4]

Either in the late nineteenth century or after the farm was sold out of the family, both sections of the house were drastically remodeled with alterations to the fenestration and heightening of the building by a full second story. In the mid-twentieth century, a fire destroyed the entire kitchen wing, weakening the structure to such an extent that it had to be completely demolished. Paneling from the hall was able to be salvaged and has been installed in another Kent County residence.   K-473

1. Land Records, Lib. JNG 5, fol. 14.
2. 1852 Tax Assessment.
3. Land Records, Lib. JKH 4, fol. 588.
4. Land Records, Lib. RRA 1, fol. 424.

Yeates House Site

Turner's Creek
c. 1740

Yeates House, c. 1740. This was the main house of a once thriving river village. In 1938 the house still had its front stoop with benches. Historical Society of Kent County, Delphine S. B. Kelly Collection.

THIS SMALL FRAME HOUSE ONCE STOOD ON A NARROW peninsula of land which juts eastward into Turner's Creek (the present location of Turner's Creek Picnic Pavilion). It is reputed to have been the home of Donaldson Yeates between the years 1770 and 1796.

Yeates, a merchant from New Castle, Delaware, together with Tobias Rudolph, a merchant from Cecil County, purchased the seven acre parcel called Knocks Folly in 1770.[1] The land had been surveyed in 1738 and patented in 1753, just after Thomas Crosby had purchased it from Henry Knock.[2] Yeates and Rudolph had acquired it from Crosby's heir, who resided in England. The house had been constructed by Henry Knock after the survey.

The house stood on a stone basement and had two brick chimneys, the east one within the structure and the west built outside its walls. From the evidence in the west chimney, the original kitchen or service wing was located on the west side of the building, but in the nineteenth century a board and batten kitchen was installed on the east gable. The entrance in the center of the three-bay facade was flanked by a pair of seats, a practice found throughout Kent County. The south side apparently always had a porch or piazza. That undoubtedly helped to preserve the original beaded featheredge clapboard siding, although the north side retained its beaded weatherboard.

The *A* roof had two hip dormers on each side, a feature it had in common with the Hynson-Ringgold House (c. 1743). The plan of the first floor was a hall-parlor plan with winder stair behind the paneling in the hall. The second floor plan consisted of a corridor with two tiny rooms on the north (one unlighted) and a large room on the west end. The small east room had a fireplace. All of the partitions throughout the house were beaded vertical boards with double beads, similar to those at the Buck-Bacchus Store and the Buck-Chambers House, both built soon after 1735.

The hall paneling had an elliptical headed fireplace opening surrounded by bollection molding with tall thin panels flanking the fireplace, suggesting pilasters. This was further emphasized by the crown molding breaking out only above the panels. The entire first floor was paneled, with fielded panels east of the entrance doors and vertical boards to the west.[3]

In the 1783 Tax Assessment, Yeates' real estate holdings at Turner's Creek are listed with 14 acres and the notation *"Good Buildings and several of them."* Elsewhere he held 1792½ acres with 56 slaves and sixty white inhabitants thereon.

Not only was Donaldson Yeates a successful merchant at Turner's Creek, but he was actively involved in the Revolution, serving as a colonel in the Kent County Militia, 27th Battalion. He was appointed Deputy Quartermaster General of Maryland in 1780 and appears

regularly in the correspondence concerning supplies for the troops. He was a member of the Lower House in the State Legislature, served as a justice of the Orphan's Court and associate judge for the County, resigning in 1794. One year prior to his resignation, he advertised in The Apollo that he was closing his accounts and transferring his business to his nephews John Lathim and James Corrie.[5]

In February of 1796, Yeates wrote his will leaving his estate to his wife, Mary Syng Yeates for the education of his children, and the choice of his Turner's creek real estate to his son George or John. In a codicil written about a week before his death, he stated,

"It is my will and desire that the building that I am about projecting shall be fully finished and this to be done at the expense of my estate."[6]

This is a reference to the brick structure known as Knocks Folly, at the top of the hill.

Yeates' inventory lists store goods and two vessels held in partnership. The vessels consisted of a sloop called *"The George and Eliza"* (after two of his children) and a schooner called *"Nancy."* Debts due his estate amounted to over £3000, a third of which was due from *"the United States of America"*—most likely debts from the Revolution.[7]

After his death, Donaldson Yeates' body was buried at nearby Shrewsbury Churchyard, where he had been a vestry member in 1793 and where his son George who took over the Turner's Creek properties was to serve likewise in 1803 and 1804.

In 1970, the Yeates house was dismantled and reconstructed in Baltimore County.   K-116

1. Land Records, Lib. DD 3, fol. 530.
2. Forman, H. C. Early Manor and Plantation Houses, 1934.
3. Certificates, Lib. GS No. 1, fol. 178; Patents, Lib. BY & GS No. 3, fol. 473.
4. Abel, Mary E. A., "Colonel Donaldson Yeates," unpublished article prepared for the DAR, Old Kent Chapter.
5. The Apollo or Chestertown Spy, August 3, 1793.
6. Wills, Lib. 7, fol. 547.
7. Inventories, Lib. 10, fol. 453; Lib. 11, fol. 607.
8. DeProspo, Katherine M., A History of Shrewsbury Parish Church, Chesapeake College Press, Wye Mills, 1988.

The Reward

Quaker Neck
c. 1742

CHARLES TILDEN EMIGRATED TO MARYLAND IN 1677 AND within a short time (1681) acquired The Reward.[1] The Reward had originally been surveyed in 1668 and was described as being "*situated in Langfords Bay at Walsford Creek, next to land lately laid out for John Tully.*"[2] Tilden, like several of his contemporaries, became very active in the development of Kent County. He was a judge in the Kent County Court in 1685-86, and in 1693, he was a founding vestryman of St. Paul's Parish and also held the office of High Sheriff of the County.

When Tilden died in about 1698, his land descended to his son Marmaduke, who resided at Great Oak Manor.[3] Nothing more regarding the property was found in the records until Marmaduke's death in 1726. His will stipulated that the Langford Bay Plantation be rented until his son, Charles, reached age 21 (in 1742).[4] It was at that time that Charles took possession of the farm[5] and soon thereafter began to build his dwelling house.[6]

The house that he constructed was unlike any other built before in Kent County. A 39' x 37', two-story, brick structure, with a four-room plan, its facade was laid in Flemish bond with glazed headers, while all other walls were laid in English bond. A classic ovolo and caveto molded water table jogged up and over the basement windows and down on the sides, corresponding with the change in floor levels within. There were segmental arches of lightly rubbed brick above the first story openings of the south half of the building. The rest were jack arches. A belt course between stories was interrupted by the back window of the second story and

stopped where it joined the rear slope of the catslide roof. In scale, the windows resembled the original windows in the Custom House in Chestertown, with 12/12 sash on the first floor and 6/6 sash on the second. Original door and window frames in the south portion of the house were made of walnut. Where the chimneys pierced the apex of the asymmetrical roof, the mason used weatherings and withes to suggest the number of flues within. This feature was also used at Violet Farm

(1762), Comegys Bight (1768) and Springfield Farm (1770), suggesting the possibility that they were built by the same hand. The rear of the building had only two openings, a window and a door.

The original plan of the first floor consisted of four rooms and a corridor which separated two rooms in the rear. Access to three of the four rooms was gained from the corridor which ran from the back door to the basement door. One room appears to have been used as a

The Reward, c. 1742. The facade is laid in Flemish bond brick with glazed headers and has both water table and belt course. The relationship of first and second story windows is the same as the Custom House (1745).

The Reward, c. 1742. The closed string stair ascends from the living room to a central hall above.

The Reward, c. 1742. The living room possesses paneled walls and glazed cabinets above the bolection molded fireplace surround.
C. Engstrom photographs, 1977.

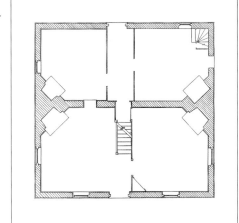

The Reward, c. 1742. The den is paneled with vertical feather edge boards except for the diagonal chimney breast, which has cabinet doors and a single raised panel. The library is nearly identical. C. Engstrom photograph, 1977.

The Reward, c. 1742. Conjectural first floor plan at the time of completion. Michael Bourne.

diate scantling for support. The same roof structure was found in Sterling Castle, 103 Mill Street, Chestertown.

In the Lord Proprietor's Debt Books, it appears that Tilden acquired Garnett's Meadow, a 41 acre tract adjoining The Reward, in 1760. Nine years later, he not only owned the above, but also parts of High Park, King's Prevention and Scott's Lott, all situated across Langford Creek on Broad Neck. After a survey undertaken for Tilden in 1774, his farm became known as Tilden's Farm and included parts of The Reward, Tully's Fancy and Garnett's Meadow. By 1783, Tilden owned a total 607 acres and by this time his holdings were listed as Tilden's Farm, High Park and Presbury's Discovery. These were not patented until after his death, and they were then done so to his son, Marmaduke.[7] In the will of Charles Tilden it is stated that his real estate had been transferred to his children, Marmaduke, Charles, John, and Edward.[8] The deeds, however, were not recorded.

Jeremiah Nichols owned the farm until 1805, when he sold it to William Trew of Providence Plantation. In 1808, William bequeathed it to his son, Bartus, whose heirs sold it in 1932 to Agnes Langhorne Johnson. It was she who built the one-and-a-half-story kitchen wing on the east side and made other improvements as well. From 1940–1966, Colonel and Mrs. Edward Hurd owned The Reward and it was during their ownership that the pool and pool house were constructed. Finally, in 1970, The Reward was purchased by its present owners who have created an estate of extraordinary beauty.   K-90

kitchen, as its fireplace possessed a wooden lintel and lug pole from which pots could have been hung. The principal stair was situated in the main room, opposite the front door and led to a second floor hall with four doors and the stair to the attic. Leading to quarters for the help, a secondary stair was located in the kitchen's northeast corner.

When the house was first finished, three of the four first floor rooms and one on the second had corner fireplaces. Also, three of the downstairs rooms were finished with walls of raised paneling and feather-edge boards. The living room was the most sophisticated with bolection molding around the fireplace, glazed cabinets above and a chair rail. The attic was unfinished, revealing the roof structure—a basically common rafter arrangement, 4' on center with very thin interme-

1. Land Records, Lib. 1, fol. 266.
2. Patents, Lib. 13, fol. 95; Rent Rolls, Lib. 5, fol. 46.
3. Land Records, Lib. BC, fol. 249.
4. Wills, Original No. 1252.
5. Rent Rolls, 1736–1769.
6. Charles Tilden is known to have been a builder, for he entered into a contract with the vestry of the newly organized Chester Parish in 1768 to construct their new parish church near I. U. Crossroads. From the initial descriptions in the vestry minutes, it appears that he was thought of as capable and as being able to produce carpentry and masonry of good caliber.

The vestry was apparently impressed enough to award him another contract to build the Vestry House as well. However, during the construction of the latter, Tilden was interrupted to reconstruct the roof of the Church, as the vestry thought it inadequate. These circumstances may explain why the contract for the construction of the chapel proposed for Chestertown was awarded not to Tilden, but to William Ringgold, another contractor.

7. Patented Certificate No. 583.
8. Wills, Lib. 9, fol. 316.
9. Land Records, Lib. BC 4, fol. 445.

Caulk's Field

Near Fairlee
1743

Caulk's Field, 1743. The house was built for William Moore, the second generation to own part of Arcadia. Tyler Campbell photograph, 1995.

Caulk's Field, stair door with original thumb latch and later bolt and knob. Gene Johnstone photograph, 1995.

THE ONE LAND BATTLE TO HAVE OCCURRED IN KENT County between the American Militia and the British Navy was fought in a field west of the Caulk's Field House on 31 August 1814. Familiar with the terrain of the area, the Regiment had held maneuvers there in the past. By the time of the battle, the seventy year old house had only been in the possession of Isaac Caulk for two years. The nephew and heir of John Moore, Jr. (d. 1812), Caulk had earlier been a captain in the 21st Regiment under Philip Reed.[1]

Caulk's uncle, John Moore, was the third generation to own and reside on the 300 acre part of Arcadia which had first been purchased by his grandfather, John Moore, in the early eighteenth century.[2] Moore's father, William, had inherited the farm in 1728 from his father,[3]

Commemorative plaque near the site of the Battle of Caulk's Field. Gene Johnstone photograph, 1997

Caulk's Field, closet window set within glazed headed Flemish bond brickwork. Gene Johnstone photograph, 1995.

Caulk's Field, 1743. The hall paneled fireplace wall is one of the best of the period, with break in the chimney breast and cornice above, bolection molded chair rail and fireplace surround, and original hardware. Tyler Campbell photograph, 1995.

and in 1743, had built the house that stands today.

William Moore had apparently prospered, as the house he built was larger than those of most of his contemporaries. Although it had a typical hall-parlor plan, the house had a full second story and attic, plus a two-room service wing. The main part was built of brick

on a full basement. Both the east and west facades, as well as the south gable, were laid in Flemish bond. Glazed headers were used on the west and south throughout. However, on the north gable, the only glazing is found in the date, 1743, which can be seen above the kitchen roof. A champhered water table separates the English bond basement from the Flemish bond above, and like several buildings of the period, it jogs above the basement windows. Both sections have central entrances with two flanking windows on both facades. The detailing on the main section is obviously more refined, with alternating glazed segmental arches over the openings. A small window on the south gable lights a closet next to the fireplace.

The interior is still largely intact, with the hall wall being paneled. It encloses two closets and the stair to the second story. The fireplace surround has bolection molding similar to that at The Reward. Above the molding there is a bold shelf with moldings like the cornice.

Original four-panel doors hung on wrought HL hinges remain in place, and around the two closet doors is a narrow backband molding like that at Piner's Grove and Marrowbone. Isaac Caulk farmed the land of his great grandfather until his death in 1837. Thereafter, the farm was sold out of the family to people who lived elsewhere. The house and farm were then tenanted. Because of this situation, the house has changed very little over the years.

Since 1940, Caulk's Field has been owned by the Tulip Forest Farming Corporation. The name Tulip Forest was derived from an adjoining farm which was patented in 1790.   K-93

1. Information from Dr. Stanley Quick who is presently preparing a book on the War of 1812.
2. Land Records, Lib. 1, fol. 429, 525; Lib. 2, fol. 547.
3. Wills, Lib. 1, fol. 302.

Dougherty-Barroll House

High Street, Chestertown
c. 1743

JONATHAN PAGE, BLACKSMITH, PURCHASED FIRST LOT NO. 12 from Daniel Perkins in 1710 and Lot No. 34 in 1733 from Simon Wilmer II.[1] This made him, at the time, sole owner of the High Street block between Front and Queen Streets. He sold the northwest half of Lot No. 34 in 1735 to John Buck and the southeast half in 1743 to Walter Dougherty. Dougherty paid £90 for the lot, a price which may have been sufficient to include a small frame house. However, what might have been there was replaced soon thereafter with a more substantial brick building.

In 1743 Walter Dougherty petitioned the County Court for a license renewal to operate an ordinary in Chestertown.[3] His name appears several times in the Maryland Gazette, first in 1746 to offer a reward for anyone finding a silver snuff box lost between Cecil County and Kent Island,[4] and later offering rigging and other nautical items for sale at the *"House of Walter Dougherty in Chestertown."*[5]

In March of 1751, he advertised that he intended to 'leave the province' and wished to settle his accounts. In this advertisement there is also mention of his house: *"The said Dougherty has a large brick house to dispose of very conveniently situated near the water-side, fit for any Gentleman and also a parcel of very good household furniture ... ."*[6]

Actually, Dougherty did not leave the province. His house is mentioned again in 1759 in the Maryland Gazette: *" ... persons indebted to Messrs. Cunliffe ... are desired to meet Mr. John Glassell, factor at the House of Mr. Daugherty at Chestertown ... ."*[7] Indeed, Walter Dougherty remained in Maryland until his death in 1761.

Dougherty's house, along with the Dr. Murray House and the Custom House, is considered to be one of the best houses built in Chestertown in the 1740s. While all three have central halls, in the Dougherty House the stairhall is flanked by two generous rooms, rather than by one large room and two smaller rooms as in the others. Since the house was built close to the southeast boundary of the lot, its kitchen would have had to have been located out the back or at the opposite end of the building where a two-bay, brick extension was later built.

Its High Street facade is laid in Flemish bond with glazed headers above a molded water table which jogs up and across each of the four basement windows. There is a simple gable roof with three dormers facing the street. Its northwest chimney had a weathering and withes, which is now partly concealed by the later addition. The windows have segmental arches composed of alternating stretchers and double headers, the lower header being glazed. There is a string course between floors. Originally, the central entrance had a double door.

The interior possesses one completely paneled room on the first floor and a paneled partition between the stairhall and second room. Unlike the majority of buildings

Dougherty's Tavern, c. 1743, flourished for the first twenty years of its life, then became a private residence, best known by its occupant in the early nineteenth century, William Barroll. Michael Wootton photograph, 1996.

of this size, there are no interior brick walls. The close-string stair possesses handsome turned balusters. King of Prussia marble fireplace surrounds and hearths were used, but they may have been installed later in the century.

Walter Dougherty died intestate in 1761. His estate was administered by his widow Mary, and before the estate was settled she had remarried—this time to John Higgins.[8] An inventory which was made of Dougherty's personal belongings amounted to £295.17.5 ½, an amount less than the value of his real estate.[9] Apparently, he owned many merchants in Chestertown.

It is uncertain if the Higgins continued to operate the ordinary in the house. Mary outlived her second husband, who died in 1767, and made her his sole heir.[10] She must have died, however, before 1770, for in that year the property was sold by *"Henry Dougherty of the City of Philadelphia, Mariner and cozen that is the Elder Brothers only son and heir at Law of Walter Dougherty late of Chestertown."*[11]

Joseph Nicholson, Jr., *"Gentleman and Attorney"* was already residing in the house when he purchased it for £500 in 1770. Joseph was the son of Joseph and Hannah Nicholson, who lived at the White Swan Tavern. He had been admitted to the Kent County Court 13 years earlier and was to become active in the Legislature in the 1770s and '80s. In 1783, he was taxed on the property valued at £600 in Chestertown.[12] He died in Queen Annes County in 1786, leaving a personal estate in excess of £1000. It is interesting to note that Nicholson's wife, Elizabeth Hopper, was the sister of his father's second wife, Mary.[13]

Elizabeth and her son Joseph Hopper Nicholson inherited the Chestertown house after her husband's death. They in turn sold it in 1793 to John Scott, attorney, for £1000. Scott was already renting the house when he purchased it from the Nicholsons. The property was mortgaged to Joseph Hopper Nicholson.[14] John Scott was a member of Washington College's first graduating class in 1783. He continued to reside at the Dougherty House until he sold it to William Barroll, who had been a classmate at college.

Either Nicholson, Scott or Barroll built the two-bay enlargement onto the northwest gable of the house. Although the mason laid the front facade in Flemish bond, he did not use glazed headers to match the rest. It is uncertain if the addition had its own entrance from the beginning, since the arch over the door is higher than the lintel, with brick infill between the two. The addition had a single room on each floor with a winder stair in the north corner adjacent the fireplace. It was well-finished with baseboard, chair rail, mantel and other trim.

William Barroll resided in Chestertown from the time he purchased the house in 1797, until he purchased Fancy Farm from John B. Bordley in 1802. Thereafter, he appears to have resided in both places. Like his predecessor, Joseph Nicholson, Jr., William Barroll was not only an attorney, but actively involved in the Maryland Legislature in the late 1790s. He was instrumental, along with several of his contemporaries, in building the first bridge over the Chester River in Chestertown. Barroll was in fact the president of the building corporation and its largest stockholder. He was also an active member of the Episcopal Church, Chester Parish, and a member of the Board of Visitors and Governors of Washington College.

In a family history written by Wethered Barroll, the following description occurs:

"On the south side of the house on the site of the residence now occupied by William R. Aldridge was a small one story and half frame building which he (William Barroll) occupied as his law office. This law office now forms the rear part of the Aldridge residence. In those

William Barroll purchased Dougherty's Tavern in 1797 and died in 1834. Historical Society of Kent County Collection.

Dougherty's Tavern, c. 1743. The central stair hall seen from the southeast room. Note the similarity of the balustrade to the Custom House (1745). The hall side of the raised panel walls have a small bolection molding around what would usually be recessed panels. Michael C. Wootton photograph, 1997.

Newtown

I reached Newtown att 12 o'clock and put up att Dougherty's, a publick house there. I was scarce arrived when I met severall of my acquaintance. I dined with Dr. Anderson and spent the rest of the day in a sauntering manner. The northeren post arrived att night. I read the papers but found nothing of consequence in them; so after some comical chat with my landlord, I went to bed att eleven o'clock att night.

Sunday, June 3d. I stayed all this day att Newtown and breakfasted with Th. Clay, where I met with one W––b, a man of the law, to appearance a civil, good natured man but set up for a kind of connoiseur in many things. I went to visit some friends and dined att the taveren where I was entertaind by the tricks of a female baboon in the yard. This lady had more attendants and hangers on att her levee than the best person (of quality as I may say) in town. She was very fond of the compliments and company of the men and boys but expressed in her gestures an utter aversion att women and girls, especially negroes of that sex—the lady herself being of a black complexion; yet she did not att all affect her country women.

Att night I was treated by Captain Binning of Boston with a bowl of lemmon punch. He gave me letters for his relations att Boston. Whiele we put about the bowl, a deal of comicall discourse pass'd in which the landlord, a man of a particular talent att telling comic storys, bore the chief part.

Monday, June 4th. The morning being clear and somewhat cool. I got up before 5 a'clock and soon mounted horse. I had a solitary route to Bohemia and went very much out of my way by being too particular and nice in observing directions.*

*The Travels of Dr. Alexander Hamilton, 1744; Cecil County, Maryland 1608-1850, G. E. Gifford, Jr.

days, prior to 1850, the members of the bar in Chestertown had their offices either in their residences or in small one and two-story buildings as near their homes as possible."[15]

If this statement is correct, William Barroll must have rented his office from Samuel Wallis, who at that time, owned the property where it was located. That property was later purchased by Barroll's son, William Hands Barroll, in 1825.[16]

William Barroll was married to Lucretia Edmondson for ten years before the marriage was annulled by the Maryland Legislature in 1798.[17] He then married Sarah Hands and their first son was the aforementioned William Hands Barroll. William Barroll (Sr.) died in 1834 and the administration of the estate was undertaken by another accomplished Chestertown attorney, John Bowers Eccleston. William Barroll's inventory consisted of household furnishings from both Fancy Farm and his house in town. He also had a granary in town that contained more corn than the one on the farm and there were ice houses listed in both locations. The latter, however, was actually on Lot No. 73, which Barroll's widow purchased from the estate in 1834.[18] Title to the house lot was not cleared until 1840–41.[19]

Sarah Hands Barroll is listed, in 1841, as owner of *"House & Lot pt No. 34; occupied by I. T. Freeman in tolerable repair."* She was also listed as owner of her son's office:

"House & Lot pt No. 12 occupied by Permetia Bowan." [20]

It is unclear from the above if Mrs. Barroll lived in part of the family residence or elsewhere. After her death in 1855, the house was bequeathed to her daughter-in-law, Rebecca Johnson Barroll. William Hands Barroll had died on Long Island in 1849.[21] Two years later, Rebecca Barroll sold the property to Rebecca Ringgold who immediately resold it to George W. T. Perkins in 1857.[22]

Perkins was only to hold the Barroll House for three years before selling it and buying the old house next to the bridge. It was sold to Joseph Wickes who lived next door. In Wickes' will, he left the house to his son, Joseph Augustus Wickes who had returned to Chestertown from Cumberland in 1860 and had resided there since.

After the death of his mother, Joseph Augustus purchased the Wickes House from his brother and sold the Barroll House to Emma P. France, wife of Thomas B. France. Mrs. France then bequeathed the house to her two daughters. By 1919, when the daughters sold the house to William G. Smyth and Thomas B. Kilbourn, the property was undoubtedly being treated as a double residence. Legally divided into two properties in 1923, it remains as such to this day.[23]   K-31

Dougherty's Tavern, c. 1743. The original section consisted of the five bay section on the right. The other two bays were added by a later owner. M. Bourne photograph, 1977.

1. Land Records, Lib. 4, fol. 343.
2. Land Records, Lib. 5, fol. 585.
3. Court Records, November 1743, ff.
4. Maryland Gazette, January 14, 1746.
5. Maryland Gazette, November 11, 1746.
6. Maryland Gazette, March 13, 1751.
7. Maryland Gazette, May 3, 1759.
8. Administration Accounts, Lib. 4, fol. 291.
9. Inventories, Lib. 5, fol. 232, 233.
10. Wills, Lib. 4, fol. 286.
11. Land Records, Lib. DD 3, fol. 262.
12. Tax Assessment, 1783, Chestertown.
13. Papenfuse, Maryland Legislators, p.614.
14. Land Records, Lib. BC 3, fol. 476, ff.
15. Wethered Barroll, The Barroll Book, p. 74, ff.
16. Land Records, Lib. TW 4, pt 2, fol. 597.
17. Maryland Gazette, January 25, 1798.
18. Inventories: Lib. 21, fol. 196; Land Records, Lib. JNG 5, fol. 401.
19. Land Records, JNG 7, fol. 268, 270.
20. Tax Assessment, 1841, Chestertown.
21. Barroll, p. 86, ff.
22. Land Records, Lib. JFG 4, fol. 459.
23. Land Records, Lib. RRA, fol. 347, ff.

Hynson-Ringgold House

Water Street, Chestertown
c. 1743

NATHANIEL HYNSON PURCHASED LOT NO. 6 IN 1735. Three years later he sold the western half, bordering Cannon Street and in 1743 he sold the other half, bordering lot No. 7.[1]

Dr. William Murray purchased the western half of the lot in 1743 and began building a large brick residence on the corner.[2] The house which Murray constructed was essentially the same as the existing front section, a rectangular plan, two-and-a-half-story building with hip roof. Its facade, laid in all-header bond, is the first use of the pattern in Chestertown. The five bay facade had 12/12 sash windows, no exterior shutters and jack arches over the first floor windows which were rubbed and gauged. The corners were slightly rubbed. Its central entrance may have had double doors originally, like the Customs House built a few years later in the same block. When built, the plan of the Hynson-Ringgold House was identical to that of the Dickinson Mansion, Kent County, Delaware. It had a central stair hall with one large parlor on the west and two smaller rooms with corner fireplaces on the east. Unlike the symmetry of the facade, the chimneys pierced the roof in atypical fashion, with the east chimney rising in the usual location on the narrow end, but the west chimney rising from the back wall, centered between the two front windows.

Kitchen and service rooms were located on the rear of the east side of the building with a short *A* roof hyphen and one-and-a-half-story kitchen, both probably frame.

In 1759 William Murray purchased the eastern half of lot No. 6 bordering his own property.[3] Thus, after 21 years lot 6 was again a single property. Murray kept the house and lot another eight years before selling it to Thomas Ringgold for the sum of £800 sterling. In the deed it states

" ... all that Brick Tenement Houses Gardens and Lott of Ground in Chester Town afsd wherein the said William Murray lately dwelt ... ,"[4] so there can be little doubt that the tenement was not only built for, but occupied by William Murray.

Dr. Murray moved from this house into a house on Princess Street (South Queen) and within two years died. It is interesting to note that he left one of four rental houses on Cannon Street, opposite

Hynson-Ringgold House, c. 1743 and 1770. The hip roof Front Street section was built by Dr. William Murray. Senator James Alfred Pearce added the Greek Revival porch and renewed the window sash and shutters. Tyler Campbell photograph, 1995.

rental houses on Cannon Street, opposite his former brick house, to each of his four daughters.

Thomas Ringgold V, son of Thomas Ringgold IV, had married Mary Galloway of Tulip Hill, Anne Arundel County in 1764. They apparently lived in the Murray house, for his father's will, written in 1768, states that the house in which Thomas V was living, purchased of William Murray, was to go to his wife, Anna Maria.[5] Perhaps the senior Ringgolds had planned on a more convenient house but his early death, altered his plans.

It is unclear from the records when the remodeling was planned, or for whom. We know from the date inscribed in the paneling at the Baltimore Museum of Art that it was made in 1771. And we know that Thomas V reversed his father's will when he drew up his own will in 1774, giving the Custom House to his Mother and the Ringgold House to his wife. His will was upheld by both Mother and Wife when they transferred their properties to Thomas VI.

Whichever Ringgold planned the extension and remodeling of the house was also responsible for tripling its original size and subsequently creating a mansion more impressive than any other dwelling of its day in Chestertown.

In reworking the house, the two original east rooms were combined into one, the old chimney was pulled down, and a new chimney was constructed in the same position as the west parlor, on the back wall. The room was paneled in the late Georgian style. The stair was removed from the center hall and the service wing moved to the back yard. Along Cannon Street a four-bay extension was constructed, nearly equal in size to the front. It contained a huge stair hall with *antler* stair, a passage and dining room. Built on a smaller scale, but contemporaneously, was another four-bay addition (5 on garden) two stories tall housing three service rooms and passage on the first story with bedrooms and servants rooms above. Cellars were constructed under all but the actual kitchen, which had its floor close to grade. There was a sub-cellar vault under a portion of the service

Hynson-Ringgold House. The east rooms of Murray's original house were made into one in 1771. Paneling from this room was sold to the Baltimore Museum of Art in 1932. Library of Congress, Historic American Buildings Survey, c. 1936.

Hynson-Ringgold House, Thomas Ringgold's stair was the most ambitious of Kent County. There was originally a side entrance beneath the stair in the place of the fireplace that was installed in 1916. Tyler Campbell photograph

wing, extending toward Cannon Street. Probably the original Murray kitchen was moved to the end of the new kitchen and served in a different capacity. The outline of the steeply pitched A roof can be discerned in the gable as well as a bricked-up door between it and the new kitchen. The result of this building project took the house out of the realm of a vernacular dwelling and placed it into the late Georgian style. The number and function of the first floor rooms was the same as Widehall, Chestertown, and Pratt Mansion in Queen Anne's County. The number of service rooms was the same as the latter.

Either at this juncture or earlier there were limestone steps at the front entrance, fragments of which remain next to Front Street and in the garden. Along Front Street, a six foot high brick garden wall was constructed to provide privacy to the garden.

Thomas Ringgold IV was listed as an attorney, in various deeds, but he was most successful in trade. He handled not only his own business, but was agent for British firms serving the needs of Marylanders, as well as the local parish of the Anglican Church. He was in business with his brother William, and later with his son and his son's father-in-law, Samuel Galloway. The Ringgolds apparently saw the benefit of advertising in the Maryland Gazette. Their names appear more frequently in the Gazette than any other Kent Countian of the period. These two gentlemen were the most successful businessmen of the pre-revolutionary period and were the most respected in their work and personal lives.

The Ringgold children moved to lands in Baltimore and Washington Counties which their father had left them. In 1808, after Mary's death, the Ringgold heirs sold the house and lots to Richard Snowden Thomas of Baltimore.[6] Richard probably never resided in the house, nor at the William Ringgold house on Front Street which he also owned, but rather rented them.

In 1811, in the deed to Isaac Spencer, Spencer is recorded living in the house prior to the deed.[7] Mary, his wife, was a Ringgold, but not in the line of the builders of the house (Isaac's sister Charlotte had married William Ringgold, nephew of Thomas IV). Isaac Spencer was owner of large farms up river which his father and grandfather had owned, as well as a store in New Market which he rented out. The Spencers are not known to have remodeled or improved the house during their twenty five year occupancy.

James Edmondson Barroll, a prominent lawyer, son of William Barroll, owned and lived at the Ringgold House for 18 years before selling it to the Honorable James Alfred Pearce in 1853.[8] In her history of the house, Elizabeth Duvall states: *"While occupying the Hynson Ringgold House, he (Barroll) filled in lots 20 and 21 Thereby turning an unsightly and unpleasant dock which was exposed at low tides into what was then a beautiful and attractive outlook."*[9] When U.S. Senator Pearce purchased the house it probably need-

Hynson-Ringgold House. Detail of roof truss needed to span the depth of the 1770 addition. Tyler Campbell photographs, 1995

Hynson-Ringgold House. The rear slope of Dr. Murray's hip roof is covered by the Ringgold addition. Note original cricket!

Left: Hynson-Ringgold House. Detail of 1771 overmantel carved garland. The carving in the Ringgold House parlor has been attributed to William Buckland, but it has recently been studied in relation to the Stamper-Blackwell parlor at Winterthur. That study concluded that the carving was imported from Philadelphia, although Buckland may have been responsible for the design. Baltimore Museum of Art.

ed a face lift. The Pearces set about bringing a new look to the house by adding Greek Revival porches to the Front and Cannon Street entrances and a new door at Front Street. They also replaced all of the sash visible from Front and Cannon Streets on the major part of the house, replacing old sills with stone. They also installed a new mantel and/or coal stove in at least the principle parlor. Late alterations would remove the Pearce interior remodeling.

James Alfred Pearce was the most politically active of all the residents of the Ringgold Mansion, being a U.S. Senator and active in many of the nation's problems of the pre-civil war period. Despite his activities in Washington, he remained committed to his home county, his church and Washington College. After Senator Pearce's death in 1864, the house remained in the possession of the family, probably inhabited by Senator Pearce's widow and youngest daughter. It is known to have been rented between 1882-90 to Jervis and Martha Spencer, grandson of Isaac, who owned the house earlier in the century. Senator Pearce's youngest daughter Minnie married Josiah Ringgold and purchased the house from her half brother, the Honorable Judge J.A. Pearce.[10]

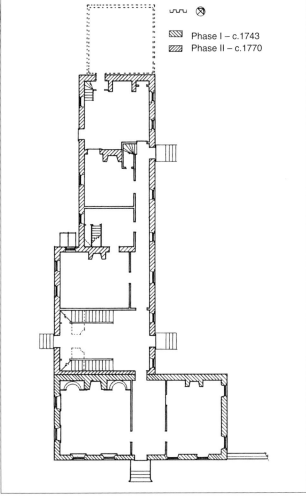

**Hynson-Ringgold House.
Detail of 1771 overdoor
carving. "The voluted
ends of several of these
acanthus leaves have
two or three trailing
lobes which are fluted
like the scroll ends on
the central panel of the
chimney piece in the
Stamper-Blackwell Par-
lor." Beckerdite, Luke,
William Buckland Recon-
sidered: Architectural
Carving in Chesapeake
Maryland, 1771-1774,
Journal of Early South-
ern Decorative Arts, Vol.
VIII, No. 2, 1982. Balti-
more Museum of Art.**

**Hynson-Ringgold House,
Chestertown. The rear of
the house with porch
constructed for Mr. and
Mrs. Catlin. Historical
Society of Kent County,
Usilton Collection.**

**Hynson-Ringgold House,
Chestertown. First floor
plan of house c. 1771.
Michael Bourne.**

In 1916 Minnie sold the house to Ilma Pratt Catlin and her husband Henry, who was a native of Chestertown, but had gone to New York in search of his fortune.[11] The Catlins began an extensive remodeling of the house that included central heat, electric wiring, and plumbing. They replaced the plaster throughout the living area and installed a lavatory in a portion of the original service passage and installed the kitchen in the central service room, turning the original kitchen into a garage. The old frame extension on the end of the kitchen was removed and in its place was built a pergola with posts set on the old limestone steps. A large porch was also constructed on the back of the house overlooking the lawn. To further enclose the yard, a brick wall was constructed along Cannon Street and across the back of the lot.

In 1932 Mrs. Catlin sold the paneling in the east room which was installed at the Baltimore Museum of Art and replaced it with a mediocre replica.

Through the efforts of Wilbur Ross Hubbard, the house was purchased from Mrs. Catlin in 1944, after years of neglect, and given to Washington College. It has served as the official residence of the Presidents of the College since.[12]

Phase I – c.1743
Phase II – c.1770

K-8

1. Land Records, Lib. JS 18, fol. 220; Lib. JS 22, fol. 134.
2. Land Records, Lib. JS 24, fol. 466.
3. Land Records, Lib. JS 29, fol. 141.
4. Land Records, Lib. DD 2, fol. 453.
5. Wills, Lib. 5, fol. 73; Lib. 5, fol. 230.
6. Land Records, Lib. BC 5, fol. 258.
7. Land Records, Lib. BC 6, fol. 461.
8. Duvall, Elizabeth S., Three Centuries of American Life: The Hynson-Ringgold House of Chestertown, Washington College, 1988.
9. Ibid, p. 57.
10. Land Records, Lib. SB 13, fol. 72.
11. Land Records, Lib. APR a, fol. 363.
12. Land Records, Lib. RAS 35, fol. 350.

Stanley's Hope

Near Still Pond
1743

STANLEY'S HOPE OR JACOBUS CREEK Farm is one of two brick houses in Kent County which bears a glazed date of 1743 (the other being Caulk's Field). When originally constructed, Stanley's Hope was a three-bay, one-and-a-half-story, brick building, approximately 20' x 40'. Beside the date on the gable laid in glazed brick, there is a diagonal row of glazed headers on each side, indicating the pitch of the original roof. The plan of the house at this period consisted of a hall and parlor, with the hall including the central entrances and westernmost windows. An enclosed stair was located in the northwest corner of the hall. The basement contained the original cooking fireplace, in the same manner as at Redmore's Supply and Lamb's Meadow nearby.

The house was constructed by one of the sons and heirs of Phillip Rasin (John, Phillip, or Thomas), who had acquired the land in 1707.[1] By 1783, Stanley's Hope was owned by two individuals, Joseph Raisin (220 acres) and Francis Cann (105 acres). Cann's property included an *"old Brick House, Wood Kitchen, meat and corn houses, stable & orchard."*[2]

In the middle of the nineteenth century, the house underwent a major remodeling when its owner added a full second story on top of the original brick walls and changed the plan to one with a central hall and two flanking rooms. A two-story, two-bay, frame kitchen wing was built onto the east gable at the same time. Its development was similar to that of Dullam's Folly. In fact, the brickwork, its texture, bond and use of corbeled cornice was similar as well. This remodeling was probably accomplished by Henry and Martha Jump who had acquired the farm in 1845 from George W. Perkins of Chestertown.[3] The Jump's name appears on both the Martenet Map (1860) and the Lake, Griffing, Stevenson Atlas (1877).

Prior to its acquisition in 1961 by Robert and Madelaine Sparre, it had been owned by two other families, the Crew and Price families. Apparently, very little remodeling was undertaken during that period. The house had received a new porch around the turn of the century and the kitchen was covered with asphalt siding around the 1950s. The Sparres thoroughly remodeled the building between 1961-73, first stabilizing the exterior, facing the kitchen wing with brick retrieved from a well, and then adding a porch on the south side, which has consequently protected the original Flemish bond and arched brickwork from the weather.

The interior plan was changed from the three-room, mid-nineteenth century plan to one large room with stair ascending along the south wall. The kitchen was changed into a den and the basement was turned into the kitchen again. Extensive landscaping has turned Stanley's Hope into a showplace on Still Pond Neck.   K-220

Stanley's Hope, 1743. North facade after rehabilitation. C. Engstrom photograph, 1977.

Stanley's Hope 1743. North facade before rehabilitation. R. Sparre Collection.

Stanley's Hope. The date 1743 and original roof line are clearly visible on the west gable. C. Engstrom photograph, 1977.

1. Land Records, Lib. 1, fol. 746.
2. Kent County Tax Assessment, Morgan Creek and South Sassafras Hundred, 1783.
3. Land Records, Lib. JNG 10, fol. 284.

Custom House

Water Street, Chestertown
c. 1745

S IMON WILMER RETAINED OWNERSHIP OF WATER LOT NO. 18 until his death in 1737 when it was devised to his daughter, Mary along with Lot No. 7.[1] She in turn, after becoming the widow of Thomas Clay and before remarrying George W. Forrester, Rector of Shrewsbury Parish, sold water Lot No. 18 to Samuel Massey, of Chestertown, Gentleman. Massey paid sixty pounds current money for *" ... all that water lott ... next adjoining to High Street and the main warff and known by lott No. 18 and formerly devised to the said Mary by her Father in his last will together with all houses Improvements warffs profits ... etc."*[2] Massey had been an innkeeper for at least the period 1740-43.[3] When he sold water Lot No. 18, he is listed as a merchant and by the time of his death in 1758, he was living across the river in Queen Anne's County *"near Chester Town Ferry."*[4]

Custom House, c. 1745. The original river side room contained the best woodwork in the house. The four doors flanking the fireplace led to (from right to left) the vestibule, closet, private stair to second floor and a passage to the front hall. Michael Wootton photograph, 1995.

After acquiring water Lot No. 18 Samuel Massey set out building what was to be the largest building in Chestertown at that time. Built partially into a bank near the river, it stood on a very prominent location adjacent the town dock. From Front Street, its five bay facade was very similar to two other houses nearby, Dr. William Murray's house at Front and Cannon Streets and Walter Dougherty's Inn in the middle of the first block of High Street. Like the latter, Massey's new facade was laid in Flemish bond with glazed headers. The water table jogged up and over the basement windows. And like the Murray House, it had a plaster cove cornice and a partially hipped roof, i.e. the southwest wall had a gable where it joined a one-and-a-half-story brick and stone structure. Unlike either of the aforesaid buildings, Massey's house had first story windows that were twice the size of the second story windows. This ratio in window size is found elsewhere in Kent County only at the Reward, constructed during the same decade of the 1740s.

Other than the Front Street facade, the remainder of the building was three full stories plus attic. On High Street, there was a secondary entrance to the first floor located in the third bay of the four-bay facade. There must have been a long flight of steps to reach the door. On ground level there was a very wide opening, large enough to wheel in a small cart, and two 6/6 sash windows. From this facade, the roof appeared hipped on all sides with a large cruciform-plan chimney rising above, in line with the entry.

The river end of the *L* plan building had only one window on each story and probably a dormer on the hipped roof. The back of the building was constructed of stone up to the first story, and English bond above. On the ground floor was another wide opening, this flanked by two windows. Apparently, there was a porch or covered deck at the first story level where the rear door is located. (A wood stringer built beneath the three second floor windows appears to have been a nailer for the roof rafters.)

The southwest wall of the *L* had a door at ground level with adjoining window and one full size window on each of the floors above. In addition to the above, there were two small four-pane casements to throw light into the secondary stair passage.

Joining the southwest gable, the aforesaid one-and-a-half-story structure was approximately thirty two feet long with a parapet brick gable at its southwest end and built-in chimney. It is difficult to conjecture its original appearance even though the stone basement exists on the water side and one old photo seems to indicate a four-bay facade on Front Street, without dormers.

The plan of Samuel Massey's building was more developed than Dr. Murray's house. In Murray's, the building was rectangular with two rooms on one side and one on the other side of the central stairhall. At Massey's the two rooms were larger resulting in the *L* plan. Having a second facade on High Street required placing the fireplaces for these two rooms back-to-back with a small vestibule for the secondary entrance on High Street. On the op-

posite side of the chimney were secondary stair passages. For spatial reasons, the fireplace of the front corner room was placed on the diagonal whereas that in the river side room was in a usual location. The finish of the river side room was usual however, for the fireplace wall was flanked by two doors on each side.

The river side room had the best woodwork, with bold cornice breaking out and tied into the window trim, bolection chair rail, etc. With the exception of the close-string stair with turned balustrade and paneled newels, joined together above the second floor, the remainder of the house was simply finished with beaded board partitions and good raised-panel doors. The one large southwest room of the first story was completely sheathed with beaded boards. To the west of its fireplace was a door connecting it to the one-and-a-half-story addition next door.

The second floor plan differed from the first in that the space above the stair hall and southwest room was divided into three small rooms and a stair hall on the riverside. The one room at the southwest gable had a plain plastered fireplace. The opposite side of the building was the same as below, with access to the river side room and a second stair ascending from the back room below.

On the ground level, in the river side room, was the original kitchen to the house which boasted an eleven foot wide fireplace into which was later built a bake oven, reducing the fireplace width to 7' 4". There was a window on each of the three walls with an exterior door on the southwest. To the side of the huge fireplace were two doors, one to a stair ascending to the front corner room, the other to a passage to the rest of the ground floor. Beneath the corner room, was access to a stone and brick vault, located beneath a terrace of the Front Street facade. Along its High Street side was a brick retaining wall with two large vents. It was easily accessible from the wide door on the High Street side of the building. No documentation has been found as to the use of the vault. Tradition states it was for maintaining slaves until they were sold, but other similar vaults in domestic situations were for storage of wines and other food stuffs requiring a constant temperature and humidity. A second vault is said to have been located in front of the adjoining brick and stone building.

Custom House, c. 1745.
High Street facade as
initially built.
M. L. Fritz, 1976

Custom House. Built by
Samuel Massey in 1745
and enlarged by Thomas
Ringgold IV before 1772.
It was the Ringgolds res-
idence as well as their
mercantile establishment.
Kent County News
Collection, glass negative
c. 1910.

Custom House. The two bay extension was built onto the earlier house before 1772.
Michael Wootton photograph, 1995

Thomas Ringgold IV (1715-1772)
Portrait by Charles Willson Peale, c. 1773.
The Baltimore Museum of Art: Friends of the American Wing Auction Fund.

Anna Maria Earle Ringgold (1723-1794)
Portrait by Charles Willson Peale, c. 1773.
The Baltimore Museum of Art: Middendorf Foundation Fund.

In January of 1749 Samuel Massey sold *"all that water lot of Ground and Messuage House and tenement lying in Chester Town ... next adjoining High Street and Main Warff (the said lott being know ... No. 18 ...) together with all Houses outhouses foundations walls stones warffs ways easements improvements profits advantages and Hereditaments whatsoever to the same lott of ground and messuage House and tenement belonging ... ."* to Thomas Ringgold.[5] In all probability, the buildings were not finished by the time of this sale. There is no reason given for the sale of the lot and buildings but probably Massey was running out of funds.

Thomas Ringgold, *Attorney at Law* was the most well respected attorney in the period of the 1740s to 1772 in Chestertown. From the land records of the period, he was very active buying and selling real estate.

He was a member of the House of Burgesses periodically during those years and was a member of the Continental Convention and was intimately involved with the affairs of the Church, first with St. Paul's Parish and after 1766 with the newly formed Chester Parish. His firm, including his brother William and son Thomas, were the bookkeepers and bankers of the day. From his home and adjoining main wharf, he was able to keep an eye on the ships for his own mercantile concerns as well as providing an office for the District Customs Collector. In a report by a supervising inspector he states that *"the Customs House is a seperate Building from the Collectors House, and I think five pounds starg. p. Annm is a very reasonable Charge for the office and firing etc ... ."*[6] From this scant information, it has been conjectured that the Customs Office was perhaps the building adjoining Thomas Ringgold's residence, the aforementioned brick and stone building.

When Thomas IV died in 1772, his house was to go to his son Thomas V and his widow, Anna Maria Earle Ringgold was to have *"the Tenement Houses lott; ground and garden I bought of Doctr William Murray ... in which my son now lives ... ."*[7] This bequest was to be reversed by his son when he wrote his twenty page will only two years later. He also revealed other facets of his business and the building which were not contained in other documents.

"And I do also give and devise to my Mother the House in which she now lives not only the old part but the addition made thereto in my Father's life together with all the Cellars belonging to it. And I do give and devise to my Mother the Lot No 7 opposite to the said House together with all the Houses erected thereon ... "[8]

This is a clear indication that the two bay wing added toward the River was constructed prior to 1772, the year the Senior Ringgold died. The addition was the same height as the earlier structure. In order to have a continu-

ous roof however, the early hip roof was eliminated. Its High Street facade was laid in Flemish bond, but there was no effort to copy the decorative glazed headers of the older part. It has neither water table nor belt course and the windows don't correspond in size or position to the others. Moreover, all header bond was used on the back of the addition which had the only exterior entrance. The addition consisted of a stair hall and one room on each floor. On the ground floor was a second kitchen with large arched fireplace having double cranes, a feature also used at the Hynson-Ringgold house up the street.

The first floor room had a plain dado with plain pilasters beneath the window trim. Its fireplace wall was paneled and had flanking closets. On the floor above, presumably Mr. and Mrs. Ringgold's bed chamber, there was the same arrangement, but the vertical board wall was plastered on the outside, probably to show off some fine wall paper. At each level, a door was broken through the old wall for easy access between the two sections. The doors are constructed in much the same manner as the doors at Widehall built in 1769-70.

Thomas Ringgold V gives farther instructions to his executors pertaining to the house that his Mother occupied:

"It is my will and I do direct that any Executors or Executor for the time being shall rent out my dry good store the Computing House adjoining commonly called Bath House and the Cellars and Vaults underneath the same the Coopers Shop on the two wharves with the

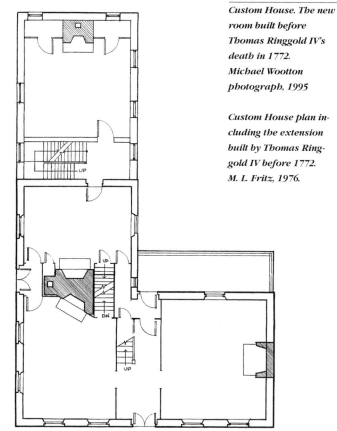

Custom House. The new room built before Thomas Ringgold IV's death in 1772. Michael Wootton photograph, 1995

Custom House plan including the extension built by Thomas Ringgold IV before 1772. M. L. Fritz, 1976.

Custom House, c. 1745.
The vault built under the
Front Street terrace.
Michael Wootton
photograph, 1995.

Custom House after
Wilbur W. Hubbard re-
modeled it into "modern"
apartments in 1923. Li-
brary of Congress, His-
toric American Buildings
Survey, 1930s.

Large Granaries or Store Houses thereon on the best terms they can first enclosing at the expense of my Estate such a yard and in such Manner as my Mother shall choose before her Kitchen door and carefully stipulating with their tennant or Tennants every matter or thing that may be thought necessary to prevent my Mother from being inconvenienced by such tenant or tenants themselves or servants and out of the rents and profits shall keep the same in good repair ... ."[9]

From this document there can be little doubt that much of the Ringgold business was carried on in the residence of the senior Ringgolds. From structural evidence found in the building during restoration, it was apparent that both front rooms of the first floor were cut into two oddly-shaped spaces and they were the dry good store or perhaps room where they sold the *"over quanity of nails"* and other goods advertised in the Maryland Gazette on June 13, 1771. With the premature death of Thomas V in 1774 it was not to be until 1791 that Thomas VI came of age and assumed the management of the family fortune.[10] But Thomas did not remain in Chestertown for long. His Grandmother died in 1794 and he sold the house she had occupied the last 45 years of her life.

William Sluby, another merchant and also co-bondsman with Thomas VI of his father's estate, purchased water Lots Nos. 18, 19, and part of 20 and Lot No. 7 across the street for the sum of £2250, a price indicating the extent and value of that real estate.[11] Perhaps Sluby had rented the premises previously. Thomas VI had moved to Baltimore County by the time he executed the deed in 1796. The other Ringgold House was not sold out of the immediate family until 1808.

When William Sluby died three years after acquiring the property, it had to be sold in order to pay his debts, which were considerable. William had been executor of his brother-in-law's estate and *"although that Estate is fully paid away and settled yet a considerable balance still stands against me on the books of the Register."*[12] His estate was brought before Chancery Court and in the proceedings is listed *"two water lots in Chestertown on which are erected a large Brick House, a Store and small Brick House, two granaries and some other improvements. One lot or part of Lot No. 7 on which are a stable Carriage House and meat house."*[13] As a result of the sale in 1801 the house was sold to William Jones, Sluby's nephew, and did not include the wharf, Store, small brick house or Lot No. 7 across the street. Prior to 1805 Jones sold the house to Simon Wickes, for in another deed to the wharf in that year it refers to the *"large brick house of Simon Wickes."*[14]

The old house remained in Simon's family until Simon Wickes, Jr. (actually the third) sold the property in 1853 to Joseph Usilton who turned it over immediately to Senator James Alfred Pearce. Pearce who had occupied the Custom House since at least 1841, owned the

house for only one year before purchasing the other Ringgold House across the street.

Hiram Brown purchased the house in 1854 and married Mary Elizabeth Merritt of Godlington Manor the following year. The Browns lived at the Custom House until they purchased River House in the next block of Water Street in 1877. But, even while residing at the Customs House they rented out rooms or apartments. After their move to River House a major remodeling was undertaken. The huge central chimney was dismantled and replaced by a small single flue chimney. The resulting space was incorporated into the several apartments. The building continued in use as apartments until after if was purchased by Wilbur W. Hubbard in 1909.[15]

Within a short time Mr. Hubbard had purchased and begun the remodeling of Widehall. He also purchased the old wharves and warehouse which were located on both sides of the public wharf as well as the rest of water Lot No. 18, and all of water Lot No. 19. Within the year he had taken down the old Custom House, or Store as it was called in the Sluby disposition, and the adjoining Redue House on water Lot No. 19. Apparently the basements were left and on them four adjoining three story frame houses were built. In 1923 Hubbard remodeled the large brick building into *modern* apartments which would appeal to a better clientele. He added a two-story frame wing in the south west corner, for kitchens and baths, and a porch along High Street. An entrance to the addition was opened on High Street, after rebuilding the first flight of stairs inside. The unique small rooms of the second floor were drastically altered. In all he had four apartments and one efficiency. Twenty years after Mr. Hubbard's death in 1938, Mrs. Hubbard deeded the Custom House to their son Wilbur Ross Hubbard.[16]

In 1975-76 Mr. Hubbard began a project of bringing the building back to an earlier appearance. The central chimney foundations were discovered and the five fireplaces and cross-plan stack were reconstructed. Woodwork was restored or duplicated and the entire building was converted into a guest house and apartment. The Custom House remains one of the most important 1740s period buildings in the county and one of the most visible. K-9

1. Wills, Lib. 2, fol. 58.
2. Land Records, Lib. JS 25, fol. 338.
3. Kent Co. Court Records, 1740-1743.
4. Maryland Gazette, Dec. 4, 1755; July 6, 1758.
5. Land Records, Lib. JS 26, fol. 282.
6. Papers relating to officers of the Customs in North America, Md. Hist. Mag. Vol. XXVII, No. 3, Sept. 1932, p. 233.
7. Wills, Lib. 5, fol. 73.
8. Wills, Lib. 5, fol. 231.
9. Wills, Lib. 5, fol. 241.
10. Bonds, Lib. 7, fol. 164.
11. Land Records, Lib BC 4, fol. 475.
12. Wills, Lib. 8, fol. 22.
13. Chancery, Lib. 47, fol. 459.
14. Land Records, Lib. BC 3, fol. 258.
15. Land Records, Lib. JTD 19, fol. 195.
16. Land Records, Lib. WHG 59, fol. 427.

Custom House. Anna Maria Ringgold's kitchen fireplace in the new wing with double cranes and iron arch support. Michael Wootton photograph, 1995

Custom House, c. 1745. Second story hall taken from the landing. Michael Wootton photograph, 1995.

Cedar Hill

Quaker Neck
c. 1750

CEDAR HILL FARM, LOCATED NEAR CHESTERTOWN AT THE northern end of Quaker Neck, was associated with the Garnett, Perkins and Thomas families in the eighteenth and nineteenth centuries. The house associated with the farm is located on the part of Kemp's Beginning which Joseph Garnett, saddler, acquired in two separate purchases, the first in 1748 and the second in 1751.[1] He had, in 1744, already acquired 250 acres of an adjoining tract called Sanford.[2]

According to the date over the basement entrance (scratched in twentieth century concrete!), the house was built in 1747. The land, however, was not acquired by Garnett until the following year. By the time of his death in 1758, the property was referred to as his *"dwelling plantation"* in his will. This places the construction date of the house somewhere in the ten year period of 1748-58.

Cedar Hill, c. 1750. Built for Joseph Garnett, a Chestertown saddler turned planter. The facade originally was a broad gambrel, like Saulsbury, Talbot County. Tyler Campbell photograph, 1996.

When originally built, the house was similar to Saulsbury in Talbot County. Measuring 18' 6" x 28', a gambrel roof extended over the longer dimension creating a broad gable entrance facade. Its two rooms were heated by corner fireplaces located on the back wall. The stair was located in the northeast corner where there was an outside basement entrance as well.

In Garnett's will, the *"dwelling plantation"* was bequeathed to his son, Joseph, Jr., when he came of age. In the meantime the lands were to be rented for the benefit of the estate. To his wife, Sarah Piner Garnett, he stipulated that a brick house, nearly equal in size to the farmhouse, should be built on his lot in town (present location of Chesapeake Bank and Trust). He appointed his daughter and son-in-law, Mary and Daniel Perkins guardians to the minor children until they reached twelve years of age. At that point his son Joseph was to be given two years schooling under the guardianship of his brother-in-law, Thomas Wilkins.[3]

After coming of age, Joseph, Jr.'s name appears in various land transactions, in each case as a farmer. When the Tax Assessor visited Cedar Hill in 1783, he assigned 97½ acres of Sanford and 250 acres of Kemp's Beginning to Joseph Garnett. Also listed were the following: *"one brick dwelling house, an old kitchen, four outhouses and one small orchard."*[4] Garnett was appointed trustee of Mary Hanson's *Tolchester* farm in a premarital agreement with Isaac Cannell in 1785. But within five years he must have fallen on hard times. In 1790, in order to have liens removed from his plantation, he sold 167½ acres to John and Anna Maria (Frisby) Rowles for their new home (Airy Hill).[5]

The sale to the Rowles was enough to see Joseph, Jr. through the 1790s, for when he wrote his will in 1797, he bequeathed the farm to his son, Joseph III, provided that Joseph be executor to his estate and guardian to the minor children.[6]

Joseph III sold the farm nine months after his father's death in 1800 to his uncle Daniel Perkins.[7] Cedar Hill remained in the possession of the Perkins until 1835 when Daniel's heirs sold the farm to John Thomas (son of Richard Snowden Thomas).[8] In 1878, the heirs of John Thomas sold the farm to William B. Usilton.[9]

In 1910, *Cedar Grove,* as it was called in the deed, was purchased by Harry Nichols [10] who undertook the major remodeling that changed the old brick one-and-a-half-story gambrel house into a two-story brick residence with hip roof (1916). The two story back wing was built at the same time. Mrs. Nichols survived her husband (d. 1961) by 13 years, at which time the farm was devised to two friends. The house and two-and-a-half acres were sold in 1988 to the present owners who have undertaken a general rehabilitation, adding a new wing in 1995.   K-80

1. Provincial Court Records, Lib. EI 8, fol. 422; Land Records, Lib. JS 27, fol. 16.
2. Land Records, Lib. JS 25, fol. 216.
3. Wills, Lib. 4, fol. 52.
4. 1782 Tax Assessment.
5. Land Records, Lib. BC 3, fol. 28.
6. Wills, Lib. fol. 57.
7. Land Records, Lib. TW 1, fol. 487. Daniel owned another part of Sandford, the Mill & Millhouse about a mile southwest of Cedar Hill (later called Brice's Mill).
8. Land Records, Lib. JNG 4, fol. 83.
9. Land Records, Lib. DCB 3, fol. 551.
10. Land Records, Lib. JTD 20, fol. 247.

Broadnox

Near Rock Hall
c. 1750

THE UNSAVORY CHARACTER OF THE SEVENTEENTH CENTURY Thomas Broadnox has been thoroughly exhausted in other histories. Suffice it to say that the man was a scoundrel. In 1659 the land on which Poplar Neck was built was patented to Broadnox who lived on Kent Island at the time.

In the eighteenth century 640 acres of this tract came into the possession of the Dunn family, early members of St. Paul's Church. When the house was actually built has not been thoroughly researched.

By the time of the 1852 Tax Assessment, the farm was in the possession of James E. Barroll, one of Chestertown's prominent lawyers, who resided at the Hynson-Ringgold House. Like his father before him, Barroll probably enjoyed life on the farm as much as life in town. By 1860, Poplar Neck, as it had become known, was owned by C. M. and E. Deputy and by 1877 it was in the occupation of R. H. Rouse.

In 1940, the farm was purchased by Glen L. Martin who employed the architectural firm of Clyde and Nelson Friz of Baltimore to draw up the plans for renovating the building.[1] Whatever remained of the old house was destroyed, except the floors in two rooms. The lovely paneling and other details all date from the 1940-41 renovation.

The original house had a very typical form, but the scale and fenestration was unique. Five bays distinguished the Flemish bond with glazed header facade. The five bays, however, were not evenly placed and there were two doors and three windows. The center window was one pane narrower than the outer two. Two dormers in the steep A roof were placed symmetrically on both the front and the back. There was no door on the first story of the back facade.

A slight difference in size and color of the brick between the main section and the four-bay kitchen wing suggests that the latter was built after the initial building. The wing was constructed several feet narrower than the main section, however, the roof was made as wide (similar to the treatment of the kitchen wing at Hinchingham).

In form and plan, as well as in regard to some other details, Broadnox is similar to Clarke's Conveniency on Quaker Neck. The house is currently used as a guest house.

Broadnox, the mid-eighteenth century plantation house of the Dunn family. Historical Society of Kent County, the Usilton Collection.

Broadnox after it was remodeled for Glen L. Martin. Tyler Campbell photograph, 1996.

1. Johnson, Robert, J. Gravesend, Serene But Still Profound. Rock Hall American Revolutionary Bicentennial Committee, 1975.

K-98

Clark's Conveniency

Quaker Neck
c.1750

IN 1707, A 196 ACRE TRACT OF LAND ON QUAKER NECK was granted to a planter named Dennis Clark.[1] It is located at the headwaters of Philip Creek and was first known as Clark's Convenience. Over the years the name has changed to Clark's Conveniency. The one-and-a-half-story brick house which exists on the property today is most likely the work of Thomas Wilkins who purchased the tract in 1749-50.[2]

Wilkins was both a shipwright and planter and lived on the tract until his death in 1769. At that time his property was appraised at £1600, an enormous fortune in a period when a person worth £1000 would have been considered wealthy.

The house in which Thomas Wilkins lived is an extraordinary example of vernacular architecture. It contains many masonry features used in larger houses of the county such as the Reward, Violet Farm and Comegy's Bight. Those include a molded water table which jogs up and over the basement windows, sloped weatherings on the chimneys, and withes, those pilaster-like protrusions which divide the stack in two. The facade was laid in Flemish bond and the arches over the 9/9 sash windows are segmental. The principal facade arches of the central door and two flanking windows are rusticated wooden jack arches with keystones and do not date from the original construction. The fenestration of

Clark's Conveniency, c. 1750, was probably built for Thomas Wilkins, shipwright and planter. The right wing was built in mid-twentieth century.

Clark's Conveniency, c. 1750. Dining room paneling. Original fireplace was nearly the same size as the wood surround.
Tyler Campbell photographs, 1995

the kitchen wing has also undergone change. Originally there was a central door with flanking windows on its principal facade.

Clark's Conveniency was built as a hall-parlor plan and was very well finished. Both hall and parlor had fully paneled fireplace walls. The paneling in each case was recessed from the face of the adjoining closets and stair by about six inches (similar to the treatment at Dullam's Folly in the upper part of the county). Paneled wainscoting was installed in the hall and all four first floor windows had paneled jambs with trim that tied into the cornice, like those at the Custom House.

The overmantel panel arrangement was the same in both rooms, but the hall fireplace opening was rectangular and trimmed with crossetted trim, whereas the parlor fireplace opening was arched with small triangular panels within the rectangular panels. The former was like that found at neighboring Providence (1781) and the latter more like that at Violet Farm (1762) and Rose Hill (c.1760). In both rooms the stairs are partially enclosed having five steps within the room before running behind the paneling. In both instances there is a handsome balustrade with turned columnar newels with ball finials.

On the second floor there are three small chambers, two with fireplaces and paneling. The middle chamber being divided from the others by vertical boards.

The kitchen wing was at ground level and probably had a brick floor when built. Its plan consisted of a passage, pantry and kitchen, all divided by board walls. In the kitchen there was a very large fireplace with iron crane. On the north side of the building there was a dove-tailed plank smokehouse which has disappeared along with other original outbuildings.

Clark's Conveniency is on the National Register.   K-92

Clark's Conveniency, c. 1750. Dining room chamber paneling. C. Engstrom photograph, 1977.

1. Patents, Lib. PL 2, fol. 311.
2. Land Records, Lib. JS 26, fol. 280, 459.

Bedingfield Hands House

Queen Street, Chestertown
c. 1750

FOR MANY YEARS THE OLD FRAME HOUSE ON THE NORTHwest side of Queen Street, between High and Cannon, has been called the Murray House after its supposed builder, Dr. William Murray. However, Dr. Murray never owned the western half of Lot No. 79 on which this house was constructed. Records of property transfers found in the County Courthouse tell of the Murrays moving from Front Street to Lot No. 10 on Cannon Street.[1] This places their residence across the street from the subject of this investigation.

When Lots Nos. 78 and 79 were originally sold by Simon and Dorcas Wilmer in 1726 and 1730, neither lot was sold as laid out (extending from High Street to Cannon Street), but in two halves. Each purchaser bought a one acre lot, one on High Street and the other on Cannon.[2]

In 1730, John Spencer, a joiner, purchased the acre lot on Cannon Street,[3] but sold it two years later for a £10 profit.[4] In the latter deed, Spencer sold it to Alexander McGachan, a Chestertown merchant, who had purchased Water Lot No. 17 in 1730.[5] When McGachan wrote his will, he specified that his property was to go to his wife Sarah, and after her death, to their daughter Sarah.[6]

In a deed for Water Lot. No. 17 (1765), it mentions Sarah as the only child of Alexander McGachan and as having married Bedingfield Hands, an important attorney and

Bedingfield Hands Office, Chestertown. This brick building, with its all header bond facade is reputed to have stood near the sidewalk east of the house. Maryland Historical Society Collection.

Bedingfield Hands House, Chestertown. Seen here with dormer windows, it changed very little until 1960, when it was completely remodeled. Kent County Historical Society, Usilton Collection, c. 1930s.

Bedingfield Hands House, Chestertown. Michael Wootton photograph, 1996.

businessman in mid-eighteenth century Chestertown.[7] The existing house was probably built for Sarah and Bedingfield Hands soon after their marriage. With a lack of references to Lot Nos. 78 and 79 and a lack of wills for either Sarah or Bedingfield, it is only assumed that Lot Nos. 78 and 79 descended to Bedingfield Hands, Jr. However, an agreement written in 1811 between Mary Hands (Bedingfield Sr.'s second wife) and Bedingfield Hands, Jr., specifies that Mary Hands was in possession of the half lots and Lot Nos. 70 and 71 at that time.[8] She apparently deeded the lots to Bedingfield Jr., in exchange for £40 yearly stipend provided that he pay the taxes and keep the buildings in good repair.

Bedingfield, Jr. married Catherine Thompson in the first decade of the nineteenth century and died in 1821, leaving the *"house lots and all real estate in Chestertown"* to her for her lifetime, after which the properties were to descend to his brother, Alexander.[9] Two years after his brother's death, Alexander mortgaged the property to Philemon Thomas of Talbot County, where he was also living.[10] Thereafter he disappears from the real estate records of Kent.

After Bedingfield Hands, Jr.'s death, Catherine married Richard Ringgold, who died in 1841. In that year the tax assessment stated that parts of Lot Nos. 78 and 79 were occupied by Mrs. Richard Ringgold and on part of Lot Nos. 70 and 71 there was an old stable. All together these properties were valued at $1,800.00. Mrs. Ringgold also had seven slaves, $300 worth of house-

hold furniture, 96 ounces of silver and two gold watches.

Is is interesting to note in the assessment that Mrs. Ringgold's sister, Caroline Thompson, owned part of Lot No. 10, the lot which her grandfather, Dr. William Murray, had owned in the eighteenth century.

Catherine Ringgold died in 1849 and the properties went to her sister Caroline Thompson, for her lifetime with the stipulation that they would descend to her niece, Emily Ann Spencer.[11] Miss Thompson, however, outlived her niece and the property descended instead to thirteen great nieces and nephews who later sold it to Charlotte R. Spencer,[12] who resided therein until 1916, when it was sold out of the family.

In the first of several deeds to Charlotte Spencer prior to Miss Thompson's death in 1885, the deed gives a good description of the property *" ... lot on North east corner of Cannon Street in Chestertown now occupied by said Caroline Thompson including the Brick Office in connection therewith ... ."*[13] This deed not only confirms the fact that Caroline Thompson lived in the subject property, but that it had a brick office. A probable illustration of the office was found at the Maryland Historical Society.

Miss Thompson bequeathed money to Emmanuel Church, which was used in 1905 to construct the bell tower on the Cross Street facade. A tablet in the narthex commemorates the fact that it was erected through her generosity and the fact that she died in her 100th year.

From the early twentieth century photographs of the house, it appears to have changed little over at least the last 70 years. The house is a two-and-a-half-story frame structure. Its proportions are similar to Worrell's Tavern which once stood nearby. The earlier photographs do indicate a roof of slightly steeper pitch.

The brick office, mentioned in the description of the property after Caroline Thompson's death in 1885, was apparently built by Bedingfield Hands, Sr. It was built with a facade of all header bond and had an external chimney on its southwest gable. Flanking the chimney were two full-size windows, similar to the Smith-Ringgold House and others on Water Street. The three-bay gambrel roof building was demolished in the early twentieth century, probably by Charlotte Spencer.

Since 1915 there have been ten owners. In 1960, completely remodeled due to extensive termite damage. The roof was reconstructed with a lower pitch and no dormers.   K-28

1. Land Records, Lib. 29, fol. 381.
2. See plat enclosed.
3. Land Records, Lib. 4, fol. 27.
4. Land Records, Lib. 4, fol. 166.
5. Land Records, Lib. JS 16, fol. 233.
6. Wills, Lib. 1, fol. 385.
7. Land Records, Lib. DD 2, fol. 169.
8. Land Records, Lib. BC 6, fol. 485.
9. Wills, Lib. 10, fol. 225.
10. Land Records, Lib. TW 4, fol. 214, 216.
11. Wills, Lib. JFB 1, fol. 275.
12. Land Records, Lib. SB 3, fol. 521.
13. Land Records, APR 1, fol. 211.

Scotch Folly

Shallcross Neck
c. 1750

ONE OF THE EARLIEST HOUSES ON SHALLCROSS NECK IS Scotch Folly, a two and one half story, three bay brick house with matching twentieth century wings. Thomas Hynson (d. 1748) bequeathed parts of Scotch Folly, Castle Carey, Simpson's Addition and other parcels on the Neck to four of his five sons in his will. William received that portion of land that became known as Woodland Hall. Andrew Hynson, the oldest son, inherited the other part of Scotch Folly on which the house stands.[1]

Andrew's house was a substantial brick structure with the facade and west gable laid in Flemish bond with glazed headers above a full basement with a champhered watertable. There was a pent eave across the front and back of the building with a two brick belt course beneath the second story windows. The pent eave stopped about two-and-a-half feet from the ends and the belt course jogged down three courses, like the Buck-Bacchus Store in Chestertown and Labadie Mill Farm in Cecil County. A kitchen wing was attached to the east gable.

Scotch Folly's plan was composed of two rooms, hall-parlor, with hall having an enclosed stair in one of its corners, adjacent the fireplace. The chimneys at both ends of the house were built within the gables.

Andrew Hynson died in 1779 intestate and his wife Mary followed soon thereafter. George Wilson, his administrator and others had to post a £1000 bond for settling the estate. By 1822, the property was owned by a distant relative, Isaac Freeman, who lived at Tibbalds at the end of the neck.[2]

When Martenet printed his map in 1860, the house and surrounding land was owned by Lewin Wethered, but it is not clear if he in fact lived there. R. Comly was recorded as the owner by 1877.[3]

In the late nineteenth century, the house was gutted and the plan was changed to conform with most of Kent's farmhouses, a central stairhall and two rooms. The pent eave was removed and the old kitchen wing was replaced with a two story frame structure which remained until the present owners acquired the land in the 1940s. At that time, the house was remodeled and the two wings were added, one at each gable end.

Scotch Folly is one of only five buildings in northern Kent county to have had a pent eave and one of only two with a jogged belt course.   K-143

Scotch Folly, Shallcross Neck, c. 1750. Probably built for Andrew Hynson. The house originally included a pent eave. Maryland Historical Trust, M. Q. Fallaw photograph, 1986.

1. Wills, Lib. 3, fol. 78.
2. 1822 Tax Assessment.
3. Lake, Griffing, Stevenson Atlas, 1877.

brick, was of the walk-in variety, another feature it shared with Marrowbone. Judging from the width of the arch support in the basement, the parlor fireplace was narrower.

When Holman Johnson died in 1767, his estate was handled by his widow, Hannah. The worth of his personal estate totaled £488.10.5.[4] Before the estate was actually settled (1769), Hannah remarried. Her new husband was Benjamin Parsons, one of Holmon Johnson's creditors.

From the records, it is not clear if Samuel Johnson was in

Long Meadow

Near Massey
c. 1750

Long Meadow Farm was created in 1720 by the sale of 200 acres out of a 3000 acre patent called Partnership.[1] William Johnson purchased it from the well-known merchant and statesman, Richard Bennett of Queen Annes County. When Johnson died the following year, his wife, Katherine, was named administrator of his estate.[2] From their son, William, the farm was bequeathed in 1749 to his brother Holman Johnson.[3] The construction of the brick house dates from the time of Holman's ownership.

Long Meadow Farm. This photograph taken c. 1941, before the old kitchen was replaced. Dorothy Durham Collection.

Long Meadow, c. 1750. This small house near Massey retains original paneling with bold bolection molding around the fireplace. Maryland Historical Trust, M. Q. Fallaw photograph, 1986.

It was like many houses built in Maryland in the early to mid-eighteenth century. It was a one-and-a-half-story brick house, three bays long with symmetrical fenestrations. The original service wing is thought to have been that pictured above. After 1941 it was replaced with another unit in which both the cornice and roof lines match the original.

The building resembles Marrowbone in its use of Flemish bond on the facade and English bond elsewhere. It retains its hall-parlor plan, along with the hall paneling which encloses a newel stair to the second story. The original hall fireplace opening, although filled with a massive block of twentieth century

fact the son of Holman and Katherine. In 1787, Johnson acquired a small section of land adjoining the original 200 acre farm.[5] Like two of his ancestors, Samuel Johnson died intestate and Long Meadow Farm descended to his four children. In 1831, Hannah Johnson and her husband, Richard Corbaley, purchased another quarter share from her brother.[6] Thirty years later, the Corbaleys bequeathed the farm to their children, Samuel J. and Richard H. Corbaley.[7] Samuel sold his half interest in 1867 to Richard C. Johnson. Richard, however, retained his ownership and resided at Long Meadow until the Johnson heirs sold the farm to another heir, Lee Carroll Clark, in 1936.[8] It was finally sold out of the family to Anthony and Dorothy Durham. The farm was acquired by Quail Run Nursery in the 1980s and the house remains, surrounded by fields of shrubbery and trees.   K-165

1. Partnership was patented to Daniel Toaes in 1684 (Patents, Lib. Y & S, No. 8, fol. 50), Land Records, Lib. BCW, fol. 109.
2. Bonds, Lib. 2, fol. 198.
3. Wills, Lib. 3, fol. 73.
4. Inventories, Lib. 6, fol. 106.
5. Land Records, Lib. EF 7, fol. 230.
6. Land Records, Lib. JNG 2, fol. 527.
7. Wills, Lib. JF 1, fol. 163, fol. 198.
8. Land Records, Lib. RAS 15, fol. 370.
9. Land Records, Lib. RAS 32, fol. 297.

Whichcote Castle

Near Fairlee
1750

Paul Whichcote (1685-1757) purchased 100 acres of *Perch Meadow* and *Woodlands Intention* in 1739 located on the side *"of the main road that leads from the church (St. Paul's) to Worton Creek and near the said Paul Whichcote's Plantation"*.[1] Whichcote's name appears as a witness to several wills earlier than 1739, and later in 1744, he purchased another 150 acres of the same tracts mentioned above.[2] In the late 1740s and early 1750s he was appointed Commissioner of the Peace and Justice for Inspection of Tobacco, along with Bedingfield Hands, Jervis Spence, Hugh Wallis and others, all prominent business men of that period.[3]

In 1752, *Paul Whichcote, Marriner* wrote his will which was probated in 1757. He appointed his wife Mary, and son Paul, to be co-executors. He bequeathed his plantation to be equally divided between his son and daughter, Sarah, and 50 acres to his grandson Benjamin Wright.[4] The appraisers of Paul's estate included John Wickes and John Carvill. His personal inventory amounted to £436.10 and included several books, shoemaker's tools, seven Negroes and an indentured servant, beside the usual items found on a modest plantation which grew primarily tobacco and wheat.[5]

The house which Paul built on his plantation had a very common form for eighteenth century dwellings throughout the Chesapeake area. However, its roof slope was a little steeper than most remaining dwellings of this period. An outstanding feature is its brickwork. Three sides are laid in all header bond. It is reputed to have a glazed date of 1750 in its gable, but due to the fact that it has been whitewashed and the all header bond, it is impossible to determine without removal of the whitewash. The initials WPM can be determined, even without cleaning. These are the initials of the builders—Paul and Mary Whichcote.

From an outline in the north gable, it is clear to see that the original kitchen was located there. Undoubtedly, this is the reason that common bond was used on this gable.

Around the turn of the century, a two-story frame wing was constructed on the east side of the house. Judging from the description in the WPA Guide, the house had a plan which consisted of hall-parlor

Whichcote Castle, 1750, was built for Paul Whichcoat on land called Perch Meadow. C. Engstrom photograph, 1977.

Whichcote Castle, near Fairlee, was constructed in 1750 by Paul Whichcote. A glazed date is located beneath the white paint on the gable. Gene Johnstone photograph, 1997.

Buck Neck Site

Near Worton
c. 1750

Buck Neck is the name of a tract patented in 1666 to Joseph Hopkins.[1] During the eighteenth century it appears to have been owned by two or three generations of the Graves family. It was resurveyed in 1737 for 493 acres for Sarah Graves, wife of William Graves.[2] Its position at the headwaters of Worton Creek was ideal for shipping since it was close to the Chesapeake Bay. In the mid-eighteenth century it is known to have been the location of one of the county's tobacco warehouses.

Uphill from the landing stood one of the farmhouses which is mentioned in the 1783 Tax Assessment in the ownership of Richard Graves:

"Buck Neck 493 acres at £616.15
pt. Conny Warren 163 acres at £203.15
Prince Wm. 90 acres at £112.10
Pt. Doe Neck 27 acres at £33.15
Wye Hill Downs 50 acres at £62.10
Two Brick Dwelling Houses and one kitchen
Nine out houses and one barn
One young orchard and one old orchard"[3]

An old photograph of the house shows a three-bay, two-story whitewashed brick house with small kitchen and out-building. The overhanging roof of the kitchen is similar to the kitchen wing at Broadnox and Hinchingham.

In the early 1960s the area was developed into a housing development called Chesapeake Landing. Only the large frame barn remained and was initially used as a clubhouse for the residents.   K-263

in the brick section, two rooms in the kitchen wing and the aforementioned two story east wing. Each of these five rooms had stairs to the chambers above.

When the kitchen wing was removed, the connecting door was converted into a window. About the same time, the interior was gutted and a new stair was installed in the living room in such a way as to ascend between the two bed chambers above. Little, if any of Paul Whichcote's interior remains in the house. The house is the product of successive remodeling caused by periods of neglect.

The descendants of Paul Whichcote retained title to the farm until 1791 when the grandchildren sold the property to Peregrine Letherbury, who later transferred it to Fray and Thomas.[6] In the 1852 Tax Assessment, John S. Thomas is listed as owner of forty acres of *"Peach Meadow,"* an obvious misspelling of Perch on which there was an *"Old Brick House in Bad Repair."* On the 1860 Martenet Map, Thomas is still listed in this location, but by 1877, when the Lake Griffing Stevenson Atlas was printed, the farm was owned by Robert Nicholson, a nurseryman whose residence was located on an adjoining farm. Although it left the Nicholson family for many years, the current owner is Robert Nicholson's great granddaughter.[7]   K-237

1. Land Records, Lib. JS 22, fol. 449.
2. Land Records, Lib. 6, fol. 188.
3. Commission Records, Maryland Hall of Records, Nov. 9, 1747, p. 82.
4. Wills, Lib. 30, fol. 311.
5. Inventories, Box 19, folder 60.
6. Land Records, Lib. BC 3, fol. 212, 214, 215.
7. Most of the research has been accomplished by James E. White III, New Bern, NC.

1. Patents, Lib. 11, fol. 24.
2. Patents, Lib. E. I. 6, fol. 107.
3. 1783 Tax Assessment.

Buck Neck Site. This house was one of two brick houses listed on the 1783 Tax Assessment. It was the seat of the Graves family in the eighteenth century, and home of James and Elizabeth Shuster in the nineteenth century. Frances Lamb Collection.

Kinsale Site

Quaker Neck
c. 1750

KINSALE HAS THE SAME EARLY HISTORY AS ADJOIN-ing Providence Plantation. In 1671, William Trew and William Davis purchased 350 acres called Comegys Choice from Cornelius Comegys. Davis sold his half of the farm to Edward Brown and in 1720, Edward Brown's grandson, Morgan Brown, along with William Trew II petitioned for a division of that land. From the records it does not appear to have been divided finally until 1747, two years after the farm had been re-patented under the name of Providence and at which time it contained a total of 420 acres. In the document of division it states that it is "to be divided so that each one's house is on his property ... divided by a cove ... ."[1]

From the late seventeenth century until 1932, Brown's Part of Providence remained in the family. In 1932, Col. John DeCoursey purchased the property[2] and began its renovation. Tragically, however, in 1966, the house caught fire on an icy morning. Fire engines were unable to reach the house before it was totally lost. Just prior to that time Mr. Rolph Townsend had begun a photographic recording project in Kent County and had documented the building on film. From that photograph and the description relayed by the present owner, its appearance has been fairly well discerned.

The house, before its destruction, had been a two-and-a-half-story brick structure with the front and rear

Kinsale, Quaker Neck. Probably begun by Morgan Brown, c. 1750, it was a one-and-a-half story brick house on part of Providence. Maryland State Archives, Jeddie deCoursey Collection.

Kinsale, Quaker Neck. The second story facade was bricked up after 1932 and an extension built on the end. Maryland State Archives, Jeddie deCoursey

second story walls built of frame, suggesting the distinct possibility that it began as a one-and-a-half-story residence. It had a central stairhall plan, but in the twentieth century, the stair had been removed and reinstalled in a back wing, creating a single large living room as was done at King's Prevention on Broad Neck.

It is said that the original kitchen was free standing, but was moved to the rear of the house, heightened and enlarged. The entrance prior to 1966 was into the area of the old kitchen, even though the original main entrance remained in place on the southwest facade. It had a wide paneled door, crosetted trim, paneled jamb and brass lock. Other features included original mantels, doors and trim.

The development of Kinsale is similar to that of Depford, Stepney and Dullam's Folly, each of which began as a one and a half story structure before it was heightened and additional bed chambers were created.   K-282

1. Land Records, Lib. JS 8, fol. 150.
2. Land Records, Lib. EHP 84, fol. 356.

Sterling Castle

Mill Street, Chestertown
c. 1756

IN 1730, EBENEZER BLACKISTON PURCHASED LOT NO. 84 from Simon Wilmer.[1] Eight years later, Blackiston sold the southwest half of the lot to Charles Scott,[2] who, prior to his death in 1756, sold it to his son-in-law, Robert Sterling.[3] Sterling was a *"Lieutenant in His Majesty's 48th Regiment of Foot, now in America"* and was married to Ann Scott, daughter of Charles and Ann Scott, who owned The Manor of Stephen Heath and other properties on the road to St. Paul's Church.[4]

The house which the Sterlings built on the half lot was a one-and-a-half story frame dwelling, three bays long and one deep. Both facades had an off center six-panel door flanked by two 9/9 sash windows with louvered blinds. On the steeply pitched *A* roof there were two 6/6 sash dormers on each side.

Its plan originally consisted of two rooms in a hall-parlor plan, with an enclosed winder stair in the east corner, adjacent to a fireplace. Framing members flanking the doors, plates, and corner posts were all exposed and covered with beaded boards. In addition to the plates, there was a crown molding which together created a well proportioned cornice. Vertical beaded board walls divided the two rooms on both floors.

It is not known if there was a second chimney to supply heat to the parlor or smaller room. Evidence of a window centered in the gable upstairs, would make it highly unlikely. The location of the kitchen is also unknown. The existing addition was probably not installed until the McClean occupancy beginning in the 1820s.

In 1759, Sterling was forced to sell the house to satisfy his debts. The new owner, Richard Porter *"chirurgeon of Chestertown"* bought not only the house, but its contents as well for £100.[5] M. P. White points out in his research that ever since that transaction the house has been known as *Sterling Castle.* White felt this to be a mockery of its former debtor/owner.[6]

In 1771, Emmanuel Josiah, a Philadelphia merchant, sold Sterling Castle for £100, a £40 loss from his initial acquisition cost in 1759.[7] The purchaser, Ralph Story, was a Chestertown Shipwright. When he wrote his will in 1783, however, he was listed as a resident of Fells Point. The will in which the house was described as *"wherein a certain Barrel now lives,"* stated that it be left to his eldest son, William.[8] When William died before his father, without heirs, the house and lot became the property of William's niece, Elizabeth Jones and her husband John. According to their deed to Margaret McClean some forty years later, they had resided in Baltimore County and had retained the house as a rental property.[9]

As mentioned above, McClean was probably responsible for the construction of the one story, two bay kitchen wing. Its plan consisted of an entry with a ladder stair to an unfinished attic and kitchen lit by a large 12/8 sash window in front. A porch or leanto was located to the rear of the new wing. The kitchen mantel was crudely worked with gouge carving, typical of the first quarter of the nineteenth century.

Margaret McClean wrote her will in 1830 and died eight years later in 1838. She designated the house and lot be given to her sister, Anna Maria *"during her natural life and after her death to Thomas Lorain McClean ... ."* [10] At the time of the 1841 Tax Assessment, Anna owned, but did not reside at Sterling Castle, it was instead inhabited by the Reverend G. Heritage.

The next transaction recorded is the purchase of the property by Charles Davis. While Davis may have lived at Sterling Castle, by 1866 he

Sterling Castle, Chestertown, c. 1756. Built for Robert Sterling, "a Lieutenant in His Majesty's 48th Regiment" and his wife Ann Scott. It remained their home for a very short time before it was sold to satisfy their debts. Tyler Campbell photograph, 1996.

Sterling Castle, Chestertown, c. 1756. The snapshot was taken before it was rehabilitated by Adelaide Shaughnessy. The tallest section is a separate dwelling. M. Bourne photograph, 1963.

had built and was living in a new duplex next door (105 South Mill Street). When he died that same year, he bequeathed the *"old house"* in which his son John was living to his two daughters, Sally and Mary Anna.[11]

In Sally's will, written in 1916, she mentions that her duplex adjoined the property of her brother John. Apparently the Davis girls had given or sold the house to their brother.[12] Sterling Castle remained in the heirs' names until 1941 when it was sold to Frank B. and Sarah Shinn.[13] In the meantime another dwelling had been constructed on the northeast side of the old house. It, however, remained a separate dwelling and was willed to their son, Ralph, in 1959. The Shinn's daughter, Helen Burris received the old house, now part of three duplexes on Mill Street. Five years later it was sold to Adelaide K. Shaughnessy and her sister, Josephine Carvell.[14]

Sterling Castle, one of the most picturesque houses from mid-eighteenth century Chestertown. Michael Wootton photograph, 1996.

In 1964, Mrs. Shaughnessy renovated the old house and added a new wing onto the back of the house. In the process, the former entry in the 1820s wing was made into a corridor to the back porch and a Federal mantel from Mrs. Shaughnessy's former home in Frederick County was installed in the *hall*. Plumbing was installed in one of the two second floor rooms. The house remains today, one of Chestertown's small pre-Revolutionary vernacular dwelling houses, which possesses an extraordinary framing system and a largely original facade.   K-73

1. Land Records, Lib. 4, fol. 36 (JS 16/33).
2. Land Records, Lib. 5, fol. 71 (JS 22/114).
3. Land Records, Lib. 8, fol. 33 (JS 28/247).
4. Ann Scott, widow of Charles Scott, sold their part of the Manor of Stephen Heath to James Frisby in November 1756. It was to become known thereafter as Violet Farm.
5. Land Records, Lib. LR 8, fol. 236.
6. White, M. P. Jr., Unpublished paper "Sterling Castle" and Land Records, Lib. 8, fol. 236 (JS 28/444, 451; 29/103).

7. Land Records, Lib. DD 3, fol. 452.
8. Baltimore County Wills, Lib. 3, fol. 534. Alexander Danskin or Danskin appears in the 1783 Tax Assessment as owner of more lots in Chestertown than anyone else on the list. His name does not appear on the Index to Land Records!
9. Land Records, Lib. TW 4, fol. 278.
10. Wills, Lib. JFB 1, fol. 43.
11. Wills, Lib. JF 1, fol. 376.
12. Wills, Lib. JRC 1, fol. 338.
13. Wills, Lib. EHP 8, fol. 129.

Bungay Hill

Near Rock Hall
1757

CHARLES AND PHOEBE CARVILL HYNSON, WHO WERE married at St. Paul's Church 30 November 1739, owned Bungay prior to the construction of the existing house. All six of their children were born prior to its construction as well. In 1757 the Hynsons constructed their house and installed the date and their initials on the west gable by means of glazed headers in a pattern between the casement windows. Their house was anything but ordinary.

Bungay is a three-bay, two-and-a-half-story brick building facing a small creek called Bungay Creek to the south. It is 47' 9" long with an asymmetrical facade, with entry in the center bay. The entry is unique in the county with a semi-circular arch and double doors. The keystone is one large ten-inch brick protruding from the facade of the glazed Flemish bond brick; the imposts of the arch also protrude from the face, but they are composed of two courses of ten-inch brick. This arch and the segmental arches above the basement and first story windows are composed of alternating courses of stretchers and double headers. The watertable is molded like a bed molding and encircles the four sides of the building, jogging up and over the south basement windows. Unlike the north side of the house, the south facade has a string

Bungay Hill, 1757. The south facade. The left wing was added in 1960. Tyler campbell photograph, 1995.

Bungay Hill, 1757, has a unique semicircular headed double door, possibly copied from the porch tower of Phoebe Carvill's childhood home. Historical Society Kent County, Usilton Collection, c. 1940.

Bungay Hill, 1757. The off-center door leads into a stairhall with brick partition walls on both sides. Tyler Campbell photograph, 1995

Bungay Hill, 1757. The dining room paneling contains a door to the kitchen and another to the kitchen porch. Tyler Campbell photograph, 1995.

course between stories. Although the windows and doors of the north facade are similarly positioned in the walls, the details are much plainer. The first floor arches are made of one row of headers and the door has a flat jack arch.

The brickwork of the chimneys is extraordinary. Where they emerge from the roof, the stacks are not flush with the gable walls, but set in by sloped weatherings and there are decorative mullions or pilasters in their centers which extend to the tops. Such detail can be found at three other houses in the vicinity: The Reward, built in the 1740s by Charles Tilden (a second cousin of Hynson); the Violet Farm, built in

1762 by James Frisby; and Comegys Bight house, built in 1768. The last two also have glazed initials and dates.

With off-center facades like Bungay, the plan is usually easy to determine. Most frequently, the door and window closest to a gable indicates that the door opens into the hall of a hall-parlor plan house, like Providence Plantation. At Bungay Hill, however, the door leads into a stairhall and the stairhall is separated from that logical space by a solid brick partition which extends to the third floor—obviously an original feature.

Another interesting peculiarity of the plan is the fireplace positions on the end walls. Off-center placement of a fireplace is most often due to the existence of an enclosed stair on the same wall. While this is true in Bungay's east room, the fireplace in the west room is also off-center and yet there is no trace of the existence of such a stair in that position.

There is an early brick kitchen built onto the east gable and its north wall is flush with the wall of the main house. The south wall, however, is set back about six feet. Within that space on the east gable of the main block there is an original doorway. It opened onto a porch created, at least in part, by an asymmetrical roof over the kitchen with a very wide cantilevered overhang, similar to that at Thornton and Hinchingham, but lacking their outer posts. The kitchen itself is one-and-a-half stories and is constructed of smaller brick than the main dated section. Its south facade is laid in Flemish bond with burnt headers. Fenestration has been altered, but the north side has two windows.

Both of the original first story rooms contain very fine paneled chimney walls. The hall with its asymmetrically placed fireplace, has fluted pilasters flanking the overmantel, similar to the treatment in the early room of the Hynson-Ringgold House in Chestertown. Plain closet doors and paneling continue to the outside walls. There is also matching paneled dado on the other three walls.

In the dining room, the former enclosed stair is located on the north side of the wall with closet beneath (now a door to the kitchen). The plane of the paneling steps back about one foot to the fireplace and continues to the south wall, without pilasters and with a slightly different overmantel panel arrangement than in the living room. A Federal period reeded mantel has been added to the fireplace. There is a doorway through the paneling to the aforementioned original doorway in the gable leading to the kitchen porch.

The stair rises in the northwest corner of the eight foot wide passage. Its balustrade is very delicate, composed of plain square walnut newels with caps shaped like the handrail. Each open step has two delicate rectangular balusters per step and bold curved step ends. The spandrel is one flush panel with beaded surround. The closet door is board and batten. The balustrade on the second floor extends around the stairwell, the hall being wide enough for passage to the attic stair which was probably enclosed originally. There were two major chambers above the first floor room and a smaller room over the front door. An original vertical panel wall separates the hall chamber from the stairhall, although it is plastered on the stair side.

The dining room chamber has no exposed fireplace and only closets flanking the chimney. It is the only room to have window and door trim from the 1830-40 period. The opposite chamber has no original features other than the wall mentioned above.

With the puzzling layout and details it is difficult to determine if the interior was finished in 1757, gradually over the years, or remodeled later.

Charles and Phoebe Hynson lived in the house more than twenty years after the date on the gable. Charles deeded *Bongy* to his son, Charles, in 1781[1] and wrote his will a year later, spelling out all of the items of value which were to be given to his children and grandchildren. It is of interest that he left a trunk marked with I. C. M. to his son, John Carvill Hynson, for the initials are those of Phoebe's grandparents, John and Mary Carvill.[2]

Charles, Jr. was taxed on 300 acres of Hynson's Chance in 1783. He had seven whites and eight blacks living on the plantation and his assessment was on a total of £697, a sharp contrast to the personal estate of his father the preceding year of £88.7.9.[3] But, his father had given away all of his real estate by deed and much of his personal estate before his death.

Charles lived only twelve years beyond his father, dying at the age of 53. In his will, he specified that his widow, Closhe, was to have use of the *"Lodging room and room upstairs over the lodging room to her own separate use ... ."* and the rest in common with the family.[4] They had three sons, John, Thomas and Richard. To Thomas he left the home plantation with the obligation of maintaining his mother and brother, Richard. His personal estate was valued at £625.11.3 and included seven slaves and the furniture, tools and livestock necessary to carry on a successful farming operation.

His creditors were his wife and brother, Richard.[5] Closhe died ten years later.[6]

Thomas carried on the farming operation until his death in 1830[7] and bequeathed the farm to his son Charles R. Hynson, charging him with the same obligations of maintaining siblings, but Charles died before completing the executorship of his father's will, unmarried and intestate which left his two brothers and two sisters equal owners of the family farm.[8] The girls, after marrying two brothers in the Carville family, sold their shares to their brothers, Thomas and George in 1834.[9]

Thomas and George sold the farm to the first non-family member in 1845.[10] In 1852, part of Hynson's Chance was taxed to John C. Willson who had purchased it from the Hynsons. It lists a *"Brick House and other buildings in tolerable repair."* After Mr. Willson's death the court ordered the farm to be sold to Elizabeth McCoy in 1867. At this time it was referred to as *Bongy* or *Oakland,* the latter name probably coming from the Willson period.[11]

In 1877 the farm is listed as belonging to Charles

Bungay Hill, closeup of dovetail joint in plank smoke house. Gene Johnstone photograph, 1995.

Bungay Hill Smoke House. All plantations had at least one smoke house. Their roofs were more frequently gabled. Gene Johnstone photograph, 1995.

Bungay Hill first floor plan. M. Bourne.

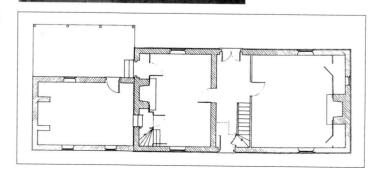

Geekie who also owned a *"Stock Farm"* at Drayton Manor between Still Pond and Churn Creeks. After a few more transfers *"Bungy"* or *"Oakland"* was advertised for sale in the Kent County News, 29 June 1886, to be held at the courthouse. In 1889, the farm was purchased by Chestertown lawyer, Richard Hynson.[12] His wife and administrator bequeathed the farm to her daughter Augusta E. Slay in 1917. The will describes the property as being tenanted by William E. deFord.[13] Mrs. Slay's heirs sold the farm in 1943.

Since 1943 the farm has been sold five times. Between 1951 and 1959 the original house was partially restored by Clifford and Carrie Nuttal.[14] In 1960 the new owners added a family room wing on the west gable, partially obscuring the glazed initials in the gable, and making an extension to the kitchen on the east. Several other alterations at this time changed the appearance of the farmhouse to that of a country estate. K-104

1. Land Records, Lib. EF 6, fol. 61.
2. Wills, Lib. 7, fol. 21. (For more information about the Carvills, see Carvill Hall).
3. Inventories, Lib. 8, fol. 188.
4. Wills, Lib. 7, fol. 469.
5. Inventories, Lib. 10, fol. 302.
6. Inventories, Lib. 11, fol. 447.
7. Wills, Lib. 11, fol. 180.
8. Inventories, Lib. 20, fol. 409.
9. Land Records, Lib. JNG 3, fol. 484.
10. Land Records, Lib. JNG 10, fol. 134.
11. Land Records, Lib. JKH 6, fol. 578.
12. Land Records, Lib. SB 11, fol. 598.
13. Wills, Lib. JRC 1, fol. 294.
14. Land Records, Lib. RAS 32, fol. 25.

"Hugh   O'Neal, Innkeeper."[1] Worrell's Tavern, however, was most likely built some thirty years later by James Porter who acquired the property in 1758.[2]

The property is named for Edward Worrell, gentleman, who purchased both halves of Lot No. 9 in 1770 for the sum of £600.[3] He did in fact run the tavern which bore his name and which is mentioned in the diaries of George Washington. In debt to William Sluby, merchant, Worrell sold his establishment to him for £1144.3.4 in 1786.[4]

From the photograph made into a post card at the turn of the century, it can be deduced that the tavern was a substantial frame structure, two-and-a-half-stories tall with an *L* plan. With its principal facade on Cannon Street, its basement windows lined up with

Worrell's Tavern historical marker. Michael Wootton photograph, 1996.

Worrell's Tavern stood on the corner of Cannon and south Queen Streets until c. 1902. Apparently, this site had a tavern from as early as 1735. Historical Society of Kent County, Post Card Collection.

Worrell's Tavern Site

Chestertown
c. 1758

WORRELL'S TAVERN WHICH STOOD on this site from the mid-eighteenth to early twentieth century, was important from an architectural standpoint for a number of reasons. Atypical for the period in form and fenestration, it also boasted a pent eave across its gable, making it unique.

Located on Lot No. 9, at the corner of Cannon and Princess Streets (now Queen Street), Worrell's, built in the late 1750s, may have replaced an earlier establishment of similar purpose as there is reference in a deed of 1735 to the property being leased to one

those above on the first story which had 12/12 sash. The four-bay facade included the main entrance in the third bay. The first bay appears to have originally been a window which was later replaced by a door.

Likewise, the first of the five-bay Princess Street facade had a later door inserted in place of a previous window. That window and another had flanked an exposed fireplace back. The middle bay was also an original entrance with transom.

In the photograph, the roof of the Cannon Street facade was pierced by two nineteenth century dormers and the gable end on Princess Street had two 6/6 sash windows flanking the chimney on the third floor. Again, the presence of the pent eave on the gable made Worrell's unique.

After William Sluby's death in 1803, Worrell's Tavern was sold. For the next 100 years it passed through several hands, including Joseph N. Gordon, a Clerk of the Court who had resided at Stepne, Nathaniel Hynson, Samuel Baker, who leased it to the Reverend Clement Jones, Rector of Chester Parish from 1832-1854, and Charles Westcott.

After Westcott sold the property in 1902 to Samuel and Sarah Pfeffer,[5] the building was demolished and replaced by the triplex which stands today. Recently, the triplex has been rehabilitated and turned into a condominium.   K-515

1. Land Records, Lib. JS 18, fol. 149.
2. Land Records, Lib. JS 29, fol. 100; Lib. JS 29, fol. 163.
3. Land Records, Lib. DD 3, fol. 273.
4. Land Records, Lib. EF 7, fol. 71.
5. Land Records, Lib. JTD 6, fol. 202.

Boxley

Near Rock Hall
c. 1758

Boxley, a 300 acre parcel of land, was acquired by Ebenezer Blackiston, a planter from Cecil County in 1674. It had previously been owned by Laurence Symonds and William Davis.[1] The Blackiston family retained ownership for over a hundred years, as it passed from one family member to another. In the mid-eighteenth century, Michael Blackiston (grandson of Ebenezer) commenced the construction of his brick dwelling house.

Although a typical one-and-a-half-story, hall-parlor plan, Boxley possesses a few features which make it different from others. It lacks a basement and is built relatively close to the ground, like Marrowbone (K-179). Its south facade is laid in Flemish bond with glazed headers and the two windows and door have segmental arches above. Common bond exists on the other three walls, but on the west gable a little lower

Boxley, near Rock Hall, was probably built by Michael Blackiston but not finished before his death in 1758. "Twenty sashes for glass" mentioned in his inventory corrresponds to the number needed for its windows. Tyler Campbell photograph, 1996.

than the cornice level, there are two glazed diamonds flanking the chimney. There is a tiny window to light a closet and sloped weatherings at roof level. Michael Blackiston left his mark on the building, as he scratched his cypher in a brick on the facade.

When Michael Blackiston wrote his will, a year before his death in 1758, he left the 200 acre farm to his wife for her lifetime and then it was to go to William, his son (his namesake, Michael, received half of Lot 13 in Chestertown).[2] There was no mention of a building project, but the listing of *"H and HL hinges"* and *"20 sashes for glass"* (the number which exists in the building) point to a house not yet finished at the time of his death.[3]

When the farm was sold to William Crane in 1805, the grantors included the heirs of Richard Blackiston and James Blackiston of Fayette County, Pennsylvania.[4] Crane's son, William Bowers Crane, owned the farm in 1852,[5] but it was tenanted by Gary H. Leaverton.[6] The buildings were listed as *"in bad repair."* In an 1858 equity case, the farm was sold to Richard Hynson, the Chestertown lawyer who was to build his residence next to River House in 1870.[7] Boxley remained in the Hynson family until the 1940s. In the 1970s the house was rehabilitated and again occupied by its owners.   K-103

1. Land Records, Lib. JS 18, fol. 149.
2. Land Records, Lib. JS 29, fol. 100; Lib. JS 29, fol. 163.
3. Land Records, Lib. DD 3, fol. 273.
4. Land Records, Lib. EF 7, fol. 71.
5. Land Records, Lib. JTD 6, fol. 202.

The Smith-Ringgold House

Water Street, Chestertown
c. 1759

Smith-Ringgold House, Chestertown. The two building phases are clearly discernible in the gable. Both chimneys are distinguished by withes. Michael Wootton photograph, 1996.

ONE OF THE MOST PROMINENT HOUSES VISIBLE FROM the Chester River Bridge is the Smith-Ringgold House, a two-part brick residence which sits on the highest part of North Water Street. On the first plat of Chestertown, this property was designated Water Lot No. 8. In 1732, it was purchased from Simon Wilmer by Henry Rippon for the sum of £10.[1] Rippon was a mariner who operated a ferry from Chester Town to Kings Town starting at least in 1739 and most likely continuing until his death in 1741, as the ferry is mentioned in the inventory of his personal property.[2]

Janie and Sarah Rippon, daughters and only heirs of Henry Rippon, along with their husbands James Porter and John Eccleston, sold their two half interests in the property to William Smith in 1754, and his father James in 1759. Only two years after having inherited his father's half interest in 1760, William sold the property to Peregrine Frisby for £600, a price large enough to suggest that half of the house facing Front Street was constructed by the Smiths during their ownership.

The house the Smiths built was the first of three Water Street houses to have the same plan and form. The other two are the Simon Wickes House and the McHard House. The Smith house had a one-and-a-half-story frame kitchen wing, unlike the other two which had kitchens in the basement. The explanation of this difference lies in the fact that the other two were built on smaller lots and were the product of one period of building. In the case of the Smith-Ringgold House, the kitchen wing was most likely the original frame house built by Henry Rippon which remained in good enough condition to use with the new brick wing.

The Smith house was three bays long and two stories tall, and constructed of brick above its stone basement. The facade was laid in Flemish bond and had a molded water table which rose up over the basement windows. The first story windows all had segmental arches. The unique feature of the house was the use of full size windows flanking the chimneys, on its southwest gable, a feature that was intended to bring light and warmth into the room. The plan consisted of a central stair hall with two flanking rooms.

William Ringgold, brother and partner of Thomas Ringgold, who resided at the Custom House, purchased the house and lot in 1764, for the same amount that Frisby had paid.[4] During his ownership (1764-1789) William Ringgold built the addition on the water side of his house. In form, it was very similar to the addition built on the Buck tenement by Benjamin Chambers after 1786. Its plan was two rooms with a central passage on each floor, all divided by vertical board partitions. Even though there were only fireplaces on the first floor rooms, the chimney stacks were constructed the size of a two flue stack. It was during the ownership of William Ringgold that the cove, indicated in the early plat of Chestertown, was filled in and the entire yard terraced to the water, the only instance of terracing or falles in Chestertown.

Smith-Ringgold House. The stair was built by G. W. T. Perkins after his acquisition in 1860.

Smith-Ringgold House. A view of living room from the parlor, through double doors installed during the Carvill occupancy. Tyler Campbell photographs, 1995.

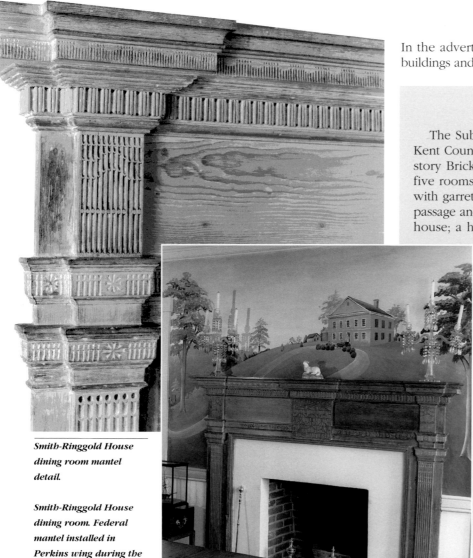

Smith-Ringgold House dining room mantel detail.

Smith-Ringgold House dining room. Federal mantel installed in Perkins wing during the Bacchus occupancy. Jack Schroeder mural painted during Huber ownership. Tyler Campbell photographs, 1995.

In the advertisement for the sale of the property, the buildings and use of the property are well described:

"FOR SALE

The Subscribers Property in Chester Town, in Kent County, which consists of a convenient two story Brick House, four rooms on the first floor, five rooms with store room on the second floor, with garret rooms, dry cellars under the whole, a passage and pantry to a large kitchen adjoining the house; a high paled in poultry and woodyard, a granary with two lower rooms and floor, a stone stable for four horses with beds and a carriage house under the same roof. Those improvements stand on Water Street, and all fronting on said street, its two sides included under paleing forms a spacious and well improved garden to the river, in which, and near the dwelling house, is a dry brick well originally built for an icehouse, but finished and now used as an office, with a framed cow shed placed in the middle of the north west line of the lot, which is divided into three parts for cultivation and grazing.

The situation of this property is pleasant and dry, and in prospect and healthyness not exceeded by any in the town. – The Terms of Sale may be known by applying to Mr. Richard S. Thomas, Baltimore, or the Subscriber.

JAMES RINGGOLD

N. B. The above property, if not sold at private sale by the 20th July next, will be sold at public vendue in Chester Town, and possession given in all the month of November next.

May 1, 1797 6 x 60 J. R."[7]

William Ringgold was the contractor for building the new Chapel of Ease for Chester Parish in Chestertown (1768-72). When he had finished building the new chapel he purchased Pew No. 4, even though he owned two-thirds of Pew No. 9 in the Parish Church at I. U. He was one of the members of the Committee of Safety during the Revolutionary War, a member of the convention which formed Maryland's Constitution in 1776, and received a military commission from Matthew Tilghman. His first wife was Sarah Jones, whom he married in 1750, and his second wife was a relative, Mary Wilmer, whom he predeceased. [5]

Upon his death in 1789, Ringgold left his three sons a comfortable inheritance. The house on Front Street was bequeathed to his son James, who was also the executor of his will.[6] James also succeeded his father in the Maryland General Assembly. By the time James sold the house eight years later, the property also included three adjoining water lots and Lot No. 16 across Water Street.

It is interesting to note that the property was purchased by Richard Snowden Thomas, the contact in Baltimore, who also purchased the Hynson-Ringgold House. Thomas was a cousin of George Washington Thomas, who was to live at River House and Airy Hill in the next century. It appears that Thomas did not live in either of his Chestertown houses, but rather rented them.[8]

When Thomas sold the property in 1802 to John Carvill, it was to remain in his family for 54 years. John Carvill IV had grown up on Fairlee Creek in the family home, Carvill Hall, a plantation that his great-great grandfather, Thomas, had patented in 1682 calling it Salters

Load. The family amassed about 2,000 contiguous acres and had a grist mill at the head of Fairlee Creek. The Smith-Ringgold House was to become their town house while they continued to maintain the farms. John died young in 1806 and left three minor children and Sarah, his widow.[9] His personal estate was appraised for $3,986.89 and the possessions were clearly of an upper class, well furnished house and farm, including the unusual entry *"26 views of Philadelphia."*[10] He also owned fifteen slaves to work the town home and his plantation.

In 1825, Carvill's holdings were distributed among his three children. His daughter Caroline received the town house as well as part of Salters Load.[11] In an equity case dated 1855, after the death of Caroline Carvill Holliday, the town house was re-conveyed to Caroline's three children.[12] Caroline's two sons conveyed their parts to their sister, Caroline, who with her grandmother, Sarah Carvill, joined in a deed to Joseph Usilton in 1856. In just three years Usilton turned it over for a tidy profit.[13]

During the ownership of Caroline Carvill Holliday, both front rooms in the old brick house were remodeled, with new window and door trim and mantels. Like Nicholson House, Airy Hill and the Geddes-Piper House, double doors were introduced between the front and back parlors. The change was in the empire style and resembled the remodeling undertaken by Joseph and Elizabeth Wickes at their home on High Street.

William Vannort and his wife Catherine, who lived diagonally across the intersection, owned the Smith-Ringgold House for less than a year before selling it to George Washington Thomas Perkins in 1860.[14] Perkins had inherited a sizable fortune from George W. Thomas, his name-sake, so he set about updating the house that was now at least partly one-hundred years old.

Perkins removed the old frame kitchen wing from the end of the first brick structure and then replaced it with an up-to-date, two-story, stuccoed brick wing, overlapping both sections. He added an overhang to the roof which was supported by brackets with drop finials. Around the majority of the house there was a one-story porch. Inside, he removed the original central stair and the north partition, converting the two spaces into one gracious entry/stair hall with curved stair. All rooms were fitted with current style mantels and stoves.

In the 1877 Atlas, GWT Perkins is listed as owner, not only of the lots previously owned by the Carvill/Holliday family, but also Lots No. 17 and 21 and parts of Water Lots No. 9 and 10, where he had his office. He also owned Hopewell Farm on Morgnec Road. By the time of his death in 1886, Perkins was in debt to two prominent merchants and an attorney, so much so that his property had to be sold to pay his debts.[15] In 1890, the house and lot, now considerably reduced in size, was sold to William F. Hines.[16]

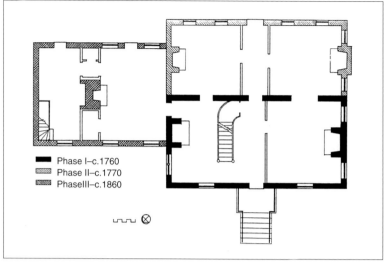

Phase I–c.1760
Phase II–c.1770
PhaseIII–c.1860

Smith-Ringgold House first floor plan. Michael Bourne.

Hines did very little to the house, other than change some mantels and install electricity. He is responsible for the construction of the existing brick garage on the north end of the property.

Avis Louis Bacchus, wife of Jefferson Bacchus, purchased the house in 1908 and it remained in the Bacchus family until 1965 when it was sold to Aubrey and Mary Romine.[17] The Romines removed the extensive porches from around the house, but it was not until 1973 that the interior was remodeled by Thomas and Mary Huber.

The 1973 remodeling included the removal of the stucco and whitewash from the exterior walls, and the installation of a new roof and chimney lining. All fireplaces were opened and old period mantels installed in several locations. The second floor plan was changed the most, with the installation of private baths for each of three bedrooms.

The house remains one of the outstanding eighteenth century vernacular dwellings of Chestertown.   K-19

1. Land Records, Lib. 4, fol. 228.
2. Wills, Lib. 2, fol. 127; Inventories, Hall of Records, Box 11, folder 43; Court Proceedings, Hall of Records, Nov. 1739; Testamentary Papers, Hall of Records, Box 43, folder 6.
3. Land Records, Lib. JS 27, fol. 393; Lib. JS 29, fol. 86; Land Records, Lib. DD 1, fol. 306.
4. Land Records, Lib. DD 1, fol. 474.
5. Papenfuse, p. 696.
6. Wills, Lib. 7, fol. 245.
7. Maryland Herald and Eastern Shore Intelligencer, Easton, May 1, 1797.
8. Land Records, Lib. TW 2, fol. 325.
9. Wills, Lib. 8, fol. 269.
10. Inventories, Lib. 11, fol. 684.
11. Land Records, Lib. TW 4, fol. 619.
12. Land Records, Lib. JNG 3, fol. 158, ff.
13. Land Records, Lib. JFG 4, fol. 37.
14. Land Records, Lib. JKH 1, fol. 750.
15. Chancery, Lib. SB 14, fol. 18.
16. Land Records, Lib. SB 14, fol. 18.
17. Land Records, Lib. JTD 18, fol. 49; Land Records, Lib. EHP 13, fol. 169.

The Bolton House

Queen Street, Chestertown
c. 1759

JOHN BOLTON'S SECOND LAND ACQUISITION AFTER COMING to Chestertown from Philadelphia was to purchase most of Lot No. 23 on the corner of Queen and Fish Streets (Maple Ave.) in 1759.[1] It is difficult to determine from the £28 purchase price whether or not the lot was improved with a dwelling. We know from the structural evidence that the oldest section of the Bolton house was a 21' x 18', one-and-a-half story structure, but whether it was standing in 1759 or was built soon thereafter may never be answered. The question is further complicated since the basement was constructed at the same time as the first addition. (Conjectural plans and elevations are based on what little evidence exists.) The first building was sheathed

Bolton House as enlarged by William Dunn after 1786. The original section is left of the porch. The Greek Revival porch was added in the third quarter of the nineteenth century. Tyler Campbell photograph, 1996.

with feather edge shiplap siding painted the typical red of the period. In the south corner there was an enclosed stair to the second story. The interior wall finish appears to have been vertical feather-edge boards. Interior partitions and placement of the fireplace in the floor plan are conjectural.

When Bolton enlarged the building, he dug a basement under both the original 21' x 18' section, and the ten foot extension on the rear. The original back wall was removed and a new feather edge vertical panel partition was installed four feet in from the former wall, creating two nearly equal size spaces with corner fireplaces. The stair remained in the same location. Probably the rear roof-pitch was altered to cover the extension. The kitchen location is unknown. *"John Bolton was an eighteenth century activist, who played a significant role in Chestertown's commercial life, as well*

Bolton House. Southwest gable of Phase I house. Michael Bourne.

Bolton House. Southwest gable of Phase II house. Michael Bourne.

Bolton House. First floor plan of Phase I house. Michael Bourne.

Bolton House. First floor plan of Phase II house. Michael Bourne.

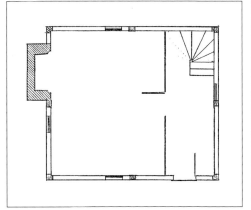

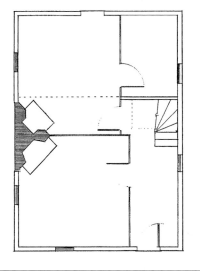

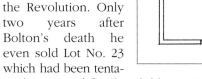

as in Kent County's participation in America's War for Independence. He was born in Philadelphia June 20, 1726, the son of Robert Bolton ... and Ann Curtis Clay."[2] Not only was he an active merchant, he was county coroner in 1770 and 1773 was executor to various estates and member of the Sons of Liberty. At the beginning of the war, he was appointed Commissary for Kent County, an appointment which cost him much of the fortune he had accumulated as as merchant. He was a pew holder of Chester Parish's Chapel of Ease in Chestertown (No. 28) as well as the parish church at I.U. and a vestryman between 1779 and his death in 1784.[3] Only a year before his death his real estate was listed in the 1783 Tax Assessment. In town, he owned seven lots worth £700 including improvements. He also owned 344 acres near Worton worth £516. In addition to the real estate there were eleven slaves in Chestertown and five on the plantation.

In his will he directed that his property, with the exception of the Queen Street house, was to be sold to settle his debts. The Queen Street house and contents were to be reserved for the support of his remaining minor children, under the guardianship of his sister-in-law Jane Dougherty.[4]

He appointed Thomas McClure executor of his estate who provided an inventory of his personal belongings first. The inventory obviously included the contents of his store, as there are numerous items of dry goods, kitchen wares, hardware, etc.[5] The total value was £1262.9.9 1/2.

Apparently McClure sold much of Bolton's property in order to settle the debts Bolton had sustained as a result of the position of Kent County Commissary during

the Revolution. Only two years after Bolton's death he even sold Lot No. 23 which had been tentatively reserved for the children. McClure sold the lot and house on Queen Street to William Dunn.[6]

William Dunn undertook the enlargement of Bolton's house and construction of his own dwelling adjoining. The extent of Dunn's building activities is discussed in Chapter IV, along with the chain of title from Dunn until the present.   K-21

1. Land Records, JS 29, fol. 213.
2. McCall, Davy H. "John Bolton," a lecture. Feb. 1993, sponsored by the Historical Society of Kent Co.
3. Chester Parish Vestry Records, Hall of Records.
4. Wills, Lib. 7, fol. 53.
5. Inventories, Lib. 8, fol. 229-233. Included in the inventory were five large pictures and four small ones. This entry may have included the one portrait of John Bolton which was advertised for sale at the Kennedy Gallery in recent years. Also included was "old map of the Town," an item which has not survived to the present day.
6. Land Records, Lib. EFG, fol. 552.

Rose Hill

Near Chestertown
c. 1760

R OSE HILL IS LOCATED ON THE old road between Chester-town and Georgetown. The house itself is a forty foot square two story brick structure that was probably built around 1760 by Alexander Calder on property he had inherited from his father, James in 1752.[1] Rose Hill is unique in Kent County in that it was designed with a gable facade, like Waterloo in Somerset County.[2] The entrance is located in the center of the five-bay Flemish bond facade. Originally, the entrance was composed of a door with a ten lite transom above set in a wide frame within the thick brick wall. A similar entry still exists on the four bay east facade, which was laid in all-header bond. Above the doors and the sixteen over twelve pane sash windows of the aforesaid two facades are two belt courses, one directly above the window openings, and the other one course below the twelve over twelve second story windows. The cornice extends around the facade and two sides, but the gable lacks the elements which would make it a full pediment, terminating instead in a plain barge board. The west and north facades are laid in English and common bond respectively and are devoid of either water table or belt course, but the first story north windows do have segmental arches which are lacking elsewhere. A unique entry is located in the center of the north facade containing a door with single sidelight.

Little has come to light on the financial resources of Alexander Calder, who was listed as a gentleman in subsequent deeds, but for some reason, the large house he was building was not finished, except for the back two rooms and stair. Those rooms were finished in the best vernacular tradition, with raised panel chimney walls, baseboard, chair rail and cornice. The fireplaces were large segmentally arched openings with off-set fireboxes that are seen in several houses constructed in the 1760s. Like the Adventure and Dullams Folly, the paneling con-

Rose Hill. The restored south facade laid in Flemish bond, with double belt course. Michael C. Wootton photograph, 1995.

Rose Hill, c. 1760 before restoration. First front door had a transom like the one in the all header bond east facade. Library of Congress, Historic American Buildings Survey, R. Langenbach photograph, 1973.

formed to the arch within a rectangular bolection molded surround. The stair was designed with an easy rise in two runs, a bottom landing and intermediate landing. The closed string balustrade was composed of bold turned newels with flattish finials and rectangular balusters.

In 1779, Calder sold the house and his inherited property to his brother-in-law, Anthony Banning (1741–1787).[3] Banning had married Ann Calder (1751–1773) around 1769 and in 1771 moved from Talbot County and established himself in Chestertown as a merchant a year after the birth of their only daughter, Catherine (1770–1855). During the ownership of the Bannings, the house appears to have been occupied and the fireplace in the southeast corner of the house, in an essentially unfinished room, was used since the cheeks of the fireplace were smoothly worn and soot was present on the brick chimney breast and joists above.[4] In 1783 the tax assessor listed Banning's property as follows:

> *"part of Dalington, 181¼ acres £362*
> *part Swersten 40¼ acres 80*
> *part Triangle 109 acres 95*
> *One large Brick Dwelling House & small Kitchen two out Houses & small log House near Chester Town."*[5]

From additional information in the tax assessment, it seems likely that Banning and his daughter were living at Rose Hill in 1783. Two whites and five blacks were listed residing on the farm, with fifty one ounces of plate, nine horses and twenty three head of black cattle. The total value of Anthony Bannings holdings amounted to £950, excluding a lot and house he owned in Chestertown.

Anthony Banning died in 1787 and bequeathed all of his property to his daughter Catherine, who married Benjamin Chew, Jr. (1758-1844) the following year.[6] Benjamin Chew appears to have been active in the community and served as Chairman for the Town Meeting until he and his wife moved to Philadelphia in 1793.[7] Thereafter they purchased Cliveden, the house his father had built in Germantown before the Revolution. While they were still in Chestertown, Rose Hill was brought to a state of completion it had not known since it was initially begun by Mrs. Chew's uncle.

As finished about 1790, the plan of Rose Hill remained the same as had been established thirty years before. The two northerly rooms and central stair hall retained original millwork finishes. The southerly room with two fireplaces backing up to the aforementioned north rooms was finished with strapwork mantels, strapwork cornice, chair rail and baseboard. The finished room measured twenty feet by thirty seven feet and was the largest residential room in Kent County in that period. The room had only two doors, the entry and a door to the stair hall, opposite. The large fireplaces were lined with brick and plastered, covering up the worn cheeks and soot that preceded the new finish. The single largest alteration to the exterior was the installation of a classical pedimented architrave at the front (south) entrance, necessitating the removal of the original transom. The architrave was designed with paneled pilasters and carved consoles supporting the pediment, a treatment similar to Thornton nearby. It was probably at this period that terracing was introduced on the south and east sides of the house.

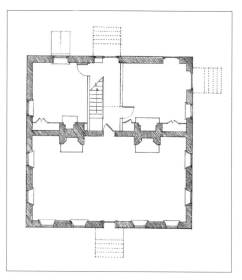

Rose Hill floor plan after the large south room was finished, c. 1790. Drawing by M. L. Fritz.

Rose Hill. The restored south room completed c. 1790, with twin fireplaces, paneled window seats, and strapwork cornice and mantels. Michael C. Wootton photograph, 1995.

Rose Hill. The northeast room (kitchen) paneling c. 1760, with later mantel shelf.

Rose Hill. Detail of cornice, mantel, and window. Michael C. Wootton photographs, 1995.

Biddle.[13] Thereafter it was mortgaged and came into possession of Robert T. Cochran by foreclosure. Cochran lived near Middletown, Delaware and was one of the most prosperous farmers in that area. Rose Hill was tenanted during this period by members of the Biddle family and was locally referred to as the Biddle Farm. During the Biddle occupancy the house received other changes. A two story porch was built across the entire facade and a second partition was installed in the south room, creating a corridor running from the entry to the stair hall, making the plan identical to the second floor. The carpenter was not as mindful of the original work as the one who installed the first partition.

Rose Hill remained in Cochran Family ownership until 1940.[14] In 1951 the farm was sold to Marion and Margaret Crew who made Rose Hill their home and operated the farm.[15] It was sold to Edwin C. Fry in 1963 and thereafter was transferred to Edwin R. and Marian Fry who undertook the restoration just before the birth of their first child.[16] It was finished in 1981 and has been open to the public on many occasions since. It was listed on the National Register in 1976.   K-119

The Chews retained Rose Hill Farm for several years after they moved to Philadelphia. The 1807 agreement for the sale of the farm is recorded in the Benjamin Chew, Jr., ledger.[8] In 1808 the deed to Samuel Ringgold was recorded in the county courthouse.[9] One alteration which occurred during the Ringgold occupancy was the installation of a partition in the large south room, creating two handsome rooms with their own fireplaces. The carpenters were very careful in copying the details of the cornice, chair rail and baseboard which had been established by the Chews.

In Mildred Schock's genealogy entitled *"Ringgold in America,"* a letter from a fourth generation descendant describes Samuel Ringgold as a *"stern aristocrat"* who resided on a large and glamorous plantation. It was said that when Samuel turned seventy years old, the birthday dinner was served on the lawn with seventy Ringgold relatives in attendance. When the family members assembled for church, some went to the Episcopal Church and others went to Methodist Meeting.[10]

The Ringgolds resided at Rose Hill until 1849 when they sold the farm to Frances Biddle, along with other land they had acquired, totaling eight hundred acres.[11]

Frances Biddle lived at Broad Neck, the old Gleaves Farm about a mile north of Rose Hill. When she wrote her will in 1863, she stipulated that Rose Hill be given to her son Stephen who was already residing on the farm.[12] Stephen Biddle, however, moved to Baltimore within the decade and sold it to David

1. Wills, Lib. 3, fol. 318.
2. The proportions of the building were analyzed for the Historic Structures Report, Bourne & Fritz, 1978, Maryland Historical Trust. "The geometrical construction is set upon a forty foot square plan. The base line is assumed to be the bottom of the basement window frames. Upon the base is constructed an equilateral triangle, its apex being the roof peak. The unusual central position of the chimneys is established by drawing a circle, the radius of which is formed by the distance (31.5') from the center of the base line to the edge of the cornice. The outside edge of the chimneys are located where this arc intersects the roof slope." The tops of the chimneys are forty feet high, completing a hypothetical cube.
3. Land Records, Lib. 5, fol. 258, 260.
4. Investigations of the house prior to restoration revealed the fact that the southeasterly fireplace was heavily used, with the edges of the fireplace jamb being severely worn and soot covering the brick chimney and exposed ceiling joists. These were covered over when the house was finally finished c. 1790.
5. 1783 Tax Assessment, Chester & Worton Hundreds.
6. Wills, Lib. 7, fol. 198.
7. The Apollo or Chestertown Spy, 1783, Maryland Historical Society.
8. Chew Papers, Pennsylvania Historical Society, Benjamin Chew, Jr. Ledger, 1793-1833.
9. Land Records, Lib. BC 5, fol. 269.
10. Schock, Mildred Cook, Ringgold in the United States, privately printed, 1970.
11. Land Records, Lib. JNG 12, fol. 119.
12. Wills, Lib. JF 1, fol. 216.
13. Land Records, Lib JKH 7, fol. 534.
14. Land Records, Lib. RAS 24, fol. 239.
15. Land Records, Lib. WHG 18, fol. 93.
16. Land Records, Lib. EHP 1, fol. 93.

Townside

Near Crumpton
c. 1760

ACROSS THE CHESTER RIVER FROM the town of Crumpton, Townside or the Comegys House is one of the early houses on the river's upper reaches to have attracted the attention of historical writers in the past. It was thought that the original house was built in 1708 for William Comegys, son of Cornelius, the immigrant. However, in an effort to locate the tracts called Presbury and Vienna, which were deeded to William Comegys by his father in 1690,[1] those parcels were found to be located to the east and north of the Comegys House (William's residence being located on Presbury).

Presbury was a 150 acre tract bordering Burris or Presbury Creek (the present eastern boundary of the farm), extending from the Chester River northward.[2] Vienna was a 600 acre inland tract which extended in the forest to the north of Presbury and contiguous thereto, and includes parts of present day farms extending from Route 290 to beyond Chesterville.

From the 1690s to the 1730s, William Comegys continued to buy and sell land along the Chester River. He purchased parts of Littleworth, Benjamin's Lott, Buck Hill, Chance, and other and had them resurveyed and some renamed. When he died in 1736, his *"dwelling plantation"* consisted of Presbury, Littleworth, and Chance and he devised it to his youngest son, Edward.[3]

The Comegys House is actually located on a single tract called Buck Hill & Billy's Lott which was resurveyed from Benjamin's Lott and Buck Hill in 1730.[4] William Comegys devised that part of his property to his son William, Jr., who had it resurveyed once again in 1745.[5] In 1746, William, Jr. sold 21 acres of his property to a Liverpool merchant, Foster Cunliffe.[6] From the deed description of the parcel, it appears that the Comegys House stands on that part of Buck Hill & Billy's Lott which was acquired by Cunliffe. His £36 purchase price, however, would not have been sufficient to include a house, especially one the size of Comegys House. Cunliffe had three acres of his parcel patented under the name Townside in 1747.[7]

Townside became a very popular place of commerce for the surrounding community during the next few years. Henry Callister, formerly of Oxford in Talbot County, was the representative of the Cunliffe firm and apparently did well enough in this service to purchase the 21 acres from *"Sir Ellis Cunliffe of Liverpool, Knight and Baronet,"* the heir of Foster Cunliffe.[8] He paid £170 for the property in 1760, *"with buildings thereon erected."* For the next four years, however, Callister did not fare well. He sold Townside in 1764 to a group of London merchants,

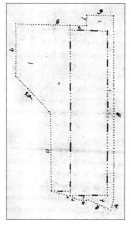

Comegys House or Townside. Enoch Pratt Free Library, photograph c. 1920; Maryland Room Collection.

"Plott of the Resurvey of Buck Hill and Billy's Lott Resurveyed for William Comegys ... containing 333 acres ... 1740." Maryland State Archives, Land Office, Patent No. 99, February 10, 1745.

Bacon, Franklin and Richardson, for £500.[9] Five years later, in 1769, this group sold the property to John Comegys, the oldest son and heir of William Comegys, Jr.[10] Thus, the entire farm was again in the ownership of the Comegys.

The sale price of £500 certainly indicates substantial improvements since the transfer of 1760. The house was most likely constructed by either Henry Callister or John Comegys between the years 1760 and 1774. In 1774, John Comegys had a four-and-a-half-acre parcel surveyed under the name of Townside Rebuilt.[11]

The first phase of construction consisted of a hall-parlor plan dwelling, one room deep, covered by a gambrel roof. It had a two-part kitchen wing built closer to the ground. Flemish bond with glazed headers distinguished the south facade of the three-bay structure. One half of the service wing was constructed of planks, the other of brick.

In his will, John Comegys (d. 1775) appointed his brother, Nathaniel, and his brother-in-law, Isaac Spencer, guardians to his four minor children and divided his land between the sons, Samuel and John. Samuel was to get the land which included the house and John was to get the land to the west. His wife was to have the use of the house for the remainder of her widowhood.[12]

Comegys House or Townside with original plank kitchen.

Comegys House or Townside. A nineteenth century brick dairy was built near the kitchen porch.

Comegys House or Townside showing the line between the original house and the early nineteenth century addition. Shed dormer added in early 1950s. C. Engstrom photographs, 1977.

Comegys House or Townside. A mid-eighteenth century center of commerce operated by agents for the firm of Foster Cunliffe of Liverpool. Henry Callister operated the business until 1764 and possibly built part of the brick house. He also operated a ferry across the Chester River. Michael Bourne photograph, 1963.

By 1783, Samuel (b. 1758) had reached his majority and is listed as owner of a *"Good Brick and wooden dwelling, Barn and outhouses."*[13] Little else is mentioned about him. His father had been a member of the vestry of Shrewsbury Parish where the births and deaths of the family were recorded. Samuel was married to a woman named Mary and together they had five children to reach majority as his heirs in 1812.[14]

It was probably Samuel who was responsible for enlarging the house and creating the unusual form which has characterized it for years. The enlargement was on the north side and consisted of a nearly equal size first floor plan of two rooms with corner fireplaces and a center passage—the entire being covered by a cat slide roof which is a continuation of the upper slope of the gambrel. After his death, the inventory of Samuel Comegys' estate was appraised by Philip Brooks and Lambert Veasey. His personal estate was appraised for $4058.01, a large inventory, even for the early nineteenth century.[15]

Washington Comegys, one of Samuel's heirs, began acquiring the other four parts that had been left to his siblings beginning in 1825.[16] Washington was not the businessman that his father had been. He defaulted on a mortgage which he executed in 1836 and the farm was sold in 1846 to Henry B. Slaughter.[17]

Slaughter fared no better than Washington Comegys, although he did establish a sawmill, cannery, and tenant houses at the foot of the hill. He was responsible for the construction of the large bank barn northeast of the house and for buying the eastern part of the farm, Presbury, where William Comegys, Sr. had lived.[18]

In 1874, Dr. Francis N. Shepherd acquired part of the Slaughter lands at auction[19] and the other part by purchase four years later.[20] Mrs. Shepherd was a Comegys descendant, so in a way it was a homecoming for her. In the nineteenth century, prior to the erection of a bridge across the river, the farm had been referred to as Ferry Farm.

Fred W. Stevens purchased the Comegys House in 1917 from the Shepherds and operated the farm with his wife, Mary Tarbutton, until he retired in 1954.[21] The Stevens retained a lot on the river and built a house where they lived out their lives. The rest of the farm was sold to Frank and Reba Peacock who renovated the old house and installed the shed dormer on the roof.[22] The old brick house stands as a reminder of a bygone era of farming, transportation and commerce.   K-118

1. Land Records, Lib. B, fol. 277.
2. Patents, Lib. 15, fol. 478.
3. Wills, Lib. 2, fol. 33.
4. Patents, Lib. SD No. A, fol. 49.
5. Patents, Lib. PT No. 2, fol. 204.
6. Land Records, Lib. JS 25, fol. 356.
7. Patents, Lib. TI No. 4, fol. 381.
8. Land Records, Lib. JS 29, fol. 414.
9. Land Records, Lib. DD 1, fol. 555.
10. Land Records, Lib. DD 3, fol. 245.
11. Rent Rolls, Lib. 5, fol. 88, 98.
12. Wills, Lib. 5, fol. 208.
13. Kent County Tax Assessment, Chester Hundred, 1783.
14. Kathryn DeProspo, History of Shrewsbury Parish, pp. 111, 149, 205.
15. Inventories, Lib. 12, fol. 458.
16. Land Records, Lib. TW 4, fol. 723.
17. Land Records, Lib. JNG 11, fol. 34.
18. Chancery, Lib. JKH 6, fol. 26.
19. The Slaughter lands were subdivided into several parcels that did not follow original patent boundaries. This is the time when the original William Comegys house on Presbury became part of Buck Hill & Billy's Lott.
20. Land Records, Lib. JKH 12, fol. 444.
21. Land Records, Lib. APR 2, fol. 113.
22. Land Records, Lib. WHG 31, fol. 539.

The Adventure

Near Sassafras
c. 1760

THE ADVENTURE IS SIGNIFICANT AS AN EXAMPLE OF MID-eighteenth century Georgian architecture and as the home of Alexander and Elizabeth Ellis Baird, tobacco planters and prominent members of their community. It is located south of the Sassafras River, facing the main road.

After Alexander and Elizabeth were married in 1746, Elizabeth's father, William Ellis, assigned a warrant for 200 acres of Moreton to the couple, who were then residing in Cecil County. It was patented in 1749.[1] The land adjoining, on which they built their house was patented in 1753 under the name—The Adventure.[2] The larger part of Moreton, 400 acres, was acquired in 1761 from James Louttit of Mount Harmon Plantation in Cecil County.[3] Soon after these three parcels of land were amassed, the Bairds built their house. They would stay here for the next forty years, with the farm as their livelihood.

The Bairds chose a design for their house similar to that of Bungay Hill and the Violet Farm located in the lower part of the County—a plain, rectangular two-story structure with two-story kitchen wing. Its southeast facade was laid in Flemish bond above a molded watertable and employed a decorative string course at second floor level, the center course being all header bond. Segmental arches were used above all of the openings, except above the attic gable windows where vertical headers were used. The northwest facade and southwest gable were also laid in Flemish bond, but burned and glazed headers were used throughout.

Flanking both center entrances, benches were let into the brick walls. The front entrance had a large eight-panel door with five pane transom within a wide frame. Windows on both stories were the same size and had 12/12 sash with paneled shutters on the first floor only. The lower two-bay kitchen wing had a door and three windows with 6/6 sash. Its facade was laid in glazed-headed Flemish bond.

The Adventure's floor plan consisted of a central stairhall with one room on each side, and a kitchen. Its architectural millwork was amongst the best in the County. The living room fireplace wall was fitted with paneling executed in the Doric order. Fluted pilasters on

The Adventure built for Alexander and Elizabeth Ellis Baird c. 1760 is a well constructed dwelling with extraordinary interior. Michael C. Wootton photograph, 1995.

paneled bases flanked the large arched fireplace. Beyond the pilasters, arched cabinets were installed, one paneled and one glazed, with superb architectural shell cabinet within. A metope beneath the cornice ran the full length of the wall, and the cornice 'broke out' above the pilasters, keystones of the cabinets, and above the windows in the flanking walls.

The windows had splayed window jambs and crossetted trim which was attached to the cornice like those at the Custom House in Chestertown. The fireplace surround had a bolection molding with small panels in the corners conforming to the arch of the fireplace. On each side of the fireplace there were plaster coves which reduced the size of the firebox. Both of the above features were similar to the treatments at Rose Hill and the Violet Farm—both of which date from the 1760s.

The stair was a bold three-flight composition with square-paneled newels and a close-string balustrade with turned balusters and drop finials. In general, the form of the stair was similar to Tibbalds, the home of Baird's co-parishioner Isaac Freeman. Another feature similar to Tibbalds was the placement of a secondary winder stair behind the paneling in the dining room.

Both second story rooms were well finished, with paneled fireplace walls, but with less detail than the rooms below.

During his lifetime, Alexander Baird acquired about 2500 acres of land near Head of Sassafras where he lived and owned a grist mill and a saw mill, as well as a wharf from which the crops were shipped to market. In 1783 his name was listed as a subscriber to Washington College in Chestertown.[4] In the same year his holdings included 1040 acres on which were four houses, two brick and two frame. He owned 25 slaves, six of whom were elderly and were not included in the valuation. His personal estate at that time was £3007, a huge fortune for the day when £1000 was considered the low end of *wealthy*.[5]

Alexander and Elizabeth Baird had eleven children, six of whom lived to maturity. All six were daughters and they married into the Keene, Hanson, Johns and Stoops families. At the time of his death in 1792, Alexander Baird passed the Adventure onto his daughter Ann Stoops.[6] It remained in the family until Ann's daughter Elizabeth Thomas sold the farm.[7] Elizabeth and her husband Charles lived in New Castle and he became the Governor of Delaware in 1830.

The Adventure, c. 1760. The paneled living room west wall is finished with Doric elements. Michael C. Wootton, photograph 1995.

The Adventure, c. 1760. The interior of the glazed cabinet was sold to H. F. duPont in 1923. James O. Reynolds Collection.

The Adventure, c. 1760. Detail of fireplace and paneling in living room. Michael C. Wootton photograph, 1995.

Joseph Griffith, who changed the name to Rich Hill, purchased the farm from the Thomases in 1839.[8] Two of Joseph's sons established themselves on the other parts of Baird's lands and built substantial houses as a result of the successful farming operations. During the

ownership of Joseph Griffith, an 80' long frame bank barn was built west of the house which remains standing today, a lone survivor of a once common form of farm structure.

Griffith sold the farm in 1859 to his son Robert who undertook the remodeling of the old house.[9] Robert must have appreciated the quality of the interior, for nothing was removed. The house, however, did receive new window frames and sash and an overhanging eave and dormers on the roof. A larger porch was built on the front facade.

From the time the Griffiths lost the property in the late nineteenth century, the house was occupied by tenants until purchased by Waldo Hagelgans, an antique dealer, in 1968.[10] Mr. Hagelgans installed a central heating system, but within a year sold it to St. Augustine Parish for use as its rectory.[11] Under the direction of its rector, The Rev. J. O. Reynolds, the house was gradually refurbished. It remained the rectory for St. Augustine Parish until sold at auction. Since that time there have been two owners, the last owner being responsible for the restoration of the great barn.   K-127

1. Warrants, 17 March 1748,
2. Patents, Lib. BY AGS No. 3, fol. 508.
   Certificate, Lib. GS 1, fol. 179
3. Rent Rolls, Lib. 5, fol. 164.
4. Barroll, L. Wethered, "Washington College, 1783," Maryland Historical Magazine, Vol. VI (June 1911), p. 169.
5. 1783 Tax Assessment.
6. Land Records, Lib. JNG 6, fol. 177.
7. Land Records, Lib. WS 3, fol. 294.
8. Land Records, Lib. JNG 6, fol. 177.
9. Land Records, Lib. JKH 1, fol. 560.
10. Land Records, Lib. EHP 27, fol. 365.
11. Land Records, Lib. EHP 29, fol. 259.

The Adventure, c. 1760. Detail of Doric capital and Metope.

The Adventure, c. 1760. Detail of original cabinet door and glass.

The Adventure, c. 1760. The dining room from the stair hall with glimpse of secondary stair.

The Adventure. Joseph Griffith purchased the farm in 1839 and changed the name to Rich Hill. The eighty foot long bank barn was built for the Griffiths. Michael C. Wootton photographs, 1995.

Tibbalds

Shallcross Neck
c. 1760

TIBBALDS WAS PATENTED TO PHILLIP HOLLIGER IN 1671 and consisted of 550 acres on the south side of the Sassafras River adjoining land that was *"taken up by Godfrey Harman."* [1] Both Tibbalds and Harman's land were purchased by William Pearce, the latter renamed Marshy Point Resurveyed.

When William Pearce died in 1720, Marshy Point was his dwelling plantation. He bequeathed it to his son Daniel after the decease of his wife Isabella.[2] Daniel did not survive his father by many years, for he died in 1727. Daniel left his dwelling plantation to his wife, Mary for her lifetime and then it was to go to his son Andrew including a part of *"Tibbolt."* [3] When Mary died in 1743, Andrew became master of the plantation.[4] Between 1747-49, through a series of three deeds, Andrew Pearce sold the two plantations, Marshy Point and Tibbalds to his neighbor Isaac Freeman. One of the witnesses

Tibbalds. Built soon after 1758 for Isaac Freeman, Jr., bears similarities to other Sassafras River houses. Michael C. Wootton photograph, 1995.

to the first deed was Jervis Spencer,[5] Isaac's brother-in-law. Freeman and Spencer had married daughters of William Comegys, Hannah and Ann.

Isaac Freeman had established himself on the west side of Terson's Creek (Freeman Creek), opposite Tibbalds, on a tract called Verina. At the time of his will in 1756, he and Hannah had four living sons and one daughter. To his second son, Isaac, Jr. he bequeathed Tibbalds and to his oldest son Abraham he bequeathed Marshy Point where Abraham was then living.[6] Isaac owned around 2,000 acres at the time of his death.

Andrew Pearce issued another deed in 1758, for *"all the lands previously conveyed to Isaac Freeman Sr.,"* to Isaac Freeman, Jr., clearing title to the same. The exact date of the construction of the house at Tibbalds is undetermined, but because of the relatively small purchase price, it appears that there was nothing substantial prior to 1749 when Isaac, Sr. originally purchased the land from Pearce. It is assumed that the house was built by Freeman's heir.

When constructed, the house on Tibbalds was a relatively large brick residence measuring nearly 24' wide by 48' long. Its two story south facade was five bays long with central entrance. Benches flanking the door and a pent eave between floors made it look more like a Cecil County, or Northern Delaware house than one typical of the remainder of the county. (Only five existing houses in the northern part of Kent County had pent eaves, but all have been removed.)[7] Its pent continued around three sides of the building.

Tibbald's floor plan consisted of two rooms flanking a central stair hall. The west room was the smaller of the two and had an enclosed stair behind a wall of paneling, in the same manner as Rich Hill up river. In both rooms the fireplace was off-center, a condition caused by the location of the structural girder below into which minor joists (18" O. C.) were mortised and tenoned. The paneling in the principal room on the east end was removed in the nineteenth century, but the splayed paneled-jamb window seats are still in place.

A choice feature of the house is the stair; a three flight open-string stair with turned walnut balustrade having three balusters per step, turned newels and drop finials. There is a raised panel spandrel beneath the first and second flight, which encloses the basement stair. A facia board attached to the upper newel finial indicates that a cornice had once continued around all four sides of the hall, just as it still does on the second floor, and similar to Rich Hill and the Reward.

The second floor plan consists of a central room, now a bath, over the entrance, with one room on the west and two rooms on the east. The bath retains original two-part cornice, bolection chair rail and baseboard.

Originally the corridor connecting the rooms to the stair would have had an *L* plan, probably having a section of balustrade adjacent the top flight of stair. The plan is similar to the second floor of Violet Farm in the lower part of the county, constructed in 1762. Only one of the east bedrooms had a fireplace.

The stair continued to a large open hall on the third floor which was originally lit by two dormers. The balustrade around the stairwell was simplified into a handrail and intermediate horizontal board. Two outer rooms were separated by vertical beaded board walls, with board and batten doors which opened from the hall. Both were lit by front and rear dormers. There were no windows in the gables.

Originally, Tibbalds had a kitchen fireplace in the west room of the basement. How long the kitchen remained here is unknown. By the time of the 1783 Tax Assessment however, there was a brick kitchen listed as attached to the house.

Isaac Freeman, Jr., like many of the gen-

Tibbalds. The open string stair has a superior walnut balustrade and the remains of a cornice similar to the treatment at The Adventure.

Tibbalds. Detail of open string stair with classically turned walnut balusters. Michael C. Wootton photographs, 1995.

try of his day, was involved in the revolutionary cause. He was also committed to the promotion of education in the county as evidenced to his commitment of £12 to the founding of Washington College in 1782. He was also active in the affairs of Shrewsbury Parish serving on the vestry 1760–1762, 1768–70, and 1778–87.[8]

In his will, written in 1795, he left his *"dwelling plantation"* to his son Isaac III. He specified that no valuation be made of his personal estate, but judging from his bequests, he had acquired an additional 600 acres beside his home plantation. Isaac III was appointed executor of his father's will, a duty which he handled until his own death in 1808.[9] Martha Freeman and Thomas Carvill were the administrators of Isaac III's will, a duty made more complex by the fact that Isaac had been executor of his brother's estate too.

Tibbalds or *"the Mansion Farm,"* was sold from the estate to William Redding in 1819.[10] He sold it in 1824 to Colin Ferguson, son of the second president of Washington College, bearing the same name.[11] The Fergusons owned the farm until 1851 when trustee George Vickers, sold it to Serek F. Shallcross. At that time it consisted of 375 acres.[12]

During the ownership of the Shallcross family Tibbald's house went through a series of alterations which simplified its appearance. The exterior pent eave was removed and the interior lost much of its chair rail, cornice and paneling to the ever-popular plaster-covered walls covered with wall paper. The stair, current bath and third floor were not appreciably altered and it is the examination of these features which help us understand its original appearance.

The *Mansion Farm* stayed in the Shallcross family between 1851 and 1895, when it was mortgaged a second time to Andrew Woodall.[13] Woodall assigned the mortgage to William Beck who sold it to the Kent Land Co. in 1914.[14] President J. Waters Russell sold the farm to Harry Willis in 1917.[15] The Willis family resided there between 1917 and 1927, at which time the father of the present owner purchased Tibbalds as a hunting preserve.[16]

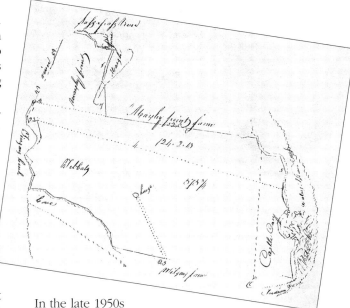

In the late 1950s the old brick kitchen wing was removed and rebuilt a little shorter than it had been originally. Some of the old bricks were reused in the reconstruction, but the plan is modern. A two-car garage was also built north of the house.

The house is surrounded by large linden trees and is situated on the highest ground before the fields slope toward Freeman Creek to the west and the Sassafras River to the north.   K-142

Tibbalds. Plat prepared for the estate of Isaac Freeman III, 1819. Chancery, Lib. WS 3, folio 48.

Tibbalds. First floor plan, Michael Bourne.

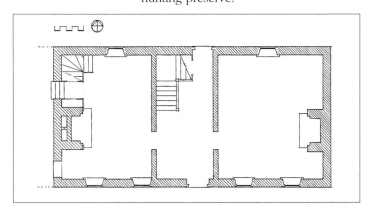

1. Patents, Lib. 14, fol. 312.
2. Wills, Lib. 1, fol. 207.
3. Wills, Lib. 1, fol. 307.
4. Wills, Lib. 2, fol. 207.
5. Land Records, Lib. JS 26, fol. 98.
6. Wills, Lib. 4, fol. 6.
7. Other buildings which had pent eaves are: Locust Hill, Scotch Folly, Partners Addition, Ryley's Farm and Shepherd's Delight.
8. DeProspo, K. M., A History of Shrewsbury Parish p. 25.
9. Wills 7/505.
10. Land Records, Lib. TW 4, fol. 543. A detailed description of the farm is found in the Guardian Bonds of 1809 (Lib. 6, fol. 414.) "On the Mansion Farm we find the following improvements 1 brick dwelling house 44 by 23 feet with new cedar roof, 2 storys high and cellar under the whole in good order - 1 brick kitchen 30 by 24 feet with cedar roof in tolerable order 1 workshop sawd poplar logs, cedar roof + cellar 18 by 14 ft in tolerable order; 1 log Poultry House 15 by 14 ft old + in bad order 1 Brick oven in good order; 1 new

Brick milk house 8 by 10 ft with cedar roof in good order; 1 old frame meat house 12 by 12 in bad order; 1 frame Barn and Granary 40 by 30 feet with good cedar roof, otherwise in bad order; one poplar log and frame stable, with carriage house 40 by 27 ft cedar roof over the whole in tolerable order; 1 sawd poplar log corn house with cedar roof 19 by 11 ft in tolerable order; 1 carriage house with cedar roof 20 by 10 ft in bad order; one large garden enclosed with paling in tolerable order, 1 old apple orchard containing 134 trees … etc."
11. Land Records, Lib. TW 4, fol. 543.
12. Land Records, Lib. JR 2, fol. 177. Prior to the Sale, it was advertised in the Kent News, July 1850.
13. Land Records, Lib. JTD 29, fol. 414.
14. Ibid.
15. Land Records, Lib. Apr 2, fol. 48.
16. Land Records, Lib. RRA 8, fol. 428.

Partner's Addition

Gregg Neck
c. 1760

PARTNER'S ADDITION WAS A ONE HUNDRED FIFTY ACRE tract patented originally in 1674 to Richard Bower and Francis Robinson.[1] One hundred acres of the tract came into the possession of John Browning in 1737,[2] who bequeathed it to his third son, Thomas.[3] Once Thomas reached his majority, he began building a good brick house on his inheritance close to " *... the post road leading from George Town Cross Roads to Head of Sassafras ... .*"[4]

Thomas Browning's house was a two-and-a-half-story, brick dwelling, three bays wide by one bay deep (33' x 21'). The placement of its kitchen is unknown. Both north and south facades had central entrances with transoms and originally pent eaves between the tall first and second story windows. All windows had 9/9 sash. Those on the first floor had paneled shutters. The south and west walls were laid in Flemish bond with glazed headers but the other two walls were laid in common bond. The six-panel doors had the smaller panels in their centers and on the interior they were covered with three thin vertical beaded boards which had been applied with rose-head nails.

The house plan consisted of a hall and parlor. A large 5' 3" wide fireplace with wooden lintel was the heat source for the hall—possibly it doubled as the kitchen fireplace. When the house was in derelict condition, it was possible to examine areas which would have otherwise been hidden from sight. Traces of soot from the fireplace were seen on the brick chimney breast and the ceiling joists above. Obviously, the house had been occupied prior to its completion. When the house was finished, a wall of raised paneling with cabinet was added to the north side of the fireplace. The fireplaces and millwork details were similar to The Adventure and Dullam's Folly.

In the southeast corner was a winder stair which continued to the unfinished attic. A two-piece cornice and chair rail and a beaded baseboard were used throughout the first floor. Even after the installation of paneling there was no door at the stair. In order to supply more headroom, the underside of the joist above the stair was undercut. There was a stair door located on the second floor.

The parlor or inner room had a 5' wide fireplace in the northwest corner which had a segmentally arched head. Like the fireplaces at Rich Hill, there was a vertical plastered cove on each side which consequently reduced the width of the firebox to about 3' 6". There was a bold trim around the opening with plaster above.

The second floor had an unconventional plan, with passage and three bedrooms. In order to access the northwest bedroom, a passage was carved out of the northeast bedroom. The former was the only second

Partners Addition, built for Thomas Browing in the 1760s, had pent eaves originally. Maryland Historical Trust, M. Q. Fallaw photograph, 1985

Partners Addition in 1995 after the arch in the basement collapsed under the weight of the two corner fireplaces. It was demolished in 1997. Michael C. Wootton photograph, 1995.

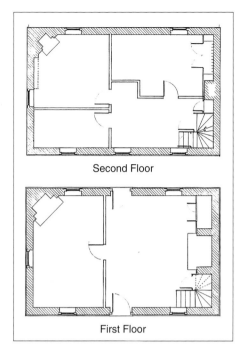

Second Floor

First Floor

floor room to have a fireplace. It was similar to those below, but the coves were half the size and instead of plaster above, there was paneling with a cabinet door which enclosed three shelves. The space for the three shelves was created by the chimney flues being carried across the wall to emerge from the roof in the center of the gable—a device which balanced the hall chimney. In the second story passage, two doors closed off the stairs. The northeast chamber appears to have had paneling on the east wall, creating closets flanking the chimney flue.

There were no windows in the attic gables, but the uniformly joined rafters were spaced for two dormers. It is of interest to note that the joists as well as rafters were quite uniform and well-joined.

When *"Thomas Browning, hatter"* sold the property to *"John Maxwell, gent"* in 1769 the consideration was £500, a sizable price for only 100 acres.[5] George Browning had purchased twice the acreage adjoining four years before for only £350.[6] The difference between the two sales indicates that John Browning's property had been improved by the construction of the brick house.

John Maxwell purchased 223½ acres adjoining Partner's Addition, to the east, in 1788.[7] Maxwell bequeathed the land to his son, Dr. John Maxwell, who obtained a quit claim deed to the same property in 1797.[8] He then sold the 333 acre farm in 1801 to *"William Palmer, farmer of Kent County."*[9] Palmer apparently did not pay for the farm, so John Maxwell sold it again in 1814 to William Pryor of Queen Annes County.[10]

William Pryor appears as the owner of the property in 1822 when the Tax Assessor made his rounds. In this record, the original tract is mistakenly called *"Partner-*

ship Addition." Pryor also owned another parcel of land, the two totaling 600 acres which together were appraised at $2,700.00.[11] John Bowers Eccleston was appointed trustee to sell the *home farm* of William Pryor in 1828, but it was subject to the life estate of Pryor's widow, Elizabeth. Upon her death, the farm was sold to Samuel D. Woodland in 1831.[12]

At some time in the nineteenth century, a curious thing happened to the house. The original south front stoop was replaced with a porch having a flat roof with railing. The central window on the second floor was lengthened and converted into a door with transom. This probably occurred at the same time that the pent eaves were removed and the kitchen wing added to the east gable. In the process of adding the wing, a passage had to be made through the cabinet in the hall paneling, requiring the rail between the upper and lower doors to be removed, as well as all of the shelves.

After an equity case in 1851, the farm was sold to John Nevin and Bronaugh M. Deringer, the latter being Woodland's son-in-law.[13] Deringer then bought out Nevin's half interest[14] and probably resided therein. His widow is listed as the owner of the farm and appears to have resided at Partner's Addition when the 1877 Atlas was printed. The farm remained in the family until 1948 when it was sold to Roy C. Mitchell.[15] It had been a tenant house until in recent years it was vandalized and stripped of its fine woodwork. In 1994 the northwest corner of the building collapsed, exposing the remainder of the interior to the elements. It was demolished in 1997. K-152

1. Patents, Lib. 5, fol. 23.
2. Land Records, Lib. DD 3, fol. 129.
3. Wills, Lib. 2, fol. 169.
4. Land Records, Lib. BC 8, fol. 128.
5. Land Records, Lib. DD 3, fol. 129.
6. Land Records, Lib. DD 2, fol. 188.
7. Land Records, Lib. EF 7, fol. 319.
8. Land Records, Lib. BC 4, fol. 624.
9. Land Records, Lib. TW 1, fol. 646.
10. Land Records, Lib. BC 8, fol. 124.
11. 1822 Tax Assessment, Third District.
12. Land Records, Lib. JNG 2, fol. 437.
13. Land Records, Lib. JR 1, fol. 423.
14. Land Records, Lib. JFG 4, fol. 257.
15. Land Records, Lib. RAS 36, fol. 543.

Lathim House

Turner's Creek
c. 1760

IN HIS RESEARCH OF THE SETTLEMENT AT TURNER'S CREEK, L. Wethered Barroll referred to the building near the granary as *"that which was occupied in the late eighteenth century by John Lathim, nephew of Donaldson Yeates."*[1] The two had been in business together and toward the end of Yeates' life, Lathim handled many of his affairs.

There is an unfortunate lack of information about the settlement at Turner's Creek. It is known that the entire area was owned by Yeates and that he had conducted a prosperous mercantile establishment there between 1768 and 1796.

Part of the building which remains may have been used for the store which Yeates operated as part of his business. Interior and exterior details are similar to the Spencer Store, another late eighteenth century structure, located at Chesterville. The window shutters were made to be locked from inside and the ceiling had exposed beams. While neither of these features is a definite indication of the building's use, they are both common to other business structures of the time.

When first constructed, the plank wing was a freestanding building approximately 16' x 20', with exterior walls extending about 2½' above the second floor level. It was covered with an *A* roof. There was a stone basement underneath and a fireplace within the south gable. Adjacent to the fireplace, in the southwest corner, there was a winder stair to the second story. This building may have been constructed soon after Yeates purchased the property in the 1760s.

Later, in the 1780s or 90s, the brick extension was built. Accessible from under the front porch, it too had a stone basement. The brick part was not as long as the existing structure. It had a door and window on the first story and two windows above. On the north gable, the stepped chimney protruded from the wall and had one window beside it. There was one window on each floor on the west wall.

Inside, there was one room with a stair on the west or back wall. The stair had a board spandrel which hid the way to the basement. Its balustrade was a simple, close-string affair and had a crudely turned newel and square balusters set on the diagonal, somewhat like the stair in the Eltonhead Manor Room at the Baltimore Museum of Art. The ceiling beams were exposed, beaded and painted. There was a simple mantel.

On the second floor, details were similar, but the attic stair was enclosed behind a beaded board partition and located on the south side of the room. Even though enclosed, the stair was built with a newel. Very short and octagonal, it looked more like a bedpost than that for which it was intended. There was a door into the second story of the plank section. There was also a fireplace on the second level.

Later, in the nineteenth century, the plank wing had its roof removed and its walls heightened. This made it equal in height to the brick section. Its second floor was divided into three cells and a passage.

The building remained relatively unchanged until the late 1960s when the property was first sold out of the family. At that time, the Yeates House was moved to Baltimore County and restored as a guest house and the Lathim house was partially demolished. When the property was purchased by the county to be used as a park, the building was stabilized, but the brick section had been reduced to one story. It now houses a park office and public facilities. K-115

1. L. Wethered Barroll, The Barroll Book.

Lathim House, Turners Creek, still occupied in 1938, was composed of plank and brick sections and probably always had a porch. Delphine S. B. Kelly Collection.

Lathim House, Turners Creek. The exposed plank construction is similar to Knocks Folly at the top of the hill. It was probably built for Donaldson Yeates in the 1760s

Ryley Farm

Gregg Neck
c. 1760

THE LAND ON WHICH THE RYLEY HOUSE WAS BUILT WAS patented to William Palmer as *"Plum Park"* in 1667.[1] It was 350 acres and adjoined Indian Range, a tract of 250 acres patented in 1671 to Jarvis Morgan. In the early eighteenth century, when this area was part of Cecil County, John Riley (or Ryley), Jr. purchased 50 acres of Plum Park and established himself thereon.[2] With additional purchases of 100 acres in 1708[3] and 150 acres in 1725[4] John Riley's farming operation had become significant. By 1730 he was able to purchase 250 acres of Indian Range adjoining his other holdings.[5] This tract was located on both sides of Mill Creek (formerly known as Palmer or Quidley Creek).

In John Riley's will of 1733, he bequeathed his dwelling plantation to his wife, Indian Range to Isaac Riley (probably his nephew) and the remainder of his holdings to his brother Nicholas.[6] Isaac and Nicholas died within a very short time of one another in 1745. Not long after, inventories were made of their personal estates. Neither had a value which could possibly correspond to the caliber of the house which has most recently been known as Heritage Farm.[7]

After his father's death, Nicholas had his inheritance surveyed under the name of *"Ryley's Land Resurveyed."* It totaled 561 acres.[8] Nicholas' will is not as specif-

Ryley Farm, Gregg Neck c. 1760, was built for Nicholas Ryley, Jr. on land originally patented in 1667 called Plum Park. Michael C. Wootton photograph, 1995.

ic as one might wish, for he left to his son Nicholas *"all my lands in Riley's Neck on Sassafras River with all the premeses and appurtenances ... (except 100 acres with premeses belonging to be laid out 75 perches from the River adjoining on Indian Range and running south with said Indian Range to make up the said 100 acre) ... ."* To son Benjamin he bequeathed his dwelling plantation after the death of his wife Mary. There is some question as to whether or not his *"dwelling plantation"* and *"Ryley's Land Resurveyed"* are not the same.[9]

It seems most likely that Nicholas, Jr. constructed the brick house (he had inherited the land from his father in 1745). The details of the Riley House are similar to other mid-eighteenth century houses remaining in this part of Kent County, such as The Adventure, Partners Addition and Tibbalds.

In form, his house was remarkably similar to that of his neighbor Thomas Browning, a house on land called Partners Addition. Both houses were two full stories with attics, they were built in a combination of Flemish and common bond, and had central entrances on their three bay facades. Both had pent eaves on the two long facades between floors. And while the fenestration of the rear of Browning's houses included two windows on the second floor, this feature was repeated on both facades at Riley's. The exterior basement entrance was located through the fireplace arch at the north end of the house similar to The Adventure.

Inside, the house was more conventional than Browning's, with hall-parlor plan and centered fireplaces. Both rooms had enclosed winder stairs behind a paneled wall. The configuration of the fireplaces is basically the same as at Browning's, but more like The Adventure, where the same bolection molding surrounds the fireplace and the panel arrangement above is similar. In the hall, the stair had a turned balustrade with square fluted newel, like Dullam's Folly nearby. On the opposite side of the fireplace there was a closet. The parlor wall on the other hand had an exterior door to the kitchen and it lacked a balustrade.

Whether the kitchen was attached or not is unknown. It was surely off the south gable since an original door remains in place and the majority of eighteenth century houses had kitchens in a similar location.

Relatively brief in nature, the will of Nicholas Riley, Jr. sites William as executor and bequeaths monetary amounts to Araminta and Nicholas.[10] There is no mention made of real estate. Two months after his death, an inventory of Nicholas' personal property was taken. Here we find a large amount of household furniture, farm tools and seven slaves, all valued at £594.15.2. His nearest kin were Benjamin Riley and Sarah Huff, probably his siblings. Two additional inventories brought Nicholas' worth to £941.2.17, a large increase in comparison to his father.[11]

William Riley survived his father by only nine years. In the meantime, he had married Rachel Stockton and had had two children. Soon after their marriage, Rachel was paid a visit from a friend, Philip Vickers Fithian, while he was traveling across the Eastern Shore. Fithian, a tutor to the children of Robert Carter of Nomini Hall in Virginia, made his way to New Jersey in the spring of 1774 and wrote in his diary of his stay at Georgetown and of his visit with Rachel Riley:

"In this Town & the neighbouring Country rages at present a malignant, putrid Fever, & what is generally called the spotted Fever!—From Chester Town I rode to George-Town, 16 miles—The Land levil, fertile, & vastly pleasant—in this Town I visited Mr. Voorbees, an eminent Merchant here, & he seems to be a Gentleman of peculiar smartness Industry & Oconomy—The Fever I now mentioned, is also here, & the whooping-Cough is very general & malignant—I lodged with this Gentleman—We had Evening prayers—Since I left Cohansie I have not heard the like—This is a small Town, & lies on a fine River, which divides it from another small Town directly opposite call'd Frederick."

Friday, April 15, 1774 (p.132)

"I rose early—After Breakfast I rode to see Miss Rachel Stocktin, now Mrs. Ryley; She lives on this River, about a mile higher up, in a large very elegant brick House; in considerable grandeur—Poor Girl She herself is much indisposed either of a bad Cold, (as She thinks) or of this epidemical Fever; Mrs. Ryley introduced me ceremoniously to Miss Ryley her husbands Sister. She has a small handsome Fortune, & is perhaps agreeable—I returned to Town, and dined with Mr. Voorbees, & immediately after crossed over the Ferry for Port-Penn. Expence at George-Town for my Horse 2/3 to Boy 4d. I rode next to a small village called Warwick, a pitiful place indeed ... ." [12]

In his will, written in 1782, William Riley appointed Rachel and merchant friend and creditor John Vorhees of Georgetown to be executors. He bequeathed the plantation to his son Nicholas, but Nicholas was a young boy and was not to receive the plantation until the year 1800. Two children and *"the child or children my wife now goes with"* were mentioned in William's will.[13] The unborn child turned out to be Mary for whom Rachel took out guardian papers in the fall of 1783.[14] John Bantham was appointed Guardian for Nicholas in 1786 and he in turn had Nicholas' inheritance appraised for the court.

"Whereas we the subscribers being appointed to vallue the Lands and plantation belonging to Nicholas Rily, an Orphan, unto John Bantham his guardian, we do therefore vallue the

Ryley Farm, Gregg Neck, c. 1760. Phillip Vickers Fithian describes the Ryley house as "... a large very elegant brick house; (and his friend, Rachel Stocktin Ryley as living) ... in considerable grandeur.

Ryley Farm, Gregg Neck, c. 1760. Fireplace and paneling in the dining room are nearly identical to the living room. Michael C. Wootton photographs, 1995.

said Lands, Houfis, & Out Houses at the following Rates or forces to wit—one tract of Land Called Plum Park supposed to contain 250 acres of land with 65 apple trees thereon & 60 peach trees one & ahalf Acres per year to be cleared & no more & not more than one third of sd. land to be turned in any one year, the land to be cleared is on the south End sd. tract enclosure of all dead timber which the sd. guardian has a right to make use of. The plantation in Medling good Repair orphans ⅔ vallued to—one Brick Dwelling Hous 36 by 21 feet in good repair. one Barn 30 by 25 feet. in good repair— with a 10 foot shed one stable 20 by 18 in tolerable repair & 2 8 foot sheds one Corn Hous 18 by. 9 in tolerable dᵒ one Quarther 20 by 18 in Bad dᵒ one Meat Hous 10 by 10 in ditto dᵒ one Milk dᵒ 10 by 10 tolerable dᵒ one Kitchen—24 by 18 tolerable—dᵒ one Pailed garden in Bad repair NB There is no allowance or deduction for the orphans Maintenance or education or assesments or any publick dues but that all such amounts shall be deducted out of the afsd valluation—Kent County To wit— we do Hereby certify that we the subscribers have made the above valluation on the 14th day of August 1786 witnefs our Hand & Seals

    Robert Moody (seal)

    Daniel Cornelius (seal)" [15]

In 1800 John Bantham and his wife Rachel (*"formerly Rachel Riley, wife of William Riley late of Kent County Dec'd"*) sold Rachel's dower right to Nicholas for £200.[16] Later that year Nicholas sold the farm out of the family to John Allen of Fredericktown, Cecil County.[17] Little is known about the ownership of John Allen, but he did acquire the rest of the Riley lands before it passed to his son Mordicai who died in 1829. Ezekiel Forman Chambers was appointed trustee to sell the lands of

Allen which he did in November of 1829 to John and Alexander Gregg of Baltimore. By the time the deed was recorded in 1836, Alexander Gregg was the surviving partner in the transaction.[18] The purchase included 515 acres, nearly the same amount as Nicholas Riley had owned in 1734.

Alexander Gregg's widow, Harriett and their children sold the farm in 1848 to Isaac Lum of New Castle County, Delaware.[19] Lum's only heir was his daughter Clara who married Richard R. Cochran. During the ownership of the Lum or Cochran families, the pent eaves were removed from the front and back of the house and the west facade received a full porch. At the same time a two story frame kitchen wing was constructed on the south side of the house. In a turn-of-the-century photograph, in the possession of the family, Mr. Cochran can be seen sitting on the porch with his family.

The house and farm remained in the family, tenanted after 1907, until 1946, when the farm was sold to J. Early and Mary E. Wood from New York City.[20] Prior to their purchase, however, many lots had been sold along the waterfront, beginning in 1931.

Mr. and Mrs. Wood remodeled the old house, upgrading all of the mechanical systems, installing baths, etc. They removed the partition between the hall and parlor and exposed the ceiling joists which had been plastered originally. Chair rail was removed and window trim renewed. On the outside of the house a small six-pane window was installed on each end of the facade to light a lavatory and stair. A small round window was placed above the entry to light the bath. On the east side, overlooking Swantown Creek, the Woods added a two story porch. They also remodeled the kitchen.

The Woods lived in the old house until 1959 when they moved into a modern house nearby and sold the rest of the farm, then consisting of 380 acres to Harry and Helen Heston.[21] The Hestons transferred the property to a limited partnership from which the house and twenty-three acres were later sold to Richard and Joanne Reevie in 1977. The Reevies lavished much care and attention on the house and property before selling it to the present owners.[22]   K-153

1. Patents.
2. Cecil County Land Records.
3. Land Records, Lib. JS, fol. 58.
4. Land Records, Lib. JS, fol. 554.
5. Land Records, Lib. JS 16, fol. 14.
6. Wills, Lib. 1, fol. 391.
7. Inventories, Lib. 3, fol. 404, Lib. 3, fol. 402, 459.
   Isaac's inventory totaled @53.19.3 3/4 and Nicholas' inventory amounted to @178.17.5 plus the crops of the following year for an additional @43.3.0 3/4.
8. Certificate.
9. Wills, Lib. 2, fol. 239.

10. Wills, Lib. 5, fol. 126.
11. Inventories, Lib. 7, fol. 143.
12. Journal and Letter of Philip Vickers Fithian, 1773-1774: A Plantation Tutor of the Old Dominion. Edited by Hunter Dickenson Farish, Colonial Williamsburg, Inc., 1943, pp. 131, 132. Fithian may have known Rachel from when he was at College in Princeton, Rachel's home town. "Miss Ryley" was William's sister Araminta who had received a @300 bequest from her father. Then William died and the inventory of

his personal estate was appraised, in 1782, "Araminta Bantham" was listed as next of kin. Apparently, she had married John Bantham, soon after Fithian's visit.
13. Wills, Lib. 7, fol. 12.
14. Guardian Bonds, Lib. 1, fol. 277.
14. Guardian Bonds, Lib. 2, fol. 277.
15. Guardian Bonds, Lib. 2, fol. 28.
16. Land Records, Lib. TW 1, fol. 464.
17. Land Records, Lib. TW 1, fol.

538.
18. Land Records, Lib. JNG 4, fol. 342.
19. Land Records, Lib. JNG 12, fol. 46.
20. Land Records, Lib. RAS 41, fol. 394.
21. Land Records, Lib. WHG 60, fol. 511.
22. Land Records, Lib. EHP 14, fol. 810. Col. and Mrs. Reevie are responsible for the majority of the research on the farm which they have named Heritage Farm.

Dullam's Folly

Near Massey
c. 1760

THE FIRST RECORD IN THE COUNTY COURTHOUSE OF PHILIP Davis owning Dullam's Folly is a land division of 1727.[1] In his will probated in 1740, Philip bequeathed 100 acres of Dullam's Folly to his son Samuel Davis. The first bequest, however, was Blackhal's Hermitage, near Chestertown, to his eldest son, Philip. It is probable that he lived near Chestertown.[2]

Samuel Davis was the same man who was contracted to underpin the Chapel at Shrewsbury Parish in 1745 (near Massey's Crossroads). He was church warden in 1748 and again in 1757. About the time he was vestryman for the first time, Davis built his dwelling on part of Dullam's Folly which his father had left to him.[3]

It was a one-and-a-half-story, hall-parlor plan brick house with principal facade laid in Flemish bond with glazed headers above a champhered water table—a superbly uniform accomplishment. The central door was set in a wide frame and had six panels, with the center panels being square. Flanking the entrance were two 9/9 sash windows with paneled shutters. Each of the openings had segmental arches. The rear facade had the same arrangement, but the brickwork was common bond and the arches were made of a row of vertical headers.

The gables had a moderately steep pitch. The northeast gable had a fireplace within and the southwest had a fireplace that was mostly outside the walls. The outline of an early service wing indicates a roof pitch about the same as the main house, but lower on the southwest gable. Since the gables had no windows, it is safe to assume that the second floor was lighted by dormers only. It would have been very similar to Long Meadow Farm south of Massey.

Beneath the main floor there was a full basement with access from the northeast gable. It was divided into the same spaces as above by a brick partition which extended to the second floor. The northeast chimney had a large deep semicircular arch that supported not only the fireplace above, but also the hearth. Between the two rooms there was a lattice door.

On the first floor, the hall was trimmed out in good eighteenth century fashion. The

northeast wall on which the fireplace was located was fully paneled. To the east of the fireplace there was an enclosed stair and to the west, an arched cabinet. The fireplace itself was large and its arched opening was surrounded by a bolection molding with two small panels which reflected the arch as well. The striking similarities in craftsmanship here to the woodwork found at the Adventure, Partner's Addition and Rose Hill raises the possibility that they were in fact the product of the same craftsmen.

The parlor was finished with a plainer two-part cornice in contrast to the five piece cornice of the hall. The chair rail was higher than the window sills and jogged down to continue across the edge of the sill. The fireplace was finished with only a mantel or molding around its opening. Southwest of the fireplace there was a door to the service wing.

On the second story there was a corridor and two chambers, the smaller one having a fireplace.

Samuel Davis II, grandson of Philip, died in 1790 having two daughters, Frances and Tabitha (the latter being named after his mother) and one son, Samuel. Hannah, his wife and his son-in-law, Nathan N. Wright were executors.[4] The inventory taken in December of 1790 included 28 slaves, lots of silver and 17 horses, along with a copy of *"Bacon's Laws"*, an indication of his profession. The total personal property amounted to £1428.8.5.[5]

Samuel Davis III, an attorney in Kent County, mortgaged his inheritance, totaling 460 acres, in 1799,[6] but defaulted in payment thereof. It was sold by order of the Chancery Court in 1811, to Dr. George Gillasspy, a physician who had purchased the mortgage in 1806.[7] In 1826 Dr.

Dullam's Folly, c. 1760. The hall paneling, contained the stair to the second story.

Dullam's Folly, c. 1760. Samuel Davis built the original one-and-a-half story structure. The second story was probably added during the ownership of Commodore Jacob Jones. M. Bourne photographs, 1964

Gillasspy sold 254 acres of the farm to Jacob Jones of Washington, D. C. [8]

Jones was to establish himself at the Anchorage, a farm north of Cecilton, which he improved after he had distinguished himself in the Navy. His widow and son sold Dullam's Folly in 1867 to John Benson,[9] a farmer, who appears on the 1877 Atlas.

In the 1883 deed, the proceeds of the sale were to be used to purchase a farm in Queen Annes County for John A. Benson, son of the aforesaid John. In that year, the farm was purchased by Samuel Cacy.[10] Cacy died intestate and it descended to his children who sold it in 1900 to Isaac Gibbs.[11] In 1927 Dullam's Folly was purchased by the grandparents of the present owners.[12]

K-157

1. Land Records, Lib. JS 23, fol. 124.
2. Wills, Lib. 2, fol. 141.
3. DeProspo, p. 67, 205, 209.
4. Wills, Lib. 7, fol. 294.
5. Inventories, Lib. 9, fol. 207.
6. Land Records, Lib. TW 1, fol. 385.
7. Land Records, Lib. TW 3, fol. 477.
   Land Records, Lib. BC 6, fol. 505.
8. Land Records, Lib. TW 4, fol. 845.
9. Land Records, Lib. JKH 6, fol. 413, 509.
10. Land Records, Lib. SB 5, fol. 293.
11. Land Records, Lib. JTD 3, fol. 131.
12. Land Records, Lib. RRA 10, fol. 357.

Presbyterian Church Site

Georgetown
c. 1760

WHEN GEORGETOWN WAS FIRST laid out in 1736, Gideon Pearce, the owner and developer of Colchester, deeded Lot. No. 77 for the purpose of building a Presbyterian Meeting House.[1] In addition to the land, he gave the congregation:

" ... the timber for framing for a house which is to be built upon the said lott."[2]

The land records are quiet after 1736, except for the purchase of Lot. No. 100 in Chestertown for the same purpose. If buildings were constructed on either lot, there is no specific mentioning of their construction in the records for the years immediately following. However, in November 1761 a notice was placed in the Maryland Gazette regarding a lottery sponsored by the Presbyterian Church whose purpose it was to raise funds for the construction/completion of two brick meeting houses, one in Chestertown and the other in Georgetown.

Westminster Presbyterian Church, Georgetown. The third church built on the site since 1736. It was demolished in 1941. c. 1920 photograph; Collection of Merrick Huyett.

SCHEME OF A LOTTERY

The Members of the Presbyterian Congregation in Kent County, Maryland, find themselves under the Necessity of solliciting the Favour and Assistance of the Public in the Way, in order to enable them to compleat and finish their two Meeting-Houses now building, and also to purchase a Parsonage or Glebe: that they may be enabled, with Decency, to worship GOD, and in a becoming Manner to support a Gospel Minister among them, according to their own Persuasion ...

The Drawing will begin at George-Town, the Fourth Tuesday in November next ... or sooner, if sooner full. The Prizes will be published in the Maryland and Pennsylvania Gazettes ...

The following Persons are appointed Managers, viz. John Hepburn, Esq. Messrs. William Rasin, Dennis Dulany, James Louttit, Charles Gordon, John Maxwell, James Pearce, John Schaw, James Harrison (Susquehanna Ferry), Hugh Wallis, and John McDuff ...

TICKETS are now selling by the Managers ... and by ... Messieurs Thomas Ringgold, and Thomas Smith, in Chestertown ... .'[3]

Some 60 years later, a letter written by Dr. Edward Scott indicates that the Presbyterian Meeting House at Georgetown had survived the burning of the village by the British in 1812.[4] And almost 50 years later, the "Old Presbyterian Church" is indicated on Martenet's Map. Within the decade, however, church records indicate that the buildings in both Chestertown and Georgetown were in such a state of disrepair that there was a desire to replace both with new brick meeting houses.[5]

In 1871, reorganized under the name of Westminster, the congregation built a new church on the same site. The new frame church, while a basic meeting house with a central gable tower, was built in a combination of styles, having elements of Gothic, Georgian and Stick Styles. It was a significant statement of taste, but like its predecessor, it too watched the congregation decline in numbers to such an extent that the building was abandoned in 1934 and demolished in 1941.   K-583

1. Land Records, Lib. JS 18, fol. 253.
2. Ibid.
3. Maryland Gazette, November 12, 1761.
4. Research supplied by Marge Fallaw.
5. Ibid.

Dunkan's Folly

Near Worton
c. 1760

Dunkan's Folly was the product of a resurvey of part of Worth's Folly executed for George Dunkan in 1719. By 1783, his son, James Dunkan (born in 1727) is listed as owner of 192 acres of Worth's Folly in the Tax Assessment of that year. Further description of his holdings lists: *"2 brick dwellings, kitchen, corn and meat houses and stable."* One of the brick houses was undoubtedly the building remaining on the farm today.[1]

Which one of the Dunkans actually built the house is a question for further research, but it appears to date from the third quarter of the eighteenth century. In form it is similar to Caulk's Field (1743) and to some extent the exterior details are similar as well, i. e. the facade is laid in Flemish bond with glazed headers and the first floor and basement windows have segmental arches. It is like Dullams's Folly in the respect that its chimney on the west gable is on its exterior. Interior woodwork, however, appears to date from the post-Revolutionary period. These apparently conflicting signs may be an indication of a house which was completed over a number of years—a frequent occurrence in Kent County.

A feature which is unique to this house and its neighbor, Worth's Folly, is the location of the attic stair. It was built in the center of the house instead of above the corner stair. The location precluded installing a center window on the second story of the north facade.

The kitchen wing had exposed and beaded ceiling joists and there were fireplaces in both the kitchen and the adjoining room of the wing. There was an enclosed stair to the rooms on the second floor. The fenestration of the kitchen wing is different than most. The kitchen had a center door with flanking windows and the other room has one door and one window. The plan is somewhat similar to Thornton.

Because the kitchen wing has three walls abutting the main house, it is obvious that it was built at a later date. The brick work, however, is relatively similar which indicates that it was probably added no more than 20 years after the initial construction of the house.

In the early nineteenth century, Dunkan's Folly was the property of John and Deborah Turner. Thereafter it was referred to as the

"Turner Farm." In John Turner's will of 1838, he left it to his wife and after her demise it was to go to his nephew, Thomas Owen Edwards, son of his sister Mary Edwards.[2] In 1864 Deborah sold her interest to John T. Edwards of Allegany County.[3] Thereafter it was owned by members of the Nowland, Fenimore and Chapman families.[4] Since 1938 the house has been occupied by tenants.   K-107

1. Kent County Tax Assessment.
2. Wills, Lib. JFB 1, fol. 71.
3. Land Records, Lib. JKH 4, fol. 204.
4. Pinpointing the early tract name and esurvey was supplied by Carolyn Cooper.

Dunkan's Folly c. 1760.
Probably built for James
Dunkan, a member of the
nearby Cecil Quaker
Meeting.
C. Engstrom
photograph, 1977.

Dunkan's Folly, c. 1760.
Since 1977 the house has
been rehabilitated, re-
vealing the original Flem-
ish bond with glazed
headers. Michael C.
Wootton, 1996.

Brice Mill Farm

Near Chestertown
c. 1761

BRICE MILL FARM IS LOCATED ON THE UPPER REACHES OF the east branch of Langford Creek on land that was called Mill Ford. Matthias Harris was the owner of the property prior to 1752 when it was purchased by Daniel Perkins, Jr.[1] Perkins was the son of Daniel Perkins who had established a saw mill, grist mill and fulling mill on Morgan Creek in the early eighteenth century.[2] Apparently Daniel, Jr. prospered at the new mill, for he purchased 13 acres of Wheatfield on the west side of the mill pond in 1765, along with two seats at St. Paul's Church.[3] He died only three years later with the instructions that the properties were to be sold at public auction under the direction of *"my Friends Thomas Ringgold and William Ringgold ... ."*[4]

The property was purchased by the Ringgolds' cousin, Thomas Smyth in 1769, but was later sold back to Daniel Perkins III in 1781, including 284 acres of Millford and 15 acres of Wheatfield, and including the *"Grist Mill or Water Mill."*[5]

The buildings which remain on the property today are largely the product of

Brice Mill Farm, built for Daniel Perkins, Jr. and remodeled by his son who was a miller and planter. The house was enlarged and remodeled around 1930.

Brice Mill Farm, c. 1761. Rear facade had no central entrance. Michael Bourne photographs, 1995

Daniel Perkins III and include a brick house, brick stable, and the foundation of the former mill. The house, when built, was a two-bay, two-story structure with enclosed gable-end chimneys and a central entrance. The brickwork is irregular, looking as though part of an earlier building was included in the new. It apparently had no wing originally, as there is a fireplace in the basement. The arrangement of the house was a standard hall-parlor plan, but the rear facade had no central entrance, indicating the probable location of an original stair between the rooms.

South of the house, a brick stable was built for the horses. It was a simple brick structure with gable-end doors flanked by two long slits in the walls for ventilation. Beyond the stable, south of the mill dam was the mill, a structure not much larger than the stable.

Daniel Perkins III was even more prosperous than his father had been, increasing his land acquisitions with the purchase of more of Wheatfield and the Garnett property, Cedar Hill, both in 1800.[6] He died around 1826 and bequeathed the family properties to his children, who sold Cedar Hill the following year.[7] The chil-

Brice Mill Farm. Eighteenth century brick stable stands near the ruined foundation of the old Mill. Michael Bourne photograph, 1995.

Gilpin's Mill

Millington
c. 1762

dren, however, kept the family farm, even though they lived in Chestertown. They leased the mill to James F. Wilkins in 1843[8] and finally sold it to John W. Jones in 1855, reserving the graveyard.[9] Jones is listed on the 1860 Martenet Map. Sarah, Eliza and Caroline Perkins are buried in the family graveyard between the house and the mill pond.

In 1865 Jones sold the farm to Benjamin F. Beck who resided at Stephney Farm on Broad Neck.[10] It is Beck's name which appears in the 1877 Atlas. In 1882, Beck sold the 160 acre property to John Brice for whom the property is named.[11] After his death in 1900, the property was acquired by his son Joseph Brice, who continued to operate the mill until it burned around 1910. Thereafter, Joseph moved to Chestertown and the mill was never rebuilt. He sold the property in 1930 to S. Arthur Eastburn.[12]

The Eastburns were responsible for adding the current kitchen wing, remodeling the stable and building a new dairy barn. Between 1937 and 1966 there were six owners of the farm. In 1966, the parents of the present owner purchased the farm, some of which they later sold.[13]

Brice Mill farm stands today as a reminder that the Perkins family was important to Kent County by establishing not just one, but two mills.   K-96

THE MOST NOTABLE LANDMARK IN MILLINGTON IS THE OLD brick mill which stands at the edge of the bridge over the waters of the upper Chester River. Thomas Gilpin, a Philadelphia merchant, took out a writ of ad quod damnum on Cypress Branch, a northerly branch of the Chester River on January 8, 1762.[1] The dammed water would cover land that he and Daniel Massey owned northeast of the proposed mill site. Two years later, an exchange of land between the two resolved the situation caused by the writ. In essence, Massey was paid back for those lands condemned.[2]

In the Tax Assessment of 1783, Gilpin's widow, Lydia, was taxed on:

"2 Grist Mills fulling Do
and Saw Mill
Brick two story House
Framed Do & some other Do." [3]

Whether or not the brick mill was in existence at the time of the Tax Assessment is not mentioned in contemporary records. It is known that the Gilpins lived in Philadelphia and leased the mill to various operators during their long ownership. Willson & Hooper are mentioned in a deed to an adjoining property in 1793.[4] Justice's Mill is mentioned on a map of 1795.

After Gilpin's death, the land stayed in the ownership of his widow who sub-

Gilpin's Mill interior with late nineteenth century machinery. C. Engstrom photograph, 1977

1. Land Records, Lib. JS 27, fol. 241.
2. Wills, Lib. 3, fol. 36.
3. Land Records, Lib. DD 2, fol. 120.
4. Wills, Lib. 4, fol. 325.
5. Land Records, Lib. EF 6, fol. 22.
6. Land Records, Lib. TW 1, fol. 343; fol. 487.
7. Land Records, Lib. JNG 4, fol. 83.
8. Land Records, Lib. JNG 9, fol. 150; fol. 152.
9. Land Records, Lib. JFG 2, fol. 555.
10. Land Records, Lib. JKH 4, fol. 611.
11. Land Records, Lib. SB 3, fol. 481.
12. Land Records, Lib. JTD 14, fol. 331; Lib. RAS 5, fol. 308.
13. Land Records, Lib. EHP 16, fol. 57.

Gilpin's Mill was built by Thomas Gilpin after taking out a writ of ad quod dammum on Cypress Branch, but the mill was built on the edge of Chester River. C. Engstrom photograph, 1977.

Gilpin's Mill, Millington. Millstone with the dates the mill was in operation. Shirley Hunt photograph, 1996.

Gilpin's Mill overshot wheel adjacent the mill. Shirley Hunt photograph, 1996.

sequently sold several lots in the southeast sector of the town. In a deed dated 1783, the village is referred as *"Gilpinton,"* but the remainder refer to it as either *"head of Chester"* or *"Bridgetown."*[5]

In 1806, Thomas Seegar of Queen Annes County made an agreement to purchase: *"a certain Brick Mill, Brick dwelling and sundry lands, meadows, mill ponds, mill races, et cetera … "* from Joshua and Thomas Gilpin, Lydia Gilpin's sons. The deed was recorded only when Seegar made an agreement to sell it to William Farrell in 1813.[6]

Farrell defaulted in his mortgage payments to Seegar and the property was sold Samuel and Nathaniel Cacy of Queen Annes County in 1821.[7] Bequeathed to J. E. Cacy in 1834, it is his name which appears on the Martenet Map of 1860. After J. E. Cacy's death, it was sold to John Hanna who in turn sold it to John Wesley Jarman in 1866. The description in this deed is nearly identical to that found in the deed of 1806.

In 1872 the mill suffered a fire, but was put back in operation as Jarman advertised in the 1877 Atlas:

"J. W. Jarman, Proprietor of Millington Merchant Mills, Manufacturer of Finest Brands of Flour, Meal, &c."[9]

Between 1889 and 1892, the mill was owned by William Reese who sold it to Edwin W. Spear.[10] Spear was probably one of the six children of James Spear who owned farms north of Millington in the late nineteenth century. In 1905, James E. Higman purchased the mill and had his sons John and Harry manage the operation.[11] By this time, the original 16 acres had been reduced to 10½, which is shown on a plat of the property. The other portion had been sold after the railroad purchased a parcel in 1869.

In 1946, John Higman sold the property to J. Karl Bauer, who later sold it to Robert O'Dell. O'Dell was the last operator of the historic mill before moving his expanded operation to the edge of town, near the old pond. The mill remains well tended and possesses some of the machinery it had acquired over the years.

K-175

1. John McGrain, The Molinography of Kent County, 1971. (This list of the mills of Kent County is the basis for this history of Gilpin Mill.)
2. Land Records, Lib. DD 1, fol. 490.
3. Kent County Tax Assessment, 1793, Morgans Creek and Lower South Sassafras Hundreds.
4. Land Records, Lib. BC 3, fol. 527.
5. Land Records, Lib. BC 5, fol. 358.
6. Land Records, Lib. BC 8, fol. 142; Lib BC 7, fol. 417.
7. Land Records, Lib. JNG 1, fol. 159. (The Cacy name appears in the 1822 Tax Assessment.)
8. Land Records, Lib. JKH 5, fol. 472. (" … all that Grist Mill at Millington … with the Brick Dwelling adjacent, together with the frame House near the Brick Dwelling and lying between it and the Brick Mill … ").
9. Lake, Griffing & Stevenson, Atlas of Kent & Queen Annes Counties, First District.
10. Land Records, Lib. SB 13, fol. 88; Lib. SGF 1, fol. 90.
11. Land Records, Lib JTD 12, fol. 163.

The Violet Farm

Near Fairlee
1762

O N THE 15TH OF FEBRUARY 1659, THE MANNOUR OF Stephenheath, a one-thousand acre tract, was patented to Samuel Pensax.[1] While the name of the patented land remained a constant in subsequent deeds, the property was broken up into several farms by the middle of the eighteenth century.

In 1756, *"James Frisby, Gentleman"* purchased 300 acres of the farm from Ann Scott, widow and executrix of Charles Scott.[2] Frisby, born in 1725, was the son of William and Jane Frisby. By the time he purchased the land, his first wife, Sarah Gresham, daughter of John and Hannah Hynson Gresham, had died and he had married again, this time Rebecca Ringgold, daughter of Thomas and Rebecca Wilmer Ringgold.[3] It was with Rebecca that James Frisby first settled on the part of the Mannour of Stephenheath bordering the upper reaches of the west branch of Langford Bay. The Frisbys built the house which survives to this day.

The house which James and Rebecca built is a five-bay, two-and-a-half story, brick building with a one-and-a-half story brick kitchen wing. It is similar to Bungay Hill in form and in the use of glazed headers on the gable which commemorate the date of construction and the initials of the builders (1762 IFR). It also possesses sloped weatherings and withes, features found on Comegys Bight (1769), Springfield (1770), and the Reward (c. 1745). Glazed headers are present on both facades, even on the kitchen, and like many houses in Chestertown, the water table rises up and over the basement windows. The rear, or north facade possesses a central door and a basement door at ground level, a feature also found at Comegys Bight in its original form. Both facades have a three-brick string course and a plaster cornice. The latter can also be found at the Custom House which was owned by Rebecca Frisby's brother, Thomas Ringgold IV.

The plan of the Violet Farm, as it was called in the nineteenth century, is very similar to the Murray House (later purchased by Rebecca's brother and in which her nephew, Thomas Ringgold V was to reside)—a central stairhall with one large room on one side and two rooms on the other. The chief difference in plan between the two is the placement of the fireplace. At the Frisby house it is located on the gable, where in the Murray House it is situated on the back wall. In both houses the two other rooms had corner fireplaces and both were supported on corbelled brick. Since the Murray House stair was removed in 1770, the stairs cannot be compared, but the one installed in the Frisby house is oddly vernacular. It is very wide and has a handsome turned, close-string balustrade. This treatment, however, continues only to the newel

The Violet Farm built in 1762 on part of The Manor of Stephenheath. Both front and rear facades are laid in Flemish bond with glazed headers and possess plaster cove cornices. C. Engstrom photograph, 1977.

The Violet Farm. The initials are those of James and Rebecca (Ringgold) Frisby. Tyler Campbell photograph, 1996.

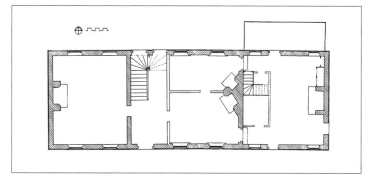

The Violet Farm. The two corner fireplaces are supported on corbeled brick bases. C. Engstrom photograph, 1977.

The Violet Farm first floor plan. Michael Bourne.

The Violet Farm living room c. 1920, was paneled on all four walls, the fireplace and cabinets flanked by naively executed fluted pilasters. Harriet Louisa Skipp Collection.

where the steps revert into a winder to the second floor.

Both first floor rooms open into a kitchen wing. On the east gable of the kitchen there is a large cooking fireplace. An enclosed stair to the servants' room located in the northwest corner of the kitchen is probably an indication that the kitchen was originally divided into pantry and kitchen. This theory is also suggested by the asymmetrical positions of the entry on the south facade.

The second floor plan is similar to the first, with a fourth room over the front entry. The narrow northeast bedroom was unheated and served a dual purpose as corridor to the servants' wing. An enclosed stair leads to an unfinished third floor which is lighted by six original dormers.

The interior of the house was finished in a spectacular manner for 1762. The living room was fully paneled with glazed cabinets flanking the fireplace. The overmantel panel had a unique design with each of the four corners forming a separate triangular panel with the inner side being an arc of a circle. Pilasters flanked the fireplace, the cabinets, door, and windows (with window seats). The bases of the fluted pilasters were naive in design with a recessed panel base and fluted sub-base.

The two rooms across the hall had paneled window seats, baseboard and chair rail and paneling across the diagonal fireplace walls. Paneling was also used in the entry/stairhall and on the second floor.

The large living room chamber had a different wall treatment. The fireplace wall had paneling across the entire expanse with closets flanking the fireplace. There were pilasters only flanking the fireplace of this wall and the two-part bases were both fluted. The windows were treated like those below, but the walls were 'paneled' with plaster, i.e. there were stiles and rails with recessed areas of plaster, a rare treatment similar to some of the work at Fair Hope, a frame house on Stratford Manor and in several houses on the Western Shore.

The Frisbys were obviously people for whom design possessed a certain significance. Not only were they responsible for an aesthetically fine house, but also for the well-planned ground which surrounded it. A large rectangular grass terrace on the south side of the residence can still be traced. Similar terracing can be found at Rose Hill, Trumpington and the Smith-Ringgold House in Chestertown.

Unfortunately for James, his second wife, Rebecca, died only a few years after the house was finished. Together, they had produced four children. Their first child, James, was committed to the care of the Pennsylvania Hospital before 1790 (his brother William asked his widow to pay half of James' care in his will).[4] Their fourth child, Anna Maria, was to marry John Rowles and build Airy Hill.

When James Frisby married a third time it was to Margaret Moore, daughter of James Moore of Arcadia. Together they built Hinchingham on the Bay in 1774 and probably resided there. James and Margaret produced two children, Sarah and Margaret. In 1777, after Margaret's death, James married, one last time, Ann Wilmer, daughter of William and Rose Wilmer and together they had another four children.[5]

In 1783, James Frisby owned 1674 acres of Kent County farmland. The tax assessment of that year lists nine white inhabitants living on the home farm, referred to as *"Stephen Heath Manor."* Frisby owned 139 ounces of plate and was assessed £61 on his total worth of £4880.[6]

By the time of his death in 1807, the plantation was referred to as *"Stephney Heath Manor"* in Frisby's will.[7] To his daughters, Margaret, Mary and Rebecca, he left the plantations, with over 700 acres. When Samuel Beck

The Violet Farm living room c. 1920, had paneled window seats flanked by pilasters, the most richly decorated room in Kent County from the 1760s. It was sold to H. F. duPont in the 1920s, who installed it in his Southampton Long Island home called Chestertown House. Harriett Louise Skipp Collection.

The Violet Farm principal bedroom c. 1920 was also paneled. The fireplace was flanked by closets which were lighted by small windows below the glazed date and initials of the builders. Harriett Louisa Skipp Collection.

The Violet Farm, had a single flat terrace in front of the house. Tyler Campbell photograph, 1996.

and Robert Dunn assessed his personal estate, he owned 38 slaves, 9 beds and several pieces of silver including a silver teapot, totaling $9,508.54. At the sale which followed, $3,578.30 of the property was sold, the proceeds being distributed to his children.[8]

After James Frisby's death, Dr. Morgan Brown and his wife, Margaret Frisby purchased her siblings' shares. Dr. Brown was a prominent physician in Kent County. It is not known if he and Margaret lived at the Violet Farm, but from the wording in his will, it seems probable.[9]

Violet Farm passed first to Dr. Brown's son, James F. Brown, before it was bequeathed just five years later to James' wife, Ann.[10] In the 1852 Tax Assessment, the following entry can be found:

> *"Brown Mrs. Ann*
> *Lands Violet Farm 200 acres*
> *Brick House & other Buildings*
> *in good repair. Formerly to*
> *Dr. Morgan Brown etc."*

After Ann E. Brown died in 1857, Richard Hynson, attorney, was appointed to sell her real estate. He sold Violet Farm to Alexander Willson in 1859, but the deed was not recorded. On the 1860 Map, Willson appears as owner and the wharf is referred to as *"Brown's Landing."* Apparently Willson mortgaged his farm to Richard Hynson, but defaulted on the payments. Richard Hynson then became the owner of the Violet Farm, though the date is uncertain. The 1877 Atlas does not help to pinpoint this transition since the house was omitted from the map, even though the road to the landing was dotted in.

Richard Hynson bequeathed everything he owned in 1893 to his wife Carolene,[11] who apparently was a very capable manager. After his death, the inventory of his estate included the contents of his office on Court Street, his horses, carriages, sleigh, and the produce from his six farms.[12] From the inventory it is not possible to determine who the tenant was on the Violet Farm.

In Carolene's will, written in 1908 and probated in 1917, the tenant on the Violet Farm was C. M. Brown, possibly a relative of the preceding owners. Since her daughter, Augusta E. Slay, who was a beneficiary in the will, died before 1917, Carolene bequeathed the Violet Farm to her grandchildren, Mary and R. Hynson Rogers.[13] Shortly thereafter R. Hynson Rogers purchased Mary's part of the farm.[14] It was Mr. Rogers who sold most of the interior of the house to Henry Francis duPont in the late 1920s.[15] Since then the house has continued to be tenanted. When Mr. Rogers died, he, like his grandmother, skipped a generation and left the farm to his grandson, the present owner.

Sadly, the house has suffered lack of care for several years and is well on its way to dereliction. If the Violet Farm were to receive the care and respect its history warrants, a great piece of Kent County's architectural history could be preserved.   K-97

1. Patents, Lib. 4, fol. 528.
2. Land Records, Lib. JS 28, fol. 342.
3. Maryland Genealogies, Vol. I, Genealogical Publishing Co., Inc., 1980, p. 461.
4. Wills, Lib. 7, fol. 274.
5. Maryland Genealogies, Vol. I.
6. 1783 Tax Assessment, Lower Langford Bay Hundred, James Frisby.
7. Wills, Lib. 8, fol. 366.
8. Inventories, Lib. 12, fol. 238.
9. Wills, Lib. JFB 1, fol. 92.
10. Ibid, p. 225.
11. Wills, Lib. TRS 1, fol. 40.
12. Inventories, Lib. JCS a, fol. 561.
13. Wills, Lib. JRC 1, fol. 294.
14. Land Records, Lib. APR 6, fol. 369.
15. The elements of paneling were reworked and installed at "Chestertown House," duPont's summer home in Southampton, New York. The house has since been demolished.

Deptford

Near Chesterville
1764

NEAR THE HEAD OF NEW BRIDGE BRANCH, A 300 ACRE tract called Deptford was surveyed in 1724 for William Comegys and John Tennant. One year later, Tennant became the sole owner when Comegys sold his interest to him. During a fifteen year period, the property was transferred to and from Edmund Huff, a Philadelphia merchant, three times.[1] Tennant died in the 1740s, after which time Deptford passed to his son John.[2] It was John and his wife Elizabeth who constructed the brick house, which in its original form had a gambrel roof. Using glazed headers, they placed their initials and the date 1764 in the west gable wall.

When first completed the house had a hall-parlor plan with the hall on the west end. Both rooms on the first floor had one large window on the north and south walls each. Like the Plains, built around the same time, the exterior was laid completely in Flemish bond with glazed headers above a molded water table which jogged up and over the basement windows.

Apparently Tennant predeceased his wife, for in 1783, Elizabeth Huff was listed as the owner of the 300 acre farm

Deptford, originally a gambrel roof house constructed for John and Elizabeth Tennant in 1764. The date and initials are still visible on the west gable. M. L. Fritz photograph, 1979.

with brick house.[3] It later passed into the hands of her son James Tennant. In the first decade of the nineteenth century, James acquired a 67 acre parcel of Killingsworthmore which adjoined Deptford on the west.[4] James died c. 1846 and bequeathed the farm to William Rayne. It was in possession of the Wallis family between 1850 and 1856,[5] after which time it was owned by John Hurlock and family until 1883.[6]

It was most likely during the ownership of Lewin J. Usilton, after 1883, that the house was completely altered into what has come down to the present day.[7] His remodeling involved the removal of the gambrel roof, raising of the walls to two full stories and the installation of a gable in the center of a new *A* roof. It was fitted with a front porch facing north over the road, and a bay window on the south. A three-bay, two-story kitchen wing was also constructed on the east gable.

In several of the land records, the original tract name was corrupted to *"Dedford"* or *"Deadford"* and after 1910, the name *"Hibernia"*, as well as *"Hurlock Farm"* and *"Tenant Farm"* is used.

Other twentieth century owners have included members of the Bennett, VanDyke and Fox families, the last two owning the farm for 84 out of 95 years.   K-190

1. Rent Rolls, Lib. 5, fol. 16.
2. Wills, Lib. 2, fol. 228.
3. 1783 Tax Assessment.
4. Land Records, Lib. WS 2, fol. 30.
5. Land Records, Lib. JR 2, fol. 325.
6. Land Records, Lib. JFG 4, fol. 104.
7. Land Records, Lib. SB 5, fol. 94.

The John Lorain House, Chestertown was constructed in the decade of the 1760s with a gambrel roof. It is now a duplex. Michael C. Wootton photograph 1996.

In 1782 when business was beginning to wane in Chestertown, John Lorain advertised his house and store in Baltimore:

> TO BE SOLD
> A Lot of Ground, situate in ChesterTown Maryland, with buildings thereon, consisting of a good and roomy dwelling house, the storehouse adjoining, with other accessory buildings; the situation pleasant, and equal to any in the place for mercantile business.
> *John Lorain*[4]

Lorain House

High Street, Chestertown
c. 1765

Due to the many alterations this house has experienced, coupled with only vague references to any edifice existing on Lot No. 7 in the earliest deeds, pinpointing the exact date of its original construction is difficult.

Thomas Lorain, mariner, purchased Lot No. 7 from William Wilmer in 1765 for the sum of £2501—an amount which could be indicative of substantial improvements. However, when William Wilmer inherited the lot, at the time of his father's death (Simon), there is reference only to the storehouse.[2]

It is not until 1776 when Lorain's son John leased 50' from the neighboring lot belonging to Sarah Cruikshank that reference is made to a building constructed during Thomas Lorain's ownership.[3] Considering this reference and a number of architectural details in the house typical of the period, the house most likely dates from the third quarter of the eighteenth century and was certainly built by the Lorain family.

The house and store were not sold, however, until fourteen years later. It was in 1796 that the property was sold to William McKenny, a Queen Annes County gentleman who owned other properties in town as well.

As there is very little change in the sale price before the latter half of the nineteenth century, it is likely that Joshua Thomas Twilley who owned the house from 1864–1912 was responsible for its remodeling into a two-and-a-half-story, five-bay house.

During a recent remodeling the remains of a gambrel roof were found on the northwest end of the building suggesting that Thomas or John Lorain had constructed a framed one-and-a-half-story dwelling originally. The northwest chimney remains from that period and possesses a wide arch in the basement and a large elliptical arched fireplace on the first floor. All of the other finishes appear to date from the Twilley occupancy.

Since 1912, the property has been two separate residences with service wings to the rear.   K-343

1. Land Records, Lib. DD 2, fol. 393.
2. Wills, Lib. 2, fol. 58.
3. Land Records, Lib. DD 5, fol. 238.
4. Maryland Journal and Baltimore Advertiser, Tuesday, October 8, 1782 and October 29, 1782.

The Plains

Near Fairlee
c. 1766

The Plains was built by John Ringgold (d. 1780), son and heir of James Ringgold (d. 1766). It originally had a gambrel roof.

The Plains was enlarged by Thomas Carvill, grandson of the builder. The rear wing was added in the early twentieth century. Tyler Campbell photographs, 1996.

JOHN RINGGOLD WAS BEQUEATHED PART OF THE Plains by his father James in 1766. He is the likely builder of the house which stands on the property today. In its original form the house was a one-and-a-half-story gambrel roof structure, built of brick and laid in Flemish bond with glazed headers. The plan was a simple hall-parlor plan. Like many houses in Chestertown, its water table jogged above the basement windows. These windows, as well as those of the first floor and the entry were topped by segmental arches and the west gable had a decorative brick pattern running along the pitch of the roof. Two small windows flanked the chimney which was built within the west wall. On the opposite gable there was a kitchen wing, probably made of frame or log.

The entry opened into the hall and on its west wall, beside the fireplace, a winder stair was partially enclosed behind a paneled wall. The windows here had splayed jambs and it is likely that there was originally a bold cornice, as well as chair rail and baseboard. The parlor also had a fireplace and a door to its south side which led to the kitchen wing.

John Ringgold and his wife had only one child, Ann, who married John Carvill III. Upon her father's death in 1780, Ann inherited the Plains.[1] In her will, written that same year, she directed that her mother continue to live at the Plains and that after her own death, it was to become the property of her son, Thomas Carvill. Ann lived until 1801.[2] Thomas, as a citizen of Kent County, fought at the Battle of Caulk's Field. He married Mary Ringgold, his second cousin and had several children. In 1835, after the death of their father, the Carvill children sold 197 acres to Bartus Trew of Providence Plantation.[3] Within four years, Trew died without having paid off the mortgage, and the Carvill heirs, Mary Freeman and Harriett Carvill were subsequently in a position to sell the farm again—this time to Edward Ringgold, a relative.[4]

It was most likely during the ownership of Thomas Carvill that the original house was altered. The remodeling involved the removal of the gambrel roof and the heightening of the brick walls to two-and-a-half stories. The entire main block was then covered with a steeply pitched *A* roof. It was this house which Edward Ringgold purchased in 1839.

When Ringgold died in 1854, the farm passed on to his son John Fletcher Ringgold and it is his name which appears on Martenet's Map of 1860.[5] Before the Atlas was printed in 1877, however, John had died and the farm was in the next generation of the Ringgold family (John Edward Ringgold).[6]

In 1880, Charles H. Baker was a trustee in the sale of John Ringgold's real estate. He sold the farm to William Vannort who lived on Front Street in Chestertown and who owned several other farms in Kent County.[7] This farm has remained in the same family ever since, continually being used as a tenant farm. In the early twentieth century, a large frame wing was added behind the parlor and the old kitchen was removed. In the late 1920s, the paneling was sold to Henry Francis duPont, who incorporated it into his summer house in Southampton, New York.   K-83

1. Schoch, Mildred C. Inggold in America.
2. Wills, Lib. 8, fol. 114.
3. Land Records, Lib. JNG 4, fol. 130.
4. Land Records, Lib. JNG 6, fol. 151.
5. Wills, Lib. JF 1, fol. 23.
6. Wills, Lib. JF 1, fol. 34.
7. Land Records, Lib. SB 1, fol. 173.

Emmanuel Episcopal Church

High Street, Chestertown
1768

WHEN CHESTERTOWN WAS LAID OUT IN 1706, IT WAS within the area which made up St. Paul's Parish. How soon thereafter a chapel was built on the public lands of the Courthouse has not been definitely determined, but in 1720 a new Chapel of Ease was erected to replace the old one. By 1766, the county population had grown to such an extent that a group of people from both Shrewsbury and St. Paul's parishes petitioned the General Assembly for the creation of a new parish between the two old parishes that had been established in 1692.

In order to construct the new Parish Church, the inhabitants of both previous parishes were taxed 100,000 pounds of tobacco, with 80,000 pounds of tobacco to be collected as the work progressed. It took 130,000 pounds of tobacco for the construction of the new parish church. An allocation of 50,000 pounds of tobacco was set aside for an addition to the Chapel of Ease in Chester Town.[1]

The vestry and inhabitants of Chestertown, however, decided that a new church would better fill their needs.

" ... *and whereas upon inspection into the said Church, the Vestry and Inhabitants of Chester Town, and other the Parishioners are of Opinion, that the said sum of Tobacco will not be significant to make an Addition large Enough for the people, that the old parts will soon want. large repairs and that therefore it will be better to Build a large new Chapple Intirely, if Money can be raised for it, making use of the Bricks and Materials of the old Church, as far as they will go, giving the proprietors of the Old Church, seats in the new, as they had in the old, and allowing seats, also in the lower parts of the said Church, as it will be then much larger that the old one with such Addition, as could have been made of the Money. To such other persons, owners of lotts in the said Town and not having pews in the old parts of said Building, and other Freeholders in the said Parish convenient to the said Church and contributing their Proportion to the cost of the said new pews, and as many well Disposed people will with a View to have the said Church large*

Commodious and Sufficient to hold the greatest parts of ye Parishioners, have Voluntarily Subscribed large sums of Money to be paid towards the Building the said Church, and it is thought that with the said Tobacco Raised by Act of Assembly, Money Subscribed, and the sale to the Highest Bidders of such pews exclusive of a Sufficient Common Gallery, that may be made in the Second Story of the Chapple to use of the Freeholders of the Parish as shall not have pews in the lower part of said Church may be built Two Story high and of good and large Dimensions, they therefore agree and enter

on the same on the Register. That with the said Fifty Thousand Pounds of Tobacco the Materials of the Old Church, the Voluntary Subscriptions as Aforesaid and the payment of the Costs of Erecting the Pews in the lower floor as a good and Handsome Brick Chapple Sixty Six Feet long and forty feet wide, two Story high with a Stone Foundation shall be built and Compleated in Chester Town, and they Request Mr. William Ringgold to

Emmanuel Episcopal Church. A classical Georgian meeting house with bellfry atop the roof. The projecting central pavillion with pediment was omitted in the sketch. Drawing from 1860 Martenet Map of Kent County; Jane B. Sprinkle Collection.

Emmanuel Church, Chestertown. The church was completed in 1772 and remodeled in 1880 with the 1905 tower. Michael C. Wootton photograph, 1996.

Emmanuel Church from the west, after the re-modeling of the 1880s, soon after the tower was built (1905) and the hall enlarged. Kent County News collection.

Plaque installed in 1932 commemorating the naming of the Protestant Episcopal Church. Michael C. Wootton photograph, 1996.

purchase Materials and Contracts with workmen to do the same in the Cheapest and best manner, and the Vestry will Confirm all such Contracts as you shall so make ... ." [2]

The above resolution in August was the result of the Vestry previously making arrangement with Charles Tilden, builder of the Parish Church at I. U. to add fifteen feet and twelve pews onto the existing chapel and advertising for workmen in *Jonas Green's Paper* (Maryland Gazette) (May 1767).

The next entry in the Vestry Minutes pertaining to the Chestertown *"Chapple"* is the distribution of the pews five years later, in August of 1772. Neither the contract with William Ringgold, nor the specifications were recorded as had been done at the Parish Church at I. U. The *"Chapple"* was, however, built as outlined in the Vestry resolution quoted above.

It was constructed upon a stone foundation and measured 66 feet long and 40 feet wide. Its five-bay facade and three-bay gables were laid in all header bond, the same bond as used on William Murrey's residence and several other buildings in town, most notably Widehall, built in 1769. The central bay of the facade contained the principal entry which was located in a projecting pavilion and was embellished with a classical pedimented architrave.

From the 1860 Martenet Map, the church appears to have had the same size windows throughout, all with rusticated jack arches except for a Palladian window above the entry. At the corners of the building there were broad pilasters terminating at the cornice, the latter continuing around the gables to form full pediments. Even the minor entrances on the gables appear to have had classical architraves.

It would be fairly safe to assume that the interior was as well finished as the exterior. From the plans recorded in the Vestry Minutes, there were thirty-six pews on the ground floor and thirty-two in the three-sided balcony above. Stairs thereto were located in the north and east corners, both having a pew beneath. The pulpit and altar were located in the center of the northeast facade. It had a barrel-vaulted plaster ceiling.[3]

In 1780, Dr. William Smith, rector of the Parish, called a meeting to convene at the Church in Chestertown at which the name

"Protestant Episcopal Church of the United States of America"

was officially adopted in place of the Anglican Church or the Church of England. This was done because of the ongoing war with England which was not to be resolved until 1783. Two years after this meeting, Dr. Smith initiated the formation of Washington College over which he presided until his return to Philadelphia in 1789.

In 1785 a group of inhabitants of Chestertown purchased an or-

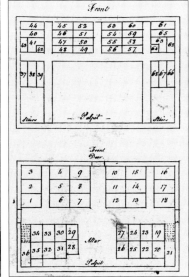

Emmanuel Church, Chestertown. Faux painting adjacent former gallery window, before the 1880 remodeling. Only a small section of the painting exists in the northwest gable above the ceiling.

Pew Plan of the "Chappel in Chester Town" taken from the vestry minutes, August 14, 1772.

Emmanuel Church. Detail of original roof tress. The mortise holes at the bottom of the member held scantling for the arched ceiling.

Emmanuel Church. Detail of joinery on original roof tress.

gan and it was to be placed in *"the vacancy under the bellfry,"* i. e. pews Nos. 66-68. Vacant pews were offered to those who owned pews Nos. 66-68. To this extent Tobias Ashmore, who had received No. 68 from Joseph Garnett, was assigned No. 53.[4]

In 1800 the parish registrar recorded that the *"Churches of the Parish are so out of repair and unprovided with stoves—they cannot be used during winter season … therefore Service will be held at Courthouse once a fortnight and Mr. Dashiell will not preach at I. U. Church til April next."* [5]

With the steady decline in Church attendance and the rise of Methodism, I. U. Church became redundant and the parish church moved to Chestertown. This occurred during the tenure of the Rev. William H. Wilmer around the year 1809.

The single most outstanding change to the Church prior to the major remodeling in the early 1880s was an interior decorating job around the mid-nineteenth century. Only a small amount of that paint remains on the gable above the existing ceiling. This treatment was not to last long as *"the Vestry passed a resolution on May 4, 1880 approving a subscription to raise funds for the building's reconstruction using plans presented to the Vestry by the architect, J. C. Nielsen."* [6]

Mr. Nielsen's plans changed the Georgian meeting house into a Romanesque chapel. His plans called for tall semi-circular headed windows in place of the old double hung sash, removal of the balcony and lowering the roof by twelve feet. This was done without disas-

sembling the trussed structure. Nielsen reoriented the building by closing the High Street entry, building a sanctuary on the southeast gable and installing an entry/vestibule on the opposite end. The interior was then finished with stained dado, the walls plastered and the vaulted ceiling replaced with an *A* shaped board ceiling. The old box pews were removed and replaced with walnut congregational pews. On the east side of the building, a small structure was built to house the new organ. It was during the dedication of the new Church that it was formally given the name, Emmanuel Church.

In 1905, the Romanesque design was enhanced by the construction of a bell tower and adjoining Parish Hall. A larger parish hall was constructed in 1969.

Throughout the period after the remodeling in 1880, minor changes have taken place inside and out, many of which are recorded in the History of Emmanuel Church, written by Fred W. Dumschott in 1972.

In 1990, the Vestry voted to raise funds for a new organ to replace the electronic one installed twenty years before. The committee formed to look into the issue recommended the installation of a tracker action pipe organ made by the firm of Harrison & Harrison of Durham, England. While preparing for its installation, termites were discovered throughout the 1880s floor system. In the process of re-installing the floor system, the chancel and sanctuary were redesigned to conform to the Present Book of Common Prayer.   K-51

1. Dumschott, F., p. 5.
2. Vestry Minutes, 4 August 1767.
3. See Plan and Appendix for owners of pews.
4. Vestry Minutes, June 11, 1785; June 1786.
5. Vestry Minutes, Dec. 1800.
6. Dumschott, p. 13. Rev. Wilmer was one of the sons of Simon Wilmer IV (d. 1798) who owned Stepney adjoining town. He is known for establishing the Virginia Theological Seminary while presiding at St. Paul's Church, Alexandria, and later as the President of William and Mary while presiding at Bruton Parish Church, Williamsburg. One of his holdings was the White Swan Tavern (from 1814-1854).

Comegys Bight

Quaker Neck
1768

COMEGYS BIGHT HOUSE IS NAMED AFTER THE BAY OR *bight* of the Chester River into which the waters of Comegys and Fore Creeks flow. It was erected on a tract called Sewell, patented in 1660 to James Sewell, and later purchased by and re-patented to Cor-

Comegys Bight, 1768. The main elevation faces the bight of Chester River. By the time this photograph was taken, the kitchen had already been heightened about three feet. Maryland State Archives, Don Swan Collection.

Comegys Bight, Quaker Neck. 1768 is clearly visible on the gable, but Edward and Mary Comegys initials were partly concealed when the kitchen was heightened. C. Engstrom photograph, 1977.

nelius Comegys. In the process of acquiring Sewell, Comegys discovered an error in the original survey and eventually acquired 1224 acres which he renamed Utrick after the city of Utrecht in his native Holland.[1]

Cornelius Comegys became a well respected citizen of seventeenth century Kent County, both politically and economically. He worked with other influential citizens of the period—men like Joseph Wickes, Michael Miller, Charles Tilden, Simon Wilmer and others. Though his inventory was not large (£332.9.4) after his death, his land holdings and gifts of land to his children totaled 3340 acres.[2] The inventory sheds light on the configuration of his house, as the items are listed by room. It is clear that Comegys' house had a typical hall-parlor plan, with kitchen and leanto room. *Utrick* was left to Comegys' third wife, Rebecca, for her lifetime, after which it was to go to Edward, their son.[3] Edward Comegys married Mary Thraul at Utrick on October 15, 1737, as recorded in the Quaker records. The birth of their first child (Edward II) was also recorded the following year. When Edward I died in 1761, the plantation was left to his first-born son, and very little was bequeathed to the remaining seven children.

Edward II, grandson of Cornelius, was responsible for erecting the house which continues to stand today. Like Charles and Phoebe Hynson at Bongay and James and Rebecca Frisby at Violet Farm before, Edward and Mary Comegys had the mason install the date (1768) and their initials in the gable above the kitchen roof. There are other similarities to the Hynson and Frisby houses as well. Their chimneys have sloped weatherings at roof level and withes. They are each laid in Flemish bond, though Comegys Bight has no uniform glazed headers. Both Comegys Bight and Violet Farm had a central stairhall with flanking rooms; two rooms on one side, one on the other. The unusual placement of a corner fireplace in the larger room has no parallel in Kent County. When constructed, Comegys Bight had a back entrance to the stairhall with a second entrance at grade level for access to the basement, a feature shared with Violet Farm. In the first one hundred years there were no dormers in the low-pitched *A* roof. About the same time, the fireplace mentioned above was demolished and relocated in the center of the gable.

Comegys Bight, 1768, has the best stair of the three nearby houses, with dated gables. C. Engstrom photograph, 1977.

Comegys Bight, Quaker Neck. When first finished there was an at-grade basement entrance, like the Violet Farm (1762). C. Engstrom photograph, 1977.

Comegys Bight, 1768, with twentieth century additions. Tyler Campbell photograph, 1996.

Of the three houses, Comegys Bight possesses the best stair. It ascends with shallow risers in three flights to the second story and boasts paneled wainscoting on the wall and spandrel and balustrade with turned columnar newels and three rectangular balusters per step. The flanking rooms were most likely finished in a similar manner; however, they have been altered since. Two cabinets in the living room were sold to Henry Francis duPont for his home on Long Island, and the dining room appears to have been reworked around 1800.

In general it is the kitchen wings of older houses that are most frequently changed. In this respect Comegys Bight is no exception. The once ground level kitchen was raised about two and a half feet to be level with the floor of the main house in about 1920-30. Its original entrance was the center of three bays on the river side, the formal entrance to Comegys Bight.

In 1783, Edward Comegys was assessed on 1000 acres, but the assessor used the old name to the tract— Sewell. The *"Brick Dwelling"* was mentioned.[4] Sixty-nine years later, another Edward Comegys was listed as owner of *"Utrick, alias Sewell."*[5] This Edward, born in 1788, was probably the grandson of the builder. By this time, 180 acres had been separated from the original tract and a brick house was constructed to the east of the old house on the Chester River. Edward owned both, totaling 800 acres of the original plantation. In addition to the above, he owned two other farms, New York and Mount Pleasant, the two in excess of 800 acres. Before he died around 1865, Edward had acquired yet another 800 acre tract called Big Fairlee, and the Carvill Hall farm on Fairlee Creek. The 1852 Tax Assessment also listed $33,000 in securities, one of the largest amounts in the District. He probably used his securities to purchase Big Fairlee and Carvill Hall.

By 1877 the same two parts of the home farm were owned by Mrs. M. E. Jones.[6] In Usilton's History of Kent County (1916), Comegys Bight is pictured before the kitchen wing was heightened. It also had a veranda across the river side of the house. H. M. Baker was the owner in 1916.[7] By the time H. C. Forman photographed the house for his first publication in 1934, the kitchen had been changed in both height and length. In the 1940s, however, the house was remodeled and enlarged with pedimented architraves at the doors and elegant brick steps. An extension on the east side of the house nearly doubled its size. Since then, it has seen another remodeling in the early 1980s by the present owners.   K-91

1. Warrants, WC 2, 1679-1681, Lib. 5, fol. 116, 219, 412; Lib. 2, fol. 185.
2. Inventories & Accts, 1708, Lib. 28, fol. 275.
3. Wills, Lib. 1, fol. 92.
4. 1783 Tax Assessment.
5. 1852 Tax Assessment.
6. Lake Griffing Stevenson Atlas.
7. Usilton, Fred, *History of Kent County*.

Widehall

Water Street, Chestertown
1769

SOMETIME PRIOR TO 1769, THOMAS Smyth entered into an agreement with William Granger to buy from him Water Lot No. 16 in Chestertown for the sum of £100.[1] Lacking a deed of record, Smyth petitioned the General Assembly of Maryland in December of 1769 for clear title. In the act granting him such, there is clear indication that he had already begun the construction of the grand brick house known today as Widehall.

"No. 9 An Act to secure to Thomas Smyth the Right in a Lot of Land in Chester Town

Whereas Thomas Smyth of Chester Town in Kent County, Mary Granger Mother of William Granger and the said William Granger have by their Petition to this General Assembly set forth That the said William Granger is seised and Possessed of a certain Lot of Ground lying and being in Chester Town aforesaid known & Distinguished in the Plott of the said Town by the Number sixteen as one of the Water Lots of the said Town which of itself is not of much Value but being Convenient to the said Thomas to erect and build a House on, the said William Granger being now but Twenty Years of Age had with the Advice and Consent of his said Mother agreed and [consented] to sell the same to the same Thomas for the Valuable Consideration of one Hundred Pounds secured to be paid to the said William. In Consequence whereof the said Thomas Smyth hath erected on the said Lot a Large and Valuable Brick House and Kitchen which he was Desirous of finishing and compleating immediately but being unwill-

Widehall 1769. The name for the house was derived from the size of the second story hall. Tyler Campbell photograph, 1994.

Widehall, 1769. Dining room chimney breast is the most original in the house. Flanking cabinets were remodeled in 1938 for the collection of Chinese Export porcelain. Tyler Campbell photograph, 1994.

Opposite: Widehall, 1769, was built on Water Lot No. 16 for merchant Thomas Smyth. Both principal walls were constructed in all header bond. Winants Bros., Inc. photograph, 1967

Widehall, 1769. The street entrance was built with a terrace and clairvoire between it and the street. Its Doric architrave with engaged fluted columns is the best in Kent County. Library of Congress, Historic American Buildings Survey, 1936.

ing to risque so valuable a part of his Property without securing his Title to the said Land which could not be done whilst the said William was under Age the said Petitioners have prayed that an Act of Assembly might pass to enable the said William Granger tho' under Age to convey to the said Thomas Smyth all his the said William Grangers Right Title and Estate in the said Lot of Land in as full and ample Manner as if he was of full Age,

And Whereas Inquiry has been made into the Truth of the ffacts in the said Petition and it appearing that the Price agreed to be given for the said Lott of Ground doth Considerably exceed what the Lotts in the said Town of much Larger Contents have usually been sold it is judged that the said Sale is Advantageous to the said Minor the said Petition is therefore granted so as that the Consideration Money shall be Secured to be paid to the said William if he arrives to full Age and if not to his Heir at Law." [2]

Wideball, 1769. The stair hall is separated from the passage by a series of three arches. Tyler Campbell photograph, 1994.

Thomas Smythe was born in Kent County on April 12, 1730. By 1769 he had begun construction of his house, known today as Wideball. After a long active life, he retired to Trumpington and died there on March 19, 1819 just fourteen days short of his ninetieth birthday. This portrait of Thomas Smythe, done in 1802, hangs in the main entrance ball at Trumpington. Courtesy of Mildred Willson Strong, a descendant.

The house Thomas Smyth built was an ambitious building for its day in Chestertown. There was no attempt to build onto an existing building, as was done later at the Hynson-Ringgold House, a block away, it was instead built from the ground up, possibly employing designs, if not craftsmen themselves from Annapolis or Philadelphia.

To set the house off from the street and also to make the house seem less tall, Smyth built a terrace with retaining wall and clairvoire which had four brick columns with stone finials. The center had a pair of gates and flanking it was a decorative paling between the columns. From the sandstone paved terrace, a second set of sandstone steps ascended to the central entrance with a

classical pedimented Doric architrave with fluted engaged columns.

The two principal walls of the house (northwest and southwest) were laid in all header bond, a uniform treatment found on many Maryland houses, but seldom in combination with rusticated wood window jack arches. For such a bold treatment over the 12/12 windows and the entrance architrave, the single ovolo molded brick watertable was understated. Two dormers were located on the front and back slopes of a hip roof. Its cornice had heavy modillion or mutule blocks.

When the petition for clear title to Water Lot No. 16 was granted, a kitchen was mentioned in the Act. That kitchen was located on the eastern side of the river facade. It was a two story three bay brick building constructed near grade level. Off the gable end of the kitchen there was a square stone smokehouse.

Originally, Thomas Smyth finished the house with the best materials and craftsmanship. Its plan was nearly identical to Henry Pratt's mansion in Queen Anne's County (built about four years before). The main entry opened onto a passage which was separated from the stairhall by a series of three arches, the center one being larger and more finished. A fourth arch separated the front and back halves of the passage. The other three rooms which were entered from the passage were finished in a similar manner—the chimney breasts having Tabernacle overmantels flanked by cabinets, bold chair rail and baseboard on wainscoting, interior window shutters and bold cornice. Each of the rooms, however, varied slightly. For example, the west parlor had window trim with crossettes at the top and rounded consoles at the chair rail, while the south parlor had squared consoles and the dining room had neither.

The west parlor had bead and reel molding on the cornice while the south parlor had none. The dining room had Wall of Troy molding cut on the diagonal and the stairhall had intermittent Wall of Troy cut perpendicular to its face. The dining room was the only room on the first story to have raised paneled dado and the south parlor was the only room to have mahogany used for the top element of the chair rail. Each of the three doors had overdoors to match the modillion cornice of the passage, while the interior overdoors matched the room cornices. The dining room, however, lacked an overdoor, due undoubtedly to the presence of a boxed stair descending from the second story to the kitchen along the passage wall.

Unlike the other three rooms, the dining room had two windows on the northeast wall only, due to the presence of the kitchen wing on the river side. From the dining room there were several steps down to the brick floor of the kitchen wing. In all likelihood, the steps entered a passage to the kitchen. A pantry opened from the passage. The kitchen fireplace was probably like that in the Ringgold House, a wide arched opening with double cranes. On one side of the fireplace was a winder stair to the servants' rooms on the second story.

The main stair was a well-executed piece of workmanship, which ascended on three walls and cantilevered from the upper two. Its railings, fluted newels, turned balusters (three per step), rectangular step ends and half-rail and fluted pilasters on the wall opposite, were all made of mahogany. The bottom of the balustrade had a large volute beginning on a newel surrounded by five turned balusters, all standing on the gracefully shaped lower step. The stair ascended to a large second story hall, the same size as the stair hall and passage below.

Three bed chambers opened onto the wide hall and passage. Like the rooms below, the fireplaces were trimmed with

Wideball, 1769. Under the direction of architect, Howard Sill, the house was reoriented to the river for Mr. and Mrs. Wilbur W. Hubbard in 1911. Tyler Campbell photograph, 1984.

Wideball. In 1870 Robert Clay Crawford rebuilt the roof in the second empire style. He stayed only two years before the building was turned into Brown's Hotel. Kent News collection, c. 1909.

Widehall. The elaborate and refined mouldings in the dining room and hallway frame this interesting view of the back parlor. Tylor Campbell photoograph, 1994.

King of Prussia marble, but the overmantels were paneled in a less formal manner. Likewise, the window trim was plainer, the paneled shutters had raised panels and the cornices were without carving. In addition to the three large bed chambers there was a small unheated room above the back door and a stair to the third floor, as well as one to the kitchen wing. The attic rooms were probably unheated and the only finish would have been plaster with baseboard and door trim.

There is record of the birth of Thomas Smyth as occurring on 12 April 1730 at *"his father's plantation."* Whether he was born at Trumpington or Radcliffe Cross (his father owned both) in uncertain. When his father died in 1741, it was stipulated that Thomas was to study under James Calder, a prominent lawyer of Kent County. He married Sarah Gresham (1730-1761) at St. Paul's Church on 12 March 1752. In the following year Sarah gave birth to their first son, Thomas Jr. A second son was born in 1755 and he was named Richard Gresham after Sarah's father. After Sarah's death in 1761, Thomas married Margaret Hands (1745-1794), daughter of Thomas Bedingfield Hands (d.1768). They proceeded to have more children, including Maria (1784-1823) who was to reside at Trumpington.[3]

One year after Thomas' second marriage to Margaret Hands he purchased Water Lot No. 17 from his father-in-law. Three years thereafter he began the construction of his mansion on Water Lot No. 16. By the time he began this endeavor, he had become a very successful merchant, had been Sheriff of Kent County in 1764 and was active in political affairs of the day. Concurrently with his building activities, Smyth was in business with Emory Sudler, his brother-in-law. In August of 1769 two advertisements in their names may be found in the Maryland Gazette, in regard to runaway servants.

In 1770 Smyth was a member of a committee set up to investigate the increase in taxation on many English imports. He appears as executor to many estates in the early 1770s. In the mid 1770s and through the Revolution Smyth was a member of the Council of Safety and supplier of arms, meat, flour and at least two galleys from his shipyard.[4]

By 1783, when the tax assessment was made, Thomas Smyth was assessed for 2354 acres of land extending from Chestertown to Eastern Neck Island. In 1784 he purchased Water Lots No. 12 and 13 from a Delaware merchant. Three years later he sold the same (River House), to his son, Richard Gresham Smyth.

Beginning in the late 1780s, Smyth's business began to fall off and he began to sell real estate to offset his losses. On 24 February 1790 he sold Widehall and his wharfs to Robert Anderson for £3250.5 Like many others in the depressed post Revolutionary period, Smyth was unable to keep up with his creditors and declared bankruptcy in 1792. His brother-in-law, Bedingfield Hands, appears to have come to his aid by purchasing Trumpington. By 1808, however, Thomas Smyth had regained title to Trumpington and continued to live there until his death in 1818 at age ninety. His body is buried in the family plot south of the house.

Widehall passed from Robert Anderson, at the time of his death, to his brother Thomas, who was responsible for the construction of the neighboring house (the Anderson/Aldrich House).[6] Anderson in turn sold Widehall to Robert Wright, then U.S. senator from Maryland.[7]

Wright had begun his law practice in Chestertown before the Revolution and later served as a captain under Col. William Richardson. In 1784 he was elected to the Maryland House of Delegates and in 1786 re-elected to the same. In 1806 he was elected Governor of Maryland and subsequently resigned from his position with the Senate. After three years as Governor, Wright decided to return to Washington where he was a Representative for seven years.

At the beginning of his last stint in Washington, Wright sold the Smyth mansion to Elizabeth Chambers, wife of the Clerk of the Court, Benjamin Chambers.[8] The Chambers moved from their vernacular residence on Queen Street (Buck/Chambers House) and remained in residence at Widehall until their deaths.[9]

Widehall continued to be owned by the Chambers family, passing first through the two daughters, Augusta (widow of Judge James Houston) and Elizabeth, wife of Joseph Wickes, to end up in the hands of their brother, Ezekiel Forman Chambers (1788-1867).[10]

Ezekiel Forman Chambers was educated at Washington College and in 1808 was admitted to the Maryland Bar. In 1822 he was elected to the Maryland Senate and between 1826 and 1834 served Maryland in the U.S. Senate. In 1834 he was appointed Chief Judge of the Second Judicial District and Judge of the Court of Appeals. He lived in Chestertown until his death in 1867.[11]

In his will, Ezekiel made provisions for his *"unfortunate son, James"* (a reference to his mentally retarded child). Another reference to the trials which Ezekiel endured is found in the diary of Martha Ogle Forman, his cousin:

"July 25, 1835 ... we reached Chester about 6 o'clock. It was the most distressing scene I ever witnessed. The Judge with his seven motherless children round him, three of them infants. O, my god, it was heart rending, such trials make people die before their time. Of what materials can a mother be made, who could desert her infant children, her husband, and everything comfortable around her, and give herself up, to infamy, and wretchedness for the sake of an abandoned man?" [12]

A detailed description of Widehall during Ezekiel Chambers' occupancy is found in the fire insurance policy which he took out in 1842 with the Franklin Fire Insurance company:

"Survey made Nov 18th 1842 and reported to the Franklin Fire Insurance Company of Philadelphia.

For the Hon Ezekiel F. Chambers

A two Story Brick Dwelling house & back Building Situated between front Street & the Chester River & East of high Street in Chestertown Kent County Maryland

Dimensions: the Mansion house is 50 feet from front & 41 ft deep having an Entry Acrofs the middle 6 ft wide with two Rooms on the right & a Hall & one Parlor on the left, in the first Story, 2nd Story divided Similarly with an additional Small room taken off the end of the Entry, the outer walls are brick 22 in thick & the partition ones 12 in thick, Stone Cellar high Rooms all communicate with the Entries by 1¾ in framed doors with brafs locks & knobs or handles, two stacks of chimneys in the partition walls running East & west with a fireplace to each room. Marble Mantels 1 St Story & breast frame over, & Meat Wood Mould Mantels to fireplaces in 2nd Story, Side closets by fire places both Stories, front & back Entry doors same as to the Par-

Widehall has a stair that rivals the contemporary antler stair of the Hynson-Ringgold House.

Widehall. Second story chimney breasts are considerably simpler than those below. Tyler Campbell photographs, 1994.

Widehall 1769. Its original floor plan as recorded in 1842 by the Franklin Fire Insurance Co., policy #4307. Pennsylvania Historical Society.

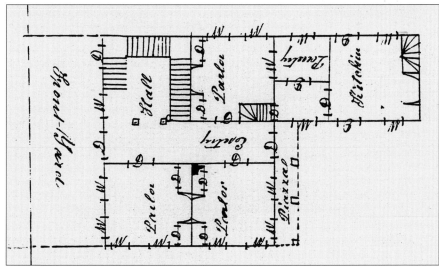

lors with outside Vinitian doors front, wood block cornice to the Entry, & wood mould cornice to hall & Parlors with dental bed moulding, and mould cornice in 2nd Story. Cornice heads to the doors in the first Story. With 6 in plasters - 1st Story 12 feet high Ceiled, 2nd Story 10 ft. & ceiled, 13 windows to first story and 15 to 2nd 2 11 light each 10 by 12 glafs. Outside Vinitian Shutters & inside folding panel Shutters with revealed frames best Carolina 1¼ in heart pine floors. Oak Joist & Rafters, a Barrack Cedar Shingle roof Overlaid with tin back & front tin gutters & conductors lightning rod, heavy block cornice, the Garret is divided into 4 parts by Stud partitions & framed doors. Ceiled 7 ft. in the clear, two 12 light dormant windows back & front 10 by 12 glafs; there is a private Stairs from the 2nd Story to the back kitchin below, & a boxed winding Stairs from the Entry in the 2nd Story to the Garret, & an open Stairs in the Hall 4½ ft. wide quarter based, Mahogany - railing Scroll, Posts balustrades, & Yellow pine plank steps There are 3 archways from Entry to Hall in the first Story & one in the Entry Way to 2nd Story, rooms lined between the Washboards & surbaces & recefs under the windows Turned pilasters in front to entry door with Cornice head & dental block moulds, Stone Sill & Step; front Yard Walled in with pailing on top. The Mansion house is built in the best & most SubStantial Manner of the best Materials & painted wood work throughout.

On the South is a Piazza 6 ½ feet wide with a Cedar Shingle Shed roof, lath & plastered ceiling Yellow pine floor and three turned posts, Oak Sill & Joist & Stands on brick pillars, & flight of Steps to the ground.

The back building is brick two Story, 20 by 35, two rooms & a pantry in first Story & 4 rooms in 2nd plastered Ceilings two windows both sides both Stories, panel Shutters, Stud & brick partitions, a ledge door each side & to each room inside brick floor to 1st & pine plank to 2nd A fireplace in South end & Stairs to 2nd Story, loft over Not plastered Cedar Shingle ridge roof Oak Joist & Rafters,

A Stone Smoke house about 10 feet South of Kitchin, the Buildings Stand Alone, the Nearest being brick

$3000 Insured at 3½ per cent
Robt Buchman Surveyor
E. F. Chambers" [13]

After Chambers' death, the house was sold to one Robert Clay Crawford, an entrepreneur, who stayed less than two years.[14] It was, however, during this time that the roof was restructured into the Second Empire style. The property was then purchased by George B. Westcott, one of Kent County's largest land owners of the time.[15] Westcott never lived at Widehall, but apparently leased it to someone who turned it into "Brown's Hotel." Two years after Westcott's death Widehall became the property of Mr. and Mrs. Wilbur W. Hubbard.[16]

Hubbard was also a substantial property owner. Besides Widehall, he owned wharf property on Water Lot No. 17, the Thomas Anderson House next door and the Custom House across the street. Under the direction of Howard Sill, a prominent Baltimore architect, the house was remodeled and reoriented to the river. Part of Thomas Anderson's lot was used for a kitchen and the wharves on Water Lot No. 17 were demolished. Once the old kitchen was removed from the river side of the house, a Doric Portico with double porches was built facing the river. A driveway with wrought iron gates at High Street was installed for family use, the entire river side was bulkheaded and the lawn graded.

Other exterior work included the roof being changed from the mansard Crawford had installed to a hip-on-hip and refurbishing the brickwork, windows and doors. Interior changes were done with respect to the original woodwork that remained, but great emphasis was placed upon accommodating modern amenities. By 1913, the house was occupied and ready to receive guests. After a visit to Widehall (the name originating with the Hubbard's), Susan Brooks wrote in her diary:

" … Our literary meeting at Mrs. Hubbard's she certainly has made a lovely place out of the Chambers property. Where once stood a granary & the wharf is now in the yard. She got the Chester River Co. to paint the wharf building, has renovated the Custom House & rebuilt the houses adjoining." [17]

From that time until her death in 1959, Mrs. Hubbard presided at Widehall, entertaining guests from around the world and maintaining the grandeur which she and her husband had created. Wilbur Ross Hubbard, their son, became the owner of Widehall before Mrs. Hubbard's death. From 1958 until his death in 1993, Mr. Hubbard made some minor changes to the house, always trying to improve its appearance and convenience.   K-10

1. William Granger was the son of Thomas Smyth's step mother, who married William Granger, Senior after the death of Smyth's father in 1741.
2. Archives of Maryland, Vol LXII, Assembly Proceedings, 1769-70, p. 124f.
3. Brown, B. B., Biographical Sketch of Thomas Smyth and family, found in Vertical Files, Enoch Pratt Library and in Hubbard Collection, Historical Society of Kent County.
4. Revolutionary Papers, Hall of Records, Box 15, folder 8; folder 2; Box 10, folder 7; Box 11, folder 5; Box 12, folder 2; folder 34; and others.
5. Land Records, Lib EF 7, fol. 534.
6. Wills, Lib. 7, fol. 309.
7. Land Records, Lib. TW 1, fol. 658.
8. Land Records, Lib. BC 6, fol. 204.
9. Wills, Lib. 10, fol. 222.
10. Land Records, Lib TW 4, fol. 96.
11. Biographical Cyclopedia; Representative Men of Maryland, p. 97; also in the Wilbur Ross Hubbard Collection, Historical Society of Kent Co.
12. Forman, Martha Ogle, Rose Hill Diaries, p. 350.
13. Franklin Fire Insurance Co, Policy #4307, Historical Society of Pennsylvania, Philadelphia.
14. Land Records, Lib. JKH 9, fol. 202.
15. Land Records, Lib. JKH 10, fol. 302.
16. Land Records, Lib. JTD 18, fol. 565.
17. Diary of Susan Massey Brooks, (1913) Manuscript in possession of Jane Brooks Sprinkle.

Wallis-Wickes House

High Street, Chestertown
c. 1769

THE WICKES HOUSE STANDS ON LOT NO. 12 OF THE original town plat. The first recorded deed is dated 1710 when Jonathan Page, blacksmith, purchased it from Daniel Perkins, stonecutter, for nearly £15. The deed states that there was a house, well and oven on the property at the time.[1] Jonathan's son John, a planter, sold the lot in 1749 to *"Hugh Wallis, Gentleman."*

The year before, however, John Page had met with the Justices for Inspection of Tobacco concerning the erection of a tobacco warehouse on Lot No. 12. It was to be the largest of the six county warehouses measuring 30' x 60'.[2] It is not recorded that it was constructed, and Wallis purchased the lot only three months after the above mentioned meeting. In 1752 moreover, the proceedings of the General Assembly states *" … Read the Petition of the Justices of Kent County Praying that Hugh*

Wallis-Wickes House. A view from the hall into the dining room.
Wallis-Wickes House. The closed string stair with walnut balustrade in the central hall.

Wallis may be obliged to build a Wharff & erect a Cran Adjoining to the Warehouse at the end of the Main Street in Chestertown in the said County ... ." [3] which only confuses the issue. Whether Wallis lived in Chestertown or at his farms near Morgan Creek or both remains unanswered. He was a member of Shrewsbury Parish and a vestryman between 1751-53. He also loaned the parish 600 pounds of tobacco to complete the addition built on the church in 1751.[4]

In the Bond taken out by executors John and Samuel Wallis in 1766 it states that there was a will.[5] It is, however, not listed in the County Index of Wills, but the executors did make an inventory of his personal belongings which totaled in excess of £3000,[6] a phenomenal amount for 1767. This would place him on par with other successful merchants of the day such as Thomas Smyth and William Ringgold. As part of the settlement of the estate, Lot No. 12 in Chestertown was deeded to Samuel Wallis by co-executor John Wallis, both listed as merchants, for the meager sum of £20.[7]

Whether Samuel Wallis was the builder of the large brick house, now called Wickes House, after he acquired Lot No. 12 in 1769, or it was begun by his father may be resolved with further research. If the tobacco warehouse had been built on the lot, it burned nine years before Samuel came into possession of the lot, so there would have been time for ei-

ther father or son to build the new 51' x 43' double pile brick mansion in its place, partially into a bank, just as Samuel Massey had done at the Custom House. Like the latter, the basement was built of stone with two doors opening at grade toward Water Street. There were no other openings on this wide expanse of brick except in the third floor. Its principal entrance faced High Street and was a typical five bay Flemish bond facade with central entrance. There was a molded water table, but no belt course. The windows probably had 12/12 sash and there were three dormers on the tall *A* roof. The rear facade was nearly identical to the front. The plan of the house consisted of central stair hall with four rooms opening therefrom. All of the rooms had diagonal fireplaces, a total of fifteen. The plan is identical, but on a much larger scale, to the Archibald Wright House in Georgetown (the upper section of the Kitty Knight House). The same plan existed in the basement where three of the four rooms had fireplaces, for the kitchen and other functions. Only the third floor level retains board partitions and four-panel doors of the early period.

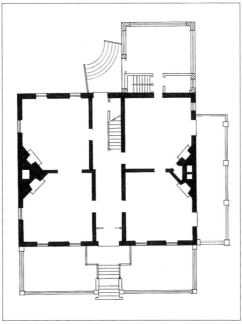

Samuel does not appear to have married but did *cohabitate* with Bersheba Cosden, widow of Jessie Cosden, after 1790. Certainly as a single man he did not need such a large residence, but it is possible he used his residence, like Thomas Ringgold, as a combination business property, store and residence. There is a later reference in Dr. Peregrine Wroth's memoirs that the building was used at one time as an Inn or Tavern.

Samuel's will was written shortly before he died in 1807. To Philip Wallis *"my son of Bersheba Cosden of Chestertown I bequeath all the residue of my estate of what kind soever it be both real and personal ... ."* [8] Samuel stipulated

that Philip was not to sell any of the real estate until after he was thirty years old.

It is stated in the Barroll family history that William Hands Barroll and Elizabeth his wife, after their marriage in 1822 lived for a while in the *"brick dwelling near the northeast corner of Front and High Streets."* [8a] A photograph of the house taken in the 1890s, with the caption *"Residence of William Hands Barroll"* has an interesting discoloration around the window left of the entrance. On closer examination of the actual brickwork, it appears that that window was at one time a door, a very curious oddity on such a symmetrical facade. This may give credence to the hypothesis that the house was more than a residence before the Wickes family acquired it.

Philip Wallis, then living in Baltimore, sold a 48' parcel of Lot No. 12 in 1825 to William Hands Barroll adjoining the residence of William Barroll.[9] Three years later in 1828 he sold the remainder of the lot to Ezekiel Forman Chambers, including the house and outbuildings.[10] When Ezekiel sold the house and lot in 1831 to his sister Elizabeth Chambers Wickes, wife of Joseph Wickes IV Esq., he retained a small portion of the lot on the corner of high and Water Streets and built or occupied an office which he used until his death.[11]

It is from the ownership of the Wickes that the house received its name. Joseph and Elizabeth undertook the project of completely remodeling the house, inside and out. They replaced all of the original windows and doors throughout. They built the retaining wall in front of the house with its elegant fence, in the same manner that already existed at her brother's house across Water Street (Widehall). The dormers of the Wallis House, were decorated with elegant consoles on each side. It was probably the Wickes who built the ground level room off the rear northeast corner of the house, the use of

Protrait of Judge Joseph Augustus Wickes. He was born on September 27, 1826 and died May 18, 1915. Mrs. Daniel Wickes Dietrick Collection.

Wallis-Wickes House. Detail of cornice installed in the dining room. Tyler Campbell photograph, 1995.

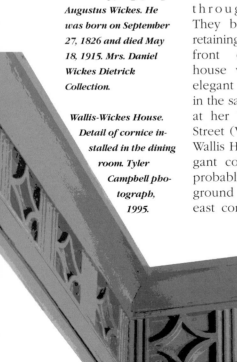

March 21, 1835

"Our friends all met and dined at Mr. Wickes, a very handsome dinner. General F. (Forman) just arrived at the conclusion. We all drank tea at Mrs. Tilghman's- spent a very pleasant evening."

Plantation Life at Rose Hill
The Diaries of Martha Ogle Forman
1814-1845

Courtesy of The Historical Society of Delaware

which may have been another kitchen or wash house.

The interior plan was already established and the Wickes could do little to change it, but on the northwest side of the house, they added tall double doors between the parlors, just as George B. Westcott was to do at the Geddes-Piper House. All of the trim and doors on the first and second floors were renewed with up-to-date woodwork. In the dining room, an empire mantel with fluted colonettes which matched the new trim was installed. Curiously enough, they did not replace the original close-string walnut stair balustrade.

When the 1841 Assessors listed the Wickes property, Joseph owned beside Lot No. 12, six other lots and the five water lots on Front Street south of Cannon. He also owned six slaves and a large amount of stock, securities and other personal property valued at $12,475.00.[12] It is interesting to compare this with the 1852 valuation of the farms he owned west of town. At that period, he owned, beside the town properties, 928 acres on four farms, including Airy Hill, left to him by Mary Thomas of River House, Piner's Grove, his grandparents farm, and a blacksmith shop at Belaire (later Fairlee). There were also twenty two slaves and his total evaluation was $25,183.00.[13]

Joseph and Elizabeth Caroline Chambers Wickes had four children, to reach maturity. Ezekiel Wickes had died before his father's will (1864) and left a widow, Ann Rebecca and four children. Joseph states in his bequests to his wife several items of interest as relating to running the house. *"Ice house, stabling, carriage house and premises adjoining the property we occupy"* and Garden lot on Queen St. *"being necessary for the benefit of the house in which we dwell."* He also mentions the right to cut firewood from Piners Grove for the Chestertown house, and he bequeathed to Joseph A. Wickes the dwelling in which he lives on High Street and frame house adjoining.[14] (The latter was the house previously owned and occupied by William Barroll.)

Elizabeth wrote her will only three months before it was probated in March of 1872. Since *Wickes* house was in her name she was able to leave it to the child of her choice. She left to her son Peregrine L. Wickes, "... *now living in York, Pennsylvania ... the house in which I now live which has fallen much out of repair ... the brick dwelling and premises adjoining in which I now live situated on High Street ... .*"[15] Peregrine however was happily established in York and was not willing to return to Chestertown, so sold the house to his brother Joseph Augustus Wickes for $4,400.[16] He also sold his interest in Airy Hill at the same time while executing his mother's will. By this time Joseph A. had been judge of the second judicial circuit for six years.[17] The move into his parents' house only improved his image at home.

What he did to *repair* his mother's house is not recorded. Joseph was married three times, first to Anna Maria Tilghman by whom he had five children and who died in 1864. The following year he married Anne Rebecca Wickes. They had two children of which only one survived, and in 1889 Anne Rebecca died. His third wife, Gladys Robinson, he married in 1893 and she had two more children. Gladys was to produce the male heir named after his father.

Joseph wrote his will in 1909 with codicils in 1910 and 1915. He devised his house to Gladys for her lifetime and then to her children. All of the rest was put into trust until Joseph reached 25 years of age, then it was to be sold and the proceeds distributed to his children.[18]

Gladys was to undertake many alterations to the house after Joseph's death. In order to obtain more light in the hall she widened the entry and installed glazed double doors with transom and huge architrave. Another glazed wall within created a vestibule similar in concept to the Beck House, a *new house* on Water Street. The three front dormers were enlarged in keeping with the scale of the architrave. Next door, Gladys had Judge Chambers' office demolished and had a square shingle house built farther back on the lot exposing for the first time, the huge gable of the house. Two French doors were broken through the first floor wall for access to a deck built over the basement entrances. Two windows were opened on the second floor. The improvements not only let in more light but gave Gladys a view to the river, partially across the newly landscaped yard of Mr. & Mrs. W. W. Hubbard. In the back, the superstructure was removed from the rectangular building which had been constructed after 1831. It was then converted into a stair, pantry, and screened porch with deck and bath above. Some of Mrs. Wickes alterations to the house were recorded in 1920 in the Diary of Susan Massey Brooks: "*Mrs. Wickes asked her (Miss Luiton) to go thru' the old Judge Wickes house. Showed her the moulding around the Judges study and two mantels she had taken from the Airy Hill Farm. She had changed the front door and put two French windows on the river side of the house.*"

Mrs. Wickes remained in residence in the newly renovated house until her death in 1944 and in fulfillment of her husband's will, the properties were sold and the money distributed to his heirs. Mr. & Mrs. O. B. Burrell who had previously resided at Rose Hill, Cecil County, purchased the property in 1946. Mrs. Burrell set about creating a flower and boxwood garden out of the whole yard. Eugene and Margaret Johnstone purchased the house in 1976 and are responsible for the installation of the new kitchen in the northeast room, and bookshelves in the northwest parlor. In the dining room the 1830s mantle was replaced by an earlier one retrieved from *Trulock* an eighteenth century house near Still Pond. Other improvements, too numerous to mention have been accomplished during their ownership, but the most visible was the reconstruction of the front stoop with side steps illustrated in a turn of the century photo. It had probably been removed by Gladys Wickes when she remodeled the front door. Since the Johnstone occupancy, the house has been open on numerous tours of historic houses and has been the scene of five of their daughters' weddings. This book was compiled and edited at Wickes House.   K-29

Wallis-Wickes House. Detail of door knocker. Gene Johnstone photograph, 1995.

1. Land Records, Lib. 2, fol. 432.
2. Proceedings of the Justices for Inspection of Tobacco. 20 Aug. 1748.
3. Wallis, Lucille, Samuel Wallis; of Kent County, Bk 1, pt 1, p. 38, Baltimore, 1992.
4. DeProspo, A History of Shrewsbury Church, p. 70, 205.
5. Bonds, Lib. 5, fol. 472.
6. Inventories, Lib. 6, fol. 141, 283.
7. Land Records, Lib. DD 3, fol. 161. The @20 sum paid by the heir does not help in dating the house or in determining the number of houses on the lot.
8. Wills, Lib. 8, fol. 345.
8a. "Barroll in Great Britain and America" p. 86.
9. Land Records, Lib. TW 4, fol. 597.
10. Land Records, Lib. JNG 1, fol. 376.
11. Land Records, Lib. JNG 2, fol. 493.
12. Kent County Tax Assessment, 1841.
13. Kent County Tax Assessment, p. 158f.
14. Wills, Lib. JPI 1, fol. 258.
15. Wills, Lib. EC 1, fol. 12.
16. Land Records Lib. JKH 11, fol. 572.
17. Portrait and Biographical Record, p. 631.
18. Wills, Lib. JRC 1, fol. 94.

Town's Relief

Near Chestertown
c. 1770

Town's Relief[1] was the ancestral home of the Wroth family of Kent County. In the memoirs of Dr. Peregrine Wroth, the immigrant James Wroth is described as follows:

"I have heard my Father say that he (James) owned 800 acres called Town's Relief, which has been the family residence ever since until 5 or 6 years ago it was purchased by Mr. Walraven—and there the family lie buried to this day."[2]

The house in which Dr. Wroth was brought up was probably constructed by his grandfather, John Wroth, in the third quarter of the eighteenth century. From what little has been uncovered in recent times, the house appears to have been composed of two sections. The main part was a three-bay, one-and-a-half-story, brick house, two rooms deep. It had a one-story, brick, one-room-deep wing, which extended along the same plane as the main section.[3]

Peregrine Wroth and his brother, Benjamin, deeded their inheritance to their older brother, John Wroth, in 1806 and 1807. John acquired a nearly equal part adjoining in 1824 and conveyed the entire 504 acres to his sons, Thomas and Edward. They, however, conveyed

Town's Relief c. 1770 was probably constructed initially by John Wroth. It was remodeled and enlarged by William Morris after 1869.
Michael C. Wootton photograph, 1995.

it to their brother, Levi, in 1838. In 1849, it was sold at a sheriff's sale for non payment of taxes and the contract purchasers sold it immediately to Joseph Walraven.[4] Twenty years later, the Walravens sold the half of the property which included the Wroth house to William Morris.

The Morrises decided to improve the old house standing on the property by bringing it up to date with others being constructed throughout the county. They squared off the original plan adding to the back of the kitchen. In the process, the old northwest kitchen wall and the fireplace were removed and the whole space became the parlor. Behind the building, a kitchen and pantry were constructed. The entire structure, when completed, was two-and-a-half stories tall with a continuous roof line. It was then stuccoed which served to hide the difference between the two periods of building. Porches were built on both sides of the kitchen and across the front.

From 1869 to 1973, the house remained in the ownership of the Morris family. In 1973, the house and three acres were sold off[6] and in 1980 the entire house was covered with aluminum siding. The present owners have made the interior a show place and are gradually removing the 1980s siding, uncovering in the process, the secrets of its construction.[7]

In a damp area, north of the house, there are the remains of a once handsome, A-roof, eighteenth century stone structure with batten door—most likely a stone dairy or smokehouse. It is one of the five remaining stone structures, the locations of which form a line in a northeast/southwest direction between here and Lynch.   K-403

1. Patents, Lib. 21, fol. 186. Patented in 1681; 800 acres.
2. Peregrine Worth, Memoirs, p. 2, Washington College Library.
3. The plan of the house appears to have been similar to the Houston House in Chestertown.
4. Land Records, Lib. JHG 12, fol. 313.
5. Land Records, Lib. JKH 8, fol. 341.
6. Land Records, Lib. EHP 53, fol. 230.
7. Land Records, Lib. EHP 132, fol. 285.

Angel's Rest

Near Massey
c. 1770

Angel's rest takes its name from a late seventeenth century 700 acre tract surveyed for Richard Angel. Together with another tract called Angel's Lott surveyed in 1684, the two totaled 1200 acres. After Angel's death, the properties, however, escheated to the Proprietor and were divided into smaller farms held in the eighteenth century by members of the Massey, McGinnis, Wilson and Wilmer families. Throughout the eighteenth and nineteenth centuries, the number of Massey kin in the immediate vicinity of the village makes it difficult to pinpoint which one was actually responsible for the construction of the house which once stood on this site.

In the nineteenth century the house and farm belonged to various members of the Benjamin Massey family. In the Tax Assessment of 1822, Benjamin and his son Ebenezer were listed as owners of Angel's Rest and Angel's Lott, along with Casparus McGinnis and Joshua Massey.

The house, which survived into the 1960s, was a two-story, three-bay, brick structure with relatively low-pitched *A* roof. It was built over a full basement and had a hall-parlor plan with winder stair in the southwest corner. During its demolition, one of its mantels which possessed a cushion frieze and crossetted trim was removed to Chestertown. When the trim was removed from around the doors, it was found to be mortised and tenoned together like a fine piece of furniture. The kitchen wing was one story when first built. It was later raised to two full stories, as can be seen from the old snapshot.

By the time Ebenezer Massey died in 1853, he was in possession of the farm and he had bequeathed it to his son, CHB Massey, referring to it as *"the Brick House Farm."* [1] Upon the death of CHB Massey in 1891, the same farm was left to his son, CHB Massey, Jr. [2]

Charles H. B. Massey, Jr. died in 1904, a single man and left the farm to his brother, E. Thomas Massey. [3] In 1936, E. T. Massey willed all of his real estate to his wife and son. [4] They joined in a deed the following year and sold Angel's Rest Farm to Charles and Marie Hadaway. [5] Since that time there have been six owners. In the 1960s, lots were sold off along the road and the old house torn down and replaced with a new residence   K-162

1. Wills, Lib. JFB 1, fol. 372.
2. Wills, Lib. TRS 1, fol. 109.
3. Wills, Lib. CHS 1, fol. 151.
4. Wills, Lib. FWS 1, fol. 346.
5. Land Records, Lib. RAS, fol. 495.

White House Farm

Massey
c. 1770

In 1822, Ebenezer Thomas Massey and his wife Emily Ann both acquired parts of Angel's Lott, Partnership and Spring Garden from their parents. White House farm was most likely included in the acquisition as well.

White House Farm was originally built as a one room frame one-and-a-half-story structure. It had exposed corner posts on the interior like Sterling Castle, located in Chestertown, (third quarter of the eighteenth century). During the Massey ownership, the small dwelling was enlarged and made into a central hall plan with gambrel roof. In its finished state, it was four bays long with four dormer windows in the roof on each side. Its form was similar to the Hendrickson House near Millington.

When E. T. Massey died in 1853, he bequeathed the use of all of his land to his widow, E. A. Massey. [1] Apparently, Mrs. Massey took the White House farm as her residence, since her name appears on the 1860 map. The farm was to go to their daughter Ellen Crane, wife of Dr. Thomas Crane, a Millington physician. However, her brother, R. B. M. Massey appears in the 1877 Atlas at this site.

The White House farm, although considerably remodeled in the nineteenth and twentieth centuries, retains its form and plan, both of which were very common in their day in Kent County.K-163

1. Wills, Lib. JFB 1, fol. 372.

Fairy Meadow Site

Near Chestertown
c. 1770

IN THE FIRST DECADE OF THE NINETEENTH CENTURY, DR. Peregrine Wroth had completed his studies at Washington College. In his diary he describes his activities which followed: *" ... soon after entered as a student of Medicine in the office of our Family Physician, Dr. Edward Worrell, two miles from Chestertown."* [1] The office was located on the Worrell farm known as Fairy Meadow which adjoined Hopewell Corner.

By the time Dr. Wroth began working at the farm, the house had seen many years of service, having been built around the time of the Revolution. The house was a large, two-and-a-half story, frame structure, five bays long and two deep. Its plan consisted of three rooms: a hall or living room into which the central door opened and which had an enclosed stair in its northwest corner

adjacent the chimney, a parlor and a stairhall, the last of which extended along the north wall to a second enclosed stair. From a photograph taken in 1980, the roof of the house appears to have had a catslide addition under which there would have been access to the mid-nineteenth century kitchen wing. This plan (with the exception of the stairhall) is consistent with many houses of Kent built in the eighteenth and early nineteenth centuries.

From another entry in Dr. Wroth's *"Reminiscences,"* the configuration of the house seems to fit. *"The office stood in such a position with respect to her (Mrs. Worrell's) sitting room that I could be*

Fairy Meadow was the home plantation to the Worrell family. Dr. Peregrine Wroth mentions apprenticing under Dr. Edward Worrell before the latters death in 1804. Maryland Historical Trust, M. L. Fritz photograph, 1980.

plainly seen at the back window. It was my duty to act as the apothecary and make up all the medicines which the Doctor prescribed for the Patients. I kept my Pitcher and wash Basin near the back window of the office and took care to wash my hands after putting up medicines." [2]

In 1804, Dr. Worrell died and so Dr. Wroth's apprenticeship and association with Fairy Meadow was cut short. The Worrell family continued to own the farm through 1881. When it was finally sold out of the family that year, the family burial ground was reserved for their sole use.[3]

It is most likely that the house was remodeled and the kitchen enlarged under the ownership of W. H. P. Worrell, the last Worrell owner. These alterations included a few elements of Italianate design.

From 1881, the farm was owned by various members of the Westcott, Price, Colescott and Crew families. In the 1940s, another remodeling altered the plan of the main house to one with a central hall. It was demolished in the late 1980s for a new house which was constructed near the old site.   K-204

1. Wroth, Peregrine, "Reminiscences" (manuscript located at Washington College).
2. Ibid.
3. Land Records, Lib. JFG 1, fol. 40; Lib. SB 1, fol. 549, 551.

Drayton Manor

Near Worton
c. 1770

DRAYTON WAS A 1200 ACRE TRACT PATENTED TO CHARLES James in 1667, in what was then Baltimore County. James' daughter married Phillip Kennard and resided on the property. In 1734, five-hundred ten acres of Drayton were resurveyed for Kennard's son, John, under the name of Kennard's Point. Kennard Point is listed in the 1783 Tax Assessment in the name of Robert Buchanan. Buchanan had married John Kennard's daughter, Mary, in 1764 and they resided on the farm.

In the third quarter of the eighteenth century, Robert Buchanan served in the Lower House for several years. He held local public offices as well and contributed £20 to the founding of Washington College. He served on the vestry of Chester Parish at I. U., where he held parts of pew No. 5. Buchanan also held pew No. 1 at the Chapel in Chestertown.

It is probable that Robert Buchanan was responsible for the construction of the *"Good Brick Dwelling and kitchen, two Barns & common Out Houses At the Mouth of Churn Between that and Still Pond Creek"* as the 1783 Tax Assessment describes Drayton Manor. Early photographs record a five-bay, two-and-a-half-story structure. In form it resembles Handy Point, which was built soon after the 1783 Tax Assessment. The decora-

tive woodwork seen in the early photographs most likely dates from after the fire of 1860 which had destroyed the original work. The fire would have occurred during the ownership of Dr. William Gemmill.

In the 1877 Lake, Griffing, Stevenson Atlas, the farm is called *"Water View Stock Farms"* and at that time it was owned by Charles W. Geekie.

A photograph from c.1920 shows Mr. and Mrs. Carson Harris relaxing on the wide verandah. From the photo it appears that the post-fire remodeling was executed in the popular Italianate style within the confines of its preestablished form. In order to conceal alterations to the brickwork, the entire exterior was stuccoed. A two-bay extension was constructed on the rear of the old kitchen.

Under the ownership of Henry Catlin, who had lived part-time at the Hynson Ringgold House in Chestertown, the house was remodeled and enlarged again. A two-story portico replaced the earlier verandah and a two-story, enclosed porch was built onto the east gable. That, however, did not survive for long.

In 1937, Mr. Wayne Johnson, a prominent New York attorney, purchased Kennard's Point and the surrounding farms. He built a Georgian Revival mansion, which reputedly incorporated remnants of the original house.[1]   K-414

1. Complete chain of title supplied by Catherine Harris.

John Williams Farm

Near Lynch
1770

THE GENERAL CONFIGURATION OF THIS FARM, AS IT HAS passed from the late seventeenth century to the present, was largely the product of George and Ann Warner, members of Cecil Quaker Meeting.[1] They acquired 150 acres called Doutch's Folly, originally surveyed for Hugh Doutch in 1682,[2] and 100 acres of Forrester's Delight, a 400 acre tract patented to Henry Trulock and Edward Trussum in 1676.[3] In 1721, the Warners conveyed their land to fellow members of Cecil Meeting, Samuel and Judith Smith.[4] In 1727, John Williams II sold 130 acres of his father's part of Wheatland on Broadneck and purchased Doutch's Folly from the Smiths.[6]

John Williams III inherited his father's land, by primogeniture. He appears to have been a planter and a member of Chester Parish after its formation in 1765.[9] Williams purchased ¼ of pew No. 26 in the new parish church.

John Williams Farm, 1770. First floor plan, no scale, Michael Bourne.

John Williams III was the builder of the brick house on Doutch's Folly in 1770. When constructed, it was a two-story, three-bay-long, brick structure with steeply pitched *A* roof. The west chimney was totally enclosed within the structure, but the east chimney was partially protruding from the gable and had irregular steps like one of the chimneys on Handy Point. It also possessed a large glazed date in the gable, but no initials, very similar in configuration to Big Meadows. The facade was laid in Flemish bond above a stepped water table; the other sides were laid in common bond. On each side of the central door there are marks indicating the position of an early porch or stoop. On the west side of the house there was a kitchen wing, which is mentioned in the 1783 Tax Assessment.

John Williams IV was assessed for the following:
"Douche's Folly–200 acres
Forrester's Delight–100 acres
Large Brick House Log Kitchen
and common outhouses
In Forest 8 miles from C. Town
Good wheat Land
250 acres arable; 50 acres woodland" [10]

The interior of the house was laid out like Rich Hill and Tibbalds, with a central stairhall flanked by two rooms. In the room nearest the kitchen, on the west side of the hall, there was an enclosed stair in the south corner. The interior was simply finished. In the living room, on the east side of the house, the fireplace had a mantel flush with the east wall. Each of the east corners had a narrow corner cupboard with glazed door, a unique feature in the County. The rest of the room had a two-piece cornice, chair rail, and baseboard. The stairhall from which the stair ascended in three flights to the second floor was finished similarly. Both walls, separating the stairhall from the flanking rooms, appear to be constructed of brick. The dining room, which contained the enclosed stair adjacent the chimney, had a door on its west wall which formerly connected it to a log kitchen.

Originally, the main stair continued to the unfinished attic. At the head of the stair, on the second floor, there was a small unheated room. The east bedroom was likewise unheated, but the west room, into which the secondary stair rose, possessed a fireplace. For a short time, the second story of the house was unfinished, and had whitewashed ceiling joists and brick walls. The roof system was composed of pairs of rafters without tie beams and whose tapered ends rested on a large continuous false plate, about 4" x 4", set on top of the joist ends. This size false plate is more frequently seen on the diagonal, but here it was set straight. One small, four-pane, casement window was located on each gable.

John Williams III died only three years after the construction of his brick house. In his will of 1773, he appointed his friend and neighbor, Macall Medford co-executor.[11] The inventory of Williams' personal property included several luxury items not frequently encountered in inventories of most farmers. There were three pair of silver buckles, and a pair of gold sleeve buttons. In total, his clothing was appraised for over nine pounds sterling. There was also an old black walnut chest, perhaps the same that his father left to his mother in 1748. When Macall Medford made the final account, £127 out of a total of £508 were owed to various merchants and friends, including his uncle, Roger Hales. Apparently, William's children, John, Samuel, Elizabeth, Mary and Sarah, were all under age at the time of their father's death. His nearest of kin were his aunts, Sarah Briscoe and Ann Howell.

John Williams IV eventually inherited his father's land, but was not as successful as his predecessors. By the late 1780s he had become indebted to 33 of the most prominent merchants and doctors of Kent County. Initially, in 1786, he sold off 100 acres close to the road.[12] Two years later, he transferred the rest of his property to a trustee appointed by the Chancellor of the State of Maryland, having been reduced to bankruptcy.[13] John disappears from the land records of Kent County thereafter.

Donaldson Yeates was the appointed trustee, but from the land records it is unclear when he sold the farm to Robert Buchanan. It was Buchanan who, in 1786, purchased the first 100 acres mentioned above, as well as the adjoining farm.[14] Doutch's Folly was bequeathed to Buchanan's son, Robert, Jr.,[15] who ten years later sold a 100 acre parcel to John Hayne. He thereafter made an agreement to sell the remaining 150 acres on which the house was situated and in which Hayne resided.[16] This agreement was not recorded until after Hayne's death at which time the farm went to his son and heir, George Hayne of Baltimore. It was either during the Buchanan or Hayne ownership that the old log kitchen, mentioned in 1783, was replaced by a two-story brick kitchen, which was set back from the face of the 1770 house and wrapped around its northwest corner forming an *L*. The roof line of the south side of the new kitchen continued in a normal fashion until it met the back slope of the main roof. From that point the roof continued downward on the same plane as the main roof, and formed a wide catslide or saltbox. The overall effect is similar to Providence Plantation but larger. When the kitchen addition was built, it contained two rooms, one small room behind the dining room and the other the kitchen itself. In the remodeling, the original doorway between the dining room and old kitchen was converted into a cabinet accessible from both sides. This shifted the doorway to the north window location. In the southwest corner of the kitchen there was a stair to a segregated second story chamber. In the west bedchamber of the main house,

in place of its north window, a doorway led to another room under the roof of the new wing.

Doutch's Folly was owned by the Hayne family from 1809 to 1836, when it was sold by George's son, William, to Hannah Riley.[17] In 1849, Hannah sold the farm to George B. Westcott.[18] On both the 1860 and 1877 Maps, G. B. Westcott is listed as owner of the farm.

After his death in 1888, the *Riley Farm,* as it was called in Chancery, was deeded to Harriett Westcott Hill, his daughter. This was one of the eleven farms which Westcott owned at the time of his death. Westcott had lived in Chestertown in what is now called the Geddes-Piper House and was one of the most successful Kent County businessmen of his day. His daughter lived in Baltimore with her husband, Thomas Hill.

Apparently, Mrs. Hill remodeled the house toward the end of the nineteenth century. Two dormers and a central gable were added to the roof, which was extended about a foot beyond the gable walls. All of the windows in the main part of the house were renewed with *modern* 2/2 sash. New porches were built in front of the main entrance as well as the kitchen. In general, it was turned into a typical late nineteenth century farmhouse.

After Doutch's Folly was sold in 1910, a two-story, frame *tower* was added to the rear of the center door which housed a new bathroom on the second floor and pantry below. During this remodeling, the original stair was removed and replaced with a plain, open-string stair which gave access to the new bath from the second landing. Instead of rebuilding the stair to the attic, a small enclosed winder was added over the earlier secondary stair in the southwest corner of the house. Many of the windows and doors were re-trimmed with millwork from the period.   K-222

1. Jacobsen, Phoebe, Quakerism on the Eastern Shore.
2. Kent Co. Patents, Lib. SD#A, fol. 272; and Rent Rolls, Lib. 5, fol. 29.
3. Rent Rolls, Lib. 5, fol. 24.
4. Land Records, Lib. JS W, fol. 212.
5. Land Records, Lib. JS P, fol. 185.
6. Land Records, Lib. JS P, fol. 78.
7. Wills, Lib. 3, fol. 193.
8. John Williams bequeathed a "black walnut chest with two drawers" to his wife, Elizabeth. In the inventory of his personal estate it is described "large chest with 2 drawers & feet." It was appraised for one pound. One of the appraisers was John Gale, who lived on Redmore's Supply, close by. By the time an additional inventory was made in 1750, Elizabeth had remarried Thomas Cully, a Quaker.
9. Chester Parish Records, original pew assignment.
10. Kent Col. Tax Records, 1783.
11. Wills, Lib. 5, fol. 129.
12. Land Records, Lib. EF 6, fol. 570.
13. Land Records, Lib. EF 7, fol. 336.
14. Robert Buchanan is discussed under Drayton Manor, his home on Stillpond Creek.
15. Wills, Lib. 8, fol. 24.
16. Land Records, Lib. BC 5, fol. 407; Lib. TW 4 fol. 534.
17. Land Records, Lib. JNG 4, fol. 209, 213.
18. Land Records, Lib. JNG 12, fol. 324.

Hepbron's Choice

Still Pond
c. 1770

EPBRON'S CHOICE IS LOCATED TO THE NORTHWEST OF the Still Pond Crossroads. The two-story brick house with one-story wing stands on a slight rise in the middle of the farm. The house is surrounded by three ponds. Its history had been obscured by time.

Sometime prior to 1718, Thomas Medford purchased Hepbron's Choice and established his dwelling plantation. In his will, written in that year, he bequeathed to his son, Thomas, *"200 acres of land with my dwelling plantation and all the appurtenances thereunto belonging ... the 200 acres to begin at the southeast of a tract of land called Hepbron's Choice ... ."* To his other three sons, Bullman, Macall and George he left, *"all the remainder part of the above said tract of land with 50 acres to be equally divided among them and that*

Hepbron's Choice, Stillpond, was built for Macall Medford around 1770. Its plan and form were similar to Piney Grove before both were remodeled in the nineteenth century.

Michael C. Wootton photograph, 1995.

"none of my above said sons shall sell or make sail of any part or parcel of the above land only to each other."[1] Thomas must have been the first generation in this country because he goes on to give to his daughter Rachel the proceeds of the shipment of *"wheat and tobacco sent home to England ... ."*

Bullman Medford apparently acquired the tract from his brother Thomas and lived thereon. When he wrote his will in 1746, he left to his son *"Macall Medford half a tract of land called Hepbron's Choice and half a tract of land called Simsis Farm and half a tract of land called Gals Addition but my will is that my aforesaid son shall have my dwelling house and when the three tracts of land be equally divided into two parts my aforesaid son shall have his half of the three tracts convenient to said house."*[2] His second son Thomas was to receive the other half, and the two youngest sons were given money. Sarah, Bullman's widow, was executrix of his will, but she died three years later and left her children and their estates in the care of George Medford, the children's uncle, and William Moore.[3]

Like his father before him, Macall Medford died leaving six minor children in 1781. After he had reached his majority, he apparently worked very hard and amassed a small fortune. He was well established in the community and had been instrumental in the establishment of Chester Parish. Macall was on the first vestry which contracted for the construction of the new parish church at I. U. in 1766, and upon completion in 1769, he shared pew No.11 with John Divine and John Gale, Jr.[4]

Soon after his experience with the construction of the Parish Church, Macall embarked on his own building project on the farm which had now seen three generations of Medfords. The house he built was unlike any other in the community. It consisted of a 30' x 32' two-story brick house with an 18' x 28' one-and-a-half-story, brick kitchen wing on the west side. Macall used field stone for the foundations of both sections, but had a basement under only the large section. It appears there may have been a change of plan by the builder because he built a bulkhead opening in the side of the cellar where the kitchen wing was to be constructed. Also, there is a seam in the brickwork between the two sections only up to the champhered watertable and then the Flemish bond brickwork of both sections is bonded together, indicating a continuous construction.

From evidence in the basement, as well as various seams on the first and second floors, the original plan emerges as being nearly identical to the original plan of Piney Grove or Tilghmans' Farm, built by Robert George a Quaker from Quaker Neck. Originally, it was a four room plan with two room kitchen wing. The south door opened into a stair hall where the stair ascended on the left side of the room to a corner landing. It then proceeded to the second floor in a second run above the door to the back room. The back room was about the same size as the stair hall, but had a fireplace on its west wall, a window on the north and a door to the northeast room on the east wall. Both east rooms were paneled to the ceiling with feather edge vertical paneling, paneled window seats and paneled jambs. Each had a corner fireplace and corner cupboard. A door in the brick partition opened between the two larger rooms. It too had paneled jambs.

The second floor had four bedrooms and the stair hall, the easterly rooms being slightly smaller than the rooms below. Only the southeast room had a fireplace.

The kitchen wing retains its original plan with the two rooms of the kitchen wing being three steps lower than the larger section. Both rooms originally had one door and one window on the south facade and one door on the north. The westernmost room of the house was the original kitchen. The ceiling joists of the wing were originally exposed and beaded, as was the underside of the flooring above. Both rooms retain their corner stairs to separate chambers. Soon after the house was built a porch was added on the north side of the kitchen. Its roof also protected the basement bulkhead from deteriorating and is probably the reason that the

original board and batten door with its arrowhead latch and spade-end strap hinges have survived.

When Macall Medford, the builder, wrote his will in 1781, he bequeathed the *"dwelling plantation"* to his two sons Macall and Unit *"... divided as follows: by a line from the Southwest corner of Thomas Medford's 50a of Hepbron's Choice to two small apple trees standing in the field to the westward of said line, then by a line to the spring I now make use of being on the Branch side to the west of my present dwelling house, then by and with said branch to the main road. I give my son Macall Medford all the land lying to the southeast of said line."*[5]*—the northwest to son Unit Medford.

After Macall's death, an inventory was made of his personal estate. It included ten slaves, and all of the usu-

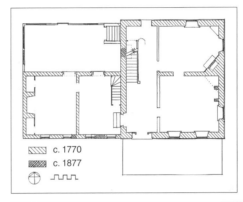

Hepbron's Choice first floor plan. Drawn by Michael Bourne, 1997.

Hepbron's Choice, Stillpond. The northeast room retains original paneled wall, corner chimney breast and glazed corner cupboard. Michael C. Wootton photograph, 1995.

c. 1770
c. 1877

al items associated with a well-run plantation and a well-furnished house. The initial inventory totaled £1426.9.6 When the crops were harvested, that produced another £192.15.3 and when the list was made of debts due his estate, there was an additional £724.3.1. Two of the interesting entries in the debts include the following: *"Money lent the State £477.14.1; money lent to Continent— £125.0.0,"*[7] an indication that he backed the cause of American Independence by putting up his hard-earned cash.

Like his father before him, Macall died leaving minor children and specified that his wife, Susannah, was to make use of the lands for educating their children until Macall, Jr. came of age. Then, the Junior Medford was to take over the operation of the plantation.

Susannah Medford was assessed in 1783 for the following:

> *"Hebbrons Choice   200 acres*
> *Gales Addition   22 acres*
> *Marshes   100 acres*
> *Long Farm   89 acres*
> • *Good Brick House and Kitchen, barn*
>   *and other necessary houses*
> • *Located in the Forest 12 miles from Chester Town*
> • *Good Wheat land, Some thin*
>   *311 acres arable; 100 woodland"*

The total valuation amounted to £1259; the assessment was £15.14.9 and seven whites were listed as living on the plantation (Susannah and her six children).[8] Susannah died in 1804 leaving everything to her son Unit.

Nothing is yet known of Macall during his younger years, but by 1811, when he wrote his will, he was living at Finsbury Square, London with his wife, Maria. The will was not probated until 1825 and in it he bequeathed to his wife *"all those lands with all houses thereon erected situated lying and being in the County of Kent in the State of Maryland in North America and which lands descended to me from my late father Macall Medford of Kent County."*[9] He did not mention any children, but by the time Maria wrote her will in 1848, two daughters, Anna Maria Hynson and Mary Louise Mann, were living, along with a grandson William Welsh. To Anna Maria she bequeathed one-half interest in the *"farm in Still Pond, Kent County, Maryland"*[10] on which she resided, and to each of the others she left one-quarter interest. She specified that her executors *"notify my trustee in England ... and Mr. Charles Warden, 334 Arch St., Philadelphia"* of her death. She died in 1855.

Anna Maria and her husband Nathaniel T. Hynson bought the other one-half interest from the other heirs, but by 1864, Nathaniel was insolvent. Later, Anna died intestate, leaving eight children. Attorney Richard Hynson was appointed trustee for the estate in chancery proceedings and finally, in 1877, he sold the farm to John F. Beeks.[11]

Beeks appears as the owner of the farm on the 1877 Atlas. During the ownership of Beeks, the house went through a major remodeling which resulted largely in the house as we see it today.

On the south facade, the Beeks replaced the two doors of the kitchen wing with windows, enlarged the principal entrance with double doors, red glass transom and sidelights, lengthened the two windows with jib doors and built a scrolled bracket porch. All original sash in the main block were replaced with 2/2 lite sash. One window on the east gable was also lengthened and the west window of the north facade was replaced

Hepbron's Choice, Stillpond. The stair was installed either by Anna Maria Macall and her husband Nathaniel Hynson or by John F. Beeks in the late nineteenth century. Michael C. Wootton photograph.

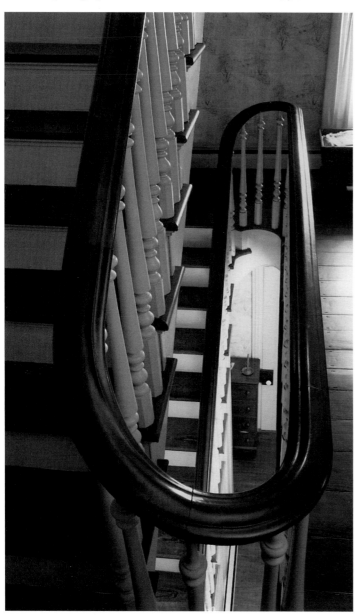

by a door. The plan of the main section was converted into a side hall plan by combining the two smaller rooms into one long space. A new, single flight stair was installed across the old fireplace in the back room. By placing the stair in this location, two rooms were eliminated, one on each floor.

In the process, the south parlor corner fireplace was disassembled and a new efficient stove and slate mantel was installed on the east wall. This room was then completely plastered, some of which was applied over the board-paneled walls. The Northeast room was not altered except for the one east window mentioned above.

The three remaining bedrooms on the second story were plastered. New doors were installed into the stair hall, but old ones were reused between the rooms. The stair continued to the third story, with headroom supplied by the large dormer on the back slope of the roof. Two smaller dormers were installed on the front slope of the roof.

In the kitchen wing, the ceilings were plastered. Any other alterations have been obscured by subsequent changes.

John Beeks died in 1888 and his widow, Sarah, died in 1904. The farm then descended to their daughter Gertrude B. Ewell and her children. The heirs, who were living in Tennessee in 1949, finally sold the farm to Norman and Bernette Baxter,[12] who held onto the farm until they sold it to Mr. and Mrs. William L. Mc-Danolds in 1964. Since their acquisition of Hepbron's Choice, the McDanolds have up-graded the house with central heat, plumbing and electrical systems. They re-built the old kitchen fireplace and switched rooms so that the kitchen is now a family room and the middle room is the present kitchen. A bath was installed off the kitchen, and the back porch, which had already been enclosed, was modernized. In the process of installing a new roof, the two south dormers were removed from the main roof. A porch over the back hall door, which at one time had benches on each side, was removed and replaced by a brick stoop. The old cornices and barge boards have been covered with aluminum and the porch brackets were removed in an effort to minimize exterior maintenance.

The house is one of the important survivors of the third quarter of the eighteenth century, being one of four in the county which had similar form and plan. It is also important because Macall Medford was an active member of the community, instrumental in establishing the third parish of Kent County and committed to the cause of American Independence.   K-217

1. Forman, Henry Chandlee, The Turner Family of Hebron and Betterton, Maryland, Waverly Press, 1933.
2. Carroll, Kenneth, "Quakerism on the Eastern Shore," Baltimore, Maryland Historical Society, 1970, p. 172.
3. Wills, Lib. 1, fol. 205.
4. Land Records, Lib. 4, fol. 358.
5. Carroll, pp. 67, 139, 154.
6. Ibid, pp. 142, 182.

Hopeful Unity

Near Lynch
c. 1770

CHARLES GROOME, ONE OF THE VESTRYMEN OF THE NEWLY formed Chester Parish in 1766, built his farmhouse on Hopeful Unity soon after the Parish Church was constructed at I. U.[1] nearby. He and fellow vestrymen McCall Medford and Dr. William Bordley built houses that were similar to one another in form. In Groome's case, the original house measured 28' 3" across its three-bay facades and 30' 6" in depth. The walls were laid in Flemish bond above the water table, which, as in several other buildings in the county, stepped up and over the basement windows. Each of the window and door segmental arches were constructed of alternating stretchers and double headers. When originally constructed, the steeply pitched A roof had no dormers, the attic being lighted by windows only in the gables. Its plan has not been thoroughly researched, but it may have had diagonal, back-to-back fireplaces in the two west rooms.

The location of the original kitchen has not been ascertained, but later in the

Hopeful Unity was built in the 1770s by Charles Groome, one of the first vestrymen of Chester Parish. Michael C. Wootton photograph, 1996.

Hopeful Unity, c. 1770. A view to the northeast shows the frame porch that was added to the service wing in the late nineteenth century. M. L. Fritz photograph, 1980.

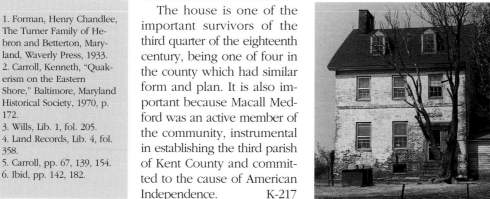

eighteenth century, a typical two-room plan, one-and-a-half-story brick service wing was constructed on the east side of the house covering a former window in the process.

Like the two aforementioned houses, Hopeful Unity underwent a major remodeling in the third quarter of the nineteenth century when in the ownership of James A. Roseberry. In this case, the fireplaces were removed and reconstructed near the center of each room on the west gable. Only the stair and walnut balustrade remained from the first period. Porches were added to the front of the house and rear of the service wing.

1. Identification of the builder from the work of Carolyn Cooper.

Hopeful Unity remains a significant pre-revolutionary house in Kent County from the 1770s.   K-231

Thomas's Hill

Near Pomona
c. 1770

K EDGERTON WAS PATENTED TO ROBERT KEDGER IN 1660 for 1000 acres. It was later acquired by William Thomas and repatented in 1719 under the name of *"Thomas's Purchase"* and included 80 acres of vacancy. For some undiscovered reason, his heirs had it repatented again in 1741, possibly to reestablish the boundaries.[1]

Part of the house on Kedgerton was probably built for one of the Thomases in the third quarter of the eighteenth century. At that point it was a two-story, three bay long, hall-parlor plan house with glazed Flemish bond brick work on its south facade and English bond elsewhere. It was built on the highest ground of the entire plantation, the boundaries of which extended to present day Pomona.

At the end of the eighteenth century a brick kitchen wing was added to the west gable, replacing an earlier structure. The house remained in this form until the late nineteenth century. In 1852, the farm

Thomas's Hill or Kedgerton was built for one of the Thomases in the third quarter of the eighteenth century. The left side of the house was the former east gable. It was remodeled and enlarged by Thomas B. Trew in the late nineteenth century. Maryland Historical Trust. M. L. Fritz photograph, 1981.

was in the ownership of Thomas W. Trew who lived at the Reward. The assessor stated that the *"Brick House and other Buildings (were) in Bad repair."* [2] Thomas Trew died intestate in 1859 and the part of the farm with the *"Brick House"* on it went to his son, Thomas B. Trew.[3] Thomas is listed as the owner in the 1877 Atlas in which the land is called *"Thomas' Purchase."*

Whether Thomas B. Trew or his successor remodeled the house is not yet known, but what was done was similar to that at Rodel Acres and Gondomah. The house was reoriented to the east (facing the road) and a central entry and two bays were added onto the north side of the old house. The gable and chimney were disassembled and two windows were installed on both floors of the former gable to balance the new wing. A pair of gables with a central dormer embellished the new *A* roof which ran perpendicular to the old roof. A porch was built on the east and south facades.

It apparently remained in the same form until 1959 when a new kitchen was built onto the north gable of the frame wing. Viewed from the land, it appears like a late nineteenth century vernacular house, but from across the creek, the impression is one of age.   K-251

1. Ruth, Grieb, Trew, Map; Colonial Quaker Neck, 1967.
2. Kent County Tax Assessment, 1852.
3. Land Records, Lib. JFG 5, fol. 120.

Maslin's Possession

Broad Neck
c. 1770

I T IS DIFFICULT TO PINPOINT the location of this early house from the 1852 Tax Assessment since the tract of Maslin's Possession is divided between three members of the family. In all likelihood, however, it was located on the 130 acre part belonging to Mrs. Eliza Maslin[1] for there is mention of an *"Old frame House in Bad Repair."*[2]

The house was a three-bay, one-and-a-half-story, frame structure with two shed-roof dormers on each side of the steeply pitched *A* roof. Within each gable is a large brick chimney which has its back exposed to the level of the second floor joists. It originally had a hall-parlor plan with the central entrance opening into the hall which was on the east side of the building. This plan is now reversed since a paneled partition has been moved.

When the house was remodeled in the 1950s, the original hall fireplace was rebuilt outside the original gable in a late nineteenth century kitchen addition. Old paneling was rearranged to such an extent that it is difficult to determine the original configuration. Brick nogging in the south wall was exposed in the dining room, along with the ceiling joists. A leanto addition was also built on part of the south side of the house. In the 1877 Atlas, the Maslin name does not appear on this tract of land. S. H. Thomas is assigned to the house.   K-255

1. Land Records, Lib. BC & GS 45, fol. 157; Lib. BC No. C, fol. 418.
2. 1852 Tax Assessment.

McHard House

Water Street, Chestertown
c. 1770

T HE HOUSE AT 110 WATER STREET WAS BUILT ON THE EASTern half of Lot No. 14 by either Samuel McHard (d. 1771) or his son, Joseph, who exchanged the house and lot in 1795 for Solomon Betts' property in Church Hill.[1] Originally the house was almost identical to Simon Wickes House located on Water Lot No. 10. Both were three bays long and two stories tall with full size windows flanking the fireplace on their southwest gables, a feature found also in the Smith-Ringgold House, built in the 1760s. Other similarities between

two of the Water Street houses include their all header bond facades, lack of original dormer windows and small double hung windows in the attic flanking the chimneys. Their floor plans are also

Maslin's Possession. The original house was a one-and-a-half story hall-parlor plan dwelling. Tyler Campbell photograph, 1996.

McHard House, Chestertown, is one of three houses on Water Street that were built with a central hall plan in the third or fourth quarter of the eighteenth century. They all were built with full size windows on the southwest gables to take advantage of the sun. Michael C. Wootton photograph, 1996.

McHard House, southeast elevation. Drawn by Michael Bourne, 1992.

the same, with basement kitchen and central stair passages. The McHard House appears to be less vertical in nature as it is located inland and has no on grade entrance at the basement level.

There were many owners of the property in the nineteenth century, including Robert Anderson, John Constable and his heirs and Rebecca Ringgold. The name of Dr. William Meeteer appears as owner on the map of Chestertown in the Atlas of 1877. At that period a long wing is shown behind the house, nearly the same size as the original block. The Atlas states that it is his residence and office at that time. After Margaret Meeteer's death, it passed to William McKenney and his son. William, Jr. sold the house, which had become a vacant derelict, in 1922 to J. Thomas and Bessie Perry Kibler.[2]

The Kiblers hired an architect to draw up plans for the house. They demolished the nineteenth century wing and replaced it with a shorter two-story frame structure which housed a den, pantry, kitchen and lavatory with back porch on the first floor. They also added a porch on the southwest gable which wrapped around the corner of the house and joined the kitchen wing. An entry of the same design was built at the central entrance. The dining room fireplace and chimney above were removed in order to make more space in the rooms on the northeast side of the house. Heating, baths and electricity were added throughout. It is said that Mrs. Kibler liked the mantel in the front parlor of the Geddes-Piper House so much that she purchased it and installed it in the living room of her own house. The property remained in the Kibler family until 1991.   K-14

1. Land Records, Lib. BC 4, fol. 303.
2. Land Records, Lib. APR 9, fol. 165.

Bordley-Usilton House

High Street, Chestertown
c. 1770

As a resident of Kent County, Dr. William Bordley was an active individual. A member of Chester Parish, he was on the commission empowered to erect a Chapel of Ease in Chestertown and later occupied Pew No. 8 there. Bordley also purchased one-quarter of Pew No. 2 at I. U., the Parish Church.[1] Involved in the revolutionary cause, Dr. Bordley is mentioned in several correspondences and other war records. After the Revolution and only a year before his death, he subscribed £18 toward the establishment of Washington College.[2]

In 1770, *"William Bordley of Chestertown, Doctor of Physic"* purchased one-half of Lot No. 57 from John Monk, son and heir of Henry Monk. Described in the deed as *"land on which Henry Monk formerly did dwell."* The £25 purchase price certainly does not point to a very substantial dwelling— at least on this half of the lot.[3] The other half was purchased by William McKenny. In 1772, Bordley and McKenny joined in a deed of partition, since both had purchased an undivided one-half interest in the lot originally.[4] There is no mention of a dwelling in this deed. However, by the time of Bordley's will in 1784, a house described as being on the lot is bequeathed to his daughter Sarah.[5]

Bordley-Usilton House, Chestertown, was built by Dr. William Bordley soon after purchasing half of Lot No. 57 in 1770. It was like Piney Grove originally, but was remodeled in the late nineteenth century by subsequent owner, William B. Usilton. Michael C. Wootton photograph, 1996.

The house was a large scale, three bay, two-story townhouse with an entrance to one side. Its facade alone was laid in Flemish bond and just beneath the first floor windows there was an ovolo molded water table. At least part, if not all, of the steps to the front door were limestone.

The plan of the house consisted of four rooms, one being the entry stairhall. The other three were of varying sizes and each had its own fireplace. The plan was similar to Piney Grove and Hepbron's Choice, two houses of Kent County which appear to have been built in the 1770s.

The house remained in the ownership of Dr. Bordley's descendants until 1834, when it was sold to Thomas E. Dugan, who with his sons Joseph and Thomas, owned several properties in the 400 and 500 blocks of High Street. The 1841 Tax Assessment in fact shows the Dugans as owners of fourteen properties valued at $4820.00. The Bordley House, at that time, was appraised at only $600 and is listed as occupied by Charles Davis, a resident of more than 26 years."[6] Later, in the 1860 Atlas, the house is listed as being the residence of Joseph Dugan.

In 1868 the house was purchased by William B. Usilton.[7] The son of Robert and Mary Lamb Usilton, he began working for the Kent News at an early age. By 1861 he and James H. Plummer had purchased the business. They continued to publish the newspaper together until Plummer's death. Continuing with his sons Fred and Wm. B. Usilton, Jr., Mr. Usilton ran the paper into the twentieth century.[8]

As a successful newspaper man, Mr. Usilton and his wife Mary Frazier Usilton were able to and did undertake a major remodeling of the house in the late 1860s. The High Street facade received a bold front porch with bracketed cornice to match the main cornice of the house. The entrance was removed to create a vestibule and the whole trimmed with an architrave with the same details as the porch. On the southeast gable a large bay window appeared and two windows were closed with brick. Inside, the floor plan was changed in the same manner as Hepbron's Choice, with a stairhall extending through the entire brick section and two rooms on the southeast side. In order to bring it up-to-date, a new kitchen wing was constructed out the rear. The basic footprint appeared in the 1877 Atlas.The Usiltons retained ownership of the house until 1942. Since that time it has had four owners and remains a private residence. K-61

1. Chester Parish Vestry Minutes, 1766-1919.
2. Barroll, L. Wethered, Washington College, 1783. Maryland Historical Magazine, p. 168.
3. Land Records, Lib. DD 3, fol 355.
4. Land Records, Lib. DO 4, fol. 17.
5. Wills, Lib. 7, fol. 169.
6. Usilton, Fred F. History of Chestertown, 1899, p. 81.
7. Land Records, Lib. JKH 7, fol. 14.
8. Portrait & Biographical Record, Chapman Publishing Co., 1898, p. 749.

Springfield Farm
Near Rock Hall
1770

SPRINGFIELD FARM WAS FIRST PURCHASED BY BENJAMIN Ricaud in 1674 from James Ringgold, the original patentee, *" ... for a considerable quantity of Tobacco and three servants ... Middle Spring ... lying in Kent County on the Eastern side of Chesapeake bay and on the Eastern side of a Creek in the said bay called Swan Island Creek respecting the land of Thomas Hynson, Senr to the Northwest ... containing ... four hundred acres ... ."*[1] Benjamin survived only ten years on his Kent County lands before leaving them to his widow Elizabeth and then to his sons Benjamin and Thomas.[2]

Thomas Ricaud survived Benjamin and lived until 1722 when he bequeathed his father's land to his wife Mary and the farm adjoining to his young son Benjamin *" ... on which Mary Davis now dwells ..."*[3] the latter was part of the lands inherited from his brother, Benjamin.

It was Benjamin Ricaud, son of Thomas, who built the brick and frame house that has survived to this day bearing the date 1770 and his initials. His wife may have died by that time, for the usual arrangement, with surname initial above the couple's initials, was not followed. It is simply *B R* below the date. Benjamin's house while one-and-a-half stories tall with dormers on both slopes of the *A* roof, had a plan similar to Piney Grove. It was two rooms deep. Springfield's fa-

Springfield Farm, west gable with 1770 and B R in glazed headers. Note double withes and weathering of chimney. C. Engstrom photograph, 1977.

cade and dated west gable are laid in Flemish bond above a champhered water table. Above the openings there are segmental arches of rubbed brick. Dentils used in the cornice are similar to the Violet Farm. The large chimney rises from the west gable and possesses two withes and a sloping weathering. The back and east gable lack the refined details of the facade and west gable.

A longer one-and-a-half story frame wing extends to the east of the main brick section. Its *A* roof also covers a narrow porch, a feature also found on the kitchen wing at Hinchingham. This section has been mistakenly dated 1698 in the past, but it appears to be contemporary with the brick section, as is the wing at Hinchingham. One of the clinchers of a contemporary date is the fact that the west wall of the frame wing is the brick gable. If it pre-existed the 1770 brick section, it should have a framed wall of its own.

The south wall of the wing is covered with riven oak clapboards secured with wrought rose head nails. The ceiling of the porch has original exposed whitewashed hewn joists. Where the porch abuts the brick house there is a basement entrance adjacent a door to the entry hall, like Airy Hill, another indication that the two sections were planned together.

Inside the brick section, the plan consists of an entry/stair hall, two living rooms on the west side with corner fireplaces and a small unheated room north of the stair. The latter acts as a back hall and connector to the service wing. There are two rooms in the service wing, a kitchen and dining room.

The interior of the brick house is well finished, with raised panel dado in both rooms. The living room has a relatively symmetrical raised panel chimney breast crowned with a five part dentil cornice. In one of the other corners of the room there is an arched cabinet said to be a reproduction of an original. The back parlor or den also has a raised panel chimney breast with an unusual panel arrangement housing two small cabinets. There are also paneled window jambs. Originally there were two small bedrooms on the second floor separated by vertical board partitions. These were converted into one room in the 1950s remodeling. At that time a third space at the head of the stair was converted into a bath.

Both rooms in the wing were gutted and renewed during the remodeling. From the floor plan in Early Manor and Plantation Houses the stair to its second floor ascended from the dining room. That space, however, was converted into a cabinet, during the remodeling, to balance a second cabinet on the opposite side of the fireplace. The current stair was reversed and the kitchen was modernized.

A once detached brick smoke house has been incorporated into a large family room which extends from the kitchen to the garage.

Benjamin Ricaud's four daughters married into the Worrell, Hatcheson, Blackiston and Bradshaw families. At his death in 1774, they were bequeathed various beds, slaves, and cattle. His one son, Richard, was to receive the real estate and all that remained.[4] Apparently Richard prospered, for in 1783 he was taxed on 669 acres of land. In 1788 his holdings were resurveyed under the name of Spring Fields.[5] He was one of the financial supporters of Washington College in its founding year, contributing £12 to its establishment. He was a member of St. Paul's Church, of which his family had been members since its founding in the seventeenth century. In 1804 he acquired 371½ acres from Benjamin Ricaud of Baltimore, possibly his son. It consisted of two parcels, Springfield Resurveyed and Dean's Adventure. He also acquired, in the same deed, eight slaves and eight horses.[6]

After his death in 1813, the farm descended to his oldest son Benjamin,[7] but the inventory of personal belongings which had not been devised to his children was sold at public venue.[8]

Apparently Benjamin lived in Baltimore and maintained the family farm. Upon his death the farm was purchased from the estate by his son James Barroll Ricaud[9] who was to become the Judge of the local Circuit Court and who was to live at Stepney in the 1860s.

When the tax assessor visited Springfield in 1852, James B. Ricaud owned 620 acres with a *"Brick House & other Buildings in Good repair."* There were 29 slaves on the plantation at this time. His personal belongings were not listed. Apparently he was renting a house in Chestertown, as he had done in 1841.[10] Judge Ricaud served on the

board of visitors and governors of Washington College and was a member of Emmanuel Church. He appears as the owner of the farm on the 1860 Martenet Map.

Just before his death in 1866, he sold half of Springfield farm with the house thereon to James Lamb, *"... reserving the graveyard on said land ... ."* [11] He bequeathed the other half to his wife and daughter stipulating that they rent it out and pay his sister Sarah $100 every year until her death.[12] His daughter and finally granddaughter kept that half of the family farm until 1918 when it was sold out of the family.

James Lamb deeded his part of Springfield to George B. Westcott in 1877. Two days later George deeded it to his son Charles Westcott.[9] G. B. Westcott's name appears on the 1877 Atlas. Charles Tilden Westcott and his wife Mary sold Springfield in 1901 to James Bramble[13] of Kent County, who owned it until 1916. In 1918 both halves of the original Springfield were again purchased by a single owner.[14] From that time until 1951, the farm suffered two mortgage defaults and was tenanted throughout the period.

In 1951 the farm was acquired by Louisa d'Andelot Carpenter[15] who had previously lived at Fairlee Manor. Mrs. Carpenter restored the old house and later added a large wing. It was open on the Maryland House & Garden Tour in the 1960s, and remains one of the show places of Kent County.   K-99

Springfield Farm, 1770. The two room deep house has back-to-back corner fireplaces on the west side of the house. The south room has a more formal overmantel and cornice than the north room. C. Engstrom photograph, 1977.

1. Kent Co. Land Records, Lib. A, fol. 359.
2. Kent Co. Wills, Lib. 1, fol. 3.
3. Kent Co. Wills, Lib. 1, fol. 236.
4. Kent Co. Wills, Lib. 5, fol. 139.
5. Patents, Lib. 1C#C, fol. 584.
6. Kent Co. Land Records, Lib. TW 3, fol. 155.
7. Kent Co. Wills, Lib. 9, fol. 241.
8. Kent Co. Inventories, Lib. 13, fol. 144, 148.
9. Kent Co. Land records, Lib. DCB 3, fol. 84.

10. Kent Co. Tax Assessment, Chestertown, 1841, p. 43.
11. Kent Co. Land Records, Lib. JKH 5, fol. 242.
12. Kent Co. Wills, Lib. JF 1, fol. 334.
13. Kent Co. Land Records, Lib. JTD 6, fol. 44.
14. Kent Co. Land Records, Lib. APR 3, fol. 324, 325.
15. Kent Co. Land Records, Lib. WHG 21, fol. 369.

Radcliffe Cross

Quaker Neck
c. 1770

IN 1659, A 500 ACRE TRACT KNOWN AS RADCLIFFE CROSS was patented to Mark Pensax. The next deed recorded is that of its sale from the estate of Peregrine Brown to Thomas Smyth II of Trumpington in 1717. When Brown had originally purchased it and how much he paid is a mystery, as there is no deed in available public records. There is reference, however, in the deed of 1717 to the sale being one to satisfy a portion of Brown's debts to Queen Anne. Apparently the title to all of Brown's lands had previously been transferred to the Queen's Surveyor General of Customs for such. Smith's purchase of Radcliffe Cross on the 8th of June 1717 included not only the usual appendages, but also four slaves and the stock of cattle, hogs, horses and sheep for £340.[1] In his will, dated 1741, he bequeathed Radcliffe Cross to be equally divided between his two daughters, Mary and Martha.[2]

Martha, who later married Emory Sudler, had the first choice of her half and chose the part bordering Radcliffe Creek and the Chester River. Mary took the other half bordering Muddy Creek (now the pond adjacent Chester River Yacht & Country Club) and the river.[3] In the 1783 Tax Assessment, Martha's farm is described as follows:

> *"One brick dwelling House & frame kitchen,*
> *7 out Houses, one young orchard*
> *Near Chester Town & on the River"* [4]

The appraisal at £1048 included 319 acres, stock and 14 blacks. As no whites were listed living on the farm, the Sudlers most likely resided at their property in Chestertown (the Buck-Bacchus Store).

The brick house mentioned in the Assessment probably included four of the five bays of the present structure, and measured 38' 8" x 24' 10". Its plan, judging from the stone foundation and first floor framing visible in the basement, appears to have been a three-room plan consisting of the large living room with a smaller dining room on the river side and a stair hall on the back. The frame kitchen could have been any form but was probably located off the south end, as it is today.

It is likely that the Sudlers first took up residence at the farm after they sold the Buck houses in town in 1785. They remained there until their deaths in the late 1790s. In Martha's will, she left Radcliffe Cross to her four daughters with the remainder to be divided between her four daughters and four sons. Martha's neighbors John Rowles of Airy Hill and Joseph Garnett of Cedar Hill witnessed her will.[5]

From the Sudler's daughters, Radcliffe Cross passed to their children, eventually being sold to Martha

Radcliffe Cross c. 1895 with the Arthur Merritt Brown family in the foreground. The house was telescopic at that period. Maryland State Archives, Dorothy Brown Day Collection.

Radcliffe Cross, built initially by Emory and Martha Smyth Sudler c. 1770. It was enlarged after being acquired in 1852 by their grandson-in-law, Samuel Spencer. Tyler Campbell photograph, 1996.

Sudler's grandson-in-law, Samuel W. Spencer in 1852.[6] By this time, however, his wife Harriett Chapman had died,[7] and he had remarried. The remodeling of Radcliffe Cross into the house as it is essentially known today was the work of Samuel Spencer. He gutted the building, with the exception of the first floor system and three of the old walls. The south wall with its chimney was completely dismantled to the first floor. The building was then lengthened by 12' 3" and heightened by about three feet which created a long five bay house with heavy Greek Revival frieze—typical of the mid-nineteenth century architectural trends and seen in the Beck houses on Broad Neck. The alterations reoriented the house to the river and the road, which had been built since the Sudlers built their house seventy or eighty years earlier. Beside the extra brick section, the

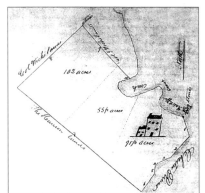 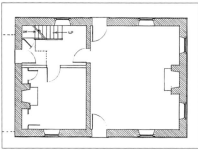

Radcliffe Cross plat from Chancery Record #177, p. 372, Maryland State Archives.

Radcliffe Cross, c. 1770, conjectural first floor plan based upon structural evidence in the framing. Michael Bourne.

Radcliffe Cross, the 1850s stair with mahogany newel and handrail, and tiger maple balusters. C. Engstrom photograph, 1977.

kitchen was remodeled and brought to the form illustrated in the old photograph, a telescoping two-part, two-story frame wing.

After Samuel Spencer's death in 1869, his widow purchased the farm from the estate.[8] When Henrietta Spencer died two years later, the mortgage had not yet been satisfied. The farm (less three acres) was sold to William D. Burchinal.[9] Burchinal appears as the owner on the 1877 Atlas.

Arthur Merritt Brown purchased one-half interest in the farm from his step-father in 1881 [10] and the other half interest after W. D. Burchinal's death in 1899.[11] Radcliffe Cross is pictured with Mr. Brown's family around 1895. The photograph shows no porch, but the two frame wings on the south side of the house.

In 1919 A. M. Brown, a widower living in Delaware County, Pennsylvania, sold Radcliffe Cross to his oldest son A. Leon Brown.[12] It was the latter who altered the house once again. Leon and his wife Helen Thomsen installed a three bay hip roof porch on the facade of the house. They also lifted the two frame wings and moved them to the west side, behind the present dining room, creating a uniform facade without the telescoping wings detracting from its symmetry.

Dr. and Mrs. G. Howard Dana purchased the farm from Leon Brown in 1947 and again altered the building to suit their needs. The front porch was removed and the frame kitchen was moved to the back of the yard and incorporated into a tenant house. They built the present four-bay brick wing, which occupies the position of the original kitchen on the south gable.

Since Dr. Dana's death, Radcliffe Cross has had four subsequent owners. In 1984, Mr. and Mrs. Daniel Brook operated Radcliffe Cross as a bed and breakfast. Most recently it has been returned to its former function as a single family dwelling.   K-86

1. Land Records, Lib. BC, fol. 295.
2. Wills, Lib. 2, fol. 160.
3. Martha Sudler was the half sister of Thomas Smyth of Widehall. Her husband, Emory Sudler was a merchant and was in business with Smyth in the 1780's Emory had purchased the Buck houses in 1771 and lived in the building on the corner of Queen and High Street.
4. 1783 Tax Assessment.
5. Wills, Lib. 8, fol. 31.
6. Land Records, Lib. JR 2, fol. 202.

7. c. 1871.
8. 12 Oct. 1869.
9. Land Records, Lib. DCB 1, fol. 598. The other three acres were sold to George A. Hansen.
10. W. D. Burchinal was the son of John Howard and Eliza Burchinal. He was born in Dover, Delaware in 1832 and served in the Civil War, earning the rank of Captain. He moved with his family to Chestertown around 1854 and became involved in many activities which

contributed to the betterment of Chestertown and Kent County. He married Margaret A. Merritt widow of Captain William H. Brown in 1868. He held several positions in the office of Customs in Baltimore, between 1869-72, 1876-81 and 1890-94, each intervening time he returned to Kent County to resume his real estate business and farming, at which time he purchased Radcliffe Cross. Between 1883-1890 he served in the Maryland Senate.

In 1895 he assumed the position of Treasurer of Kent County which he held until his death in 1899, – Biographical Cyclopedia, p. 44.
11. Land Records, Lib. SB 2, fol. 100.
12. Land Records, Lib. JTD 3, fol. 83.
13. Land Records, Lib. APR 6, fol. 89.
14. Land Records, Lib. WHG 1, fol. 513.

Hebron

Still Pond
c. 1770

ON A GENTLE RISE SOUTHEAST of the village of Still Pond stands a house known as Hebron. James Corse, a Quaker and early member of Cecil Meeting, purchased 150 acres of Hebron's Farm from Thomas and John Hebron in 1713.[1] In 1717 he became *"Overseer of Cecil Meeting"* along with George Dunkan, another influential early Quaker who had established himself south of the meeting house.[2] James Corse died in 1720 and left his land to his two sons, Michael and John.[3] In 1733, the two sons exchanged properties which placed John to the north of the division line their father had established.[4]

It was in the 1770 period that John Corse built his dwelling house. He constructed a two-story building with full basement and two-story kitchen wing. The kitchen wing was built off the west gable on the same axis, but set back about eight feet.

Hebron's facade was laid in Flemish bond with neither water table nor belt course. The windows were fitted with 9/9 sash and paneled shutters on the first floor

Hebron—the dining room possesses the only fielded paneling in the house. It conceals two cupboards. To the right of the chimney breast is a glimpse of the former pass-through between the kitchen and dining room. Michael C. Wootton photograph, 1995.

Hebron, c. 1770. The north side of the house showing the set-back of the kitchen wing. C. Engstrom photograph, 1977.

and 6/9 sash above on the second. The east gable chimney projected the length of one brick and the only windows on this gable were casements whose purpose it was to light the attic rooms. The west chimney was constructed completely within the gable wall.

In its original form, the kitchen was one room. A door on the south side opened onto the porch. Another door to the exterior was located on the east side where the wing projected beyond the main block. There was, essentially, no interior access to the main house, only a small pass-through joining the kitchen and dining area. Around 1830, the setback on the south side of the house was filled in to make a connector on both floors. It also created a cat-slide

roof from the original kitchen ridge.

The interior of the house consisted of a central stair passage with one room on either side. The stair was narrow, but possessed a fine close string balustrade with turned newels and balusters. The spandrel was paneled. Between the east room and the stair was a plastered brick partition extending to the third floor level. All of the other partitions in the house were of beaded boards. Three of the four mantels were executed with crossetted trim and mantel shelves while the fourth was made without crossettes. On both sides of the west fireplace there were raised panels concealing cupboards from the side (like Kentland, 50-60 years later). All of the rooms were fitted with chair rail and baseboard. The attic rooms were plastered.

The kitchen had exposed beams, brick floor and large fireplace on the west gable with an enclosed winder stair in the southwest corner. The second floor was divided into two rooms for servants.

During the Revolutionary War, John Corse had some of his personal property (cows, beds, blankets) confiscat-ed by the Sheriff for failing to serve in or obtain a substitute to do so in the militia. In 1774, Corse freed two slaves in a directive from the Yearly Meeting. In 1780, he was a member of the School Committee, but nothing ever came of it locally.[5]

In the 1783 Tax Assessment, John Corse was listed as owner of *"169 acres of Hebron Farm, 69 acres of Love and Friendship, 5 acres of Lamb's Meadow and 16 acres of Drugan's Discovery."* Listed on the property was a *"Good Brick Dwelling & Kitchen & other necessary Houses."*

John Corse's wife, Cassandra Rigby, was a well-known traveling Friend among the Quakers of Kent County. It is noted in 1791 that she paid *"a Religious visit to such of the black people as have been set free by Friends."* She served in Chester County, Pennsylvania. Her death in 1801 was grieved by the Community.[6]

On the 1860 Martenet Map, John J. Bowers is listed as the owner of Hebron and in 1877, J. G. Bowers is in the same location. J. L. Bowers died only a year after the Atlas was printed and was buried with other Friends at Cecil Meeting.   K-112

Hebron, c. 1770. The "Good Brick Dwelling & kitchen ... ." on Hebron Farm mentioned in the 1783 Tax Assessment, is the same dwelling that still exists near Stillpond.

Hebron, c. 1770. Corner cabinet with paneled doors in living room is a modern addition. Michael C. Wootton photographs, 1995.

1. Forman, Henry Chandlee, The Turner Family of Hebron and Betterton, Maryland, Waverly Press, 1933.
2. Carroll, Kenneth, "Quakerism on the Eastern Shore," Baltimore, Maryland Historical Society, 1970, p. 172.
3. Wills, Lib. 1, fol. 205.
4. Land Records, Lib. 4, fol. 358.
5. Carroll, pp. 67, 139, 154.
6. Ibid, pp. 142, 182.

Houston House

Queen Street, Chestertown
c. 1771

Houston House, Chestertown. Built for either William or James Houston, the house originally had a one-story wing. It was heightened in 1908. Michael Bourne photograph, 1995.

Houston House, Chestertown. The front parlor has a simple paneled chimney breast with a raised central panel flanked by recessed panels. The interior walls throughout are vertical beaded boards. Michael Bourne photograph, 1985.

WILLIAM HOUSTON, STAYMAKER, PURCHASED FIFTY feet of Lot No. 20 (adjoining lot No. 24) in 1771 and built the house which he and his descendants would own until 1908.[1] His house consisted of a three-bay, double-pile, two-story brick residence with one story brick kitchen wing on the northeast side. The plan consisted of the entry/stairhall with two rooms on the southwest and the kitchen on the northeast. Both principal rooms contained corner fireplaces, the larger having raised and recessed panel chimney breast similar to the treatment in the den at Aspendale, Kent Co. Delaware, built at the same time. All interior partitions were and still are vertical beaded boards.

When he died in 1782, his wife Susannah Wickes was administrator along with other relatives, Simon and Joseph Wickes. His inventory included items that were typical for a well furnished house of the day, and four slaves. It totaled £332.7.6, which was a sizeable estate for a tradesman.[2]

William and Susannah left two sons, Benjamin and James. James apparently acquired the house, for in a deed for the adjoining property in 1788, the property

begins *"at the southwest corner of Mr. Houston's house on Queen St. ... ."*[3] and again in 1802 James Houston acquires 21.5 feet of the adjoining property.[4] In 1806 James was appointed Judge of the U.S. District Court for Maryland by President Thomas Jefferson. In 1814 Judge Houston acquired the farm later known as Airy Hill, which he held until his death. He married Augusta Chambers, daughter of General Benjamin Chambers and had two daughters, Augusta and Elizabeth. When his inventory was appraised, it included such items as *"Passage & stair carpet + rods"* and a *"dressing room looking glass,"* items which could have been in either the Queen Street house or Airy Hill. There were many farm animals and seven slaves, most of which would have been located on the farm. His inventory totaled $3,959.32, an indication of his financial success and position in the community.[5]

James probably did little to improve his dwellings, as both were relatively new and would not need any more than routine maintenance. After his death, his widow married James Bowers. The Airy Hill Farm was sold, but the Queen Street house was to remain in the family. In 1841, the property was listed under the name of *"James Houston heirs."* The assessment states it was in good repair and included a stable on part of Lot No. 27, across the street, both occupied by Rev'd Webster. It descended to his daughters, Elizabeth, who married Thomas Patton of Philadelphia, and Augusta, who married John Bowers Eccleston, attorney of Chestertown. Elizabeth sold her half interest to her brother-in-law and he in turn bequeathed it to Augusta, who in turn left it to their son James H. Eccleston. At the time of the sale of Elizabeth's half, (1859),[6] the house was *"rented to and occupied by Richard Hynson,"* another prominent attorney who was to build a brick house on Water Street adjacent to *River House* in 1870.

Since the house remained rented for most, if not all, of the time, it is unlikely that much was done to the house until Augusta Eccleston's son and heir, James Houston Eccleston, sold the property in 1908 to Dr. Henry G. Simpers.[7]

Dr. Simpers contracted with Walter T. Pippin, contractor and builder, to remodel and enlarge the house for use not only as residence, but with an office for his medical practice. At this juncture, a second story was added to the old one-story kitchen wing, the door and window were changed to two windows and the front entrance door was moved about one foot to the right and given an architrave. A porch and porte-cochere were wrapped around three sides of the two-story section. Three dormers were added to the roof and the roof was given a wide overhang. A lean-to kitchen was also built behind the former kitchen.

Inside, the old stair was removed and replaced with a typical heavy stair of the period. New floors were applied over the old and a new heating system and plumbing were installed. The house remained essentially the same until it was acquired by Carolene Hynson Miller, granddaughter of Richard Hynson, who had rented it 117 years before.[8]

Mrs. Miller remodeled and up-dated the building extensively in 1976, cleaning the accumulated whitewash and paint from the exterior and removing the porches and adding an extension to the kitchen. She converted the office into a dining room after removing the chimney flue.

After her death, it was given to Washington College, and soon thereafter sold to the present owners. The new owners have gradually improved the house by re-building a stair which is closer to the period of the house, remodeled the dining room by re-building a fireplace with flanking cupboards and overmantel paneling. The master bedroom with adjoining dressing room and bath were rearranged and the 1908 bedroom was given a fireplace and bookshelves. Most recently, the 1908 overhang of the roof was removed and the dormers were remodeled to appear earlier.   K-23

1. Kent Co. Land Records, Lib. DD 3, fol. 413.
2. Kent Co. Inventories, Lib. 8, fol. 233.
3. Kent Co. Land Records, Lib. EF 7, fol. 286.
4. Kent Co. Land Records, Lib. TW 2, fol. 104.
5. Kent Co. Inventories, Lib. 16, fol. 142.
6. Kent Co. Land Records, Lib. JKH 1, fol. 679.
7. Kent Co. Land Records, Lib. JTD 17, fol. 116.
8. Kent Co. Land Records, Lib. EHP 68, fol. 424.

Shrewsbury Farm

Shrewsbury Neck
1772

GENERAL JOHN CADWALADER IS BEST KNOWN IN AMERI-can history as the man who *"quashed the Conway Cabal,"* that ill-fated move to have General Washington removed from his command in the Revolutionary Army (1778). While his home and personal belongings in Philadelphia have attracted the attention of cultural and architectural historians alike, his house at Shrewsbury Plantation on Turner's Creek has enjoyed little attention in the past.

John Cadwalader came into possession of the Shrewsbury Farm through his marriage in 1768 to Betsy Lloyd, daughter of Edward Lloyd III. In Wainwright's Colonial Grandeur in Philadelphia, he is described as *"an extremely active man who basically enjoyed rural life."* Wainwright goes on to say, *"Commercial business was not good and his attention began to focus more and more on his wife's Kent County plantation, which he called Shrewsbury Farm."* [1] Within a few years of the marriage, Cadwalader had begun building a residence on the farm and from his accounts and correspondences, it would appear that he continued improving not only the house, but the farm buildings as well. Although the accounts are somewhat spotty, it is evident that in the spring of 1771 he began purchasing building materials from John Vorhees, a merchant in Georgetown and continued to do so into 1784. There are receipts for labor, as well as for materials for plasterers, masons, and painters.

To his brother-in-law (Richard Bennett Lloyd) in London, he wrote in September 1772:

"I believe I had begun my house in Kent before you left us. We got finished in the summer and went down with our family to spend only two or three (but stayed) seven weeks, and have concluded to make some additions and improvements which will render the place more convenient against the next summer." [2]

Shrewsbury Farm, c. 1938. Geese, L. Wethered Barroll and the old house in the back ground. Delphine S. B. Kelly Collection.

Indeed, the next year there were more entries for materials purchased of John Vorhees.[3] His active service in the war lasted about three years. Two letters from William Gough, his overseer, in November and December of 1772, relate the struggles of building at such a distance.

"17 November 1772

The carpenters have shingled the house. They cannot do any more 'till it is underpinned and the chimneys run up. The Bricks Mr. Yeates promised you is not yet come. Oliver has brought some and halled some of them home, but the Winter setting in. The creek has frosen last night, and cannot get a Mason to underpin the house, and if we could get one I am afraid it freeses to hard for his work to stand. I shall try again and if I can get a Brick layer, and the weather should moderate shall set him to work. The carpenters will raise the quarter in a day or two. I believe Jobson would build the cowhouse for £40 … ."

"1 December 1772

The Bricklayers begun to underpin the House yesterday—we have got 4000 Bricks for the chimneys, the carpenters will finish shingling the Quarter toMorrow, Jobson said you told me that you told him not to do anything to the stable till you come down, however shall get him to board up the ends and make the sashes and doors for the House and then go on with the stable … ."[4]

References to the main house being plastered before 1772 eliminate these letters as referring to its construction. They are most likely references to the construction of an auxiliary dwelling on the property, such as the one to house the overseer.

During Cadwalader's service in the war, his first wife, Betsy, died. He married again in 1779 one Williamina Bond of Philadelphia. It was by Williamina that he had male heirs. After moving to Kent County in 1778, he became actively involved in the Legislature, serving twice. In 1780, he was instrumental in finding Dr. William Smith the position of rector of Chester Parish. He was also intimately involved with Dr. Smith in the founding of Washington College in 1782 and with the erection of its first building. Unfortunately, he was not to live

Shrewsbury Farm. The only old house on the farm was built in the mid-nineteenth century, possibly with materials from General John Cadwalader's earlier house. It was built in several stages. Maryland Historical Trust, M. Q. Fallaw photograph, 1985.

General John Cadwalader, Revolutionary War hero and benefactor of Washington College is buried in the Shrewsbury Parish Church churchyard. Michael C. Wootton photograph, 1996.

Receipt for funds received on account of Washington College, 1783. Cadwalader Papers, Historical Society of Pennsylvania.

long enough to see the building completed. He died two months before the building was dedicated, but must have taken great pleasure in seeing it rise from the foundation during his trips to Chestertown.

Before his death in 1786, he wrote a will leaving Shrewsbury Farm to his daughters, by his first wife. Witnesses to the will included Donaldson Yeates (his brick supplier) and Isaac Freeman. Both gentlemen resided on either side of his plantation. Unlike the Thomas Ringgolds of Chestertown, Cadwalader did not stipulate that there be no inventory of his estate. His belongings were recorded with other probate records at the Courthouse. The inventory, as well as a brief description by the 1783 Tax Assessor, provide a glimpse into the appearance of the plantation within a three year period:

"Bennett's Regulation 1000a
Good Wood & Brick dwelling, good outhouses
on Sassafras River
Middling Good Land some broken
1200 acres 600 acres arable"[5]

Customarily inventories were made by grouping like items together in small lists. Fortunately, Cadwalader's inventory was instead made by listing his belongings room by room or in some cases building by building. This helps to shed further light on the configuration of the house and plantation. The rooms mentioned are the *"Parlor," "Chamber," "1st Room upstairs," "2nd Room Upstairs," "3rd Room Upstairs,"* and *"4th Room Upstairs."* Also mentioned were the *"Cellar," "Cellar*

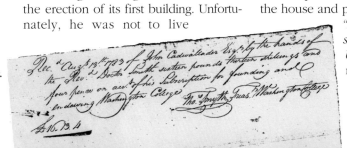

General John Cadwalader (1742-1786)

General Cadwalader died at Shrewsbury farm on February 10, 1786. Dr. William Smith conducted his funeral service at Shrewsbury Church where the general was buried. His epitaph read:

"His early and inflexible patriotism will endear his memory to all the true friends of the American Revolution. It may with the strictest justice be said of him that he possessed a heart incapable of deceiving. His manners were founded in the nicest sense of Honor and the whole tenor of his life was governed by this principle. The companions of his youth were the companions of his manhood. He never lost a friend by insincerity nor made one by deception. His domestic virtues were truly exemplary. While they serve to endear the remembrance, they embitter the loss of him to all his numerous friends and companions."

—-Thomas Paine

Kitchen," "passage," "Nursery Room," "Middle Room" and *"Upstairs over Brick Kitchen."* [6]

There are four houses in Kent County from the 1770s which have plans that this compares to, but the most similar is Piney Grove in its original form. It even had a cellar kitchen.

In June 1777, Cadwalader's account indicate that the nursery and kitchen were plastered, along with other improvements to the property. The puzzling room is the Nursery. This appears to be what in other houses of the period would have been the pantry.

It seems that Cadwalader was in the process of at least planning to build a new and more elegant house, for the inventory reads:

"NB Articles to be used in the new building proposed to be erected on Shrewsbury Farm –

33,000 3' shingles	*1380 ft cedar 1" Boards*
100,000 good bricks	*100 tons of stone*
1600 bu oysters shells	*1 Slk d Lime*
48 lb yellow oaker	*104 lb whiting*
114 lb 12d nails	*45 lb 10o nails*
172 lb 8d nails	*101 lb pewter urn*
125 lb White Lead	*articles excepted*
1 barrell Red Oaker" [7]	

This entry in the inventory, combined with subsequent entries in the accounts for work done at Shrewsbury Farm might suggest that Cadwalader's executors, his brother, Lambert, and brother-in-law, Philemon Dickenson, continued with his proposed project, even after his death. (The same sequence of events took place ten years later across Turner's Creek when Donaldson Yeates left instructions that the house he was *"about projecting"* be finished at the expense of the estate.)

Whether the *"new building"* was actually completed or not is a point for further research. If it was, it did not survive long. The older house did not survive beyond middle of the nineteenth century either.

An entry in Sydney George Fisher's diary dated November 13, 1849 describes the house in its ill-repair:

"On Sunday morning, Wister and Cadwalader took the boat and crossed over the river to the Kent side to visit the farm formerly the residence of Gen. Jno. Cadwalader of Revolutionary memory, the Genl's uncle. He had naturally a wish to see this old family, tho it has long since passed to other hands and expected to find there the tomb of his uncle in which, however, he was disappointed. He said the house is very much dilapidated and the only vestige of the family he discovered was a looking glass set in the wall on which were written with a diamond the names of various Cadwaladers, McCalls, Lloyds. Wister, whose passion is fishing, took a fine rock by trolling. Fox and myself walked over the farm. We dined and spent the evening as usual" [8]

It is likely that the house fell to ruin within a few years of General Wister's visit. Thereafter, a poorly constructed brick tenement house was built, probably using some old materials from the former residence. It was enlarged later in the nineteenth century. The majority of the farm remained in the same family until 1967. K-569

The John Cadwalader Family. In this family portrait, painted in 1772, we see General John Cadwalader with his wife, Elizabeth (Betsey) Lloyd, daughter of Edward Lloyd III of Talbot County. The General is shown presenting a peach to their first daughter, Anne. Charles Willson Peale (1741-1827). Courtesy of The Philadelphia Museum of Art: The Cadwalader Collection.

1. Wainwright, Nicholas B. Colonial Grandeur in Philadelphia, The Historical Society of Pennsylvania, Philadelphia, 1964, p. 61.
2. Ibid.
3. The Cadwalader Papers, Historical Society of Pennsylvania.
4. Ibid.
5. 1783 Tax Assessment, South Sassafras Hundred.
6. Inventories, Lib. 8, fol. 364.
7. Ibid.
8. Wilson, W. Emerson, editor, The Mount Harmon Diaries of Sydney George Fisher, 1837-1850, Historical Society of Delaware, Wilmington, 1976, p. 276.

Piney Grove

Quaker Neck
c. 1773

Situated on the Chester River between the tracts of East Huntington and Radcliffe Cross, Tilghman's Farm was patented to Richard Tilghman on January 10, 1670 and contained 900 acres.[1] Richard Tilghman died soon thereafter and left the farm to his son, Richard, Jr., who began selling off parcels beginning in 1710.[2] By 1738, William Thomas owned six hundred twenty seven acres, half of which he willed to his daughter, Mary Thomas.[3] Mary's son, Samuel Dickenson, of Talbot County, deeded 327 acres to Robert George of Kent County, in January of 1773.[4] Soon thereafter, Robert and his wife, Ann, had the original house constructed. It consisted of the southeast half of the existing dwelling.

In its original form, the house was 28' x 34', two stories tall with an *A* roof and without dormers. Two chimneys were contained within the gables, the southeast chimney being broader than the other. Since there is a large fireplace in the basement, there is some question about when a kitchen wing was constructed above ground. And, since there is an original brick opening on the northwest gable of the original house, it seems likely that the upstairs kitchen was at least planned from the beginning. Perhaps the laundry was in the basement! In the northwest basement, traces of an eighteenth century wing are visible in the front wall.

In 1783, Robert George was assessed for 410 acres of Tilghman's Farm and 140 acres of Stradford Manor. A *"Brick dwelling and other necessary houses"* are listed along with seven *"Whites"* living on the farm. The property was valued at £800.

As built, the George residence was an imposing, though vernacular form of house. The plan consisted of four rooms on the first floor, one being the stair hall on the river side of the house. The room behind the stair was of nearly equal dimensions and had a fireplace. The two other rooms were larger, the river side room having paneled jambs with two-part trim and a fireplace nearly centered. The back room had plain window jambs with backband molding and a corner fireplace. In plan the house is similar to two others in Kent, namely Springfield Farm (1770) and Hepbron's Choice, (approximately of the same date).

The second floor plan remains largely intact. Doors trim and windows remain along with some hardware. At the head of the stair is a small hall with four doors leading to the four bedrooms and an enclosure for the stair to the attic.

Of interest in the attic is the exposed roof structure which has the tie beams mortised and tenoned into the rafters and the rafters half-lapped and pegged, the reverse from usual practice. On the south side, the attic has 5" wide oak flooring whereas the other half has wide yellow pine. Three windows originally lit the attic, two in the southeast and one in the northwest gable.

By 1799, the year of Robert George's death, and two years after Ann's death, his bondsmen were required to post a bond for £10,000, a huge sum in those days. He left the majority of his land called

Piney Grove, Quaker Neck. First floor plan with two periods of construction indicated. Michael Bourne.

Piney Grove, c. 1772, consisted of the right side of the house when originally constructed for Robert George. The other half was added and the whole stuccoed around 1866 for Robert and Julianna Emory. C. Engstrom photograph, 1977.

Piney Grove, built on part of Tilghman's Farm (pat. 1670) around 1772 and enlarged c. 1866. The verandah looks toward the river and former steamboat dock with a distant view of Chestertown. Historical Society of Kent County, William Usilton Collection, c. 1940

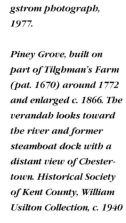

c. 1772
c. 1868
Twentieth Century

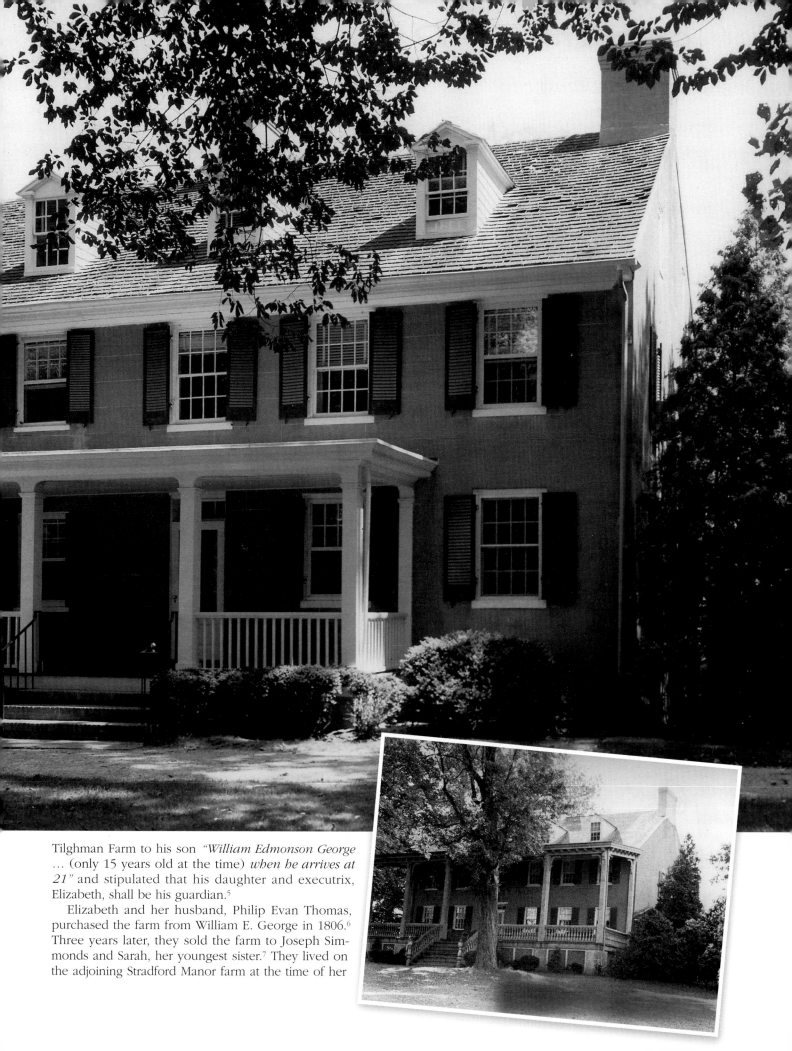

Tilghman Farm to his son *"William Edmonson George ... (only 15 years old at the time) when he arrives at 21"* and stipulated that his daughter and executrix, Elizabeth, shall be his guardian.[5]

Elizabeth and her husband, Philip Evan Thomas, purchased the farm from William E. George in 1806.[6] Three years later, they sold the farm to Joseph Simmonds and Sarah, her youngest sister.[7] They lived on the adjoining Stradford Manor farm at the time of her

Piney Grove, Quaker Neck, is the only one of four 1770s houses to retain its original floor plan.

Piney Grove, Quaker Neck. An original 1770s second story mantel.

Piney Grove, Quaker Neck, was built with a large fireplace in the basement. Like Lamb's Meadow and Tibbalds, a first story kitchen wing was added soon after initial construction. C. Engstrom photographs, 1977.

father's death. Joseph and Sarah both died in 1824, and Joseph bequeathed *"part of my Mansion Farm"* to his son Robert George Simmonds, he paying to his six younger siblings $2,000.[8] Five years later, Robert sold the farm to his sister Sarah and her husband, Bartus Trew,[9] the son of William and Mary Trew of Providence Plantation. It is not probable that the Trews lived at Tilghman's Farm, as Providence is referred to as the *"home farm"* in a deed recorded in 1840. As a result of Bartus' death, his real estate had to be sold.

Edward Comegys purchased Tilghman's Farm or the *Simmonds Farm* in 1837[10] and held it until 1848.[11] Edward owned huge tracts of land in Kent County at this period and probably lived at his ancestors' plantation known as Utrick or Comegys Bight. He sold the property to James Mansfield, a contractor, who lived on High St., Chestertown in 1841.

Mansfield was taxed on 310 acres of Tilghman's Farm in 1852, which lists *"Brick House and other buildings in good repair formerly to Edward Comegys."* It is likely that Mansfield lived here since the assessment listed livestock, furniture, plate and other property.

Mansfield sold 312 acres to Col. Edward Wilkins in 1860.[12] Col. Wilkins had married Mary A. Merritt and upon the death of her father, Joseph T. Merritt, had inherited part of Godlington Manor at the end of Wilkins Lane. Apparently, Col. & Mrs. Wilkins lived on the latter part of Godlington Manor farm, then called *Riverside* and in 1866 sold Tilghman's Farm to their daughter and son-in-law, Julianna and Robert Emory for $400 rent per annum.[13] In that deed, there is mention of a county road being laid out which *"leads to Col. Wilkins residence."*

Like his father-in-law and brother-in-law, Robert Emory was well known for his orchards. It is said in Portrait & Biographical Record 1898 that he *"Grew more pears than anyone east of California, having about 20,000 trees ... ."* In the 1877 Atlas, he is listed as *"extensive fruit grower and dealer."*

It was during the ownership of the Emorys that the house was enlarged to its present form. A nearly equal size addition was constructed over the former kitchen and houses a kitchen and pantry and large dining room on the first floor. At the same time, or soon thereafter, connection between the second floor was made, making one bedroom smaller by three feet. In order to conceal the fact that part of the old kitchen wall was incorporated into the new section, the entire six-bay structure was stuccoed and scored to resemble ashlar masonry. Two dormers in the new section were balanced by two in the old section. On the riverside a tall porch with square champhered columns and bold balustrade was constructed to take advantage of the view up river to Chestertown, as well as to keep an eye on the wharf at the foot of the property. The interior of the old section was altered very little. Chair rail was removed from the walls but window trim remained. The three fireplaces received new mantels at this time; that in the riverside parlor received a slate mantel and coal stove so typical of the latter half of the nineteenth century. One curious feature exists in that the original walnut balustrade remains, but the stairs themselves appear to have been replaced. Another handrail, dating from the 1860s, with bold newel post, and fitting the exact size of the stair was made but possibly never installed.

Since 1860, the house has remained in the same family and has become a document of one family's ties with the land. Only minor changes have occurred over the years since the major 1860s remodeling. Bathrooms were updated in the 1950s. A breakfast room was added onto part of the heightened side porch and new wallpaper and paint were applied. About the same time a large frame building used in packing the fruit before being sent down the lane to the wharf, was torn down and replaced with a three-car garage. It was stuccoed to match the house. An early brick smoke house remains between the garage and house and on the opposite side of the yard is a mid-nineteenth century ice house. Landscaping is largely the product of the 1950 remodeling.   K-242

Piney Grove, Quaker Neck. The early brick smokehouse received a coat of stucco when the house was enlarged in the nineteenth century.

Piney Grove, Quaker Neck. The roof of the nineteenth century ice house. C. Engstom photographs, 1977.

1. Patents, Lib. 14, fol. 139.
2. Land Records, Lib. JS 6, fol. 260, 264.
3. Wills, Lib. 2, fol. 103.
4. Land Records, Lib. DD 4, fol. 178.
5. Wills, Lib. 8, fol. 43.
6. Land Records, TW 3, fol. 464.
7. Land Records, BC 6, fol. 53.
8. Wills, Lib. 10, fol. 366.
9. Land Records, JNG 1, fol. 483.
10. Land Records, JNG 6, fol. 158.
11. Land Records, JNG 11, fol. 712.
12. Land Records, JKH 2, fol. 276.
13. Land Records, JKH 5, fol. 676.

The Archibald Wright House

Georgetown
c. 1773

EORGETOWN CONTAINS FOUR EIGHTEENTH CENTURY houses which survived the devastation wrought by the British when they burned the town in 1813. Two of those were joined together and remodeled after being acquired in 1924 and 1929 by Herbert G. Stine of Washington County. The southern property was built on lot No. 37 and the northern property on Lot No. 30, both being one half acre lots that are recorded on the renewed plat of Georgetown, dated 1787.

The southern property was acquired in 1773 by Archibald Wright from the heir of Edward Drugan for the small sum of £10.[1] The house was built by Wright some time after 1773 and before his death in 1783. According to the general conditions set forth for the purchasing of lots, the house should have been started within 18 months from the time of purchase in order to retain ownership.

The form and plan of the building are similar to the Wickes House in Chestertown and Worsell Manor, near Warwick, Cecil County, both of which were built before the Revolution. Some of the interior details, however, and the belt course on the Flemish bond facade appear post-Revolutionary, like Rich Level and Duck Hollow.

Wright's house was built three bays long and two stories tall over a deep basement on the top of the hill in the small village of Georgetown. Attached to its south gable was a kitchen, one bay and one story, but the full depth of the two room deep structure. Beside the aforementioned facade having central door with transom, the side walls were laid in common bond with most of the header courses laid in glazed headers which created striped gables, similar to the north gable of Trumpington on Eastern Neck. Its plan consisted of a central stairhall with four rooms, all heated by corner fireplaces. The chimney bases were corbeled out from the bottom of the cellar wall, like that at Violet Farm (1762).

The northeast room was finished with the most elaborate woodwork in the house. The diagonal chimney breast was fitted with double crossetted trim around the fireplace and overmantel panel, the panel being a raised panel with usual thumbnail molding. The combination of the panel and crossettes is a co-mingling of vernacu-

finished with very simple mantels or fireplace surrounds.

After the death of Archibald Wright in 1783, the property passed first into the hands of his son John, and subsequently in the nineteenth century, to John's daughters, Juliana Bordley, Ann Rumsey and Mary Everett. Mary Everett ended up purchasing the interests of her siblings and resided there until 1822.[2] In that same year Mary deeded it to her daughter, Mary, wife of the Reverend Purnell F. Smith, the Rector of Shrewsbury Parish.[3] The Smiths also owned Valley Cottage, the gambrel roof dwelling south of this property, on Lot No. 51.

In 1857, Mary Smith deeded the property to her daughter Serena Smith: "... *to have and to hold ... especially one brick dwelling house and several wooden outhouses erected and situated on Lot No. 37 ... .*"[4]

For the rest of the nineteenth century and up until her death in 1921, the house was referred to as the *"Serena Smith Property."* It took a decree of Chancery Court to settle Miss Smith's estate, as the heirs were numerous, all of her siblings having predeceased her, leaving many nieces and nephews.

The deed was not recorded until 1928 when it was transferred to Herbert Stine, who had acquired the adjoining Kitty Knight property four years before. Thereafter the two houses were joined and turned into the Kitty Knight House Restaurant and Inn. Since that time the two buildings have been transferred in a single deed.[5]   K-147

The Archibald Wright House, chimney wall in principal room (N. E.) with raised panel and double crossetted trim. C. Engstrom photograph, 1977.

Archibald Wright House, Georgetown, c. 1773, was occupied by his descendants into the twentieth century. In plan and form it is similar to the Wallis-Wickes House in Chestertown. The Wright and Kitty Knight House were joined together in the late 1920s and converted into the present Inn. Michael Bourne photograph, 1979.

The Archibald Wright House. Detail of the masonry and nineteenth century front door. Michael C. Wootton photograph, 1996.

lar and design book elements. Around the ceiling of the room there is a cornice that has disproportionate dentils, a vernacular interpretation that is as crude as the dentils added to the entry hall of the Hynson-Ringgold House in Chestertown. Equally naive is a corner cupboard with reeded pilasters and crudely executed arched trim with keystone.

A close string stair with paneled spandrel was built in the southwest corner of the center hall. A summer beam across the center of the hall was paneled. The other rooms were

1. Land Records, Lib. DD 4, fol. 190.
2. Land Records, Lib. BC 6, fol. 72, 74.
3. Land Records, Lib. TW 4, fol. 198.
4. Land Records, Lib. JKH 1, fol. 25.
5. Land Records, Lib. RAS 1, fol. 592.

Hinchingham on the Bay

Near Rock Hall
c. 1774

Hinchingham on the Bay, 1774, was the second dated house built by James Frisby, this for his third wife. It is sited next to the Bay and looks west to Baltimore and Harford Counties. Tyler Campbell photograph, 1995.

AT LEAST SIX HISTORIC DWELLING HOUSES REMAIN ON THE Hinchingham tract, this being the most significant and the only one listed on the National Register.

The land known as Hinchingham began as a grant of 2200 acres *"on the East Side of the Chesapeake Bay"* made to Thomas Hynson in 1659.[1] By the mid-eighteenth century the huge quantity of land had been divided into nine parcels. This parcel appears to have been owned by John Gresham who bequeathed it in 1750 to his daughter Sarah.[2] Sarah became the first wife of James Frisby III and it was through their marriage that this part of Hinchingham came into the Frisby family. The family also owned another parcel about a mile south of this site. James and Sarah may have lived on the plantations, but she died young and James was married a second time to Rebecca Ringgold, sister of Thomas Ringgold of Chestertown. Rebecca and James resided at the Violet Farm, near St. Paul's Church, which they had built in 1762.

After Rebecca's death, James Frisby married a third time, Margaret Moore, and it was for her that he built the present Hinchingham house in 1774. Interestingly, James would marry again after the death of Margaret, this final marriage to Ann Wilmer. He continued to live at Hinchingham until his death in 1807. In addition to marrying four times and fathering eleven children, James Frisby was a Commissioner for Justice in Kent County. In the 1790 Census he was listed as the owner of thirty slaves. One of his oldest daughters, Anna Maria, was responsible for the construction of another important Kent County house—Airy Hill. William, his son, lived at Big Fairlee. Three daughters by his last two wives received the majority of his lands: Margaret, who was married to Dr. Morgan Brown, received the Violet Farm, and Rebecca, wife of the Reverend Simon Wilmer V received Hinchingham.[3]

The house which James Frisby built on Hinchingham was similar to, but plainer than the Violet Farm. Composed of two parts, it had a five-bay, two-and-a-half-story main part and a four-bay, one-and-a-half-story service wing. The main part had a central stairhall with two flanking rooms. The principal room (south room) had pilasters flanking the chimney breast and arched glazed cupboards beyond them. Rather than full paneling, there was paneled wainscoting on the other walls. It had a well-developed cornice with modillions. The north room had plainer paneling with closet adjacent the fireplace.

Like the Violet Farm, Hinchingham was built of Flemish bond on the front and rear facades and English bond elsewhere. The only regular use of glazed headers was in the date 1774 in the south gable. No initials were installed with the date. The kitchen or service wing had a small porch also covered by the *A* roof, like Springfield Farm nearby.

The Reverend Simon Wilmer served as Protestant Episcopal Minister of Shrewsbury Parish from 1803-1806. In 1804 he was appointed a deputy to the General Convention of the Episcopal Church. He was later Rector of St. Paul's Church from 1808-1810. In the first year of his stay at St. Paul's he purchased Stepney, his boyhood home adjacent Chestertown. His actual place of residence has not been established. Wilmer sold Stepney in 1813 and Hinchingham later in 1819.

John E. Gale acquired Hinchingham around 1835.[4] He owned Gresham College to the north, as well as a farm on the opposite side of the main road. Gale apparently resided at Gresham College as it was in better repair than Hinching-

Hinchingham on the Bay, 1774. The south room is finished with some of the best early Georgian woodwork in the county. Tyler Campbell photograph, 1996.

Hinchingham on the Bay, 1774. Detail of glazed date on the south gable. Gene Johnstone photograph, 1995

Hinchingham on the Bay, 1774. The Bay side (west). Tyler Campbell photograph, 1995.

Muddy Branch Farm

Near Worton
1774

WHEN THE NAME ISAAC PERKINS IS MENTIONED IN REFERence to the Perkins Mills on Morgan Creek, it is usually associated with White House Farm, as he owned both. However, Perkins had actually been living on Muddy Branch Farm, a few miles away, at the time of his death in 1791.

It is reported that the date 1774 is etched in a chimney brick. If so, that would place the construction date in the year Perkins turned thirty-one. Unlike his father's house on White House Farm, his was a four-bay, two-story, brick structure which had been built over a full basement.

The south facade was laid in Flemish bond and had two doors and two windows with segmented arches above. The rear facade was similar, but with only one door. The presence of a segmental arch higher than the east window points to the original location of the interior stair.

When constructed, the plan consisted of three rooms, the hall with stair in the east end and two rooms on the west end. This plan was altered in the late nineteenth century when a central stair was built in the former hall. At that time, the old corner stair was removed and the second front door was

Muddy Branch Farm, 1774. The living room mantel. C. Engstrom photograph, 1977.

ham which was listed as in *"bad repair"* in 1852.[5] At the time of his death, Gale's son, John L. Gale became owner of Hinchingham. After his death, his widow, Araminta Harper was given use of the south rooms, a cellar and kitchen for her lifetime.[6] It was during the ownership by John L. Gale that a tall one-room addition was constructed on the south gable. It appears in Swepson Earle's Maryland's Colonial Eastern Shore.

After the Gale occupancy, the farm was acquired by George B. Westcott[7] in whose family it remained until 1931 when Carolene Hynson duPont purchased it.[8] Mrs. duPont, later Mrs. Clifton Miller, restored the house to a pristine condition which it had not seen since it was constructed. Hinchingham became a showplace, was featured in Forman's Early Manor and Plantation Houses and was frequently on the Maryland House and Garden Pilgrimage. The Miller occupancy ended in 1958 and since that time Hinchingham has had four owners. K-101

1. Certificates, Lib. 4, fol. 223; Patents, Lib. 4, fol. 302.
2. Wills, Lib. WH 3, fol. 184.
3. Wills, Lib. BC 5, fol. 405.
4. Land Records, Lib. JNG 3, fol. 654; JNG 4, fol. 235.
5. 1852 Tax Assessment.
6. Land Records, Lib. JFG 5, fol. 100.
7. Land Records, Lib. DCB 3, fol. 231.
8. Land Records, Lib. RAS 7, fol. 402.

changed into a long window. The kitchen wing was always located on the east end of the building.

One of the most unusual features of the house is the cornice which has the ends of the attic joists exposed and shaped into decorative ogee, a feature it has in common with Lansdowne in Queen Annes County.

Perkins was a member of the Lower House of the Maryland Legislature in 1777, and again from 1786–87. He was purchasing agent for the Revolutionary Army and in that position, also profited by supplying wheat to the Army.

In 1780 the mills were destroyed by fire, but Perkins rebuilt the following year. He had amassed a fortune in property and personal belongings by the time of his death. Beside being a successful owner and operator of mills, Perkins was a farmer and merchant during his lifetime.[1] His personal property was appraised for £4,123.12.4, including 19 slaves. Perkins bequeathed his estate to his two sons and five daughters.[2]   K-228

1. Papenfuse, p. 643.
2. Wills, Lib. 7, fol. 458

Muddy Branch Farm, 1774, was the home plantation of Isaac Perkins who owned and operated the mills at the upper reaches of Morgan Creek which his father had established.

Muddy Branch Farm, 1774, is the only Kent County house to have exposed decorative joists in place of a cornice. The form of the house was similar to Emory Sudler's house at Radcliffe Cross originally. C. Engstrom photographs, 1977.

William's Venture

Near Rock Hall
c. 1775

THE TRACT WILLIAM'S VENTURE WAS PATENTED IN 1725 TO William Bradshaw. It consisted then of 114 acres.[1] When he died in 1773, Bradshaw bequeathed his dwelling plantation to his son, John.[2] In 1770 and 1772, John Bradshaw sold first two, then seven and a half acres to John Page, planter, which was to be known for the next eighty years as *Page's Point*. Page paid £85 for the two parcels, which was not enough for a substantial brick house to have been standing.[3]

John Page built a house on the point soon after he purchased the land. When first constructed, the house was a four-bay, one-and-a-half-story brick house built on a high stone basement. Both facades were laid in Flemish bond and the north gable in English bond.

The plan of the house was a somewhat typical hall-parlor plan, but it differed from most in that it had nearly equally sized rooms. The stair, located in the northeast corner of the hall was a full-blown, two flight, open-string stair with finely turned walnut balustrade. It also possessed the added refinement of raised panel wainscot in both rooms and two-part cornice. Between the two rooms there was a vertical board partition with corner cupboard built into the parlor. The parlor fireplace had a mantel with dentil course beneath the shelf on a full wall of raised paneling. A kitchen wing was located off the south gable of the house.

William's Venture c. 1775, was originally one-and-a-half stories tall. When heightened in the second quarter of the nineteenth century, it had a porch which de-emphasized the lack of syummetry.1977.

William's Venture, c. 1775. The finely executed walnut balustrade stands in sharp contrast to the original form of the house. C. Engstrom photographs, 1977.

In 1783, John Page was taxed on the small acreage he had acquired from Bradshaw, along with 860 other acres. He apparently had a warehouse on one of his properties, because Benjamin Chambers was taxed on one hogshead of tobacco at John Page's warehouse in the same assessment.[4]

Page left the property to his son, Henry, but Henry lost it to the state, apparently for non-payment of taxes. In 1806, the property was sold to a Philadelphia lawyer by the name of James Vaux.[5] Vaux sold the property (which then contained ten acres) to John Humphreys in 1808.[6] Henceforth, the point became known as *Humphreys Point*. During the long ownership of John Humphreys, the second story was added to the old house. Modern brick was used and there was no attempt made to follow the Flemish bond pattern. Like many early nineteenth century brick houses, the cornice was constructed of corbeled brick. The three windows of the second story did not line up with those below. The addition of a leanto porch helped to minimize this asymmetry. The same treatment was employed at Little Neck across Swan Creek. An old photo in Robert Johnson's *Gravesend, Serene But Still Profound* shows the house with the porch.

John Humphreys died without a will in 1851. His widow, Martha declined to administer the estate, so the job was taken over by his two neighbors, Merritt Miller and

William's Venture, c. 1775. The parlor chimney wall has classically inspired details in the mantel.

William's Venture, c. 1775. Detail of paneled wainscot in parlor. C. Engstrom photographs, 1977.

John Reid House

High Street, Chestertown
c. 1775

BY TRADITION, THE TWO STORY BRICK HOUSES NUMBERED 518 and 520 High Street were constructed by members of the Reid (or Reed) family. From the land records it is difficult to pinpoint the exact date of acquisition of Lot No. 61 by John Reid, but in 1775, Robert Reid (probably his brother) acquired one-half of Lot No. 62 adjoining John's lot. The bounds of the half lot state *"beginning at the end of an old building now in the possession of Sarah Craig and running from thence up High Street 66' to a new brick building in possession of John Reid ... ."* [1]

In its original form, 520 High Street was a three-bay, two-story house built high above a kitchen basement. Like the facade of its contemporary, Hopkins House (K-66, 536 High Street), it has a central door with two flanking windows

John Reid House, Chestertown, referred to as a " ... new brick building in possession of John Reid ... " in 1775. It was a small scale vernacular hall-parlor plan house when built. Michael C. Wootton photograph, 1996.

James Page who lived up the creek. Two other neighbors, Abel Rees and Hiram Jones appraised the estate.[7]

By the time the county appraisers visited the property in 1852, it was in the name of Miss Catherine Humphreys and the house was listed in bad repair.[8] By 1877, the property appears to be in the ownership of John Humphreys' appraiser, Abel Rees.[9]

When the property was purchased in the 1950s by Berthold and Silvia Atwater Bothe, it had seen years of neglect.[10] In their renovation, an old two-story kitchen wing was replaced by a one-and-a-half story frame structure. The porches were removed, as was the north fireplace and chimney. Inside, the partition between the hall and parlor was removed, creating one large room. The fact that the house has survived its damp location is a tribute to the materials and craftsmanship of its builders.

K-260

1. Certificates, Lib. IL No. A, fol. 637; Patents, Lib. PL No. 6, fol. 131.
2. Wills, Lib. 4, fol. 319.
3. Land Records, Lib. DD 3, fol. 391; Lib. DD 4, fol. 79.
4. 1783 Tax Assessment.
5. Land Records, Lib. TW 3, fol. 349.
6. Land Records, Lib. BC 5, fol. 351.
7. Bonds, Lib. 13, fol. 68; Inventories, Lib. 27, fol. 96, 102, 126; Accounts, Lib. 20, fol. 264.
8. 1852 Tax Assessment.
9. 1877 Atlas.
10. Land Records, Lib. EHP 18, fol. 296.

and three symmetrically placed windows above. The scale was smaller and the windows had 9/6 sash on the first floor and 6/6 sash on the second. Its plan consisted of a hall/parlor plan, like the Palmer House (K-65), with a kitchen basement.

What happened to John Reid has not been documented, but the property fell on hard times under the ownership of the heirs of Robert Reid in the early nineteenth century. They were finally sold in 1823 and 1829 to Thomas Dugan, who was listed as owning two houses on Lot No. 61, along with several other properties in the area in the 1841 Tax Assessment. Emiline Dugan owned a third dwelling on Lot No. 61—this is documented in the tax assessment as well.[2]

Between 1841 and 1900 there were seven owners, the last being Enoch Pleasanton. It was probably he who was responsible for installing a front porch across the facade and a frame leanto kitchen on the back of the building. The windows were changed and the plan altered to a center stair plan. The porch remained on the house until about 1980 when it was removed and replaced by a simple stoop. At the same time the facade was painted.   K-64

> 1. Land Records, Lib. DD 5, fol. 100.
> 2. 1841 Tax Assessment.

The Hopkins House

High Street, Chestertown
c. 1777

In the 500 block of High Street, Chestertown, there are four eighteenth century masonry dwellings. Of the four, the Hopkins House is the most substantial, being two full stories tall.

Edward Hopkins purchased part of Lot No. 63 from Simon Wilmer in 1777 for the sum of £25, a sum too small to have included a dwelling. In fact, the deed says nothing about a dwelling of any sort, only that Mary Mason lived on an adjoining lot.[1]

Shortly after acquiring the lot, Hopkins built a two-story, brick house, 37' 6" by 18' 7", with a three-bay facade laid in Flemish bond above a remarkably refined molded astragal water table. The central entrance had a six panel door with transom above and a molded architrave overlapping the brickwork. Flanking the entrance were benches, like most of the contemporary houses of Chestertown. The 12/12 sash windows had no lintels or arches, only a continuation of Flemish bond supported on the frame itself. It is not known if in its original configuration there was a kitchen on the upper end, since there was also a kitchen fireplace in the basement.

The Hopkins House was built on Lot No. 63 after being acquired in 1777 by Edward Hopkins. Michael C. Wootton photograph, 1996.

Hopkins chose a central stairhall plan for his new house and, like several in the area, the interior partitions were made of vertical feather-edge paneling. The doors within are of a better quality than most, with raised panels inside, and requiring a thicker stock for the stiles and rails. They are hung on cast butt hinges in contrast to the battened exterior doors which are hung on large HL hinges.

The two rooms which flank the stair were finished with baseboard, chair rail and simple mantels, each of which has a flat frieze with shaped ends suggesting a cushion frieze. The stair itself ascends to the second floor in three runs. The closed-string balustrade is composed of turned newels and thin rectangular balusters above a single raised-panel spandrel.

The second floor had the same room arrangement, plus a small room at the head of the stair. The partitions on the second floor are composed of vertical beaded boards. With a different balustrade, the stair continues to the unfinished attic. During the recent restoration of the house, whitewash was found on the ceiling members, indicating that it was occupied prior to the second story being plastered.

Another feature discovered during the restoration of the dining room was a glazed cabinet cupboard adjacent the fireplace. It had been a corner cupboard, but was moved late in the nineteenth century to block a door to an adjoining building.

Edward Hopkins died in 1796, leaving his house and lot to Elizabeth, his wife, for her lifetime, after which it was to go to his nephew, " ... *the eldest son of my brother, William Hopkins ... .*"[2] In the inventory of debts due his estate, a curious entry reading *"Wm Bigs*

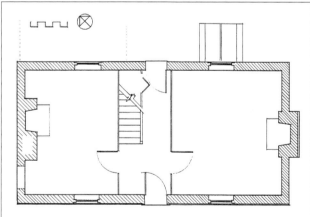

for poor House in full £55.6.9," indicating some connection with the Alms House, then being housed in the old Kent Free School.[3] After disbursements, his personal estate was worth £579.12.2, indicating a moderately comfortable household.[4]

Five years after Edward's death, Elizabeth remarried a man named William Pope from Georgetown, after a premarital contract was prepared in which everything that was owned by Elizabeth would remain her property.[5] The marriage endured for ten years before Elizabeth died in 1811. Her estate was worth $1622.39 and was distributed to three Palmers, her neighbors one being the executor.[6] Some of the belongings were sold at auction and her husband purchased a few necessities. Other items were purchased by her neighbor and heir, John Palmer.[7] In the final account, there is mention of *"... one cupboard appraised at $10.00 given to Real Property,"* which indicates that the cupboard remained in the house.[8]

The Hopkins House, Chestertown. Living room with original corner cupboard that was appraised with the real property upon the death of Elizabeth Hopkins Pope in 1811. Tyler Campbell photograph, 1995

The Hopkins House, c. 1777. First floor plan. Michael Bourne, 1997.

A long time passed before Edward Hopkins' nephew sold the property. James Hopkins of Queen Annes County sold the house and lot in 1831 to the man who was renting it, Samuel Mansfield.[9] In the 1841 Tax Assessment of Chestertown, the Mansfield heirs were taxed on *"... two houses and Lot Pt No 63 occupied by T. Dugan and I. Arthur in good repair."* They were ap-

The Hopkins House, Chestertown. The hall looking into the dining room. Feather edge partitions are used on the first story. Tyler Campbell photograph, 1995.

Simon Wickes House

*Water Street, Chestertown
c. 1780*

SIMON WICKES PURCHASED WATER LOT NO. 10 AND HALF of Lot No. 15 opposite in 1780 for the sum of *"222 bushels of Good merchantable wheat."* [1] He immediately set out building a fine brick house that would be similar to that at 110 Water Street. The house was built into the river bank and is nearly one story higher on the water side than on the street. Flemish bond was used below the water table on the facade as well as on three other walls. Glazed headers were used in the bond on the northeast gable, creating an archaic effect in relation to the all header bond on the street facade. There was a porch on the river side, probably with a stair to the ground level. There is evidence that the street entrance had a deck with benches flanking the door.

Like the house at 110 Water Street, the original kitchen was located in the basement, with access to the river side yard from a central entrance. The central hall contained the stair on the main floor and above. This stairhall was separated from the two flanking rooms by vertical board partitions. On the second floor, the northeast end of the house was divided into two separate rooms, the larger room having the fireplace. This arrangement was like the Violet Farm and Tibbalds.

In the northeast room of the first floor, the fireplace wall was originally sheathed with raised fielded paneling, a feature common throughout the eighteenth century. Flanking the fireplace were cabinets or closets. In the southwest room the fireplace is off-center because of the large flue from the kitchen fireplace below. The chimney breast had no paneling, but a mantel, corner boards and cornice forming a frame for a plaster panel. The same treatment was used on the two fireplaces on the second floor. All of the windows had splayed jambs with paneled interior shutters.

Sometime before 1805 Simon Wickes purchased the Custom House. Whether or not Mr. Wickes moved his residence there can not be ascertained from the existing records. In his will of 1813, however, he bequeathed his real estate first to his daughter Elizabeth and then to his son Simon Wickes, Jr. While Elizabeth is listed as owner of 115 Water Street in the 1841 Tax Assessment the house is further described as *"occupied by Mrs. Perkins."*

After Elizabeth's death the house was indeed sold to the Perkins family who retained ownership of it until 1942. In the nineteenth century, the Perkins family re-

praised for $1100. Mansfield was probably responsible for replacing the bottom newel and for retrimming the living room windows and possibly the ceiling of the second floor.[10]

Between 1847 and 1850, the five Mansfield heirs conveyed their interest in the property to James W. Phillips.[11] In his deed of 1865, Phillips sells the brick house, but keeps the remaining property which is referred to as *"Phillips frame house property,"* possibly referring to the building remaining on the corner of High Street and College Avenue. [12]

Henrietta Boyd and her family owned the brick house between 1865 and 1898, when it was sold to Mary Maslin.[13] One of these women is pictured in an early photograph found at the Maryland Historical Society.

Samuel E. Cooper purchased the house in 1902 and it remained in his family until 1969.[14] The recent owners have gradually restored the interior of the house to its former appearance. The cupboard in the dining room was returned to its original place in the living room where it had been when the Hopkins resided in the house 200 years ago. K-66

1. Land Records, Lib. DD 5, fol. 240.
2. Wills, Lib. 7, fol. 521.
3. Inventories, Lib. 10, fol. 478.
4. Accounts, Lib. 9, fol. 299.
5. Land Records, Lib. TW 2, fol. 140.
6. Inventories, Lib. TW 2, fol. 140.
7. Ibid., fol. 507.
8. Accounts, Lib. 13, fol. 23.
9. Land Records, Lib. JNG 2, fol. 423.
10. Samuel and Ann Mansfield were the parents of Mary Ann Mansfield, who became the wife of Senator George Vickers.
11. Land Records, Lib. JNG 11, fol. 645, 548; Lib. JR 1, fol. 65.
12. Land Records, Lib. JKH 4, fol. 613.
13. Land Records, Lib. JTD 1, fol. 524.
14. Land Records, Lib. JTD 6, fol. 362.

After their acquisition of the house in 1942, Mr. and Mrs. Richard Carvell enclosed part of the porch and made a den. The porch was also lengthened and that part converted into a screened porch with access to ground level. A small fish pond was installed between the porch and street. On the street entrance a double brick stair with wrought iron railing was installed. Other improvements to the heating, plumbing and kitchen were made at that time as well.

Silhouette of Simon Wickes, died in 1815. Son of Joseph Wickes. He married Mary Freeman, and was the father of Captain Simon Wickes (d. 1848). Mrs. Daniel Wickes Dietrick collection.

Simon Wickes House, c. 1780, was similar to the McHard House across the street, with basement kitchen and central hall plan. It too has all header bond on the facade. Michael C. Wootton photograph, 1996.

modeled the house by adding a large double dormer centered over the stair hall for extra headroom. They also added three dormers on the street side of the roof and overhanging eaves. All of the windows were replaced, including their trim. The balustrade was also replaced; however, they kept many other original features. Later in the nineteenth century, a kitchen and lavatory were constructed on the river side of the building with access from one of the gable windows in the southwest room.

In 1971, Mr. and Mrs. Charles Atherton purchased the property from the Carvells. Their occupancy only lasted until 1972, at which time they sold the house to Mr. and Mrs. William Sears who maintained the old landmark house for the next ten years. In 1982, Mr. and Mrs. George Dean purchased the house and began its restoration. They essentially brought the form and function and many of the details back to the Wickes period, while introducing modern conveniences.   K-17

1. Lib. DD 5, fol. 538.

Bolton-Anderson House

Maple Avenue, Chestertown
c. 1780

Bolton-Anderson House.
The older right part of
the house was probably
built by John Bolton (d.
1784) and enlarged by
James Anderson after
Bolton's death.
Tyler Campbell
photograph, 1996.

Bolton-Anderson House,
Maple Avenue, Chester-
town. Detail of gable,
phase II with off-set
kitchen wing. Gene John-
stone photograph, 1997.

JOHN BOLTON, MERCHANT OF CHESTERTOWN, PURCHASED lot No. 23 in 1759 for the sum of £28.[1] This price indicates that there was little in the way of improvement on the property at that time. Bolton constructed his own residence on the north side of the lot, on the corner of Queen and Fish Streets. He also built a stable or *"cow house"* in the yard, for it is described as such in his will written in 1784 and is listed in subsequent deeds as the same.[2]

In an effort to pay off Bolton's debts, Thomas McClure, his executor, sold off most of his properties. Bolton's house and its *cow house* were sold to William Dunn in 1786.[3] The southeast part of the lot, however, had been sold earlier, in 1784, immediately after Bolton's death, to James Anderson.[4] As Anderson paid nearly as much for his half lot as Dunn had paid for his (£301 and £350 respectively) it is likely that the half lot was similarly improved with a dwelling house and that Bolton had been responsible for its construction.

While the earliest part of the existing structure consists of the three most northwestern bays, the two bay extension along the same axis is nearly as old. It, as well as the one-and-a-half-story, four-bay brick wing out the back date from the late eighteenth century.

During the nineteenth century overhanging eaves and a central gable with flanking dormers were added (an addition similar to that of its neighbor on the corner of Water Street). A flat roof two bay porch was added to the front. Later, a board and batten carriage house was built in the back of the property. In 1901, a frame second story was built on to the old kitchen wing.

Around 1970, the porch was enclosed, but the original beaded weatherboard can still be seen along with the original 9/6 windows with period trim. The original section has 6/6 sash on the second story, whereas the two bay extension has 9/6. The chimneys are exposed on both gable ends of the house.   K-20

1. Land Records, Lib. JS 29, fol. 188.
2. Land Records, Lib. EF 6, fol. 377.
3. Land Records, Lib. EF 7, fol. 36.
4. Land Records, Lib. EF 6, fol. 377.

Killy Langford

Near Chestertown
c. 1780

KILLY LANGFORD IS LOCATED ON THE EAST BRANCH OF Langford Creek and possesses a combination of structures dating from three different periods. The squared log or plank one-and-a-half-story section may be the earliest. This one-room and loft structure had a fireplace on its east gable and an enclosed stair in the northeast corner. The adjoining, slightly taller, one-and-a-half-story frame section was probably constructed in the late eighteenth or early nineteenth century. It appears to have been another one-room and loft structure with its stair in the southeast corner adjacent the fireplace. Both of these sections were built facing south.

A third section, built in the 1880s, is set at right angles to the others with its west facing facade looking down the lane and across the open expanse of fields. The final wing may have been built by William Ford, who appears as owner of Killy Langford in the 1877 Atlas. The house originally had a front porch across the facade of the 1880s section and a one-story bay window on the south gable. Overall, the builder of the final section brought the farmhouse into an equal footing with most of Kent County's farmhouses of the period.   K-81

Right: Worth's Folly was built on part of a 1687 patent by that name around 1780, probably by James Dunkan who owned the adjoining farm to the north. Michael C. Wootton photograph, 1996.

Below: Killy Langford, now called Islandia, is composed of three distinct building periods, the log section presumably the oldest. M. L. Fritz photograph, 1981.

Worth's Folly

Near Worton
c. 1780

WORTH'S FOLLY WAS A 1000 ACRE TRACT FIRST PATENTED TO John Worth in 1687. In the late eighteenth century on part of that tract, a substantial brick house was constructed. In form it had a three bay two story main block with a one-and-a-half-story kitchen wing. As built, the house faced south and had a quarter round water table, but no belt course in the Flemish bond brick work. The two basement windows had three-centered arches and the first story windows had row-lock arches. The windows of the first floor had 9/6 sash with those on the second story having 6/6—a very common proportion in Kent County houses of the late eighteenth century.

The north facade was laid in common bond and was similar to the south facade, except that there were only two windows on the second story, quite like its neighbor Dunkan's Folly.

Originally the plan consisted of a hall and parlor. A full wall of paneling contained the hall stair with closet beneath, the fireplace and another closet on the opposite side.

An interesting deviation from the normal second floor plan occurs here and at Dunkan's Folly across the road. There is a passage leading to an attic stair located in the center of the build-

ing. The usual location would be in the corner above the first stair. The location of the attic stair is the determining factor in not having a central window on the north side of the house. There were two small chambers on the south side of the passage, divided from each other by vertical beaded board walls. A third chamber, above the parlor, was partitioned by a brick wall. In the eastern most chamber there was a small arched fireplace. All second floor joists were originally exposed and beaded, but the first floor was ceiled.

Early in the twentieth century, a framed second story was added over the one story kitchen wing. A straight run stair was added in the kitchen wing for access to the new room, as well as the old parlor chamber. Subsequent alterations were made in the 1970s and 1995.   K-108

Worth's Folly c. 1940. Seen here with a kitchen door in place of the present window. Maryland State Archives, Don Swan Collection.

Worth's Folly. Living room or hall with original paneled east wall. C. Engstrom photograph, 1977.

Salutation Farm

Near Lynch
c. 1780

THE LAND ON WHICH SALUTAtion Farm house sits was in the Rasin family for the majority of the eighteenth century. In 1795, when William Rasin sold it to Robert Buchanan, it consisted of parts of Forresters Delight, Hales, and Hillens Adventure and by the time of Buchanan's death, in 1799, it totaled 385 acres.[1]

In all probability, the house

Salutation Farm was probably built in the 1780s by William Raisin. It has many details that are similar to Friendship nearby. Gene Johnstone photograph, 1997.

Opposite: Salutation Farm. First floor plan. Michael Bourne.

was built by William Rasin in the 1780s as it has some of the same details as nearby Friendship, dated 1782. When constructed, it had a two-part composition with two-bay, two-story brick section and a slightly lower two-bay, two-story frame kitchen wing. The entry/stair hall and parlor were in the brick part and the kitchen was located in the frame section, three steps lower. Like Friendship, all joists were exposed and beaded, on both floors. The parlor fireplace was finished with a well-designed mantel with simple classic shelf. The stair was built with a short section of close-string balustrade, with walnut newel and handrail, before winding to the second story. Beaded board partitions were used between the stairhall and parlor and the bedrooms above. Beneath the house the basement walls were built with stone below grade and an exterior bulkhead entrance was located on the west gable. The back or north side of the house probably had the same fenestration.

The house appears to have remained essentially the same, from the time of Robert Buchanan's death in 1799 through Daniel Lamb's ownership, which terminated at his death in 1824. Lamb bequeathed this part of his large holdings to his niece, Mary Ann Alston, a

member of the Cecil Quaker Meeting where she had married John Norris. During the Norris ownership, a frame wing with stone basement was constructed on the north side of the house which covered the north windows and was connected by the original back door. It had a chimney centered on the addition which adjoined the old back wall. With the addition came the introduction of new windows north of the fireplaces on the west wall. In order to match the narrower frames of the new windows all others were renewed in a like manner with the exception of those in the attic. A bulkhead to the new cellar was constructed on the east side of the new back wing. Probably the older rooms were ceiled during the same remodeling.

The farm remained in the Norris family between 1824 and 1889, when Mary Ann's son, William Norris had to sell it to cover his debts.[2] Between 1890 and 1938 it was owned by Chestertown lawyer John D. Urie and his wife Lilian.[3] In 1953 the farm was purchased by Arthur and Lilian Montell, who remodeled the house by

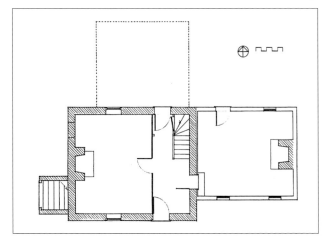

enlarging the north wing, installed bath and laundry rooms, porch and a garage.[4]

Two other owners followed the Montells in the 1960s and 70s until it was purchased in 1975 by the present owners.

East of the house is the only existing brick bank barn in Kent County. It's walls are laid in common bond and the shuttered windows have flat brick arches above bold wood frames. The principal opening to the barn is centered on the north side, which has no other openings. On the south, at a lower level, are stable doors. Two tiers of windows are centered above the doors. The original crude framing remains in place, although some flooring has been removed from the upper of the three levels. K-109

1. Land Records, Lib. EF 6, fol. 398; Wills, Lib. 8, fol. 24.
2. Land Records, Lib. SB 12, fol. 104.
3. Land Records, Lib. SB 14, fol. 177; Lib. RAS 20, fol. 561.
4. Land Records, Lib. WHG 31, fol. 188.

Peacock House Site

Millington
c. 1780

O N THE NORTH SIDE OF CYPRESS STREET IN MILLINGTON, there stood a long gambrel roof dwelling that burned in the mid 1980s. From the remains of the burned shell, it was apparent that the house was built in several stages. The eastern section was a plank building and to it a brick wing had been added on the west. It has been suggested that the plank section originally had an A roof and the whole was made a gambrel when the extension was added, similar to the development of White House Farm, Massey. Its facade was stuccoed and scored to resemble ashlar masonry.

The interior developed into a central hall with two flanking rooms on each story. Around 1890 a two story frame wing was added onto the rear of the brick section. Interior trim dated from early, middle and late nineteenth century. A photographic project undertaken during the original survey in 1977 recorded a c. 1830 mantel from the second floor and the Victorian stair balustrade.

Peacock House, Millington, was originally a one-room plank building. When the brick extension was added on the left (west), the whole roof was changed to a gambrel. C. Engstrom photograph, 1977.

On the 1860 Martenet Map, the house was listed as owned by *"T. Walker heirs."* Thomas Walker was a Kent County merchant who owned property in Chestertown, as well as Millington. In his will (1854), he bequeathed a lot near Millington to the son of a friend and ordered the rest of his real estate to be distributed between his niece and nephew.[1]

By 1877 the property was owned by C. B. Peacock. It was known as the Peacock House well into the twentieth century.[2] K-172

Peacock House, Millington, had woodwork from several periods; this second story mantel dates from around 1830. C. Engstrom photograph, 1977.

1. Wills, Lib. JF 1, fol. 4.
2. Lake, Griffing, Stevenson Atlas, 1877.

Runnymeade

Near Still Pond
c. 1780

Sᴇᴛ ᴏɴ ᴀ ʜɪʟʟ ᴀʙᴏᴠᴇ ᴛʜᴇ ʜᴇᴀᴅ ᴡᴀᴛᴇʀs ᴏғ Urieville Lake is a late eighteenth century farmhouse that was isolated from nearby roads when depicted by the mapmakers of 1860 and 1877. John Lusby and J. Vandergrift were the owners on those maps respectively. Long before the maps were made, the house's form had been established.

Like many vernacular farmhouses of Kent County, Runnymeade evolved into a two-part house. The brick section is four bays long and two stories tall. The frame section is also four bays long, but only one-and-a-half stories tall. Unlike the more usual sequence, this house began with the frame section which was built in the last quarter of the eighteenth century, and was enlarged by the construction of the brick section some 30 to 40 years later.

The alterations to Runnymeade's plan are so extensive that their sequence is difficult to ascertain. One old wall of raised paneling and a corner cupboard survive in the dining room, but the remainder of the trim has been changed.

An unusual ice house also survives near the house. It originally had a steeply-pitched, pyramidal roof, but one slope was altered when it was changed into a garage in this century.   K-227

Runnymeade. The brick section of the house is a later addition to the original frame building. c. 1780. Constance Stuart Larrabee photograph.

Runnymeade. An early icehouse, converted into a garage in the twentieth century. Constance Stuart Larrabee photograph.

Runnymeade. Paneling in the earliest part of the house. Historical Society of Kent County, Usilton Collection, 1956.

Runnymeade, c. 1780. The four bay frame section was built in the last quarter of the eighteenth century. The four bay, two story brick section was added some years later. M. L. Fritz photograph, 1980.

Broadneck

Near Chestertown
c. 1780

"*T*HORNMAR" IS A RECENT NAME GIVEN TO ONE OF the oldest houses standing along the shores of Morgan Creek. It stands on a tract called *Broadneck*, a 700 acre farm patented to John Edmondson in 1666.[1]

At least as early as 1756, John Gleaves purchased a small part of the tract.[2] By the 1783 Tax Assessment, he owned 290 acres of Broad Neck and 490 acres of the adjoining Batchelor's Resolution. On the assessment list the following items were recorded:

> "– one large Brick dwelling House & kitchen
> – one Grist Mill, 7 out houses
> – on Morgans Creek
> – soil thin
> – 350 (acres) arable; 430 (acres) woods"

The large brick dwelling mentioned above refers to the large dwelling that has stood on the land referred to as the *"Brooks Farm,"* *"Biddle Farm,"* *"Old Revolutionary"* and the *"Bonwill Farm"* in the land records.

It is moreover the same farm which first appeared in the Maryland Gazette, December 20, 1792, described as follows:

> "*One of the most valuable tracts of LAND on the eastern shore of Maryland, lying in Kent County, within three miles of Chester-town*
>
> "*this farm contains about 1000 acres of land ... there is on the premises a large brick dwelling house,*

with four rooms on a floor, a brick kitchen, a good barn, stable, and other outbuildings. There are also, on the premises, the most valuable grist-mill and saw-mill in the county, situate on Morgan's creek, which empties into Chester river, and not more than three miles distant from it. A vessel of more than 1000 bushels burthen can lay at the mill door, and receive her load. There are also, on the above farm, a most valuable shad and herring fishery, and a great abundance of natural meadow ground ... ."

Only a month later on 24 January 1793, another advertisement in the Maryland Gazette stated that the farm was part of the estate of John Gleaves, but within the month one half of the tract had been purchased and the part remaining had been reduced to 500 acres. "*William Barroll became purchaser of the House and Lot with five hundred acres ... part of Bluff Point, Worth's Folly, Broad Neck and Bachelor's Resolution ... containing 520 acres ... .*"

The transaction had been approved by the Court in 1793, but the actual deed was not recorded until 1800,[3] just prior to Barroll's sale of the farm to John Ward, son of John Ward of Cecil County.[4] A short time later, William Barroll purchased Fancy Farm which he improved and kept until the time of his death.

When Frances Biddle (widow of Raymond Biddle) wrote her will in 1861, she referred to the farm as the *"Brooks Farm"* or *"Home Farm"* and bequeathed it to her unmarried daughters.[5] In the settlement of her estate, a plat of

Broadneck, c. 1780. John Gleaves built the " ... large Brick dwelling House & kitchen" that is mentioned in the 1783 Tax Assessment. He also had a grist mill adjacent the navigable waters of Morgan Creek. C. Engstrom photograph, 1977.

Broadneck, c. 1780. The stair hall is very generous and the details well executed.

Broadneck, c. 1780. The eastern room with original classical chimney breast.

Broadneck, c. 1780. Paneled window detail. C. Engstrom photographs, 1977.

James W. Lambert owned the *Biddle Home Farm* between 1882 and 1917. Between 1919 and 1950, it was owned by Emory Bonwill and heirs.[8] In 1961 the name was changed to *Rosemont,* and in 1972 to *Thornmar.*

The house standing on Broadneck was standing by the time of the 1783 Tax Assessment. It would have been built for John Gleaves who owned farmland on both sides of Morgan Creek, as well as the grist and saw mills mentioned in the settlement of his estate. There are several unusual or unique features in the design and construction of the house.

First, the building was designed on a large scale with large rooms, tall ceilings, etc. On the exterior, the use of rubbed and gauged brick for the string course and jack arches and the semi-circular fanlight above the principal entrance are unique features on this otherwise common five-bay two-story house. Secondly, the plan and form of the building are sufficiently different to have been highlighted by previous recorders of Kent County's Georgian architecture. The plan consists of a central stairhall with large room on the west and two rooms on the east, the rear room jutting about ten feet behind the plane of the back wall. The back room is in a typical leanto, but is also two stories tall with corner fireplaces. The plan was the prototype of Bachelor's Resolution next door, but that is where the similarity ends.

Broadneck's interior possesses some original woodwork of fine quality. The stair is a large structure with raised panel spandrel under the first flight. Like Knock's Folly, the landing extends across the entire width of the hall and also like Knock's Folly, the balustrade has delicately turned newels and a railing which rises above the intermediate newels and terminates in the newel cap. It also has a corresponding half rail in the wall with paneled pilasters rather than half newels. Three rectangular balusters per step are much plainer than those at Knock's Folly.

The interior of the large room was removed and reworked in the 1930s, but the den and dining room retain original chimney breasts, recessed panel dado, window jambs and seats. The trim, however, was replaced in the early nineteenth century with reeded work having corner blocks.

In the kitchen wing, the majority of original millwork was replaced in the 1930s when the house had its one major remodeling. At that time, a two bay extension was constructed. K-202

the farm was prepared and recorded with the deed to the three unmarried daughters. In 1864, one of the three daughters sold her share to the others[6] and by 1881 it was sold out of the Biddle family. It had been reduced by this time to 338 acres.[7]

1. Certificates, Lib. 10, fol. 3; Patents, Lib. 10, fol. 132.
2. Land Records, Lib. JS 27, fol. 279.
3. Land Records, Lib. TW 1, fol. 308.
4. Land Records, Lib. TW 1, fol. 311.
5. Wills, Lib. JF 1, fol. 216.
6. Land Records, Lib. JKH 4, fol. 523.
7. Land Records, Lib. SB 3, fol. 542.
8. Land Records, Lib. APR 6, fol. 71.

***Kimbolden. The central
core of Kimbolden is an
early one-and-a-balf
story brick residence,
similar to Springfield.
Tyler Campbell
photograph, 1996.***

***Kimbolden. A nineteenth
century stair in the old
section of the house.
C. Engstrom
photograph, 1977.***

***Kimbolden. The gable
and first story indicate
its original form.
C. Engstrom
photograph, 1977.***

Kimbolden

Near Rock Hall
c. 1780

KIMBOLDEN STANDS NEAR the head waters of Davis Creek. Vastly re-modeled and enlarged in 1949, it contains in its core, a three-bay, two-room-deep, one-and-a-half-story brick house which in its original form resembled nearby Spring-field Farm (K-99). The southeast gable of this part is laid in Flemish bond above a molded water table and stands above a high basement. A large chimney rises within the southwest gable where evidence exists of former windows. The stair of this sidehall-plan house is the only piece of early woodwork to remain. It appears to date from the 1840–1850 period and is relatively plain with a moderately large newel and turned, tapered balusters. The original core appears to have built in the last quarter of the eighteenth century and remodeled in the mid-nineteenth century. The house was owned by the Burgess family in the nineteenth century.

K-267

Locust Hill Farm

Near Galena
c. 1780

T HE HOUSE AT LOCUST HILL BEGAN AS A three-bay, two-story brick house with kitchen wing and was similar to Partner's Addition, located a few miles away. It was a vernacular structure with a pent eave between the first and second stories—a detail associated with the building traditions of the Delaware Valley. The windows probably had 12/12 sash on the first story and 12/8 on the second.

Most likely built for a member of the Comegys family, it was purchased by Moses Lambson in the mid-nineteenth century.[1] By that time, however, it had undergone a major remodeling. Around 1830, the distinctive pent eave was removed and a new Federal style entry was installed. Its ellyptical-headed fanlight covered both the door and sidelights. At the same time, the stair was rebuilt with delicate close-string balustrade, turned newels, and a continuous round rail that rose in goose necks over the intermediate newels. It appears that the entire house was remodeled at the same time.

By the time the Lake, Griffing, Stevenson Atlas was printed in 1877, Moses Lambson was living on the adjoining farm where he had established a station on the Kent County Railroad Line, and Locust Hill was owned by Captain Andrew Woodall of Georgetown. It remained in the Woodall family into the twentieth century.[2] In the late 1930s, the farm was purchased by Mr. and Mrs. Kenneth Clevenger who began the preservation of the old farmhouse.[3] In 1946 it was sold to Mr. and Mrs. Frank Wisner, formerly of Greenwich, Connecticut.[4] Alterations which occurred in the 1940s and later have resulted in a more refined interior. Mantels from England and elsewhere in the United States have been installed. The farm has been open on house tours from time to time and is one of the show places of the First District. K-208

1. Land Records, Lib. JR 1, fol. 77; Lib. JKH 4, fol. 38.
2. Land Records, Lib. JTD 15, fol. 122; Lib. RRA 7, fol. 234.
3. Land Records, Lib. RAS 21, fol. 269.
4. Land Records, Lib. RAS 39, fol. 406.

Fancy Farm

Near Chestertown
c. 1780

I N 1783, JOHN BEALE BORDLEY WAS ASSESSED £70.18.9 ON 1816 acres of land, including the 500 acre tract called The Fancy.[1] Bordley had an education in law under his brother in Annapolis, was Clerk of the Court of Baltimore County and later, a member of the council under the last two Colonial Governors. Through his marriage to Margaret Chew, he came into possession of the southern half of Wye Island in Queen Anne's County and established an extraordinary self-sufficient plantation called the Vineyards which became legend in its time (1770s). He wrote treatises on several subjects published between 1784 and 1799, and was a subscriber to the founding of Washington College in Chestertown.[2] He was truly an accomplished man. It was during his ownership of Fancy Farm that the frame section of the present house was constructed. Most likely its purpose was to provide housing for the overseer.

Four bays long, two-and-a-half-stories tall, the structure consisted of a narrow stair hall flanked by one room on each side. Both of the rooms contained interior fireplaces. The stair was a close string affair with beaded board spandrel, square newel and balusters. Both rooms were simply trimmed with beaded baseboard, chair rail and ovolo-molded window and door trim. The chambers above were finished in the same manner. Its

original kitchen may have been located on the east end of the house where an addition was built by the next owner.

Bordley had all of his Kent County lands resurveyed in 1793, under the name of Kent Land. In 1802, while residing in Philadelphia, he sold 650 acres, including the 500 acres of The Fancy, to William Barroll, attorney of Chestertown, for the sum of £5031.13.9.[3]

William Barroll was one of the most successful lawyers in Chestertown from the late 1780s through the first quarter of the nineteenth century. His residence in Chestertown was located on High Street adjoining the Wallis-Wickes House and is still popularly known as the Barroll House.

Barroll added a two-part brick house onto the old frame house at Fancy Farm. It was a three-bay, two-and-a-half-story structure with a two-bay kitchen wing at ground level and because of its size, became the principal part of the house. Originally, the kitchen wing was one story in height, with a steeply pitched roof. Across the central part of the house a portico was constructed. Reminiscent of the River House porch, it was a tall open porch which extended from the ground to the roof.

The plan for the Barroll addition to Fancy Farm, consisted of one principal room with a stair hall/entry adjacent the frame structure and a kitchen at the other end. The millwork details throughout were well executed in the late Federal style, with reeding and drill work similar to Big Fairlee and Thornton Farm. The entry was the best designed of the three houses, with a flight of sandstone steps up to the reeded and crossetted architrave. Rope moldings were used on the cornices of the house and porch. The kitchen door was constructed like those at River House and Trumpington, with diamond pattern board and batten units hung on strap hinges.

In 1809, Barroll acquired 210 more acres of Kent Land[4] adjoining The Fancy which remained in his possession until his death in 1834. Barroll was another owner of exceptional character and learning and is responsible for constructing several of the outbuildings which remain on the farm (a plank smoke house, frame dairy, carriage house, barn and corn crib). Another building to remain on the property until c. 1980 was a large brick stable.

After William Barroll's death, the inventory taken of his personal belongings indicated that he was living at both his town house and The Fancy. His inventory was valued in excess of $10,000.00, including twenty one slaves. Beside being one of the most prominent lawyers of his day, he also served on the Maryland Legislature in 1795-99, was a life-long member of Chester Parish, serving as vestryman, and was on the Board of Visitors

Fancy Farm. The west room in the earliest frame section retains c. 1880 Eastlake style wallpaper.

Fancy Farm. A view from the "new" stair hall into the older section of the house. Tyler Campbell photographs, 1995.

Fancy Farm. The original kitchen door and thumb latch in the Barroll wing.

Fancy Farm. Detail of reeded crossetted trim in the Barroll wing. Tyler Campbell photographs, 1995.

Fancy Farm. A sketch of the first floor plan prepared for the Franklin Fire Insurance Company. Pennsylvania Historical Society, Special Collections.

and Governors of Washington College, his Alma Mater. Barroll was a member of the Masonic Order and was instrumental in having the Masonic Hall built in 1827. He was also one of the prime movers in having the General Assembly pass the Act for constructing the first bridge across the Chester River at Chestertown in 1820, and was the largest stock holder in the Bridge Company.[5] William Barroll's widow, Sarah Hands, retained an annual dower rent of $250.00, even though the farm was sold in 1837 to William S. Constable (b. 1806, d. 1851).[6,7]

Constable was a farmer who had large holdings in the county. He was a member of the House of Delegates from Kent County in 1839. During his ownership, Fancy Farm was insured with the Franklin Fire Insurance Company of Philadelphia. From the survey of February 27, 1844, the description and plan of the house indicate that the building has continued in use with only a few alterations:

"Survey made February 27th 1844 and reported to the Franklin Fire Insurance Company of Philadelphia

For William S. Constable

A two Story Brick Dwelling House with a two Story frame Addition and A One Story Brick Kitchen adjoining Situate on his Farm (known as the Fancy Farm) on the Belle Air Road four Miles from Chester Town Kent County Maryland

The Brick House is 30 ft. by 18 ft. having one room and an Entry 9½ feet wide on each floor and an open continued Stairs to the Garrett quarter based, Stain railing turned Posts and Sq Balustrades 1¼ in. heartpine. Steps & floor boards throughout Oak Joist and Rafters & lath A Ridge roof regular pitch. Cyprefs Shingles, trap door & Mould boxed Cornice, the first Story is 10 ft. high the 2nd 9 ft. both plain lath and plaster ceiling—a brick partition between the Entries & rooms Continued from the Cellar to the Garret, 1¼ in. panel Doors painted in imitation of Maple, in the inside with good knoblocks, a board partition in the Garret. A fire place in each Story with Side Closets, and Wooden Mantels—the Parlor Mantel being carved, two 24 light windows front and back to the first Story. 8 by 10 glafs panel Shutters & Yellow pine frames—Three 20 light windows front and back to the 2nd Story with inside folding Shutters—the Garret has three 15 light dormant windows front and two back—Garret finished 4 light gable Windows Cellars under with Outside ledge doors.

The frame addition is 38 feet long and 18 wide—divided into two rooms and an Entry 6½ feet wide on each Story & Garret—The first Story is 9 and the 2nd 8 ft. in the clear ceilings lath and plastered, fire places both ends to 1st and 2nd Story with Side Closets & Nat Wooden Mantels—All heavy oak frame Joist Rafters and lath. A Cyprefs Shingle Ridge roof Mould Cornice heart pine weatherboarding Planed Ploughed & lapped & painted, front & back Entry door, double panel doors

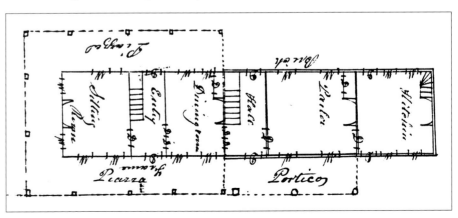

from the entry to the East room & to the Entry in the brick part—the other doors are Single panel with good knob locks; heart pine floors; Open Stairs in the Entry both Stories plain pine railing—4 windows front 3 back & two at the end to 1st Story 15 light—8 by 10 glafs and panel Shutters. The 2nd Story had 5 front 4 back windows and two in the end with Vinition blind Shutters, three front dormant windows and two gable windows—finished Garrets and Cellars under, brick Walled two feet above ground, communication with the brick house—There is a one Story Piazza on three Sides of the frame building with a Cyprefs Shingle Shed roof board ceiled Sq. Oak posts & brick floor; In front of the Brick is a Portico the Whole front 10 feet wide with three turned post two Stories high, with a Shingle Shed roof-board ceiled and brick floor—The Whole of the Buildings are finished in the best Manner and built of the best Material. The Kitchen is 18 feet Sq. having two windows front and back & a door front & back, panel Shutters, brick floor to first Story & Yellow pine to loft. A fireplace and a boxed winding Stairs loft finished & divided into rooms. A Ridge roof Cyprefs Shingles.

$3000 Insured at 65 cts pres $100 for one Year—
Robt Buckman Surveyor
I believe this to be an accurate description.
W. S. Constable"

Again, we get a glimpse of Fancy Farm in the 1852 Tax Assessment, although the house is described as a *"Frame House ... in tolerable repair,"* rather than brick and frame. Beside the 804 acres of *"Fancy Farm Resurveyed,"* the Constable estate was taxed on two other farms, being *"parts of Kenland, Queen Charlotte and Whitfield ... Formerly to John Constable"* and *"Rousby's Recovery & Thomas's Purchase ... Formerly to A + Jane Blake."*

Apparently, the family was not living at Fancy Farm since there is no furniture included in the tax list. William had died the year before, so it is assumed that his widow and children had moved to Chestertown or Baltimore. In 1866, when the estate was settled four of the six children were living in Baltimore. When the lands were sold in 1872, the estate was worth a total of $68,094.62.

Josiah Lusby (d. 1905), who later lived on the corner of High and Mill Streets, purchased 500 acres of the original Constable farm. His daughter, Sara Ida, wife of William T. Nicholson, lived on the farm in 1905, and it was either the Nicholsons or the Lusbys who installed the bathroom addition on the back of the house. The west parlor was also papered during their occupancy, and that paper has remained in relatively good condition ever since.

Fancy Farm has remained in the family of Josiah Lusby through various legacies and transactions, the last owners being Mr. and Mrs. Albert Nicholson. When Albert and Sue Nicholson acquired the farm in 1951, they

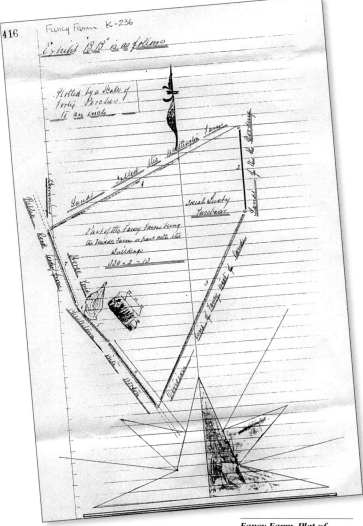

Fancy Farm. Plat of Fancy Farm prepared for the estate of John Constable in 1866. Chancery Records, Lib. JKH 3, fol. 416.

removed a part of the leanto porch on the frame portion of the house, and renewed the kitchen. During their ownership the farm became primarily a grain farm and the outbuildings became superfluous. After Albert's death, Sue provided for the continued preservation of The Fancy[8] as a farm by placing it under easement to the Maryland Environmental Trust.

K-236

1. 1783 Tax Assessment, Lower Langford Bay & Eastern Neck Hundreds.
2. Pappenfuss, Ed., *Maryland Legislators.*
3. Kent Co. Lands Records, Lib. TW 2, fol. 317.
4. Ibid, Lib. BC 5, fol. 102.
5. Barroll, L. Wethered, *Barroll in America.*
6. Kent Co. Land Records, Lib. JNG 5, fol. 80.
7. Correspondence with George W. Constable. According to Constable family tradition, Fancy Farm remained in the family of Isabella Conner Bordley Stevenson, until well into the nineteenth century. Future research may indicate that they lived on Bordley's farm, but not the part which William Barroll owned between 1802-1834. In 1837 William Stevenson Constable purchased the Barroll farm, bringing it back into Isabella's family.
8. The Fancy was patented in 1682 for John Lewellen, a tract of 500 acres. Patents, Lib. CB 3, fol. 154.

Trumpington

Eastern Neck
c. 1780

Trumpington. This fine old house at the southern end of Eastern Neck, overlooking the mouth of the Chester River and the Bay, was the last residence of merchant, Thomas Smyth. His remains are buried in the family cemetery. Trumpington has remained in the same family since the late seventeenth century. Tyler Campbell photograph, 1995.

TRUMPINGTON WAS FIRST PATENTED AS 400 ACRES IN 1658 to Thomas South. In 1687 Thomas Smyth I purchased this tract from two separate grantees who had acquired it earlier. An immigrant, Smyth (1648-1719) was a member of the Provincial Court from 1682-1719 and was Deputy Commissary General from 1707-1718. He was also one of the founding members and vestryman of St. Paul's Church.[1]

Upon his death in 1719, Trumpington passed to his minor son, Thomas II (1710-1741), who became nearly as active as his father in local affairs. But the younger Thomas was to die at only thirty-one years of age and the plantation was again passed on to a minor son, Thomas III (1729-1819).[2]

Thomas III studied under James Calder, a prominent Chestertown lawyer and soon thereafter practiced law. A successful merchant, he was in business at one time with Emory Sudler, his brother-in-law, and later with his sons, Thomas and Richard Smyth, and was also co-owner of the Chestertown Rope Walk with Dr. William Murray. From 1757-59 he was a judge of the County Court and in 1764 Sheriff of Kent County. Eleven

years later Smyth was named a delegate to the Provisional Convention in Annapolis and was a signer of the Association of Freemen. Between 1774–76 he was also a member of the Maryland Committee of Safety. In short, Thomas Smyth III was active in the revolutionary cause and served in numerous capacities during the war. When Washington College was chartered, Smyth, a benefactor, served on the first Board of Visitors and Governors as treasurer.[3]

Building was definitely in Smyth's blood for in 1769 he purchased Water Lot No. 16 adjacent the town wharves in Chestertown and built the best example of mid-Georgian architecture in the county—the house now called Widehall. In 1784, he purchased another water lot and began building River House which he later sold to his son, Richard Gresham Smyth. In 1785, he purchased the Buck houses from Emory Sudler and immediately advertised them for sale in the Maryland Gazette. His real estate transactions were many and varied. By 1783, Smyth owned over 2500 acres in the southern part of the County.

The date of construction of Smyth's project at Trumpington is not as well documented as with his other properties; judging from the various details, inside and out, the house was probably constructed in the 1780s. It was most certainly standing when the property was advertised for sale in both the Maryland Gazette and the Chestertown Apollo in 1793 due to bankruptcy:

> *"… Also, about 500 acres—Windmill in working order … Also, about 500 'Acres of Land,' consisting of several adjoining tracts. … there is on said Land a two-story Brick House and Kitchen, and other necessary Farm buildings, with a Wind Mill in working order … ."*[4]

As it turned out, Trumpington was not sold, but mortgaged to his brother-in-law, and remained his home until his death in 1819.

Smyth's country house was not as grand as the houses he had built in Chestertown, but it did possess the same number of rooms on the ground floor as Widehall. The plan of the house was nearly the same as James Frisby's Violet Farm, with central stairhall, one large room on one side and two smaller rooms on the other. The kitchen wing, however, was closer to the plan of his house in Chestertown, with a large kitchen and a breakfast room.

Trumpington's five-bay, two-story facade faced the Chester River and Chesapeake Bay beyond. Originally, there were no dormers on the roof; only the full size windows on the gables lighted the attic rooms. On the northwest gable, the common bond is laid with dark or glazed headers creating horizontal bands similar to the south gable at the Archibald Wright House (Kitty Knight House) in Georgetown.

While the kitchen is early, neither its brick walls nor chimney are bonded into the main house, indicating a later date of construction. One of the interesting features of Trumpington's kitchen wing is the board and

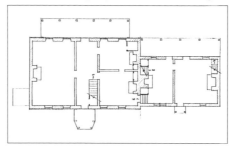

Trumpington. First floor plan, measured and drawn by Orlando Ridout V, 1979.

Trumpington. Paneled chimney wall in the north living room. The painted panel is a reproduction of an original at the Maryland Historical Society. Tyler Campbell photograph, 1995

Trumpington. The two original kitchen doors were nearly identical to the kitchen door at River House, a house Smyth built in Chestertown for his son, c. 1784-87. C. Engstrom photograph, 1977.

batten doors with diamond pattern on the exterior, a feature Smyth employed at River House in Chestertown.

The stair has an open string with turned newels and balusters and a simple walnut railing. It appears to have been reconstructed in the second half of the nineteenth century. The balustrade from the second floor to the attic is totally different.

There are five rooms on the second floor, all finished with chair rail and baseboard. Only one room has a paneled wall, like the two below.

On the third floor, the space is divided into three rooms and stairhall. It is the reverse of the first floor plan. The arrangement probably dates from the time the dormers were installed in the late nineteenth or early twentieth century.

An extraordinary feature exists in the basement in the use of a lattice partition which encloses the southwest half of the central passage as a storage room. This room is exceptional in the quality and construction and in the fact that it has survived the years in good condition. Two small window openings in the interior brick walls have wooden frames with riven slat-like vertical bars.

Trumpington. The central room in the basement has an extraordinary original slat partition and brick floor. Tyler Campbell photograph, 1995.

Trumpington. An original wooden latch in the basement. Gene Johnstone photograph, 1995.

While in the process of restoration, the footings of an earlier house were located enclosed in the dimensions of the existing basement. In relaying the floor, the outline was marked out in a different brick pattern. It measured approximately 22' x 32'.

Southeast of the house there is a small cemetery where the remains of Thomas Smyth III are buried along with other family members.

Upon his death in 1819, the farm was purchased by Smyth's son-in-law and daughter, Thomas and Anna Maria Willson, who had previously lived in Queenstown.[5] Dr. Willson's will of 1859, leaves Trumpington to his son, Richard Bennett Willson (1817-1901).[6] R. B. Willson is listed as owner of Trumpington on both the Martenet Map and the 1877 Atlas. In 1902, the property was divided between Richard's two children, Julia Willson Ringgold and Notley Oswald Willson.[7] In 1923, Notley devised his half to his wife, Mary, who sold it to Julia's daughter and son-in-law, Mary and James Ernest Willson.[8] When Julia Willson Ringgold died in 1936, the other half came into the possession of her daughter, Mary, reuniting the two shares. After the deaths of Ernest and Mary Willson, the property was purchased by their daughter and son-in-law,[9] who have gradually restored the house on this farm, which has remained in the same family for over 300 years.

Trumpington is on the National Register and is a Bicentennial Farm.   K-271

1. Papenfuse, P. 750.
2. Wills, Lib. 2, fol. 160.
3. Papenfuse, p. 756; White M. P. "Washington College."
4. Maryland Gazette, October 10, 1793, The Apollo, October 4, 1793.
5. The deed for this transaction is unrecorded in the courthouse, but family history confirms the transaction.
6. Wills, Lib. JS 1, fol. 171.
7. Wills, Lib. JTD 1, fol. 1.
8. Wills, Lib. RRH 1, fol. 436, Land Records, Lib. RRA 2, fol. 210.
9. Land Records, Lib. EHP 11, fol. 169.

Camelsworthmore

Lynch
c. 1780

CAMELSWORTHMORE FARM INCLUDES ONE OF TWO FIELD-stone dwellings remaining in Kent County. Unlike the Palmer house in Chestertown, this stone building is actually an addition to a one-and-a-half-story brick building. The brick section was a four-bay structure with facade laid in Flemish bond and other walls in common bond. The stone addition is two bays in length and appears to have carried the same roof line as the brick section, like Long Meadow farm near Massey.

Camelsworthmore. The brick and stone farm house was engulfed by the 1920s enlargement. This view shows the brick end of the house. Maryland State Archives, Don Swan Collection.

Camelsworthmore, a view from the fieldstone kitchen end shows the unique development of the house.

Camelsworthmore. First floor plan. Drawn by M. L. Fritz, 1980.

Many alterations have been made to the building over the years with the result that little original material remains. The biggest alterations occurred in the 1920s when a second story was added not only above the masonry section, but above an eight foot porch-like area as well.

This house is important as an early example of a common house type and because of the use of fieldstone in its kitchen wing. Because fieldstone is more durable in moist locations than brick, it was most frequently used for foundations when available. It is said that there were two stone outbuildings adjacent the kitchen until recently.

The house stands on part of Camelsworthmore, a large seventeenth century tract. On both the Martenet Map of 1860 and the 1877 Atlas, the farm is listed as owned by *"Miss Sutton."*   K-416

Lyons Hall

Quaker Neck
c. 1780

THIS OLD BRICK HOUSE, WHILE CALLED REARDON, IS ACTU-ally located on the tract called Lyons Hall and dates from the last quarter of the eighteenth century. Originally, its southeast facade was nearly identical to Providence Plantation only a mile up Quaker Neck, a three-bay, two-story main house with a two-bay, one-and-a-half-story brick kitchen wing. Both houses have Flemish bond brickwork and asymmetrical door placement. The plan differed in that it was of the more common vernacular form of hall-parlor with attached kitchen, lacking the leanto room found at Providence Plantation.

Originally, the enclosed winder stair was located in the north corner of the hall, and like Providence, there

was probably a wall of paneling across the chimney breast and adjoining cabinet. The parlor may have had a paneled chimney breast too. The kitchen was located down four or five steps and had a brick floor on grade. Its ceiling joists were originally exposed as they are at present.

In the 1783 Tax Assessment, Morgan Brown is assessed for the property, but there is no improvement schedule for Quaker Neck, making it more difficult to pinpoint the date of construction. In his will, probated in 1800, Brown left *"all my land which belonged to my grandfather, Morgan Brown, and 100 acres that belonged to my father, Edward, called Lyons Hall"* to be divided between Edward and Morgan, his sons.

In another tax assessment of 1852, the owner was Captain Morgan Brown and the parcels of land and improvements were listed as follows:

> *"Pt. Providence, Price's Lot*
> *Lyons Hall, Batchelor's Hope*
> *Reardon & McConican*
> *Brick House & other Buildings*
> *in good repair, formerly to*
> *Edward Brown   281 acres"*

Strangely enough, this man whose ancestors were Quakers, possessed two slaves along with livestock, furniture, two watches, etc., totaling $6,088.

According to local tradition, the house was struck by lightning in the late nineteenth century and burned, leaving only the brick shell. The Browns rebuilt within the old shell, changing and simplifying as was necessary. Instead of rebuilding the corner stair, they built the new one in a narrow center hall, making it more like other farmhouses of the time. All of the windows were

changed to 6/6 sash with louvered blinds, and dormers were built on the roof to light the attic bedrooms. The property remained in the Brown family until 1932.

The house appears to have remained essentially a typical nineteenth century farmhouse until it was purchased in 1935 with fourteen acres by Mr. and Mrs. Walter Roach. The Roaches undertook the next major alteration by adding a one-and-a-half-story brick wing on the northeast side of the house, installing a kitchen in what was the living room and converting the old kitchen into a den. By raising the kitchen walls a half story, they created a master bedroom adjacent a dressing room in what was the parlor chamber. Other amenities changed the old farmhouse into an attractive estate overlooking the waters of Comegys Bight.

The present owners have recently remodeled the house within the general confines established in the 1930s

Lyons Hall or Reardon was built by Morgan Brown in the last quarter of the eighteenth century and was enlarged c. 1934. Kent County Library, M. L. Fritz photograph, 1981

Lyons Hall or Reardon, photographed soon after the 1934 wing. Historical Society of Kent County, Usilton Collection.

Providence Plantation

Quaker Neck
1781

THE EARLIEST LAND RECORD IN THE KENT COUNTY Courthouse which indicates that the Trew family owned Providence is an agreement for the Division of Land between William Trew and Morgan Brown, dated 1720.

"Know all men by these presents that my Father William Trew and William Davis did joyntly and severally buy of Cornelius Comegys a certain tract of land called by the name of Comegys Choice in the year 1671 and the above said Wm Davis sold his part unto Edward Brown grand father to old Morgan Brown deceased and the said Edward Brown gave the said moiety of land unto his Grandson Morgan Brown being the lower part of the said tract of land ... ."[1]

The land purchased by Trew and Davis in 1671 was a 350 acre tract which Cornelius Comegys had patented in 1669. In the agreement quoted above, the northern half of the tract went to William Trew and the southern half to Morgan Brown.[2]

In the will of William Trew, father of the above petitioner, there is no specific bequest of the above land, only a reference to his son William having received *"the rest."* In the father's inventory, made after his death in 1713, personal items were listed by room in his house which is presumed to have been on the property. Trew's house included an *"Outter room,"* as well as an *"inner room,"* *"Chambers"* above each, and a *"Kitchen."* This is a clear indication that the house had a hall-parlor plan. This house has not survived.[3]

In March, 1747, another division of land was agreed upon, the two parts being divided by a cove. The same division line exists to this day. In the same year William Trew II died and bequeathed his dwelling plantation to his nephew, William, son of his brother John.[4]

In 1760, William Trew III acquired 150 acres adjoining Providence called by the names of *Hansford* and *Hatchberry.* With that purchase, his holdings amounted to 360 acres. In his will, written in 1765, he refers to a resurvey of *Providence Plantation* and bequeaths it to his son William IV. The 150 acres of Hansford and Hatchbury he left to his son John.[5] William Trew IV was a minor until 1772. His marriage and the birth of his son William, was recorded in the Quaker Records in 1774. In 1781, a year after the birth of his second son, Bartus, William and his wife,

Providence Plantation. William and Mary Trew's initials and the date of construction are clearly visible on the north east gable of the house.

Providence Plantation. The living room has a paneled fireplace wall with cupboard and closet and paneled wainscot. Tyler Campbell photographs, 1995

Providence Plantation, looking at the north corner of the house across the Trew family grave-yard. The catslide roof section was original to the 1781 construction date, but both dormers were added in the nineteenth century.
Tyler Campbell photographs, 1995.

Providence Plantation. The corner cupboard in the original dining room with a glimpse of the living room. Vertical board paneling in the old dining room is similar to the Reward.

Mary, built their new brick house on Providence Plantation and recorded the date and their initials in the northeast gable for generations to see (1781 WTM). Their mark is the clearest of the dated gables of Kent County.

The house was a two-story, three-bay-long, brick structure with a two-bay, one-story, brick kitchen. The plan consisted of a hall and parlor with a third room behind the parlor. The kitchen opened from the parlor, but was situated on grade. The form of the building was unusual in that the roof over the third room was a continuation of the main roof, creating a second story room with sloping ceiling.

Its interior was very well finished with paneled chimney wall with a glazed cabinet, fluted pilasters and a mantel with double crossett trim. In the north corner an enclosed stair was located within the paneling. The other three walls had paneled wainscot and cornice.

All five walls of the parlor were paneled, the diagonal chimney breast with fielded panels, the others with vertical, feather-edge paneling. A glazed corner cabinet was located in the north corner. The back room was finished with a combination of features found in the preceding two rooms. It had both a paneled, diagonal chimney breast and paneled wainscot. This back room also had an enclosed secondary stair in the east corner which had a small closet beneath. Many features of the interior finish of Providence are similar to the earlier Reward Farm, which was built by Charles Tilden, who is known to have been a building contractor. Perhaps Tilden had a hand in the construction of Providence as well.

The kitchen, according to Forman, had a walk-in pantry in the north corner where it abuts the main house.[6] It also had a brick floor, exposed beam ceiling and a pyramidal fireplace similar to those at Godlington Manor and Hinchingham Farm. There was a ladder to one side of the fireplace for access to the servants' quarters above.

Although not as highly finished as the first floor, the second floor was fitted with a paneled wall and fireplaces in both main rooms. Otherwise, there was simply chair rail, baseboard and window trim. Access to the originally unfinished attic was not in its usual place, above the first stair, but rather on the opposite side of the paneled wall.

When Providence was taxed two years after its construction, it was comprised of about 200 acres. But when William died in 1815, it then contained about 325 acres, an indication that William had acquired his brother's share of the property by inheritance. It is interesting to note that William had also purchased the Reward Farm in 1805, which he left to his son Bartus. Providence was bequeathed to his wife and their son Thomas Wilkins Trew.[7] As Bartus did not agree with the terms of his father's will, he and Thomas switched properties.

Bartus did not marry until 1823, when he was forty-three years old. He had spent his youth working very hard. By the time he died in 1837, he owned about 2,000 acres. It is assumed that Bartus Trew always remained at Providence, since it is referred to as the *"Home Farm."* It was during his ownership that the house received two dormer windows on the south facade and two on the back, one being lower and lighting the room occupied by sisters Mary and Deborah. One of the attic rooms was finished at that time. Bartus left no will and was in debt for some of his acquisitions so all his lands were sold. Providence was purchased by his widow Sarah and as before, the two back rooms were reserved for his maiden sisters.[8] Prior to the 1852 Tax Assessment Sarah had married her neighbor, Edward Brown, who lived on the southern part of Providence. Edward was assessed for the Trew lands on which is listed *"Brick House and other*

Buildings in good repair formerly to Sarah S. Trew."[9] Sarah deeded her lands to her son Bartus Trew II, in 1865, reserving the wood lot on the opposite side of the road.[10] In her will, dated five years later, she mentions that her *"whole estate is comprised in obligation of my Son Bartus Trew and a little household and bedroom furniture and the tract of woodland on the east side of the road."* She then bequeathed the woodland to Bartus. Sarah died in May of 1874 and her sister-in-law Deborah Trew, died in the fall of the same year, ending a fifty year entail on the property.[11]

No sooner had one entail ended, when another began! Although Sarah S. Trew had sold the farm to her son Bartus, she held the mortgage and upon her death, her equity in the land had to be divided between her seven children. Bartus protested sharing it with his half sister's only child, but the courts ordered the farm sold and proceeds dispersed. Bartus II's wife Sarah C. Trew was the purchaser.[12]

The heirs of Sarah and Bartus sold the farm to a man from Swarthmore, PA in 1921, but he defaulted and the property was foreclosed. The Court ordered the farm to be sold again. Walter Trew first purchased it and then, in 1924, transferred it to his cousin, Henry Brown. It remained in the family for only nine more years before it was sold to *outsiders*.

Meredith and Elizabeth Gardiner, purchased Providence and began to spruce it up. Evidently their luck was down during the depression years and they finally listed it for sale.

Providence was once again to come into the possession of the Trew family, as the advertisement was seen by Bartus Trew, grandson of Bartus Trew II who had owned it in the last quarter of the nineteenth century. In 1938, Bartus and Clementine Trew purchased Providence Plantation[13] and set about restoring the buildings and generally improving the property. The first thing they did was to install a new roof and then a driveway. Since neither of them knew farming, they hired a cousin, another Henry Brown, to keep the farm in production. Prior to 1946, they removed the early twentieth century porch and installed an elaborate Doric Architrave around the original front door. Since the house was only to be used in summer, central heating was not installed, but plumbing and electricity were. A bath was installed in a portion of Deborah and Mary's second story room and a door was cut through the wall so that both bedrooms could have private access to the bath. The final addition included the construction of a new kitchen with gun room, servant's room and baths. The Trews also created a terrace off the new gun room and built a short brick retaining wall around the north corner of the house. A similar wall was constructed around the old family graveyard, in which the remains of Mary and William Trew, the original builders of Providence, lie along with those of many of their descendants.

Providence Plantation. The secondary stair in the back room and the room above were reserved for the use of William's daughters, Mary and Deborah. C. Engstrom photograph, 1977.

Providence Plantation. This plank smokehouse was found in an overgrown thicket beyond the graveyard in 1992. It originally stood near the back kitchen door. Gene Johnstone photograph, 1995.

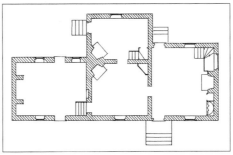

Providence Plantation. First floor plan of original part of house. Drawn by Michael Bourne.

In 1992, Providence was purchased from the Bartus Trew estate by George and Jane Dean, who had previously restored the Imperial Hotel and the Simon Wickes House on Water Street, Chestertown. Providence was once again restored, and a new wing was added to the back. The farm was subdivided and two parcels were sold. The current property consists of about eighty acres. K-84

1. Kent Co. Land Records, Lib. JS 8, fol. 150.
2. Even though the land had been divided in 1720, both parties had the land patented in 1745 under the new name of Providence. It included 420 acres.
3. Inventories, Lib. 1, fol.149. It is interesting to compare this inventory with that of John Trew, William's bachelor brother, who lived on part of Stratford Manor, the room names are the same.
4. In John's will, (Lib. 2, fol. 159, 1741), he anticipates that his son, William, will inherit his brother's farm. It is uncertain, from either will, if William II had direct heirs.
5. Hansford (one-hundred acres) was patented in 1673 to Hans Hanson; Hatchbury (fifty acres) was patented 1683 to Philip and Joseph Everett. Wills, Lib. 4, fol. 264.
6. H. C. Forman, Early Manor and Plantation Houses of Maryland, privately printed, Easton, MD, 1934, p. 234.
7. Wills, Lib. 9, fol. 316.
8. Land Records, Lib. JNG 6, fol. 484.
9. Tax Assessment, 1st District, 1852.
10. Land Records, Lib. JKH 5, fol. 163.
11. Wills, Lib. EC 1, fol. 112; Lib. EC 1, fol. 222.
12. Chancery, Lib. DCB 1, fol. 617.
13. Land Records, Lib. RAS 20, fol. 406.

Chapter 4
The Federal Period 1783–1820

The Colonies found that winning the revolution and gaining independence created many responsibilities along with unexpected changes. The merchants and farmers of Kent County were left to their own resources to find a market for their products.

IN 1783, THE FIRST GENERAL TAX ASSESSMENT WAS LEVIED on the people of the new nation in an attempt to pay for the cost of the Revolution. While portions of this assessment for Kent County have been lost, fortunately nearly two-thirds have survived. It has proven to be a vital resource and research aid regarding Kent's early buildings, as the assessments generally include brief descriptions of structures existing at the time. A similar assessment was made in 1798; however, this assessment for Kent is missing in its entirety.

1783 Tax Assessment

In the 1783 Tax Assessment, the enumeration of buildings in the eastern half of the county is extensive and fairly complete. Only a small number of structures are listed in the southern half and none are listed in Chestertown. Not until 1841 was there a complete assessment made for Chestertown in which the basic building materials were indicated.

From these surviving descriptions, it is possible to draw some conclusions regarding the mix of brick, frame and log construction. For example, of 133 buildings listed in the Chester and Worton Hundreds (an area roughly corresponding to the Third Election District), about half are simply described with the following phrases: *"small old house," "very bad house"* or *"old dwelling."* Of

Opposite: Methodist Meeting House, c. 1803. During the post-revolutionary period the Methodists were the only religious denomination to embark on a major building campaign. Their accomplishment was recorded by Francis Asbury as "elegantly planned." Michael C. Wootton photograph, 1996.

the remainder, about one-fifth are brick, one-fifth frame and three-fifths are log. Only one stone building is listed, along with two grist mills, five quarters and three steward's houses.

In the Morgan Creek and Lower South Sassafras Hundreds, a relatively large area, the descriptions

are more detailed. There are 161 frame or wooden houses listed, with 41 of them having log kitchens. There are 24 brick houses with brick kitchens listed and 23 structures which are described as combinations of either brick and frame or brick and log. Only four houses are listed as being constructed of log alone. This unusually small number may indicate that the assessor was unaware of original log structures

A page from the 1783 Tax Assessment. Microfilm No. 872, Maryland Historical Trust

which had subsequently been sheathed in clapboard and/or whose interior walls had been plastered.

In the hundreds corresponding closely to the First District and part of the Second, log buildings outnumber both frame and brick. In all, 95 log houses are listed, along with two brick buildings which are listed as having log attachments. The assessment, includes 80 frame houses and 21 constructed of brick. As in the previous district, there is one house listed as having been built with stone walls. It was located in Georgetown.

By comparing the building descriptions included in the 1783 Tax Assessment with surviving structures in the above mentioned hundreds, it is safe to say that there were more log buildings in the eastern sector of the county than in the center or lower sections. It can also be surmised that a large number of those log buildings were replaced in the second and third quarters of the nineteenth century with more substantial brick or frame dwellings as improvements in agricultur-

al practices made for more prosperous times. This is especially true for the first district.[1]

LOG AND PLANK STRUCTURES

While it can be surmised that log buildings were plentiful in eighteenth century Kent County, only a handful have survived. Each is a one room, one story structure which has subsequently been incorporated into a larger and later dwelling. There is no evidence of there having been any two-story log structures in Kent.

The thoroughness of the assessor's descriptions appears to have waned as he arrived at Turner's Creek, for there he stated only that Donaldson Yeates owned *"good buildings,"* and several of them, and failed to describe the bounty of the village that stood above the creek. One of the houses owned by Yeates was located up the hill from the village. A nearly square, one-and-a-half-story, log structure, it was later incorporated into the residence of his widow. This small log building with its two rooms and central chimney became the kitchen and dining room of Knocks Folly when it was constructed at the end of the century. The beaded ceiling joists were exposed and the log walls were covered with vertical beaded boards in the better room and whitewashed in the kitchen and rooms above. It was probably built in the 1760s since the fireplace configuration followed the design that was used in that decade.

The records of the Orphans Court also point to an abundance of log structures in both the eastern part of the county and along the Bay. In 1779, part of the large Hinchingham tract was recorded by Marmaduke Tilden for the orphan, Joseph Frisby. The record includes the following description:

" ... one sawed log dwelling house with brick chimney two plank floors breast work and stairs 20 feet long and 18 feet wide with bad roof 1 old log ditto 18 feet long and 16 feet wide covered with featheredge shingles 1 old log house clapboard roof 1 sawed white oak log corn house with shingle roof good 24 foot long and 12 foot wide 1 old tobacco house posts in the ground 40 foot long and 22 feet wide pritty much shuttered 1 old log dwelling house 20 foot long and 16 foot wide 1 log Granary weatherboarded and shingle roof good 16 foot long and 15 foot wide and all the cultivated land is under a low fence and we permit the said Guardian to get timbers anywhere on the said lands for repairing the houses and fencing on the same and that the yearly value of the said lands and plantations is two hundred and fifty pounds ...

Michael Miller
Nathaniel Miller'[2]

At Hinchingham Farm, the original plank kitchen exists now as the den of the present house. Here, the planks are mortised into the corner posts from which the down braces extend to the sill. This type of construction is mentioned in a 1784 description of a small Methodist meeting house which had formerly stood on Handy Point Road.[3] It can also be seen in the original wing of Fairlee Manor Camp. Other log/plank buildings in the county are built with dove-tailed corners.

At Pine Point, the house is actually made up of two log structures connected by a framed stairhall, not un-

Hinchingham Farm. Part of the last section of Hinchingham Farm is built of sawn planks, mortise and tenoned into corner posts with diagonal down bracing. Similar construction was mentioned on a small Methodist Meeting House which stood on Handy Point Road in the late eighteenth century. Maryland Historical Trust, Michael Bourse photograph, 1969.

Hinchingham Farm. The old log kitchen is constructed of planks mortised and tenoned into braced corner posts. C. Engstrom photograph, 1977.

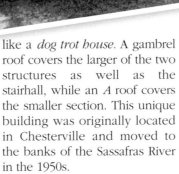

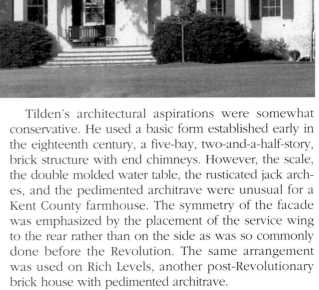

like a *dog trot house*. A gambrel roof covers the larger of the two structures as well as the stairhall, while an *A* roof covers the smaller section. This unique building was originally located in Chesterville and moved to the banks of the Sassafras River in the 1950s.

Log and/or plank construc-tion continued to be employed into the nineteenth century in Kent. The latest example found thus far occurred at the Myers House, a small dwelling which formerly stood at Hanesville. In the 1845 deed to Hill Top Farm, two acres were men-tioned as having been sold to Turbutt Betton and were further described as *"on which … a small house has been erected."* This building which was in an advanced state of decay in 1970, was a sawn plank structure, with dovetailed corners. It contained two rooms and a leanto kitchen with a dirt floor.

It is unlikely that log structures were built much af-ter the late nineteenth century, as both framing materi-als and prefabricated building materials had become readily available.

The 1780s and 1790s

HANDY POINT, RICH LEVELS, ROSE HILL AND THORNTON

As tax assessor for Worton Hundred, Marmaduke Tilden described the house on his own plantation, Handy Point, as *"one very bad House & kitchen."* From another description in his mother's will (1774), it is clear that the building had a hall-parlor plan with a leanto room off the parlor. After the Revolution, Tilden demolished the house and built anew. What exactly led him to do so remains a mystery. It is known that he was involved in Revolutionary activities before and during the war.

Tilden's architectural aspirations were somewhat conservative. He used a basic form established early in the eighteenth century, a five-bay, two-and-a-half-story, brick structure with end chimneys. However, the scale, the double molded water table, the rusticated jack arch-es, and the pedimented architrave were unusual for a Kent County farmhouse. The symmetry of the facade was emphasized by the placement of the service wing to the rear rather than on the side as was so commonly done before the Revolution. The same arrangement was used on Rich Levels, another post-Revolutionary brick house with pedimented architrave.

Thornton on Morgan Creek, and Rose Hill, an earlier farmhouse near Chestertown, had similar architraves. The construction of Rose Hill had begun in the 1760s, however, it was not finished until after the Revolution. Thornton differed from Handy Point in that its service wing was on the same axis as the main house. Like Hinchingham on the Bay and Springfield, the roof of the service wing at Thornton continued on to cover a porch from which there was access to the basement.

Thornton, Handy Point, and Rich Levels were all fin-ished in the late Georgian style. Flush paneled chimney breasts with applied crossetted moldings are used in their principal rooms. Two have broken pediments in the principal rooms. All possess center halls with open-string stairs. The balustrades have turned newels and railings which ascend over the newels.

THE BOLTON-ANDERSON HOUSE AND THE DUNN HOUSE

In Chestertown, during the decade after the Revolution, commerce was brisk and houses were built by successful merchants and speculators, though most were slightly less sophisticated than those discussed above. Houses were also remodeled and augmented. The Bolton-Anderson House, which began as a three-bay, frame structure was enlarged to five bays and a brick service wing was built to the rear. Located on the same lot, the Dunn House was built

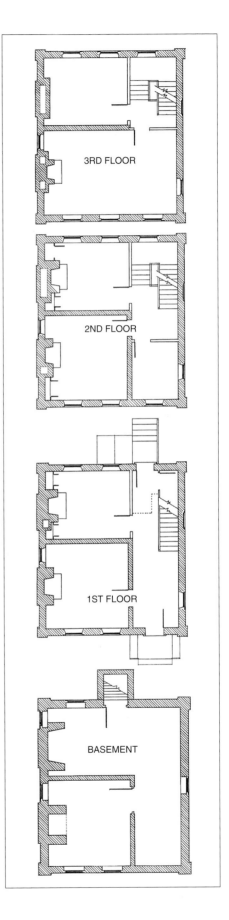

*Geddes-Piper House.
The post-revolutionary
period saw the introduc-
tion of the townhouse
plan, initially in Chestertown and later carried
out to the farms. The
Geddes-Piper House
originally had a kitchen
in the basement. Library
of Congress, Historic
American Buildings
Survey, 1936.*

*Geddes-Piper House.
Floor plans before 1830.
Michael Bourne.*

with a central passage plan, but was only four bays long
and the service area was located in the cellar. It adjoined
the earlier Bolton house (not to be confused with the
Bolton-Anderson House). In the parlor of the Dunn
House, the cornice has a course of dentils, a feature that
is repeated in the mantel and one which was used in a
number of other houses in Chestertown and the county
(Buck-Chambers House, Nicholson House, River House
and Miller's Purchase).

Townhouse Plans

GEDDES-PIPER HOUSE, NICHOLSON HOUSE,
DR. THOMAS HOUSE, THE KITTY KNIGHT HOUSE
AND THE CHAMBERS HOUSE

The first use of the townhouse plan in Kent County appears in the post-Revolutionary period in the design of

the Geddes-Piper House in 1784. Here, the entrance is located on one side of the three-bay facade. In most instances, the plan is similar in form to the earlier 1770s four-room plan, differing in that the two smaller rooms were being incorporated into one space with a stair. The Nicholson House, built after 1788, had such a plan with its original kitchen located in the cellar.

Other examples include the Dr. John Thomas House, constructed circa 1787 in Millington and the house built by John Henry circa 1784 in Georgetown which was later occupied and owned by Kitty Knight. Interestingly, the fireplace configuration differs in each of these houses. In the Chestertown examples, the fireplaces were centered on the two rooms, while at The Kitty Knight House back-to-back corner fireplaces were used. At Dr. Thomas' house there is a combination of the two.

A unique use of the townhouse plan can be found at the Chambers House (1786), a one room deep building with only a stairhall and one room. Like some other townhouses in Chestertown, it had a basement kitchen. Both the Chambers House and the adjacent Nicholson House are the first buildings in the county to have molded brick cornices. The Nicholson House has the more elaborate of the two, with a row of dentils in the otherwise classical cornice.

Newmarket

CHESTERVILLE STORE, POST OFFICE AND HOTEL

New Market, later called Chesterville, had its major building boom during the decade which followed the Revolution. The most impressive building was construct-

The Nicholson House and Chambers House, c. 1788. Both houses had basement kitchens, but most importantly they possess the earliest use of brick cornices in the county. Maryland Historical Trust, c. 1975.

Dr. John Thomas House. By the late 1780s the townhouse plan had reached Millington. Dr. Thomas built his kitchen wing behind the house. C. Engstrom photograph, 1977.

ed circa 1785 by merchant, Isaac Spencer, Jr., presumably to serve the residents of east central Kent County. Here, as at the Buck-Bacchus Store (1735), the plan followed the general practice of having two rooms on the ground floor, one heated and one unheated. The four-bay, two-story, brick building has Flemish bond with the use of glazed headers being limited to its east gable. At the time it was built, the interior had exposed beaded ceiling joists and an enclosed stair which was accessible from the heated room. Paneled shutters were installed on the exterior of the windows with diagonal iron bar hardware that could be locked from the inside.

Across the street from Spencer's Store was another commercial building with a similar plan and detail, but it was only one and a half stories tall. It was constructed by John Woodall who owned Vianna nearby. On a

Chesterville Crossroads. The Chesterville Hotel (left), Spencer Store (center) and Chesterville Store and Post Office (right) in their original locations. This community was called New Market until the postal system changed its name to Chesterville in the 1840s. The photograph was taken prior to all three historic buildings being moved by the State Highway Administration. Library of Congress, Historic American Buildings Survey, 1973.

Spencer Store, c. 1785. It was built with two doors into the store room and one into the residential part. Glazed Flemish bond was used only on the original east gable. This photograph was taken soon after being moved from its original crossroad location. Library of Congress, Historic American Buildings Survey, c. 1976.

Opposite: River House—the stair hall is separated from the central passage by an elliptical arch. Tyler Campbell photograph 1992.

cluded in the Kent County Farm Museum. However, the building was later destroyed by fire.

WASHINGTON COLLEGE AND RIVER HOUSE

The culmination of the ideals of Georgian architecture in Kent County was displayed in the massive main building of Washington College constructed in 1784. In a county where the largest residence measured 50 feet across, the college building must have appeared huge as it measured 160 feet long and four stories high. Its use of a Palladian window was an architectural detail it shared solely with the Episcopal *Chapel* in town. Actually, these buildings were similar in several details, even though the *Chapel* had been constructed some fifteen years earlier. Unfortunately, neither of the two great Georgian buildings have survived. The main building at Washington College burned to the ground in 1827 and the Episcopal *Chapel* has suffered multiple remodelings which have obliterated most of its Georgian detail.

At the same time as Washington College was being constructed, Thomas Smyth, the college secretary who had built Widehall in 1769, purchased another water lot and began building a residence for his son. This home, which has become known as River House, is a transitional piece of domestic architecture which bridges the gap between the late Georgian style and Federal period architecture in Kent County. Here, the brickwork of the facade is uniform in color and laid with a thin mortar joint which creates the impression of a single plane on which the windows and doors are drawn. At Smyth's house limestone is used for the molded water table, belt course, rusticated jack arches and the capitals of the flanking brick pilasters. The door is framed with a simple, well-proportioned pedimented Doric architrave and the cornice is composed of shaped brackets, dentils and mutule blocks. All of the cornice elements are carved above the pilasters. On the river

third corner of the crossroad there was a frame, one-and-a-half-story building also dating from the late eighteenth century which appeared to have been intended for residential use. It had a hall-parlor plan with an attached kitchen which carried the same form one bay further. The kitchen fireplace backed up to the parlor chimney and possessed a small wrought iron crane In the nineteenth century it was referred to as a hotel in the records, and in the early twentieth century it was a store. In 1973 this building was moved to Turners Creek where it was to be in-

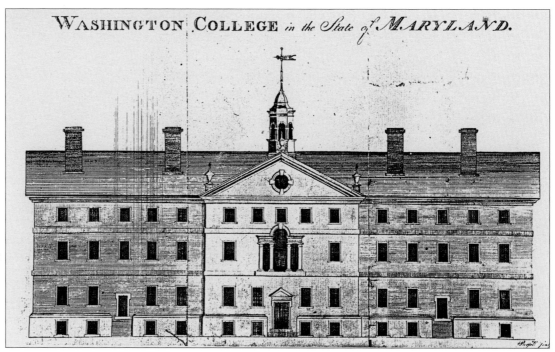

River House. The back porch or gallery overlooking the Chester River. Maryland Historical Trust, Miss Marian Weeks Collection, c. 1911.

River House, 1784-1787. The best example of an early Federal period townhouse in the county, with very uniform brick on the facade, the use of limestone architectural elements and carving in the cornice. The Greek Revival porch was added in the third quarter nineteenth century. Library of Congress, Historic American Buildings Survey, 1936.

Washington College, 1784. The engraving of the proposed building was included in Dr. William Smith's pamphlet entitled An Account of Washington College. *It is depicted in the overmantel painting featured on the dust jacket of this book.*

side, a three-level porch affords its inhabitants an unobstructed view—perhaps intended to provide a place from which an eye could be kept on the commercial activity along the river.

The first floor rooms are simply finished, while those on the second floor are finished in grand style with overmantel designs taken from earlier design books. The balustrade is the first to lack newel posts. Instead, the builder installed an iron baluster at each turn, to provide stability. It begins at the bottom with a volute supported on thin square balusters and continues unbroken to the third floor. The position of the stair is also unusual. Located to one side of the central passage, the

Airy Hill, c. 1790, was built by a niece of the builder of River House. The left side of the frame service wing predates the rest. Library of Congress, Historic American Buildings Survey, 1936.

Woodland Hall c. 1790, was originally two stories tall. The service wing is located behind the dining room wing. C. Engstrom photograph, 1977.

two are separated by an elliptical arch. This feature can be seen in several later houses, i. e. Bloomingdale (1792) in Queen Anne's County, and in Cecil County at Holly Hill (c. 1810) and Mount Aararat (c. 1800).

TRUMPINGTON

Thomas Smyth appears to have begun the replacement of his ancestral home at Trumpington in the same decade. This project, however, was not completed before Smyth went bankrupt in the early 1790s. The plan and form for the farmhouse were very different from either of Smyth's townhouses. At Trumpington, there is no architrave at the front door, no elegant cornice and no attempt to create a totally symmetrical facade. Instead, an earlier form was used with service wing built on the same axis with the main house. The plan is similar to the Violet Farm built twenty years earlier. Flemish bond with glazed headers is used only on the south gable. Here, as at River House, Smyth used a wide batten door with diamond and herringbone pattern on the exterior kitchen door. Although the principal room is simply finished, the details of the mantel with undercut brackets are similar to Thornton and Handy Point.

1790s

During this period, less successful farmers were building in the same manner as their fathers had, following vernacular forms and plans for their houses or farms in both the countryside and in town. While features such as the use of a dentil cornice or certain molding profiles aid the architectural historian in dating these houses, no more obvious or certain feature can be found than the common practice of installing the date and owners initials in gable walls. In the last decade of the eighteenth century the differences in style are subtle, which can make the dating process more difficult. However, iden-

tification and classification can usually be accomplished with the use of deeds, wills and family histories.

AIRY HILL, MONTEBELLO, WOODLAND HALL

In 1790, John and Anna Maria Rowles purchased a part of Kemp's Beginning. In the 1783 Tax Assessment no previously constructed buildings were listed in this location. It is assumed that the construction of their house was begun soon after their acquisition of the land. The frame kitchen which predates the larger section of the house could either have been built between 1783 and 1790 by the previous owners, or by the Rowles before they proceeded with the construction of the brick section. Architecturally, the house possesses a townhouse plan, as well as millwork details often associated with the previous decade. Of the buildings attributed to the 1790s, Airy Hill is the most sophisticated, along with Montebello (Duck Hollow) and Woodland Hall. At Montebello the service wing is a full two stories tall. The plan at Woodland Hall is more developed with the

States Adventure, c. 1797, has a longer service wing than Mt. Herman and interior details like Knocks Folly. Michael C. Wootton photograph, 1996.

Knocks Folly's log wing was built in the 1760s and the brick section after 1796, when its planning was written in the will of Donaldson Yeates. The modillion cornice with drill and gouge work decoration are unique and match some of the interior decorations. Michael Bourne photograph, 1964.

Mount Herman, c. 1794, possesses the popular form of Kent County farmhouse with details similar to Airy Hill. Like Hebron and Thornton, the service wing is set back from the facade. Jack R. Schroeder, 1976.

Opposite: Comegys House, Millington (foreground). This two part c. 1790 house contains a central stairhall and two flanking rooms. Its stair is similar to the Dr. John Thomas House a block away. Jack Schroeder, 1964.

Shepherd's Delight was originally built by John Angier with a hall/parlor plan. It was enlarged c. 1800 by John's son, Unit Angier, with central stairhall and additional leanto room. The porches are extraordinary and have aided in the preservation of the building. C. Engstrom photograph, 1977.

States Adventure has a brick in the west gable bearing the inscribed date 1797. The plan is the same as at Mount Herman; however, here the service wing is longer and on the same axis as the main section. The interior possesses gouge and drill work detailing which is also found at its contemporary, Knocks Folly.

KNOCKS FOLLY

In his will, written in 1796, Donaldson Yeates instructed his executor to build the house he had been planning.[6] That house is now known as Knocks Folly. When the house was completed was not documented. The detailing at Knocks Folly is of fine quality. A modillion cornice with gouge work on the facia decorates the main facade of the house. Inside, the gouge work is repeated in the cornice of the main room. The living room mantel is a masterpiece of fine carving and that on the floor above possessed a painted scene of presumably Turner's Creek and the Sassafras River. The form of Knocks Folly is unusual, since the log wing existed before the three-story brick section was built. The brick wing consists of a stairhall and one room. That juxtaposition of form created a unique combination of materials and styles. Another extraordinary feature of the addition is the delicacy of the stair's turned balusters which ascend to the attic and produce a dramatic effect from any angle.

dining room and passage located in the usual space for the service wing and the actual service wing extending to the rear of the passage.

MOUNT HERMAN AND STATES ADVENTURE

Mount Herman, near Chesterville, is reputed to have been built in 1794. Several of its details support such a date. Its cornice is similar to that at Airy Hill, with shaped modillions. Its two-story service wing is set back from the facade, like those at Thornton and Knock's Folly, which creates a space for a porch off the kitchen. Here, the plan is a central stairhall flanked by two rooms.

Shepherd's Delight

The plan at Shepherd's Delight has developed over the years. Beginning in the 1760s as a hall-parlor house, it was augmented around 1800 with an addition which converted it into a central hall plan with leanto off the rear of the inner room. The original house was one-and-a-half-stories tall and had pent eaves beneath its cornice. There is an original one-story, two-room service wing. The interior possesses many fine details. The stair balustrade is similar to that at Knocks Folly, but here it ascends only one flight. And the living room is decorated with very fine millwork with gouge work, drill holes and carving. As a whole, the farm represents one of the best preserved complexes of agricultural

Other Houses of the 1790s

Greys Inn Point Farm, Standaway, and the Hosier Farm are all examples of the central hall plan, but due to the characteristics of the service wing or the interior details, these three-bay-long dwellings all appear to be different. Hosier Farm is the only one of the group to have a small band of reeding in its baseboard and Standaway is the only one to have recessed panel dado.

As in the previous generation of buildings, the familiar hall-parlor plan continued to be built primarily in the country. The Moody Farm and McKay's Purchase are two such buildings, but they were two full stories plus an attic in height. They also had ample service buildings in the county, including a stable, granary, smokehouse, dairy and a reconstructed slave cabin.

Hosier Farm on Great Oak Manor has a closed string stair with unusual turned newels and a shadow rail with pilasters along the wall. C. Engstrom photograph, 1977.

Greys Inn Point Farm, c. 1790, from the back. The asymmetry of the center bay is caused by the placement of the stair landing. This was the home of three generations of Greshams. Michael Bourne photograph, 1982.

Trulock, near Stillpond. the asymmetry of the south facade is due to the fact that it has a hall/parlor plan with nearly equal size rooms. Its stair is a small enclosed winder in the south east corner of the hall. Michael Bourne photograph, 1968.

COMEGYS HOUSE

Closely akin to Dr. John Thomas' house in Millington, the Comegys House was probably constructed for Samuel Osborne, a Millington merchant, around 1790. The plan consists of a central stairhall with one room on each side and a service wing to the rear. The unique form of this two-story house is derived from the fact that one room is about four steps lower than the stairhall, creating the appearance of a two-part house. The stair is nearly identical to that in Dr. Thomas' house, with close-string, turned balusters and paneled spandrel. Crossetted trim on the mantel and doors gave a degree of elegance to this once fine building.

wings. Both are traditionally said to have been built in the 1790s. Trulock, Blackhall's Hermitage, London Bridge and Travilla are other hall-parlor, one-and-a-half and two-story buildings, each having individual characteristics which make them unique.

1800-1820

The decade following the turn of the century saw little building in Kent County. The economic condition was stagnant with many of the merchants having relocated to the new and thriving metropolis of Baltimore or to the old established mercantile center of Philadelphia. Houses of the second decade were as likely to have hall-parlor plans as they were to have central hall plans and are perhaps the most difficult to date with any accuracy.

THE HARRIS HOUSE

In 1801, William Harris, a merchant who stayed in Chestertown despite the economic slump, purchased that part of Lot No. 7 which was part of William Slubey's estate. On it he built a two-story, three-bay, frame, vernacular house with a hall-parlor plan. The symmetry of that first facade is apparent when looking at the second floor windows which were left unchanged when he added a nine foot extension about fifteen years later. At that time, a central hall was created with an open stair to the second story. Harris used vertical beaded board partitions to divide the rooms in both the original construction and the remodeling. The profile of the handrail and shape of the turned newel posts is identical to the work at Carvill Hall, when it was remodeled after 1814.

METHODIST MEETING HOUSE

In 1801, the Methodists were successful in obtaining a lot on the town square where they built a two-story, brick meet-

Harris House, Chestertown, c. 1801. The symmetry of the three second story windows marks the original section of the house. A nine foot extension created the fourth bay. Michael Bourne photograph, 1980.

Methodist Meeting House, is lined up with the Episcopal Church across the square. It originally had one central double door facing High Street and a smaller door facing the square. Michael C. Wootton photograph, 1996.

Blays Range, c. 1809, has a plan and form similar to Montabello in Georgetown. It stands on the opposite side of the ravine from Shrewsbury Church. Francis Lamb Collection, c. 1900

Locust Grove Farm, c. 1804. James Corse purchased part of Bachelors Resolution in 1804 and built a house with the same plan as Shepherds Delight. It was a tenant house for most of its life and thus the majority of the original interior remains intact. C. Engstrom photograph, 1977.

LOCUST GROVE AND BLAY'S RANGE

In 1804, James Corse purchased part of Batchelors Resolution and proceeded to build a good farmhouse which was later called Locust Grove. The house was a near duplicate of Shepherd's Delight as enlarged a decade before. Its main section is a frame, one-and-a-half-story, four-bay edifice. There is also a smaller, two-room service wing and a leanto located behind the middle room. Flanking the chimney in the living room there are two closets, neither of which was fitted for decorative display. The newel post with bulbous turning is perhaps the most unusual feature of this otherwise vernacular house.

Blay's Range is reputed to have been built in 1809, but due to a twentieth century fire and replacement of the windows, the date is not easily discernible. The plan and form appear to have been similar to Montebello in Georgetown, but the four-bay, two-story service wing was reduced to half of its original size after the fire. The unusual feature here is the double chimney with curtain wall connecting the two stacks.

Big Fairlee, c. 1815. The older house on the property was destroyed by the British in 1813. This tenant house replaced what was lost. Even though it was built for tenants, no money was spared on the interior woodwork. C. Engstrom photograph, 1977.

ing house. Like the Episcopal Chapel of Ease across the square, it was oriented to both the square and to High Street. Considerably plainer than the Episcopal Chapel, the only decorative devices used were the wide frame windows fitted with louvered blinds. Inside, the meeting house was just as plain, there being no window or door trim. Initially the building had an arched ceiling, but when the roof trusses were replaced within a short time after its construction, a typical flat ceiling was reinstalled.

How to make Whitewash

" ... Whitewash, a receipt obtained from Miss Anna Pierce: The proportions producing the whitest covering that will remain hard on walls are—3 Gallons of white wash (lime), 3 pounds of salt, and one pound of sugar, an increase of sugar will strengthen the cement but will injure the colour. The wash should be made of the best lime, and slacked with enough water to cover the lime and make it of the consistence of good thick paint, if it thickens as you use it, thin with boiling water."

from Plantation Life at Rose Hill,
by Martha Ogle Forman
Diary entry for May 7, 1821

Other Houses of the 1810s

Other buildings from the first decade of the nineteenth century include Rosedale, a hall-parlor plan house on Swan Creek, part of the Rees Corner House, the Urieville Miller's House, the Miers-Pennington Farm and Toll Inn Farm. One interesting feature of the two-story Urieville Miller's House is the use of exposed beaded ceiling joists. This occurs on two other frame, one-and-a-half-story structures near Worton and Lynch, one now being a part of Sandy Hill. These buildings resembled contemporary work in Caroline and Dorchester Counties.

BIG FAIRLEE

When the British attacked the Bayside in 1813, they burned one of the most significant new houses to have been built in the first decade of the nineteenth century. The house which had been built for Henry Waller on

Big Fairlee was completely destroyed. Waller sold the property and a new house was erected soon thereafter. The details in the entry architrave and the overmantel of the hall include a profusion of reeding and gouge work details that, while similar to some work executed ten to fifteen years earlier, could not have survived the War of 1812. Big Fairlee, as the new house was called, was built with a hall-parlor plan in a standard two-story, brick form with lower, smaller service wing. Grantham and Forest, near Millington is essentially a four-bay-long version of Big Fairlee.

THORNTON FARM

On a larger scale and with more emphasis upon the overmantel, Thornton Farm had a similar profusion of reeding and gouge work. In 1809, Thomas Brooks and his brother Philip had exchanged their farms (Thornton and Thornton Farm). While Thomas received the home farm with its house near Morgan Creek, he chose also to build a new house near the center of the farm. Built c. 1815, Thornton Farm is exemplary of the late Federal style. While its form, center hall plan and pedimented tabernacle overmantel design are nearly identical to Thornton, the reeding and gouge work place it in a different period altogether.

Closely akin to the millwork of Big Fairlee and Thornton Farm is that in the brick addition built onto the eastern end of Fancy Farm by William Barroll. There he installed a naively executed, pedimented architrave with reeded trim on the main doorway. Reeding and gouge work decorated the inside, but with less

Urieville Millers House was probably built after the Revolution when all of the Perkins Mill complex had been burned by a Tory. It has exposed beaded ceiling joists and brick nogging in the walls. The stone basement may be the remains of the pre-revolutionary house. Marsha Fritz photograph, 1980.

Thornton Farm, c. 1815. This house was built by Thomas Brooks, a bachelor, who had exchanged his paternal inheritance with his brother in 1809. The two houses are similar, except for the profusion of reeding originally in Thomas's house. Note the brick fill beneath the kitchen windows, indicating that the floor level was raised after the house suffered a serious fire in 1926. Historical Society of Kent County, Bill Usilton Collection, c. 1930.

Fancy Farm was built in two stages. The first frame part built around 1780 and the brick addition built by Attorney William Barroll around 1815. The brick addition has many reeded features that are similar to Big Fairlee and Thornton Farm. Tyler Campbell photograph, 1995

Millington Academy was built in 1813 to serve the educational needs of the growing community. It is reported to have begun life as a two story structure, perhaps like the Academy in Middletown, Delaware. After a fire late in the nineteenth century it was reduced to one story and lengthened. Postcard collection, R. Dennis Hager, c. 1900.

profusion than the two aforesaid buildings.

SHREWSBURY AND MILLINGTON ACADEMIES

Public education in Kent County was established by law in 1723 and in 1728 the Kent Free School was established adjoining Chestertown. After that school became Washington College in 1782, the primary school continued on a less formal basis until smaller schools were established in outlying areas and villages. In 1759, a one-room school associated with Shrewsbury Parish was established in Sassafras. It did not long endure and in 1817 Shrewsbury Academy was established in Galena. Four years before, Millington had established Millington Academy for which they built a two-story, brick structure which probably resembled a residential structure, like the academies at Middletown and New Castle, Delaware. Later that building was lengthened and then after a fire reduced in height. The latter two schools remained independent until after the Civil War, when they were amalgamated into the county system.

Footnotes:
1. Kent County Tax Assessment, 1783, Microfilm No. 872, Maryland Historical Trust.
2. Guardian Accounts, Lib. 1, fol. 49.
3. E. C. Hallman, Garden of Methodism.
4. Kent County Tax Assessment, 1783, Microfilm No. 872, Maryland Historical Trust.
5. Wills, Lib. 5, fol. 164.
6. Wills, Lib. 7, fol. 547.

Washington College

Chestertown
c. 1782, 1844, 1854

THE FIRST CONCRETE SIGN OF ANY INTEREST OR ABILITY TO establish a school in Kent County occurred on August 21, 1728, when Simon Wilmer sold part of Stepney to the Visitors of the Free School. The parcel was described in the deed as *" ... beginning at the mouth of a Gutt of Marsh lying on the northernmost of Chester Town ... containing one hundred Acres of Land ... ."*[1]

The General Assembly had passed an Act for the Establishment of Schools in each county in 1723, but it took five years to get the Kent County Free School to this point. Records of the Free School are few. The only verbal description appears in an advertisement in 1797 after it had been replaced by a new structure on *"the Hill"* nine years earlier:

"To be leased for a Term of Years, that large and commodious Building known by the name of Old Kent Free School. It contains four spacious, airy rooms on the first floor, five on the second, with two small lodging rooms at the head of the stair, and a well fur-nished garret. It has a convenient brick kitchen with a good oven, a stable, meat house, etc. and about six acres of ground of the first quality for a garden or grass lots. On the premises and within forty yards of the House is a spring, famed for the abundance and salubrity of its waters. There is also a good situation for an ice house which might be erected at a trifling expense. These advantages with its proximity to the Court House and Market, render it the first situation in town for a tavern, and is presumed that a person acquainted with the business might here fix himself much to his satisfaction and with certainty of profit."[2]

Doctor William Smith, D. D. was born near Aberdeen, Scotland in 1727 and died, age 76 years, in Philadelphia. He was the founder of Washington College and was chosen as its first president in 1782. Portrait by Gilbert Stuart. Courtesy University of Pennsylvania. A copy of this painting by an unknown artist hangs in the president's office at the college.

Etching of Washington College showing all three buildings constructed prior to the Civil War. Martenet Map of Kent County, 1860

During the same decade, an unknown artist had painted a view of Chestertown from the home of Simon Wilmer IV. This may, in fact, include the only existing depiction of the building. Even after the establishment of Washington College in 1782, the old Free School building maintained its usefulness. Classes were held in it until the new building was opened in 1786. For some time thereafter the Free School was still used by the younger students, but in 1790 it was leased to the Trustees of the Poor until such time as they could build on a lot located between town and Wilmer's Mill, purchased of Simon Wilmer.

Dr. William Smith, former Provost of the College of Philadelphia, and one largely responsible for its formation, came to Chestertown in 1780. Within a short time after his arrival, he became the headmaster of the Free School and within two years he had convinced members of the Maryland General Assembly (with the great assistance of

General John Cadwalader) that the time was right to charter a college in Chestertown. The Charter was signed in June of 1782 and the college was to be named in honor of General George Washington. To this purpose, Smith wrote to Washington seeking permission to use his name. In Washington's response, he accepted the honor and pledged fifty Guineas toward this purpose. Dr. Smith then had to raise the money stipulated by the charter. With the help of many associates of the various counties of the Eastern Shore, this was accomplished within the year.

The next major task was to raise enough money to build the structure itself. This step proved to be more difficult than the first. In 1784, Dr. Smith wrote a pamphlet entitled *"An Account of Washington College"*—for the dual purpose of attracting students as well as sponsors for the building project. The pamphlet included an elevation drawing of the proposed building and a brief description:

"... the Building ... which will be large and commodious, being One Hundred and Sixty feet in Length ... and capable of containing near Two Hundred Students ... ."[3]

In the same year, a lottery was initiated to help in raising funds. It was advertised in two or three newspapers and representatives were appointed in each of the Eastern Shore counties and in the cities of Baltimore, Annapolis and Philadelphia.

By the spring of 1788, the building had progressed to the point that an official dedication was given during commencement. While at this time the building was used to house both students and classrooms, it was not yet finished. An interesting description of the College is found in the writings of Peregrine Wroth who had been a student there between 1795 and 1803:

"The Old College Edifice which was destroyed by fire in 1827, was a magnificent building. It consisted of a large Central Hall, in which Comedies were sometimes acted by the Students with an East and West wing, joined to the Hall and a large Chapel at the rear of the Hall. The whole presented a front of 150 feet long, by 45

or 50 wide, besides the chapel. It was three stories above the Basement. There were 24 rooms in the wings—above the basement. The Hall had not been finished and above the Theatre there was no floor. The roof was seen from the lower floor through two stories of joists—The present College buildings are not half the size of the original building."[a]

Even before a minor fire in 1817, the College had been granted permission to have a lottery in order to raise more funds to complete the building. How much had been completed has not been further documented, but as mentioned by Wroth, the fire of 1827, which started in the basement, consumed the building in its entirety. The event was described in the January 12 edition of the Telegraph that year:

"Our village engine arrived on the spot a few minutes after the alarm was given, and while the flames were confined to the cellar, but owing to a scarcity of water, could not extinguish them.

Winter on the Hill, Washington College. *Painting courtesy of the artist, Harry Lloyd Jaecks of Millersville, Maryland. c. 1996.*

A welcome sign to all passers-by in Chestertown. Tyler Campbell photograph, 1996.

The fire continued to increase with redoubled fury, ascending through the common hall to the roof, and from thence extending along each wing, the whole building was soon wrapt in one sheet of vivid flame. We never witnessed a more awful and sublime sight. In a little while more than two hours the whole building was destroyed."[5]

The conflagration must have been so intense and the light it created so bright that it was seen for miles around. Martha Forman who was living at Rose Hill, Cecil County, some fourteen miles away recorded her impressions of the spectacle in her diary:

"This evening the College of Chestertown was burnt, we saw the fire here very distinctly."[6]

Initial efforts to reconstruct the college building were unsuccessful, but its charter remained in effect and the institution carried on in rented quarters. While discussions started as early as 1835, it was not until 1844 that a new building was finally erected on *College Hill*. The designer and builder was one Elijah Reynolds of Havre de Grace. Before the building was ready for occupancy, Mr. Reynolds wrote a thorough description of it for an insurance policy with the Franklin Fire Insurance Company of Philadelphia:

"Survey made August 8th 1844 of the Washington College building on College Hill near Chester Town

Dimensions and specifications as follows

The Building 57 feet fron(t) by 45 ft deep a hammer dressed Granite Basement wall 10 feet high in the Clear Principal Story 12 feet in the Clear Brick wall 18 inch thick faced outside with Best prefs Brick. 2nd Story 10½ feet in the Clear wall. 14 inch faced as the first story with prefs brick attic 4½ feet in the Clear at the sides Brick wall 14 inch Covered with an entabliture of wood outside in which is placed 18 two light hinged sash fastened with Brafs Buttons The Roof is framed Square or Castle form with a wooden Cornice X Tin Gutters & Conductor The whole covered with Best Susquehanna Blue Steel. There is a Balistrade Sypported with Irons The Peak of the Roof is Surmounted with an oblong Square observatory, 19 x 7 four Glafs windows of 12 lights each side & 2 in each end The Roof of Tin all the outside neatly painted with 3 Coats White Lead. a Portico Back & front 10 x 15 feet 4 Doric columns Supporting an entabliture floors & Steps north Carolina pine Roof Tin

Interior

Basement Floor 2nd quality north Carolina pine 5/4 in laid on 3 x 10 white oak Joist 11 windows 12 lights 10 x 14 Glafs Pannall shutters 6 Blank windows pannall shutters divided into 4 Rooms and pafsage 2 east Rooms are connected by a set of Sliding doors placed on Brafs Rail ways fastened with

George Washington, cast in bronze, stands in front of Middle Hall overlooking the campus at Washington College. It was a gift to the College by the sculptor, Lee Laurie, in 1957. Tyler Campbell botograph, 1996.

Middle Hall, built in 1844 by Elijah Reynolds of Havre de Grace. Historical Society of Kent County, Usilton Collection, c. 1910.

Opposite: This is a model of the first building at Washington College based on details in Dr. William Smith's An Account of Washington College, 1784. The replica was constructed by Knoll Architectural Models under the supervision of Professor Robert J. H. Janson-La Palme. It was funded by the Historical Society of Kent County and presented to the college in honor of its bicentennial anniversary. Photograph from Robert Janson-La Palme Collection.

Left to right: Middle Hall, built in 1844; East Hall and West Hall, built in 1854. Tyler Campbell photographs, 1996.

Long Boults Lock & 6 and are intended for Recitation Rooms

West Rooms are to be occupied for Kitchen & Dining Room the pafsage is for Stairs at one end a cellar at the other the middle for entrance to the Rooms 2 of the Partitions are Brick the others wood an outside Door wile lead from the kitchen where there is a small granite flight of Steps all the Doors are pannal 7/4 in Carpenter Pattent Locks four fire places with plain wooden mantels the Stairs are of yellow pine closed up and lead to the principal story pafsage Plaistering & painting 3 Coat

Principal Story Floor 1st quality north Carolina pine laid on 3 x 12 in Joist divided into 4 Rooms and pafsage 2 Rooms on east side of the pafsage and have folding Doors 8 pannal furnished with flush boults Rabited mortice Lock Partition Stud four fire places with neat wooden mantles 12 twelve light windows glafs 13 x 20

Sash Hung Venition shutters outside plain pillasters all Doors 7/4 in Mortice Locks Stair open newall, Mahogany newall, Rail & Balustrade, North Carolina Steps, 5/4 in thick Plaistering & Painting 3 Coats

2nd Story Floors Joist Stain divisions partition Mantles Painting Plaistering windows and Doors as below except there is no folding Doors and the Glafs is 13 x 18 and a venition window over front Door and one over Back door. Door 7/4 in pannall mortice Locks.

Attic White pine 3 x 10 Joist division and partition, as below Doors 6/4 pannal tin carpenter, Locks Plaistering 2 Coats painting 3 coats a winding Stair Leads up to the observatory

The whole work plain but neat & substantially done of the best materials.

The above is the description of the building when finished it is now in progrefs the walls Cornice & roof is finished the frames have the Shutters fit in but not hung the Joist floors and partitions are all done except Basement and 2 upper Stories ready and principal Story nearly ready for plastering the attic in 3/4th latched.

The building stands alone near it is an excellent well of water with a good pump in it.

Elijah Reynolds
Builder"[7]

The construction of the new building ushered in a time of rebirth for the College. Enrollment grew and degrees were conferred after a 22 year dormancy. This growth soon created a need for even more space. Two additional buildings were constructed on the Hill in 1854. They flanked the 1844 structure which then became the central focus and after which time came to be known as Middle Hall. The College was contained essentially within these buildings until the 1890s. They remain three of the best examples of Greek Revival architecture in the County today.[8]   K-1

1. Land Records, Lib. JS 10, fol. 267.
2. Maryland Herald and Eastern Shore Intelligencer, February 11, 1797.
3. William Smith, *An Account of Washington College*, 1784. Washington College Library. Rakestraw and Hicks of Philadelphia drew up the plans for the new building, which was called the *Common Building* in early records. The actual construction was undertaken by Robert Allison, who with many of his craftsmen and laborers also came from Philadelphia.
4. Peregrine Wroth Memoirs, manuscript, Washington College Library.
5. Chestertown Telegraph, January 12, 1827.
6. M. O. Forman, The Rose Hill Diaries of Martha Ogle Forman, p. 228.
7. Fire insurance Policy #5357, 1844, Franklin Fire Insurance Company Records, Historical Society of Pennsylvania.
8. Three works on Washington College have been of great assistance:
*Barroll, L. Wethered, "Washington College, 1783," Maryland Historical Magazine, Vol. VI, p. 164 ff. (A typed copy is in the collection of the Historical Society of Kent County.)
*Dumschott, Fred W. Washington College, Chestertown, 1980.
*White, M. P. "An Account of the First Edifice of Washington College, Chestertown, Maryland," masters thesis prepared for the University of Delaware.

Robert Reed House

High Street, Chestertown
1782

I N 1775, ROBERT REED ACQUIRED THE HALF LOT (ON WHICH he most likely built his house) from Elizabeth Tuille,[1] cousin and heir of James Harris (d. 1766). He was a gunsmith by trade and, due to the work required of him during the revolution, he did not build his home until 1782, a date found etched in an attic brick.

The house abuts 520 High Street, which was built around 1775. At the time it was built, its facade had only one window and an entrance door, the former with 9/6 sash and shutters and a gauged brick arch. Beneath the window, was a bulkhead entry to the basement. The second floor had two windows placed symmetrically above the first floor openings, but they were shorter, having 6/6 sash and no shutters. There were no dormers on the roof, the attic received light only from

Robert Reed House, 518 High Street, was built by a revolutionary period gunsmith around 1782. It was originally only two bays, but a nineteenth century owner bricked up the original window (Jack arch still visible between the windows) and added two windows. Michael C. Wootton photograph, 1996.

the gable end. To the rear of the brick structure was a two-story frame wing which housed a kitchen.

The original two room plan consisted of an entry/stairhall with a parlor to the northwest, separated from the former by a feather-edge board partition. The parlor was lighted by only one window. It was heated by a fireplace which had a cabinet on its north side. The configuration of the frame wing is unknown.

On the second floor the same arrangement was repeated. The stairhall, however, was about two feet wider than that on the first floor. The ceiling was exposed and whitewashed. The stair continued to an unfinished attic where the gable end of the adjoining house was visible and where there was one boarded up window. A brick in that gable displayed the scratched-in numerals *1782.*

From the profile of the moldings of the front door, the brickwork on the southeast gable, and the second story mantel, the house appears to have been significantly altered in the 1840s or 1850s. At that time, the house was owned by Ann Rollins and her son-in-law John Russell.[2] The remodeling they undertook involved rebuilding the southeast gable above grade, bricking in the single window on the facade, and installing two flanking windows on both stories. A dormer was added at this time and the entire interior was plastered, both the ceilings and board partitions. The second story partition was moved, narrowing the hall to the same size as the one below and a new mantel was installed.

A large increase in sale price was recorded in a 1920 deed by Hallie C. Kelly.[3] Her grandfather had purchased the house in 1879, and bequeathed it to his son Amos, who died around 1908. Amos' heirs sold it to Kelly. Kelly was probably the next major remodeler, installing a porch across the facade and rebuilding the back frame wing. The wing was to house a kitchen and dining room with narrow stair in the latter. A buffet mantel with mirrored overmantel was installed in the parlor and a tiny bath at the head of the stairs.

The house remained in that configuration until Preservation, Incorporated purchased it in 1975.[4] The facade was restored to its 1840 appearance. Mrs. Horace Havemeyer undertook a major rehabilitation of the interior and back wing. Since that time there have been three owners and several tenants, the present owner being responsible for the most recent remodeling.[5] K-63

1. Land Records, Lib. DD 5, fol. 100.
2. Land Records, Lib. JNG 8, fol. 36; Wills, Lib. JFB 1, fol. 174.
3. Land Records, Lib. APR 6, fol. 404.
4. Land Records, Lib. EHP 70, fol. 137.
5. In the late eighteenth century the deed descriptions are often vague and sometimes misnumbered. Many times a chain of title can only be completed by combining information from neighboring buildings/lots with what extant information there is on the subject. In the case of 518 High Street, such methods were used to identify its original owner/builder.

The Palmer House

High Street, Chestertown
c. 1782

THE PALMER HOUSE STANDS ON THE NORTHWESTERN HALF OF Lot No. 62 in Chestertown. The entire lot had been sold by Simon Wilmer II to Joseph Everett for £10 prior to August 10, 1737. On that date Wilmer entered into a sale of the same lot to Joseph's two sons and heirs, St. Leger and Abraham.[1]

Abraham received the northwest half of Lot No. 62 and kept it until 1756, when he and his wife Margaret transferred it to Mary Stanton for £20.[2] Mary's daughter, Sarah and her husband Henry Hynson of Queen Annes County sold the lot to John Palmer for £75 in 1782.[3]

Palmer built the existing three-bay stone structure over a full basement. Either contemporarily or soon thereafter, the space between it and the Hopkins House to the west was filled with a stone wing having the same roof line. Old photos of the house show a room at ground level with a window above, and a small dormer on the back of the roof. This structure was probably a

John Palmer House. The southeast gable of rubble stone construction. Michael C. Wooton photograph, 1996.

John Palmer built the stone house after he acquired the lot in 1782. In its original configuration it had a kitchen between it and the Hopkins House next door. Maryland Historical Society Collection, c. 1900.

John Palmer House without the fence. The seats on front stoops appear to have been a common feature of early Kent County houses. Kent County News Collection, c. 1910.

John Palmer House. The small stoop was later replaced by a larger covered porch. At the same time, the old kitchen was removed and a new lean-to was attached to the back. Historical Society of Kent County Usilton Collection, c. 1940.

kitchen wing and access from the main house was probably gained via a door where the present west window is located. The presence of brick down to the floor level in the west gable might be explained by the fact that the kitchen fireplace was connected to the main flue and the irregularities were left when the wing was removed after 1903. After the old kitchen was removed, a frame leanto was added on the back of the house.

John Palmer sold the house and lot in 1811 to his son Edward for £200 ($533.50 is also stated in the deed).[4] During the same year, Edward was the administrator of his neighbor's estate.[5]

Apparently Edward sold the property to Thomas Edwards without recording the deed. After Thomas Edwards' death, the chancery court ordered the property be sold to William Sappington, which was recorded in 1836.[6]

The 1841 Tax Assessment lists Sappington residing on Lot No. 62 with *"Buildings in tolerable Repair"* and as owning two houses on part of Lot No. 89 and a blacksmith shop occupied by William Webb and G. Usilton in bad repair. Both properties were valued at $700.00.[7]   K-65

1. Land Records, Lib. 4, fol. 709 (for St. Leger Everett see *Big Meadow*).
2. Land Records, Lib. 8, fol. 28.
3. Land Records, Lib. EF 6, fol. 112.
4. Land Records, Lib. BC 6, fol. 358.
5. Inventories, Lib. 12, fol. 507. (Elizabeth Hopkins Pope). At the public sale of Pope's personal property, John Palmer purchased several items. Both John and Edward were heirs of Mrs. Pope, receiving $540.79 3/4 each. (Administrative Acts, Lib. 13, fol. 23.)
6. Land Records, Lib. JNG 4, fol. 251.
7. The house is also known as *Rock of Ages* and is depicted on the Silver Service which once graced the officers dining table on the USS Maryland. The service is now on display at the State House, Annapolis.

Friendship

Lynch
1783

W HEN FRIENDSHIP WAS IN THE PROCESS OF RESTORATION by its present owners, it became quite evident how the house developed over the years and that it was probably planned accordingly from the beginning. In 1783, the western half of the house was constructed and consisted of a one-bay kitchen section two stories tall and a one-bay living room section also two stories, but taller. Both had chimneys in their west gables. The south facade was laid in Flemish bond with water table and no belt course. Inside, both rooms had exposed beaded ceiling joists and enclosed stairs. The kitchen stair was in the southwest corner and the living room stair was in the southeast corner.

According to tradition, the house was built by George Lamb, but on the 1783 Tax Assessment Daniel Lamb was listed as having an unfinished house located on part of Warner's Addition. The fact that the house belonged to Daniel is corroborated in a history of the Lamb family by James G. Lamb.[1]

A brick dated 1783 was found during the restoration and subsequently incorporated into the cheek of the reconstructed kitchen fireplace. A second brick dated 1792, still located in the east gable, indicates when the two eastern most bays were constructed. This addition is the same form as the taller part of the 1783 structure and it would appear that an effort was made to match the earlier section stylistically, as the south facade is also laid in Flemish bond and the joists are also exposed and beaded. Its plan includes a stair hall separated from the east parlor by a beaded board partition. The new addition created a plan that was to become the most popular for Kent County farmhouses.

Whether the living room stair was removed in 1792 has not been determined, but it was certainly gone when the house received its first major embellishments in the late 1830s or 1840s. At this period, all of the windows and doors were retrimmed, the ceilings and board walls were plastered and three dormers were installed on each side of the moderately pitched *A* roof. At that time, a porch was also added to the north entry.

Family tradition also states that Friendship was owned by Sarah Lamb Bowers Parrott and later by James Lamb Bowers. If so, that would have been prior to 1860 when Josiah Massey appears to be owner.[2] William Hepborn acquired the farm thereafter and owned it for several years. In the 1877 Atlas, J. T. Willis' name appears on the farm, but in 1884 Robert Rouse purchased the farm from Willis. A plat of Robert Rouse's land appears in a chancery case after his death.[3]

In the late 1950s, the house was remodeled by removal of the old kitchen fireplace and installation of a modern kitchen. An enclosed porch was built on the south side of the kitchen and a bath was installed on the second story. The dormers were also removed at this time.

In the 1980s, the house was totally gutted and restored to its conjectural appearance of the 1790s. The fireplace was reconstructed in the kitchen section, plaster was removed from the ceiling joists and board partitions and windows were replaced. A new kitchen wing was added south of the old kitchen and a porch was added across part of the south facade.

The details of Friendship and Salutation Farm are very similar. Both houses were built by Quakers.   K-230

Friendship was built for Daniel Lamb in 1783, initially as the two bays on the right. In 1792, he added the other two bays which created a central passage plan. Michael C. Wootton photograph, 1996.

1. Courtesy of Francis Lamb.
2. Martenet Map 1860.
3. Chancery, Lib. SB 4, fol. 182, 184.

River House

Water Street, Chestertown
1784

R IVER HOUSE WAS BUILT ON WATER LOTS NOS. 12 AND 13 ON THE ORIGINAL PLAT of Chestertown. John Tennant and Jude Clarkson were the first record-ed grantees, but the lots had apparently previously been sold to William and Hannah Trew and Thomas Garnett.[1]

Thomas Garnett described the house he was constructing on his water lot in his 1730 will in which he bequeathed to his son, George:

" ... the water lot in Chestertown whereon the frame of my designed Dwelling House stands ... ."[2]

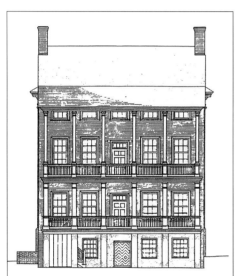

River House, 1784-87, was built by Thomas Smyth for his son Richard. The primary occupant was Peregrine Letherbury, one of the principals in the estab-lishment and manage-ment of Washington College. River House is the only Kent County house to have limestone water table, belt course, rusticated jack arches, and pilaster capitals. Tyler Campbell photo-graph, 1978.

River House. The River facade with its two story "piazza" as reconstruct-ed c. 1970. Historic American Buildings Sur-vey, 1973.

It was undoubtedly the same house referred to in a later deed to William Timbrell. Timbrell died in 1743 intestate and his affairs were settled by Richard Button, a Barbados attorney who was given the power to sell the Chestertown property. Initially, there was a sale to one John Kennedy,[3] but this was never finalized. There is a record, however, that in 1778, Eleazer McComb, mer-chant, petitioned the General Assembly for a clear title to the property.[4]

McComb was an important merchant in Chestertown before and during the Revolution. He was Clerk for the Council of Safety in 1775[5] and served in various capacities with Thomas Smyth, Emory Sudler, Donaldson Yeates and others.

McComb continued to petition the General As-sembly in 1780 and 1782, but it was not until 1784 that he finally obtained clear title to Water Lots Nos. 12 and 13. By that time he had moved to New Castle, Delaware and proceeded to sell the property to Thomas Smyth.[6]

In the 1783 Tax Assessment, the property had been assessed at £50, £20 less than Timbrell had paid some 46 years earlier. However, in the 1784 deed from McComb to Smyth, the recorded sale price is £300, a huge increase, one either indicative of substantial improvements, or of a big spender. (The latter was the case when Thomas Smyth pur-chased Water Lot No. 17 from his stepbrother and built Widehall.)

Smyth deeded the property to his son, Richard Gresham Smyth, in 1786, for the same amount he had paid McComb in 1784.[7] However, only nine months later, Richard Smyth in turn sold the property to Peregrine Letherbury for the sum of *"£1200, lawful money of Mary-land,"* indicative of vast improvements. Those vast improvements in-cluded the existing house with its handsome facade laid in an even color brick with convex mortar joints, highlighted by limestone water table belt course, and rusticated jack arches. The facade was further delineated by corner pilasters with sandstone capitals. Both the stone capitals and their corresponding wood cornices are embellished with carving the likes of which has never been repeated in Kent County. The river facade and gables were laid in less regular brick, but over-looking the river was a *piazza* that was accessible from the ground, first and second stories.

Its floor plan was similar to Mount Pleasant, Philadelphia, with cen-tral passage flanked by one large room on the northeast and a smaller

is Kent County's finest remaining example of Federal period architecture.

Letherbury was an attorney in late eighteenth century Chestertown. The son of Jonathan and Mary Letherbury, his birth is recorded in St. Paul's Parish on 1 August 1752.[9] His father was a bricklayer and had owned a lot in the upper part of Chestertown. He had one sister, Sarah, who had married a Piner, and had probably lived at Piner's Grove. In 1775, Letherbury was admitted to the Kent County Court[10] and in the same year is listed as Captain in the Ninth Company of the Militia.[11] Only two years later he is listed as a Major and it was in this year that he began a long stint in the Maryland Legislature, including being a presidential elector in 1792.

Peregrine Letherbury appears to have represented the State in the sale of confiscated properties after the Revolution which may have become the basis for his fortune.[12] He was extensively involved with Washington College—first in its founding, then later as secretary, law professor and President of the Board of Visitors and Governors.[13] He was also active in Masonry and became the second Grand Master in Maryland.[14]

When Letherbury died in 1801, his property was transferred to his daughter, Mary, who soon thereafter married George Washington Thomas, a local physician and attorney.[15] After their marriage, the property was advertised for sale:

For Sale or Exchange, THE elegant three story Brick HOUSE in which the subscriber now resides, situated on Chester river, in Chester-town. The water lot on which the building is erected, is upwards of one hundred and twenty-five feet in front, and one hundred in depth, and is inclosed chiefly with brick and stone

River House. The easterly room of the second story was removed to Winterthur in the 1920s. Its design has been attributed to Plate XXIII in Abraham Swan's Designs in Architecture (London, 1757). Courtesy, The Henry Francis duPont Winterthur Museum.

River House, from the garden, showing the two-story piazza. The patched windows had been installed when the house received its river side addition in 1912. Marion E. Warren photograph.

River House. First floor plan. Historic American Buildings Survey, 1973.

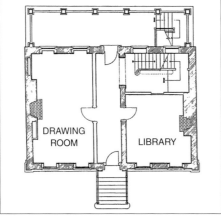

DRAWING ROOM

LIBRARY

room and stairhall on the southwest. River House is much smaller in scale and has less architectural sophistication. Two of the second story bed chambers were finished by a craftsman with references to designs taken from contemporary design books.[8] Like the exterior, the interior detail was not repeated in any other surviving house in Kent County. It

walls and buildings. *The house is forty-two feet by twenty-eight, has two kitchens, a close and open pantry, two servants' rooms, with the necessary closets. On the first floor are two commodious rooms, with a passage through the center, another, including a staircase leading into the kitchens and upper part of the building, a piazza looking to the south-east, and commanding a fine prospect of the river. In the second story are three neat commodious rooms, and another piazza over that of the lower floor. In the third or attic story are four rooms and a clothes press, with passages as in the second story, and a flush garret above. The house is composed of the choicest materials, and finished according to the most approved style in modern*

architecture. On the premises are a meat house, a garden formed on piles, and on the opposite side of the street is a stone stable and coach house, thirty feet by twenty, and stands on the front of a beautiful garden, containing one third of an acre, with delightful fruit trees, &c. The subscribers rather exchange the premises for lands either in Kent or Queen Anne's, but if sold, will give a reasonable credit, securing the annual payment of the interest ... George W. Thomas and Mary S. Thomas[16]

The house, however, remained in Thomas ownership and occupation until their deaths in 1842 and 1850. It is interesting that in 1827, Mary and George Thomas did purchase a farm, Airy Hill, a few miles from town. Thereafter, they spent time in both places, but stipulated in their will that their remains be buried at Airy Hill. Dr. Thomas had indeed been successful, as is evidenced in the 1841 Tax Assessment in which he is listed as owner of some eight other lots in Chestertown.

The property is described again in Mary Thomas' will of 1849:

"I give and devise and bequeath to Peregrine Letherbury Wickes, son of Col. Joseph Wickes, the three story house on front street in which I reside with all its contents ... also the garden with stone stable on it on the opposite side of the street. The lot in front of my house now timothy grass between the property where Mrs. Elizabeth Walker resides and the stone wall on my garden line ... ."[17]

After graduating from Princeton, Wickes studied with Severn Teakle Wallis, a prominent Baltimore barrister. He initially settled in Chestertown, but later moved to York to be nearer his wife's family. In 1860, he sold River House to his brother, Ezekiel Chambers Wickes, also an attorney.[18]

Detail of carved pineapple in corner of cornice. Karl Miller photograph, 1972

River House, detail of capital and carved modillions and mutule blocks above the corner pilaster. Library of Congress, Historic American Buildings Survey, 1970.

River House. The Greek Revival porch was added around 1860 when in the ownership of Ezekiel Chambers Wickes. Ward Allen Howe photograph, c. 1950.

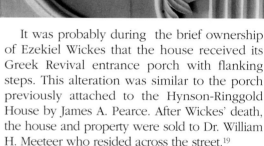

River House. The west room, second story, retains original panelled dado with mahogany cap. The overmantel design is taken from Plate I of the eighth edition of Salmon's Palladio Londonensis.

Detail of the foliated roundel in the overmantel.

River House. Library, first floor.

When the paint was removed on the original mantel of the library, the outline of a Chinese fret was found and renewed. Maryland Historical Trust photographs.

It was probably during the brief ownership of Ezekiel Wickes that the house received its Greek Revival entrance porch with flanking steps. This alteration was similar to the porch previously attached to the Hynson-Ringgold House by James A. Pearce. After Wickes' death, the house and property were sold to Dr. William H. Meeteer who resided across the street.[19]

After Dr. Meeteer sold River House in 1870 to Richard Hynson, Hynson kept the part of the property northeast of the stone wall to which Mrs. Thomas had referred as the *"lot in timothy grass."*[20] During Hynson's ownership, he erected another house on the adjoining Water Lot No. 13, into which he moved upon its completion. River House was sold at that time to Mary E. Brown, widow of Hiram Brown.[21]

In 1884, Mrs. Brown transferred River House and her childhood home of Godlington Manor to her children. However, she continued to reside at River House until her death.[22] In 1912, River House was sold out of the Brown family to William W. Beck.[23]

During the Beck occupancy, the riverside porch was replaced with a two-story, stucco structure. On the first floor this housed a kitchen, pantry, and dining room above which were two bedrooms and a bath. Since such an addition blocked much of the natural lighting, windows were added on the first and second stories of the gable ends.

From Beck, River House was left to his wife, Mary Page Beck, who sold it to Elizabeth G. Brown. In 1938, Harry B. Cannon, a local contractor, purchased River House from Mrs. Brown,[24] owning it for three years during which time he removed the second story of the 'new' porch.

In 1941, Miss Frances B. Denton, retired secretary of Colonel Edward House (1859-1938), Advisor to President Wilson, purchased the property. It was she who first referred to it as *"River House."* At the time of her death, River

House became the property of her niece, Miss Marion Weeks, a retired librarian. Miss Weeks' interest in River House and concern for its future was manifested in her donation of the property to the Maryland Historical Trust in 1968, just prior to her death.[25]

Since that time, the Maryland Historical Trust restored the exterior to the pre-1912 period and the interior was restored by Irma and Karl Miller in exchange for life tenancy. During the tenancy of the Millers, River House became a focal point of the ever-popular Candlelight Tour sponsored each year by the Historical Society of Kent County. It became the stimulus for other preservation/restoration projects in Chestertown. After Mr. Miller's death, Mrs. Miller relinquished her life tenancy and the Maryland Historical Trust sold the property and house as a private residence.[26]   K-12

1. Land Records, Lib. JS 16, fol. 292; Lib. JS 18, fol. 371.
2. Wills, Lib. 1, fol. 407.
3. Land Records, Lib. EF 6, fol. 100.
4. Maryland Gazette, September 15, 1780.
5. Maryland Gazette, November 23, 1775.
6. Land Records, Lib. EF 6, fol. 277.
7. Land Records, Lib. EF 7, fol. 89 (Original in vertical files at Washington College).
8. In a room analysis made by John Snyder in May of 1969, he attributes the design of the chimney breast to Plate XXXIX of William Pain's "The Practical Builder" (London, 1774). The design of the surviving west chamber on the second floor he attributed to Salmon's "Palladio Londonensis" (1773).
9. St. Paul's Parish Records, Kent County, p. 60.
10. Papenfuse, p. 532.
11. List of Militia and Oaths of Allegiance, June 1775, for Kent County, compiled by Mrs. William G. Buckley, 1952. Also, Army Accounts, No. 1, fol. 51.
12. Hall of Records, Intendants Letter Book, No. 12, pp. 2554-60; Agents Letter Books, No. 1 pp. 1 & 34.
13. Washington College Files: Contract for Brick Manufacturing; George Washington Diploma; Lottery for Tickets—all signed by Peregrine Letherbury. Also—An Account of Washington College in the State of Maryland, Philadelphia, 1784.
14. Maryland Gazette, January 3, 1793; Edward T. Schultz History of Free Masonry in Maryland, Vol. I, p. 396.

15. Wills, Lib. 8, fol. 107. Mary was the natural daughter of Peregrine Letherbury and Mrs. Margaret Amery. They were ordered to appear before the Vestry of Chester Parish 6 March 1780 for *cohabitation,* but apparently did not respond.
16. The Republican Star or Eastern Shore General Advertiser, Easton, Maryland, August 20, 1805.
17. Wills, Lib. JFB 1, fol. 305. The stone walls remain a division line to this day. The stone stable was replaced with a frame structure early in the twentieth century and was recently converted into a residence.
18. Land Records, Lib. JKH 1, fol. 775.
19. Land Records, Lib. JKH 9, fol. 453.
20. Land Records, Lib. DCB 5, fol. 371.
21. Land Records, Lib. DCB 3, fol. 390.
22. Land Records, Lib. SB 5, fol. 586.
23. Land Records, Lib. JTD 13, fol. 516; Lib. JTD 25, fol. 27.
24. Land Records, Lib. RRH 2, fol. 568; Lib. RAS 19, fol. 525. Mrs. Brown was responsible for selling the east chamber paneling to Henry Francis duPont in 1926. It was installed in his residence, Winterthur, and was first called the Breakfast Room. After Winterthur became a museum, the name was changed to the Chestertown Room.
25. Wills, Lib. WPJ 1, fol. 169; Deeds, Lib. EPH 26, fol. 7.
26. River House was the scene of a Decorator Showcase in 1992 sponsored by the Historical Society of Kent County which in turn raised funds for this publication.

Spencer Store

Chesterville
c. 1784

ABOUT TWO MILES NORTH OF CRUMPTON, CHESTERVILLE IS located at the line which separates the First and Second Election Districts. Until the middle of the nineteenth century, it had been known as New Market (the earliest reference being a deed dated 1728). However, in 1844 when the Maryland Postal System was created, it was renamed, as there were several New Markets in the state.

In 1773, Isaac Spencer, a successful farmer, merchant and large landowner, purchased a ¾ acre lot which faced south and was located on the north west corner of the roads which led to *"Georgetown Crossroads (Galena) and Chester Town."*[1] It was on this lot that his son Isaac constructed this substantial brick building for his business.

The two street facades were laid in Flemish bond, the east gable having glazed headers. Both first and second floor windows had 12/8 sash. The first floor had paneled shutters which could be barred shut for security. The south facade had two entrances, one into each of

Spencer Store from the northwest, prior to demolition of wing and moving brick section. Maryland Historical Trust, 1973.

Spencer Store, Chesterville, in its original location on the northwest corner of the village crossroads. Flemish bond with glazed headers was employed only on the east gable. Library of Congress. Historic American Buildings Survey, c. 1972.

*.Spencer Store, Chester-
ville, now called Brick
House, in its post 1973
location, with a new
kitchen wing.*

*Spencer Store, Chester-
ville. The original "store"
room, with exposed
beaded ceiling joists and
two exterior doors, now
the living room.
Michael C. Wootton
photographs, 1995.*

*Spencer Store, Chester-
ville, conjectural first
floor plan. Michael
Bourne.*

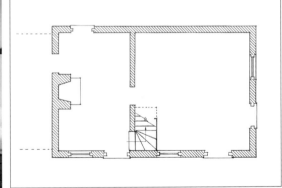

the two rooms. A third door on the east gable opened into the larger room which was originally the store-room. The *A* roof had no dormers and only one chimney in the west gable. It was flanked by two four-pane casement windows. On the east gable, third floor, there was a window with 6/6 sash. There was undoubtedly a kitchen, but nothing is known about its appearance.

The interior plan consisted of a large, unheated storeroom and a small room with fireplace. Both rooms had exposed, beaded, ceiling joists and whitewashed brick walls. Centered in the brick partition, which separated the two rooms, there was a door. Another interior door located near the south door of the small room led to a winder stair. The space for the stair was actually taken from the storeroom.

On the second floor, the plan was somewhat standard for the period—two rooms, center hall and a small room at the north end of the hall.

Some years after its construction, the walls were plastered. The small first floor living room had baseboard

Spencer Store, Chesterville. The "heated" room in the brick section of the house as seen through the door in the "store" room.
Michael C. Wootton photograph, 1995.

Chesterville Store and Post Office Site

Chesterville
c. 1784

JOHN WOODALL ACQUIRED 1½ ACRES OF LAND, PART OF Vianna, from William Woodall in 1780, for *"£30 in gold."*[1] In the deed recording this transaction, the property is described as being bounded by the *"Duck Creek Road and the George Town Road"*[2] (which places it on the northeast corner of the Chesterville crossroads). While John lived on his nearby farm (on another part of Vianna), he was responsible for the construction of the brick building which he later bequeathed to his son, Edward Woodall, a blacksmith.[3]

One-and-a-half stories tall with gable entrance, the building measured 18' x 30' 7" and had a full basement. On the second story there was a wide door for ease in lifting merchandise to the second floor storage area. The west side originally had a 5' x 10' 7" porch recessed beneath the symmetrical roof of the building. There was a six-panel door that opened into the back room of the two-room building. All of the windows on the first story were fitted with shutters which had iron security bars with which they could be fastened from within, just like those at the Spencer Store across the road.

The interior was divided into two rooms by a vertical beaded board partition. In a recess on the west side of the back room, there was an enclosed winder stair. The back room had a fireplace in the northwest corner of the room near the batten door to the porch. Opposite the door was another, which led to a part of the living quarters that was replaced with a 14' x 14' leanto in the nineteenth century. Both rooms had exposed beaded ceiling joists.

and chair rail installed, as well as a mantel. The third floor rooms were not finished until later.

When purchased by Aaron Gooding and his wife, Rebecca, in 1857 (the fifth owners since Isaac Spencer),[2] the building saw its biggest changes. The Goodings replastered, trimmed all of the windows and doors, constructed the dormers in the roof and probably built the two-room kitchen wing which lasted until 1973. They also constructed a porch along the two sides which faced the crossroads.

For the next 39 years, the Goodings operated their store in the building. It was sold out of the family in 1896. On the insert map of Chesterville in the 1877 Atlas, the name is misspelled as *"Mrs. Goodwin's Store."*

Nine other owners in the twentieth century preceded its being acquired by the State Roads in 1973. Demolition of the house began earlier that year with the destruction of the frame wing, but was halted by the intercession of Representative Clayton Mitchell on behalf of concerned local citizens. Two other buildings at the intersection were moved by the Kent Museum. Only the Spencer or Gooding Store remained to be restored in Chesterville. It is now the focal point of the crossroads village. It was entered on the National Register in 1978.   K-182

1. Land Records, Lib. BC 8, fol. 176.
2. Land Records, Lib. JKH 1, fol. 87.

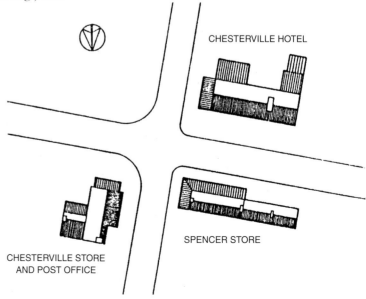

CHESTERVILLE HOTEL

SPENCER STORE

CHESTERVILLE STORE
AND POST OFFICE

Chesterville Store and Post Office. The little brick building was built on the northeast corner of the crossroad village in the 1780s by John Woodall. Historic American Buildings Survey, c. 1973.

Chesterville Store and Post Office, from the northwest. A porch was located in the 'L' originally. Historic American Buildings Survey, c. 1973

Chesterville Store and Post Office. Elevations drawn by J. A. Norfolk for the Historic American Buildings Survey. Note: board partitions, composed of board and panel.

Chesterville Store and Post Office. First floor plan. Like the Spencer Store across the street, the ceiling joists were beaded and exposed. Historic American Buildings Survey, drawn by J. A. Norfolk, 1973.

Edward Woodall resided and worked on his property in New Market (Chesterville) until his death in 1815. In his will, he bequeathed *"all my lott or lotts of ground together with the houses and other improvements thereon lying on the north side of the main road leading from New Market to the Head of Chester whereon I now live to him (Thomas Woodall) and his heirs and assigns forever."*[4] Edward had also purchased a field across the road from his brother, which he bequeathed to his second son, John.

When the Tax Assessor visited New Market in 1822, Thomas Woodall owned three lots, totaling 1¼ acres. Together, they were appraised for $550.00 and it was estimated that they would yield $65.00, $50.00, and $25.00 in annual rent.[5] In 1826, Woodall sold the corner lot to John Thomas Numbers, whose daughter and heir sold it in 1849 to Caleb W. Spry.[6]

Caleb Spry established a store, which is depicted on Martenet's Map of Kent. New Market lost its name in the 1840s due to the proliferation of *"New Markets"* in Maryland. Thereafter, it became known as *"Chesterville."* In 1866, it became the property of Spry's son after whose death it was sold to G. Allen Jarman. In the 1877 Atlas, the property was called a *"Store and Post Office."* Since the Jarman ownership, there were only three owners until the State Highway Administration purchased it in the 1960s.   K-183

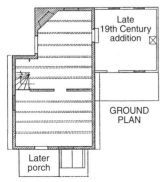

GROUND PLAN
Late 19th Century addition
Later porch

BOARD PARTITION

SOUTH ELEVATION

WEST ELEVATION

1. Donna Hole, Williamsburg's Four Original Stores: An Architectural Analysis, Colonial Williamsburg, Inc., 1980.
2. Land Records, Lib. DD 5, fol. 505.
3. Wills, Lib. 8, fol. 120.
4. Wills, Lib. 9, fol. 327.
5. Kent County Tax Assessment, 1822, First District.
6. Land Records, Lib. TW 4, fol. 727; Lib. JR 1, fol. 11.

Chesterville Hotel

Chesterville
c. 1784

THE ONE AND ONE-HALF STORY FRAME STRUCTURE WHICH once stood on the southwest corner of the Chesterville crossroads was moved in 1973 to the grounds of the Kent Museum, Inc. where it remained until it was consumed by fire in 1991. It had been built like a typical small hall-parlor plan house with an attached kitchen. The hotel was nearly identical in form and size to the Stephens House which once stood in Galena and which was photographed in the 1930s for HABS.

Its hall was on the east end of the structure and was separated from the parlor by a board partition. The winder stair was enclosed in the southeast corner adjacent an interior chimney. Whether the kitchen was late eighteenth century or later is not known, but it was constructed with its fireplace backing up to the parlor fireplace with a seam between the two. The kitchen fireplace was fitted with a plain iron crane and had a c. 1830 mantel which has been preserved in the addition to the Spencer Store. South of the kitchen fireplace, there was another winder stair to the room above.

The second floor was composed of three small rooms. Those over the hall and parlor were separated by a board partition with door in the center. The parlor chamber had a small fireplace, north of which there was a very small two board and batten door hung on H hinges for access to the kitchen chamber. On the south side of the kitchen and overlapping part of the parlor there was a lean-to of undetermined date, with an additional room further to the south. Both were unfinished.

The builder of this structure has not been established, but it is listed on the 1860 Martenet Map as a hotel, owned by Joseph Morris. On the 1877 Atlas it was listed as the *"Chesterville Hotel,"* under the ownership of James Carey. In 1871 Carey mortgaged not only the land, but the furniture, livestock and liquor.[1] It remained in the same family until the land was purchased by the State Highway Administration in 1972.

Within memory of many still living, the building was used as a general store and was run by Mrs. Messick. By this time, the hall and parlor had been converted into one large store room. A storage room was built on the south side and a tin covered porch was built on the east gable. A new entrance and window for the store and a door above were added on the east gable where the former chimney and stair had been located.

Even though this building would be considered cramped today, this was the form and size of many early Kent County dwellings, beginning in the seventeenth century and continuing well after the mid-nineteenth century in many areas.

K-184

1. Land Records, Lib. JKH 11, fol. 24.

Chesterville Hotel. In the 1877 Atlas this building was referred to as the Hotel. It was built in the last quarter of the eighteenth century. Historic American Buildings Survey, c. 1973.

Chesterville Hotel, after its move to the Kent Farm museum. Brick nogging was visible after the shed was removed. The building was lost to fire in its new location. Maryland Historical Trust, James Kilvington photograph, 1974.

Geddes-Piper House

Church Alley, Chestertown
c. 1784

JAMES MOORE, BRICKLAYER, WAS THE INITIAL PURCHASER OF Lot No. 26 in 1730.[1] The lot measured ninety-nine feet on High Street by two hundred seventy-six feet, six inches on Queen Street. In the 1735 deed for the lot across Queen Street to John Buck, the following quotation referred to James Moore's building on Lot No. 26: "lying & being in New Town or Chester Town ... opposite to a dwelling house there lately built by one James Moore ... ."[2]

Moore probably built his house on High Street in the same manner in which John Buck had his principal house constructed. Early brick foundations, which may date to Moore's ownership, are still visible beneath the existing frame structure on the corner of High and Queen Streets now called the Evans Building. In his will, dated 1754, Moore bequeathed the house and lot in Chestertown to his wife for her natural life, then to his daughters Mary, Rebecca, Margaret, Sarah, Dorcas, and Closke.[3] In 1771, the Moore ladies made an agreement with William Geddes, Esq. to sell the house and lot for £350 to be paid within a year and a half, but the agreement and the deed were not recorded until 1784.[4] Two months later, Geddes, then living in New Castle County, Delaware, agreed to sell Lot No. 26 to local merchant, James Piper and his wife Tabitha for the large sum of £800, an increase of £450 in thirteen years.[5] This

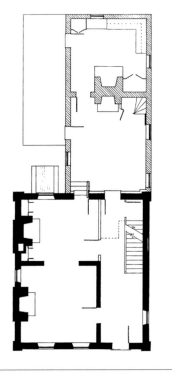

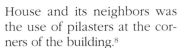

Geddes-Piper House kitchen fireplace. It remained in the basement until the new wing was built at grade by G. B. Westcott in the 1830s.

Geddes-Piper House first floor plan, as restored by the Historical Society of Kent County. Michael Bourne.

Geddes-Piper House. The back parlor was finished with built-in cabinets. Michael C. Wootton photographs, 1995.

increase may represent the cost of the building now referred to as the Geddes-Piper House, or the cost of building more commercial or residential structures along High or Queen Streets. The deed, stating that the full amount had been paid, was recorded in 1789.

On the same day in 1789, James Piper sold 62' 4" of Lot No. 26, along High Street and the full depth of the lot along Queen Street, to Jeremiah Nichols, Esq. for the same amount, £800.[6] This left him a little over a third of the lot: 36' 8" on High Street, including that part of the lot on which the Geddes-Piper House stands. With a third of a lot and £800 to spend, it is more likely that the Geddes-Piper House was built by Piper.[7]

The house was similar in plan to two houses across Queen Street: The Houston House (c. 1771) and the Nicholson House (c. 1788). When completed, the house had its kitchen in the basement, like the Nicholson House. The plan is two rooms deep with side stair hall. The plans of the floors above were similar, although the third floor rooms were apparently not finished until the 1830s. A major difference between the Geddes-Piper

House and its neighbors was the use of pilasters at the corners of the building.[8]

Like many of Chestertown's merchants after the Revolution, James Piper began to look elsewhere for business opportunities. Soon after settling on his one-third part of Lot No. 26, he moved to Baltimore, which was thriving by comparison to Chestertown. In July of 1793, Piper put an ad in the Maryland Gazette stating: *"Notice is hereby given that the subscriber proposes to remove to Baltimore Town ... To be rented, his dwelling house, and other improvements thereunto belonging, also the Store Houses and Granary. Merchandise now on hand, will be sold at the most reduced prices."*

His house was apparently rented until his death in Baltimore in 1802, when he devised it to his two daughters, Harriet and Sophia. In 1818, Sophia and her husband William Medcalf of Baltimore sold their half interest in the property to Edward Anderson.[9] Edward and Matilda Anderson sold their half interest to Samuel Ringgold in 1827[10] and he in turn sold it, in 1828, to Robert Constable.[11] Finally, in a series of deeds dated 1834, 1835, and 1837, the property was transferred to George B. Westcott, including not only the two half interests from James Pipers heirs, but also about half of adjoining Lot No. 35 bound by Court Street and Church Alley.[12] In 1873, Mr. Westcott purchased 105 feet of the adjoining parcel, bounded by Church Alley and Queen Street, thus giving him the entire frontage of 198 feet on Church Alley.[13]

The Westcotts improved their residence soon after acquiring the property in the 1830s by constructing a one-and-a-half story brick wing off the back of the original house, containing a kitchen and family dining room. It was the Westcotts who also broke a large opening between the two original first story rooms and who finished plastering and trimming the third floor rooms. They introduced three dormers in the attic and finished that space as well, possibly to house some of the house servants. The kitchen wing had two second floor rooms which were accessible from separate corner stairs.

George Burgin Westcott, not to be confused with his nephew of the same name, was one of the most successful merchants and businessmen in mid-nineteenth century Kent County. When the tax assessor recorded Westcott's holdings in Chestertown in 1841, he owned most of Lot No. 26, which contained his residence and a house occupied by Charles Stanley, a cabinetmaker. It was assessed for $1550. On adjoining Lot No. 35, he had a stable and blacksmith shop. He owned a tavern on Lot Nos. 44 and 45, the most valuable of his town holdings, and three houses on Lot No. 80, occupied by E. Carty, S. Barret and S. C. Tooker. Westcott owned $5,000 worth of private securities, but only $300 worth of household furniture. Westcott was the first Secretary of the Mutual Fire Insurance Co. of Chestertown, founded in the 1840s. In the 1877 Atlas, Chestertown Business directory, he was listed as the President of the First National Bank. By the time of his death he owned eleven farms totaling 2717 acres, twelve lots in Chestertown in various states of improvement and four lots in Baltimore.[14]

Upon the death of George Burgin Westcott, the residence passed to his widow, Mary Tilden Westcott, his

Geddes-Piper House. The second story stair looking into the second story of the 1830s wing. Maryland Historical Trust.

second wife. Later it was the home of their son Charles Tilden Westcott, and Mary, his wife, until 1913, when Charles died.

In 1905, Charles Westcott sold a part of Lot No. 35 bordering Court Street and Church Alley to Thomas G. Wroth, on which Wroth built a large one-story brick building for his business and office.[15] In 1908, the High Street part of the Westcott lot was sold to Wilbur W. Hubbard on which he had built the Imperial Hotel.[16] Finally, after Westcott's death, his heirs sold the house and lot on Church Alley and Queen Street to A. W. Culp.[17] Culp built a duplex and single residence facing Queen Street and kept the brick house, which he converted into thirteen apartments. It remained a tenement until 1958, when the property was purchased by the Historical Society of Kent County and subsequently refurbished. It has served as the headquarters of the Historical Society ever since. K-24

1. Kent Co. Land Records, Lib. 4, fol. 60.
2. Kent Co. Land Records, Lib. 4, fol. 542.
3. Kent Co. Wills, Lib. 3, fol. 242.
4. Kent Co. Land Records, Lib. EF 6, fol. 322.
5. Kent Co. Land Records, Lib. EF 6, fol. 336.
6. Kent Co. Land Records, Lib. EF 7, fol. 388, 390.
7. Maryland Gazette, 17 March 1767. William Geddes' name first appeared in the Maryland Gazette, announcing his appointment as *"Collector of his Majesty's Customs for the District of Chester"* in March, 1767. In May 1773, he again advertised in the Maryland Gazette that he had lost " ... off Barren Island ... a large new Pine Canoe." He had married Mary Wilmer, daughter of Simon Wilmer (of Sassafras River) and had eight children living at the time of writing his will in 1794. By that time, he had removed to New Castle County, Delaware (Kent Co. Wills, Lib. 8, fol. 207). Both Will and

Codicil [1795] were witnessed by Eleazer McComb, a merchant who had lived in Chestertown before and during the Revolution and was very active in the Revolutionary cause. His portrait hangs in the Corbit-Sharp House, Odessa, Delaware.
8. Pilasters were used on River House in the next block and at Rye Hall, across the river, both of which were built in the 1780s.
9. Kent Co. Land Records, Lib. WS 2, fol. 238.
10. Kent Co. Land Records, Lib. JNG 1, fol. 42.
11. Kent Co. Land Records, Lib. JNG 1, fol. 285.
12. Kent Co. Land Records, Lib. JNG 3, fol. 467, JNG 4, fol. 57, JNG 4, fol. 453.
13. Kent Co. Land Records, Lib. JKH 12, fol. 19.
14. Chancery, Lib. SB 4, fol. 409.
15. Kent Co. Land Records, Lib. JTD 11, fol. 402.
16. Kent Co. Land Records, Lib. JTD 18, fol. 151.
17. Kent Co. Land Records, Lib. JTD 29, fol. 367.

The William Henry House

Georgetown
c. 1784

The north section of the *"Kitty Knight House Inn"* was originally a three bay wide, side entrance town house, similar to the large part of Montebello, across the street. A house is mentioned in a mortgage drawn up on the property in 1784 between William Henry and two Baltimore merchants. The amount of the mortgage is £1126.13.9, and included a *"sloop named Poly and two negroes named Matt and Moses"* as well.[1]

Like the neighboring Wright house, the facade was laid in Flemish bond and the other walls in common. When it was originally constructed it had an *A* roof with two dormers on each slope. Its north gable had two windows on each floor, including the basement and attic. One large chimney rose from the center of the gable. On the rear there were two bays like the Houston House in Chestertown.

Similar to both the Houston House and the Wright House adjacent, was the use of corner fireplaces on the outer wall. And also like both, the chimney breast was more finished in the front room than in the back. In the case of Mr. Henry's house, the chimney breast was fitted with a naively executed tabernacle overmantel with crossettes around a central raised panel, a cushion frieze and broken pediment. A mantel with crossettes and cushion frieze finished the fireplace while a chair rail and cornice tied the room together. In the corner opposite the fireplace, Mr. Henry installed a corner cupboard. Its original configuration may have been different than the existing scalloped arch opening.

The back parlor was later fitted with a Federal period mantel with reeded pilasters and plinth blocks. Between the 1780s and 1920s the building remained basically unchanged, with two parlors and stairhall. Throughout that period, the kitchen was located in the front room of the basement.

William Henry died in the 1790s, and left several heirs. The heirs apparently rented out the property, for there is mention, in the deed of 1809 for the adjoining property, that Mrs. Henry's house was occupied by Philip Rasin.[2] How soon thereafter the house was rented to Kitty Knight is not known, but in 1803 she had purchased lot No. 13 from a free black man named Stepney Congo – a lot on the River, just below the Henry lots. In 1839, 26 years after the British burning of Georgetown, she purchased the house in which she was then living, from the Henry heirs.[3]

Traditionally, Kitty Knight was supposed to have saved this house and the one next door from the hands of the British. The land records shed no light on this story. If indeed Miss Catherine Knight was responsible for saving the houses in question, she may also be given credit for saving Montebello and Valley Cottage as well as the Presbyterian church to the south.

The William Henry House front parlor. The raised central panel of the overmantel is akin to the work in the Wright House. The design, however, is even more naive. Library of Congress Historic American Buildings Survey, 1936.

A commemorative bronze plaque is located at the juncture of the 1784 William Henry House and the addition installed around 1907 by Andrew Woodall, Jr. Gene Johnstone photograph, 1997.

IN HONOR OF
MISTRESS KITTY KNIGHT
REVOLUTIONARY BELLE AND BEAUTY
A FRIEND OF GENERAL GEORGE WASHINGTON.
WHEN THE BRITISH BURNED GEORGETOWN IN 1813.
HER HEROIC EFFORTS SAVED THIS
HOUSE WHICH LATER BECAME HER HOME.
PLACED BY
LONDON BRIDGE CHAPTER, D.A.R.

Catherine Knight deeded her lot, which she was still occupying in 1855, to her nephew William Knight, only a year before her death.[4] The residue of her estate was also passed to the same nephew. Like the Henry heirs before, William, who was living in Cecil County on his wife's farm, must have rented the house until 1870, when he sold it to Sophie Betton, the wife of William T. Betton.[5] The latter appears on the 1877 Atlas, as did William Knight on the 1860 Map.

Andrew Woodall held the mortgage on the Betton property and it was to his son, Andrew W. Woodall that Mrs. Betton sold the property in 1906.[6] An-

View of Georgetown, c. 1880. Gables of the Henry and Wright house are visible in the upper center of the photograph. National Building Museum.

The William Henry House. A. W. Woodall's enlargement included a bay window on the original facade. Jane Brooks Sprinkle Collection, c. 1910.

The William Henry House, Georgetown. The enlargement made by Andrew W. Woodall, re-oriented the house to the River and created a full third floor. Michael C. Wootton photograph, 1996.

drew's widow, Alice, sold the house in 1924 to Herbert Stine of Washington County.[7]

After it was acquired by Mr. Stine, a large brick wing was added including a dining room and kitchen. The original back parlor was turned into an entry when a door with leaded sidelights and transom was added on the river side. A porch was also built on the river side and a gambrel roof added across the original section and new addition, reorienting the house 90 degrees to the River.

A two story connector was constructed which joined the Henry and Wright houses, enabling the two properties to be used as a large inn. From that time until the present, it has had many changes, as the business has had its ups and downs. Since 1939, there have been nine owners. During some of that time the business was operated by a restaurateur while the property was actually owned by others.   K-146

1. Land Records, Lib. EF 6, fol. 397.
2. Land Records, Lib. BC 6, fol. 74.
3. Land Records, Lib. JNG 6, fol. 214, 373.
4. Land Records, Lib. JFG 2, fol. 532.
5. Land Records, Lib. JKH 8, fol. 581.
6. Land Records, Lib. JTD 13, fol. 479.
7. Land Records, Lib. RRA 4, fol. 99.

Big Meadows

Near Worton
1784

W HEN GALLOWAY'S CHANCE WAS patented to William Galloway in 1684 the 200 acre parcel was then within the boundaries of Cecil County.[1] A warrant and resurvey were granted to Joseph Everett in 1734 for the same 200 acres plus 22 additional acres of vacancy under the name of Everett's Double Purchase.[2] Everett died in 1750 leaving the farm to his three sons, but Augustine died young and John sold his half interest to his brother Benjamin. In the same year, 1753, Benjamin purchased 45 acres adjoining called Rich Meadows.[3] Benjamin's son, Hales, acquired the property from his siblings in 1783 consisting then of 293 acres.[4] The following year, Hales built the house for his family, recording the year of the event, 1784, in large glazed headers on the southwest gable.

The Everett house was constructed similarly to the John Williams House, a 1770 three-bay brick house east of Lynch. Each of the two houses has a large glazed date in the gable opposite its kitchen. At Big Meadows the 8 is on the face of the protruding chimney, whereas the 1770 flanks the chimney on the Williams house. Neither has initials like Bungay Hill or the Violet Farm. Big Meadows is the latest house in Kent County to have a glazed date.

Although many of the sash and frames have been altered, the sizes of the openings appear original. There would have been 12/8 sash originally on the first floor with 6/6 sash on the second. The northeast gable had a 2/2 sash to light the attic. Possibly the house began life with a hall-parlor plan and continued with an enclosed corner stair until the present central hall was installed in the 1830s. At that juncture, another window would have been added at the stair landing on the northeast side of the house. The dormers were probably added to each side of the *A* roof at the same time.

Big Meadows was built in 1784 by Hales Everett. The glazed date is located on the gable, the latest use of this dating device in the county. Gene Johnstone photograph, 1997.

Big Meadows. The 'gooseneck' handrail of the early nineteenth century stair. Gene Johnstone photograph, 1997.

The former kitchen was a one-and-a-half-story leanto structure, nearly square. It appears to have been early twentieth century and most likely replaced an earlier structure. One of the original outbuildings, a plank smokehouse with *A* roof, remains behind the house today.

In addition to entries in the land records of the county, the name of Hales Everett occurs in the records of I. U. Church in 1768 as having acquired one third of Pew No. 30 in the newly constructed church. Everett's daughter, Mary Everett Walker inherited the farm from her father and maintained it until 1816 when she sold it to John Bowers. Bowers owned several farms in the immediate vicinity. Upon his death, the farms were resurveyed and distributed amongst his children. The *Walker Farm* went to son James L. Bowers in 1841, the same man who owned what is now called Friendship. Since J. L. Bowers' ownership, the farm has been the subject of multiple transactions. Beginning in the 1860s the name *Big Meadows* appears along with earlier names.[5]   K-232

1. Patents, Lib. 22, fol. 342.
2. Warrants, Lib. EI 5, fol. 310.
3. Land Records, Lib. 7, fol. 401.
4. Land Records, Lib. EF 6, fol. 177.
5. The author would like to express his gratitude to Carolyn Cooper for the research she has provided on Big Meadows.

Brice-Johnson Farm

Near Galena
c. 1785

IN THE NORTHERN PART OF THE FIRST ELECTION DISTRICT, stands an early brick house that has suffered at the hands of insensitive owners. It is referred to as the Brice-Johnson Farm because the Brice family gravestones were located in the north yard, and its ownership by the Johnson family in 1986.

When the house was first built at the end of the eighteenth century, it was composed of a two bay long, two story brick dwelling, facing south, with a frame or log kitchen wing on the east. The brick part had a basement and one room and stairhall above. The main room had a fireplace in its northeast corner, similar to Partner's Addition's west room. Both facades were laid in Flemish bond.

In the first quarter of the nineteenth century, a two bay extension was built on the west side of the stairhall, creating asymmetrical four bay facades. The new addition contained only one room per floor. The first floor had paneling across the west fireplace wall and paneled wainscot on the other three walls. Both the mantel and flanking glazed cabinets had fluted pilasters, a sophisticated architectural treatment of the Federal period.

"W. A. Brice" was printed next to the house on the 1860 map and in the 1877 Atlas—"the Est. of W. A. Brice." During the Brice occupancy the facade was reoriented to the north with the addition of a full-length porch with period brackets to match the overhanging eave. It was probably during its reorientation that a two-story plank wing was moved south of the house. It was reputed to have been a dwelling for hired hands who assisted with the operation of the farm. Once the old kitchen wing was removed, it was pressed into service as a kitchen, attached with a small hyphen to the south entry.

The house has been crudely remodeled in recent years and the Brice family gravestones have been removed.   K-156

Brice-Johnson Farm. The west room has a Federal period wall of paneling. It is similar in basic design to the Adventure, built about fifty years earlier. Marge Q. Fallaw, 1986.

Brice-Johnson Farm was built in two nearly equal sections at the end of the eighteenth century and beginning of the nineteenth. Its road side was originally the back of the house. Marge Q. Fallaw photograph, 1986.

London Bridge

Near Millington c. 1785

I**N THE LAST DECADE OF THE SEV-**enteenth century, there was already a tavern and a ferry across the Chester River at Head of Chester, as Millington was then called. The land on which the tavern was located was called *London Bridge.* It was a large tract which extended northward and on which the crossroad village was to be established.

The farmhouse which bears the name of London Bridge is located on the northern part of the tract and was built about 100 years after the establishment of the ferry. It was a three-bay, two-story brick house with the road front facade laid in Flemish bond and the other walls in common. It had a two brick string course between windows, but was otherwise typical of the last quarter of the eighteenth century – virtually a plain vernacular structure. Its kitchen wing was located off the south gable.

Inside the brick house, the plan was originally the typical hall-parlor plan. The central entrance opened into the hall and to the south there was a partition dividing it from the parlor. The hall contained a winder stair in the northeast corner which was partially enclosed behind the wall of paneling which extended across the chimney breast as well. There was a fireplace in both rooms, but the south room lacked paneling, which was similar to Dullams' Folly, north of Massey.

In the 1822 Tax Assessment, Elizabeth Comegys was taxed on 204½ acres of *"London Bridge Renewed"* which had been appraised for $818.00. The property was later acquired by D. Ford in whose estate it appears on the 1860 map. By 1877, William Ford was the owner.[1]

London Bridge was built around 1785 on a large tract of land north of the crossroad village now called Millington. Historical Society of Kent County photograph. The Usilton Collection.

Alterations were made to the house periodically, but its character was totally changed in the late 1950s when a major remodeling was undertaken by Arthur and Lillian Montell who had previously lived at Salutation Farm near Lynch. In the remodeling project, which lasted several years, the entrance was moved to the south window and embellished with a classical architrave. The interior was changed into a center hall plan with the second room being in a two story frame wing. On the east side of the house was the kitchen. Later, a large family room was added at a lower level to take advantage of the pond created by the damming of Long Meadow Branch. The house is now the center of a large nursery operation.   K-169

1. Lake, Griffing, Stevenson Atlas, 1877.

Banning House

Queen Street, Chestertown
c. 1785

THE BANNING HOUSE IS LOCATED ON THE CORNER OF Queen and Cannon Streets—Lot No. 10 of the original plat of Chestertown. This location has an interesting history, as its owners include some of the most prominent figures of eighteenth and nineteenth century Chestertown.

Dr. William Murray, who had built and occupied the front section of the Hynson-Ringgold House, purchased Lot No. 10 in 1761 from merchant, William Ringgold.[1] By the time he wrote his will in 1768, he was residing there and bequeathed it, after his wife's widowhood, to his sons, William and Alexander.[2] In 1777, William Murray, Jr. purchased his brother's half interest and in 1785, sold it to Anthony Banning, another merchant.[3]

Later that year Banning sold the northeast quarter of Lot No. 10 to Alexander Murray, including the store and meathouse which Murray was occupying. It is probable that Banning built or remodeled the house soon after his acquisition of the property. After Banning's death in 1789, his real estate, which consisted of the Rose Hill Farm and at least three-fourths of Lot No. 10 in Chestertown, descended to his daughter Katherine. She and Benjamin Chew, Jr. were married shortly thereafter and may have occupied the house on this corner of the lot, as well as Rose Hill. By the time they sold the lot in 1802, they had been living in Philadelphia for a number of years.[4]

James Carson, Schoolmaster of Philadelphia, purchased the lot in 1803 and mortgaged it to the Chews. In 1816 a confirmatory deed stated that the mortgage had been paid.[5] It remained in Carson's ownership and was passed on to his heirs. They, however, failed to pay the taxes and the house was subsequently purchased by Miss Caroline Thompson from the Tax Collector.[6]

The house was tenanted during Miss Thompson's ownership, from at least 1841 to her death in 1885. She bequeathed it to her niece Lottie Spencer (Roberts),[7] who sold it in 1916 to the recently widowed Mrs. Joseph Wickes. Since that time the house has had many owners. Prior to its recent rehabilitation, it had been an apartment house.

During the rehabilitation, evidence of several additions and alterations was discovered. The changes spanned its 200 plus years of occupation. The plan of the original two-story, two-bay house consisted of an entry hall and parlor, like the Chambers House, plus a one-story service wing which may have housed a dining room in addition to the kitchen. The second story of the main section originally contained two chambers and a stairhall. All interior walls were of vertical beaded boards, with the beads occurring on both sides of each board. This curious feature had been found at the Buck-Bacchus Store, as well as other buildings dating from the 1730s. Another inconsistency in dating the building is the heavy framing members with gunstock corner posts, a feature usually found in early to mid-eighteenth century buildings of the area.[8]   K-534

The Banning House, Chestertown. Anthony Banning, a merchant, purchased the lot in 1785 which included at least one house. The double porch is a mid-nineteenth century addition. Michael Bourne photograph, 1996.

The Banning House. Detail of the porch brackets and balustrade. Michael C. Wootton photograph, 1996.

1. Land Records, Lib. JS 29, fol. 381. The sale of this lot for £340 coincides with William Ringgold's purchase of the Smith House on Water Lot No. 8 (see Smith-Ringgold House). The sale price indicates a substantial house or more on the property at the time. In the Ringgold to Murray deed, it mentions that the lot faced Cannon Street, whereas the house faces Queen Street. This slight discrepancy along with the remaining fabric of the building points to a date of construction after the Revolution, perhaps after the lot was purchased by Anthony Banning in 1785.
2. Wills, Lib. 4, fol. 352.
3. Land Records, Lib. DD 5, fol. 241; Lib. EF 6, fol. 486. William Murray was listed as a physician living in Annapolis. Anthony Banning lived in Talbot County previously, but came to Kent during its pre-Revolutionary prosperity and purchased the Rose Hill Farm from his brother-in-law, Alexander Calder.
4. Land Records, Lib. BC 8, fol. 452.
5. Land Records, Lib. TW 2, fol. 517 ff; Lib. BC 8, fol. 452.
6. Land Records, Lib. JNG 9, fol. 285. The deed was recorded in 1843, but in the Tax Assessment for 1841, Miss Thompson was already in possession of the house and lot. It was occupied by S. & H. Wilmer and the house was appraised for $700.00. Mrs. Thompson was a granddaughter of Dr. William Murray and lived with her widowed sister across the street in the Hands House.
7. Land Records, Lib. JNG 9, fol. 285.
8. The house was restored through the efforts of Dr. Davy H. McCall, co-contributor to this book.

Handy Point

Fairlee Neck
c. 1785

GREAT OAK MANOR WAS A 2000 ACRE PATENT TO GOVernor Josias Fendall dated 16 August 1658. It comprised most of present day Fairlee Neck, bounded by the Chesapeake Bay and Worton Creek and a line drawn from the mouth of Fairlee Creek to the head of Worton Creek and adjoining a later patent called Packerton.[1]

The first Marmaduke Tilden to reside on Great Oak Manor was the son of Charles Tilden, an early patentee of the Reward on Quaker Neck. Marmaduke Tilden married Tabitha Harris, daughter of William Harris (1644–1712) who owned 300 acres of the Manor in the late seventeenth century. It is most likely that the land

came to Marmaduke through a bequest from William Harris. Marmaduke's second wife, Rebecca, was the daughter of Lambert Wilmer.

Marmaduke Tilden, who was a member of St. Paul's Parish as his father had been, served in the capacity of Church warden (1715) and vestryman (1718). He was a member of the Lower House the year he died, 1725. He left his dwelling plantation to his son and namesake Marmaduke II.[2]

Marmaduke II (1714–1767) who, first married Susanna Lanham, purchased 670 additional acres of Great Oak Manor between 1751–1768. When he wrote his will in 1767, he bequeathed his plantation to his second wife

Handy Point was built after 1783 by Marmaduke Tilden. At the time it was called Green Hill. Tilden used some of the most sophisticated architectural elements for post revolutionary Kent County: rusticated jack arches, circular beaded transom, and medallion cornice. The portico and balcony are twentieth century embellishments. C. Engstrom photograph, 1977.

Sarah for her widowhood and then it was to descend to his son Marmaduke III.[3] The personal property listed in the inventory of his estate amounted to £960.10.3.[4]

Sarah's will was probated in 1774 and she bequeathed many specific items which she listed by room. To daughter Martha, she bequeathed *"one featherbed standing in the hall shed room ..."* and *"... one looking glass ... in my lodging room."* Tabitha received *"one feather bed standing in the room upstairs."* Tabitha and her brother Marmaduke received a pair of *"gilted looking glass(es) standing in the hall."* To grandson John Waltham she bequeathed *"my chimney glass standing in my Hall as also the New York Map in Sd Hall hanging over said glass ... ."* In her husband's will, there was mention of a Corner Cabinet that be kept part of the house and not be appraised with his personal property.[5]

When Marmaduke III's farm was listed in the 1783 Tax Assessment, it included 455 acres of Great Oak Manor with *"one very bad house, kitchen, outhouses and orchard ... ."* on Worton Creek. In all probability, Sarah's dwelling was a frame, story-and-a-half, hall-parlor plan house with a leanto off the hall; the lodging room corresponding to the 'parlor' in the plan, in the same manner that Mrs. Bowles' accommodation is listed in 1727 at Sotterley in St. Mary's County. By 1783 the house had fallen on hard times. Also in the 1783 assessment there were nine slaves, fifteen horses, thirty five cattle and 16oz. of plate, for a total valuation of £682.10.

If the present house was not standing in 1783, it seems likely that Marmaduke III began designing and building his plantation house, which he named Green Hill, soon thereafter. The house he built was a large scale farm house with many sophisticated features including a semi-circular fanlight above the door with pedimented architrave, rusticated jack arches above the windows, and a well-executed modillion and Wall-of-Troy cornice. Its west facade was laid in Flemish bond above a molded, two-course, water table. Although the facade appears symmetrical, the south windows are slightly closer to the gable than the north windows and the south chimney projects 5" beyond the face of the gable as opposed to the north gable being on one plane. Unlike the west facade, the south gable windows have rubbed and gauged brick jack arches. The south wall is on the same plain as the four-bay, two-story ser-

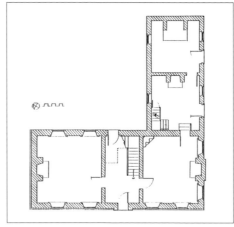

Handy Point. An original corner cabinet was built into the parlor. Paneling of the walls is twentieth century. C. Engstrom photograph, 1977.

Handy Point. Conjectural first floor plan, c. 1785. Michael Bourne.

vice wing, built considerably lower. The house plan consisted of a central stairhall with one room on each side. To the rear of the south room and three steps lower, there was a heated room and beyond it was the original kitchen. (see plan) Although it possesses the same number of rooms as many of Kent County's farmhouses, it is atypical in having the rooms arranged in an *L*, rather than in a straight line. *L* plan dwellings are much more common in the nineteenth century and

through hard times as well as good times.[8] In the Tax Assessment of 1852 Luther is listed with 261 acres of Great Oak Manor with *"Brick House and other buildings in good repair."* After his death the house probably remained untouched and tenanted until it was purchased by Elizabeth Dixon, in 1927,[9] who gave it to her daughter and son-in-law in 1932.[10] At this juncture, a large portico/porte-cochere was constructed on the west facade and if anything else was undertaken, it was all to be changed after 1940, when F. Bramwell Geddes and his wife Alice purchased the farm and enlarged the house.[11]

After 1940 the porte-cochere was converted into a porch and the drive was carried to the back of the house. On the back of the house a two story four-bay long and one-bay deep extension was constructed extending from the first bay of the service wing.

Paneling and bookshelves were added to the north and south rooms, the old kitchen was enlarged into a dining room. A new kitchen and servants' quarters were added to the east end of the house. The Geddes carried on a full farm operation until their deaths in the early 1960s.

Eight of the original acres remain with the house, the remainder is still in cultivation and under an agricultural easement.   K-106

Handy Point's central stair has a simple but well defined balustrade and corresponding paneled dado with an easy rise. C. Engstrom photograph, 1977.

Handy Point. The design of the living room chimney breast is the most developed of the post revolutionary farm houses. Only River House was more refined. C. Engstrom photograph, 1977.

tend to focus more attention on the principle facade. In its original form, Rich Level and Widehall in Chestertown had such an arrangement, with their kitchen wings to the rear.

Marmaduke Tilden III and his wife Mary lavished great detail in the north room and stair hall. In the former there is a classical chimney breast with pedimented overmantel flanked by fluted pilasters with double-crossetted inner panel. The design for the chimney breast was certainly copied from a contemporary design book, as it is well proportioned and well executed. The north parlor also had raised panel dado, window jambs and window seats. The paneled dado is carried into the stairhall and up to the top of the stair. The south room had no dado, but had a chair rail between the otherwise identical window seats and a built-in corner cupboard.[6]

Green Hill Farm passed from Marmaduke III in 1816 to his daughter Mary, who had married Dr. Geo. D. S. Handy.[7] Upon Mary's death in 1850, the farm was to be sold, but her youngest son, Luther Handy, purchased the farm from the heirs and carried on operations,

1. Patents, Lib. Q, fol. 423; Rent Rolls, Vol. 1, fol. 6,8,81.
2. Papenfuse, E., Maryland Legislators.
3. Wills, Lib. 4, fol. 341. Marmaduke Tilden petitioned the Court in 1747 to have his lands resurveyed. The two witnesses were his neighbors William Graves, aged 31 and John Carvill, aged 40. (Land Records, Lib. JS 26, fol. 100).
4. Inventories, Lib. 6, fol. 208.
5. Wills, Lib. 5, fol. 164.
6. Marmaduke Tilden III was a member of Chester Parish and occupied pew No. 43 at the church at I.U. He was vestryman in 1780-81. He was a member of the Lower House, 1781-82; tobac-

co inspector at Worton Creek Warehouse 1773; Justice for nine years. In his will of 1815 he manumitted *"My Negro Man Cuff and my negro woman"* and stipulated that over the next 31 years, 13 other slaves be set free, (Wills, Lib. 10, fol. 23). His total personal estate was appraised for $3,387.99.
7. Wills, Lib. 10, fol. 23.
8. Land Records, Lib. JFG 1, fol. 563.
9. Land Records, Lib. RRA 9, fol. 67.
10. Land Records, Lib. RAS 8, fol. 40.
11. Land Records, Lib. RAS 23, fol. 405.

Hinchingham Farm

Near Rock Hall
c. 1785

Hinchingham was a 2200 acre tract granted to Thomas Hynson in 1659, one of the earlier patents in present day Kent County. Undoubtedly the name is derived from *Hynsonham*, meaning Hynson's home or village. In 1675, a part of Hinchingham and some vacancy totaling 700 acres were purchased by Michael Miller and at that time renamed Miller's Purchase.[1] He also acquired the 1000 acre tract on the upper end of Quaker Neck known as Godlington Manor.

Michael Miller was a significant resident of late seventeenth century Kent County. He was elected as one of the County Burgesses is 1685 and was appointed vestryman of St. Paul's Parish in 1693-94. In his will witnessed by his friend Simon Wilmer, he bequeathed Miller's Purchase and lands on Kent Island to his son Michael Miller, Jr. and Godlington Manor and 1200 acres nearby to his son Arthur.[2]

The property called Miller's Purchase Resurveyed passed from Michael Miller, Jr. in 1738 to his son Michael III (d. 1746)[3] and two other brothers.[4] How the land was divided later during the eighteenth century has not yet been determined.

By 1783, when the tax assessor visited Swan Creek, Miller's Purchase was divided between Michael, Walter (probable builder), Samuel and Richard Miller.[5]

In 1852 that part of Miller's Purchase which contained the house was owned by Merritt Miller, Walter's grandson and valued at $4500 with *"Frame House and other Buildings in good repair."*[6] On the 1860 Martenet Map, Merritt Miller was still listed as owner but in the 1877 Atlas the farm was listed as belonging to the Estate of Walter Theodore Hodges Miller, Merritt's son. Hinchingham remained in the Miller family until 1951, when it was sold by Severn A. Miller.

The house is traditionally said to have been built in the seventeenth century, but from structural evidence, as well as millwork details, it appears to date from the last quarter of the eighteenth century or later. The three bay, two story section has the earmarks of late eighteenth century work, with original ovolo window

Hinchingham Farm, was remodeled around 1940, but the telescopic form is the same as it appeared in 1900. Michael Bourne photograph, 1969.

Hinchingham Farm, Swan Creek, with Walter H. Miller in the front yard. Note the door in the center section and lack of windows in the kitchen. Michael Miller Collection. c. 1900.

final room, the old or original kitchen. The latter is constructed of planks, mortised and tenoned into braced corner posts. It has hewn and champhered joists and a brick floor. The pyramidal fireplace and the floor are mid-twentieth century replacements.

By the time the original building project was completed, the Millers possessed a telescopic farmhouse, with a plan that was the epitome of a Kent County Farmhouse … a central stairhall flanked by a single room on each side with two-room service wing, all in a straight line.

Hinchingham Farm is the best preserved telescopic house remaining in Kent County—an obvious example of one of the basic elements of vernacular architecture—one that is able to be enlarged.   K-100

Hinchingham Farm. The stair has a walnut balustrade and newels with board wainscoting.

Hinchingham Farm. The dining room mantel has Greek Revival moldings on an otherwise Federal style design. C. Engstrom photographs, 1977

Hinchingham Farm. The Swan Creek facade, with the earliest section being in the foreground. Michael Bourne photograph, 1969.

trim and a well executed walnut balustrade. The plan of this section is like the Chambers House, built in the late 1780s in Chestertown—a stairhall and parlor. A kitchen wing probably abutted the east gable, but it was replaced by the present dining room section in the 1820–30 period. This is immediately evident in the delicacy of the woodwork. This section also possesses a basement and the brick walls are built abutting the west section's walls. The latter wall, facing into the newer basement space has very rough joints, like walls intended to be back-filled.

Located several steps lower than the dining room, the kitchen or service wing is composed of two rooms, one the present day kitchen, built of frame and the

1. Miller, John Haskel, A Family Chronicle, unpublished family history (courtesy of Michael Miller).
2. Wills, Lib. 1, fol. 57.
3. From the files of Michael

Miller; Wills, 1738.
4. Wills, Lib. 2, fol. 271.
5. 1783 Tax Assessment, Lower Langford Bay Hundred.
6. 1852 Tax Assessment, 1st District.

The Dunn (and Bolton) House

Queen Street, Chestertown c. 1786

IN HIS FIRST RECORDED LAND TRANSACTION IN 1778, William Dunn is called *"Joiner,"* and leased a property near St. Paul's Church to John Fitzgerald, a schoolmaster. In subsequent deeds, he is referred to as a *"Farmer"* or *"Planter."* Finally, in 1782 he is called *"Innholder."* He was undoubtedly of the Dunn family which owned Poplar Neck, now part of Remington Farm. His earlier deeds refer to property in the vicinity of St. Paul's Church. In 1786, William Dunn purchased for £350 the northwestern half of Lot No. 23 on which John Bolton had resided. He undertook a major project of remodeling and enlarging the Bolton House and building a second dwelling for himself adjoining.

Dunn added a stair hall/entry and living room on the southwest side of Bolton's house and raised the entire roof above a full second story, producing an asymmetrical five bay dwelling. Simultaneously, he built his own four bay house adjoining, utilizing the new center chimney to serve two back-to-back fireplaces in each dwelling. He used the same roof line across both houses, producing an eighty-six foot long facade along Queen Street. The interiors of both houses were finished in a similar manner. Both stairs were composed of three flights to the second story and contained a paneled spandrel housing a basement stair. They both had a closed string balustrade with turned newels and intermediates and delicate rectangular balusters. The principal room in each house was trimmed with baseboard, chair rail, mantel and cornice. In the Dunn House a dentil course was added to the mantel and cornice similar to the Buck-Chambers House.

For his own house, Dunn installed the kitchen fireplace in the southwest side of the basement. To light the basement stair he installed a small two-pane horizontal window at the head of its stair, a unique feature in Chestertown. Both stories had the same floor plan of two rooms flanking a central stair hall. On the second floor was a small room at the head of the

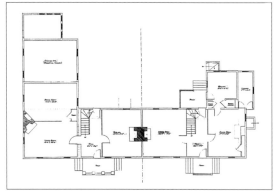

stair, over the entry. Most interior partitions were vertical beaded boards and all doors had six panels. The stair originally continued to a board enclosure at attic level, but later, in the nineteenth century the closure was brought closer to the second floor level.

In Bolton's house, beside the addition of the stairhall and living room mentioned above, the original enclosed stair

Dunn House with attached Bolton House, Queen Street, Chestertown. After 1786, William Dunn constructed the building we see today, both houses being center hall dwellings. Dunn's own house had a basement kitchen until a new structure was built around the turn of the twentieth century. Gene Johnstone photograph, 1997.

Dunn and Bolton Houses, first floor plans, Michael Bourne, 1994.

Dunn and Bolton Houses, Queen Street elevations, Michael Bourne, 1994.

Dunn House. Detail of original H hinge on door to the basement. Gene Johnstone photograph, 1997.

was removed, creating more space in the back room. Since the ceiling height of the first floor was lower than the new addition, and the entire structure had the same roof line, the second story rooms over the old section had higher ceilings than elsewhere. Without the old stair, access to the back bedroom was obtained by making a corridor on the far side of the new attic stair. The first four steps were open on both sides, requiring balustrades on both sides of the first four steps, another unique feature in an otherwise simple late eighteenth century dwelling. Interior partitions in the house were a mixture of vertical beaded board and stud walls with plaster. Like the neighboring Dunn House, the stair originally continued to a board wall closure at attic level, but in the nineteenth century the closure was brought closer to the second floor. Both attics were left unfinished and were lighted by a single small casement at the two gables.

William Dunn sold the Bolton House in 1790 to John Scott for £400. From the description in the deed, Scott appears to have already been residing in the house and Dunn was living in the adjoining house. In the transaction, Scott received the *"cow house"* mentioned in Bolton's will, but it is also called the stable in that deed.[1]

Later in 1790, William Dunn sold his own house and lot to William Ringgold for £250. It was then being rented to Joseph Williams.[2] No other real estate transactions are recorded in Kent County under the name of William Dunn. It is thought that he moved to Philadelphia.

Between 1790 and 1828, the two houses were owned separately. The Bolton House was owned by John Scott and his heirs. The Dunn House was sold twice until it was purchased in 1819 by Robert Constable. Constable also purchased the adjoining house in 1828 from the Scott sisters, who were then living in Baltimore.[3] The Scotts had advertised the house for rent and finally for sale in the Transcript in the late 1820s.

Between 1828 and 1867 the two houses were owned jointly by four different owners, including the aforementioned Robert Constable and his daughter, Margaret Ann Osborn. In 1841, she sold the two houses to John McKenny a farmer, from Queen Anne's County.[4] He is listed as the owner of the houses in the 1841 Tax Assessment: *"Two Houses + Lot. Pt. No 23–in good repair ocd by Dr. Wroth + Dr. Whaland."* He also owned the other house on Lot No. 23 fac-

ing Maple Avenue, the Bolton Anderson House, and a stable on Lot No. 22 worth a total of $3,200.00. The two occupants of the houses were probably Dr. Peregrine Wroth and Catherine his wife, and Dr. Thomas Whaland, all of whom appear on the same assessment without owning town land.

John McKenny, by then a merchant in Centreville, sold the properties in 1846 to Dr. James Bordley, also from Queen Anne's County.[5] Dr. Bordley's name appears on Martenet's Map of the county printed in 1860. Dr. Bordley sold the properties to William H. Lambert in 1867.[6] Lambert then sold the Dunn House to John K. Willis[7] within a few days and kept the Bolton House himself which he deeded to Mary J. Lambert in 1901.[8] Mary Lambert died in 1903 and the executors sold it to Cora Baldwin in 1910.[9]

In the meantime, a similar fate occurred to the Willis family next door. John Willis died in 1880 and the property descended to his daughter Mary. Mary mortgaged the house and lot to Harrison Vickers but could not keep up the payments, so it was sold to Thomas Wickes in 1893. Wickes is mentioned in the Lambert deed in 1901. Fred G. Usilton owned the Dunn House for a year before selling it to Emma and Mary Knight in 1903.[10] The Knights sold it to Cora Baldwin in 1917.[11]

From 1917 to the present the two properties have had four owners. In 1926, Mrs. Baldwin had two large two story additions constructed behind the Bolton House, creating six apartments in the enlarged building. The Baldwins continued to live next door in the Dunn House. Possibly at the same time as the Bolton House enlargement, a kitchen addition with leanto was built onto the Dunn house, and the old basement kitchen fireplace and chimney were disassembled and replaced with a simple brick stack. Above the new kitchen, a bath and small bedroom were added. The property remained essentially unchanged, even after it was sold in 1973 to Lester Carpenter Leonard.[12] Leonard allowed the buildings to deteriorate to such a point that they became nearly uninhabitable. Preservation Incorporated purchased the two houses in 1989[13] and began their restoration, first removing the 1926 addition followed by an exterior restoration. When completed, the houses will be sold as two separate dwellings reflecting primarily their 1790 appearance, with later porches.[14]   K-22

1. Land Records, Lib. BC 3, fol. 4.
2. Land Records, Lib. BC 3, fol. 91.
3. Land Records, Lib. JNG 1, fol. 444.
4. Land Records, Lib. JNG 7, fol. 515.
5. Land Records, Lib. JNG 11, fol. 158.
6. Land Records, Lib. JKH 6, fol. 114.
7. Land Records, Lib. JKH 6, fol. 161.
8. Land Records, Lib. JTD 5, fol. 166.
9. Land Records, Lib. JTD 21, fol. 52.
10. Land Records, Lib. JTD 8, fol. 402.
11. Land Records, Lib. RAS 20, fol. 154.
12. Land Records, Lib. EHP 50, fol. 775.
13. Land Records, Lib. EHP 280, fol. 148.
14. The porches were added at two distinct times, the Greek Revival Porch on the Bolton house was probably installed by Dr. James Bordley before selling it in 1867. The Dunn House porch was probably installed during the Willis ownership between 1867-1893.

Dr. John Thomas House

Millington
c. 1787

Tʜᴇ ᴍᴏsᴛ ᴘʀᴏᴍɪɴᴇɴᴛ ᴏʟᴅ ʀᴇsɪᴅᴇɴᴄᴇ ɪɴ Mɪʟʟɪɴɢᴛᴏɴ ᴡᴀs called Sunset Hall by its mid-twentieth century owner. While it is not the only brick residence in town to remain from the eighteenth century, it is indeed the most significant.

Isaac Spencer, a gentleman, planter and merchant, lived at Marrowbone three miles down river. He purchased a ten acre parcel of London Bridge Renewed from the town developer, Gilbert Falconer, in 1776.[1] By 1783, the year of Spencer's will and the County Tax Assessment, the property included a log building. In 1785, after Spencer's death, the ten acres became the property of his daughter, Charlotte.[2] In 1787, the ten acre parcel was purchased by Dr. John Thomas for £300, a substantial sum for such a small parcel with only a log building on it.[3]

It is assumed that Dr. Thomas began building his new brick residence soon after his acquisition of the land. The house was on par with several new dwellings in neighboring Chestertown—a three-bay, two-story, two-room-deep residence with attached kitchen wing in the rear. Like the Nicholson, Houston, and Geddes-Piper Houses, Dr. Thomas' house had an entrance door on one side of the three-bay facade flanked by benches that were partially embedded in the wall. The door led into a long stairhall from which the two parlors were accessible.

The facade of the Thomas House was classically simple with brick laid in plain Flemish bond without decorative water table or belt course. Moreover, there were no decorative arch supports above the openings. The facade had the classic window relationship between floors with 9/9 sash on the first story and 9/6 sash on the second.

The west gable was built adjoining the log building that had been listed in the tax assessment of 1783. The kitchen which was constructed perpendicular to the house and street, was bonded into the west gable, on the same plane. Originally, the kitchen was two bays with a door and window on each side. The width of the kitchen wing was determined by the placement of the back door of the hall which is the only opening on the first floor of the north facade. Unlike the south facade, its northern counterpart's second floor had only one window, making a stark statement.

As mentioned above, the plan was a typical townhouse plan of the period, but unlike the referenced Chestertown houses, Dr. Thomas' was planned with a fireplace centered on the west wall of the south parlor and a diagonal or corner fireplace in its southwest corner of the north parlor. The same plan was used on the second story. The flues were joined above the attic and exited the roof as a single stack.

The south parlor was originally finished with a wall of paneling over the fireplace, with flanking cabinets or closets. Only the shadows left on the walls and ceiling are evidence of its original presence. Similar lines in its north parlor indicate a paneled wall over the fireplace and a corner cupboard in the northwest corner. One curious feature in the north parlor is the existence of a small window adjacent to the kitchen door. It may have been a pass-through from the pantry or kitchen, like the opening which existed at Hebron.

Dr. John Thomas House, Millington, was built soon after his acquisition of the ten acre lot in 1787. The house originally had a small log office wing for the doctor. It was removed around c. 1945. Michael C. Wootton photograph, 1995.

Dr. John Thomas House, Millington. The closed string stair has very good turnings and was not altered when the house was remodeled around 1860. The paneling enclosed a basement stair. C. Engstrom photograph, 1977.

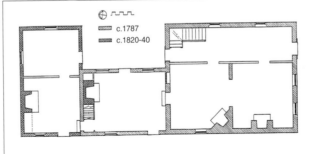

c.1787
c.1820-40

Dr. John Thomas House. First floor plan. Michael Bourne, 1997.

actly happened to the bricks has not yet been ascertained from the records, but it is not unlikely that they were employed to build the later addition to the kitchen.

The kitchen addition is a little smaller than the original kitchen. Two bays long, with a chimney in its north gable, the addition also included a small leanto on its east side. The loft was unfinished and contained two small casements flanking the chimney.

Nearly 50 years after Dr. Thomas had first purchased the property, Mary Cosden Thomas (probably his daughter-in-law) sold the property to Ebenezer Massey. While his main residence had been Gondomah (located near the village of Massey), he is known to have been living in Millington at the time the insurance policy on Gondomah was written.

Eleanor F. Horsey purchased the house and land in 1844 and lived there until her death in 1858. Because she died intestate, the court appointed George Vickers as trustee to sell her real estate. Via Mr. Vickers, the house was sold again to another physician, Dr. Edward Rasin. Before Dr. Rasin could obtain title to the property, he passed away and the house and property were passed on to his family.

It was during the Rasin occupancy that the house was remodeled. At this point the house was about 70 years old and was most likely in need of some attention. The Rasins made changes to the facade by replacing the windows, adding a wide overhang to the roof with bracketed cornice, and adding a new front door with architrave and front porch. The porch necessitated the closing of the cellar bulkhead.

Inside, paneling was removed from the chimney breasts and the corner cabinet was removed, creating clean surfaces which could then be finished in the fashion of the day with wallpaper. The Rasins also enlarged the opening between the first floor rooms to a double door and converted the first kitchen into a dining room. Virtually nothing was changed upstairs.

On the second floor, instead of paneling over the fireplaces, there were fireplace surrounds similar to the door trim. Window trim was only the width of the backband. At the head or south end of the hall, there was a small unheated room with the window centered above the front door.

Board partitions were used to separate the same number of rooms on the third floor. The doors were board and batten.

At the time of Thomas' death, an inventory was made of his personal belongings. It included enough furnishings for the house, tools for the garden, medical books, instruments, and medicines. Interestingly, Thomas also had 20,000 bricks, scantling and 17 slaves (an increase of 14 slaves since the Tax Assessment of 1783).[4] What ex-

The house remained in the possession of the Rasin heirs until 1940 when it was sold to Elizabeth Collins, an antique dealer. By this time the lot had been reduced to just 1.9 acres. Miss Collins lived there for the next 27 years and ran a fine antique shop from her home. It was she who removed the old log wing, as it had been consumed by ivy. Miss Collins also removed the porch which the Rasins had installed across the front facade. Since her death in 1967, the house has passed through three owners and to its present owners in 1987.   K-174

1. Land Records, Lib. DD 5, fol. 154.
2. Land Records, Lib. 7, fol. 109.
3. Land Records, Lib. EF 7, fol. 125.
4. Inventories, Lib. 13, fol. 159.

Thornton

Morgan Neck
c. 1788

Surveyed and patented in 1664, Thornton was originally a 1000 acre tract located on Morgan Creek.[1] Within four years of the patent, it had passed through as many owners. Philip Hopkins acquired the lower half of Thornton in 1693 when the area had just become part of Kent County.[2] Upon his death in 1712, Hopkins described it as, *"the Plantation whereon I now live,"* and bequeathed it to his cousin Philip Brooks.[3] In his inventory completed by William Comegys and Samuel Wallis, his belongings were listed by room, including the *"Hall, Parlor, Parlor Chamber, Blue Room and White Room."* With his personal estate valued at over £600, it is obvious he had a good house.[4]

The upper part of Thornton was purchased by Elizabeth Lowe in 1717 and sold in 1723 to John Johnson, a relative of the Brooks mentioned above.[5] When Johnson's son, Richard, prepared his will in 1753, he left his part of Thornton to his wife for her lifetime and *"then to my two cousins John and Philip Brooks, sons of Philip Brooks."*[6] By the time the will was probated a year later, Philip Brooks had married *"Mary, sister ... of the deceased."* Since both Philip and John died intestate in the early 1760s, it is difficult to determine how the property descended or how much they owned. Philip's personal estate however was three times the value of John's so it is probable that Philip was the owner of a major part of Thornton.[7] By 1783, when the tax assessment was compiled, the lower part of Thornton was owned by John Brooks and the upper part was in the *"occupation of William Ringgold."*[8]

Houses listed in the assessment included a frame dwelling on Morgan's Creek on John's part, and an old brick house on William's. On John's part there were 21

Thornton, Morgan Creek. The house was built by Philip Brooks after the Revolution. When he died in 1801 he bequeathed it to his nephew Philip Brooks. The farm has remained in the same family since the early eighteenth century. Michael C. Wootton photograph, 1995.

Thornton, c. 1890. A family group seated on the front porch. Jane Brooks Sprinkle Collection. Maryland State Archives.

Thornton. The dining room in the wing was finished later than the rest of the house.

Thornton. The parlor overmantel is similar to others at River House and Handy Point.

The master bedroom was equipped with built-in closets from the beginning. Its fireplace, like most second story fireplaces is off-center in order to accommodate the flue from below. Michael C. Wootton photographs, 1995.

ever the initial circumstances of Ringgold's involvement in the property, they were all resolved in the wills of Philip's children, John (d. 1792) and Philip (d. 1801).

John bequeathed his lower part of Thornton, the dwelling plantation to his son Philip, and to his son, Thomas, he left the *"reversion of part of a tract of land called Thorntons which William Ringgold now occupies and all my right and title to the same."*[10] But, in three deeds executed in 1808, it mentions that their uncle Philip Brooks made a will 11 April 1801 and in it bequeathed his part of Thornton (the upper part) to nephew Philip provided Philip deed his father's legacy (the Home Farm) to Thomas. Apparently both agreed to the terms of Uncle Philip's will and exchanged farms in 1809, along with the widow's dower.[11]

During the restoration project of the 1980s, many components of the kitchen wing showed signs of having been reused from an earlier structure. There were footings for a previous fireplace nearly centered in the wing and overhead joists were beaded, whitewashed and extended through the wall and over the built-in porch. However, since the existing walls are bonded into the main house, it is believed that the kitchen structure was rebuilt at the same time the main house was constructed.

When built, the house was five bays long and two stories tall with the central entry having a pedimented architrave supported on recessed panel pilasters with

slaves and 5 whites, whereas there were no whites listed as living on William Ringgold's part. In the accounts of Philip Brooks' estate, prepared by Risdon Bishop and his wife, Mary (former widow of Philip Brooks) in November, 1793, there is an interesting entry which might help to shed light on Ringgold's relationship to the property. *"Of Tob. due from the dec'd to William Ringgold, Jr. as per amount proved for half law charges and pd. by these accountants as p. Rent ... 712."*[9] What-

triglyphs, a unique treatment in Kent, but bearing some similarities to Rose Hill. The majority of the brick work on the north facade was laid in Flemish bond. However, beneath the quarter-round water table the bond is English and the basement windows had four-pane sash behind iron bars. Flanking the entrance there were two 12/12 sash windows with paneled shutters. On the second floor, there were five 12/8 sash windows which lacked shutters. Each floor had jack arches one brick in height. The south facade was very similar, except that the center door and window were located so as to best serve the position of the stair. In each gable there were two small, four-pane casements flanking the chimney. Originally there were no dormers.

Set back about six feet from the north wall in order to create enough space for a basement bulkhead in the west gable, the service wing is very similar to that at Springfield Farm. It has an asymmetrical A roof with the longer side extending over the six foot porch. The five brick posts which support the roof have the same molded water table as the main block. There were originally four openings on the north facade, two doors and two windows with 9/6 sash and shutters. Above, there were two dormers east of the central chimney and one west of it. The same fenestration occurred on the south side. In the west gable flanking the chimney there were two full-size windows with 6/6 sash, just as all the other windows in the second story of the kitchen wing.

The interior of Thornton had the most popular plan for Kent County farm houses, a central stair passage with room on each side. The kitchen wing had two rooms with the outer room having the cooking fireplace.

In the east parlor, the most formal room of the house, there is a tabernacle overmantel with crossetted central panel. Crossettes are also used around the fireplace opening, windows and door. The mantel shelf is supported on undercut ogee consoles. There are recessed panel jambs in all of the windows, molded baseboard, chair rail and cornice, creating a well finished room of the period. The west room has a less formal arrangement, a paneled chimney breast with cabinet adjoining. There are crossettes over the plain over-

mantel panel only at the top and nowhere else in the room. The paneled wall is the only one to possess a cornice.

The front and back doors in the entry are flush with the interior wall, with paneled jambs which correspond to the door panels outside. Wide horizontal boards cover the inside of the doors and, with their large H hinges, they look identical to the original front door at the White Swan Tavern.

The open string stair rises in three flights to the second story. Its newel and intermediate are turned in the form of a doric column and its hand rail rises up and over each intermediate post. There are well-designed, scrolled step ends, a paneled spandrel, and half hand rail and half posts in the walls which provide a fine degree of finish.

Both second floor chambers are finished with paneled closet walls flanking a plaster chimney wall with mantel around the off-center fireplaces. There is no cornice in either room and the window trim consists only of the backband and board jambs.

There is some speculation about the original appearance of the rooms in the service wing. The original arrangement may have had a stair in each of the rooms which ascended to two private chambers. Around 1820 however, the east room was finished with reeded plinth mantel and adjoining board wall pantry closet. At that time, a stair was installed between the two rooms for access to the two bedrooms above.

One of the interesting entries in the inventory taken of Philip Brooks' estate is *"the remains of old brick kiln"* valued at $6.00.[12] This reinforces the supposition that Philip

Thornton, porch detail. The brick piers have the same molded brick as the main part of the house. Michael C. Wootton photograph, 1995

Thornton, c. 1890, from the west gable. Jane Brooks Sprinkle Collection. Maryland State Archives.

was the builder of the house, for there would be no other reason to have a kiln on the property. Besides, the architectural features and the delicacy with which they are executed suggests the 1780–90 period.

Philip's nephew, Philip Brooks lived at upper Thornton until his death in 1837. He died intestate, so the farm became the property of his widow, Araminta Angier Medford Brooks and their three children. In 1850 Thomas Brooks, brother of Philip, who had exchanged farms with him in 1808, died with a will and bequeathed his land to Philip's children.[13] The estates were finally settled after Araminta's death in 1858.[14] The division of the farms was recorded in the land records in 1862.[15] The three remaining Brooks children had inherited over 1000 contiguous acres, which were divided into three parcels in order that each receive an equal share of the family farm. Upper Thornton went to George Courtland Medford Brooks. Lower Thornton (Thornton Farm) went to his sister, Mary Araminta Brooks (the wife of William B. Wilmer. Another part of the farm went to their sister, Grace Brooks Hildebrand, and has since been called the Hildebrand Farm.

George C. M. Brooks installed dormers on the main house. He may also have built the front entry porch and replaced the window above with a door, as depicted in the old photograph. After George's death in 1863, the farm descended to his son, Philip A. M. Brooks, who with his wife, lived on the farm for a few years before moving into Chestertown. While residing in town, the farm was tenanted until the 1880s, when they returned. After his death, the property was owned by his widow, Susan E. Massey Brooks, and later by their son, Philip Medford Brooks.[16]

When the P. M. Brooks' estate was settled, the house and farm went to Jane Brooks Sprinkle. She and her husband, John H. Sprinkle, have restored the house, bringing to perfection one of the architectural treasures of Kent County.   K-195

1. Rent Rolls, Lib. 5, fol.55.
2. Land Records, Lib. C, fol. 23. In this article Thornton (K-195) is referred to as upper Thornton; lower Thornton refers to Thornton Farm (K-196).
3. Wills, Lib. 1, fol. 140.
4. Inventories, Lib. 1, fol. 125-130.
5. Land Records, Lib. BC 1, fol. 315; Lib. JSB NW, fol. 451.
6. Wills, Lib. 3, fol. 228.
7. Inventories, Lib. 5, fol. 94; Lib.

5, fol. 118.
8. 1783 Tax Assessment.
9. Accounts, Lib. 4, fol. 329.
10. Wills, Lib. 7, fol. 351.
11. Land Records, Lib. BC 5, fol. 387; 432; 433.
12. Inventories, Lib. 11, fol. 329.
13. Wills, Lib. JFB 1, fol. 308.
14. Wills, Lib. JF 1, fol. 117.
15. Land Records, Lib. JKH 3, fol. 51 ff.
16. Land Records, Lib. RAS 30, fol. 545.

John Nicholson House

Queen Street, Chestertown
c. 1788

JOHN NICHOLSON, SON OF JOSEPH NICHOL-
son, Sr., had been active in the War for
Independence, rising to the position of
Captain in the Continental Navy. After
the war, upon his return to Kent County,
he became Register of Wills and resided
in Chestertown before moving to Baltimore County in 1801.

In 1788 John Nicholson purchased
part of Lot No. 25 from Thomas Smyth
for the sum of £137 and soon thereafter
improved it with the construction of a
large townhouse.[1] Like its nearby neighbor the Geddes-Piper House, the house
was of a tall design allowing for room in
the basement for the kitchen. The floor
plan was also the same as the Geddes-
Piper House, only in reverse, and on a
larger scale.

For the three bay facade, Nicholson
chose common bond, with cove water
table. It lacked a belt course and decorative window heads above the large
12/12 sash. The single decorative feature
of the facade was its cornice. Molded
brick was used to imitate crown and facia, beneath which was a row of brick
dentils, supported on a cove molding.
Short cornice returns wrapped around
the gables. The Nicholson House and its
neighbor, the Chambers House possessed the earliest examples of brick cornice work in Kent County. They are the only such
examples to use molded brick.

Its interior was well finished with baseboard, chair
rail and cornice. The two parlors have dentil cornices
similar to rooms in River House, Dunn House and the
Buck-Chambers House. Many of the window and door
openings are trimmed with double crossetted trim.

After John Nicholson departed for Baltimore County, he sold his residence to Margaret Forman, mother
of Elizabeth Chambers her neighbor, and widow of
Ezekial Forman, earlier Clerk of the Court.[2] In 1802,
Mrs. Forman sold twenty five feet of her lot to her
neighbor James Houston and in 1808 she sold another
portion to her son-in-law Benjamin Chambers for a
stable.[3] At that time she was living in Cecil County.
When she finally sold her house in 1820, she was in

*The Nicholson House. By
1936 it had a semi-octag-
onal front stoop with
built-in benches. Library
of Congress. Historic
American Buildings
Survey.*

*The Nicholson House
front parlor has double
crossettes (or dog ears)
in the mantel and win-
dows. Dentil molded cor-
nices are used in many
contemporary houses in
Kent County.*

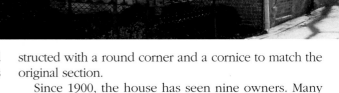

*The Nicholson House,
c. 1788. It was built for
John Nicholson, a
Captain in the Continental Navy, after his return
to Chestertown. The
large scale townhouse
was the first to employ
molded brick for
the cornice.*

*The Nicholson House
stair from second story
with a glimpse into the
back wing.*

*Detail of window trim
and cornice in the front
parlor of the Nicholson
house. Michael C. Wootton photographs, 1997.*

1. Land Records, Lib.
EF 7, fol. 286.
2. Land Records, Lib.
TW 2, fol. 97.
3. Land Records, Lib.
BC 5, fol. 374.
4. Land Records, Lib.
WS 3, fol. 425.

fact living in Adams
County, Mississippi.
The following year
Mrs. Forman's granddaughter, Elizabeth
Chambers Wickes repurchased the house
and resided there with her husband
Joseph until they acquired the Wickes
House in 1831.[4]

It was possibly during the Wickes
tenure that the facade was improved
by the addition of wooden lintels with
corner blocks over all of the openings.
Inside, large double doors between
parlors were installed, creating, when
needed, a huge double room.

In 1841, the lot was owned and occupied by Joseph N. Gordon, Clerk of
the Court. In the Tax Assessment, the
house and lot were assessed for $1,600.

On the Map of Chestertown in the
1877 Atlas, the house is drawn without
additions. Apparently, it was not until
the 1890s that the two story brick wing
with matching brick cornice was constructed off the back of the stairhall.
The wing included a dining room and
kitchen which moved the location of
the latter from the basement. Charles T.
and Mary Westcott were responsible for
the addition. The addition was con-

structed with a round corner and a cornice to match the
original section.

Since 1900, the house has seen nine owners. Many
alterations have been made during this century, most of
which have occurred during the past ten years.   K-310

Ferguson House

High Street, Chestertown
c. 1788

ONE OF CHESTERTOWN'S EIGHTEENTH CENTURY DWELLINGS located in the 300 block of High Street is currently used as an office. The story of its structural development, physically now hidden beneath both modern and historic fabric, has recently come to light as a result of research in its chain of title and structure.

The High Street half of Lot No. 84 was purchased in 1764 by George Laybourn, merchant, for £90.[1] Laybourn also owned adjoining Lot No. 83. After his death, the High Street half of Lot No. 84 was sold for £275,[2] an amount which indicates the presence of at least one substantial dwelling there, if not two.[3] In 1788, half of lot No. 84 was purchased by Rev. Colin Ferguson, rector of Chester Parish, and second President of Washington College.

The earliest of four buildings currently on this half lot is numbered 357 High Street. It was constructed on

a fieldstone foundation, without basement. A late 1960s fire, which originated in an adjacent building, revealed that the original siding was beaded riven oak, a feature usually associated with buildings constructed before 1765. In form and plan, the original house was similar to the Banning House, with a two-story, one room deep front section and a service wing behind. Here, the service wing was two stories tall. A subsequent addition of a small leanto room in the space created by the *L* was also two stories tall. The plan which was revealed on the second story, was composed of a stair/entry on the westernmost side with one room on the east. The wing contained two rooms and the leanto may have been accessible from either section.

Around 1817, the half lot appears to have been divided into four parcels, after which it is difficult to trace with certainty since the lot sizes are not stated. In the 1841 Tax Assessment, two parcels of Lot No. 84 were owned by James Mansfield and John W. Carroll, with the latter occupying the former's house. For most of its existence, the house appears to have been a rental unit. In the third quarter of the nineteenth century, a bracketed cornice was added to the front and the siding was either covered or renewed.

In the twentieth century, the first floor was lowered bringing the entrance closer to street level. Store windows were installed, the stair was removed to the exterior and the small leanto was incorporated into the back room along with an equal depth section of the wing. From that time on, the first floor has been used as offices or commercial space, with an apartment above.   K-56

Ferguson House, Chestertown. Colin Ferguson owned this lot and may have been responsible for the construction of 357 High Street. Michael C. Wootton photograph, 1996

Silhouette of Colin Ferguson (1751-1815), who was the second president of Washington College as well as rector of Chester Parish. Historical Society of Kent County Collection.

1. Land Records, Lib. DD 1, fol. 507.
2. Land Records, Lib. EF 7, fol. 359.
3. Fred Usilton, History of Chestertown, p. 67. Usilton mentions a one-story building set back from the street which was the rectory for Chester Parish. It was demolished in 1857 when the Lusby House was built. It was on the corner of Lot No. 84, and may have been built by George Laybourn.

Stephens House Site

Galena
c. 1789

T HE STEPHENS HOUSE HAD STOOD ON THE SOUTHWEST corner of the crossroads of present day Galena. Originally part of a tract called McCay's purchase and owned by Robert Maxwell, Sr., this lot and others were sold by Maxwell in the 1780s and 90s. At the time of its first transfer to Garrett Vansant in 1789[1] the purchase price was a mere £50. When he sold the property just four years later to Joshua Vansant the price had increased to £200, a likely indication that the house had been constructed during his ownership. Between the 1780s and the 1840s there were several owners, but when the Stephens family purchased the property in 1843,[2] they would continue to own it for a hundred years.

The sole existing photograph of the Stephens House was taken by the HABS photographer in the 1930s. The house appears to have been a twin to the former Chesterville Hotel located on the corner of that crossroad village. The form and fenestration of the building suggests that it had a hall-parlor plan with attached kitchen, all under the same roof. The one room kitchen addition on the end of the house may date from 1796–1799 when there was another increase in the purchase price.[3] Soon after the photograph was taken, the house was demolished.

K-526

The Stephens House, probably built by Garrett Vansant between 1789-93 was located in Galena. It was very similar to the "Chesterville Hotel." Library of Congress, Historic American Buildings Survey, c. 1936.

Stephens House, Galena. A unique date brick taken from the house during demolition. The initials GV may be those of Garrett Vansant, cooper, who acquired the property in 1789, perhaps after he had built his house. Gene Johnstone photograph, 1997.

1. Land Records, Lib. DD 5, fol. 381.
2. Land Records, Lib. JKH 1, fol. 824.
3. Land Records, Lib. BC 4, fol. 411.

The Ireland-Ruth House

Galena
c. 1789

T HE IRELAND-RUTH HOUSE STANDS ON THE NORTH SIDE OF the Chestertown Road in Galena. Like the Stephens and Sutton Houses in Galena, this house also began as a one-and-a-half story frame house with a hall-parlor-kitchen plan beneath the same roof line. It was most likely built during the last quarter of the eighteenth century, when the village was called first Down's Crossroads and later Georgetown Crossroads.

The Ireland-Ruth House, Galena. Possibly a contemporary of the Stephens house, the Ireland-Ruth House began as a one-and-a-half story building which was heightened in the late nineteenth century. Gene Johnstone photograph, 1997.

The Ireland-Ruth House, Galena, 1916, with Emma Pettebone, Elizabeth H. Ruth, Frances I. Ruth and Lena R. Shallcross standing in front of the old iron fence and the elegant porch. Ruth G. Othoson collection

Frank Ruth, who lived a few doors west of the Galena crossroads drew the above sketch of Down's Inn from memory in 1932. The old Inn was the first building to be constructed at the crossroads in 1763. It probably began as the one-and-a-half section with south facing porch. The two-story wing to the north was probably a later addition. The building was known as Farmer's Inn in 1792 and as Pennington Hotel in 1848. It survived until March 31, 1893 when it was consumed by fire.

In 1867, the property was purchased by Malvina Ireland and her husband Samuel, from John and Laura Caldwell of Baltimore. The Irelands enlarged the house by building a second story above the small early house and adding a dining room and kitchen wing out the back. This enlargement also gave the owners the opportunity to install a central stair in what was the *hall,* creating a thoroughly modern house for the late nineteenth century.

The house has remained in the family of Malvina and Samuel Ireland, becoming the property of Frank and Lena Ireland Ruth,[1] then to their daughter and son-in-law, Frances and Warren Gillespie. Today the house is in the ownership of their daughter and her family and has been thoroughly remodeled, incorporating the lot formerly occupied by the Cochran House. On the 1860 Martenet Map the property is owned by Laura McGee.   K-535

I. U. Sexton House

Near Worton
c. 1790

N ORTH OF CHRIST CHURCH, I. U., IS A PICturesque one-and-a-half-story brick and frame house that has been owned by the Vestry of I. U. since 1877, when that body purchased it at a tax sale. The building is a vernacular structure that appears to have been assembled and finished at one time, possibly using an earlier frame section. It possesses a central hall plan with two small chambers on the second floor. Remains of a paneled stair enclosure and closet can be found in the western room of the first floor, while the east room has the remains of an early Federal style mantel with Wall of Troy molding under its shelf. The house is typical of those of smaller land owners or tenants of eighteenth century Kent County. Most of these were replaced with better dwellings as farming methods improved in the nineteenth century.   K-134

I. U. Sexton House, photographed during restoration. Gene Johnstone photograph, 1997.

I. U. Sexton House. The frame half of the house (left) probably pre-dates the c. 1790 brick extension. The original chimney with exposed back of fireplace is visible on the gable. Katherine Hepbron Harris Collection, Maryland State Archives.

1. Frank Ruth remembered the early Down's Tavern that stood on the northwest corner of the Crossroads and drew a sketch thereof which first appeared in Usilton's History of Kent County (1916) and which appears elsewhere in this book.

DOWN'S INN, 1763 — FARMERS INN, 1792 — PENNINGTON'S HOTEL, 1848.
DOWNS + ROADS, — GEORGETOWN + ROADS, 1803. — GALENA, 1858.
STATION (TRACKS) BY FRANK H. RUTH.
GALENA, MD. — 1932.

The Knock Farm

Near Millington
c. 1790

The Knock Farm stood on the west side of the Millington-Massey Road, about a mile north of Millington. The house, mentioned as *"unique"* in H. Chandlee Forman's Early Manor and Plantation Houses of Maryland (1934), was a frame dwelling composed of three parts. The largest section was a three-bay, gambrel-roof structure with two end chimneys. It was the arrangement of the chimneys which set this building apart from others. The east chimney was built outside of the gable and the west chimney was built in the northwest corner of the house. This is the only known example of a gambrel-roof house with corner chimney to have existed in Kent County.

With the placement of the chimneys and windows, it would appear that the stair was located on the hall side of the partition which separated it from the parlor. Located several steps lower, on the west end of the house, there was a one-and-a-half-story building sheathed with vertical board and batten siding (probably the siding concealed an earlier log or plank building). It had a fireplace in its western end, but there would have been enough space for two rooms, probably the kitchen and either a pantry or dining room. Attached to the west end of the house there was a leanto addition.

Prior to his death in 1855, Jesse Knock, a farmer and local Justice, purchased the farm that was either part of London Bridge or Partnership, or both.[1] He bequeathed it to his son, Samuel Henry Knock.[2] Samuel, his wife, and his mother apparently grew greatly in debt and had to sell it in 1872 to Peregrine Hendrick-

The Knock Farm. This late eighteenth century house stood north of Millington until it was demolished in the 1950s. It had a unique corner chimney on a gambrel roof. Jane Eliason Collection, Maryland State Archives.

The Knock Farm, east gable. The width of the chimney indicates fireplaces on both floors. Jane Eliason Collection, Maryland State Archives.

son.[3] The farm remained in his family until 1946. In 1954, it was purchased by the present owners who replaced the old house with a modern brick rancher. The Knock and Hendrickson graveyard remains north of the site of the former farmhouse.   K-168

1. Land Records, Lib., fol.
2. Wills, Lib. , fol.
3. Land Records, Lib., fol.

Hodges Bar Farm

Near Rock Hall
c. 1790

Hodges Bar Farm takes its name from a large oyster bar lying off-shore, named for the Hodges family, who owned the farm during the first half of the nineteenth century. While the tract is also, sometimes, referred to in the records as Bayside Farm, Hodge's Farm or Driftwood, it is the reference to it as *"part of Hinchingham"* which points to its origins.

Hinchingham was a 2200 acre parcel patented to Thomas Hynson in 1659. In the eighteenth century Hynson's granddaughter, Mary, married William Glanville. Throughout the eighteenth century the Glanvilles owned that *"part of Hinchingham"* which would later be known as Hodges Bar Farm (approximately 216 acres). In the nineteenth century the farm was purchased by Samuel Hodges who was probably responsible for enlarging the house to its present form and finishing the interior.

The farm house appears to have begun life as a one-room *A* roof dwelling, composed of the present middle room. After being used for some time, the stair hall and west room were added with a gambrel roof covering both structures. Service rooms located on the east side of the building were later enlarged, and survived into the 1960s.

When the house was restored after a severe fire in the late 1960s the structure was exposed, revealing that the now middle room was a separate structure. It had a door and window on the north wall and two windows on the south. It also indicated that the entire roof had been built at one time, in the same manner as the roof of Godlington Manor. Moreover, whitewashed studs and ceiling in the west room revealed that the *new* room had been used prior to being plastered. The close string stair was similar to several in Chestertown constructed between the 1790s and 1820s. Second floor partitions around the stair were all made of vertical beaded boards. Both rooms on both floors were constructed with fireplaces. Moreover, sufficient headroom existed in the attic for a ladder stair to be installed in the northeast closet, the possible location of the first stair.

A curious anomaly in the structure is the use of a brick partition between the two sections which rises

from the basement to the second floor. Since the brick wall is the only wall between the old and new sections, and it rises on the new basement walls, that alone would suggest that the middle section was brought up to the new structure from elsewhere. This is one structural mystery which will probably never be solved.

Samuel Hodges lived at his bay side plantation until his death in 1851. The inventory of his estate indicates the possessions of a prosperous mid-century farmer. After the death of his second wife, Mary, the following year, the farm became the inheritance of Walter T. H. Miller, nephew of Hodges' first wife, Sarah Miller. Walter T. H. Miller owned and had probably grown up at Miller's Purchase nearby. On Martenet's Map (1860) Walter N. Miller is listed owner.

After Col. Miller died in 1868, the farm was sold to pay his debts. Between 1868 and 1930 it passed through eleven owners. In 1930 Mr. and Mrs. George Debnam purchased the farm and raised their family in the old Hodges House. They built several buildings on the property, but only the large dairy barn remains. Mr.

and Mrs. Thomas Page purchased Hodges Bar from the Debnams in 1948 and lived there until 1966. In that year a disastrous fire consumed the kitchen wing and part of the gambrel roof.

Dr. Davy McCall undertook a gradual restoration of the house after the fire and eventually constructed a one-and-a-half-story wing in place of the old kitchen using architectural elements from an old house near Dover, Delaware and bricks from Wilmer's Mill house which stood near Chestertown.[1] K-102

1. McCall, Davy H., "Hodges Bar Farm," *The Kent Shoreman* Vol. 10, No. 12, 1976, p. 9 ff.

Hodges Bar Farm was built in the late eighteenth century on part of Hinchingham. It began life as a one-room, one-and-a-half story structure that was enlarged and covered with the gambrel roof, a development similar to Godlington Manor. Tyler Campbell photograph, 1996.

Hodges Bar Farm. The two-story wing burned in 1966, damaging part of the gambrel structure as well. Photograph from the collection of Mr. and Mrs. George Debnam, 1940.

Trulock

Near Still Pond
c. 1790

LOCATED BETWEEN STILL POND AND THE HEAD OF STILL POND Creek, Trulock stands today as a mere brick derelict. Dating from the late eighteenth century, it was most likely built by Thomas Trulock who is listed in the 1783 Tax Assessment as having been taxed on 409 acres consisting of Bears Green or Hales, Nancy's Choice and Trulock's Adventure. When the house was first finished, it was a three-bay, two-story building which faced south with a one-and-a-half-story kitchen wing on its east gable. The southern facade was laid in Flemish bond without water table, but with a two brick string course. While the east chimney was constructed completely within the gable, the west chimney was built partially outside. The windows probably had 12/8 sash on the first story and 8/8 on the second. The north facade of Trulock had only two windows per floor and no back door, similar to Broadnox.

The interior was composed of a hall-parlor plan with the usual location of the rooms reversed, i. e. the hall was located between the parlor and the kitchen rather than at one end. The parlor was well trimmed with crossettes at the windows, door and mantel. The mantel shelf, with dentil molding was supported by fluted plinth blocks or consoles, above a paneled frieze. The larger hall, had an enclosed stair in the southeast corner adjacent to the fireplace. Between the stair door and the fireplace opening, there was a cabinet above a plain panel. The space behind the panel was needed for head room for the stair from the kitchen wing to the basement.

On the second story the plan was the same except for a corridor along the south front which was unusual in that it was wider at the stair end than it was at the other, having a partition wall set on the diagonal. Both chambers had small fireplaces with simple mantels.

There is evidence that the door between the hall and parlor was originally grained to look more elegant than the yellow pine from which it was made. Other details may have been painted decoratively as in Knock's Folly and Shepherd's Delight.

In the late nineteenth and/or early twentieth century, the old kitchen was removed and a two-part, two-story, frame wing was built in its place. Windows throughout were removed, enlarged and replaced. Dormers were added to the roof, and the small gable casements were bricked in. The hall was remodeled, but the old stair remained, and the parlor was untouched except for the window trim. A porch was added in front of the new south entry and all windows were embellished with shutters. In both periods the farmhouse was a significant statement of the aspirations and achievements of its builder/remodeler.

The farm was owned by G. W. Crossley in 1860, before Clark Road was made a public thoroughfare. By 1877 the road was marked on the map and the farm was assigned to A. Clemens.

No one has lived in the house since before 1960. The wing has completely collapsed, as has the roof of the brick section.

Trulock, c. 1790. This small hall-parlor plan house was well finished with crossetted trim, paneled stair enclosure, and grained doors. It is now in an advanced state of ruin. Marsha L. Fritz photograph, 1980.

Trulock from the back. There was no rear door in the brick section. The dormers were added and the gable windows were bricked in when the frame wing was constructed. Michael Bourne photograph, 1968.

K-110

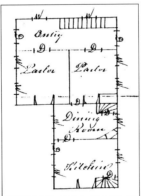

transformation that could have been used to exemplify the trend to remodel *dull old houses* promoted by nineteenth century designers.

A few excerpts from the diary of Susan Massey Brooks bring the house alive with the people who lived there:

"In 1855 Mary Amanda Oldham was married at Montebello, to Dr. D. H. B. Massey and went to live across the street in the Kitty Knight House where she stayed three years, where her son George Oldham was born and possibly her second son Beauregard. Then they moved to the "Brick House Farm" or "Angel's Rest", as the bachelor place of C. H. B. Massey's place was called, where Susan Emily was born.

After the death of Geo. W. Oldham (1865) the family moved back to Montebello, where was born, Mary Ella, Herman Biddle and E. Thos. and where they all lived until moving out to Belmont, the house bought of H. Clinton Massey, when that family moved to Phila."6

In another entry in the Brooks diary, Montebello is mentioned again. This time in reference to her aunt, Mary Ella Emory. After moving to Centreville, she returned to Montebello and remained in residence there until her death in 1918.

When Montebello was purchased in 1940 by Walter and Chiquita Burns, the house was stripped of its Gothic detail and returned to near the simplicity it had possessed when first constructed. In about 1961, a gas leak in the frame wing built during the Oldham/Massey occupancy caused it to explode. Only minor damage was done to the original house. The Burns renamed the property Duck Hollow during their ownership. The present owners constructed a modern wing on the north side of the house, making the entrance hall the center of the house. It was designed to take advantage of the two levels the site afforded, as well as the exquisite view to the northeast over Mill Creek and the Sassafras River.   K-117

1. Land Records, Lib. JS 18, fol. 248.
2. Land Records, Lib. EF 6, fol. 540, 543.
3. Land Records, Lib. WS 3, fol. 364.
4. Republican Star, Easton, MD, 7 April 1812.
5. Franklin Fire Insurance Policy #4042, Pennsylvania Historical Society, Philadelphia.
6. Diary of Susan E. Massey Brooks, unpublished. Courtesy of Jane Brooks Sprinkle.

Montebello, Georgetown. This Federal period house was vastly remodeled in the late nineteenth century, although the interior remained intact. Harry Armstrong Collection, c. 1890

Montebello. The floor plan as sketched by Robert Buchman for the Franklin Fire Insurance Co. of Philadelphia in 1843.

The Chambers House

*Queen Street, Chestertown
c. 1790*

THE CHAMBERS HOUSE WAS BUILT ON PART OF LOT NO 25 which was first acquired by Emory Sudler in 1771, sold to Thomas Smyth in 1785, and finally sold to Benjamin Chambers in 1786.[1] Chambers' purchase also included a building on Lot No. 34 which he was to enlarge and occupy as his own dwelling (see K-27, Buck-Chambers House).

Benjamin Chambers was an attorney in Chestertown who later served as Clerk of the Court and was a general in the militia during the battle at Caulk's Field. He and his wife, Elizabeth Forman, raised two daughters and a son to maturity before moving to Widehall in 1810.

The first mention of a brick house on Chambers' part of Lot No. 25 occurs in a deed of 1811, when the house and lot were transferred by Chambers to his son, Ezekiel Forman Chambers. In that deed it is mentioned that the house was *"lately occupied by James Arthur."*[2] Due to its similarity to the Nicholson House, however, it is likely that it was built between 1788–90.

As described in 1811, the house consisted of the 28' x 21', two-story, three-bay, brick structure with the unique floor plan of stairhall and living room. (The current street side of the house.) The exterior cornice was also different as it was composed of four courses of molded brick which together formed a classi-

The Chambers House, Chestertown, appears to have been constructed at the same time as the Nicholson House next door. Both houses have molded brick cornices and similar millwork details. Michael C. Wootton photograph, 1996.

cal Doric capital. This is one of the first two uses of a molded cornice in Kent County. The other is found in the Nicholson House next door. There was apparently no other attached structure originally, since the kitchen was located in the basement and was accessible from beneath the main stair. Like other Chestertown dwellings of the 1780s and '90s, the interior was well-finished but simple, with a close-string stair, chair rail and cornice. In the living room, there were paneled, recessed window shutters. The second floor plan consisted of three rooms, a

The Chambers House. First and second floor plans of original house. Michael Bourne, 1996.

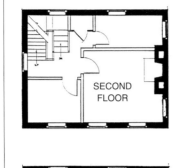

SECOND FLOOR

FIRST FLOOR

closet and stair to the attic. Only the largest of these rooms was equipped with a fireplace. The attic was divided into two rooms by a board partition.

Ezekiel F. Chambers is best known as having lived at Widehall and as an important attorney and distinguished judge. He may have lived here as a young man, but during his residency at Widehall, after 1822, the house was primarily a rental property. Mentioned in the 1841 Tax Assessment with other Forman properties, it was appraised for $1,000.00. Chambers sold the building and lot in 1865 to John Greenwood, a local carpenter/contractor, who according to the deed, had previously rented the property *"for several years."*[3]

The nearly three hundred percent difference between the sale price in the deed to Greenwood and that of the following year to the Vestry of Chester Parish suggests that it was in 1865 that the 28' x 16' brick wing was constructed. It added a first-floor pantry and dining room and two additional bedrooms above. Dormers were also added on the old roof and the basement was equipped with another fireplace to augment the original cooking fireplace located in the front portion of the house.

For forty-four years (1866–1910), the property was owned by Chester Parish and the house occupied by the rectors of Emmanuel Church and their families. These included the Reverends Edward H. G. Goodwin (1866–1870), Stephen C. Collins, D. D. (1871–1899), and Henry B. Martin, D. D. (1899–1919). Harry and Martha Hughes purchased the property[4] in 1921 and lived there until 1956. The house was then sold to Mrs. William Dixon. After her death it was sold to Dr. and Mrs. Guy Goodfellow, and they resided there from 1963 to 1990.[5] The present owners, Mr. and Mrs. David Singer, who bought the house in 1994, are currently restoring it.

K-26

1. Land Records, Lib. DD 4, fol. 25; Lib. EF 6, fol. 486; Lib. EF 7, fol. 77.
2. Land Records, Lib. BC 7, fol. 51.
3. Land Records, Lib. JKH 5, fol. 87.
4. Land Records, Lib. APR 8, fol. 203.
5. Land Records, Lib. EHP 3, fol. 296.

Rich Levels

Near Sassafras
c. 1790

IN 1771, AT THE TIME OF THE DEATH OF HIS FATHER, AUgustine Boyer III inherited 300 acres of Rich Level.[1] The Boyer family had been substantial landowners, holding over 1000 acres in Kent County, as well as land in Delaware. Rich Level had been in their ownership since the early eighteenth century.

As the Boyers were obviously prosperous in their farming operations and in other business ventures (a mercantile business in Georgetown run in conjunc-

Rich Levels. The stairhall has a well executed balustrade with shadow rail in the wall. The turned balusters are similar to those at the Dr. John Thomas House in Millington. C. Engstrom photograph, 1977.

Rich Levels. Both bedrooms have recessed paneling across the fireplace wall.

Rich Levels. Dining room paneled wall is composed of raised and flush panels with built-in cabinets. This is similar to the living room wall pictured in Chapter IV. C. Engstrom photographs, 1977.

Advertisement for Sale of Farm in The Telegraph. Nov. 14, 1828.

Trustee's Sale

BY virtue of a decree of Kent County Court, sitting as a court of Equity, I will expose at public sale on Tuesday, 2d December next, at 11 o'clock, A. M. on the premises, a

Valuable Farm,

lying and being in Kent county, one mile from the Head of Sassafras, on the road from that place to Smyrna, Del.—It contains about five hundred acres.—The improvements consist of a Brick Dwelling, Meat House, Stables, Corn Houses, &c. Further particulars can be had, by application to the subscriber residing on the property.

The Terms of Sale are, that the Purchaser or purchasers shall pay a full amount of the purchase money, in cash, on the day of sale.

E. WARD BOYER, Trustee.
Nov 7—3w.

tion with John Rumsey), the construction of a fine brick residence on their plantation was a logical development.

Late in the eighteenth century, Augustine Boyer III built his house. Five bays long and two stories tall, the plan is one of a center hall with two flanking rooms. The exterior has a two-course molded water table and a three-course belt course in which the uppermost course protrudes from the others. The pedimented architrave has fluted pilasters. The windows have 12/12 sash on the first floor and 12/8 on the second.

Inside, the detailing is of excellent quality and remains intact today. The stair boasts turned balusters and a shadow rail with recessed paneled pilasters. Also, each of the four principal rooms is paneled. In the living room, the paneling is limited to the chimney breast with dentil molding in the mantel, and Wall of Troy molding elsewhere. Each of the three other rooms, however, has a complete wall of paneling. In the dining room, the fireplace is flanked by paneled china closets with crossetted trim. On the second floor,

the fireplace end walls have large recessed panel over their respective mantels. Set back about four inches, the flanking paneled walls contain closet doors, also with recessed panels.

The original service wing, located to the rear of the main block, has not survived. A replacement was constructed in the 1950s.

At the time of the 1822 Tax Assessment, Augustine Boyer III was in his heyday. In addition to his home farm, he owned an additional 288 acres, 8 slaves and

53 oz. of plate. However, by the time of his death just six years later, the picture had changed entirely. In debt to two banks and seven individuals, Boyer died intestate. In the accounts of his estate, $151.00 was paid to two lawyers *"for prosecuting suit against asignees of Caverly and Boyer in Philadelphia."*[2] In the November 14 issue of The Telegraph (Kent County's weekly newspaper) that year, the farm was advertised for sale:

" … Valuable Farm, Lying and being in Kent County, one mile from Head Of Sassafras, on Road from there to Smyrna, Del.—It contains about five hundred acres … The improvements consist of a Brick Dwelling, Meat House, Stables, Corn Houses, etc. … ."

The outcome of this sale was not available from the records, but by the time of the Martenet Map in 1860, Edward Boyer appears as the owner. Boyer and his sister, Anna Maria Boyer sold the farm to one Joshua

Clayton in 1870, but reserved the family graveyard.[3] Clayton retained ownership until his death in 1892, but never lived on the farm. After his death, his executor sold the farm to Nathaniel J. Williams.[4]

Sometime after the house was acquired by the grandfather of the present owner, the *A* roof was removed and a third story was added with shallow-pitched roof. The overall effect was reminiscent of the earlier Italianate style. At the same time, or possibly earlier, a porch was built across the facade. This was removed when the farm was acquired in the early 1960s by its present owners. K-129

Rich Levels, c. 1790, has many characteristics in common with Thornton. The third story was added in the late nineteenth century. C. Engstrom photograph, 1977.

1. Wills, Lib. 5, fol. 87.
2. Accounts, Lib. 15, fol. 26.
3. Land Records, Lib. JKH 9, fol. 565 ff.
4. Land Records, Lib. SGF 1, fol. 453.

Woodland Hall

Shallcross Neck
c. 1790

REFERRED TO IN THE NINETEENTH CENTURY AS *"THE MANsion,"* Woodland Hall was built by Edward and Araminta (Hynson) Wright in the last decade of the 1700s. The land on which they made their home was an amalgamation of properties inherited by Araminta (of her father) and land which Edward Wright had previously purchased.

Similar in form to Duck Hollow in Georgetown, the house had a 31' x 37', two-story main block, with a 24' x 20', two-story side wing. To the rear of the wing there was an additional 27' x 18' plank, one-and-a-half-story wing which contained the kitchen and pantry.

The plan consisted of a side hall and two parlors in the main block, a passage and dining room in the brick wing, and as mentioned above, a kitchen and pantry in the plank wing. At present, the two-story wing is the least altered part of the house. Its southwest facade retains the original six-panel entry door and trim, 9/9 sash, and paneled shutters.

The original Flemish bond brickwork can still be seen through the many coats of paint applied over the years. While the house lacks a water table, there is a two-brick string course. Only the basement has jack arches above its windows. The remainder of the building was simply finished with two chimneys rising from its southwest gable. Only one chimney rises above the wing and kitchen gables.

In the 1790 census, the Wright household is listed as containing only one male and one female, with seven slaves. Edward Wright is known to have subscribed £9 toward the founding of Washington College and was a vestryman at Shrewsbury Parish from 1786–87, in 1799, and again from 1803–1808. In his final year on the Shrewsbury vestry, Wright was responsible for the installation of a brick wall around the church yard.[1] One year before, Wright was in William Spencer's 33rd Regiment and had earned the rank of Colonel.

At the time of the 1804 Tax Assessment, Edward Wright's property was appraised for $4836. This amount places him in the company of some of the wealthiest land owners in the county. By 1822, his properties were each listed by name in the tax records. They amounted to 882⅓ acres, a 500 acre increase from his holdings at the time he and Araminta Hynson were married.

Together, Edward and Araminta had three children. After Araminta's death, Edward remarried her remote

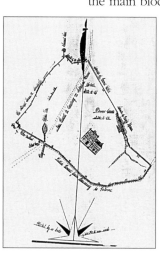

Plat of Woodland Hall, the "Mansion Farm," prepared for the estate of James Freeman Woodland, 1860. Chancery, Lib. JKH 2, fol. 237.

Woodland Hall, Locust Grove, was built around 1790 by Edward and Araminta Hynson Wright. Both sections were originally two stories. James Woodland heightened and remodeled the house in the 1850s. Michael C. Wootton photograph, 1995.

cousin, Phoebe Hynson, daughter of John Carvill Hynson of Edesville. They in turn had an additional six children.[2]

When an inventory was taken of Edward Wright's belongings in 1825, his personal property amounted to $5084.40 and included a large sum of cash in the house—$534.38. His personal belongings were typical of a gentleman of his standing. The farm included many livestock and ten slaves.[3]

Woodland Hall was bequeathed, in equal parts, to the two children of Edward and Araminta, and their granddaughter. In 1827, Dr. Thomas Hynson Wright purchased the other two thirds of the farm from his sister Julianna Wright Ellis and his niece, Malvina Wright.[4]

In 1840, Dr. Wright and James Freeman Woodland entered into an equity case which resulted in the sale of the farm to Mr. Woodland.[5] The major remodeling of Woodland Hall in the 1850s was his doing. In keeping with the stylistic trend which swept Kent County in the antebellum period, Woodland raised the entire house by one story and installed nearly flat roofs throughout. Italianate brackets were added to the cor-

The stair was replaced during the 1850s remodeling with a fine example of the period. C. Engstom photograph.

Woodland Hall, first floor plan, Michael Bourne, 1997.

Woodland Hall. During the 1850s the old mantels were replaced with cast iron mantels which were equipped with coal stoves. The mantel at the front of the living room has eglomise work in the spandrels. C. Engstrom photograph, 1977.

nices and French doors were installed to gain access to the porches which were constructed across both facades. A belvedere with balustrade was added atop the main section.

J. F. Woodland's remodeling was extensive to say the least. All of the windows and entrances of the main section were changed. The stair was renewed from the first to the third floor. Fireplaces were dressed with mantels of the period—cast iron in the rococo style. And the old wing to the southeast side of the house was changed, with a fourth bay being added, the ground floor enclosed with lattice and a bathroom installed, which received its water from a cistern on the top floor—a very early instance of indoor plumbing in Kent County.

Woodland Hall, with members of the Woodland and Hurtt families and their household around 1870. Mary Woodland Gould Collection, Maryland State Archives.

Having inherited the *"Mansion Farm"* from her husband, along with Marsh Point and a small island to its east, Margaret Travilla Wilson Woodland later sold the farm to her stepson-in-law, James W. Hurtt, in 1866.[6] A farmer from the age of 18, Hurtt first purchased his parents' farm, then Marsh Point (where he and his wife, Mary Elizabeth Woodland Hurtt resided for 9 years) before buying Woodland Hall. Together, the Hurtts raised seven of their ten children there. James was a member of the Maryland Legislature in 1872, and active in Shrewsbury Parish Church from 1872 until his death in 1908.[7]

In 1914, Woodland Hall was transferred by the Hurtts to their youngest son, Edmon S. Hurtt.[8] He and his wife, Sophie Scott, in turn, transferred the farm in 1939 to their son-in-law, Simon Wickes Westcott. The property was transferred again from Simon and his wife, Elizabeth Hurtt Westcott to their daughter, the present owner.[9]

After the porch had become dilapidated, the present owner removed it, and utilizing a few of its elements, they built a smaller porch in front of the entrance bay. The windows on both floors were returned to their earlier configuration with 12/12 sash. Numerous other alterations were made to make the house more convenient to twentieth century living.

As Woodland Hall celebrates its bicentennial, it stands as a reminder of the efforts and foresight of two families.   K-144

1. Kathryn DeProspo, A History of Shrewsbury Parish Church, 1988, Chesapeake College Press, P. 206.
2. Wills, Lib. 9, fol. 332.
3. Inventories, Lib. 17, fol. 391.
4. Land Records, Lib. JKH 1, fol. 201.
5. Chancery, Lib. JKH 2, fol. 237, ff.
6. Land Records, Lib. JKH 5, fol. 649.
7. Portrait and Biographical Record of the Eastern Shore of Maryland, Chapman Publishing Co., New York, 1898, p. 889.
8. Land Records, Lib. JTD 29, fol. 503.
9. Land Records, Lib. RAS 21, fol. 387, ff.

Comegys House

Millington
c. 1790

THE DISASTROUS FIRE OF MILLINGTON IN 1904 LEFT FEW structures standing which have their roots in the eighteenth century. Sunset Hall and Comegys House appear to be the only surviving structures from that period. The Comegys House is especially notable because it was built so close to the road that the original front entrance and basement bulkhead are now inaccessible. Two other curious features involve the lower story of the east part of the building. There is a vertical joint between the two sections to the top of the windowheads. From that point the Flemish bond continues uninterrupted across the entire five bay facade. The other feature is an in-fill of old brick between the two east windows, indicating a former door. The two features together suggest an earlier structure.

Although the form is not the same as the Logan House, the plan is, with a stairhall and parlor in the taller part and a dining room in the lower. Behind the dining room a kitchen and pantry are

Comegys House, Millington, from the rear. From the stair landing there is access to the second story of the dining room wing.

Comegys House, Millington, from the side, showing the original two-room kitchen wing. C. Engstrom photographs, 1977.

Comegys House, Millington, was built around 1790, probably for merchant Samuel Osborne. When constructed it had the same number of rooms as the Dr. John Thomas House, only in a different form and plan. C. Engstrom photograph, 1977.

Vianna

Near Chesterville
c. 1790

JOHN WOODALL, SR. BEQUEATHED HIS HOME plantation to his son William in 1800, provided that he allow his mother to have the use of one room.[1] The home plantation consisted of parts of Vianna, Stepney and Stepney Fields. In the 1822 Tax Assessment, it appears that William owned 218 acres of Vianna and 124 acres of the other two tracts combined. Both of the Woodalls were farmers.

The earliest part of the existing house was standing in the late eighteenth century and may have been constructed by John Woodall, Sr. It consisted of a frame, three-bay, gambrel roof structure which had been built over a full basement. There was an attached one-story kitchen wing on the west gable. Both north and south facades were identical, with two windows flanking a central door on the first story and two dormers in the roof above. A brick chimney had been built within the west gable. The kitchen possessed a door and window with no dormers and a brick chimney within its west wall.

Vianna, the tract, was a six-hundred acre patent to Cornelius Comegys in 1683. Part of Vianna came into possession of John Woodall, Sr. one-hundred years later on which he built his dwelling house.

Vianna, c. 1790, began as the three-bay central section. It was enlarged soon thereafter by John Woodall, Sr. The farm remains in the same family (1997). Michael Bourne photographs, 1995.

housed in a one-and-a-half-story frame, three-bay structure which was built contemporaneously with the front.

The stair in the entry hall is nearly identical to Sunset Hall, with turned newels and balusters on a closed string. The spandrel has recessed panels instead of raised. The door and window trim has crossetted heads. The parlor mantel has the same crossetted trim with paneled frieze and a course of dentils. The chamber has a simpler treatment.

The dining room has no trim dating from before the nineteenth century, but the chamber above retains an original enclosed winder to the attic, as well as a closet and plain fireplace trim. The attic over the kitchen and pantry opens from the aforementioned chamber.

Originally the dining room chamber was divided into a passage, two small rooms and the pantry chamber, and was accessible from the stair landing. The kitchen chamber, half of the present space, was accessible from a ladder adjacent to the fireplace. This arrangement produced five sleeping rooms plus two attics, an arrangement for a large household.

In the mid-nineteenth century, possibly when owned by J. H. Harle,[1] the Greek Revival architrave was added and the windows were all changed to 6/6 sash with paneled and louvered shutters. Only the dining room was altered at that time.

The name given the house is that of the owners between 1950 and 1985—Irvin and Pearly Comegys.[2] K-171

1. Martenet Map, 1860.
2. Land Records, Lib. EHP 189, fol. 339.

All of the corner posts and plates of the gambrel roof section mentioned above were exposed in the single room. In its northwest corner there was an enclosed stair adjacent to the fireplace which led to the two chambers above—one with fireplace. In its earliest stage, the kitchen framing was unplastered and whitewashed and its floor level was several steps lower than the upper part.

During the occupancy of William Woodall, an east extension was added continuing the line of the cornice and gambrel roof. Its facade had a door on the west and window on the east with two dormers above. In the east gable there was another chimney stack. The foundation of this section was built without basement and butted up to the older part of the house.

In its original form, the doors led to a corridor from front to back, off of which there was a parlor on the east and the old room on the west. Instead of installing a stair in the central hall, as would be expected for this period, a second enclosed stair was built in the northeast corner of the new room which led to a corridor and two chambers. (An attempt at more privacy over the old section.)

William Woodall died in 1845 and left the farm to his son Jesse.[2] His neighbor, Hezekiah Masten, who lived north of New Market on another part of Vianna, was a witness to his will. After Jesse took over the farm, he bought additional acreage, thereby extending the boundaries from the Chestertown-Millington Road on the south to the Chesterville-Millington Road on the north. Jesse Woodall appears on the 1860 map.

Soon after the map was printed, Jesse died and the farm descended to his daughters, Sara and Mary. Mary bought Sara's share in 1865[3] and apparently later married a Pennington, for *"Mrs. Pennington"* appears on the 1877 Atlas. Mary Woodall Pennington's only heir was Sarah V. Moffett, who in turn had three heirs. Jesse Moffett bought the other two thirds in 1923[4] and the farm has remained in his family ever since.

The name, Big Marrowbone, by which it is known to the family, is probably derived from the fact that Pearly Moffett, Sarah's husband, owned Marrowbone the farm adjoining to the south. They used *big* and *little* to differentiate between the two farms, until Marrowbone was sold in the 1950s. This farm is one of about a half dozen that has remained in the same family for over 200 years in Kent County.

1. Wills, Lib. 8, fol. 120.
2. Wills, Lib. JFB 1, fol. 292.
3. Land Records, Lib. JKH 4, fol. 675.
4. Land Records, Lib. RRA 2, fol. 511.

K-181

Ryley's Beginning

Near Still Pond
c. 1790

WHEN THE HOUSE WAS BUILT ON RYLEY'S BEGINNING IN the late eighteenth century, it was a simple vernacular brick building, three bays long and two stories tall, built over a full basement, with a two-bay, one-story log kitchen wing on the west side. The door was originally in the central bay, flanked by two windows, and there were three windows placed symmetrically above. The house had three chimneys one on either end of the brick section (the west chimney later removed) and another at the western end of the kitchen. (The arch for the west chimney of the brick section remains in the basement, as does the finishing board which outlined the hearth on the first floor.) Basically, the plan was a hall-parlor with a one room kitchen.

Ryley's Beginning was originally a hall-parlor plan house, two stories tall with a central entry. It was remodeled in the late nineteenth century into a side passage plan. Marsha L. Fritz photograph, 1980.

The house appears to have remained unaltered until the late-19th century when the original A roof was replaced by a mansard. During the remodeling, the central entrance was bricked in and turned into a window and the west window was converted to an entrance. The plan was then changed to a stairhall and parlor on the first floor, with the old kitchen becoming the dining room. A new kitchen was added onto the back of the dining room and the whole addition became two stories. A porch was built across the brick section.

It remained essentially unchanged until the late 1970s when the old wing was replaced by a new one and a leanto was added off the north side of the brick section.

On both the 1860 map and the 1877 Atlas, the farm appears to have been in the possession of the John Wilson family.

K-215

Toll In Farm

Near Still Pond
c. 1790

Nᴏʀᴛʜ ᴏꜰ Sᴛɪʟʟ Pᴏɴᴅ, ᴛʜɪs ʟᴀᴛᴇ ᴇɪɢʜᴛᴇᴇɴᴛʜ ᴄᴇɴᴛᴜʀʏ, brick, farmhouse has seen many changes over its nearly 200 years of life. When first built, it was similar to many other Kent County farmhouses of the period. Its five-bay facade was constructed of Flemish bond brickwork above a champhered water table. The plan consisted of a central stair passage with two flanking rooms. The original size and height of its kitchen is unknown, but several other buildings in the area are known to have had two-story service wings, e.g. Maxwell's Purchase and Lavenham.

Toll In Farm is a typical late eighteenth century farmhouse built for a prosperous family, possibly one of the members of the Medford family. It was called Green Wood Farm in the 1870s. Marsha L. Fritz photograph, 1980.

The signs of a fire are discernible in the roof rafters. (This may have been the cause of the destruction of the kitchen wing.) After the fire, the exterior and interior finishes appear to have been replaced with *up-to-date* materials from the late nineteenth century. At that time, the cornice was replaced with a bracketed one of a Victorian Italianate nature. A wide porch was constructed across its facade.

On the two maps of Kent County which designate owners of various properties, G. M. Brooks is listed as owner in 1860 (Martenet), and T. Rasin, Sr. appears in 1877 (Lake, Griffing, Stevenson Atlas).   K-216

King's Grant Cottage

Near Fairlee
c. 1790

Oᴠᴇʀʟᴏᴏᴋɪɴɢ ᴛʜᴇ ʜᴇᴀᴅᴡᴀᴛᴇʀs ᴏꜰ Wᴏʀᴛᴏɴ Cʀᴇᴇᴋ, ᴏɴ part of the original Great Oak Manor, King's Grant Cottage is a two-and-a-half story, three-bay, brick house. It is nearly contemporary with its neighbor, the Hosier Farm and has some features in common. King's Grant Cottage, however, has suffered the misfortune of remodelings which have left few original features. The central stair is a close string affair with turned newels, rectangular balusters and a paneled spandrel. Original 12/8 sash remain in the second story windows. The first story would have originally had 12/12 sash.

The principal facade of the building faces Worton Creek, to the east, and is laid in Flemish bond in contrast to the common bond elsewhere. A cheaply constructed one-story wing was added to the south gable of the building in the twentieth century; at the same time two huge shed dormers were added to the main roof.

On the 1852 Tax Assessment this farm is listed under the ownership of Anthony Bell with the following information:

> *"Pt. Great Oak Manor Brick House & other Buildings in tolerable repair, formerly to Philip Reybold."*

"A. Bell" is also indicated as owner in the 1877 Atlas.   K-238

King's Grant Cottage, Great Oak Manor. This c. 1790 brick farmhouse was similar to the neighboring Hosier farmhouse. It has had insensitive additions built onto it during the twentieth century. Gene Johnstone photograph, 1997.

Miller's Purchase

Near Rock Hall
c. 1790

Miller's PURCHASE WAS A 900 ACRE TRACT FIRST ACQUIRED by THE Miller family in the seventeenth century.[1] Starting with Michael Miller I, the property remained in the family's ownership over the next three generations. The house in question was constructed by Thomas Miller in the late eighteenth century.

Miller's Purchase, in its original form was a three-bay, one-and-a-half-story, well-constructed frame house. Erected over a tall brick basement, the gables were also built of brick laid in Flemish bond, but only to the height of the second floor where they turn to frame. The large windows of the south facade have 12/12 sash, while those on the north have 9/9 and the central door has a rectangular transom. A two-room kitchen wing of nearly equal size exists on the west side of the building. And while it is of some age, it is most likely a nineteenth century replacement of an earlier structure. At present, two double shed dormers pierce the *A* roof on each side of its slope. These replace earlier single dormers. In plan, the house would have been similar to Godlington Manor, the home of some distant cousins of the Millers.

Miller's Purchase. The rear windows are one pane narrower than the creek side windows. Double dormers were added to both sides of the roof in the early twentieth century. Michael Bourne photograph, 1995.

Miller's Purchase, c. 1790, was constructed by Thomas Miller on land his great grandfather had purchased in the seventeenth century. Its one-story brick east gable wall is only one of the unusual features of the hall-parlor plan house. Michael Bourne photograph, 1969.

Miller's Purchase. At the head of the northeast stair is a unique balustrade that has no equal in Kent County. Michael Bourne photograph, 1995

The plan consisted of a hall-parlor plan in the main section, and a pantry and kitchen in the kitchen wing. The hall was well-finished with an enclosed stair in the northeast corner, a fireplace with dentil-molded mantel and a closet to the south. This room had a dentil cornice which matched the mantel, and the windows and doors had crossetted trim. The millwork was similar to that at the Dunn House, River House and the Buck Chambers House, all in Chestertown, and all of which were constructed in the late eighteenth century. The remainder of the house while well-trimmed, is not exactly of the same caliber as the hall. The parlor and parlor chamber both had fireplaces, and like the east side, the chimney was constructed within the house.

The house probably remained in much the same condition throughout the nineteenth century, or at least throughout the Miller ownership, which continued to the third quarter of the century.

By 1877, the farm is denoted as the property of Wm. R. Jones in the Lake, Griffing, Stevenson Atlas. In the 1911 will of Richard W. Jones, the *"Thomas Miller Farm"* is listed as the residence of his grandson, Ringgold Jones, to whom he bequeathed the same.[2] Jones had owned two other farms across Swan Creek, one of which was Rosedale, his home farm. The Miller Farm remained the property of Ringgold and Nellie Jones until sold by their trustee in 1973[3] Since then, the farm has been known as Heatherfield.

K-261

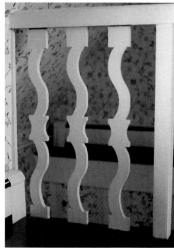

1. Wills, Lib. 1, fol. 57.
2. Wills, Lib. JEM 1, fol. 475.
3. Land Records, Lib. EHP 50, fol. 289.

Koppelman Farm

Near Kennedyville
c. 1790

THE KOPPELMAN FARM, NORTH OF KENNEDYVILLE, IS A frame, gambrel roof farmhouse, the first part of which dates back to the late eighteenth century and the other, larger part to 1926. When the latter three-story structure was constructed, the old kitchen was removed and the former hall-parlor plan house was converted into what would be the kitchen and dining room. In 1926, and in subsequent remodelings, original features in the hall and parlor were removed, however, the second floor plan was left intact.

That plan contains a unique feature in that the stair is located between the fireplace and the original exterior gable. Placing it in this location, rather than in the corner results in a stair without winder steps and makes the ascent to the corridor and three bedrooms above easier.

On the second floor, the corridor and one small bedroom are located on the west side of the house. A medium size chamber is located in the southeast corner and the largest of the three is adjacent to the corridor and stair and retains remnants of the old fireplace that heated the room. All of the interior partitions are vertical beaded boards and the doors are board and batten. Those board walls still carry a whitewash finish, the only finish that they have had.

In 1926, the three-story addition was built on the south side of the old gambrel roof house. It dwarfed the original structure. This newer structure has some features associated with the late nineteenth century Colonial Revival and shingle styles. There are a pair of two-story bay windows which terminate in a gambrel roof, dormer-like projection from the side of the larger gambrel roof. The plan of this early twentieth century building includes a stair/entry hall and two parlors with interior corner fireplaces. The plan is similar to 103 South Queen Street in Chestertown, a late nineteenth century townhouse.

In the 1877 Atlas, the farm is owned by George W. T. Perkins, who lived at 201 Water Street, Chestertown. It was undoubtedly tenanted at the time, which is probably the reason that the second story is still intact.   K-392

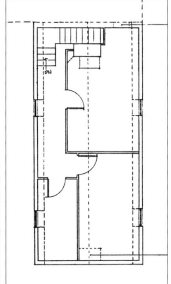

Koppelman Farm has an early gambrel roof wing on the north side of the 1926 house. Marsha L. Fritz photograph, 1980.

Koppelman Farm. Second floor plan of early wing, a unique placement for the stair. Marsha L. Fritz, 1980.

Tilghman House Site

High Street, Chestertown
c. 1790

The Tilghman House was built in the late 1790s. While it is unclear if it was constructed by William Slubey, William Baker, or William Burneston (all merchants), it is documented that between 1801 and 1824 Burneston and his wife (later widow) lived in the house on Lot No. 78. He also owned a storehouse on the corner of High and Princess Streets (Lot No. 79).[1]

In 1825, a deed recording the transfer of the property to Matthew Tilghman was recorded with a sale price of $2410.00.[2] Son of Richard Tilghman IV (d. 1805) and his wife, Margaret, Tilghman was a merchant in Chestertown, as well as a member of the legislature in 1815. Tilghman was twice married, the second time to Harriett Hynson, daughter of Richard and Araminta Hynson. Together they had nine children, one of whom was born after his death in 1828.[3] Tilghman's wife lived at the house until her death c. 1870.

After Harriett Tilghman's death, her real estate was advertised for sale in the Kent County News of 21 November 1874:

"Town Property
at Trustee's Sale
Large and Valuable
Brick Dwelling House
formerly the residence of Mrs. Harriett Tilghman and the lot there to attached situated on High Street in Chestertown near the Bank. The Dwelling is two stories in height with basement kitchen and servants rooms, and a well plastered attic which makes comfortable sleeping apartments. The house is well built, roomy and in very fair condition. Its central and convenient location makes it desirable either for a private residence or boarding house, in which capacity it is now used.
The lot attached affords ample space for gardening purposes and as such is a valuable appendage to the house.
C. T. Westcott, trustee"[4]

From the description of the basement rooms in the advertisement and from the scale of the building on the 1908 Sanborne Insurance Map, the house appears to have resembled River House.

The Reverend Samuel W. Thomas, Methodist minister, living in Philadelphia, purchased the building in 1876, and subsequently turned the first floor into commercial space.[5] In the process, he probably dropped the floor level so that it was convenient to the sidewalk as the old photographs show tall store front windows. The building served commercial purposes until it was acquired by the Chestertown Bank of Maryland, after which time it was demolished and replaced with the Beaux Arts style bank in 1929.   K-504

Tilghman House, Chestertown, is so named for a later owner, Matthew, son of Richard Tilghman IV, who purchased it in 1824. It is unclear from the land records if the house was built by William Slubey, William Baker or William Burneston, all merchants, including Tilghman. Kent County News Collection, c. 1929.

1. The two half lots were initially purchased in 1726 by James Cruikshank, Chirurgeon (Lib. JSP, fol. 23). Cruikshank's heirs sold the property in 1777 to William Slubey, merchant (Lib. DD 5, fol. 209). Slubey sold the same property in 1795, for about eight times what he had paid in 1777 to William Baker and William Burneston (Lib. BC 4, fol. 275). Slubey was probably the builder of the house. The following year he purchased the Custom House. Burneston bought Baker's interest in 1801 (Lib. W 1, fol. 670).
2. Land Records, Lib. TW 4, fol. 629.
3. G. A. Hanson, Old Kent, reprint, 1936.
4. Kent News, 21 November 1874.
5. Land Records, Lib. DCB 2, fol. 156.

Standaway

Near Rock Hall
c. 1790

For the past two generations this house has been referred to as the Jacquette House and has been owned in conjunction with the Shipyard Farm on the east side of Route 20 and Shipyard Creek.

Between 1882 and 1947 the two parcels were the property of Columbus Leary and his descendants. Well known in Rock Hall, the Leary family owned and operated the saw mill and basket manufacturing business at Greys Inn Wharf and George Leary was pastor at M. E. Church in the 1870s.

On the 1860 Martenet Map, W. B. Everett is listed as the owner of the property, and in the 1852 Tax Assessment, Mrs. Henrietta Everett was taxed on 161 acres of *"Stan(a)way"* and 25 acres of *"Gresham's Levels."* A *"Brick House & other Buildings in Tolerable repair"* were listed and the whole appraised for $5022.00.[1]

The house, that was then occupied by Mrs. Everett, was at that time about 60–70 years old. It may have been the home of one of the Hynson family, for there is mention of Standaway in Mary Hynson's will of 1807, where she bequeaths it and part of Arcadia to her son Ringgold Hynson.

The form of the house is similar to other buildings in the area, specifically, Rosedale, Greys Inn Point and to some extent, Bungay. Like the last two, the plan consists of a central stairhall with one room on either side and a service wing of two rooms. Its woodwork is well-executed, beginning with the paneled front door with paneled door jambs and transom, and continuing into the stairhall. The stair has a three-run, open-string

Standaway, near Rock Hall. "Stan(a)way" was owned in 1852 by Mrs. Henrietta Everett and the "Brick House & other Buildings" were listed in "Tolerable repair" in the tax assessment. The house had been built about sixty years earlier. Gene Johnstone photograph, 1995.

balustrade with delicately turned newels, square balusters and turned drop finials at the bottom of the upper newels. On one side of the stairhall, the room has recessed panel dado and a mantel with crossetted trim and a shelf supported on small consoles. To the right, the mantel is slightly more refined, with dentil molding added. The house contains many original features typical of late eighteenth century vernacular interpretation of Federal period trim.   K-492

1. Land Records, Lib. EF 7, fol. 286.
2. Land Records, Lib. TW 2, fol. 97.
3. Land Records, Lib. BC 5, fol. 374.
4. Land Records, Lib. WS 3, fol. 425.

Grey's Inn Point Farm

Piney Neck, Rock Hall
c. 1790

Grey's Inn Point Farm is significant in two respects. First, it is situated on part of what is possibly the earliest land patent in present day Kent County, and second, because it possesses the late-eighteenth century farmhouse built by Thomas Gresham and in which three generations of Greshams lived.

Grey's Inn Point Farm. The original Flemish bond facade had been partly concealed by a 1920s wing. It was restored during the 1980s remodeling and enlargement. Michael Bourne photograph, 1996.

In 1658, a 1500 acre tract was granted to John Langford by Lord Baltimore. Possibly this was an expression of gratitude for Langford's treatise, in defense of Baltimore, in response to the Puritans views on Baltimore's position in the Colonies.

A large section (1040 acres) of the tract was resurveyed in 1735 for John Smithers who later sold parcels to Slippers, Hanson, and Gresham. In 1748, Richard Gresham, who lived at Gresham Hall on the bayside, advertised in the Maryland Gazette. The advertisement spoke of the baking business operated by William Ossen at Gresham's plantation which was described as being on *"Grasing Creek, near the mouth of the Chester River."*[1] This would have been the eighteenth century equivalent of food services which provide goods for public transportation today.

Richard Gresham died in 1773 and bequeathed *"Grazen Point"* and the remainder of Langford's Neck (as his parcel was called) to Thomas Gresham, *"son of Sophia Whalon, dec'd and grandson of Edward Whalon, living, all of Langford's Neck."*[2] Thomas Smyth, Gresham's son-in-law was the executor of the estate.

After Thomas Gresham came of age in the 1790s, he built the brick house which remains on the land. He died in 1814 and left the farm to his son, Thomas P. Gresham, *"the natural son of Susanna Wharton ... ."* (a second generation of illegitimacy).[3]

Grey's Inn Point Farm, c. 1790, was built for Thomas Gresham on part of the 1658 patent of Langfords Neck. It remained in the family until 1881, at which time the house was extensively remodeled. Michael Bourne photograph, 1982.

Grey's Inn Point Farm. The south gable was built with windows flanking the chimney to take advantage of the sun and the view to Grey's Inn Creek. Michael Bourne photograph, 1996.

Gresham's house was a three-bay, two-story brick structure with frame kitchen wing laid in Flemish bond, its principal facade facing east to the Chester River. The central entry door had a rectangular transom which lined up with the tops of the flanking 12/12 sash windows. Three symmetrically placed windows on the second floor had 12/8 sash. There were no dormers originally. The west facade was similar with the exception of the central bay which was off-center and its door lacked a transom. Basement windows on both facades had horizontal bars in front of the sash. The south gable, which faced Greys Inn Creek, had windows flanking the chimney on each level, with 9/9, 9/6 and four-pane casements respectively. The cornice had bold crown and bed moldings.

In its original state, the brick section had a central hall from which the stair ascended to the second floor. The stair itself had three separate runs, with the middle section being adjacent to the west wall. The balustrade was walnut. Flanking the hall there were two rooms,

each with tall mantels, splayed, un-paneled window jambs, chair rail and baseboard.

The second floor was similar, but the fireplaces were off-center and there was also a small room at the head of the stair. From this level, the stair to the attic rose three steps before being enclosed for the remainder of the flight.

The original kitchen was built on the northernmost gable of the house. No other building remains from the Gresham period other than a small plank smokehouse, covered with vertical boards.

In the 1852 Tax Assessment, Thomas P. Gresham is listed as *"farmer"* and his properties included *"pt Greys Inn & Langford Neck 485 acres Brick House & other Buildings in Bad Repair ... ."* His total worth at that time was assessed at $9,910.00, a modest fortune.[4] When he died in 1865, Gresham left everything to his wife Ann, for her widowhood.[5] After Ann's death, the estate was settled in an equity case between their children (1873). Consequently, the farm was sold to Edwin R. Hoffman of Baltimore in 1881.[6] In 1906 Mr. Hoffman bequeathed the farm to his nephew's wife, Rose Strong. For nearly 100 years, the Hoffmans and Strong family remained in possession of at least half of the original purchase.

During the Hoffman period, the house was remodeled extensively, with the addition of porches on both facades, dormers on the roof and a new kitchen wing, one and a half stories in height. The stair was rebuilt in the hall going in the opposite direction from the original. This necessitated changing the door to the living room to the west side. The stair to the attic remained in the same location, but the enclosure was removed. Only the window trim in the living room remained untouched; all other was renewed, including doors, mantels, etc.

The kitchen was built at the same level as the main house, over a full basement which had its own fireplace. The first floor plan of this part consisted of a kitchen, pantry and corridor with stairs to the separated rooms above the kitchen and pantry.

Around 1920, a wing was attached to the original front of the house. It contained a gun room on the first floor and a communal bathroom on the second, accessible from the landing. During this period part of the house was used as a lodge for a gun club.

In 1982, Grey's Inn Point Farm was purchased by the present owners who undertook the rehabilitation of the old brick house and construction of a new wing.[7,8]   K-537

1. Maryland Gazette, 30 November 1748.
2. Wills, Lib. 5, fol. 105.
3. Wills, Lib. 9, fol. 264.
4. Kent County Tax Assessment, 1st District, 1852.
5. Wills, Lib. JF 1, fol. 291.
6. Land Records, Lib. JF 1, fol. 291.
7. Land Records, Lib. EHP 131, fol. 251.
8. For more information on the history of Langford Neck, see K-268, Belle View.

Airy Hill

Near Chestertown
c. 1790

Airy Hill stands on a small rise of ground on a tract surveyed for Simon Wilmer in 1688 called Kemp's Beginning.[1] Broken up into several parcels in the early eighteenth century, there are a number of properties today which contain sections of the original tract.

By the mid-eighteenth century, a major part of Kemp's Beginning had been reassembled by Joseph Garnett, a saddler, who had lived in Chester Town.[2] Upon his death in 1758, the farm descended to his son, Joseph Jr., who is referred to as a farmer in subsequent deeds.[3] After the Revolution, Joseph, like so many of his contemporaries, had financial difficulties and, in order to pay the creditors, he sold 167½ acres of Kemp's Beginning to John and Anna Maria Rowles.[4] He kept the land with the house that his father had built, the only house listed on the 1783 Tax Assessment.

John Rowles was also listed on the Tax Assessment of 1783 as an able bodied male living on the Bay Side. Anna Maria was either living with her father, James Frisby, at his new house Hinchingham or at the Violet Farm, the older house he and Anna Maria's mother had built near St. Paul's Church.

It is apparent from the records that Anna Maria was well connected and had a small fortune of her own, as she was an heir to her uncle James and mother, Rebecca, both Ringgolds, siblings of Thomas Ringgold (d. 1772) of Chestertown. After purchasing the farm, John Rowles appointed Thomas Anderson trustee of the property for his wife's benefit.[5] Soon after purchasing the land, they began constructing what would become one of the finest Federal style houses in Kent County.

Airy Hill is composed of two seemingly distinct sections, a five-bay, one-and-a-half-story, frame wing and a three-bay, two-story, brick, Federal style main section. Traditionally, the frame wing was thought to have been built early in the eighteenth century, and examination of the structure revealed that it was constructed in two sections, the land records indicate that

Airy Hill was built by John and Anna Maria Rowles soon after acquiring part of Kemp's Beginning in 1790. They began by constructing the first half of the frame section followed by the remainder of the building. Library of Congress, Historic Americn Buildings Survey, 1936

Airy Hill. The doric architrave is one of the most developed in the county. C. Engstrom photograph, 1977.

Airy Hill. The back (south) side of the building lacks the architectural elements of the north and west sides. The contemporary smokehouse is the only original outbuilding remaining. Maria Boria photograph, 1996.pb.

the same time, as it is bonded into the brickwork of the taller brick portion.

The main brick house is a large (35' x 32'), two-story structure built over a full basement. Its principal facade (north) has a well-designed Doric architrave around the wide, six-panel entrance door which has a rectangular transom. Each of the five windows of the facade have wooden rusticated jack arches, 6/6 sash and louvered blinds. The basement windows originally had the same type arches, but they were replaced with plain brickwork after having rotted. The cornice has well-executed modillion blocks and bold moldings. The north and west sides of the building are laid in Flemish bond with molded water table and a three-course belt course, the latter painted white to resemble stone. The west facade windows are treated like those of the north facade, but the rear or south facade is devoid of ornamentation.

Airy Hill's plan consists of a large side hall and two parlors to the west. The delicate stair ascends along the east wall to a landing and then to the second story balcony. It is situated so the second flight divides the hall visually into a front and back hall. The balustrade consists of turned column newels with a handrail that ascends up and over each intermediate newel. An engaged half-rail and half-newels mirror the balustrade along the walls. A delicate double-ogee fret design decorates the open-string step ends. The wall plane created by the spandrel continues on the same plane to the rear wall, creating space for two closets and headroom for the basement entrance below. The stair ascends to the second floor in such a way as to leave enough space for a small room over both the front and back halls beside two rooms over the parlors. This creates a grand stairwell that is finished on the third floor with an arched ceiling.

When the north parlor was completed, it boasted a superior Federal mantel with fluted pilasters and decorative swags in the frieze. The south parlor was similar, but both were removed to the Wickes House in the early twentieth century. In their place are other mantels of similar period, but less sophisticated in design.[6] A cabinet was built-in left of the north parlor fireplace and a small cubby hole was fitted into the right cheek of the chimney. Like many Federal houses, the windows had panels beneath them which were recessed into the depth of the brick wall. The chair rail, with its gouge and drill hole design of flutes and swags, forms the base on which the window trim rests. Paneled shutters are folded into the window jambs. A boldly molded baseboard and a dentil cornice, similar to those on the first story of River House, complete the room.

A wide opening with double doors was installed with the same crosettes as the hall doors, but the moldings are a little later than the originals. The south parlor was well-finished, and the chair rail has fretwork design.

there were no houses on the property except the Garnett house, listed in the tax assessment of 1783.

It is a possibility that the older section of the wing was constructed initially as a temporary residence for the young couple, John and Anna Maria Rowles. That section appears to have been divided into two rooms with a stair to the attic between. The newer section of the wing is contemporary with the brick section of the house, as it possesses only two framed walls which extend from the kitchen to the brick section. Moreover, the chimney which serves the two rooms of this section was clearly built at

Like the north parlor, the north chamber is the better of the two rooms on the second floor. Across the chimney breast is a wall of raised paneling with slightly later mantel supported on fluted plinths with gouge work frieze. When the mantel was installed, the fireplace was filled in and an iron stove plate bearing the date 1769 was inserted. Both parlor chambers were finished with two closets flanking the chimneys. The inner closets were originally fitted with shelves, but the outer closets had pegs on which to hang clothing. Each of the latter also contained a full-size window. Like the rooms below, the windows have shutters folded into the jambs. Chair rail and baseboard are simpler than those on the first floor.

Both smaller rooms had a vertical board wall inside, with the outside being plastered. Without fireplaces, the rooms were devoid of a focal point. The south room

has been converted into a bath and the north room into a sewing room. The north room has always had access to the west room of the wing via a small batten door.

When the house was completed, the two rooms in the kitchen were converted to one and a stair was built in the northeast corner, adjacent to the broad cooking fireplace with its wooden lintel. The fenestration of the frame wing was made into a nearly symmetrical five-bay arrangement with central door (with transom) and three dormers above. The door actually opened into the corner of the old kitchen, so a vestibule of vertical boards was built to screen it from the kitchen. Doors then opened into the two flanking rooms. The ceiling joists were always exposed, but the vestibule was ceiled with plaster. There is one small step up into the middle room.

The middle room was probably the last to be finished and may be contemporary with the double doors between the parlors. It was finished with beaded board enclosure around the chimney breast, with stair in the southwest corner, and cabinets on the north cheek. There were chair rails and baseboard. Like the rest of the house, the flooring was yellow pine. Both this room and the kitchen opened onto a back porch from which there was access to the basement.

Above the middle room there was a corridor and two rooms, one with a fireplace. The partitions were like the beaded enclosure below. There was a third room over the kitchen which was not accessible except from the kitchen. This original arrangement has been altered, by the previous and present owners, into two bedrooms with bath and passage between.

From the time it was finished, Airy Hill must have been considered a very desirable farm. Two years after John Rowles' death in 1802, Anna Maria sold the farm to a remote cousin, Samuel

Detail of double ogee fret on step ends.

Airy Hill. The stair ascends near the center of the house, enabling there to be four rooms on the second story rather than the usual three. Library of Congress, Historic Buildings Survey, 1936.

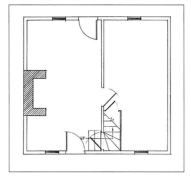

Airy Hill. First and second floor plans, as originally completed. Michael Bourne, 1995.

Airy Hill. With the exception of the Somerset County mantel, the remainder of the trim is original to the north parlor. Michael Bourne photograph, 1994.

Airy Hill. Conjectural plan of the first section of the house. The stair and partition were later removed, creating the existing kitchen. Michael Bourne, 1995.

Ringgold for three-and-a-half times what she and her husband had paid for it in 1790.[7] It is not likely that he lived at Airy Hill, as Rose Hill was his principal residence. He sold the farm in 1813 to Jonathan Harris,[8] who was then residing there. But Harris sold it the following year to James Houston, one of the leading attorneys of Chestertown and later Judge of the United States District Court for Maryland.[9]

The Houstons most likely resided both at Airy Hill and at their residence in Chestertown on Queen Street. This was a common practice for the period. After his untimely death in 1817, Airy Hill was sold to Thomas Worrell.

Worrell had been Clerk of the Court and during his ownership of Airy Hill he was Sheriff of Kent County and Judge of the Orphans Court. He also owned property on Piney Neck and Eastern Neck Island, so it is not known if he resided at Airy Hill, in town or on his other properties. He however defaulted on his loan, then died intestate, so the farm was sold by order of the Court. It was actually sold in 1827, but the deed was not recorded until 1834.[10] George W. Thomas was the purchaser.

When George Thomas and Mary Letherbury were married in 1804 or 1805, they were living at River House and advertised that they were interested in either selling or exchanging River House for a fine farm. Their search took over twenty years, but by that time, they no longer needed to sell their residence in town. They

kept both River House and Airy Hill and like the Houstons, resided in both. The Thomases became so fond of Airy Hill that it was there that they wanted their remains to be buried.

Since the Thomases had no children, Mary bequeathed Airy Hill to her cousin Joseph Wickes (d. 1864), who lived up the street in town and who owned Piners Grove close to Airy Hill.[11] The farm remained in the Wickes family until the early 1920s, when it was sold to Henry S. deFord.[12]

During the ownership of Mr. deFord, the kitchen wing deteriorated to such an extent that it appeared to be collapsing according to its next owner, Elizabeth Sterling. Mrs. Sterling depicted the end of the kitchen in a state of disrepair, in a sketch she made prior to settlement.[13] The Sterlings began the process of preserving Airy Hill, which has been carried on since by each subsequent owner.[14]   K-94

1. Patents, Lib. NS No. B, fol. 522.
2. Land Records, Lib. JS 25, fol. 216; Provincial Court Records, Lib. EI 8, fol. 422; Land Records, Lib. JS 27, fol. 16.
3. Wills, Lib. 4, fol. 52.
4. Land Records, Lib. BC 3, fol. 28.
5. Land Records, Lib. BC 3, fol. 137.
6. In her unpublished memoires, 1877 to 1934, Susan Emily Massey Brooks made an entry for November 6, 1920 (page 24) in which she states:
" ... Miss Luiton, of Georgia came to see records, Mrs. Wickes asked her to go thru the old Judge Wickes house, showed her the moulding around the Judge's study and two mantles she had taken from the Airy Hill Farm,

she had changed the front door and put two french windows on the river side of the house ... ." Jane Brooks Sprinkle Collection.
7. Land Records, Lib. TW 3, fol. 194.
8. Land Records, Lib. BC 7, fol. 278.
9. Land Records, Lib. BC 7, fol. 513.
10. Land Records, Lib. JNG 3, fol. 359. This deed mentions the previous sales, but gives no references to the court records.
11. Wills, Lib. JFB 1, fol. 305.
12. Land Records, Lib. RRA 1, fol. 434.
13. Land Records, Lib. RAS 12, fol. 488.
14. For more detail see "Airy Hill," a publication by Michael Bourne and Dr. James J. Berna, 1996.

Mount Herman

Near Chesterville
c. 1794

O N THE 28TH OF APRIL 1730, *"CHEAPSIDE,"* AN 890 ACRE parcel extending to the Chester River was resurveyed under the new name of *"Mount Herman"* for William Thomas.[1] It was patented on the 1st of September 1732. From that time until 1919, the farm remained in the Thomas family.

According to family tradition, the present house was built for William and Elizabeth Thomas in 1794-95. The details of the house certainly suggest the same general date, since the cornice is similar to Knocks Folly and Airy Hill, both built in the 1790s. Like those two houses, the central entrance of the five bay facade was originally designed for a pedimented architrave, although the existing architrave is a naive copy of the original. Its original might have been similar to either of the above or that of Thornton, only a few miles to the west. Like Thornton, the service wing is set back from the plane of the facade, leaving enough space for a porch, but here, the service wing is two stories tall.

Mr. Thomas' floor plan consists of a central stairhall with two flanking rooms and a one room kitchen in the wing, similar to the plan of The Adventure. Interior details are similar to Thornton and Rich Level, both of which were built in the same period.

William Thomas, for whom the house was built in 1794-95, died in 1808. The farm descended to his son William, who in 1822, was taxed on 565¾ acres composed of the following:

Part Killingsworthmore	*105 acres*
Mothers Plains	*75 acres*
Kilherrins	*1¾ acres*
Pt. Harman	*143 acres*
Pt. Ratlif	*241 acres[2]*

In 1860 the property was owned by Miss E. Thomas, and in the 1877 Atlas, by her heirs. In the latter, it was listed as the residence of C. L. Wallis, apparently the nephew of Miss Thomas. In 1919, the property was sold out of the family and deteriorated for a number of years before being rehabilitated by the present owners.

Mount Herman is the best example of a Federal style farmhouse in the Chesterville area.   K-189

1. Rent Rolls, Lib. 5, fol. 122.
2. 1822 Tax Assessment.

Mt. Herman, near Chesterville was built for William and Elizabeth Thomas in 1794. Some of the details of this farmhouse are similar to Airy Hill. Margaret A. Fallaw photograph, 1985

The Anderson-Aldridge House

Water Street, Chestertown c. 1795

IN THE MID 1790s, THOMAS ANDERSON purchased part of Water Lot No. 13 and all of Water Lots Nos. 14 and 15. On Water Lot No. 14 he built a fine brick residence, two and a half stories tall, laid in Flemish bond with molded water table and three-brick string course.

Anderson's house was similar to those located at 110 and 115 Water Street in plan (central stairhall with rooms on either side). Like 115 Water Street it is built high enough to have the basement open at grade level on the river side. In all these houses, the kitchens were located originally in the basement. On the second story an original back door remains, evidence of a former river side porch like that documented to have existed at the Custom House. Such a porch would have provided an open air shaded work place at ground level near the kitchen.

In the early nineteenth century Dr. Morgan Brown acquired the property.[1] Dr. Brown also owned the Violet Farm near Old St. Paul's Church, Fairlee, but used the Water Street house as his town home in winter months.

The house survived with few known changes for nearly eighty years and through six owners until it was purchased by John K. Aldridge in 1876.[2] Aldridge gutted the house, removed the A roof and raised the roof to form a full third story which he covered with a shallow-pitched tin roof. He added a two-story brick kitchen wing on the northeast side and a two-story porch on the river side. He then decorated the windows with cornices and added a flat roofed front entrance. On the southwest gable Aldridge added a two-story oriel window

The Anderson-Aldridge House, Chestertown, built in 1795 by Thomas Anderson. It was originally a two-story building above a basement kitchen. In 1876 John Aldridge remodeled, heightened and enlarged the house, covering the whole with scored stucco to resemble ashlar masonry. Michael C. Wootton photograph, 1996.

The Anderson-Aldridge House. The two-story bay window was installed c. 1876. Maryland Historical Trust.

decorated with fish scale shingles. The string course was cut back flush with the plane of the wall and then the entire structure was stuccoed and scored to resemble ashlar masonry. The interior was renewed with 1870s millwork, including stair, doors, trim and flooring on the first and second floors. Today, only the third floor retains original 1790s doors and trim.

In 1911, Wilbur W. Hubbard purchased Aldridge's property in order to acquire part of Water Lot No. 15 upon which he would construct a new kitchen wing to Widehall.[3] He subsequently sold the Aldridge House in 1920 with less land.[4] Since that time it has passed through eleven more owners.

In 1966 the stucco of the facade was removed revealing the old brickwork and in 1972 the interior was remodeled and updated.

K-11

1. Land Records, Lib. BC 5, fol. 378.
2. Land Records, Lib. JKH 2, fol. 13.
3. Land Records, Lib. JTD 23, fol. 351.
4. Land Records, Lib. APR 6, fol. 400.

McCay's Purchase

Galena
c. 1796

To the casual observer, Buttonwood appears to be a handsome Victorian house of the Civil War era. On closer examination, however, the brick core is actually the remains of a much earlier house—one of the earliest remaining in Galena today.

William Maxwell owned McCay's Purchase (as it was originally called) in the late eighteenth century and it was he, who sold off the first lots along the road from Georgetown Cross Roads to Chester Town in the 1790s.[1] In 1796, he sold the remaining 121½ acres to William Armstrong, a merchant from Chestertown.[2] According to family tradition, soon after his acquisition of McKay's Purchase, Armstrong moved his business to Georgetown Cross Roads.

The house which Armstrong built was a three-bay, two-story, brick structure with north facade laid in Flemish bond above an unmolded water table. Like most of the houses of the Federal period, the brick was fairly uniform in size and color on the main facade. There was a two brick belt course running between the first and second floor windows. Within each gable there was a brick chimney which serviced two fireplaces in each. The house, in its earliest form, was similar to Trulock near Still Pond.

William Armstrong's name appears on the 1822 Tax Assessment with properties consisting of 143½ acres, plus two lots appraised for a total of $1898.00. He owned three slaves and fifteen ounces of silver as well.[3] William Armstrong, Jr. was the next owner of the farm and after him, his son, John Medford Armstrong. It is the name of J. M. Armstrong which appears on the 1860 Martenet Map and in the 1877 Atlas as well.[4]

J. M. Armstrong was responsible for the major remodeling which converted the vernacular Federal farmhouse into an up-to-date Victorian *mansion* in the 1870s. In the process of remodeling, the house was totally gutted of its Federal woodwork. Windows and

doors were enlarged and a large frame wing was built on the south side of the house. Millwork of the period was installed, including a two-story, bay window similar to the one installed by J. K. Aldridge on his house next to Widehall in Chestertown. Gables were built in the center of both the brick house roof and the new wing. In many respects, the house was more completely remodeled than Montebello (now called Duck Hollow) in Georgetown, where the majority of its interior was left intact.

In the backyard, a fenced area contains the remains of the Armstrong family and several gravestones.   K-151

McKay's Purchase, Galena, is the earliest remaining brick house in Galena, having been built in the late 1790s by William Armstrong. He was a merchant who had operated in Chestertown before moving his business to Georgetown Crossroads. Historical Society of Kent County, postcard collection.

McCay's Purchase (Buttonwood), Galena, was built by William Armstrong soon after buying the farm from William Maxwell in 1796. The Gothic remodeling was undertaken late in the nineteenth century, at about the same time as Montebello was remodeled. Gene Johnstone photograph, 1997.

McCay's Purchase, Galena. The west gable has original size windows on the old brick walls. Note the use of string course at second floor level. Gene Johnstone photograph, 1997.

1. Land Records, Lib. DD 5, fol. 341.
2. Land Records, Lib. BC 4, fol. 502.
3. Kent County Tax Assessment, 1st District, 1822.
4. Martenet Map, 1860; Lake Griffing Stevenson Atlas, 1877.

Knocks Folly

Turner's Creek
c. 1796

K NOCKS FOLLY AT TURNER'S CREEK IS AN UNUSUAL COM-
bination of a mid-eighteenth century log building
and a turn of the nineteenth century Federal
brick townhouse. The one-and-a-half stories and steeply pitched A roof with leanto porch of the early vernacular structure
contrasts dramatically with the narrow
verticality of the three story Federal style
building. This difference is a reflection of
the economic condition and social status
of the two men who built the structures.

*Knock's Folly. The plank
house was built around
1760; the brick section
was begun in 1796 by
Donaldson and Mary
Yeates. Michael C. Woot-
ton photograph, 1995*

*Knock's Folly, Turners
Creek, suffered a devas-
tating fire in 1977, de-
stroying part of the plank
structure. Preservation
Inc. photograph, 1977.*

When Donaldson Yeates purchased
this property in the 1770s, the log building was standing at that time.[1] Its appearance was considerably different
than it is at present. The 25 by 30½ foot
building was covered with beaded
shiplap on the exterior and the door was

short and all other openings were windows. No dormers existed on the roof, but there was a single window
in each gable. Its interior consisted of two long narrow
rooms, heated by back-to-back fireplaces in a chimney
slightly west of center. The south room was a kitchen
and had exposed whitewashed plank walls and beaded
ceiling joists. The north room walls were sheathed with
vertical beaded boards and had exposed beaded joists.
East of the fireplace was a stair to the second floor
which had similarly shaped rooms. Their fireplaces had
arched heads and back-set fireboxes like those found at
Rich Hill, Partner's Addition, and other buildings which
date from the 1760 period.

Yeates is believed to have lived in the house closer to the landing, simply referred to as the Yeates House. Its interior was better finished than the log house on the hill and it was closer to the landing and the storehouse.

In the 1783 Tax Assessment for Kent County, Donaldson Yeates had 1792½ acres and 56 slaves. There were 60 white inhabitants living on his lands, including the settlement at Turners Creek. He died in 1796, by then a resident of Kent County, and left his three sons their choice of the different properties he owned.[2] George Yeates, his eldest son, chose to take possession of his father's land in Kent County, including Knocks Folly. A statement in the supplement to the will indicates that the construction of the brick wing of Knocks Folly was initiated by him and probably completed by his wife, Mary, after his death. In this supplement he wrote,

"It is my Will and desire that the building that I am about projecting shall be fully finished and this be done at the expense of my Estate."[3]

The brick portion of the house is very significant, being a good example of Federal architecture with well executed detail. It was built about 14 feet forward of the old log house and on its north side. The entrance on the south side of the west facade had a fine architrave with fluted, entasized pilasters, paneled jambs, and a series of gaugework, rope, fluted and drill-hole carving beneath the semi-circular fanlight with swag muntins. There was a pediment as part of the architrave with the same refinement. The main cornice had shaped modillions and a facia consisting of gougework rosettes separated by vertical rows of drill-holes. The facade is laid in Flemish bond and the other sides in common. The sash decrease in height on the second and third floors, there being 12/12 on the first, 8/12 on the second and 8/8 on the third. Two chimneys centered on the gables give even more height to the tall house. The south chimney is decorative. Two small, four-pane casements flank the chimneys in the gables. The north gable wall also has two windows on each story, probably placed to take advantage of the superior view over Turner's Creek and the Sassafras River. The basement entrance is located on the east side of the building.

The interior of the Federal portion of the house is divided into stairhall and parlor. The stair ascends to the attic, commencing on the south wall to a landing extending across the east wall and a short flight on the inside (north) wall. The triangular wall enclosing the basement stair has three recessed panels. The stepends have wave like fretwork applied to the facia. The balustrade has turned newels, very thin, turned balusters, a natural finished poplar handrail over the newels and a half rail along the inside wall supported by fluted pilasters. The half rail is used as a chair rail in the stairhall only. A large window on the south wall with recessed paneled jambs lights the

Knock's Folly, Turners Creek. Detail of cornice on 1796 wing.

Knock's Folly, Turner's Creek. Perhaps the best federal architrave in Kent County. Michael C. Wootton photographs, 1995.

Knock's Folly, Turner's Creek. The original mantel in living room had tiny carved pineapples between dentils and egg, and dart carving around the paneled pilasters. It was stolen about 1973. M. Bourne photograph, c. 1970.

Knock's Folly, Turner's Creek. The stair was severely damaged in the 1977 fire, but restoration was undertaken through the efforts of the Kent County government with funding from the Maryland Historical Trust and the current curators, Mr. and Mrs. Jon Mullin. Michael C. Wootton photograph, 1995.

hall. Carved keystone and impost blocks add refinement to the arched door trim. Brass box locks were used on the first floor doors.

All six windows of the parlor have trim and jambs extending to the floor with raised panels beneath the windows. The mantel was the best in the building, having a series of small carved pineapples between dentils in the molding of the shelf, recessed panel pilasters boasting egg and dart molding around the panels, rows of flutes between the pilasters and shelf, and three blocks between, filled with gougework carving. Although the cornice of the room is bold, its gougework rosettes and flutes appear weak in comparison to the superior workmanship and profusion of detail on the mantel. The second story floor plan is identical to the first. The window jambs and trim rest at the chair rail and the mantel has a painted scene between the fluted plinth blocks. The third floor has three small rooms, each with closet except the east room which has two. Door and window trim is simpler than that of the first and second stories. In the attic there is an open space at the head of the stair and a partially finished storage area.

In 1807 George Yeates, then a merchant living in Baltimore deeded a half share in Knocks Folly to his cousin,[4] John Lath-

im of Kent County, as security in a business dealing. Five years later he sold the other half to Lathim's daughter,[5] Elizabeth Medford, who in turn left it to her daughter Hannah in her will of 1827.[6]

Hannah Medford married Peregrine Wethered shortly after her mother's death. The Wethereds were a well-known family in Kent County. Peregrine farmed the land on Turner's Creek, while maintaining close ties with his relatives and the business world in Baltimore. He died in 1858, and left his property at Turners Creek to his daughter Mary Elizabeth, later Mrs. William Janvier. In his will, the property is described as:

"consisting of the Granary, wharf, store house, dwelling houses, lots, gardens and all other out houses thereon with the brick Mansion House and all the lands,

houses, and appurtances thereto attached and belonging ... "[7]

Peregrine and Hannah Wethered were responsible for improving the house by installing dormers on the roof of the old log wing and remodeling the interior and installing the porch on the west side. They also had a large bookcase installed in the second story hall and filled it with books, many of which have descended to their progeny.

During the ownership of their daughter, Mary Wethered and her husband William Janvier, a porch with ogee tin roof was installed across the face of the brick portion. The interior paneled areas beneath the west windows were renewed with double doors for easy access between the porch and drawing room. At this period, all of the exterior woodwork was painted chocolate brown, even the new blinds that had been installed on all of the windows, including the dormers.

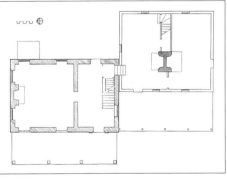

Knock's Folly, Turner's Creek, the second story mantel possesses a unique painting in the friese, perhaps Turner's Creek harbor.

Knock's Folly, Turner's Creek. First floor plan. M. Bourne.

Knock's Folly, Turner's Creek. Detail of porch brackets, c. 1870. Michael C. Wootton photographs, 1995.

The farm was left to Mrs. Janvier's nephew, Dr. J. L. Wethered upon her death in 1918.[8] From that point on the house was primarily used in the summertime. In 1947 it was bequeathed to his nephew L. Wethered Barroll, a lawyer in Baltimore and the son of Margaret Spencer Wethered and Hope H. Barroll of Byford Court, Chestertown.[9]

After Mr. Barroll's death the house and twenty acres were acquired by the County,[10] but in 1977, the house suffered a fire which destroyed half of the log wing, the stair and roof of the brick portion. All of the work has been duplicated and the exterior remains in good condition. The interior restoration is being carried on privately. The surrounding property is used as a county park.

Footnotes:
1. Land Records, Lib. DD 3, fol. 528.
2. Wills, Lib. 7, fol. 547.
3. Ibid.
4. Land Records, Lib. BC 5, fol. 16.
5. Land Records, Lib. BC 7, fol. 205.
6. Wills, Lib. 11, fol. 20.
7. Wills, Lib. JF 1, fol. 103.
8. Berringer, Brandon, Barroll, L. Wethered, *The Wethered Book*, Peterborough, New Hampshire; Richard Smith, Publishers, 1967.
9. Ibid.
10. Land Records, Lib. 60, fol. 1.

States Adventure

Near Kennedyville
1797

STATES ADVENTURE STANDS ACROSS THE HIGHWAY FROM Shrewsbury Protestant Episcopal Church. A large brick farm house, it is composed of two sections plus a one story frame wing. The house faces north, with a view of Shrewsbury Church in the distance.

The facade is five bays long and two and one half stories tall, laid in Flemish bond with both water table and string course. The wing facade is four bays long and two stories tall and is laid in the same manner as the principal section. The remainder is laid in common bond with less uniform brick, some glazed. In the west gable there is a date plaque with initials and the date 1797.

Like many of Kent's farmhouses, States Adventure has a central stairhall with flanking rooms. At the lower level of the wing there were originally two more rooms (now one large *country*

States Adventure, 1797, was built for Alexander Briscoe, possibly incorporating part of an earlier house in the service wing. The central hall house has superior woodwork with gouge carving, like Shepherds Delight. Michael C. Wootton photograph, 1996.

kitchen). The interior is noted for its fine Federal period carved woodwork, similar to Evergreen Farm. It also boasts some original marbleized baseboards, like Shepherd's Delight and Knock's Folly, all of which date from the same period.

In the deed to Lambert Wickes of Cecil County in 1816, the following reference points to the builder of the house:

"Whereas Alexander Briscoe formerly of Kent County … died seized of a tract of land lying in Kent County aforesaid called States Adventure granted to him by Patent dated the fourth day of December in the year of our Lord one thousand seven hundred ninety two … containing 277 acres … ."[1]

Alexander Briscoe's heirs sold the property to Lambert Wickes, but it is uncertain whether Wickes lived on the farm or remained in Cecil County. After his death, it descended to his daughters, one of whom sold her half to her sister and brother-in-law, Louise and Peregrine Wethered, not to be confused with Peregrine who owned Knock's Folly.[2]

Lewin Wethered, trustee of Peregrine Wethered's estate, sold it to Samuel Wethered of Baltimore (probably the son of Samuel) and he in turn sold it in 1847 to William Maxwell.[3] Maxwell sold the 277 acre farm to Margaret B. Polk, who had owned part of the Cadwalader farm down Shrewsbury Neck.[4] Mrs. Polk appears as owner on the 1860 Martenet Map, but by the time of the 1877 Atlas, she had willed it to her daughter. The Atlas actually lists the name of her son-in-law, C. Beaston, as owner.

From the time of the Briscoe ownership this house on States Adventure has been used more as a tenant house than a primary residence. It is most fortunate that the exquisite woodwork has survived.   K-138

1. Land Records, Lib. BC 8, fol. 514.
2. Land Records, Lib. JNG 11, fol. 520.
3. Ibid.
4. Land Records, Lib. JFG 1, fol. 501.

Ingleside Site

Eastern Neck Island
c. 1797

INGLESIDE WAS BUILT ON PART OF HYNSON'S DIVISION, THE name given to the northern half of Eastern Neck Island in 1680, at the time of the death of its owner, Thomas Hynson. From 1659 until that year, Hynson had owned the island in conjunction with Joseph Wickes. On the northern half, the earlier patents of Market Place and Elke Point were resurveyed and incorporated into Hynson's Division.

Hynson's Division remained in the Hynson family through several generations, until 320 acres were sold to John Stoops, a Cecil County farmer in 1771.[1] Three years later, Stoops sold the land in two parcels to Richard and Ann Jones (probably his daughter and son-in-law).[2] By 1783, Richard Jones had died and Ann had married again, this time to Charles Chambers.

Through a series of mortgages involving the estate of John Hynson, the final deed was recorded in 1796.[4] It is unclear from the records who was actually responsible for the construction of the house on the property in the 1790s, since David Jones, his mother, and his step-father were all listed as joint owners of the farm.

The house, built by either Jones or Chambers, was a substantial brick house, composed of two sections. The tall, three-bay, two-story section was built over a full basement, and had windows flanking the chimney stack on the west gable. The one-and-a-half-story wing was built close to ground level. Both sections measured about 20' x 28'. In form it was nearly identical to Rosedale, located north of Rock Hall. At some period in its development, a small shed-roof addition was constructed on the north side of the wing, creating a plan that was identical to Godlington Manor. At another time a frame section

was attached to the east end, but it was moved away after 1957.

When Charles Chambers died in 1801, there was no mention of real estate in his will. And, when David Jones died, there was no will.[5] In 1830, the Sheriff sold a half interest in the farm to Hiram Jones, since Jesse, David Jones' son, was bankrupt.[6] The second half interest in the farm was purchased from Jesse Jones' sister and niece in 1834.[7]

After Hiram Jones' death, the *Island Farm* as it had come to be known, was purchased by his son, David Jones.[8]

His name appears on both the 1860 Martenet Map and the 1877 Atlas.

In the twentieth century, the farm was owned by the Johnston and White families, who used the farm for a private gunning preserve. The property was acquired in the 1960s by the U. S. Government as part of the Eastern Neck Island Wildlife Preserve.   K-272

1. Land Records, Lib. DD 3, fol. 393.
2. Land Records, Lib. DD 4, fol. 317, 318.
3. Kent County Tax Assessment, Lower Langford and Eastern Neck Hundred, 1783.
4. Land Records, Lib. EF 7, fol. 73, 165; Lib. BC 4, fol. 385.
5. Wills, Lib. 8, fol. 99.
6. Land Records, Lib. JNG 2, fol. 254.
7. Land Records, Lib. JNG 3, fol. 503.
8. Land Records, Lib. JFG 4, fol. 93.

Moody Farm

Near Galena
c. 1798

ROBERT MOODY, RESIDENT OF CECIL COUNTY, PURCHASED the first portion of this farm in 1768. He continued to acquire small portions of the adjoining lands and by 1806 had amassed 331 acres.[1] In 1798 Moody had built the existing house. It is a three-bay, two-story brick

The Moody Farm, near Galena, also called the Cosden Murder Farm, was built in the last years of the eighteenth century for Robert Moody, a successful farmer. Its hall-parlor plan house originally had enclosed stairs in both rooms. In the early nineteenth century the stairs were removed and installed in the wing.

The Moody Farm. The south facade was laid in Flemish bond. This facade was intended to be the front. Michael Bourne photographs, 1996.

structure built above a high basement with a lower two-story, two-bay brick wing nearer the ground.

When constructed, the first story had 12/12 sash windows and the second story had 8/12. On a smaller scale, the kitchen had 6/6 and 3/6 respectively. The principal facade is laid in Flemish bond and faces south, away from the road, a puzzling arrangement since the road was in place before the house was built. Both facades had two doors and an extra window east of the three bays, allowing access to both interior rooms.

The principal rooms had enclosed stairs, adjacent to the fireplaces, leading to one room above each. At a very early date (c. 1820), the stairs were removed and replaced with cabinets that matched the original mill work. A new stair was constructed in the wing from which there was access to a new corri-

dor along the north wall. Both bedrooms are accessible from the corridor.

The finishes throughout the house are of good quality, design and workmanship. The mantels are similar to the Welch Farm, in the Second District, with recessed panel pilasters supporting a broken shelf with a course of gouge-carved flutes and swags.

In his earliest land transactions, Moody is referred to as a farmer, but prior to his death in 1815, when he acquired a third lot in Georgetown Cross Roads (Galena), he is referred to as gentleman. He was mentioned as principal grantee in 1802, when Cornelius Comegys sold one acre to the trustees of the Methodist Protestant Church.[2] The same lot was transferred to the Trustees of Olivet Chapel in 1808.[3] The church is located south of the crossroads.

Upon his death in 1815, the farm was bequeathed to his daughter, Sarah Elizabeth.[4] It was still listed, for tax purposes, in his estate in 1822. The 311 acres were composed of parts of Hangman's End, Hangman's Folly, Browning's Discovery and Partner's Addition and were appraised for $1400.00. The estate continued to hold a quarter-acre lot at Georgetown Cross Roads.[5]

The farm was later acquired by James F. Woodland who owned Woodland Hall. While owned by Woodland, the most brutal murder in the history of Kent County occurred in the house on February 27, 1851. Mr. William Cosden and his family were resting in front of the fire, when someone shot him from outside. The perpetrators then forced their way into the house, and shot Mrs. Cosden, her sister, Mr. Cosden's sister and a black servant. Recorded in the Kent County News, the story was repeated in the paper several of the following weeks.

At the time of Mr. Woodland's death, George Vickers was appointed trustee of his estate. The Moody farm was sold from the estate in 1878 to Dennis McCauley,[6] who later defaulted on his mortgage at which time, it was assumed by Carolene Hynson, more often associated with farms in the lower part of the county.

In 1898, she sold the Moody Farm or *Cosden Murder Farm* as it had come to be known, to James E. Hurlock, in whose family it remained until 1946.[7] Since that time, the farm has had six owners, many residing elsewhere.   K-154

1. Land Records, Lib. DD 3, fol. 75.
2. Land Records, Lib. TW 2, fol. 83.
3. Land Records, Lib. BC 5, fol. 234.
4. Wills, Lib. 9, fol. 293.
5. Kent County Tax Assessment, First District, 1822.
6. Land Records, Lib. DCB 3, fol. 548.
7. Land Records, Lib. JTD 1, fol. 27.

Shepherd's Delight

Near Still Pond
c. 1799

SHEPHERD'S DELIGHT IS ONE OF THE MOST PICTURESQUE farms of Kent County. One of several farms situated on an 1100 acre tract once called *Camel's Worthmore,* it is the most memorable of the group.

After the initial grant (then in Cecil County), to William Marr and Thomas Collins,[1] the property was broken into smaller parcels. One of those parcels was acquired by Richard Bennett, keeper of the Rent Rolls for the Eastern Shore, and devised to his cousin Edward Neale in 1749.[2] Neale sold the land to James Tilghman, an Eastern Shore attorney, then living in Philadelphia.[3] John Angier, a Kent County farmer, purchased the land in 1767 and before 1783 had built a house thereupon for his family.[4]

The house, only briefly mentioned as a *"Good Wooden Dwelling"* in the 1783 Tax Assessment, was an unusual building for Kent at that time. It was a true one-and-a-half-story structure, with the walls continuing above the second floor. The second floor joists continued through the front and back walls and supported a small roof or pent eave.

Before his death, John Angier sold the farm in two parcels to his sons, Thomas and Unit.[5] In 1799, Unit purchased Thomas' share which

Shepherd's Delight was built by John Angier and enlarged by his son, Unit. The farm has been in the Hepbron family since 1828. Nancy Hepbron Ash Collection, c. 1870.

Shepherd's Delight, near Stillpond. The west gable with both north and south porches. Begun in 1767 and later enlarged by Unit Angier and Sewell Hepbron, Sr. It remains in the Hepbron family. Gene Johnstone photograph, 1997.

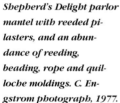

Shepherd's Delight parlor mantel with reeded pilasters, and an abundance of reeding, beading, rope and quilloche moldings. C. Engstrom photograph, 1977.

Shepherd's Delight. A view from the west side of the house with glimpse of south porch and leanto with brick smokehouse and reconstructed quarter in the background. Gene Johnstone photograph, 1997.

Shepherd's Delight. The farm bell on east end of porch, probably installed c. 1880 when the porch was extended to this point. Gene Johnstone photograph, 1997.

included the buildings.[6] Soon thereafter, Unit decided to remodel his house and bring it up to the standard of the day. He accomplished this by adding about ten feet to the west end of the house with end chimney and making a central stair hall out of part of the original hall. He also added a leanto room onto the back of the parlor, and installed dormers on both sides of the A roof, eliminating the pent eaves in the process. He added porches on the front and the back of the house. The result was a house, which resembled the plan of Bounds Lott in Wicomico County.

The alterations to the house were undertaken with great detail. Although the stair is small and the ceiling height near standard, the stair details are remarkably similar to Knock's Folly, i.e. turned newel and very delicately turned balusters with shadow handrail and pilasters along the wall. In the parlor, the mantel is the chief architectural element. It is richly executed with reeded pilasters, oval panels surrounded with bead,

rope and quilloche moldings. The chair rail and trim is decorated with reeding and gougework carving. Original marbling and graining exist on the baseboard and door respectively, with original brass lock on the latter.

In each of the other principal rooms, there is some type of reeding on the mantels, either vertical or horizontal and there are overmantel surrounds with crossetted trim and plaster panels.

It seems likely that the kitchen wing was part of the original dwelling built by John Angier,

but the two story granary, brick stable, meat house, dairy and quarter were the product of Unit Angier's desire to upgrade the farm. When Unit died intestate in 1824, his property was sold for the benefit of the estate.

Thomas Hepbron, Jr. purchased the property from Ezekiel Forman Chambers for $4001.00 in 1828.[7]

After his death, Shepherd's Delight, by which name it was called during the Hepbron ownership, was bequeathed to Reverend Sewell Stavely Hepburn who was rector at St. Paul's Church between 1874–1881 and later Christ Church I. U. [8] Mr. Hepburn also served as interim at Shrewsbury in 1918–19 and 1928. Shepherd's Delight remains in the ownership of Rev. Hepburn's descendants.   K-111

1. Patents, Lib. SDA, fol. 248.
2. Wills, Lib. DD 7, fol. 447.
3. Land Records, Lib. JS 27, fol. 226.
4. Land Records, Lib. DD 2, fol. 455.
5. Land Records, Lib. EF 7, fol. 383.
6. Land Records, Lib. TW 1, fol. 216.
7. Land Records, Lib. JNG 3, fol. 45.
8. Wills, Lib. JCS 1, fol. 16.

Page-Hines House

High Street, Chestertown
c. 1800

Lot No. 12 remained undivided from the time Chestertown was laid out until 1825 when 48 feet of it was sold to William Hands Barroll by Philip Wallis.[1] The property adjoined that of Barroll's father's house on Lot No.34 and it appears that young Barroll's house abutted that of his father, as there is evidence of such on the outside gable of the Barroll House. The sale price of $1250 was comparable to the $1300 sale price paid for the William Harris House across the street four years earlier. This would confirm that a building was on the lot at the time of the sale.

The house originally measured 48 feet long (four bays) and was one-and-a-half stories tall. It contained two rooms on the ground floor, with a partial basement beneath. After the building was acquired by William Hands Barroll it was used for his law office, and may have been in the occupation of his father before. In the fall of 1825, when the Chestertown Telegraph was a new weekly publication, it mentioned that the Telegraph was printed on High Street, one door down from the office of William Hands Barroll.[2] By 1841, however, the building was occupied by Permetia Bowan.

In 1864 the property was acquired by John Hines, who mortgaged it, along with his farm in the first district, two years later. Another mortgage recorded in 1888 probably refers to the major remodeling which he undertook in that decade. It consisted of constructing a new front block and moving the old dwelling perpendicular to High Street behind the new structure. He also raised one half of the old section to two full stories. By

placing it on the southeast edge of the lot, Hines was able to create a space between his house and the Barroll House, part of which he paved with brick. The new front structure had all of the earmarks of an 1880s residence, with front porch, side bay windows, brackets and fretwork. It is similar to several dwellings in town constructed by H. M. Stuart, a Chestertown contractor of the period.

John Hines suffered a series of financial setbacks and was unable to keep up payments on his mortgage. This resulted in the property being sold in 1891 to William R. Aldridge.[3]

K-30

1. Land Records, Lib. TW 4, fol. 597. The history of this lot before the above cited deed is the same as the Wallis-Wickes House. The presence of a basement that does not relate to the Barroll office or the Hines addition may be part of an earlier structure associated with the Page occupancy.
2. This may refer to the small building which stood next door in the twentieth century, that was Joseph Wickes office and later a private school.
3. Land Records, Lib. SB 15, fol. 2.

Page-Hines House. The back wing originally stood along High Street and was standing when William Hands Barroll purchased the forty-eight foot wide lot from Philip Wallis in 1825. In 1888 John Hines built a new front section and moved the old house to the rear. Tyler Campbell photograph, 1978.

Urieville Miller's House

Near Kennedyville
c. 1800

ANIEL PERKINS ACQUIRED THIS SITE IN 1710 and the right to dam the stream to power a grist mill. It is conceivable that he lived in a structure at this site until he built a new brick house in 1721 on the hill, over-looking the mill, called White House Farm. During the revolution, however, the mill was burned and probably the adjoining structures. The mill was rebuilt the following year but there is no documentation concerning the rebuilding of the house. It is also conceivable that the stone basement beneath the existing house predates the frame structure above, but how early it is cannot be determined by visual inspection alone. The existing three bay, two-story, brick-nogged frame structure appears to date from either the last quarter of the eighteenth or very early nineteenth century. Like several early nineteenth century houses in Kent County, the Miller's House at Urieville boasts beaded ceiling joists in the hall-parlor plan house. Its asymmetrical three-bay north facade retains an original board and batten door, with later window cut therein. The broad windows with 6/6 sash appear to be replacements of earlier 12/8 sash. A second door on the south side gives access to the parlor, although the present plan has kitchen and dining room in the parlor.

In the late nineteenth century, Urieville was a small community of shops and houses. It is depicted in the Lake, Griffing, Stevenson Atlas of 1877 with a number of houses beside a grist mill and saw mill. Samuel Hopkins advertised his flour in the Kennedyville business directory along with J. P. Pote, Blacksmith, and A. Strong, Wheelwright, all in Urieville.[1] In 1902, the property was listed for sale in the Kent News:

Urieville Miller's House, c. 1800. The hall of this hall-parlor plan house possesses good post revolutionary vernacular millwork, exposed beaded ceiling joists and a plaster panel over the mantel, like the Simon Wickes house in Chestertown.

Urieville Miller's House. Detail of brick nogging in frame wall.

Urieville Miller's house. The stone basement walls may have belonged to the pre-revolutionary house on the site. Michael C. Wootton photographs, 1997.

"This property consists of a flour and feed mill, a two story dwelling with kitchen and stable and carriage house. The dwelling is old and in fair condition. The mill was remodeled last year to the latest improved system of grinding, scalping and bolting, and is now almost new throughout. Power is supplied by two turbine wheels under 12 feet head. The water is abundant at all seasons. There is no better water pow- er or more desirable milling property in Kent County. It is situated in one of the finest grain sections of the State, and has local demand for all its product, being close to several thriving towns and villages, and has paid a good profit for many years. The Mill is now idle, due to a break in the dam during the recent heavy rains. It can be put in condition for operations in a few days."[2]   K-291

1. 1877 Lake Griffing Stevenson Atlas.
2. Kent County News, October 11, 1902.

Ivingo Site

Near Kennedyville
c. 1800

Ivingo is the name given to a 210 acre parcel taken from Kent Manor in 1708.[1] One half of Ivingo was sold in 1769 to William Merritt by James Burgan, heir of the original patentee. The other half came into Merritt's possession by his first wife, who was a Burgan.[2]

Merritt was one of several revolutionary heroes to be buried at Shrewsbury Church to the north. He was Sheriff of Kent County in 1779 and was also a vestryman and church warden of Shrewsbury Parish. After his death at Ivingo in 1793, his second wife, Martha Vansant, was named administrator of his estate. The estate, however, was not settled until after her death in 1808. Her son, Benjamin Merritt, completed the administration.[3]

The property remained in the family for another one hundred years before being sold in 1908 to Robert R. Hill, in whose family it remained until 1951.[4] The old house was tenanted during their ownership, as Mr. Hill built the house which stands across the road.

Only the Historic American Building Survey photograph of the old house remains. But from the memories of two res-

Ivingo stood near Shrewsbury Church Lane before its demolition in 1951. It is associated with the Merritt and Burgan families from 1708 to 1908. This photograph was captured near the end of its useful life. Library of Congress, Historic American Buildings Survey, c. 1936.

idents of Kent County, the plan was apparently somewhat unconventional—a hall-parlor with stair in the center of the building. The wing had a stair in each of its rooms. From the descriptions of the interior, as well as the photograph, the house was probably built close to the time of William Merritt's death in the late 1790s. It was demolished in the mid-1950s. K-524

1. Hall of Records, Index to Patents.
2. Mary Elizabeth Appleby Abel, "Ensign William Merritt," (D. A. R.), 1992.
3. Ibid.
4. Land Records, Lib. JTD 18, fol. 165.

Essex Site

Near Worton
c. 1800

The single extant photograph of the house which once stood on Essex, portrays a three-bay, two-story brick dwelling with attached one-and-a-half-story wing. Built by Thomas Bowers in the late eighteenth century, little is known of its plan as it burned in 1916.

Thomas Bowers (1741-1784) was a member of the Quaker sect. Four years before his death he deeded 150 acres of Essex to his brother, John Bowers (1766-1820).[1] At the time of his death, John left a widow, Rosamund, and seven children. Of his real estate holdings, Essex was assigned to his daughter, Mary Ann Bowers, in 1840.[2]

In a deed dated 2 March 1880, Essex was transferred to George T. Williams[3] in whose family the farm remains today. According to Williams family tradition, George T. Williams (seated center in the photograph) had purchased the farm from his brother-in-law who had previously owned the farm, but could no longer pay the taxes.

From the photograph, the house appears to have been similar to Worth's Folly and Duncan's Folly in form. Both of these houses had hall-parlor plans and similar chimney treatments, i. e. one chimney within the gable and the other partially protruding from the shared gable of the service wing. K-518

1. Land Records, Lib. TW 1, fol. 424.
2. Land Records, Lib. JNG 7, fol. 271.
3. Land Records, Lib. DCB 5, fol. 583.

Essex stood near I. U. Church until 1916 when it burned and was replaced by Red Acres House. The proportions of the main house are similar to Worths Folly and Hepbron nearby. Pictured here is the George Thomas Williams family with Sally and Joe Ringgold in the kitchen door. Mr. and Mrs. Harry T. Williams Collection, c. 1900

Boyer-Williams House

Rock Hall
c. 1800

For all intents and purposes, the Boyer-Williams House appears to be a modest late nineteenth century dwelling. However, upon closer examination it is apparent that the house encompasses a late eighteenth century, one-room, plank structure. Made of yellow pine, a material which rarely survives in plank buildings, this small old house would most likely have gone the way of many others if the present structure had not been built around it.

In its original form, the little plank house had a central door with two flanking windows. The chimney was located on the north side of the room and the ceiling joists were exposed and beaded. In a photograph taken during a remodeling in the 1970s, the dove-

The Boyer-Williams House, Rock Hall contains a one room yellow pine plank structure dating from around 1800. Like Urieville Millers House, the ceiling joists were originally beaded and exposed. The house was enlarged around the turn of this century. .

Detail of J. W. Boyer's name chiseled in a barn member. Michael Bourne photographs, 1996.

tail corner construction can be seen. At present, the only place where the planks are visible is in a closet beneath the stair. It appears that they had been whitewashed and that the gaps had been neatly filled with a plaster-like mortar.

On the property there is also a small barn for horse and carriage. The name of the owner was chiseled into one of the horizontal member: J. W. Boyer, Rock Hall. The house was built on the large tract called Prevention of Inconvenience.   K-510

Parsons Farm Stone Smokehouse

Near Worton
c. 1800

This ten foot square fieldstone smokehouse accompanies a twentieth century farmhouse and other buildings. Its walls are about two feet thick and there is a board and batten door. The rafters are half-lapped and pegged, suggesting a construction date before the mid-nineteenth century. It is one of at least four stone outbuildings in the vicinity suggesting the presence of stone in the soil in the same way as was found in Talbot and upper Dorchester Counties where other early stone outbuildings occur.   K-395

Parsons Farm Stone Smokehouse, near Worton. This small stone building is an indication of the use of natural resources in vernacular architecture. Marsha Fritz photograph, 1980.

Napley Green

Eastern Neck
c. 1800

Napley Green was patented in 1669 to Nathaniel Evetts, whose name appears in other early patents on Quaker Neck as well.[1] In the eighteenth century, Napley Green was owned by the Williamson family who were allied with other prominent families on Eastern Neck. Two parts of the tract were in the possession of Jarvis and John Williamson in the 1783 Tax Assessment.[2] Since the Williamsons were connected socially and politically, it is fair to assume that they had good dwellings on their farm. The only historic building to remain, however, is not the principal dwelling, but a small, one-story, plank building which was built originally as quarters for either slaves or farm hands. It is a one-room and loft structure with a three-bay facade.

In 1852, Thomas W. Ringgold was listed with 450 acres of Napley Green on which were " ... *Frame House & other Buildings in good repair.*"[3] In the twentieth century, the main house was replaced by a new structure, but the old plank out building was saved and restored. K-275

Napley Green, a plank building located on the shores of Greys Inn Creek, is a rare survivor of a once common form of construction.

Napley Green. This plank building contains a large fireplace with double cranes.

Napley Green, detail of heart-end strap hinge. Rock Hall Museum Collection.

1. Patents, Lib. 10, fol. 326.
2. 1783 Kent County Tax Assessment, Eastern Neck & Lower Langford Bay Hundreds.
3. 1852 Tax Assessment, 1st District.

Rosedale

Near Rock Hall
c. 1800

Located on the upper reaches of Swan Creek, Rosedale is a telescopic Federal period brick farmhouse. Similar in proportion to the Moffett House on Quaker Neck, the main section is two and a half stories tall with dormers. Here, however, there are two dormers rather than three. There is also a one-and-a-half-story kitchen wing and a new one-story wing as well. The brick is light in color and the window arches are gauged brick with mock keystones.

The plan of Rosedale consists of hall and parlor in the main block and one room in the old wing. (Originally this wing had a kitchen and pantry.) The stair in the hall is located in its northeast corner and allows access to the rooms above. Trim details included reeded and rope moldings.

The house may have been built by John Bradshaw or his son, James, to whom he bequeathed the farm in 1788.[1] In the 1812 will of James, his property is described as on the *"south side of Swan Creek from the road to Paiges Point to Swan Creek Bridge."*[2]

On the north side of the house there are two period outbuildings; one a brick smokehouse, the other a pyramidal roof brick dairy. Both were stabilized in the 1980s.

In the 1852 Tax Assessment, Hiram Jones owned 383 acres called Pages Farm on which a *"Brick House & other Buildings in good repair"* are listed.[3] Richard W. Jones appears on both the 1860 map and in the 1877 Atlas. In 1957, at the time of Rock Hall's 250th Anniversary Celebration, Rosedale was owned by Hiram Jones. K-259

Rosedale. A smokehouse and dairy stood behind the house where the remainder of the farm buildings once stood. Michael Bourne photograph, 1969.

Rosedale, near Rock Hall, was built around 1800 for John or James Bradshaw. It has classic proportions and details of a Federal period farmhouse. Mr. and Mrs. Roger Mangels Collection, c. 1980.

1. Wills, Lib. 7, fol. 221.
2. Wills, Lib. 9.
3. 1852 Tax Assessment.

Grieb Log Smokehouse

Quaker Neck
c. 1800

I N 1938, THIS LOG OUTBUILDING WAS MOVED TO ITS PRESENT site from a farm near Betterton by W. Clarke Grieb, a Chestertown realtor. Grieb incorporated the 10' 6" x 12' 0" smokehouse into his residence which he had constructed at Deep Point at the northern end of Comegy's Bight, on the seventeenth century tract called Sewell or Utrick. The building itself is a typical log walled smokehouse with *A* roof and one door centered on the twelve foot wall. Its logs are dove-tailed at the corners. K-246

Grieb Log Smokehouse. This log smokehouse was moved to its present site at Deep Point in 1938 from a farm near Betterton.
Marge Q. Fallaw photograph, 1986.

Hosier Farm

Fairlee Neck
c. 1800

O F THE THREE FARMS LYING ON THE EAST SIDE OF GREAT OAK Manor, the Hosier Farm is located between the other two and overlooks Worton Creek. When constructed, the house was oriented to the creek. Its symmetrical three-bay facade was laid in Flemish bond above an ovolo molded water table. There was also a two-bay, two-story service wing which was constructed without a basement and lacked the decorative quality which the Flemish bond gave to the main block. The wing, however, did have a pent eave between stories. Due to the placement of the stair, the approach side appears asymmetrical.

The plan of the house consists of a central stair passage with two flanking rooms. Much of the woodwork within is original. The main door with transom retains

Hosier Farm, or Great Oak Manor has its three-bay principal facade facing Worton Creek. It was built for Henry Hosier sometime between 1790 and 1810.

Hosier Farm. The original six-panel front door retains its original vertical battens. The nail pattern on the battens outlines the panels. Original penny-end strap hinges and iron rim lock remain in use.
C. Engstrom photographs, 1977.

original battens, strap hinges and large iron box lock. One room has a strip of reeding in the baseboard and the stair is completely original with turned newels and close-string, rectangular balusters above a paneled spandrel. There is also the added sophistication of a shadow rail with paneled pilasters along the stair wall.

Hosier Farm. The closed string balustrade, with its single panel spandrel is similar to Kings Grant Cottage on the adjoining farm. C. Engstrom photograph, 1977.

Locust Grove Farm

Near Chestertown
c. 1800

ONE OF THE MOST PICTURESQUE HOUSES REMAINING IN AN extraordinarily unspoiled part of Kent County is Locust Grove Farm. While it sits within sight of the main road, it is not only attractive, but is an excellent example of the most common house form in Kent County in the eighteenth and early nineteenth centuries. The long one-and-a-half-story frame dwelling is composed of two four-bay sections with the service wing being lower and smaller in scale than the main block. Its plan and fenestration is nearly identical to Shepherd's Delight, even to the extent of the extra room added behind the middle room. The height of Locust Grove, however, is lower.

The exterior retains several original features which are unique. The living room possesses a wall of vertical beaded boards enclosing two closets and the fireplace. Its mantel is a fine piece of Federal design and craftsmanship. The stair has extraordinary vase shaped turned newels and delicate drop finials on an otherwise simple balustrade.

In the mid-twentieth century, some feather-edge boards and the corner cupboard which had been re-

It is conjectured that the house was built by Henry Hosier, sometime between 1790 and 1810. In his will, written and probated in 1826, Hosier bequeathed his Great Oak Manor farm to his nephew, William H. Dorsey (son of Ann Hosier Dorsey). He bequeathed a farm located on Worton Point to the same nephew and stipulated that he pay his mother (Hosier's sister) $200 per annum from each farm and give her the right to reside in his dwelling house.

Between 1826 and 1852, the farm was acquired by Samuel G. Kennard who later sold it to William Vannort. Vannort was taxed on the farm in the 1852 Tax Assessment where it is described as:

> *Lands Pt Great Oak Manor   213a $3834*
> *Brick House & other Buildings*
> *in good repair, formerly to*
> *Samuel G. Kennard"*

'On the 1860 Martenet Map, the farm was referred to as the residence of Joseph Usilton, but in the 1877 Atlas, it is under the name of Samuel Vannort and includes a panoramic view of the property looking from the lane northward.

The main part of the Hosier Farmhouse is very similar to the house on the adjoining farm, now called King's Grant Cottage.   K-239

moved from the Mill House at Chestertown were installed in the dining room.

Locust Grove Farm is part of an early tract called *"Batchelor's Resolution."* In the late eighteenth century, the farm was part of the lands of John Gleaves, lands which were advertised for sale in 1792.[1] Five hundred ninety-one acres of the tract was acquired by James Corse of Richard M. Gresham in 1804.[2] Both Gresham and Corse were listed as farmers on the deed. It was one of these two men who was responsible for the construction of the house.

The house has survived well into the twentieth century with few alterations. This is most likely due to the fact that for over a hundred years the house was owned by one family and they chose to keep it as a tenant house. Jacob Raymond from Smyrna, Delaware purchased the farm in 1830.[3] He and his family owned the farm until 1946. During this entire period few, if any, alterations were made. From the deeds and wills within the family very

little about the farm was gleaned. In the will of Jacob's daughter, Susan (1870),[4] there was mention that it was occupied by Robert H. Loud, which corresponds to the 1877 Atlas.

In 1946, the farm was purchased by the present owner[5] who was responsible for rehabilitating the house and installing the woodwork from the Mill House mentioned above.

K-201

Locust Grove Farm was probably built after 1804 when James Corse purchased 591 acres of Batchelor's Resolution. The form and plan are nearly identical to Shepherd's Delight. Michael C. Wootton photograph, 1996.

Locust Grove. The living room retains original paneling and a Federal style mantel. The ceiling was originally plastered. C. Engstrom

Locust Grove. The newel posts of the closed string stair are the most articulated in the county. C.Engstrom photograph.

1. Maryland Gazette, Jan 24, 1793.
2. Land Records, Lib. TW 3, fol. 196.
3. Land Records, Lib. JNG 2, fol. 239.
4. Wills, Lib. EC 1, fol. 217.
5. Land Records, Lib. RAS 41, fol. 41

The brick section of the house is composed of a stairhall and dining room and is similar in form to the Edick Farm at Chesterville. Mr. Welch's farm is earlier, however, having been constructed in the late 1790s or early 1800s. The stair and dining room mantel are the extraordinary features of the house. The close-string stair is built with three flights to the second and attic stories, and has a paneled spandrel with delicate balustrade. The newel posts have a slightly exaggerated entasis, and look similar to bed legs of the period. There is a half-rail in the wall mirroring the handrail. Each of the drop finials, in the shape of an elongated grape, remain in place.

Original crossetted trim survives in the dining room, as does a superb mantel. It is very tall with paneled pilasters supporting a well-executed shelf with course of dentils and swags of drill holes. The same swag motif is found in the chair rail. Adjacent to the chimney breast is a built-in cabinet.

Welch Farm

Near Kennedyville
c. 1800

JAMES WELCH BEGAN ACQUIRING small parcels of adjoining land in 1797.[1] By 1822, he had acquired 859 acres, about three quarters of which were contiguous.[2] Welch appears to have been a farmer, as did his son and grandson who were subsequent owners of the properties. In 1823 he sold all of his lands to his son William. At that time, the home farm is described as consisting of parts of the following tracts: Agreement, Welch's Purchase, Mount Hermon, St. Patrick's Garden, Graham's Purchase, Graham's Addition, Long Neglect and parts of Kent Manor.[3] When James Welch died in 1828, the only legal instrument recorded was a bond for $10,000 taken out by his sons William and Ebenezer Welch and Joseph Moffett.[4]

The house which Welch constructed was composed of the existing three-bay, two-story, brick section with frame wing on the west gable and a wing further south of the west wing. The original wing burned in 1943 and was not replaced at that time. A new kitchen was built on the east gable thereafter and in 1964 a new west wing was constructed.

Welch Farm was constructed for James Welch, a successful planter who had amassed 859 acres by the time of his death in 1822. Originally his house consisted of the brick section with a 'T' addition on the right side. After the wing burned, it was replaced by the wing on the left. A new smaller addition was added later in place of the old one.

Welch Farm. Small windows on the back of the house pinpoint the stair landings. Michael Bourne photographs, 1996.

It wasn't until William Welch died in 1837 that there was a will and inventory. In his will he bequeathed the farm to his son, John D. Welch.[5] His inventory, taken by his neighbors, Samuel Comegys and Daniel Jones, mentioned *"Carpet in the Parlor ... Cane carpetting in passage ... (and) cane carpetting in parlor chamber ... ,"* referring to the present dining room and hall. He owned 14 slaves and 12 ounces of silver (old silver spoons), with a net personal worth of $5,730.00.[6]

John D. Welch died in 1857, leaving his real estate to his son, William, but providing for his wife, Sarah, to have enough furnishings for the house that William was then occupying.[7] As a result of an equity case between Mary L. Welch and Andrew Woodall in 1881, the farm was sold by the trustee to Thomas W. Eliason, merchant in Chestertown.[8]

Since 1881, the farm has remained in possession of four generations of Eliasons, during which time it has always been tenanted.   K-211

1. Land Records, Lib. BC 4, fol. 597.
2. Kent County Tax Assessment, 1822, First District.
3. Land Records, Lib. TW 4, fol. 200.
4. Kent County Bonds, Lib. 11, fol. 54.
5. Wills, Lib. JFB 1, fol. 28.
6. Inventories, Lib. 21, fol. 438.
7. Wills, Lib. JF 1, fol. 73.
8. Land Records, Lib. SB 2, fol. 460.

Travilla Farm

Near Morgnec
c. 1800

TRAVILLA STANDS ON WHAT WAS ONE of the main landings of the Chester River. The derivation of its name points to Phillip Travilla who occupied the house/farm in the early nineteenth century. Travilla was a man of local prominence, who at one point in his life was the County Tax Collector.

The house at Travilla Farm was similar in form to Marrowbone further up the Chester River, being a three-bay, one-and-a-half-story brick structure with a one-and-a-half-story service wing on the east gable. Unlike Marrowbone, its principal facade, laid in Flemish bond, was the north wall, facing the lane rather than the River, reflecting a change in the importance of the road system over the old water way. Its watertable rose above the basement windows like Deptford, located upon higher ground about a mile and a half away. Travilla Farm, however, used no glazed headers in any uniform patterns. From photographic and millwork evidence in the house, it was either built or remodeled in the early nineteenth century.

From Phillip Travilla, it passed into the hands of John W. Walker, a local merchant who had acquired many properties in Kent County before his death in the mid-century. Walker's widow and daughter sold the farm to Jonathan Slaughter of Delaware, in whose ownership it remained until 1875.[1] In that year, it was purchased at public sale by David Clements who had built the Italianate house, Darby, east of Prickle Pear Mill.[2]

Mr. Clements transferred the farm to his daughter Margaret, the wife of William E. Jarrell in 1899.[3]

Until the house was acquired in 1938, and subsequently remodeled by Clarence Jenkins,[4] it had been either a tenant house or vacant since Phillip Travilla's ownership. With the help of an architect, Mr. and Mrs. Jenkins took the little derelict house and turned it into a comfortable modern dwelling using the old house as the center of a five part composition. Since 1937, it has remained in the same family.   K-197

Travilla Farm, c. 1800, is located near the Chester River where there was once a prominent local wharf. The house originally had a hall-parlor plan in the one-and-a-half story central section. It received hyphens and wings in the 1930s. Michael C. Wooton photograph, 1996.

Travilla Farm. An early photograph of Travilla taken from the same angle, with the river in the background. Mr. and Mrs T. Allan Stradley Collection, c. 1930.

Travilla Farm. The riverside, with bay windows added in the 1930s. C. Engstrom photograph, 1977.

1. Land Records, Lib. JFG 3, fol. 233.
2. Land Records, Lib. DCB 2, fol. 130.
3. Land Records, Lib. JTD 2, fol. 376.
4. Land Records, Lib. RAS 19, fol. 469.

Miers Farm Site

Near Galena
c. 1800

THE MIERS FARM, LOCATED OFF DUCK PUDDLE ROAD, is now but open fields. In the 1960s, the farmhouse was dismantled and part of it was moved to Sandy Hill where it was incorporated into a house there. Used as a wing to the three-part house at Sandy Hill, only its form and frame remain; all other elements of its past have been either covered or rearranged.[1]

The Miers Farmhouse had been a two-part, frame dwelling composed of a three-bay, gambrel roof section built over a full basement, and a four-bay, two-story wing. Originally, this two-story wing had been one-and-a-half stories, but it was raised to a full two stories around the turn of the century. There were two chimneys within the gables of the gambrel roof section and one within the outer end of the wing. Access to the basement was in the northeast gable, north of the chimney. There had been an enclosed leanto porch across the northwest side of the wing.

There were two rooms in the gambrel roof part. Each had an enclosed stair in its northern most corner with a closet beneath, adjacent the fireplace. There was a cabinet in the northwest room on the opposite side of the fireplace from the stair. A door to the wing in the inner room occupied the corresponding space. Both rooms had simple early nineteenth century mantels.

Lower by three or four steps, the first floor of the wing had been used in the 1950s as a dining room and kitchen. The kitchen had a pyramidal brick fireplace. There was wainscoting of horizontal boards to the height of the window sills. An enclosed stair was located in the south corner of the kitchen.

In his will, written shortly before his death in 1841, William Parker bequeathed all of his real estate and personal property to his wife, provided that she support her mother, Ann Myers. The will goes on to explain that the farm was entailed and also stipulates that it go to William D. Salisbury, his brother-in-law, after his wife's death.[2]

The farm later came into the possession of Katherine Parker's brother, John G. Miers.[3] When he wrote his will in 1886, he in turn bequeathed it to his niece, Annie Maria Pennington, *"formerly Annie Maria VanSant."*[4] Mrs. Pennington was the daughter of Mary Ann Miers Duyer and George VanSant. She had married James Thomas Pennington in 1871 and together they ran a successful farming and mercantile operation, living in a grand house in Galena.

In 1907, the farm was left to Mrs. Pennington's half-brother, Lawrence Rochester VanSant.[5] It remained in the VanSant family until 1955 when Mr. VanSant's daughter, Catherine LeCates, sold it.[6] The house was moved after the present owner purchased the farm in 1964. The graveyard, barns, and kitchen wing were all demolished, an unfortunate loss to the history of Kent County.   K-188

1. Sandy Hill is located at the head of Still Pond Creek and is found herein under that name.
2. Wills, Lib. JFB 1, fol. 91.
3. Wills, Lib. JR 1, fol. 472.
4. Wills, Lib. TRS 1, fol. 212.
5. Wills, Lib. CHS 1, fol. 374.
6. Land Records, Lib. WHG 40, fol. 407.

Sandy Hill

Near Worton
c. 1800

TOAD HALL ON SANDY HILL FARM IS COMPOSED OF THREE late eighteenth century frame houses originally located in the second, third and sixth election districts. These were moved to the site in the 1960s when Toad Hall was first assembled. The individual parts of Toad Hall are highly representative of vernacular building forms which would have been encountered in late eighteenth century Kent County. Each of the structures is three bays long and each was originally the principal part of the farm house from which it came.

The eastern most section is one-and-a-half stories tall and

Sandy Hill or Toad Hall is situated on high ground above the head waters of Stillpond Creek. It is composed of the principal parts of three early frame Kent County farmhouses. The gambrel roof section is the Miers Farmhouse (K-188); the middle section a house on Gresham Hall property and the lower section from near Worton. Marsha L. Fritz photograph, 1980.

came from a farm on the southeast side of Worton. The central two-and-a-half-story section came from Gresham College on the Bay near Tolchester. And the final section with gambrel roof, originated from a farm on Duck Puddle Road (K-188).

The latter two parts have been encased in a shell of old bricks taken from other old buildings in Kent and Queen Annes Counties. Each of the original two room structures has been altered to meet the needs of the owner, using fragments of old woodwork from several more old dwellings.

From an architectural standpoint, the building must be viewed from the perspective of a 1960s project that incidentally incorporated several old buildings and not as an historic structure in and of itself.

In the 1783 Tax Assessment, Sandy Hill and the adjoining Mill at the head of Still Pond Creek were owned by John Eunick. K-132

Blackhal's Hermitage

Near Chestertown
c. 1800

BLACKHAL'S HERMITAGE HAD A LOCATION SIMILAR TO THE ADjoining Hopewell Farm, on a ridge a little less than a mile back from the Chester River. It was situated so as to look over at least half of the farm. When constructed, either in the late 1790s or early 1800s, it was similar to Boxley and Marrowbone, both three bay, one-and-a-half-story dwellings. Its principal facade was laid in Flemish bond above an unmolded water table. The house was 33' long by 20' 8" wide and had a hall-parlor plan with chimneys built within the rectangular plan.

In the late nineteenth century the house was remodeled to resemble a Gothic cottage. At that time the roof and gables were pulled off and a short second floor was built. A projecting gable with porch below was added to the river side. This addition boasted two windows in the Gothic style. While the addition may have originally been sheathed in weatherboard, shingles survived into the 1980s.

With the replacement of the fireplaces by chimney stacks, the interior space was large enough to install a center stair. A small *T* wing was added to the rear.

In the 1860 map printed by Simon Martenet, the property was listed in the ownership of Levi Fiddis who owned the property to the west as well. In 1877, the Atlas bears the name of Rev. T. N. Frazier. The house and all but one barn were demolished in the early 1980s to increase the area of productive land on the farm. K-121

Blackhal's Hermitage was built around 1800. It was originally one-and-a-half stories in height and similar to the adjoining Hopewell Farm. It was demolished in the 1980s. M. L. Fritz photograph, 1980.

Wesley Manor Site

Near Rock Hall
c. 1800

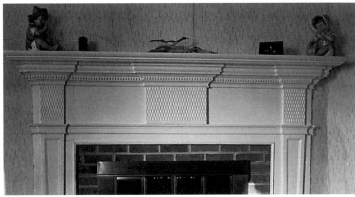

BEFORE IT WAS CONSUMED BY FIRE, AN ACCURATE picture of this frame house that stood near Rees' Corner was obtained by the field surveyor. The four-bay, two-story, frame structure was a product of at least two periods. The north half was constructed in the early nineteenth century and was a one-and-a-half-story structure with tall *A* roof over two back-to-back rooms with corner fireplaces. Its stair was located in the rear room. There was probably an attached kitchen originally on the south side, but it was removed later in the nineteenth century when the owner enlarged the house. This enlargement was done by adding the same amount of space to the south, raising the entire structure to two full stories and building a kitchen wing out the back or east side of the new section.

In the process of enlarging the building, the original mantels and other period details were maintained. The principal mantel was a well designed, country style Federal piece with tapered columns, gougework plinths and dentil molded shelf. In general form it was similar to two other Eastern Shore mantels; that at Jarvis Hill, Dorchester County and that at Sewell Mill, Caroline County. The evolution of this frame house was very similar to the brick house called Town Relief, owned by the Wroths and enlarged by the Morrises.   K-490

Wesley Manor. The northern half of this old house dated from early nineteenth century. It's early roof was like Springfield or Kimbolden, a steeply pitched one-and-a-half-story 'A' roof covering the two-room depth.

Wesley Manor. The mantel in the front room was a fine piece of Federal craftsmanship.
Marsha L. Fritz photographs, 1981.

Methodist Meeting House

High Street, Chestertown
1801

METHODIST MISSIONARIES HAD BEGUN TO VISIT the Delmarva peninsula before the Revolution of 1776. By the close of the century these itinerant preachers had become so influential that chapels were built in the countryside so that the locals could have places to gather other than in private dwelling houses. Apparently all of the chapels were built in rural areas except for the one in Chestertown.

The first Chestertown chapel may have been built as early as 1784 and was most likely a wooden structure. By 1799, however, the Chestertown congregation had become so strong that they prevailed upon the State Legislature to secure a lot in the town square where upon they could build a new meeting house. Two years later the Legislature appointed five gentlemen of Kent County to lay out a place for erecting the new building, which they did the following year.

Apparently the fact that a relatively new organization had been successful in obtaining public land was considered an extraordinary accomplishment by Francis Asbury, as he recorded it in his diary in the following manner.

"Mon 12 April, 1802—That evening I came on to Chester Town, the wind at East; cold and damp.

Tues 13 April, 1802. We had a rainy day, but we attended the house of God, noon and night. Our brethren in this town are about to build: by a train of strange persons, providences, and things, they have a place in the public square, where the market house stood: the chapel will be in line with the Episcopal Church; its size, forty by forty-eight."[2]

When Asbury returned to Chestertown, the new chapel was already in use.

"The new chapel in Chester Town is elegantly planned: Brother Whatcoat first preached in it."[3]

The *"New"* chapel Asbury visited was remarkably similar to, though plainer than, the Episcopal Chapel with which it stood *"in line."* Basically it was a five-bay long, three-bay deep structure with principal facades, on High Street and the Town Square, laid in Flemish bond. The windows were classically larger on the first floor than those on the second; 16/12 sash on the lower story and 12/12 on that above. The principal entrance, like its Episcopal neighbor was located in the central bay on the High Street facade and possessed a double door with transom. All windows were fitted with louvered blinds.

There is no contemporary record of its interior, but from a remaining patch of plaster in the attic in the form of an arc and a difference in the brick work near the roof, it can be deduced that its original ceiling was arched like the Episcopal chapel, and the roof pitch was

The Methodist Episcopal Church, Chestertown, as depicted on Simon Martenet's Map of Kent County, 1860.

The old Methodist Meeting House, now called the Kent and Queen Anne's Hospital Auxiliary Building. Much of this book was researched by the author in his office on the second story. Michael C. Wootton photograph, 1996.

The old Methodist Meeting House after it had been converted into a commercial building with offices on the ground floor and Odd Fellows Hall above. Later, it was the telephone building, until the 1960s. Note the original front door. Kent County News Collection of glass negatives, c. 1915.

" … I went to Sunday School every Sunday in the Old Brick Church in front of the Voshell House, and the only living person that I can find that went to Sunday School with me is T. W. Eliason, Sr. … ."

The Eighth Decade of a Wandering Boy, *personal recollections of Thomas William Hepbron, 1910.*

lower than that which exists today. The reworked brickwork is visible only on the Town Square gable, suggesting it was repaired due, perhaps to a structural failure. When the roof was changed, the ceiling was reinstalled without an arch.

Two small areas of patched brickwork centered on the northwest gable at the second floor level indicate the original presence of two small windows. Their placement may suggest the location of the pulpit and table on the northwest side of the building. This hypotheses would include the placement of a gallery at the opposite end, like Barrett's Chapel. If this were the case, it would have differed from the Episcopal chapel which had an altar on the long axis with gallery on three sides.

Not long after the chapel was erected, divisions in the Methodist Church occurred. By 1830, the New Methodist Protestant Church had been established sufficiently to buy a small parcel of land at the corner of Cross and Cannon Streets.[4] The original Methodist

Episcopal Church retained ownership of the *Chapel* until they built a new church one block up High Street in 1870. Thereafter, the old *Chapel* was purchased by Reverend Samuel Thomas, a Methodist minister from Philadelphia, who also owned the Tilghman House and a farm on the Fairlee Road bordering Bakers Lane.[5]

After Reverend Thomas' acquisition, the building was remodeled into offices. In the early twentieth century, the second story was used by the C & P Telephone Company for many years. It is now owned by the Kent and Queen Anne's Hospital Auxiliary.

K-52

1. Land Records, Lib. TW 2, fol. 219.
2. Elmer T. Clark, editor, Journals and Letters of Francis Asbury (Nashville: Abbington Press, 1958), Vol. II, p. 334.
3. Ibid., p. 387.
4. Nancy Harrington and Robert Sutton, "The History of Christ Methodist Church – 1773-1988," p. 9.
5. Land Records, Lib. DCB 1, fol. 622.

Blay's Range

Near Kennedyville
c. 1809

Blay's Range and Blay's Addition play an important part in the history of Shrewsbury Church. In 1710, after the first South Sassafras Parish Church had been constructed, Edward Blay gave two acres of Blay's Addition to the Vestry.[1] Ninety years later, in 1800, Blay's grandson William Blay Tilden devised to his son Charles:

"all the Church Plantation ... Blay's Addition, Blay's Range, Ivingo and Stanaway ... 415 acres ... except four acres most convenient to Shrewsbury Church ... ."[2]

In 1809, Dr. Charles Tilden petitioned the Kent County Court to resurvey the property. This was done and is recorded in the land records. From that survey, it appears that Dr. Tilden built his house on Blay's Addition.[3] The earlier generations had most likely resided on Blay's Range, closer to the creek.

Typical of the first quarter of the nineteenth century, Dr. Tilden's house possessed the same form and plan as Tolchester, Joseph Mitchell's house on the Bay. The largest deviation from the Mitchell house was the placement of the stair in the hall rather than in a separate appendage. When finished, it had a three bay, two room deep main block with a four bay two room long wing. Both facades were typically laid in Flemish bond. One of the outstanding features at Blay's Range is the use of a curtain wall between the two west gable chimneys. It stops short of the tops of the chimneys, giving it another feature which differs from the Mitchell house.

Dr. Charles Tilden was a local physician and planter. He was also a member of Shrewsbury's vestry, as had been his father and great-grandfather. After his death the farm was purchased by Dr. William Gemmill, whose name appears on the 1860 map. In 1863 the farm was purchased by Charles Beaston who owned States Adventure as well.[4]

Early in the twentieth century, the house suffered a fire which destroyed the kitchen to such an extent that it was removed. Consequently, the existing wing is only half of its original size. About the same time the windows in the main house were replaced with narrower units and the remaining space was bricked in.

The present owner has lived on the farm for at least the last fifty years. K-137

1. DeProspo, Katherine Myrick, A History of Shrewsbury Church, Wye Mills, MD: Chesapeake College Press, 1988.
2. Wills, Lib. 8, fol. 49.
3. Land Records, Lib. BC 6, fol. 447.
4. Land Records, Lib. JKH 3, fol. 649.

Blay's Range. The house built by Dr. Charles Tilden was two rooms deep. Its double chimneys are joined by a curtain wall.

Blay's Range and Blay's Addition play an important role in the history of Shrewsbury Church of South Sassafras Parish. Two acres of the later were deeded to the vestry on which to build a church by Edward Blay. One-hundred years later Dr. Charles Tilden a descendant, built the present house on Blay's Addition. The service wing was originally twice as long as it appears in the photograph. C. Engstrom photograph, 1977.

Cacaway Farm

Broad Neck
c. 1810

Cacaway Farm is located at the southern tip of Broad Neck. Incorporated into the present house which dates from the 1930s, is an early one and a half story brick structure which would have contained one room on each story originally. The two-bay south facade was laid in Flemish bond; the other sides were all laid in Liverpool bond. The chimney on the west gable contains two flues which suggests the possibility of fireplaces on each floor. When the house was augmented in the 1930s, the interior of the early section was completely renewed.

Cacaway Farm, located on the site of seventeenth century Gloucester Town. It is the earliest survivor on the tip of Broad Neck, where the two branches of Langford Bay join. Tyler Campbell photograph, 1996.

The Moffet House was constructed around 1810 with a one-story kitchen wing built on the north gable (blocked by the holly tree). Around the turn of the twentieth century a new kitchen was built along with the front verandah. Tyler Campbell photograph, 1996.

The southern tip of Broad Neck was the site of Gloucester, a town established by the General Assembly in the 1680s. In 1685, 400 acres of Gloucester was owned by William Comegys, son of Cornelius Comegys.[1] When the latter wrote his will in 1707, he bequeathed a 300 acre tract to William *"in Piney Neck over against him in Chester River."*[2]   K-256

1. Rent Rolls, No. 12-A-137.
2. Wills, Lib. 1, fol. 92.

Moffet House

Near Pomona
c. 1810

When originally constructed, around 1810, the Moffet House consisted of the existing three-bay, two-story brick house with a one-story frame kitchen addition on its north gable. The first alteration (or perhaps completion) probably occurred around 1830 when the parlor (south room) was trimmed out with Empire woodwork, typical of the period with gougework corner blocks. It was probably at the same time that the mantel with its sunburst design, gougework and reeding was installed. Three dormers were added to each side of the *A* roof. From that period, until around 1900, the house remained unchanged. Its open string stair in the central hall and all the plainer mantels of the other three rooms were not altered.

Around the turn of this century, the old kitchen wing was removed and its door was converted into a window. On the north half of the west side a two-bay two-story frame wing, was added. Across the facade a shallow hip roof porch with turned posts and decorative scrollwork brackets was also added. The one room leanto off the new kitchen was probably added at the same time.

During its second phase, the house and farm were owned by Francis Baker. On the 1852 tax assessment, he is assessed with two farms, both consisting of parts of *"Thomas Purchase"* and *"New York."* One of the farms had a *"Brick House in good repair"* and the other had a *"Brick House in tolerable repair."* Since the Moffet House is still in good repair, it seems that Francis might have lived in this early nineteenth century dwelling. On the 1860 Martenet Map, his name appears at this location with two houses, however, in the 1877 Atlas, the name Francis Baker appears with only one house. The farm adjoining to the south is owned by James Baker and is illustrated as a great new farm elsewhere in the Atlas. At the latter period, the hamlet of Bakerville grew up around the three roads. Today it is called Pomona. K-249

Lavenham

Near Still Pond
c. 1810

LAVENHAM, LOCATED ON STILL POND NECK, IS A WELL-DE-signed brick house of the Federal period. It is composed of two sections, the larger of which is a five-bay, two-story structure which was built over a full basement around 1810-1820. The smaller section is a four-bay kitchen wing which was built about ten to twenty years later and is near ground level. The north facade is distinguished by its use of Flemish bond brickwork. All other walls were constructed with common bond.

In the main section, the fenestration is classic in that the second floor windows are one pane less in height than those below. The windows in the wing, however, are all the same size. The two sections also differ in their cornices, with a simple wooden box cornice on the main section and a corbeled brick cornice on the wing.

Lavenham's plan consists of a central stair hall with two flanking rooms in the main section. The wing, originally two rooms, has been made into one. The interior is simply finished with

Lavenham, named after a town in Suffolk, England, was constructed during the first quarter of the nineteenth century. The product of two periods of building, it is the typical residence of a prosperous Kent County farmer. Marsha L. Fritz photograph, 1980.

Federal mantels, chair rail and baseboard. Some of the woodwork was removed and reused at Sandy Hill.

The land now called Lavenham was originally a 300 acre tract surveyed in 1659 for George Goldsmith. At that time it was called George's Town.[1]   K-219

Rent Rolls, Lib. 5, fol. 164.

Kentfields Site

Quaker Neck
c. 1810

BUILT IN THE EARLY NINETEENTH CENTURY, KENTFIELDS HAD stood on a part of Stratford Manor on the west side of Jarrett Creek. The house was a four-bay frame structure which was one room deep—a form typical of Kent County's earliest farmhouses. Local recollections tell of a building originally constructed in two sections. This would not be difficult to believe, as many of Kent's houses are the product of successive additions. In the early twentieth century, a third construction phase produced a square one-and-a-half-story wing on the south side of the older section. Since the building was demolished in the 1960s, it is impossible to determine its exact age, but the author recalls details which were plain and quite typical of simple late Federal interiors. In the 1877 Atlas, the farm is listed as owned by T. W. Toulson.   K-243

McHenry Farm

Kennedyville
c. 1810

THIS HANDSOME BRICK HOUSE STANDS ON A HILLOCK SOUTH of Kennedyville on land once known as Hudson Hills & Germany. It is composed of two, two-story sections, both built at the same time. The taller of the two is three bays long with a hall-parlor plan, while the lower section is two bays long and is currently limited to one room. Originally this would have included a pantry.

McHenry Farm, Kennedyville. This Federal period farmhouse stands on a hill south of town. It was built on early lands patented under the names: Hudson, Hill, and Germany. Marsha L. Fritz photograph, 1980.

The least altered of the first story rooms is the hall which retains an enclosed stair, mantel and cabinet from the Federal period. The parlor also has a cabinet adjacent its fireplace. The second story contains first period fireplace surrounds, doors and trim. The plan of the second floor was originally a corridor with two bedroom chambers.

Early in the building's history, perhaps during the ownership by William Kennedy, the windows were replaced with narrower units necessitating an in-fill of brick on one side of each opening. At the same time, the interior window trim was replaced.

The plan of the kitchen contains an enclosed straight-run stair adjacent the main section. Its arrangement is similar to Lamb's Meadow. The kitchen, like those in many old houses, has been the subject of the greatest alterations as cooking techniques have changed so much over the years.

Between 1860 and 1877, the farm was acquired by John Kennedy, the founder of Kennedyville. He, however, did not reside here, but in a large Italianate house located at the north end of town.   K-213

Tavern Creek Farm

Near Rock Hall
c. 1810

TAVERN CREEK FARM WAS PART OF THE MID-SEVENTEENTH century tract patented under the name of Hinchingham. The Swan Point area of the tract remained a 1000 acre estate into the nineteenth century when it was in the possession of Benjamin Chew of Philadelphia. In 1831, the tract was sold to James E. Barroll, attorney of Chestertown who later exchanged it for Poplar Neck (now part of Remington Farm). In 1852, the farm was listed in the ownership of Daniel Diehl, with *"Brick House and other Buildings in good repair."*

The house, probably built in the first decade of the nineteenth century, is composed of a two-bay, two-story, brick section with two frame telescoping wings. Its plan and form are similar to nearby Hinchingham Farm. A mid-twentieth century remodeling removed most of the original features.

An early barn, sixty feet long, remains north of the house. It appears to be a forerunner of the great bank barns of the mid-nineteenth century in Kent. K-262

Tavern Creek Farm. Although this house has been extensively remodeled in the twentieth century, many details remain that can be related to other vernacular houses in the neighborhood. Michael Bourne photograph 1996.

Harris House

High Street, Chestertown
c. 1810

PRIOR TO THE DEATH OF SIMON WILMER II IN 1737, ONE-quarter of Lot No. 7 was occupied by his son, William, who had a warehouse there. Simon Wilmer bequeathed the remaining three-quarters of Lot No. 7 to his daughter Mary.[1] In 1754, Thomas Ringgold IV purchased that lot, five years after having acquired the water lot and house which was his home, the Custom House.[2] For the next fifty-two years, the lot remained in the possession of the Ringgold family and was used as a service area for their residence as well as the Ringgold residence located on Lot No. 6.

In 1796, Thomas Ringgold VI sold the Custom House property and his part of Lot No. 7 to William Sluby, Jr.,[3] a noted merchant. At one time Sluby was in partnership with Benjamin Morgan and the business was called Morgan and Sluby and Sluby and Company. Sluby was a member of Chester Parish and joined with others of similar stature in Kent County to aid in the founding of

Washington College. He pledged £55, a sum that was only exceeded in Kent County by John Cadwalader.[4] Later in life, however, he was deeply in debt as a result of having assumed the debts of his brother-in-law, David Jones, as well as being in debt to Ann Carvill and James Ringgold. Due to the economic condition of his estate, the Chancery Court made a final distribution of his real estate holdings in 1801. Those holdings included the buildings on Lot No. 7. The lot was sold to William Harris as part of the settlement. At that time it included *"a stable, Carriage House and meat house."*[5] Apparently there was no residence standing on the property.

William Harris purchased the lot for £500, a large amount for no house, and owned it between 1801 and 1821. He is responsible for erecting and probably enlarging the house which remains to-

Harris House standing on lot No. 7 in Chestertown, was built soon after 1801 for William Harris, a local merchant. His first house stands to the right of the seam in the foundation wall. The nine foot extension was added around 1815. Tyler Campbell photograph, 1995.

Harris House. Conjectural elevation of Harris' first house. Drawn from original by Jim Wollen, 1974.

Harris House. The central stair hall was produced by the c. 1815 enlargement. The details of the stair are nearly identical to the early nineteenth century stair at Carvill Hall. Tyler Campbell photograph, 1995.

Harris House. The living room mantel is a mid-nineteenth century piece brought in when the old mantel was removed. Tyler Campbell photograph, 1995.

Conjectural first floor plans: phase I (c. 1801) and phase II (c. 1815). Drawn from original by Jim Wollen, 1974.

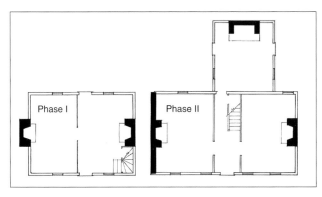

£165 and £130 respectively. In 1821, Harris sold his house for $1300.[6]

By 1841, the property had come into the ownership of Richard Baker, another merchant. The tax assessment valued the house at $1400. Baker also had stock in trade valued at $1000, household furniture worth $700, twenty-six ounces of silver, a silver watch, a seventy-one ton sloop called the *"General Lafayette"* and a thirty-five ton schooner called the *"John N. Steel."* The sailing vessels, although appraised, were not taxed.

During the ownership of William Conyer (1859-1887), a shoemaker, who is reputed to have carried on his business from his home, the house received a face-lift with the addition of pilasters at the front corners, a bracketed cornice and dormer windows in the unfinished attic.[7] By tradition, Conyer is said to have created a door in the upper bay of the first floor which was used as the entrance for his business. Conyer also advertised his trade and wares frequently in the local newspaper.

In 1888, Mary Ayres Wheatley (widow of A. B. Wheatley), purchased the house from the sale of William Conyer's estate. The deed was not recorded until 1893, when she transferred the property to her daughters, Mary M. Sherwood and Kate Wheatley.[8]

Between 1922 and 1945, the house was owned by Margaret R. Massey, the State Health Nurse for Kent County.[9] Between 1945 and 1958 there were six owners, Dorothy D. Molloy being the purchaser in 1958.[10] Mrs. Molloy made several alterations to the house, but grew more fond of it as the years passed. She transferred the house and lot to the Maryland Historical Trust in 1971 and upon her death, bequeathed some funds towards its restoration. Since then, the exterior has been restored and the property sold. It remains a private dwelling.   K-33

day. Initially the house was built as a three-bay, two-story, frame structure with central entrance, 24' 6" in length. Its plan was of the hall-parlor type with the hall being on the town end and the stair being in its north corner adjacent the chimney. The location of the kitchen wing at this stage is unknown. Judging from other houses in Chestertown, it was most likely located either facing High Street on the river end of the house or out the back. If indeed it was built along High Street, it was removed when a 9' extension was added to the house. At that time, it is certain that the wing was out the back, as it is today.

When the nine foot extension was added, c 1815, the plan was rearranged to include a central stairhall. First-story windows and the front door were relocated, but the second-story windows remained in their original locations. The weatherboarding was replaced uniformly across the lengthened facade.

In 1807 and 1808, two small lots were divided off and sold from Harris' original purchase. They sold for

1. Wills, Lib. 2, fol. 58.
2. Land Records, Lib. 7, fol. 482
3. Land Records, Lib. BC 4, fol. 475.
4. Wethered L. Barroll, "Washington College, 1783," *Maryland Historical Magazine,* Vol. VI, p. 164 ff.
5. Chancery, Lib. 47, fol. 459, June 1801.
6. Land Records, Lib. BC, fol. 167,
178; Lib. WS 3, fol. 420.
7. Land Records, Lib. JKH 1, fol. 702; Lib. SGF 1, fol. 511.
8. Land Records, Lib. SGF 1, fol. 511, 515; Lib. APR 6, fol. 509.
9. Land Records, Lib. APR 9, fol. 541; Lib. RAS 35, fol. 563.
10. Land Records, Lib. WHG 54, fol. 311.

The War of 1812

Kitty Knight: Kent County Heroine

IN SEARCHING THE RECORDS TO OBTAIN RELIABLE INFORMATION about Kitty Knight, one will find many variations whether passed on by word of mouth or revealed in what printed matter was available two hundred years ago. This account of our heroine has been told many times before and in many different ways.

Catherine Knight was born in 1775. Her father, John Leach Knight, and her mother, Catherine Matthews, were both from old Kent families. Kitty grew up in a socially prominent family and enjoyed its amenities. As a young girl she spent many winters in Philadelphia where she met distinguished people of the day. On one of these visits, she had an experience which she found memorable, for she was fond of telling it as long as she lived. Benjamin Harrision, former Governor of Virginia, had escorted Kitty to the theater. This is her story, in her own words:

"I must explain the manner in which the theater is built. The stage proper could be removed in sections, disclosing a circus for giving performances, in which horses and other animals were used; this was protected by heavy iron bars so that the horses could not jump into the space allotted to the audience. General George Washington who was in attendance, speaking pleasantly to his personal friends, possibly noticing that I was with Mr. Harrison, said to me, passing his hand down these iron bars, 'You are well guarded, Miss.' Then I said to him, 'I am surely, sir, in your presence,' and curtsied." Kitty was then twenty-three.

No portrait of her has been located but it is a known fact that she was very pretty and equally intelligent. She never married and there are no reports of romance in the surviving records of her life.

Saint Frances Xavier Church (1704), now known as Old Bohemia, near Warwick, Maryland was the church where Kitty Knight attended mass. It is recorded in the Jesuit records, under the date of July 15, 1794 that Father Ambrose Marechal baptized seven of Miss Knight's slave children and that she was their Godmother. Also, the story goes that Miss Kitty would arrive at the Bohemia Church *"very much dressed,"* and that a young Negro boy would accompany her. He would stand by her in the front pew, and fan her during the service.

In December 1812, England declared the ports of the Chesapeake and Delaware Bays under blockade. The country was at war and the British Navy was ranging the Chesapeake Bay, burning undefended settlements pretty much at will. On the 5th of May, 1813, the British had concentrated off the mouth of the Sassafras River. The next day, a detachment of about 500 men in fifteen large barges and three smaller ones, traversed the river and

The William Henry House, Georgetown. The house barely visible to the left is the Archibald Wright House. These are the two houses which Kitty Knight saved from destruction by fire in 1813. They were later joined and enlarged to form what became known as the Kitty Knight House. Old Bohemia Church Collection.

burned Fredericktown and Georgtown. We have Kitty's own words of what happened at Georgetown:

"The British after landing, commenced to burn all the lower part of the town, which was largely frame. There were; however, two brick buildings* on top of the hill, in the town, which had not yet been fired. In one of them was an old lady, sick and almost destitute, and toward that building Admiral Cockburn with his sailors and marines proceeded at a rapid gait. I followed them, but before I got to the top of the hill they had set fire to the house in which the old lady lay. I immediately called the attention of the Admiral to the fact that they were about to burn up a human being, and that a woman, and I pleaded with him to make his men put the fire out. This I finally succeeded in doing, when they immediately went next door, not over forty feet distant, and fired the second of the brick houses. I told the commanding officer that as the wind was blowing toward the other house, this old lady would be burned up anyway, when apparently affected by my appeal, he called his men off, but left the fire burning, saying, 'Come on boys.' As they went through the door one of them struck his boarding axe through the panel of the door." Kitty put out the fires.

Miss Catherine Knight died November 22, 1855. She is buried on the east side of Old Bohemia Church beside her uncle, William Knight, who was born in 1750 and died March 26, 1815.

*The two brick buildings were:
Archibald Wright House,c. 1773 (K-147), page 246
The William Henry House, c. 1784 (K-146), page 320.
Also see, Valley Cottage c. 1737 (K-148), page 119.
Montebello c. 1790 (K-117), page 347.

William Henry House, Georgetown. After 1907 Andrew W. Woodall transformed the early vernacular house into a twentieth century Colonial Revival dwelling. It remained a dwelling until being joined to the Archibald Wright House and becoming the Kitty Knight House. Drawing by John B. Moll. Ford Hall Collection.

Millington Academy

Millington
c. 1813

O N 22 FEBRUARY 1813, the Trustees of the Academy at Bridgetown (Millington) signed an agreement to purchase a lot 138' x 200' on the south side of Cypress Street from Thomas Gilpin. Gilpin, in fact, owned much of the land that the town was built upon. An actual deed was not drawn up until 1 July 1836, 18 years after the name *"Millington"* was adopted for the town and 23 years after the initial agreement.[1] By the time of the deed in 1836, a brick schoolhouse, 40' x 20' had already been constructed and the boundaries of the property were given from the corners of the building.

It was said that the original academy building was two stories tall and boasted a bell tower atop the roof, in the same manner as the academies in Middletown and New Castle, Delaware. Excluding their bell towers, both buildings possessed traits of vernacular domestic architecture of the late Federal period.

The Millington Academy, as it came to be known, was enlarged in the period of 1840–50, but in the late nineteenth century it burned and was subsequently rebuilt as a one story structure, embellished with a central gable of decorative shingles in a vernacular gothic style. Part of the remodeling at that time was a frame addition, which appears to have been demolished in the twentieth century.

After the construction of the Millington School around 1915–16, it was sold and has since been used for residential purposes. In 1957, it became the home and office of Dr. Geza Koralewski, local physician. Currently the old building is owned by the mayor of Millington (1995)   K-318

Millington Academy. The Trustees agreed to purchase the lot on which to construct a school in 1813. They built the academy soon thereafter, a 20' x 40' two-story brick building. An enlargement and later a fire with subsequent remodeling produced the building as it stands today. C. Engstrom photograph, 1977.

Part of Kentland, now called Casa Blanca, is a good Federal period farmhouse built around the same time as the extension on neighboring Fancy Farm. Only the stair remains from the initial construction. The other woodwork has been removed. Tyler Campbell photograph, 1996.

Trustees of the Academy	Building Committee 1915
Samuel G. Osborn	J. L. Smith
Jesse Knock	John P. Ahern
Henry Strong	Joseph Mallalieu
Ebenezer T. Massey	Charles M. Hurtt
George N. Newnham[2]	R. E. Feddeman[3]

1. Land Records, Lib. JNG 4, fol. 296.	2. Ibid. 3. Ibid.

Part of Kent Land

Fairlee
c. 1815

B UILT AROUND 1810–1815, CASA BLANCA IS LOCATED ON a tract of land referred to as *"Part of Covent Garden & Kent Land"* in the 1852 Tax Assessment. In that same assessment, the buildings on the farm are described as *"a Brick House & other Buildings in Bad Repair."* By the time of the 1877 Atlas, the property is listed under the name of the Rev. S. W. Thomas, a Methodist minister who was living in Philadelphia and who had purchased several buildings in and around Chestertown (the Methodist Meeting House in Chestertown and the Tilghman House, for example).

Five bays long and two stories high, the main block is augmented by a three-bay, two-story brick kitchen wing. Its south facade is laid in Flemish bond with neither belt course nor watertable.

The house was extensively remodeled in the late nineteenth century with new windows and doors and the additions of a pent eave and a one-story porch across the facade. One original feature remaining is the main entry which has a five-light transom, gouge work carving and paneled jambs and head. Local tradition tells of carved rope moldings on the chair rail and mantels. These would have survived until the 1950s when the owners removed much of the period woodwork, leaving only the original stair. It was during this same period that the two-story portico was added to the facade.

The house was probably built close to the time of the construction of the brick wing at neighboring Fancy Farm. Casa Blanca was in the Hatcherson family for four generations.   K-279

Big Fairlee

Near Fairlee
c. 1815

BIG FAIRLEE IS AN 800 ACRE FARM WHICH had been owned by the Thomas Eliason Family for nearly 130 years. Until recently, it was undivided and was thought to have contained only one house of any significance or age. In the past it has received little notice from past chroniclers of the Bay Side, which is regrettable, as it is significant for two reasons. One is that the farm played a very important part in the war of 1812, after the Battle of Caulk's Field[1] and the other is that the farm was the site of three good houses, two of which have surfaced as a result of Dr. Stanley Quick's research.

"Farley" was patented in 1659 on the west side of Fairlee Creek at the Bay Side. Little is yet known of its earliest history, but by 1764, part of the patent was owned and occupied by Col. Richard Lloyd, father of James Lloyd and Ann Nichols. In the Maryland Gazette, Feb. 14, 1764, Richard Lloyd advertised *"Flour, Manufactured in the neatest manner, either for family use, or shipping off, by the subscriber, at his Wind-Mill opposite Pool's Island."* When the tax assessor arrived in 1783,

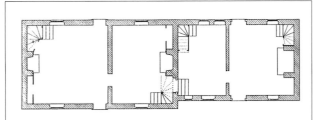

Col. Lloyd owned 712 acres, 21 slaves, 72 horses, 172 cattle and 166 oz. of plate. There were four whites living on the plantation at the time. Col. Lloyd (d. 1786) left the plantation to his wife for her lifetime and also *"my plantation on the Church road near Mr. William Moore's ... ."* (Caulk's Field). After her death, the farms were to go to his son James.[2]

James Lloyd (1756–1830) was a fifth generation legislator who distinguished himself in service to Kent County in various local offices, in the Maryland Legislature and the U.S. Congress.[3] He sold 253 acres of the farm in 1807 to Richard Frisby and Henry Waller *" ... for the use of Mrs. Melinda Waller and her children begotten by her husband Henry Waller until the said Henry Waller shall become a naturalized citizen of the United States ... ."*[4] The farm con-

Big Fairlee. The hall fireplace wall, containing an enclosed stair to the second story, crossetted trim and profusion of reeding.

Big Fairlee. Detail of reeding on the chair rail, fireplace trim , mantel and overmantel, is similar to work at Thornton Farm.

Big Fairlee. First floor plan, Michael Bourne, 1997.

Big Fairlee. The parlor wall is simpler than the hall. All four rooms of the first floor have enclosed corner stairs. C. Engstrom photographs, 1977.

"The property of Henry Waller, which was destroyed by the British sometime during the last war, consisted of one large and elegant brick dwelling house 66 feet in length, by 22 in breadth, and 23 in height—33 feet of which was of some years standing but in good repair—an entirely new front was built of brick at the time the remaining 33 feet was erected—which was in the year 1808 and composed of the best and most expensive materials and finished in the best and most costly manner. One of the rooms of the mansion house was a splendid octagonal room, and there was a neat porch and a spacious passage with a staircase. The roof was finished in a particularly expensive manner with four triangular fronts and a floor of 22 feet by 14 with palisades in front receded (?), wreathed (?) and also covered with cypress shingles altogether a superb building, perhaps the best in the county—"

Also:

- *"A new frame barn 22 feet by 40 built in 1807 of the best materials with a granary attached to it—*
- *A frame carriage house 20 feet by 16 built in 1807 of the best material—*
- *A brick dairy 14 feet square finished in an expensive manner and erected in 1807—*
- *A new frame corn house 23 feet by 12 built in 1808 of the best materials—*
- *A two story overseers house frame, about 22 feet by 16, not known in what year exactly erected but in good repair and of good materials—*
- *Two negro quarters frame, one 32 feet by 20, old, but repaired in 1808 with a cypress roof—the other a new frame quarter 22 feet by 16 built in 1814 the year in which the property was destroyed."[5]*

tained the brick house mentioned in the 1783 Tax Assessment, and that part referred to in the claim of Henry Waller for damages incurred to his house, after the Caulk's Field Battle in 1814. In the description of the house, it is mentioned that the older part of the house was 33' long by 22' deep.

After the Waller's farm was destroyed, he sold it to his neighbor, Richard Frisby, who had also lost his house in the war. Richard Frisby was the son of James Frisby and brother of Dr. William Frisby, and inherited from them the northern part of Farley.[6] (He is not to be confused with a cousin of the same name who lived on Great Oak Manor, one and a half miles to the north.)

Richard Frisby is the person responsible for constructing the brick house which remains today on Big Fairlee. Most likely, the house was constructed as either a part-time residence or as an overseer's dwelling, as Richard moved to Baltimore County soon after the War of 1812.

The house is a two-story, vernacular, brick, structure, three bays long with a two-bay-long, two-story, service wing, all constructed at the same time. Even when the house was first built, the only suggestion of decoration on the exterior was the door surround, which had reeded trim with crossettes and raised panel jambs. Inside the main part of the house, the hall-parlor plan was exquisitely detailed, with paneled west wall having an enclosed stair on the north with closet beneath. Centered in the room was the fireplace with mantel and overmantel, both with crossetted trim and a profusion of reeded detail

Big Fairlee. The back of the house, showing not only the two original brick sections, but the later hyphen and two story frame wing. C. Engstrom photograph, 1977.

that is similar to the work taken from Thornton Farm and installed in the Philip Wilmer House on Water Street. The parlor was also finished with its own enclosed stair and wall of paneling, but it lacks the reeded detail of the hall.

Originally, the lower kitchen and dining room were plainly finished, both rooms having their own enclosed stairs. The second story originally had very segregated areas, as is suggested by the four sets of stairs. Above the hall there was a corridor, a small room which had a fireplace and a larger unheated room to the east. The brick partition separating the hall and parlor below continued to the attic floor and remained unbroken by a door. The bedroom above the parlor, was fitted with a fireplace. All rooms in the main part were trimmed with chair rail. There were two other bed chambers over the kitchen and one over the dining room as well.

In 1852, the property was still in the ownership of the Frisby family. Mrs. Elizabeth G. Frisby was listed on the tax assessment with the following:

Pt. Fairlee	480a
Bought of James Bowers	19½ a
Pt. Coventry & Hills Down	243 a
Fairlee Bar	3½ a
	746 a at 25
Brick House & other Buildings in tolerable repair	
	3 225
Male Slaves under 13	5 1250
Male Slaves 12–21	1 400
Male Slaves 21–45	300
Female Slaves under 12 6	1 200
Female Slaves 12–21	2 600
Female Slaves 21–40	
Live stock	1700
	$23,325

The fact that there were no personal belongings such as furniture, stocks, silver, etc. is an indication that the house was not used by the family, at least in 1852. Only four years after the Tax Assessment, the property was sold by the Chancery appointed trustees, to Edward Comegys, a farmer and owner of several large farms in Kent County.[7]

In addition to Big Fairlee, Comegys owned Arcadia Farm at Langford, Tully's Fancy and his home farm, Comegys Bight on Quaker Neck, the latter having the house which had been built in 1768 by his grandfather. Like the Frisbys, Edward Comegys did not occupy the farm house at Big Fairlee, but leased it to tenant farmers.

Late in the nineteenth century, access doors were cut in the walls, enabling the inhabitants to get from one end of the house to the other without having to descend to the first floor. About the same time, a one-sto-

ry hyphen and two-story, frame, wing was built north of the kitchen.

Thomas W. Eliason purchased *Fairlee Farm*, 841 acres, at the sale of Edward Comegys' property held at the Voshell House in Chestertown after his death in 1866. Mr. Eliason had become the most successful merchant in mid-nineteenth century Chestertown and with the profits from his enterprises, he purchased farms around the county. Big Fairlee is one of the farms that remains in possession of his descendants.[8]   K-277

1. All of the facts around this event have been thoroughly researched and are to be published by Dr. Stanley Quick in his forthcoming book on the War of 1812.
2. The farm appears to have been acquired by Dr. William Frisby and his father James by 1790, for he bequeaths his one half interest to his wife Elizabeth (nee Hansen). Dr. & Mrs. Frisby had no children, so he devised real estate and personal items to his siblings, Margaret, Mary and Rebecca Frisby, and Anna Maria Frisby Rowles, wife of John Rowles. He was very solicitous of his brother James *"now insane in the Pennsylvania Hospital,"* and requested that Elizabeth pay for half of his maintenance out of the profits from the plantation. Elizabeth Frisby afterward married Dr. Edward Worrell, so according to the provisions of the will, the plantation reverted to William's brother Richard with a confirmatory deed by Elizabeth, who was again widowed by 1805.
Wills, Lib. 7, fol. 154.
3. Papenfuse, p. 540.
4. Land Records, Lib. BC 5, fol. 130.
5. Claims against U.S. as result of war of 1812, National Archives, Dr. Stanley Quick.
6. Wills, Lib. 7, fol. 274; Land Records, Lib. BC 4, fol. 676; Lib. TW 3, fol. 250.
7. Land Records, Lib. JFG 4, fol. 219.
8. Land Records, Lib. JKH 5, fol. 693.

Thornton Farm

Near Chestertown
c. 1815

Since 1693 the southern half of Thornton has been in the same family. In 1792, John Brooks bequeathed his plantation (the lower half of Thornton) to his son Philip. He also bequeathed his part of upper Thornton to his son, Thomas.[1] The arrangement changed, however, in 1801 when Philip Brooks, uncle to Philip and Thomas left his part of upper Thornton to Philip, provided that he exchange the land inherited of his father with Thomas, which would in turn reverse the will of their father.[2] The two sons followed the desires of their uncle, and thus in 1808, Thomas became the owner of lower Thornton.[3]

It was on the *home plantation* that Thomas built his new house. By family tradition, the old residence had been located close to Morgan Creek, on the western side of the farm, but Thomas chose a more central location for the site of his new residence. He followed the example of his uncle in that respect and must have used his uncle's house as a prototype as it possesses the same general form and floor plan. (By

this time his uncle's house was owned by his brother Philip.) Instead of a wing offset from the main house, as at Philip's house, the service wing is centered on the west gable. Otherwise they were very similar. One small glazed diamond between the attic windows in the east gable is its unique exterior mark of identity.

Thornton Farm, c. 1815. The house as remodeled in the 1980s. Note the glazed diamond in the east gable. Michael C. Wootton photograph, 1996.

Thornton Farm paneling. Prior to a 1926 fire which destroyed the house, the paneling was removed from the living room and installed in the new house being built for Mr. & Mrs. Phillip Wilmer in town. C. Engstrom photograph, 1977.

Inside, the twenty year difference in construction produced a more refined detailing. This is evident from the one room of the interior which was removed and preserved prior to the devastating 1926 fire. The room was reinstalled in the new home of Philip and Isabel Wilmer at 108 Water Street in Chestertown. Its fireplace has an extraordinary tabernacle overmantel with reeded pilasters and broken pediment. The mantel possesses double-crossette trim with three plinth blocks supporting the shelf. The whole composition is lightly decorated with reeding, gouge and drillwork and a rope molding in the cornice. The work is almost identical to that at the house at Big Fairlee, but the composition

Thornton Farm, taken in 1977, before restoration. Its form is similar to neighboring Thornton, both of which were built by members of the Brooks family. C. Engstrom photograph.

Thornton Farm. Detail of reeding in mantel and overmantel. The work appears very close to the reeding at Big Fairlee. C. Engstrom photograph, 1977.

Grantham & Forest Farm

Near Millington
c. 1815

IN 1801, JOHN WOODALL, SR. WHO LIVED AT VIANNA NEAR New Market, wrote his will. Woodall devised to his son John, the plantation *"he had purchased of Jonathan Smith, being part of Grantham and Forest."*[1] It is questionable as to how soon after John, Jr. took possession of the farm, but by 1815–20 he had built himself and his family a substantial brick house which faced the road between New Market and Head of Chester (between Chesterville and Millington).

The house was a two-story, four-bay long dwelling (36' 2" x 19' 4"; three bays on the south). The location of the kitchen is unknown. Its north facade was laid in Flemish bond above an unmolded watertable. There was no belt course and the jack arches were without sophistication. As would be expected of a hall-parlor plan house, the entry in the second bay from the west opened into the hall. A brick wall extended from the basement to the attic separating the two rooms. Like Big Fairlee, built during the same period, the two rooms were both fitted with enclosed stairs. The mantels in the house were designed in the Federal idiom, the one in the hall being more refined with gougework and reeding. The house was similar to the Robert Moody farmhouse near Galena.

The farm remained in the Woodall family until it was sold by Emily Ann

Grantham and Forest Farm was bequeathed to John Woodall, Jr. by his father in 1801. After establishing himself as a successful farmer, he built the brick house that remains to this day. In plan, it is similar to Big Fairlie, with an enclosed stair in each of the two rooms. Marge Q. Fallow photograph, 1986

is more elaborate. These two houses boast the best Federal period woodwork in the county.

Thomas Brooks died in 1840 without wife or children and willed *"the plantation on which I dwell, which was devised to me by my brother Philip in 1809"* to his niece and two nephews.[4] Philip, their father, had died in 1837. With both parts of Thornton going to one family, along with additional acreage that Philip had acquired, it was decided in chancery that Thomas' part of Thornton would go to a niece, Mary A. Brooks who married William B. Wilmer. The deeds formalizing this outcome were recorded in 1862.[5]

William Wilmer died in 1877 leaving everything to his wife, Mary A. Brooks Wilmer who died in 1896. William Blackiston Wilmer, Jr. and his wife lived on the farm until her death in 1901. Thereafter, the house was occupied by the Lamb family until 1979 when three generations after Mary A. B. Wilmer, the present owner undertook the restoration and enlargement of the family farmhouse.   K-196

1. Wills, Lib. 7, fol. 351.
2. Land Records, Lib. BC 5, fol. 387.
3. Land Records, Lib. BC 5, fol. 433.
4. Wills, Lib. JFB 1, fol. 308.
5. Land Records, JKH 3, fol. 51-60.
6. Wills, Lib. EC 1, fol. 250.
7. Wills, Lib. TRS 1, fol. 427.

Grantham and Forest Farm. The back of the house is only three-bays long. The addition is twentieth century. Marge Q. Fallaw photograph, 1986.

The Hackett House, Chestertown. This house was probably built by Charles Hackett several years after acquiring the property in 1806. Hackett was a watchmaker and silversmith. It remained in his family's ownership until 1854. The corner of the house is visible on the 1860 etching of the Methodist Meeting House. Maryland Historical Trust, 1977.

1. Wills, Lib. 8, fol. 120.
2. Land Records, Lib. 8, fol. 168.
3. Land Records, Lib. DCB 1, fol. 493.
4. Land Records, Lib. SGF 6, fol. 330.

Gamble in 1842.[2] She inherited half ownership from her father. The other half was bequeathed to her by her mother who had purchased her son's half interest. By this time, the plantation included two more tracts or parts of tracts: Woodall's Fancy and Plains.

Samuel Jarman purchased the farm from Emily Ann Gamble and subsequently left it to his sons with a dower interest to Sarah, his widow. The two sons mortgaged the farm to J. R. Lusby who sold the mortgage to George B. Westcott. In 1875, after the mortgage had not been paid off, Westcott acquired Sarah's dower.[3] Later, he acquired the remainder of the farm.

In 1883, Westcott gave the farm to his son Charles Tilden Westcott, who sold it in 1897 to William E. Jarrell.[4] In one of the later deeds, the land is referred to as *"Lewis Farm,"* an indication that it had been tenanted by a family of that name in the twentieth century. Since 1875 the house has been tenanted.   K-178

Hackett House

Park Row, Chestertown
c. 1815

Between 1765 and 1770 Lot No. 41 was owned jointly by Benjamin Morgan and William Sluby, Jr., merchants trading under the name of Morgan & Sluby.[1] Sluby acquired full title to the northwest half in 1770 and in 1783 sold it to Richard Tilghman IV of Queen Annes County.[2]

In 1806 that part of Lot No. 41 was sold to Charles Hackett for $500.[3] Hackett was a watchmaker and silversmith and it was he who was responsible for the construction of the house which stands on the lot today. Five bays long, it is a two-and-a-half-story frame structure with a service wing out the back. Hackett used a standard plan of the day, a center hall with two flanking rooms and a two room service wing. Unlike many of the other contemporary buildings in town, the ceilings are low which gives the building a small scale. The balustrade is typical of the first quarter of the nineteenth century.

In the 1841 Tax Assessment, Charles Hackett was listed as owner of the building, but it was occupied by J. T. Hall. At that time the building was listed in *"bad repair."* This Charles was probably the son of the silversmith. He sold the property in 1854 to Henry H. Simms who put it in trust for the use of his family. Simms' name is on the 1860 Martenet Map. His heirs sold the house in 1901.

Since that time it has been owned by members of the Reed, McWhorter, Green, Copper and Wright families. In 1965 it was purchased by Dr. and Mrs. Paul Noerr and was used by Dr. Noerr for his dental practice. Later, Mrs. Noerr retained it as a gift shop. Since 1965 it has seen many commercial tenants with an apartment on the second floor.   K-53

1. Land Records, Lib. DD 2, fol. 225.
2. Land Records, Lib. DD 3, fol. 334; Lib. EF 6, fol. 234.
3. Land Records, Lib. TW 3, fol. 336.

Shrewsbury Academy Site

Galena
1817

SHREWSBURY ACADEMY, INCORPORAT-Sed in 1817, WAS ONE OF the independent academies founded in Kent County after the Revolution. Like the Millington Academy, it survived until after the Civil War, when the county public school system was invigorated.

The Academy was established at Georgetown Cross Roads, the village that was later to become Galena. It was located on the west side of the main street. The appearance of the first building on the site is unknown, but around 1858 a new frame, two-story building was erected on the same site. A photograph of it, taken around 1888, shows a structure similar to other schools of the time. It is said to have had a vestibule with stair to the second floor, two classrooms on the first floor and one on the second; an arrangement similar to the Centreville Academy in Queen Annes County.

The building remained in use under the county system until it was replaced in 1916 by a new school at the south end of town. It was finally destroyed by fire.

K-600

When it was being remodeled in 1975, two original openings on its east side were clearly visible. The door was located in the northernmost bay and a small 4/4 window was located to the south. In the north brick gable there was a fireplace, but its chimney had been removed above the roof. The west side had two 6/6 windows, but these may have been later alterations to what may have mirrored the east side.

When the north two-story, frame wing was added, around the turn of the century, a leanto was added on the east side of the old brick section, slightly overlapping the frame part. The house remains essentially the same, but with various modifications over the years.

K-284

1. Land Records, Lib. 4, fol. 323.

Left: Shrewsbury Academy, Galena, is the successor of an academy of the same name that was established in Sassafras in 1758 through a legacy from William Boyer to Shrewsbury Church. The Galena academy was incorporated in 1817, similar to the Millington Academy from the same decade. The building in the photograph was built 100 years later than its predecessor at Sassafras. Courtesy of Addie H. Walters.

Yellow Brick House, Georgetown, is reputed to have been the birthplace of Andrew Woodall, the man who would bring commerce again to the once prosperous port town. It was originally a one-room, one-story building. Michael C. Wootton photograph, 1996.

Yellow Brick House

Georgetown
c. 1819

ON THE 1787 RESURVEY OF GEORGETOWN, Lot No. 7 corresponds to the location of the Yellow Brick House. Originally, the entire lot extended from Front Street to the Sassafras along King Street, currently Route 213. The first owner of the property, besides Gideon Pearce who developed the town, was George Vansant, a farmer. He purchased Lot No. 7 in 1733.[1]

According to local tradition, the house was standing in 1819 when Andrew Woodall was born therein. Whether it had survived the burning of the town by the British or was built or rebuilt afterwards has not been documented.

Masonic Building from Memorial Park.
The original entrance to the Lodge Hall
was on the left side of the gable.
Michael C. Wootton photograph, 1996.

Chapter 5
Greek Revival 1820–1860

The Industrial Revolution, the opening of the West, and a sharp decline in trade with England brought an end to the prosperity Kent County had enjoyed.

DURING THE FIRST QUARTER OF THE NINETEENTH CENTURY, Kent County suffered a fate it had in common with many of Maryland's rural counties. The hopeful prosperity of the post-Revolutionary period which had produced so many fine buildings was followed by an economic slump. Caused in part by poor agricultural practices and a decreased trade with England, this was manifested architecturally in a virtual dearth of buildings constructed during the period. The reemergence of a newspaper in Kent in 1825, after a thirty-two year absence, can perhaps be viewed as an effort to reignite both commerce and trade.

As the century progressed, scientific advances made in agricultural practices helped to bolster the failing economy. Undertaken first by the wealthy and well-educated on a relatively small scale, the new techniques became increasingly popular to the point that they soon became common practice. In 1805, the first organization dedicated to the promotion of agriculture and rural economy was founded. Formed in Easton, this society was followed by

the Maryland Agriculture Society in 1818 which had branches on both shores of the Chesapeake Bay. Members from Kent County included Thomas Walker, a noted merchant and owner of several farms, and John Bordley, son of John Beale Bordley who had created a self-sufficient plantation economy on Wye Island earlier. The improved crops, livestock and garden produce became the focus of other's visitations, observations and questioning. Figuratively speaking, these society members sowed the seeds of their knowledge throughout the county.

Advances in agriculture in the early nineteenth century led to the construction of a number of farm buildings throughout Kent County. Fancy Farm, purchased by attorney William Barroll from John Beale Bordley in

Chestertown Telegraph; One of the first issues of the newspaper reintroduced in 1825. Kent County News.

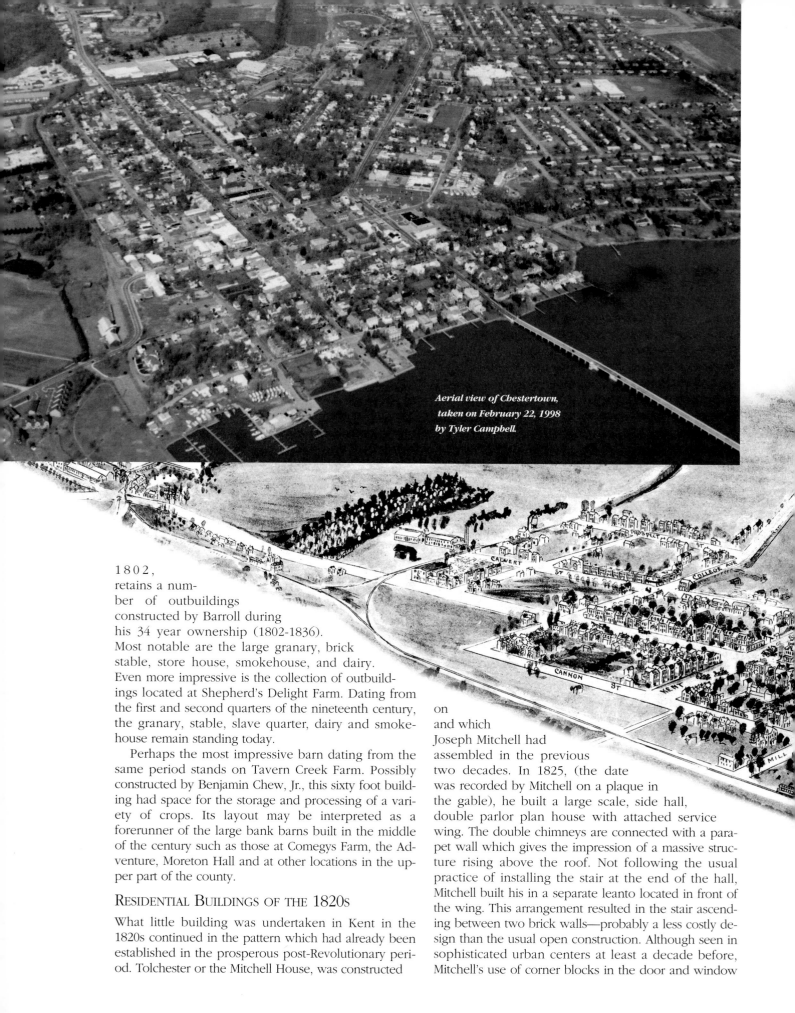

*Aerial view of Chestertown,
taken on February 22, 1998
by Tyler Campbell.*

1802, retains a number of outbuildings constructed by Barroll during his 34 year ownership (1802-1836). Most notable are the large granary, brick stable, store house, smokehouse, and dairy. Even more impressive is the collection of outbuildings located at Shepherd's Delight Farm. Dating from the first and second quarters of the nineteenth century, the granary, stable, slave quarter, dairy and smokehouse remain standing today.

Perhaps the most impressive barn dating from the same period stands on Tavern Creek Farm. Possibly constructed by Benjamin Chew, Jr., this sixty foot building had space for the storage and processing of a variety of crops. Its layout may be interpreted as a forerunner of the large bank barns built in the middle of the century such as those at Comegys Farm, the Adventure, Moreton Hall and at other locations in the upper part of the county.

RESIDENTIAL BUILDINGS OF THE 1820s

What little building was undertaken in Kent in the 1820s continued in the pattern which had already been established in the prosperous post-Revolutionary period. Tolchester or the Mitchell House, was constructed

on and which Joseph Mitchell had assembled in the previous two decades. In 1825, (the date was recorded by Mitchell on a plaque in the gable), he built a large scale, side hall, double parlor plan house with attached service wing. The double chimneys are connected with a parapet wall which gives the impression of a massive structure rising above the roof. Not following the usual practice of installing the stair at the end of the hall, Mitchell built his in a separate leanto located in front of the wing. This arrangement resulted in the stair ascending between two brick walls—probably a less costly design than the usual open construction. Although seen in sophisticated urban centers at least a decade before, Mitchell's use of corner blocks in the door and window trim was a first for Kent County. The Empire style wooden mantels with bold columns supporting a frieze and shelf were also the first of their type to be used in Kent. Similar designs were later used at the Wickes House, and at Rose Hill, Cecil County, in wood and marble respectively.

A few miles to the south, Little Neck was constructed a year or two later. With double chimneys on its gable, it lacks the parapet wall found at Mitchell House. Here, the same plan was employed with some modification due to its smaller scale. The stair is located in the side hall, but the hall is only one half the depth of the house and the back room runs the full length of the facade. Even though Little Neck is essentially contemporary

with the Mitchell House, the trim, mantels, and cabinets differed in that they were executed in the Federal style.

COMMERCIAL BUILDINGS OF THE 1820S

A major remodeling was undertaken at the Buck-Bacchus Store in the 1820s, then owned by Thomas Walker and his wife, Christianna. The old stone wing mentioned in an advertisement in the Maryland Gazette in 1768 and which contained a kitchen and family dining room, was torn down, as was the original chimney in the back of the remaining brick wing. At this time, a side passage was constructed in its place, a new chimney was built on the rear wall and the Queen Street door was reduced to a window. Also, a new frame kitchen was added to the rear of the building. Shelving was installed in the front or store room of the original brick building. The end result, as seen from High Street, was a facade with two doors, one to the store and the other to the living quarters. It was at this time that the principal second floor room with its new fireplace was papered with a handsome damask pattern wallpaper which had been manufactured in Philadelphia by H. P. Borrekins in the same decade.

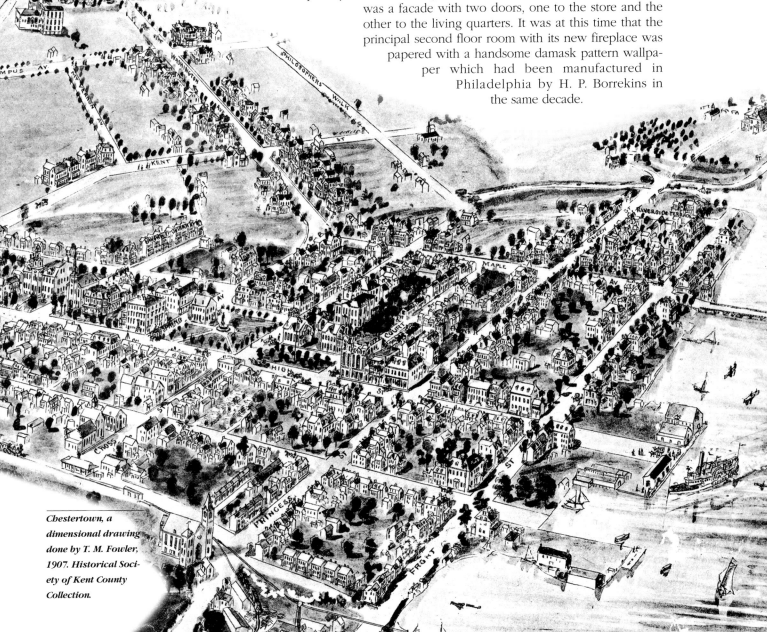

Chestertown, a dimensional drawing done by T. M. Fowler, 1907. Historical Society of Kent County Collection.

Fancy Farm
Granary/corn crib.

Fancy Farm brick stable.

Fancy Farm plank
smokehouse.

Fancy Farm dairy.
Marsha L. Fritz
photographs, 1980.

Bungay Hill log smoke-
house, the most common
type of domestic out-
building to have sur-
vived into the twentieth
century. Gene Johnstone
photograph, 1995.

Salutation Farm brick
bank barn. Here the op-
erations of stable, barn
and granary are all un-
der one roof. Marsha L.
Fritz photograph, 1980.

The Adventure bank
barn. This eighty foot
long structure is the
finest surviving bank
barn in Kent County.
Michael C. Wootton
photograph, 1995.

Shepherd's Delight. Strap hinge on smokehouse door. Gene Johnstone photograph, 1997.

Shepherd's Delight. The brick dairy, now the pumphouse. Gene Johnstone photograph, 1997.

Shepherds Delight. smokehouse and log quarter, two of the five early farm buildings remaining on the farm. C. Engstrom photograph. 1977.

Little Neck Farm, built around 1826 is located on a peninsula of land between Swan and Tavern Creeks. The porch was original to the small scale vernacular house. Michael Bourne photograph, 1978.

Mitchell House or Tolchester, built for Joseph Mitchell in 1825. This large scale Federal style house was probably the first to use corner block trim and mantels with detached columns. Bob Creamer photograph, courtesy of Tracey and Jim Stone.

The remodeling undertaken at the Buck-Bacchus Store was to become the prototype for other commercial/residential structures that were to follow including the T. R. Hynson Store (Cahall Store) built nearly forty years later across High Street.

Just one year after the Walkers remodeled their store, the Masons were granted a parcel of land on the courthouse square for the purpose of building a lodge in which to meet. The Masonic Building was constructed in 1827 and contained space for stores on the first floor and a meeting room on the second. The unusual features employed in the construction of the new building included plain stone lintels which were longer than the windows themselves and a wide central gable bearing a circular plaque with the Masonic emblem. The lintel detail was to become a very common feature throughout Maryland, though it was more often seen executed in wood. The central gable

detail was also to be seen in post Civil War architecture.

RESIDENTIAL STRUCTURES OF THE 1830s

During the decade of the 1830s, a larger number of farmhouses were constructed as an obvious result of improved farming techniques. Some of these buildings replaced earlier log structures that had come to the end of their useful lives. At least two buildings were constructed by members of the Massey family; Belmont and Gondomah. Belmont is very similar in plan and form to both Timberwick and the Logan House. Typical of the quintessential Kent County farmhouse, they are each two-and-a-half stories tall with five-bay facades and gable end chimneys. Belmont, constructed in 1832, and its contemporary, Logan House, have lintels similar to those at the Masonic Building in Chestertown. However, in these instances they are constructed of wood and have decorative end blocks. Their plans consist of a central stairhall with one room on each side. While each has a service wing, at Belmont it is located in line with the main block instead of to the rear as at Timberwick and Logan House.

Tully's Fancy on Quaker Neck and Fairlee Manor near the Bay were built around the same time. Composed of three-bay, two-story sections with one-and-a-half-story wings, they possessed essentially the same form and plan. Fairlee Manor, however, probably had a third telescopic wing from the beginning.

One very successful farmer of this period of agricultural improvement, Benjamin Howard, built Suffolk about 1830. With a main section five bays long and two-and-a-half stories tall and a four-bay, two-story wing, Suffolk's form was a repetition of that employed at the neighboring farms of Maxwell's Purchase and State's Adventure. The distinguishing features here included a corbeled brick cornice on both sections of the house and the use of both a current style Empire mantel in the living room and the more traditional Federal style mantel in the dining room, along with corner block window and door trim.

The adjoining farm, Green Forest, c. 1830, was also owned by Benjamin Howard. With the exceptions of a wooden rather than brick cornice and the elevation of the kitchen wing to the same level as the main house, it was identical to Suffolk.

Several farmhouses received additions during the prosperous years of the second quarter of the nineteenth century. Gondomah is such a house. The product of two phases of building, the second occurred in 1836 when the central stairhall became the principal feature. The house had begun as a two-story, hall-parlor plan building which faced south. In the 1836 remodeling a stairhall and parlor were added with extensive kitchens behind which faced east and incorporated one of the rooms of the previous house. The resulting plan was like a four-square plan, but the form was like the Custom House in Chestertown,

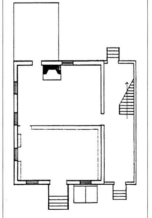

with two gables and a hip. It was a unique house built by a well-educated and successful farmer, Ebenezer T. Massey.

Kentland, an earlier frame house, received the addition of a stairhall and parlor, resulting in a central stairhall plan with attached two-room service wing. Its form, however, was not the more typical two-part form, but a telescopic one made up of three parts.

CHURCHES OF THE 1830s

With the rise of Methodism in Kent County after the Revolution, large numbers of regular church goers left the long estab-

*Gondomah, was built and enlarged by E. T. Massey. The first section was the three bays on the left. The second phase of building occurred in 1836, when he doubled the size of the original.
Marge Q. Fallaw photograph, 1986.*

Suffolk, near Kennedyville, was built around 1830 by Benjamin Howard, who followed the form and plan of his neighbors at Maxwell's Purchase and States Adventure. Maryland State Archives, Don Swan Collection

Tully's Fancy, Quaker Neck, was built in the 1820–30 period in the vernacular tradition. Michael Bourne photograph, 1983.

Fairlee Manor, near Fairlee, began life c. 1830 with the two smaller wings on the right. About 100 years later, the left side of the building received its balancing wings. Maryland Historical Trust, c. 1985.

lished Episcopal Church. As a direct result of these dwindling numbers, two projects were undertaken in 1834. The first involved the complete removal of the established parish church of Chester. The second entailed the removal of the existing structure at South Sassafras Parish (Shrewsbury) and its subsequent replacement with a smaller building. Judging from a watercolor made of the church around 1860 and the church's present appearance, the new building was a very plain vernacular structure which displayed no influence of either the preceding colonial style or the Greek Revival style which was gaining in popularity throughout the county.

THE 1840S

The most sophisticated Greek Revival style building to be constructed in Kent during the decade of the 1840s was also the first to be constructed for Washington College since the fire of 1827 took its original edifice. In 1844, prior to the completion of Mid-

dle Hall, the builder, Elijah Reynolds of Havre de Grace, penned a description of the building for the Franklin Fire Insurance Company of Philadelphia. In it he mentioned a dressed granite basement and pressed brick facade. The building measured 57' x 45' and was three stories tall. The description further mentioned the *"best Susquananna blue steel roofing"* and a 19' x 7' observatory at the peak of the roof. This building represents a first in modern building technology and was to be imitated by many later Kent County builders.

Vernacular traditions, however, are not uprooted overnight. During the decade of the 1840s, houses around the county continued to be constructed with

central hall plan, as well as with the even older hall-parlor plan. At Galena, the Orlando Sutton House was constructed around 1846. It was a one-and-a-half-story, frame, hall-parlor plan house. The Myers House at Hanesville built between 1838 and 1845, was an even more primitive log house with the same plan and form as was seen 100 years earlier.

In Chestertown, Thomas W. Eliason, the first of that name to overwhelm Chestertown with his mercantile prowess, purchased a house which Chestertown builder James Mansfield had built, around 1840, on Spring Avenue. While similar in form and plan to older vernacular buildings, the trim details consisted of machine-made stock items. In residential construction, such stock, or *imported* items were most frequently used in the construction of stair balustrades and fireplace mantels.

CHURCHES OF THE 1840S

One of the most active Methodist congregations of this period was Olivet Methodist Church in Galena which had been given land in the first decade of the nineteenth century. In 1842, the congregation undertook the construction of a new brick meeting house on the same parcel of land. The resulting structure was a simple vernacular edifice, very similar to Shrewsbury Church. The greatest difference was the use of fine uni-

Washington College reestablished itself on the Hill in 1844, with the construction of a Greek Revival style building, to be called Middle Hall after the construction of two flanking buildings in the next decade. Kent County News, Glass Negative Collection.

Mansfield-Eliason House, Chestertown, was built in the early 1840s and purchased by T. W. Eliason for his residence. He was a prominent merchant in the second half of the nineteenth century. His house originally consisted of the left three bays with back building and was located on the adjoining lot. Michael Bourne photograph, 1997.

Myers House, Hanesville, was built between 1838 and 1845. The chimney was located in the earth floored leanto kitchen and had a back-to-back fireplace. It was demolished soon after this photo was taken. Michael Bourne photograph, 1968.

Orlando Sutton House, Galena, was built around 1846, using the same plan and form as the Stephens House. The interior trim is the only indication of a later date than the late eighteenth century Stephens House. Michael Bourne photograph, 1997.

Olivet United Methodist Church was constructed in 1842 and like Shrewsbury Episcopal Church, was a basic meeting house, with two plain windows flanking the front entrance and two windows to light the loft above. The tower and other remodeling was undertaken much later. Drawing: Addie Walters Collection.

Kennard Farm, near Stillpond, has the same type balustrade as Stephney Farm. C. Engstrom photograph, 1977.

Captain James F. Taylor House, Chestertown, is one of the best Italianate style houses remaining in Chestertown. It is currently called Fort Belvedere because of the observation deck on the roof and a curious breakwater in the back yard. J. M. Kilvington photograph, Maryland Historical Trust, 1974.

form brick on its gable entrance which was laid in Flemish bond. At this juncture, both Shrewsbury and Olivet had rectangular windows with multi-pane sash. This was the last of the simple meeting house designs to be constructed in Kent. In the next decade the Greek Revival style was utilized in all of the surviving Methodist churches of Kent County.

THE 1850s

During this period, the produce industry prospered in Kent County as the demand for peaches and other crops resulted in shipments to Baltimore and Philadelphia via steamer. The 1830 opening of the Chesapeake and Delaware Canal made Philadelphia that much more accessible from the Eastern Shore. Consequently, the face of the county changed from one of a rural landscape of cultivated fields dotted with farmhouses and other vernacular structures to one with grander houses, larger barns and more fruit trees. As in previous decades, vernacular forms and plans persisted. As the century progressed, architectural details were increasingly mass produced. Catalog ordering was no longer limited to millwork, but now included specialty items such as slate and marble mantels, kitchen equipment, cast iron ornamentation, and heating devices.

By the mid-nineteenth century, agricultural production increased to such an extent that numerous farmers and merchants throughout Kent showed their prosperity by building anew or making major changes to their residence. In 1850, Benjamin F. Beck built a new house on the Manor of Stephen Heath which he called Stephney Farm. Similar to Washington College's new building in its use of the Greek Revival style, it was, however, laid out like a typical vernacular farmhouse. Here at Stephney Farm is another dated use of metal roofing on a modestly-pitched roof. The attic story is treated like a very heavy frieze. The Ionic portico of the front entrance is the best of that order in Kent County. A long porch on the wing was constructed with thin Doric columns with lozenge pattern railing, a detail used on the Kennard House near Stillpond. The Kennard House is a plainer but larger house than Stephney. Here both

the principal and service sections are two rooms deep which results in eight rooms per floor.

Another product of the 1850s, the Lusby farm near Kennedyville, represents the best example of the transition between Greek Revival and Italianate residences in Kent County. Here, the third story of the frame structure is treated with flush shiplap in contrast to the weatherboard below. The wide overhanging cornice of the nearly flat hip roof is supported on Italianate brackets that are also used on the porch.

Several other farmhouses of the 1850s combine Greek Revival boxiness with decorative Italianate brackets. The houses built for Captains Andrew Woodall at Georgetown and James F. Taylor in Chestertown are representative. Spry Landing, Doe Neck and Plaindealing were all similar, but consisted of a side rather than central hall. The first two were three stories tall and one room deep, while Plaindealing was two stories and two rooms deep. The Lusby House in Chestertown can perhaps be seen as a more decorative version of the same.

Across the street from the Lusby House was the incomparable residence of Senator George Vickers. It was a three-story, four-square plan house with Italianate details. Maple Grove, near Langford looked similar, but was only one room deep. At the apexes of their metal roofs, many of these buildings possessed observatories or belved-

advantage of the views afforded by their height. At both the Captain Taylor House and the Stephens House these observatories were of the covered variety, while at Darby and Spry Home Farm they were open. Two houses which had completely enclosed observatories were the Kennedy Farm in Kennedyville and Moreton Hall near Sassafras and in that respect they were like the 1844 building at Washington College. However, they differed from each other significantly in detail and form.

Moreton Hall, near Sassafras, is the only Italianate house in Kent to have a double porch beneath the principal roof. The pattern of wrought iron differs from the first to second stories. Michael Bourne photograph, 1997.

Detail—Cast Iron Porch at Moreton Hall, first story. Gene Johnstone photograph, 1997.

Worthmore Farm, near Stillpond, was constructed by Sewell Hepbron, Sr. in 1854-57. This vernacular brick house was enlarged with the frame wing on the west side of the house, which has since disappeared. Maryland State Archives, Kitty Hepbron Harris Collection.

Monitor on Hynson's Store. The monitor is a short version of a belvedere and was used on many antebellum houses of the area. Michael Bourne photograph, 1997.

Moreton Hall, c. 1850, possesses the grandest of cast iron porches in the county. There the hip roof covers not only the house but the porch as well. Interestingly, other houses in the county which have cast iron ornamentation on their porches are also located in the same vicinity. Both Wilson Point, c. 1850, and the Dreka Mill House, c. 1854, have such porches. Wilson Point was a four-square, three-story structure with observatory on the roof, while the Dreka Mill House was a modest two-story, hip roof house in Sassafras. In addition to the houses in this area of Kent, Ward's Knowledge, across the river in Cecil County and many contemporary houses in and near Elkton used ornamental cast iron on their porches.

Several contemporary buildings in Kent used a different form of observatory, called a monitor. Fairfield, c. 1854, Stepne, c. 1860, Middle Plantation, c. 1856, and the Hynson Store, c. 1850, all possessed a shorter version of the observatory. Around the short walls were very small windows or

louvers that could be opened in summer to increase ventilation. Middle Plantation and the Hynson Store still retain their monitors, but the other two have been obliterated by later additions.

In 1851, Joseph Turner came to Betterton from Baltimore and built Ellwood. Being a Quaker, he was not swayed by the passing styles that were being displayed in Baltimore or to a much lesser extent in Kent County. For his new residence, he chose a plain style that can be called late Georgian. The only feature of the house that was unusual was the gallery on the roof which extended from one gable end chimney to the other.

In 1854, Sewell Hepbron, Sr. built a new house on his farm, Worthmore. His accounts indicate that materials were shipped in from Port Deposit, Baltimore and Chestertown, but even with the availability of a wide

choice of materials, he built a sturdy, vernacular, brick farmhouse that had only a modest gesture of stylistically inspired materials on its porch.

In the early 1850s, Belle View, near Rock Hall, was constructed along the same lines as Federal townhouses in Chestertown, the Mitchell House and Little Neck from the 1820s. In 1854, Charles Davis purchased half of Lot No. 84 which had previously been referred to as Sterling Castle. On his lot he built a new duplex in an older style; a frame, one-and-a-half-story building with two doors, each side having two rooms on the first floor and winder stairs to the second story.

CHURCHES OF THE 1850S

With the prosperity being shown in residential structures, it is only natural that the inhabitants of Kent would want to show their prosperity in their churches as well. St. James, built in 1853, was the prototypical Greek Revival church constructed for the Methodist congregations, not only throughout Kent, but up and down the Eastern Shore. The gable facade was composed of wide pilasters at the corners of the building with central entrance flanked by two long windows. A date plaque above the door gave a certain relief to the plainness of the low-pitched gable. In 1860, Waters Chapel (later Kennedyville Methodist Church) was constructed along the same lines as St. James.

In the previous year (1859), Rehobeth Methodist Church at Sas-

Wilson Point, now called Shorewood, near Galena, was similar to the Kennedy House except for the extensive wrought iron porches which extend around three sides. It is one of four SassafrasRiver houses to have used wrought iron for its porch. C. Engstrom photograph, 1977.

The Davis Duplex, Chestertown, was built on the same half lot as Sterling Castle soon after 1854. Each half of this vernacular building has two rooms on the ground floor, but the northerly half had three bedrooms as opposed to two on the southerly half. Michael Bourne photograph, 1968.

safras was modeled on the same form. The gable facade of the frame building was flanked by pilasters and there was a full pediment. It also varied by the reversal of the window and door placement that had been seen earlier at St. James. Two doors flanked a central window.

The largest of the Methodist churches to be built in Kent County were Wesley Chapel, near Rock Hall (1852) and the predecessor to Christ Methodist Church in Chestertown (1858). Both were larger structures with gable facades. Wesley Chapel was a plain Greek Revival building. The Chestertown church possessed Italianate brackets and window ornamentation. One purely Greek Revival structure built by the Rock Hall Methodist Church in 1854 was the only temple form structure built in Kent. This classical church was similar to several buildings built in Baltimore at the same time. Unfortunately, the building burned in 1900, forty-six years after it was constructed.

The Episcopal Church experienced a rebirth in the central part of the county during the 1850s and after much planning, a new church was constructed on the site of the original Chester Parish Church at I. U. Built in the Gothic Revival Style in 1858, the new building differed from other contemporary churches with its lancet arched windows and steeply pitched roof. The interior was also more elaborate than other Greek Revival churches of the period with exposed roof trusses and sheathing.

THE 1860s

Two of the most impressive buildings constructed in Kent County before the Civil War are representative

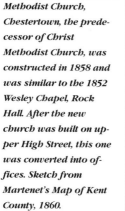

Methodist Church, Chestertown, the predecessor of Christ Methodist Church, was constructed in 1858 and was similar to the 1852 Wesley Chapel, Rock Hall. After the new church was built on upper High Street, this one was converted into offices. Sketch from Martenet's Map of Kent County, 1860.

Salem M. E. Church, Fairlee, is the least changed of the Methodist chapels that were built in the 1850-60 period. Others that originally had the same form include St. James, Waters Chapel, Kennedyville, and to some extent, Rehobeth Church, Sassafras. Michael Bourne photograph, 1996.

Christ Church, I. U., was built at the same time as the Methodist Church in Chestertown (1858) but the designer for the church used a combination of Italianate and Gothic revival details. it has remained remarkably unchanged since its construction. Kent County News Glass Negative Collection.

of the Italianate style, the Kent County Courthouse and Brampton or Fairy Hill. As progress was being made on so many fronts, the inadequacies of the colonial courthouse became increasingly evident. In 1860, a new building was constructed which addressed the various public needs under one roof. The large structure was faced with pressed brick, had tall windows with closable shutters and a series of relatively simple Italianate brackets to support the widely overhanging eave. To a lesser degree, the Courthouse had details similar to the huge contemporary Frederick County Courthouse.

Brampton or Fairy Hill was constructed by Henry Ward Carvill in 1860 after he sold Carvill Hall, his ancestral farm on Fairlee Creek. Carvill constructed a large, three-story, brick residence with glazed observatory on the roof and extensive porches. Choosing expensive materials available through catalogs, he used walnut doors with porcelain and silver plated hardware, and a walnut balustrade with a bold carved newel post. The mantels were slate with marbleized painted finish.

Like the building traditions of the past, the Italianate and Greek Revival styles did not cease with the interruption of the Civil War. These styles persisted, as can be seen in the Burchinal Building on the corner of Cross and High Streets and the Voshell House on Spring Avenue. As new economic prosperity came to Kent, those styles were modified, shifting into American Gothic and later reinterpretations of historic styles. Post Civil War architecture of Kent County and Kent's incredible growth after that period is planned in another volume by the Historical Society of Kent County.

HILDEBRAND FARM

About the same time that Thomas Brooks was building his new house at Thornton Farm, another house was being built on another Brooks farm. The Hildebrand Farm was similar to Big Fairlee in form and plan. It was a frame structure and like many others of the eighteenth and early nineteenth centuries, the chimney backs were exposed to the level of the second floor, a detail intended to reduce the chance of fire. Two contemporary

frame houses with the same detail include the Koppleman Farm, a gambrel roof structure and Wesley Manor, a back-to-back, hall-parlor plan within a one-and-a-half-story frame.

CENTRAL HALL PLANS OF THE EARLY NINETEENTH CENTURY

Fair Hope and Stratford Manor on Quaker Neck are examples of early nineteenth century center hall plans. The former was built of frame covered by weatherboards above a high brick basement. The latter was built completely of brick. Lavenham and the Bradford Johnson House are similar brick houses. The Johnson House had the same plan as nearby Adventure, i. e. the dining room had an enclosed stair to the second story in addition to the one in the central hall. It is also interesting as an example of the builder having insufficient funds to complete the house all at once. When it was being dismantled, it was evident that the living room was the last room to have been finished and the difference in the window and door trim revealed the transition to the Empire style that was made known not as a style in and of itself, but as signifying the end of the Federal style.

Another example of an originally unfinished house dating from the early nineteenth century is Hodges Bar Farm where the original stairhall and bayside room were whitewashed before the plaster was installed. Interestingly, the house was enlarged to a central hall plan and the original *A* roof was replaced with a gambrel. The stair balustrade is nearly identical in its simplicity to the Harris House in Chestertown and the newer stair at Carvill Hall, the latter two having been remodeled in the second decade of the nineteenth century.

Kent County Courthouse, Chestertown, was built in 1860 to replace the assemblage of eighteenth century structures that stood in the same area. In keeping with current fashion, it was built in the Italianate style. Birds Eye View of Chestertown, 1907.

Burchinal Building, Chestertown, stood where Chesapeake Bank & Trust now stands. It was built in the ever popular Italianate style and served the community until the great fire of 1910, which consumed a large part of the commercial district. Birds Eye View of Chestertown, 1907.

Pine Point was originally constructed in Chesterville in the early nineteenth century. It was moved to its present location, overlooking the Sassafras River, in 1951. Bart Stolp Collection, 1978.

The Woodall-Hurtt House, Georgetown, was constructed on the foundation of an earlier house that was destroyed during the British invasion of Georgetown in 1813. It grew as the family prospered through the late nineteenth century. Michael Bourne photograph, 1979.

Pine Point

Gregg Neck
c. 1820

OVERLOOKING THE SASSAFRAS RIVER AND its tributary, Swantown Creek, this old gambrel roof house was moved here from Chesterville by Mr. Stewart Huston in 1951.

Pine Point is a unique survival of a *dog trot* plan log house in tidewater Kent County, i. e. two separate log structures with space between and covered with a common roof. In this situation, the space is actually a framed stairhall. The three bay long gambrel roof section contains the larger of the two log buildings and the stairhall. An asymmetrical *A* roof covers the other log building which was enlarged after the move. The doors are batten doors, hung on cast butt hinges.

Inside, the balustrade is very delicate, with turned newel, three balusters per step and a small, nearly round handrail with goose neck at the upper newel. Some of the log walls are exposed, as well as ceiling joists on both floors.

While the house has been enlarged and changes have been made, this house would not have survived if it had not been moved in 1951.   K-530

Woodall-Hurtt House

Georgetown
c. 1820

ONE'S FIRST IMPRESSION OF THIS THREE-STORY FRAME BUILD-ing is that of a standard late-nineteenth century vernacular Italianate dwelling. On closer examination, however, it is in fact earlier. Recollections and information offered by its late owner helped to document its age.

Local tradition tells of a small dwelling with basement in this location which was destroyed when the town was burned by the British in 1813. Sometime thereafter, part of the present house was constructed as a replacement. The kitchen was located in the western basement. When Mr. James Hurtt's grandparents, J. F. M. and Emily Ann Woodall were married in 1865 and resided here, the house consisted of a three-bay, two-story rectangular dwelling with kitchen still in the basement. It was the Woodalls who added a two-story kitchen behind the east half of the house. An old photograph of Georgetown, taken from across the river c. 1880, shows the house in that configuration. The photograph included several extant structures: the stable (1874), a meathouse and shed, chicken house, and the picket fence.

The present third story was added after the photograph was taken, in the late 1880s or 1890. At the same time, a second story was added to the west porch. The Woodall-Hurtt House is a significant structure in Georgetown due to its long ownership by one family (roughly 120 years) and the fact that it represents the changing needs and tastes of that family.   K-581

Rodel Acres

Near Kennedyville
c. 1820

O N THE FARM CALLED RODEL ACRES NEAR KENNEDYVILLE stands an interesting combination of brick and frame farmhouse with an *L* plan. It apparently started as a three-bay, two-story, brick farmhouse with gable-end chimneys. Originally facing north, the front was laid in Flemish bond with a stepped watertable. Although the interior has been altered, the original plan of the brick section appears to have been a hall-parlor. It probably had a kitchen wing off the west gable.

Around the third quarter of the nineteenth century, the new owner decided to reorient the house and built a frame wing on the south side, even with the east gable. The new east facade, now facing the road and including the old brick gable, was completely covered with weatherboard. The east chimney was dismantled to the basement level and a new one built on the north side to balance that at the new south end. The east gable, above the attic floor, was also dismantled and the roof was then hipped at its juncture with the old section. The old center door of the north facade was converted into a window and a two-bay, two-story kitchen wing was

Rodel Acres. This early nineteenth century brick farmhouse was enlarged and re-oriented later in the century. The same development occurred at Thomases Hill and Gondomah. Note the former central door way

Massey Farm near Chestertown is an early nineteenth century frame hall-parlor plan farmhouse. It has a unique recessed entry which serves both the kitchen and the basement. Marsha L. Fritz photographs, 1980.

built onto the west gable. The resulting house is very similar in form and development to Gondomah near Massey.

In the deed to the property, the beginning point of the survey is the first stone of a tract called Partnership.[1] In 1877, the farm is shown in the Atlas as in the ownership of J. F. Wilson.[2] The current name is derived from the first names of the last owners.[3]   K-381

1. Land Records, Lib. EHP 95, fol. 335. Partnership was owned in the eighteenth century by Samuel Wallis and his offspring.
2. 1877 Atlas.
3. Ibid No. 1.

Massey Farm

Near Chestertown
c. 1820

T HE EARLY NINETEENTH CENTURY FRAME dwelling which stands on the Massey Farm resembles two brick houses in the County; the Costen Farm and Grantham & Forest Farm both in the First District. The similarities are in form, fenestrations, and plan. Each of the two-story buildings has a four-bay facade, and a roof without dormers. Each has a two-story wing and a nearly equal hall-parlor plan, with both rooms having its own stair and entry.

In the case of the Massey Farmhouse, the western room corner stair has been replaced with a straight run stair and the mantels and other period woodwork have been removed. One feature unique to this house is a recessed entry in the south facade which provides access to the basement as well as the kitchen. In this area original horizontal sheating boards are still exposed and not covered with asbestos shingles.

In the 1877 Atlas, the property is owned by the heirs of G. B. Ford.   K-380

The Overbeck House

Quaker Neck
c. 1820

ONLY TWO SIGNIFICANT OLD HOUSES EXIST ON CORNELIUS Comegys' seventeenth century plantation, Utrick; Comegys Bight and the Overbeck House. The description of the exterior of the two houses is similar ... three-bay facade, central entrance, two-story brick house with moderately pitched A roof. The facades are laid in Flemish bond and the chimneys within the gable have sloped weatherings. But the similarities cease there.

There is no date in the gable at the Overbeck House as there is at Comegys Bight. Most likely it dates from around 1800 and was built for the Comegys, as the entire Utrick tract was owned by the family from the seventeenth century to the 1850s.

When originally constructed, the two-bay kitchen wing was one-and-a-half stories tall and its southeast facade laid in Flemish bond, like the main part. When it was heightened, later in the nineteenth century to two full stories, the mason did not carry the Flemish bond to the second story, but used the cheaper common bond.

Inside, the house was originally divided into the hall-parlor plan with the kitchen down several steps. In the 1970s, the house was gutted and remodeled with central stair in the living room. The house is an interesting example of a vernacular late Georgian farmhouse.   K-360

The Overbeck House was built in the early nineteenth century on part of Utrick. The only feature it has in common with the eighteenth century houses of Quaker Neck is the sloped weathering of the chimney.
C. Engstrom photograph, 1977.

Stratford Manor

Quaker Neck
c. 1820

KING'S GRANT IS BUILT ON PART OF STRATFORD MANOR, A 1000 acre tract patented in 1660 to Richard Chandler.[1] The manor was later resurveyed in 1735, for George Garnett and included over 200 additional acres.[2] Garnett began selling farms soon after the resurvey.

The house on the farm is an interesting vernacular brick residence begun around 1800. It was changed during the 1820-30 period, then again in the late nineteenth century and in 1930.

Stratford Manor. The original central hall stair received a new newel post and balusters in the late nineteenth century. C. Engstrom photograph, 1977.

Only the stair and some second story trim date from its earliest period. The door trim with its incised corner blocks and late Federal trim date from the second period, along with the heavy mantels of the two rooms flanking the central stairhall. The late nineteenth century change occurred only on the first to second story balustrade where catalogue parts were used except for the handrail and intermediate newels.

In the 1930s, Mr. and Mrs. Temple Blackwood purchased the farm and turned it into an *estate*. A second wing was added to the house to balance the original brick kitchen. An enclosed one story porch was added in front of the main entry and two bay windows were installed on the river side of the house. The Blackwoods installed a swimming pool, pool house and many other buildings including barns for their fine herd of cattle. The house has remained essentially the same since that time.

In the 1877 Atlas, the house appears to be owned and/or occupied by Isaac Cordray.　　　K-283

1. Grieb, Quaker Neck Map.
2. Ibid.

Stratford Manor, Quaker Neck. This vernacular farmhouse was built on part of the seventeenth century manor granted to Richard Chandler. In the 1930s it was transformed into an agricultural estate with modifications to the house especially apparent on the south side.

Stratford Manor mantel. The late Federal design borders on the Greek Revival style that was to come in favor a few years later. C. Engstrom photographs, 1977.

Reese's Corner House

Near Rock Hall
c. 1820

Reese's Corner House.The north facade shows the position of the stair landing and extensions to the early kitchen. Tyler Campbell photograph, 1996.

Reese's Corner House was built in at least two stages, with the west (left) three bays constructed with Flemish bond facade. The two-bay extension is laid in common bond. Marsha L. Fritz photograph, 1981.

THE REESE HOUSE LOOKS VERY SIMILAR TO its neighbor to the south, Standaway. It is a five-bay, two-and-a-half-story, brick structure with three dormers on each side of the *A* roof. On closer examination, however, its evolution differs from that of Standaway. Here the house began as a three-bay, side-hall house to which two bays were later added. The facade of the original structure is laid in Flemish bond; the two other bays and all the rest are laid in common bond. The brickwork and form of the first section looks Federal but the interior details (which may be later alterations) are Greek Revival in style.

Abel J. Reese was taxed on this property in 1852, along with other land and personal property. In the Assessment the following description can be found:

> *"Lands Pt. Fair Meadows*
> *Brick Dwelling, Frame Store*
> *& other Buildings in good repair*
> *Formerly Collin F. Hale*
> *etc."*[1]

In 1877, the house and store were owned by J. Baker who apparently built a wagon shop and several other houses. In the 1877 Atlas, the business references for Rock Hall state that *"Strong Bro. ran a general store at Rees' Corner."* On the actual map in the Atlas there is a house depicted in that location.[2]   K-257

1. 1852 Tax Assessment.
2. Lake, Griffing, Stevenson Atlas, 1877.

Beck's Landing

Broad Neck

c. 1820

Horatio Beck purchased parts of Scotts Lott, High Park and Mulberry Plains around 1830. He was assessed for 483 acres in the 1852 tax assessment which included a *"Frame House + other Buildings in good repair."* He also owned eleven slaves and considerable livestock. Mr. Beck is listed as the owner on the 1860 Martenet Map, but by 1877, it had passed into the ownership of Mrs. M. M. Beck. On the latter map, it is referred to as Beck's Landing.

At least two parts of the three-part house were standing when Horatio purchased the farm, the one-and-a-half-story, three-bay kitchen wing and the three-bay two-and-a-half-story center section. Parts of the foundation of the third section appear earlier, but whatever might have been there was removed when Mr. Beck built that section. A supporting factor to this theory is the unique plan of the middle section, with a passage across the back connecting the kitchen to that other structure and then to Mr. Beck's wing.

Whoever Mr. Beck employed to undertake the construction of his house was a designer and builder of merit. Its basic form is common to Kent County, a five-bay, two and a half story, center-hall plan house, but the details are outstanding. It has a well-proportioned Greek Revival porch, similar in design to the Ringgold House, Chestertown: windows with consoles under the sills and dormers with pilasters and applied pressed tin wreaths in the tympanums, similar to those at Stepney across the road.

The interior is trimmed with architraves around each opening and the ceilings boast plaster cornices and medallions. Original graining on the doors has been restored and the whole house brought up to code as a result of the 1980s restoration which also replaced the old kitchen wing.

North of the house some eighteenth century gravestones with the names of various members of the Dunn family have been found. Through the 1930s, Becks Landing was a regular stop for ships carrying produce to the Baltimore markets. The farm is still owned by the descendants of Horatio Beck.   K-254

Beck's Landing, Broad Neck. The middle section of this house was built around 1830, with the major section being constructed in the 1850s by Horatio Beck. Tyler Campbell photograph, 1996.

Brick House Farm

Near Worton
c. 1820

T HE BRICK HOUSE WAS CONSTRUCTED BY EITHER THOMAS Maslin, Jr., or his son Jacob, in the first quarter of the nineteenth century. The tract upon which the house was built is called *Harris' Forrest* and was part of Thomas Maslin's acquisitions in 1806–07 and 1810.[1] The Maslin house was very similar to the Moffett house on Quaker Neck, a three bay long, two-story brick structure with hall-parlor plan and a kitchen

Brick House Farm, near Worton, was built in the early nineteenth century by Thomas or Jacob Maslin. In 1883 it was acquired by W. T. Morris, in whose family it remains.

Hildebrand Farm, Morgan Neck, is a simple vernacular farmhouse constructed in the early nineteenth century by a member of the Brooks family. Its history is closely related to that of Thornton and Thornton Farm. Marsha L. Fritz photographs, 1980.

wing on its north gable. This house, however, possesses a corbeled brick cornice in contrast to the wood cornice of the Moffett House.

In 1883, Walter T. Morris acquired the farm which adjoined the farm of William Morris (part of Town Relief), and the family has owned the farm ever since. In 1905, the old house was changed in a way that is very similar to Kinsale. The old kitchen wing was taken from the north gable and moved to the west side of the building with a hyphen between containing a new stair and entry. A porch was built on

the east facade of the old house and over the new entry.

The house retains many original interior features along with the 1905 alterations. A contemporary brick smoke house remains north of the house. It also has a corbeled cornice. The house is a good example of the vernacular form and plan of farm houses in Kent County which began with Caulk's Field (1743) and continued into the middle of the nineteenth century.   K-233

1. Attribution of builder supplied by Carolyn Cooper.

Hildebrand Farm

Near Morgnec
c. 1820

T HE THREE BAY LONG, TWO-STORY FRAME dwelling on the Hildebrand Farm was built around 1820 in a vernacular manner, with hall-parlor plan. Both rooms have enclosed winder stairs with closets beneath and vertical beaded board chimney breasts. The two-bay, two-story wing was constructed soon after the main house. The building is loosely related in form and plan to the miller's house at Urieville, on the property across Morgan Creek, about a half mile away.

Hildebrand Farm received its name from Grace E. Brooks who was married to Merrill Hildebrand. It was part of the division of the Brooks farms in 1862.[1] Prior to that time, the farm was in the ownership of the Brooks family and appears to have accompanied the northern portion of Thornton since the eighteenth century. G. M. Brooks appears as owner of the farm on the 1860 map. He was residing at Thornton at the time. On the same map, School No. Four is located on the Hildebrand Farm opposite the lane to Thornton.   K-194

1. Land Records, Lib. JKH 3, fol. 51.

Maxwell's Purchase

Near Kennedyville
c. 1820

ON THE EAST SIDE OF THE ROAD FROM KENNEDYVILLE TO Turner's Creek there is a tract of land called Maxwell's Purchase on which stands a two part brick farmhouse nearly identical in form and fenestration to State's Adventure two miles to the east.

Maxwell's Purchase was assembled by Captain William Maxwell. It came into the possession of John and Rebecca Maxwell and by the time of their deaths in 1829 totaled 900 acres. The house they built was typical of those built by prosperous farmers in Kent County in the late eighteenth and early nineteenth century—a culmination of 100 or more years of temporary or inadequate housing and answering to a desire for more efficiency and space.

The Maxwell's house consisted of two parts, both two stories tall, the main part being five bays long and the lower part four. Both facades were laid in Flemish bond of uniform brick, while the other walls were laid in common. Neither water table nor belt course was used, but the lintels above the doors and windows were stetcher-long jack arches.

The interior of Maxwell's Purchase is extraordinary in its use of walnut and walnut graining and fine corner block trim. Two parlors and a central stairhall comprise the main section. The wing typically contains the kitchen and dining room. One mantel removed from the house in the early twentieth century had pairs of colonettes on each leg and an impressive array of fluting and gougework. It was made of walnut, as was the balustrade which has three slender turned balusters per step and an elliptically molded handrail. Newels and intermediates are also turned as are the drop finials beneath the intermediates. Foliated tracery graces the step ends and landings. Fluted pilasters and a half rail echo the hand rail along the wall of the stair.

Various alterations were made to the house during the late nineteenth century, including the installation of new trim in the east room and the chamber above. Dormers were added to the attic around the same period. A usual occurrence in the modernization of old houses, the updating of the kitchen, took place at Maxwell's Purchase at least two times before the 1970s.

Both John and Rebecca Maxwell died in 1829 and left wills providing for the distribution of their lands and education of their one minor child. The farm was divided into three parts, two going to sons and the third to a grandson, John H. M. Wallis, son of their daughter, Sophia.[1]

By 1850, Emily Wallis had acquired all of the original 900 acres. After 1864, it began to be divided again, the part with the house having been acquired by William Welsh, another prosperous farmer. It remained the property of his descendants until 1971 when it was acquired by the present owners.   K-140

Maxwell's Purchase, c. 1820, was built by either William or John Maxwell following the form and plan of other houses in the vivinity. Marsha L. Fritz photograph, 1980.

1. Wills, Lib. 11, fol. 118.

Boyer-Johnson Farm

Near Golts
c. 1820

It appears that when the builders of the Bradford Johnson Farmhouse first constructed the dwelling they used the Baird house on the adjoining Adventure as their model. They are similar not only in fenestration, but in form and plan as well.

The south facade is laid in Flemish bond above an unmolded water table. The mortar joints were double-struck making them appear more delicate that they were. Originally the windows appear to have had 12/12 sash on the first floor and 9/9 on the second—unusual proportions in any house. The kitchen had a door and window on each facade, but the doors were asymmetrically placed, indicating the position of the interior partition. The rear facade had a different window pattern than that of The Adventure. One dining room window was eliminated from the five bays, but all five windows above are in place, including a smaller window to light the stair landing. This last window appears to have been an afterthought, because there is a filling of brick above it to the height of the other windows.

The interior of the main block had an entry/stairhall with one room on either side. The east side contained an enclosed stair in the northeast corner. Before the building was plastered, the west room, hall and east room ceiling were whitewashed. By 1830, however, the plastering appears to have been completed in the main part of the house. The kitchen wing was not finished with plaster, but only whitewashed. The two chambers and passage above the kitchen had whitewashed board walls, brick walls and exposed ceiling joists. These remained unfinished until its demolition in 1994.

When the Tax Assessor visited the Third District (present First and Second) in 1822, he found Stephen Boyer the owner of 620 acres composed of Angel's Lott, Forrest Lands and The Adventure. Boyer's property, land, slaves, etc. were appraised for $3702.00.[1] When he died intestate in 1838, his personal property exceeded $4400.00, including *"a well furnished dwelling, 14 slaves"* and a large number of livestock.[2] One of the appraisers of the estate was E. T. Massey who lived nearby. Boyer's widow, Maria was the administrator.

Apparently after Boyer's death the Farm passed to his son, Simon Wilmer Boyer, as he is listed on the Martenet Map. In Simon's inventory at the time of his death in 1869, both a cook stove and a woodstove are listed.[3] The farm was sold to Robert A. Cochran of the Middletown area. Thereafter it was a tenant farm until it was purchased by Bradford Johnson. Upon the death of Mrs. Johnson the farm was given to the present owners who subsequently demolished the house in 1994.

K-131

Boyer-Johnson Farm, near Golts, was built around 1820 but the interior was finished in stages. The well constructed house was demolished and replaced with a modular home in 1994.

Boyer-Johnson Farm had the same floor plan as neighboring Baird House, with a secondary stair in the dining room. The main stair was not finished until several years after the dining room, perhaps the reason for the in-fill above the stair landing window. C. Engstrom photographs, 1977.

1. Tax Assessment, 1822.
2. Inventories, Lib. 1, fol. 572.
3. Inventories, Lib, JP 1, Lib. 1, fol. 523.

Kings Prevention

Broad Neck
c. 1820

Kings Prevention is situated across Langford Creek from the Reward. Essentially it is an early nineteenth century farmhouse which was incorporated into a larger house in the twentieth century. In its original state, the house faced south and the drive came in from the west.

The south wall of the house had three bays and was laid in Flemish bond. The north wall lacks a center window on the second story. It, as well as the gable ends, are laid in common bond. While there is neither water table, nor belt course, there is a three course corbeled cornice, usually an indication of construction in the 1820s. The kitchen wing was most likely located on the west gable, as there is a bricked-in door on that side.

When the house was remodeled in the twentieth century, a two-story frame wing was built on the south side, concealing two of the three bays. The plan of the house was also changed to a single room in the old section with fireplace at each end, eliminating the evidence of its probable hall-parlor plan.

King's Prevention, Broad Neck, was re-oriented to the rear or north side when a twentieth century wing was built over the original facade. The hall/parlor plan became a single room during the same period. Constance Stuart Larrabee photograph during her ownership.

King's Prevention, Broad Neck. The brick patch on the right side of the gable indicates the position of the stair and basement entrance. C. Engstrom photograph, 1977.

Although built thirty or forty years later, Kings Prevention's form and fenestration resembled Dunkan's Folly and Worth's Folly near the Cecil Meeting House. On both the 1860 and 1877 maps, the property appears to have been in the possession of Joseph J. Maslin. The name *Kings Prevention* is derived from a 34 acre parcel of land patented to Elias King in 1695.[1]   K-125

1. Patents, Lib. C 3, fol. 491.

Fair Hope Farm

Quaker Neck
c. 1820

Fair Hope Farm is a twentieth century name given to an old farm composed of parts of East Huntington, Tilghman's Farm and Norris Forest. The house itself stands on East Huntington and is an early nineteenth century frame farmhouse, two-and-a-half stories tall, five-bays long, with a two-part service wing which is one-and-a-half stories tall. The entire structure is one room deep.

The house is similar to others on Quaker Neck in form and plan. Its plan consists of two rooms and central stairhall, with a dining room in

what appears to have been the service wing. These are all located on the same level. At ground level in the service wing there is a three-bay kitchen.

The dining room is reputed to be the earliest part of the house. It has a fine early nineteenth century yellow pine corner cupboard. The details of the stair in the main section appear to date from the 1840s, but the rest of the millwork is the product of Brognard Oakie, the Pennsylvania architect responsible for remodeling the house for Mr. and Mrs. Charles Stokes in 1935.[1]

The farm was owned in the early nineteenth century by Samuel Merritt [2] whose family lived on the adjoining tract of Godlington Manor. During the period between 1836 and 1880, William Lamb owned the farm.[3] In 1852 the house was listed as *"in tolerable repair"*, which meant that it was not new.[4] For thirty years before the Stokes family purchased the farm, it was the home of the William T. Maslin family.[5]   K-89

1. Land Records, Lib. RAS 13, fol. 447.
2. Land Records, Lib. JNG 13, fol. 208.
3. Land Records, Lib. DCB 1, fol. 609.
4. Kent County Tax Assessment, 1852.
5. Land Records, Lib. JTD 11, fol. 29.

Fair Hope Farm, Quaker Neck, from the approach side. Francis Lamb Collection, 1951

Fair Hope Farm, Quaker Neck, was built on part of East Huntington in the first half of the nineteenth century by either Samuel Merritt or William Lamb. It was remodeled in 1935 under the care of Pennsylvania architect, Brognard Oakie.

Fair Hope Farm, dining room corner cupboard. C. Engstrom photographs, 1977.

Middle Farm

*Near Millington
1821*

T HE BRICK HOUSE ON THIS FARM which borders Pudding Branch appears at first glance to be later than the date on the recently *discovered* marked attic rafter— 1821. All walls of this 37' x 18', two-story house are laid in common bond. Its smaller, two-story wing has a corbeled brick cornice. For the size building, it is surprising that the plan includes a central stair-hall, albeit somewhat narrow.

The stair is a very delicate, close-string stair with plain square newel, round handrail and thin rectangular balusters. Its spandrel is composed of vertical beaded boards, now enclosing a basement stair. Both rooms have plain Federal style mantels. The stair only ascends to the second floor. Like many nineteenth century farmhouses, the attic stair is a winder located in the corner of the south room.

In the 1877 Atlas, this farm and two others were owned by the Spear family. The Alexander Farm is actually referred to as *"Middle Farm."* The road on which this house is located is named for that family.   K-636

mon bond without the use of any decorative devices. The interior plan is divided into a stairhall and parlor, similar to The Agreement and the Chambers House in Chestertown.

On its west gable, a frame, central-hall plan house was added with its roof at right angles to the original. Here, the windows are paired, like the late-nineteenth century remodeling of Douche's Folly. The house represents vernacular building traditions from both periods. The Davidson family is connected with the farm in the 1860s and 1870s.   K-218

Middle Farm, near Millington. Built in 1821, is a plain vernacular house with late nineteenth century central gable and overhanging eave. Marge Q. Fallaw photograph, 1986.

Camp Tockwogh, Stillpond Neck, is the site of an early nineteenth century brick farmhouse with an 1892 frame wing. The camp is named for the Indian tribe which inhabited the shores of the Sassafras River as recorded by John Smith in 1608. Marsha L. Fritz photograph, 1980.

Camp Tockwogh

*Near Still Pond
c. 1821*

N EAR THE END OF STILL POND Neck, where it overlooks the Chesapeake Bay, this late Federal period brick house consists of a three-bay main section with a late-nineteenth century frame wing (c. 1892). The brick section was constructed over a full basement and is two stories tall with an attic beneath the moderately pitched *A* roof. The windows on both floors originally had 9/6 sash, but the first story sash were later replaced with 6/6. The brick walls are laid in com-

Gondomah

Near Massey
c. 1822

EBENEZER T. MASSEY AND HIS WIFE, EMILY ANN, THROUGH inheritance, owned nearly 550 acres of land near Massey in the early nineteenth century. It is probable that they were responsible for the construction of Gondomah.

Initially the house was a three-bay, two-story, brick dwelling with hall-parlor plan, the hall being on the east and the parlor on the west. In plan and form, it would have been very similar to Angels Rest, an earlier house on the adjoining farm. In 1836, however, the Masseys had

prospered to such a degree that they more than doubled the size of the house. They added a three-bay addition with its own kitchen wing to the north and reoriented the house to the east with a new five-bay facade. It was at this time that the entire house was gutted and fitted with new woodwork throughout.

For a time, E. T. Massey moved his family to the Dr. John Thomas house in Millington, but continued to own Gondomah and rented it to his manager, a Mr. Sewell. In 1841, he insured the house with the Franklin Fire Insurance Company of Philadelphia. In order to do so, he was required to submit a plan and thorough description of the house's interior. Massey did so with the help of his carpenter, Joseph Hill of Smyrna, Delaware. Hill's plans indicated the name and use of each of the six rooms. He also described the materials and finishes throughout.

"Above you have a ground plan of the E. T. Mafsey family residence near Mafseys Cross Roads a farm house in Kent County Maryland; a two story brick building well furnished with 1¼ in yellow pine floors below and yellow pine floors in the parlor & dining room chambers the rest of the floors white pine.

East front with 4–18 & 5–12 light windows & 2–12 light dormers front door & Portico.

South front 2–18 & 3–15 light windows & 2–12 light dormers one front door & Portico

North end of Nursery 1–18 light window below

4 windows in Kitchen & 1 dormer window

2 trap doors in house roof a pump of water within official feet of the Kitchen.

The part of the house in which the Parlor and dining room are situated has been built for Some time but under went a thourough repair in 1836 and all the other

Gondomah. The plan of the house sketched for the Franklin Fire Insurance Co. in 1841, by Joseph Hill, carpenter. The first part of the house measures 19' x 38' on the plan. Pennsylvania Historical Society.

Gondomah the 1836 addition included not only the three bays on the right but the leanto wing which was twice as long as it is today.

Gondomah, near Massey. The three-bay south part of the house was constructed around 1822 by Ebenezer T. and Emily Ann Massey. In 1836 they more than doubled its size and re-oriented it to the east.
Michael C. Wootton photographs, 1995

part of the building is an addition which was built at the same time it is all plastered and painted except the Kitchen which is plastered but not painted. This new part and as much of the old as was repared are now of modern finish and of good meterials, I believe the cost of the whole building amounted to four thousand dollars and is at this time (in consequence of the late removal of Mr. Mafsey) occuped by his overseer.

Yours Respectfully,
Joseph Hill of
Smyrna house carpenter

Millington Kent County MD Jan 1841
Gentlemen

In accordance with your mode of business I have procured from the gentleman who built my house, a ground plot—description, materials & of my house, which I wish to effect an insurance on to the amount of $2000 and for which I paid you through Mr. J. L. Boon on the 10th of Decr last the sum of $71.00.

The description given you by Mr. Boon was correct—except in the instance of its being occupied by myself, it is in the occupancy of Mr. Sewell my manager—you will please forward me a policy forthwith, directed to this office and oblige.

Yours
E. T. Massey"[1]

By 1844, the Massey family had moved back to the farm, having sold the Thomas House to Miss Eleanor Horsey. After E. T. Massey's death in 1853, Gondomah remained in his wife's ownership for the rest of her life. It was then to go to their son, Robert B. M. Massey.[2]

In 1868, Robert mortgaged the farm to William C. Eliason.[3] Four years later, the mortgage was reassigned to Jacob Tome.[4] Apparently, Robert eventually defaulted and the Circuit Court appointed trustees to sell the farm. Recorded in January 1877, the deed indicated that Gondomah was sold to Robert's brother, Charles H. B. Massey,[5] who had inherited the adjoining farm, Angels Rest, from their father.[6] Charles went on to acquire Belmont, as well as a farm across the road, one on the Chester River near Crumpton, one near Chesterville and properties in Georgetown and Massey. At the time of his death, he was living at Belmont.

The farm remained in the Massey family, passing through Herman B. Massey and E. Thomas Massey, Jr. before it was sold in 1946 to Garrett and Barbara Turner, who resided there until 1975.[7] Between 1975 and the early 1990s, it was a rental property. The current owners have refurbished the house and now make it their home.   K-160

Gondomah. The stair in the 1836 section looking toward the front door.

Gondomah. The stair between the second and third floor of the 1822 section. Michael C. Wootton photographs, 1995.

1. Pennsylvania Historical Society, Franklin Fire Insurance Co., Policy.
2. Wills, Lib. JFB 1, fol. 372.
3. Land Records, Lib. JKH 7, fol. 628.
4. Land Records, Lib. JKH 10, fol. 503.
5. Land Records, Lib. DCB 2, fol. 500.
6. Wills, Lib. JFB 1, fol. 372.
7. Land Records, Lib. RAS 41, fol. 180.

Fairlee Manor

Near Fairlee
c. 1825

Fairlee Manor stands on part of Fare Lee, a 1900 acre tract composed of four other earlier surveys patented in 1674 to James Brown, merchant.[1] Little is yet known of this part of the property for its first 125 years, but it was acquired by Philip and Jane Taylor in the late eighteenth century.

The Taylors had only one daughter, Mary Ann, who married William Blackiston Wilmer in 1816. Shortly thereafter, Philip bequeathed the farm to his daughter[2] and on that 212 acre inheritance Mary Ann and William Blackiston Wilmer built the main house.

The house that the Taylors built was composed of the present central section, the two-bay brick wing now covered with stucco, and the plank kitchen on the west. From the architectural evidence, it appears to have been built in the 1820s. When the Tax Assessor listed this farm in 1852, the Wilmers owned 268¾ acres of Fairlee on which is mentioned a *"Brick House & other Building in good repair."*[3]

William and Mary Ann's daughter, Sarah Ann, married George D. S. Handy, Jr. in 1847. Handy was brought up two miles north of Fairlee Creek on a farm called Green Hill or Handy Point, on part of Great Oak Manor. The Handys lived in Baltimore, where he was a prominent physician. Dr. Handy purchased the farm from his widowed mother-in-law in 1859,[4] but it is uncertain who lived there afterwards.

In 1867, Handy transferred the farm to his wife. Then in 1880, Sarah Handy sold it out of the family.[5] It passed

through seven owners until 1936 when it was purchased by Frances B. Jackson, a woman from Elkhorn, Wisconsin.[6]

Mrs. Jackson set about making the house grander than it had been by building a balancing addition on the east and bringing in another old plank building to balance the original kitchen. She even built a second pyramidal roof outbuilding to balance the late nineteenth century pump house on the north side of the house.

After Mrs. Jackson's occupancy, the farm was owned by Mr. and Mrs. Maurice Heckscher for five years before being purchased by Louisa d'A Carpenter.[7] Mrs. Carpenter owned the farm for seven years and then moved to Springfield Farm three miles south. At that time she gave Fairlee Manor to the Easter Seal Society (1953).[8]

The plan of the original house was composed of a central stairhall with two flanking rooms. Even though the stairhall was narrow, the entrance had double doors and elliptical transom. Both flanking rooms were trimmed with corner blocks, a feature just being introduced in Kent County at the time, and both had Empire style mantels with engaged columns. In many ways, the detailing was similar to that at the Mitchell House.

In the middle section of the house there was one room, probably used as a family dining room. The service wing was composed of a kitchen with small pantry in the corner near the dining room.   K-105

1. Patents, Lib. 15, fol. 211.
2. Referenced in Land Records, Lib. JKH 1, fol. 627.
3. 1852 Tax Assessment.
4. Land Records, Lib. JKH 1, fol. 627.
5. Land Records, Lib. SB 1, fol. 17.
6. Land Records, Lib. RAS 16, fol. 162.
7. Land Records, Lib. RAS 41, fol. 364.
8. Land Records, Lib. WHG 31, fol. 523.

Fairlee Manor front entrance has a unique elliptical headed transom.

Fairlee Manor, Fairlee Creek, was built for William and Mary Ann Wilmer on land they inherited from her father, Philip Taylor. When first built it consisted of the main block and the telescoping sections on the west (right). Balancing wings were added by a subsequent owner in 1936. Tyler Campbell photographs, 1995.

Mitchell House

Tolchester
1825

JOSEPH THOMAS MITCHELL BEGAN PURCHASING PROPERTY on the Bay Side in 1808 with his purchases of parts of Tolchester, Tomb and Arcadia from Mary Granger. Granger was his mother-in-law and widow of William Granger.[1] In 1811, Mitchell acquired an adjoining part of Tolchester from William and Martha Ringgold and subsequently mortgaged both parcels (375 acres) back to William Ringgold. The deed stated that Joseph was living on the part he had previously acquired. The mortgage was paid off in 1822.[2]

In the following years, Mitchell continued to acquire additional properties. He exchanged adjoining land with Anna Maria Rowles, widow of John Rowles. (The Rowles had built and lived at Airy Hill.) Two other land transactions involved Wickcliffe and Market Place on Eastern Neck Island, which Joseph and his brother,

Richard Bennett Mitchell, had acquired as part of the dowry of their wives—sisters, Sophia and Maria Granger. In 1824, Joseph Mitchell was appointed trustee for the orphans of Richard Miller, his neighbor to the south, who had resided on part of Hinchingham. He also held a mortgage on the lands of Mr. Ricaud, located at the head of Swan Creek.

In 1825, Mitchell built a new house on his Tolchester farm which was composed of a large, two-and-a-half-story, brick main section with a two-and-a-half-story service wing. Its form was similar to many Federal period houses—nearly square, three bays wide and two bays deep with double chimneys. Connected by a curtain of brick, the already large chimneys appeared even more massive. In form, it is similar to Wades Point, Talbot County, constructed in 1819. Their plans, however, differ. The Mitchell House has double parlors to the west. On the east side, set back even with the north wall, there is a five-bay service wing which consists of a breakfast or dining

Mitchell House, Tolchester, as seen from the pond. It was constructed by Joseph Thomas Mitchell in 1825 and remained in possession of his son until 1852. Bob Creamer photograph. Tracy and Jim Stone Collection.

room separated from the kitchen by the back stair. On the south side of this wing is a large shed-roof porch.

The main part of Mitchell's house was very up-to-date. The double parlors were trimmed identically with the flat grooved trim and corner blocks, typical of the 1820–30 period. Beneath each window, a raised panel was set back from the interior wall and their sloping jambs and trim continued to the floor to complete the window composition. Both fireplaces were fitted with mantels with two round columns supporting a paneled frieze and wide shelf. (This form is found at Rose Hill, Cecil County in marble. Here, however, it is constructed of wood.) Access from one parlor to the other was gained through double doors, a feature which slightly predates similar arrangements found at Wickes House, Geddes-Piper House and the Smith-Ringgold House, all in Chestertown. And lastly, the entry hall ran uninterrupted to the back of the house.

The stair was mostly enclosed in a narrow leanto structure which extended down from the roof of the service wing. Before entering the enclosure, it rose five steps and then continued along what would otherwise have been the outside wall. Graceful half-rails with gooseneck curves were embedded in the plaster. The stair ascended to a corridor in the service wing before it continued into the main section.

In many ways, the second floor plan was similar to Airy Hill, i.e. two chambers over the parlors with two smaller chambers above the entry hall, all opening onto a small hall. It differed in that access to the third floor of the main section was gained via a separate enclosed stair. The second floor corridor of the service wing con-

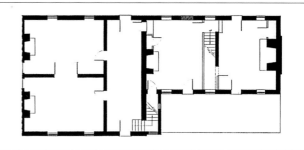

tinued along the south wall to the kitchen chamber. The two rooms each had their own fireplaces. All of the mantels were executed with the same moldings as in the main section. However, their form was more like earlier Federal mantels, with plinths supporting the mantel shelves.

Back on the first floor, the dining room was two steps lower than the entry hall and had a fireplace on the hall wall. Both its north and south walls had one window and one door. On the west wall there was a door to the back stair and kitchen beyond. The dining room trim was more like an earlier house, but with backband molding typical of the 1820-30 period.

The kitchen was another two steps lower than the dining room and it too had a door and window in the north and south walls and a large fireplace on the east gable. Beneath the back stair, there was a door to the pantry which was lighted by a full size window with vertical iron bars inside, a deterrent for anyone thinking of raiding its contents!

When Joseph T. Mitchell had nearly completed building the walls of his house, he installed a stone plaque with his initials and the date 1825 above the attic window.

After the construction of his mansion, Mitchell continued to acquire more land. In 1828, he purchased 407 acres of Gresham College to the south, and in 1829, he acquired 370 acres of Swamp Resurveyed. He was not to enjoy his new acquisitions, however, for he died intestate in 1830.

Mitchell's personal inventory, included 39 slaves and was valued at $14,562.85. When the inventory was evaluated, the appraisers listed the contents of the house by room, naming ten rooms and a curious space called *"the Entry Recess."* This could be a reference to the space beneath the stair landing.[3] Two curious entries give a glimpse into the activities in which Mitchell was involved. *"Wheat machine with grist mill and corn sheller worked by the same horse power,"* appears to have been a very modern device which would have made work easier and would have consequently resulted in greater profit. *"Set of house wheels,"* refers to the fact that he had also moved houses or other buildings.[4]

Joseph Thomas Mitchell, Jr. was the only son and heir of his father, but being a minor, his mother was named administrator of the estate. Mitchell, Jr. was to be paid $11,691.95 after all the debts were paid and to receive lands in excess of 1000 acres.[5]

Joseph, Jr. continued farming the holdings and must have done well, for the only mortgage on the farm was for $1,000 and it was paid off in a short time. In 1852, the Tax Assessment listed the following lands in his name:

Tolchester   375a
Pt Arcadia & swamp   47a
Pt Swamp lot of Dr. Brown   28a
Pt Swamp & Arcadia Resurveyed   370¾
Tract name unknown 10
1,038 acres at $22 per acre.

Joseph, Jr. had 23 slaves, but his household belongings were small, perhaps an indication of the fact that he was living in Baltimore and using Tolchester as a part-time residence. In 1852, Joseph T. Mitchell, Jr. made an agreement to sell the *"Plantation on Bayside called Tolchester supposed to contain 1050 acres"* to G. D. S Handy and J. G. Gordon for $27 per acre.[6]

When George D. S. Handy died in 1875, he was in sole possession of the farm. As part of the settlement of the Handy estate, Tolchester was sold to John and Annie Armbruster of Camden, New Jersey. They sold the farm, in 1882, to John W. Woodside of Philadelphia, but only after a thirty acre parcel had been surveyed off for Tolchester Park.[7]

The most substantial alteration to Mitchell House occurred around the turn of the century when the win-

Mitchell House, Tolchester. The double chimneys are joined by a curtain wall creating a massive structure viewed from either gable. The date plaque bearing the name Joseph Mitchell and the date, 1825, is embedded above the third floor window. C. Engstrom photograph, 1977.

dows of the south facade were lowered on both floors and new 2/2 sash and shutters were installed. A low pitch hip roof porch was also added at this time.

Between 1902 and 1922, the farm passed through three owners, all of whom had tenants living in the house. In 1927, the farm was sold to Tolchester Estates, a major subdivision which extended not only to this farm, but to the adjoining Waltham Farm as well.

In 1928, the house and several acres were purchased for Miss Katherine Dixon by her mother, Lillie Crisfield Dixon. Miss Dixon dammed the stream which drained the adjoining tract called Swamp and created ponds in which she grew water lilies for the market.[8]

By the time the Bishtons had purchased the house, the front porch had been removed so that only the outline of its roof was visible between floors. They repaired and maintained the house and during their ownership, it was one of the houses opened and featured in Rock Hall's Centennial Celebration in 1957.[9]

Between 1962 and 1971, the house was converted into a nursing home. Many alterations occurred during this period, including the installation of new bathrooms, the replacement of the dining room and kitchen floors with brick and the construction of new brick steps in the front.

Since 1982, the house has been run as a bed and breakfast with each successive owner improving the building and its grounds.   K-276

1. Land Records, Lib. BC 5, fol. 361.
2. Land Records, Lib. BC 7, fol. 39-44; Lib. TW 4, fol. 173.
3. Inventories, Lib. 20, fol. 114.
4. Ibid.
5. Accounts, Lib. 15, fol. 272.
6. Land Records, Lib. JFG 2, fol. 146.
7. Land Records, Lib. DCB 2, fol. 329; Lib. SB 3, fol. 30; Lib. SB 10, fol. 492.
8. Land Records, Lib. RAS 1, fol. 388.
9. Land Records, Lib. WHG 26, fol. 214.

Tulley's Fancy

Quaker Neck
c. 1825

Initially patented to John Tulley in 1664, Tulley's Fancy was repatented to Henry Hosier in 1671.[1] Hosier acquired an additional 100 acres the following year which he called Hosier's Addition.[2] One hundred and twenty-five years later a farmhouse was constructed in a location which most likely straddles both properties. The name *Tulley's Fancy,* however, is the one which has remained.

In plan the house is typical of Kent County farmhouses of the nineteenth century, with a central stairhall, two flanking rooms, and a kitchen located off the smaller of the two rooms. It is well finished with mantels having reeded elements, chair rail, and a period cabinet adjacent the dining room chimney. Between the dining room and stairhall, there is a vertical beaded board wall. All second story partitions were of a similar construction.

In addition to the two rooms directly above those below, the second story has a small room at the head of the stairs which is now used for a bath. Unlike the usual house of this period, the stair to the attic is located in the west corner of the house rather than being a continuation of the central stair.

In the 1950s, a two-story porch was constructed on the rear or northwest side of the house which affords a view down the east branch of Langford Creek. There had been a frame second story addition above the kitchen, but this was removed and the old kitchen roof line was reestablished in 1982 when the house was remodeled.   K-244

1. Ruth, Grieb, Trew, Map of Colonial Quaker Neck, 1967.
2. Ibid

Tullys Fancy dining room with paneled closet adjacent a simple Federal mantel. The living room mantel is more up-to-date in its use of Greek trim, combined with reeding.

Tully's Fancy dining room chamber. Although the main stair is central, the attic stair is enclosed in a chamber. Michael Bourne, photographs, 1983.

Tully's Fancy, Quaker Neck, was patented in 1664 to John Tully. The house was built between 1820–30, overlooking the upper reaches of East Langford Creek. Tyler Campbell photograph, 1996.

Hepbron Farm House Site

Near Lynch
c. 1825

Oｎｅ ｏｆ ｔｈｅ ｂｅｓｔ ｈｏｕｓｅｓ ｂｕｉｌｔ between 1820 and 1830, in the second district, was located near the village of Lynch. Between 1902 and 1942, the farm was referred to as the Hepbron Farm since it was leased during that period by William Jackson Hepbron and his family.

The house on the farm was a late example of a hall-parlor plan house, and like many of its predecessors, it had a two-room kitchen wing. Both sections were two full stories tall, but the main part was a three-bay, frame structure covered with beaded weatherboard, whereas the kitchen wing was a two-bay brick section with corbeled cornice.

The interior finish of the house was typical of the period, with well-designed late Federal style mantels and beaded trim with corner blocks. The chair rail employed intermittent reeding which complimented the reeded pilasters of one of the mantels. Both hall and parlor had their own enclosed newel stairs and both rooms in the kitchen had stairs as well.

First and second floor plans were identical to Godlington Manor (K-88), with the exception of exterior door placement. The second story division was clearly indicative of the hierarchy within the domestic operation.

Near the kitchen, there was a log or plank smokehouse with dovetailed corners. It was covered with vertical boards. Also on the property during the tenancy of the Hepbron family, was a corn fodder rick which was used as bedding for the farm animals each winter. Fodder was also used as roofing over the animal pens, which by spring had been used for additional bedding.

The farm appears in the ownership of J. M. Carron on the 1860 Martenet Map, and A. R. Tatnall in the 1877 Atlas. In the latter, it was also stated that it was the residence of W. H. Bowers. During the Hepbron tenancy, the farm was owned by Harry W. Dunlop. K-223

Hepbron Farm near Stillpond, had a combination frame and brick house. Like Big Fairlee, the Hepbron Farm had a stair from each of the first floor rooms. Maryland State Archives, Kitty Hepbron Harris Collection, c. 1930.

*Hepbron Farm. The "Hall" mantel is one of the most sophisticated combinations of Federal and Greek Revival details in Kent.
Marsha L. Fritz photograph, 1980.*

Hepbron Farm. Corn fodder ricks and cattle sheds with corn fodder roofs. Maryland State Archives, Kitty Hepbron Harris Collection, c. 1930.

Little Neck

Near Rock Hall
c. 1826

ORIGINALLY PART OF HINCHINGHAM, THE 2000 ACRE LAND grant patented to Thomas Hynson in 1659, Little Neck is the name given to a narrow strip of land situated between Swan and Tavern Creeks. A portion of this land was sold to Richard Coleman of Baltimore in 1826.[1] Richard is listed as a resident of Kent County in two deeds in 1839, but by the time of his death in the 1850s, he was again residing in Baltimore. The farmhouse at Little Neck was constructed for Richard Coleman's use.

The main facade of Little Neck appears to be the west side of the house, facing Tavern Creek. These openings are the only ones to have jack arches; all walls are laid in common bond. From the three-bay west facade, the two-story frame kitchen wing is set back. The rear walls of both wings are on the same plane. Across the entire back of the building there was a leanto porch, which included a bulkhead door to the cellar. The cellar is only beneath the east half of the house.

Because of the small scale of the building, the plan was made to take ad-

Little Neck Farm, near Rock Hall, was built soon after 1826, when the land was purchased by Richard Coleman. Its plan is a-typical of the period, having one large room across its southwest side with a stairhall and dining room on the northeast. Michael Bourne photograph, 1995.

Little Neck living room was finished very simply with plain Federal mantel and cupboard. Michael Bourne photograph, 1978.

vantage of all of the limited space. Instead of having a hall which extended through the building, the stair was located in a narrow passage in the southeast half. A dining room opened to the north and on the west side there was one large room which extended the full length of the facade. Like the Mitchell House, its grand neighbor located three miles to the north, Little Neck had a double door between the two rooms. Here, however, the opening was relatively small. Both of these rooms had well designed simple late Federal mantels and a chair rail. The living room also had a paneled cupboard to one side. The kitchen wing consisted of one space with enclosed stair adjacent the cooking fireplace. A pantry was partitioned off in the corner abutting the dining room. At one time there was also a west kitchen porch. Other similarities to the Mitchell House include the profile of the round stair rail, backband molding in various locations and an exterior corbeled cornice.

On the second floor, there were three bedrooms. The chamber above the living room had the only fireplace. The other two bed chambers were located above the kitchen. The stair as-

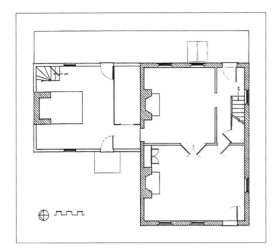

cended to the third floor, which was finished with plaster and undoubtedly used for children's accommodations. It was lighted by one window in each gable.

In the 1852 Tax Assessment, Richard Coleman was taxed on 230 acres being part of Hinchingham. It listed a *"Brick House and other buildings in tolerable repair."* He also owned 244 acres that was part of Hinchingham and Millers Purchase, on which there was a frame house, and 87 acres of *"St. Tantons."* There was no mention of household furniture or other items which might indicate he was in residence at Little Neck.

Richard Coleman agreed to sell his farm to John K. Bruff after 1852 for which he received half payment before he died. As it was not recorded, Richard's heirs had to register the deed in 1857 and were subsequently paid the other half.[2] In the meantime, Richard's widow, Sarah Coleman, married John K. Bruff. The Bruffs purchased an additional 133 acres at the southern end of Little Neck in 1859.[3] In the 1877 Atlas John Bruff is listed as owner and there appears to be another dwelling on the lower end of the Neck. Bruff had died two years before the Atlas was printed.

The farm was sold as the result of an equity case in 1880.[4] It was purchased by Thomas W. Eliason. From that time until the late 1980s, it remained in the Eliason estate. The farm was tenanted and few changes were made to the property. The kitchen wing was covered with shingles around the 1920s and a wash room was installed on the corner of the west porch.

In the late 1980s the farm was purchased by a development company and sub-divided. The exterior of the house was remodeled and placed on the market with about twenty acres.

One of the interesting structures to have remained until the subdivision was a small frame carriage house which had post-in-the-ground construction. K-264

Little Neck first floor plan, Michael Bourne, 1997.

Little Neck carriage house was the last remaining post-in-ground structure to have survived into the 1980s. It has since been demolished.

Little Neck attic balustrade. The very compact stair was more visible from the attic than elsewhere! Michael Bourne photographs, 1978.

1. Land Records, Lib. TW 4, fol. 981.
2. Land Records, Lib. JFG 4, fol. 569.
3. Land Records, Lib. JKH 1, fol. 689.
4. Land Records, Lib. SB 1, fol. 494.

Glenmore Site

Near Kennedyville
c. 1826

IN THE NORTHWESTERN CORNER FORMED BY THE Kennedyville crossroads was an old frame farmhouse which was owned by Mary E. Hurtt and her descendants between 1885 and 1979. The farm has been known as Glenmore since the early nineteenth century and has been home to the Sims and Jones families. Daniel Jones purchased the farm in 1826 from William and Mabel Sims[1] and was responsible for the construction of the oldest portion of the house. The house as it existed prior to its demolition, was the product of several additions and remodelings.

There are two theories concerning the early development of Glenmore. One is that it was similar to the first stage of the Molloy House in Chestertown, a two-story, three-bay, center-door, hall-parlor house. The other is that it was built anew after the Jones' purchase of the farm, as a three bay, two story, stairhall and parlor plan, like the tall section of Hinchingham Farm. In either case, there would most likely have been an attached kitchen.

The interior trim which was similar to the Hepbron House near Lynch, originates from the 1820s to 1830s. The mantel in the principal room had engaged columns with exaggerated entasis and each of the three plinth blocks had panels with cove-cut corners, a Federal device seen on grained doors from an earlier period. The house was finished within the period when chair rail was still in use.

Within a year of the deaths of Daniel and Catherine Jones, the farm was taken over by their son, John Wesley Jones who became secretary to the President of the Philadelphia and Reading Railroad.[2] He had worked his way up to the office of First Vice-President by the time of his resignation in 1877. His name, J. Jones, is listed as owner of the farm in the 1877 Atlas. During Jones' prosperous years with the Philadelphia and Reading Railroad, the house was enlarged to the five bay, two-and-a-half-story farm house that stood until recently. In 1885, he sold the farm to Mary E. Hurtt.[3] Her descendants built the kitchen wing and installed the segmentally arched architrave over the front door.

The house was demolished around 1980.   K-141

1. Land Records, Lib. TW 4, fol. 740.
2. Land Records, Lib. JKH 1, fol. 1.
3. Land Records, Lib. SB 7, fol. 284.

Glenmore, Kennedyville. The assymetry of the facade is the result of two or three building periods. Daniel Jones purchased the property in 1826 and was responsible for the majority of the late Federal interior. It was demolished around 1980. Maryland Historical Trust.

Masonic Building

High Street, Chestertown
1827

THE FIRST PUBLISHED MENTION OF FREEMASONRY ASSOCIATed with a Kent Countian can be found in an advertisement in the Maryland Gazette of the 25th of March 1763, in which Dr. John Scott was listed as a person from whom a lottery ticket could be purchased. The first lodge in Kent County was established at Georgetown in 1766 and known as Lodge No. 6, an offshoot from the Grand Lodge of Pennsylvania.

Lodge No. 7 was formed that same year in Chestertown. About 1780–81 dissension in the Georgetown Lodge was resolved by the Reverend William Smith of Chester Parish, who had recently come to Chestertown from Philadelphia. He was instrumental in the establishment of Washington College as well. His activities in Freemasonry culminated in his being named Master Mason in the 1780s.

Like many of the institutions of Kent County after the Revolution, Freemasonry seems to have had its ups and downs. Various lodge rooms around the county were utilized, including locations in Georgetown, Chestertown, Georgetown Crossroads and Millington. It was not until 1826 that the Maryland General Assembly granted a parcel of land to the Clinton Lodge on which they could build a Masonic Hall. It was located on the public square in Chestertown.

A notice in the May 18th issue of the Chestertown Telegraph, 1827, states:

"NOTICE
The subscribers being duly authorized by the Legislature of Maryland hereby give notice that on Saturday the 26th instant, at 10 o'clock A. M. at the office of William H. Barroll, Esq., they will open a

book receiving subscriptions to a Capitol Stock of three thousand dollars, to be expended in the erection of a Masonic Hall, on the public square in Chestertown ... .
  William Barroll
  Timothy Clowes
  George W. Thomas
  Morgan Browne
  Peregrine Wroth"

Soon after the establishment of the lottery, permission to lay the cornerstone was granted by the Grand Lodge. Apparently, the building was begun very soon after, for it was announced to the Grand Lodge of Maryland on May 15, 1828 that Clinton Lodge had completed the erection of a *"neat and elegant Masonic Hall."*[1]

Later that year, Benjamin Greenwood announced in the Telegraph that he had established a *"New Stand, having taken one of the spacious and beautiful store rooms in the Masonic Hall."*[2]

The building which was constructed for Clinton Lodge was built on a lot 40' x 60'. It was built over a full basement, and included three store spaces on the first floor and a lodge room on the second. Entrance to the lodge appears to have been gained through the last bay of the northwest gable from the Courthouse Yard. The stair to the lodge room rose within that gable. The lodge room itself occupied four of the five bay second floor and had a high tray ceiling. The original ceiling is painted black, and still exists above a dropped ceiling.

The High Street facade is laid in Flemish bond brick with plain stone lintels above the openings, each store having its own door. In the center of the facade a gable rises bearing the Masonic emblem in a circular panel. The same motif is repeated in the two gable ends. The rear elevation differs from the front in that there are three windows on the first floor with five above. Each of the windows has a standard jack arch. The front gable is a forerunner of a feature found in residential structures in the last half of the nineteenth century.

In 1836 the property was transferred to the Masonic Hall Company and remained in that ownership until the late nineteenth century when it was purchased by William B. Usilton. It remained in the Usilton family until 1933 when it was sold. Since that time there have been three subsequent owners.

In Fred Usilton's History of Chestertown (1899), several occupants of the first floor store rooms are listed, including Mr. T. W. Eliason, who after 1854 moved across the street to what had been a tavern (The White Swan Tavern). During the Usilton ownership it was called *The Kent News Building.*   K-48

Masonic Building, Chestertown, was constructed in 1827 by Clinton Lodge on the courthouse grounds. It had been authorized by the Maryland General Assembly.
Michael C. Wootton photograph, 1996.

1. Townsend, Rolph, Sr., History of Masonry in Kent County, Maryland, January 1952. Unpublished.
2. Telegraph, 14 November 1828.

Charles Joiner's Stone Dairy

Near Worton
1828

O N THE FARM ORIGINALLY UNDER THE NAME OF BROAD Neck, there is a small stone outbuilding which adjoins a late nineteenth century frame farmhouse. It measures about 10' x 12' and has walls about 1' thick. The plaster ceiling and concrete floor conceal interior structural details, but rough-hewn and round structural members project at the eaves. All of the openings have been altered and the exterior has been stuccoed. In the southwest gable there is a date, the numerals of which are unclear—either 1828 or 1858. It was originally constructed as a dairy to service a house which predated the existing residence. This building is one of five structures in the Third District which are built of stone. There was apparently a concentration of stone in this small area in the center of the county.
K-229

Charles Joiner's Stone Dairy, near Lynch, is the only early structure remaining on the farm. It is one of a string of stone outbuildings extending from Flatland Road to Lynch. Marsha L. Fritz photograph, 1980.

Charles Joiner's Stone Dairy, plan by Marsha L. Fritz, 1980.

Green Forest

Near Kennedyville
c. 1830

G REEN FOREST IS A THREE-BAY, GABLE ROOFED, BRICK house with an unusually tall two-bay wing, all built at one time. There appears to be basement under the entire building and that is probably the reason for the height of the wing. Most often, there is no basement under the kitchen wing on Kent County houses. One other exception to the rule is Stepney, which was built considerably earlier.

Like several other buildings constructed in the second quarter of the nineteenth century, Green Forest has a corbeled cornice. Its closest neighbor, Suffolk, shares this treatment. As a matter of fact, both buildings were constructed for Benjamin Howard. His son, Joseph, lived on the farm and received it upon his father's death in 1865.[1] Joseph sold it to his sister, Mary Ellen Haman, in 1871.[2] It appears to have remained in the family until after the death of B. Howard Haman, attorney in Baltimore, in 1932.

It was acquired by Glenn L. Martin, founder of the Remington Arms Corporation, who modernized the interior.[3] The only original feature of the house is the stair, with its round rail and turned newel and balusters.

Green Forest, near Stillpond, was probably built by Benjamin Howard c. 1830–40 for his son Joseph, who inherited the property in 1865. Michael C. Wootton photograph, 1996.

1. Wills, Lib. JF 1, fol. 286.
2. Land Records, Lib. WHG 15, fol. 144.
3. Ibid.

K-418

Jessup Farm

Broad Neck
c. 1830

THE JESSUP FARMHOUSE WAS CONSTRUCTED in the second quarter of the nineteenth century on part of Pentridge, a 550 acre tract patented in 1670 to William Hemsley. The house was composed of three parts, the first of which is a frame, two-and-a-half-story structure and is located on its westernmost side. About twenty years after its construction, a second section equal in size to the first was added to the east, along with a two-story kitchen.

The first section was composed of a stairhall and a living room with fireplace on the interior wall. The stair was the best feature of the house, with close-string balustrade and round handrail. The windows had 12/12 sash on the first floor and 12/8 on the second.

There did not appear to be a connecting door on the second floor between the two taller sections. The attic was only accessible from the newer section—the older stair having been removed.

In a deed, dated 1804, from Benjamin Vickers to Joel Vickers, the property was referred to as being on *"Cacaway Neck,"* an earlier reference to Broad Neck. It stated that the farm had been in the family since at least 1790.[1] Joel Vickers was listed as a resident of Baltimore County, where he apparently continued to reside until his death in 1860.

Jessup Farm, Broad Neck, was composed of two nearly identical plan sections, possibly an indication that the house was used by two generations of Vickers when it was built.

Jessup Farm, Broad Neck: the earlier part of the house had no communication on the second story.
Michael Bourne photographs, 1977.

In the 1852 Tax Assessment, the property was listed as part of *"Helston, Pentridge and Spring Garden"* and included a *"Frame house & other Buildings in good repair"* and *"ten slaves."*[2] Apparently Captain Vickers (as he was referred to on the Martenet Map) was prosperous, for he left Olney Mill to his son, George R. and Windsor Mill and a lot on Sharp Street, Baltimore, to his son Benjamin. He bequeathed to his daughter Geraldine, *"the house and lot in which I reside ... No. 71 Sharp Street."* The farm, however, he left in trust for his daughter Celeno Jessup, the trustees including his two sons and *"George Vickers of Chestertown."* He further stipulated that the farm was later to descend to his grandson, George Albert Jessup, and then to George's heirs. His brother, William, was to have the right of a home on *"Lankford Farm"* (which may explain the separation of the two sections of the house).[3] George A. Jessup is listed as the owner on the 1877 Atlas.

In 1911, after the death of George Jessup, the farm was acquired by his son, Charles, a single man.[4] Charles deeded the farm to his two sisters in 1947[5] and they in turn sold it out of the family in 1968.[6] The house and many outbuildings were demolished in 1977.

K-501

1. Land Records, Lib. TW 3, fol. 164.
2. Kent County Tax Assessment, First District, 1852.
3. Wills, Lib. JTD 1, fol. 397-413.
4. Land Records, Lib. JTD 24, fol. 171.
5. Land Records, Lib. WHG 5, fol. 307.
6. Land Records, Lib. EHP 27, fol. 460.

Poplar Hill

Fairlee
c. 1830

WHEN COLONEL JOSEPH WICKES' PROPERTIES WERE LISTED in the 1852 Tax Assessment, *"Poplar Hill Resurveyed"* (220 acres), *"Pt. St. Tantons"* (three-and-a-half acres), and *"Pt. Fairlee & Bishford"* (32 acres) were included in the 939 acres he owned. The Assessor described the houses as *"Buildings in Bad Repair."*[1]

In 1857, William Crow purchased the farm from Colonel and Mrs. Wickes. It is likely that he remodeled the house thereafter. The deed describes its location as *"on the east side of the road from Bel Air to St. Paul's."*[2] Twenty-three years later, Crow sold the farm to John Parr Nicholson, but as Nicholson's name appears next to the property in the 1877 Atlas, it is likely that he began farming the land for Crow prior to his acquisition.

The form of the house is early and resembles Locust Grove, a house northeast of Chestertown. It was one-and-a-half stories tall and five bays long with a lower service wing. Behind the room adjoining the wing there was a leanto, similar to that at Shepherd's Delight, as well as Locust Grove.

In 1905, the Nicholsons gave the old house to a person who moved it to nearby Georgetown. The house which replaced it remains on the farm today.

K-479.

Poplar Hill, near Fairlee, had the same form as Bachelor's Resolution (Locust Grove), with leanto room across part of the back left side. Pictured on the porch is the family of John Parr Nicholson. Maryland State Archives, Emily Skirven Spencer Collection, c. 1900

1. Kent County Tax Assessment, First District, 1852.
2. Land Records, Lib. JKH 1, fol. 36.
3. Land Records, Lib. SB 1, fol. 38.

Kentland

Near Fairlee
c. 1800, 1830

SOMETIME BEFORE 1783, JOHN BEALE BORDLEY INHERITED part of his father's original tract of land. In the tax assessment of that year, Bordley was taxed on a total of 1816 acres. His large holdings were patented under the name *"Kent Land"* and included Fancy Farm, Grumble, Providence, Bordley's Beginning, Coventry, Hills Down and Harris Adventure.[2]

Bordley is the likely builder of the frame tenant house which existed on Kent Land until two of its three sections were moved in 1987. Originally the two part house had a two-story frame section measuring roughly 18' x 20' with basement and winder stair. The second story was divided into two nearly equal size rooms, one with a fireplace. Both the chimney breast and partition wall upstairs were made of vertical beaded boards. The principal room appears to have had a central door with two flanking windows, but the north door had been closed when the third section was added.

The one-story section had two rooms, a kitchen and a pantry. A boxed-in, ladder-like stair was located in the southeast corner of the kitchen next to the fireplace which was built in pyramidal fashion. There was little else about this structure that was noteworthy.

William Harris, merchant of Chestertown owned the farm at least as early as the 1820s. His heirs, however, sold it in 1/5

Kentland in its original location. It was the home of William Baker who was responsible for building the tallest part of the telescopic house. Marsha L. Fritz photograph, 1981.

bedroom and small room at the head of the stair. A doorway was added to the old wall for access to the earlier bedrooms. The stair continued to an unfinished attic. The interior was finished with woodwork of the period, with molded trim and corner blocks. The second floor fireplace wall was fitted with small closets on each side which allowed enough room for full size windows on the gable. Both of the new rooms were lighted by six windows.

In 1917, the farm was purchased by Mr. and Mrs. Joseph Quinn and remains in the family to the present.

Kentland, moved to Fairlee Creek and remodeled in the 1980s. The middle section is the earliest existing part of the house. Tyler Campbell photograph, 1996.

Kentland, c. 1800. First floor plan. Drawn by Michael Bourne, 1985.

Kentland, c. 1800. Front elevation, Michael Bourne, 1985.

parts to Samuel E. Baker between the late 1820s and 1830s, finally joining together in a joint deed in 1839.[3]

It would appear that even before the final deed, Samuel Baker had built the third section onto the existing house. This addition turned his three room house into the best known plan in the county, one similar to that of Hinchingham Farm and many other houses is Kent. The new wing was taller that the other two and possessed an entry/stairhall and parlor. On the second floor there was a

In 1987, however, the old house was moved to a branch of Fairlee Creek and the site is now occupied by a new dwelling. In its new location, the old house is a three-part dwelling. The old kitchen and pantry have been replaced with a gambrel roof wing, the roof of the main section heightened, and dormers added.   K-82

1. 1783 Tax Assessment, Worton Hundred.
2. Patents, Lib. IC #G, fol. 235.
3. Land Records, Lib. JNG 5, fol. 487 (JNG 1/436; JNG 2/687; JNG 6/18).

Logan House

Millington
c. 1830

Ｏ N THE SOUTH SIDE OF CY-press Street there stands a two-and-a-half-story brick house which was built during the second quarter of the nineteenth century, quite near the time the town received its new name of Millington. Its five bay facade is very uniform dark brick laid in Flemish bond with thin white mortar joints, a uniformity which is similar to the earlier River House in Chestertown.

Like earlier houses, the five bay facade has the classical difference in window height between stories, with 9/6 sash on the first floor and 6/6 on the second. The size of the window frames, however, is narrower and the lintels are wooden with corner block applied to each end; both features more distinctive of the 1830s. The two dormers with steeply pitched *A* roof have applied trim with corner blocks, like some of the work inside. Few of the houses of Kent County boast a fanlight, but here radiating muntins like a sunburst are contained within a rectangular transom.

As can be surmised from the exterior, the plans consists of a central stairhall and two rooms with a one-and-a-half-story wing on the rear which houses a kitchen. The hall possesses a close string stair which ascends to the third story. Both living room and dining room have mantels with plinths which support a broken or three-part shelf. The living room mantel, however, is the more sophisticated with its use of corner block trim and detailed plinths and panels between. Adjacent the latter there is a cabinet with double paneled doors. Both rooms possess chair rail installed at a time when many houses were being built without.

The Logan House is one of the best examples of late Federal dwellings in Kent. In form and plan it is similar to several farmhouses located between Millington and Sassafras, but it, unlike the others, has suffered the least amount of change.   K-170

Logan House. The dining room, with built-in cabinet, chair rail, and Federal style mantel.

The living room mantel was more sophisticated, with Greek moldings on the shelf and corner block trim.

The Logan House, Millington, was built c. 1830, with Flemish bond facade. All of the windows are fit with corner blocks, including the dormers. C. Engstrom photographs, 1977.

Cummins Farm

Near Galena
c. 1830

Richard Holding purchased 210 acres of Free Gift from the heirs of George W. Forrester in 1813.[1] He is listed on the 1822 Tax Assessment owning the same parcel, which is valued at $860.00. Whether the existing house was built before or after 1822 is questionable. Is was, however, built before Holding's death in the early 1840s. Holding's daughter and son-in-law purchased it from the estate and sold it in 1849 to John H. Cummins.[2] Thereafter, it is referred to as the Cummins Farm in the land records.

The Federal style house which Holding constructed is a two-story, frame structure, three bays wide and two bays deep (23' x 30'). It has a side passage or townhouse plan, with two parlors on the east. Connected to these, the kitchen wing was later replaced by the Cummins family. It is said that the kitchen wing was one room longer than the existing two-room, two-story structure.

Holding's house has an open-string stair with delicately turned newels and intermediates and three rectangular balusters per step, beneath which there is beaded panel spandrel. The mantels in both parlors are identical. In form and plan, the Holding house is similar to two others which stood near Millington, one on the Chesterville-Millington Road and the other at Unicorn in Queen Anne's County.

In the 1877 Atlas, the Cummins Farm is owned by J. G. Black.

K-641

1. Land Records, Lib. BC 7, fol. 432.
2. Land Records, Lib. JNG 12, fol. 133.

Houghton Farmhouse

Near Morgan Creek
c. 1830

East of Morgan Creek, Houghton Farm is a five-bay, two-and-a-half story frame house with four-bay, two-story wing. The house continues to give the impression of a typical second quarter of the nineteenth century Kent County farmhouse, even though it was covered with shingles in the early twentieth century. It is similar to Sunnyside Farm a few miles to the northeast. The fact that some of the second floor windows are not placed symmetrically above the 9/6 sash windows below may be reason to question the evolution of the house. Perhaps it began as a one-and-a-half story building and is earlier than its exterior appearance. Its location may well be on a part of the original Buckingham tract, a 500 acre patent to Simon Wilmer in the late seventeenth century.   K-394

Cummins Farm, Lambson's Station, was built by Richard Holding between 1813 and 1840. The kitchen wing was replaced by the John Cummins family after 1849. Marge Q. Fallaw photograph, 1986.

Houghton Farmhouse, Morgan Neck, has the same form as Glenmore and Sunnyside. Marsha L. Fritz photograph, 1980.

W. T. Hepbron Farm Site

Near Stillpond
c. 1830

On the central neck which juts into Lloyd Creek from the south was a two-story early nineteenth century farmhouse which measured about 20' x 30'. The central bay of the three-bay facade was slightly off-

W. T. Hepbron Farmhouse. This little frame house was built in the second quarter of the nineteenth century by Thomas Hepbron and was a tenant house most of its life.
Marsha L. Fritz photograph, 1980.

Owlhurst, near Kennedyville, contains at least three building periods in the nineteenth century. There is a basement beneath the oldest part of the house.
Marge Q. Fallaw photograph, 1977.

Owlhurst

Near Kennedyville
c. 1830

OWLHURST APPEARS ON THE 1860 MAP OF KENT COUNTY as having been in the possession of Colonel E. Jefferson. The house he would have occupied was composed of a four-bay, two-story, frame section with hall-parlor plan. Attached to its western end was a two-bay kitchen wing, built over a basement. Only the basic form and a few details remain in the house today. Noteworthy is the dining room cabinet with tall paneled double doors.

Later in the nineteenth century, a third section was built on the west end. It serves as the kitchen at present. This is a survival of a vernacular form of house that was built in Kent County from the mid-eighteenth to mid-nineteenth century.

K-212

Fairview

Near Galena
c. 1830

center creating two nearly equal size rooms. Each had an enclosed corner stair adjacent its fireplace giving access to the rooms above.

The houses suffered two major fires which destroyed the majority of its woodwork. The doors that remained were from the second quarter of the nineteenth century. It had a form very like the Andelot Tenant House, although the chimneys of the Hepbron farmhouse appeared taller. Part of that phenomenon was caused by the fact that the roof, which was replaced in 1975 after a fire, was installed lower than the original. Like many houses of this period, the backs of the fireplaces were exposed outside as a fire prevention measure. On the 1860 Martenet Map of Kent County, the farm appears to be the only one in the ownership of W. T. Hepbron, who had purchased it from the estate of his father, Thomas. By 1877, W. T. owned two other farms nearby and lived on one closer to Turner's Creek. The house was a tenant house for most of its life. It was demolished in the 1980s and replaced by a new house.

K-421

THE NAME FAIRVIEW IS first mentioned in a mortgage made by William Gooding on his half interest in the farm in 1879.[1] The other half of the farm was owned by the Rev. Cornelius Prettyman and his wife. In 1880, in a lease agreement, Gooding rented his half to the Prettymans while he was out of the country. In that agreement Gooding is referred to as *"temporarily residing in Leipzig in Europe."*[2]

Slightly before the above mentioned transactions took place, in the early or mid 1870s, the farm had been leased to George and Harriett Ford who had moved from Cecil County. The Ford family remained tenants on the farm until after the deaths of Gooding and Prettyman. It was at this point that the Ford's son, Samuel and his wife Eliza Jane Spry purchased the farm. They resided here for many years, raising their children to maturity. The farm passed on to their oldest son Herbert Spry Ford, in whose family it remained until 1995. The house which George and Harriett Ford moved into had already been standing for about thirty years. It was in about the same condition as is shown in the photograph taken in 1910.

A handsome late Federal frame farmhouse, it was composed of a large five-bay block with one-and-a-half-story kitchen wing. In form and date it is similar to Timber Level, the John Carvill Sutton Farm built near Black's Station in 1838. Fairview, however, had two sophisticated dormers on the roof which had pilasters and segmentally arched roofs of their own.

The interior plan was like the earlier Mt. Herman, near Chesterville, with central stairhall, living room, dining room and kitchen with pantry. The stair is a handsome late Federal work with turned newels and round handrail which rises above each newel. Two balusters per step give an openness to the balustrade. One of the mantels is typical late Federal work while the other is more like the antebellum mantel found in a bedroom at Moreton Hall (c. 1850).

Fairview is well constructed and a house typical of the second quarter of the nineteenth century Kent County landscape. It represents the prosperity which

resulted from better farming methods introduced in the county around the turn of the nineteenth century and is probably a replacement of an earlier house that had been worn out by previous generations.   K-187

Fairview, Lambson's Station, was built in the late 1830s. It is similar to Timber Level which is dated 1838. It was owned by the George Ford family between the 1870s and 1990s. Marge Q. Fallaw photograph, 1985.

Fairview, with porches on both sections. Curved-roof dormers require metal roofing that was just coming into general use in the area. Kitty Ford Ayres Collection, c. 1900.

1. Land Records, Lib. DCB 4, fol. 187.
2. Land Records, Lib. DCB 5, fol. 623.

The Eaton Farm

Near Chesterville
c. 1830

JAMES SPEAR, WHO BUILT AND LIVED IN THE HOUSE NORTH OF Millington bearing his name, bequeathed his home farm and the *"Eaton Farm"* to his daughter Georgianna in 1874.[1] The Eaton Farm had been tenanted prior to his death. It remained so until 1921, when it was purchased by Charles and Emma Schelts.[2] It was owned and operated by the Schelts family for the next fifty years when it was sold again. In the meantime, the name of the farm had been lost in the deeds.

During all of this time, the principal residence on the farm was the existing three-bay, two-story brick house

with attached kitchen wing. It was built in the second quarter of the nineteenth century, a little later than the Edick Farm, closer to Chesterville. It had a hall-parlor plan which was actually a late use of the plan for houses of the county. Otherwise, it was similar to Angel's Rest, north of Massey, in both plan and form. Like Angel's Rest, the original wooden one-story kitchen was heightened to two full stories carrying the roof line of the main section.

After 1971, the once whitewashed brick walls were covered with formstone. The interior retains some features of the second quarter of the nineteenth century, as well as an earlier Federal Mantel.   K-186

1. Wills, Lib. EC 1, fol. 98.
2. Land Records, Lib. APR 8, fol. 288.

Edick Farm

Chesterville
c. 1830

EDICK FARM IS A NAME GIVEN TO THIS FARM IN 1946 WHEN IT was purchased by the late Edmund and Muriel Cook.[1] The farm was composed of parts of two early tracts: one being Vianna, the other being Doumford (or Rumford).

Around 1830, Hezekiah Masten owned the farm and built the existing house. Masten's house appears to have been the three-bay, two-story brick section with one-and-a-half-story brick wing. At the time of construction, there would have been a kitchen in an adjoining wing. As now laid out, the house has a living room and

The Eaton Farm, near Chesterville, was originally a brick house with hall-parlor plan. The house dates from the second quarter of the nineteenth century. Marge Q. Fallaw, 1986.

Edick Farm was built by Hezekiah Masten after 1830. In form it resembles Runneymeade but one bay shorter. The farm includes parts of Vianna and Rumford. C. Engstrom photograph, 1977.

Edick Farm. The three flight stair has a graceful balustrade with large newel post and three balusters per step. C. Engstrom photograph, 1977.

stairhall in the two story section, a dining room in the brick wing and kitchen in the frame wing—the plan which is most common in Kent. Its form, however, is not common in relation to the plan. Salutation Farm is the house that most resembles Edick Farm, and it is about 40 years earlier in origin.

The interior is well finished, with unusual incised corner block trim. The mantel shelf has a scotia molding so typical of this period. The stair rises in three flights to the second floor. The newels are simply turned, a little larger than earlier newels, but not as large as the Antebellum woodwork of the following decades. A round handrail of cherry rises over the newels and beneath are three rectangular balusters per step.

The house was modernized in the mid-twentieth century, but its basic historic character remains intact.

Hezekiah Masten was a trustee of the M. E. Church and gave a one acre parcel on the Millington Road in Chesterville in 1841:

"That they shall erect and build or cause to be erected or built thereon, a house or place of Worship for the use of the members of the M. E. Church."[2]

When Masten's estate was settled, the farm was purchased by John G. Miers who also owned Bordley's Gift. Miers' heirs sold the farm in 1940.[3]   K-180

1. Land Records, Lib. RAS 41, fol. 214.
2. Land Records, Lib. JNG 8, fol. 9.
3. Land Records, Lib. RAS 23, fol. 348.

Suffolk

Near Kennedyville
c. 1830

Suffolk has been associated with the Howard family since the house was constructed in the second quarter of the nineteenth century. Benjamin Howard began acquiring land in the vicinity in 1821, with the purchase of 100 acres of Green Forest and 200 acres of Suffolk, land that had previously been owned by Moses Briscoe.[1] An additional 106 acres were acquired in 1828 and 318 acres in 1837, the latter from his brother-in-law, Thomas Bevins.[2]

The house that Howard chose to build was very traditional in form and plan. Two other structures in the area, Maxwell's Purchase and State's Adventure share the same plan and form. These two, however, are earlier than Suffolk. At Suffolk there is a corbeled brick cornice. The main section has a center stairhall which is flanked by two rooms. There are an additional two rooms in the kitchen wing which is lower. The living room is well-finished having recessed windows with paneled splayed jambs and a panel beneath which extends to the floor. Door and

Suffolk, near Kennedyville, was built c. 1830 for Benjamin Howard. The use of corbeled cornice and Greek moldings on the dormers and mantels is a touch of period identity to an otherwise vernacular form. C. Engstrom photograph, 1977.

window trim possess corner blocks and the mantel has a horizontal fluted frieze between two engaged columns, a design that is similar to the marble mantel installed at Rose Hill, Cecil County in 1837.

Like several other houses of the period, the stair balustrade is simple, but the newel is made of tiger maple, a striking contrast to the dark mahogany handrail and a detail which is seen in furniture design of the period. This treatment can be found at Locust Hill Farm which was remodeled during the same period.

Benjamin Howard married for a second time in 1845. He first, however, drew up a premarital agreement with his bride-to-be, Augusta Eubanks of Baltimore. It stipulated that she would relinquish her dower in lieu of £200 per annum.[3] Interestingly, his will, probated in March of 1885, revokes the premarital contract and allows his widow $2000 per annum for the remainder of her life and specifies that his son should give her free board.

The inventory of Benjamin Howard's personal belongings included two interesting entries beside the usual furniture and equipment for the prosperous farm, *"20 Peach boxes"* and *"12 barrels of plaster."* Mr. Howard may have been an early peach grower, a favorite crop in the last half of the nineteenth century. The total amount of his personal belongings amounted to $9825.60.[4]

In his will he bequeathed his home plantation to his daughter, Mary Ellen Haman, Green Forest and Lower Bloomfield to his son Joseph, and Young's Neck and Upper Bloomfield to his other son George.[5] Upon the death of Mary Ellen Haman, who had resided in Baltimore, all of her earthly possessions were bequeathed to her son and daughter.[6] It is uncertain what happened to Kate Haman, but Benjamin Howard Haman of Baltimore became the sole owner. He was a prominent attorney and bachelor. He bequeathed his assets to various

Suffolk. The living room mantel has engaged columns with convex fluted friese. A similar mantel can be seen at Rose Hill, Cecil County, only in marble.

Suffolk. The stair with a tiger maple newel and mahogany rail over a paneled soffit.
C. Engstrom photographs, 1977.

friends and cousins in 1932.[7] The heirs sold Suffolk in 1951 to the present owners.[8] Since that time the house has been a tenant residence.   K-139

1. Land Records, Lib. TW 4, fol. 203.
2. Land Records, Lib. JNG 9, fol. 237; Wills, Lib. 10, fol. 352. Benjamin Howard married Rebecca Bevins, daughter of James Bevins, a prosperous farmer of the Second District. Howard was named co-executor in Bevins' will (1824), but he resigned the position for unspecified reasons. In 1840, Benjamin purchased the Notley Young Farm which James Bevins had devised to his son, Thomas, as a result of a chancery case brought to court in 1837, in which Howard was the Plaintiff. Sometime in the late 1830s to early 1840s, Howard constructed a house for his daughter and son-in-law, Mary Ellen and Dr. James Haman. Having purchased bricks from Chester Parish in 1834 (the remains of the church at I. U.), it is possible that he used these in the construction.
3. Land Records, Lib. JNG 10, fol. 330.
4. Inventories, Lib. JP 1, fol. 74.
5. Wills, Lib. JF 1, fol. 286.
6. Wills, Lib. TRS 1, fol. 280.
7. Wills, Lib. FWS 1, fol. 128.
8. Land Records, Lib. WHG 21, fol. 99.

Moffett House

Millington
1830

O N THE 1860 MARTENET MAP, THE brick duplex on Cypress Street, Millington, appears to be in the ownership of J. M. Carrew. In 1868, Richard and Emily Millington owned the entire property but deeded it to two different women in separate deeds. Annie Blackiston, who purchased the western half of the house from the Millingtons, appears as the sole owner on the Lake Griffing Stevenson Atlas (1877).

The duplex was constructed in 1830. The date is painted on a recess near the apex of the east gable. Although it is a duplex, it possesses many features in common with the Logan House, across the street and slightly to the east. Both have uniformly laid Flemish bond brick with narrow joints and neither has belt course nor watertable. Wooden lintels with bulls-eye corner blocks are found above the openings of both facades.The facade of the Moffett House is symmetrically arranged with two doors in the center of the four bays. Both gables are identical, except for the date, and have three windows per floor and one in the attic. The central window in both was originally a door. Patches in the raised seam tin roof indicate the position of former chimneys, two of which rose from each gable. Behind the building there is a one-and-a-half-story semi-detached kitchen wing, also built of brick.

The interior plan of each half of the house is identical, with two rooms separated by an enclosed stair.

Originally there were exterior doors at the bottom of each stair. These have since been filled in. The kitchen wing is also divided down the middle, although modern kitchens are in the hyphen.

Fine window and door trim exist throughout, with gothic like moldings and corner blocks typical of the 1830 period. The doors, shutters and mantels all have a series of recessed panels, the doors having vertical battens inside, like many eighteenth century doors.

Late in the nineteenth century, two dormers were added to both slopes of the roof, about the same time as the installation of the wide overhang of the eaves. The existing porch is the product of late twentieth century up-date.   K-173

Timberwick

Near Massey
c. 1830

TIMBERWICK IS A MODERN NAME GIVEN TO THIS FARM NORTH of Massey which had belonged, in the nineteenth century, to the Boyer and Cacy families. It may have been the second house built for Stephen Boyer who also owned the Bradford Johnson farm (c. 1820, K-131).

The design of the new farm house was similar to Belmont located on the opposite side of the road which had been built for B. H. C. Massey in 1832.

The house was a five-bay, two-story, brick house with kitchen wing on the back or east side. The walls were laid in Flemish bond without decorative elements, as in earlier houses in the vicinity. There was, however, a corbeled cornice. The most ambitious architectural element inside was the stair which was built with a paneled spandrel and open-string balustrade. The newels were turned and there were two delicate rectangular balusters per step. Its dark, nearly round handrail rose above each newel post, suggesting a rope draped over the newels.

When Stephen Boyer died intestate in 1838, his personal estate was appraised by his neighbors, Ebenezer T. Massey (owner of Gondomah) and Samuel E. Briscoe. The estate included items that would have been expected of a well-run farm including 19 cows, 25 head of sheep, 9 horses, lots of pigs and 14 slaves. The total amounted to $4407.05 and included some carpets in the houses, 7 beds and 4 pair andirons with tongs and shovels.[1]

The farm was to go to his children, but the court apparently saw otherwise and appointed George Vickers to sell the real estate. This was carried out in 1844 and the deed to William Cacy was recorded the following year.[2] Cacy, another successful farmer, lived on a farm south of the village and purchased the Boyer Farm in an effort to increase his farming operation. He had a frame house built on part of the Boyer Farm for his son, William E. Cacy, who died subsequently before his father.

Cacy retained ownership in all of the farms until his death in 1892, when he bequeathed his residence to his wife, Elizabeth Ann, the frame house to his grandson and this farm to his son, Samuel. William Cacy reserved the graveyards in his will for the use of his family. The family graveyard remains near the house on the farm with both Boyer and Cacy headstones.[3] K-161

Timberwick, near Massey, was built for Stephen Boyer before his death in 1838. The Flemish bond facade and corbeled cornice are the most outstanding features of the exterior.
Marge Q. Fallaw photograph, 1986.

Timberwick, c 1830. Detail of the Flemish bond facade and corbeled cornice. Gene Johnstone photograph, 1997.

1. Inventories, Lib. 21, fol. 572.
2. Land Records, Lib. JNG 10, fol. 183.
3. Wills, Lib. TRS 1, fol. 152.

Belmont

Near Massey
1832

In 1832, Ebenezer Thomas Massey built a house on his farm for his son, B. H. Clinton Massey and his family. That house was a five bay long brick house, two-and-a-half stories tall with central stairhall and two flanking rooms on each story. A cellar was built of granite under the three northern bays.

The house was trimmed with millwork typical of the period, but details were added to the stair that make it stand out from others in the community. Its spandrel has four vertical panels. The balustrade is open string with two beaded-edge rectangular balusters per step. The step ends have delicate fretwork and the newel and intermediates are turned in a simple taper. A round walnut handrail rises above and is attached to the tops of the newels and continues to the third floor.

The configuration of the original kitchen is not documented, but the present four bay long, two story kitchen covers an early window on the north gable of the main house. This indicates that the original was either semi-attached or out the back.

Before moving to Philadelphia in 1870, B. H. Clinton Massey sold the farm to his brother Dr. C. H. B. Massey, who was living at Montebello in Georgetown.[1] Dr. Massey improved the Belmont farm with a new frame kitchen wing, including not only the present structure, but an *L* out the back—like Montebello on a smaller scale. He is responsible for adding the dormer windows and for making other minor improvements before moving, with his wife, Martha Oldham and their six children, to Belmont where they remained for the rest of their lives.

In her diary, their oldest daughter, Susan Emily Massey, wife of P. M. Brooks wrote of her father:

"*Charles Henry Bedford Massey was a prominent and influential citizen of Kent County. His keen intellect, indomitable will power, rare judgment and good sense made him a born leader ... His home was on the old Massey Estate ... was born on the old Massey Farm October 4, 1828, and attended Newark College when acquiring his medical education, having finished a medical course at the University of Maryland. He was engaged in practice for a few years, but eventually gave his whole attention to the management of his whole estate. He inherited a portion of the original homestead, which has been in the family for generations. Here he passed the remainder of his busy life until he died on June 11, 1891. "*[1]

By the time Dr. Massey died in 1891, he owned six farms besides some property in the village of Massey and was able to leave a farm to each of his children. Belmont was to go to his youngest son, E. Thomas Massey, after the death of his wife.[2] The farm remained in the same family until 1996.   K-159

1. Diary of Susan Massey Brooks.
2. Wills, Lib. TRS 1, fol. 109.

Belmont, near Massey, was built for H. Clinton Massey in 1832. Its main five-bay section is similar to Timberwick nearby except the brick is laid in common bond. Gene Johnstone photograph, 1997.

Shrewsbury Church

Near Kennedyville
1834

SOUTH SASSAFRAS PARISH WAS ONE OF THE ORIGINAL ANGLI-can parishes created by the Act for the Establishment in 1692. It soon became known as Shrewsbury like the nearby town of the same name.

The first building to be constructed in fulfillment of the Act for Establishment was recorded as having been a frame structure, 24' x 30', located at the head waters of Turners Creek. By 1705, the congregation had grown sufficiently to warrant a 20' extension. This basic frame chapel was in use to the 1720s, when it was replaced by a large new brick church 44' wide by 63' long (constructed between 1722–29).

Like its predecessor, the new brick church soon became too small and in 1750–52, a 32' x 34' extension was built on its north side. It was reported that the church, at this time, could hold in excess of 700 people.

After the Revolution, Shrewsbury, like the neighboring parishes of St. Paul's and Chester, had a difficult time adjusting to the ramifications of the break from the Mother Church and its subsequent independence. Somewhat parallel to the developments at I. U. Church (Chester Parish), Shrewsbury was demolished in the 1830s. In Chester Parish this resulted in a shift of the Parish Seat to the Chapel of Ease in Chestertown. At Shrewsbury, however, the Vestry voted to build a third church on the same site. Greatly reduced in scale from that of its predecessor, this third church reflected the loss of parishioners to the Methodist, Catholic and Lutheran Churches.

In 1834, the old church was taken down. Several yards away, the new structure was a very simple one, more like

a meeting house than an Episcopal church. From a sketch of the building drawn c. 1860, the building had a gable entrance which was flanked by two windows on both levels. There were only three rectangular windows on each side and another two flanking the altar. Its similarities to Olivet Methodist Church in Galena are immediately apparent, but Olivet had a refined Flemish bond facade, whereas the brickwork at Shrewsbury was undistinguished throughout.

The church remained essentially unchanged until the late 1870s, when a chancel and vestibule were added, all of the windows changed to Romanesque openings and a small belfry added to the roof. The old box pews were discarded and replaced with congregational seating. What had been a plain, vernacular meeting house, had taken on the faint style of the Romanesque.

Later, however, in 1903, a tall bell tower with crenelated top was constructed in the center of the gable facade, a popular alteration also used at the surrounding Methodist churches in Galena, Kennedyville, Hanesville, and Rock Hall. Minor alterations and rehabilitations have occurred throughout the twentieth century, but the basic building has not changed considerably since the tower addition of 1903.

The church yard contains one of the two earliest graveyards in Kent County associated with the Anglican/Episcopal Church. Shrewsbury's most prominent parishioner of the Revolutionary period, General John Cadwalader, is buried there. Best remembered for his quash of the Conway Cabal, he had lived on Shrewsbury Farm nearby.[1]   K-136

The tomb of John Cadwalader at Shrewsbury Church. See Shrewsbury Plantation, Chapter III, for the life of General Cadwalader. Historical Society of Kent County. Wilfong Collection.

Shrewsbury Church, South Sassafras Parish, is the product of the Vestry building a smaller house of worship in 1834, followed by remodeling in the 1870s and finally the construction of a tower in 1903. It is one of the original thirty parishes established in 1692. Conjectural renderings of the eighteenth century churches are to be found in Chapter III. Michael C. Wootton photograph, 1995.

Opposite: Shrewsbury Church, showing the 1870s sanctuary and romanesque windows, along with the 1903 tower. Courtesy of Francis Lamb, c. 1920.

1. See A History of Shrewsbury Parish Church by Katherine DeProspo for an in depth history of Shrewsbury Church.

The Sutton house followed the form and plan of many residences built in Kent County in the second quarter of the nineteenth century. Its detail closely resembled the millwork at Fair View, a house near Lambson's Station. Timber Level had a central stair with two flanking rooms in the two-story, 20' x 40' section with another two rooms in the service wing. Its eastern most room is thought to have been an earlier structure. The house was demolished around 1990

K-598

1. Wills, Lib. 4, fol. 6.
2. 1822 Tax Assessment.

Timber Level Site

Near Locust Grove
c. 1838

Timber Level, near Black's Station, was constructed in 1838 for the John Carvill Sutton family. Part of the kitchen was thought to have been an earlier structure.
Marge Q. Fallaw photographs, 1985.

Glencoe, Shrewsbury Neck, was built on Verina, around the middle of the nineteenth century. It appears to have been a tenant house from the beginning.

THE DATE JULY 3, 1838, WAS SCRATCHED IN the plaster along with the contractor's name, G. M. Leary, in a second story closet when this house was completed. It was built for the John Carvill Sutton family and the Sutton name appears in conjunction with the farm on both the 1860 and 1877 maps. (The original John Carvill Sutton was named for his mother's father, John Carvill III, who had resided at Carvill Hall on Fairlee Creek.)

Glencoe

Shrewsbury Neck
c. 1840

THE PLAIN MID-NINETEENTH CENTURY FARMHOUSE CALLED Glencoe stands on a tract of land originally called Verina. It was here that Isaac Freeman, Sr. dwelled and brought up his family. Freeman also owned several tracts on the opposite side of Terson's Creek. After his death in 1756, Verina went to his son, William Freeman, and that opposite went to Isaac Freeman, Jr.[1] Thereafter, the creek became known as Freeman's Creek. In 1822, two-hundred acres of Verina were owned by William Woodall.

Whether the existing house is near the old Freeman house site is not known. The present house is two stories tall and two bays long with a two-story wing built in two sections. Its plan is one room and stairhall, with one room in the original addition. The final addition included another stair and another room. Stylistically, the house can best be classified as a vernacular late-Federal structure due to the form and general simplicity of the trim. It is similar to parts of the Jessup House, Broad Neck.

The house may have been built as a tenant house at a time when so many Kent County farms were owned by absentee landowners who lived in town or the cities of Baltimore, New Castle or Wilmington. In the 1877 Atlas, the house is depicted as occupied by R. Kumple.

K-571

Alton Site

Eastern Neck
c. 1840

Around 1944 the old house which had stood on this farm burned to the ground. One photograph and a painting of the old house have survived which indicate an unusual four-part, frame building composed of a three-bay, two-story section with a one-and-a-half-story wing on the south and a one-story wing on the north. A two-story, fourth section was constructed at right angles to the southern wing. The age of the building cannot be determined by the photograph alone, but at least part of the building was standing in 1844 when the farm was sold at auction by George Vickers.[1]

In the report prepared by George Vickers, trustee, to the State Chancellor, it states that the property was put up for sale according to accepted practice and went on to describe it as *"The Tavern and plantation lying and being in Kent County ... in Eastern Neck adjoining the lands of Doctor Thomas Wilson and commonly called Trumpington and Smith's Chance containing one hundred and forty-four acres and a half of an acre ... ."*[2]

Alton, Eastern Neck, was described as "the Tavern and plantation ... in Easern Neck adjoining Trumpington ... ." The water color was painted prior to its being consumed by fire in 1944. Courtesy Mildred Willson Strong.

Alton. Detail of front porch balustrade and bench. Courtesy Mildred Willson Strong.

Melton Point dairy. Marsha L. Fritz photograph, 1981

The land had been the property of William Browne, part of which he had acquired in 1817 from William Quinn. The same land was mentioned in the 1783 Tax Assessment in the possession of William Crabbin.

At the auction on the tavern porch of Carl Strandburg in Chestertown, the property was sold to Dr. Thomas Willson for $3310.00.[3] Thereafter, the farm has remained in the possession of the Willson family, appearing on the 1860 Map in the possession of C. Daniel Willson and in the 1877 Atlas as the residence of Alexander H. Willson. The farm was sold in 1918 to Alexander Caroll Willson by his siblings.[4] After being advertised in the Enterprise in 1948, it was purchased by J. Ernest and Mary R. Willson, in whose family it remains.[5]   K-507

1. Chancery, Lib. 162, fol. 635.
2. Ibid.
3. Ibid.
4. Land Records, Lib. APR 3, fol. 419.
5. Land Records, Lib. WHG 9, fol. 330.

Melton Point

Quaker Neck
c. 1840

Melton Point is located northeast of Quaker Neck Landing. A peninsula extending into the Chester River, it encompasses 100 acres called Skinner's Marsh,

Melton Point barn. Marsha L. Fritz photograph, 1981.

Andelot Tenant House, near Worton, was built as a tenant house around the middle of the nineteenth century. Marsha L. Fritz photograph, 1980.

patented to Andrew Skinner in 1670.[1] Samuel Milton had the tract resurveyed in 1735 for 115 acres.[2] Samuel's surname was given to the tip of the peninsula. Today's spelling is a corruption of its original name. Adjacent the Milton tract is a larger tract called Stratford Manor, one of a handful of manors in Kent County. Stratford was a 1000 acre tract patented to Richard Chandler in 1660.[3] In 1735, it was repatented to George Garrett, who began selling off farms immediately after the resurvey.[4]

On the portion of the farm called Melton Point there are two old outbuildings which survived the house fire of 1964. One is a shingle covered barn, similar in form to the old barn on Fancy Farm. This one, however, has one side with open leanto and small one leaf door and probably dates from the first half of the nineteenth century. The second is a two-story, ten-foot-square dairy dating from the end of the nineteenth century and similar to a pump house in Still Pond. Both are good examples of traditional service buildings from their respective periods.

James P. deCorse is the owner listed in the 1852 Tax Assessment, as well as in the 1877 Atlas.   K-488

1. Grieb, et. al., Quaker Neck Map.
2. Ibid.
3. Ibid.
4. Ibid.

Andelot Tenant House

Near Worton
c. 1840

FEW HISTORIC HOUSES REMAIN ON THE LARGE ANDELOT Farm, assembled in the early twentieth century by Lamotte duPont Copeland, one time President of the Dupont Company. This old house appears to date from the second quarter of the nineteenth century and may have been built as a tenant house which it is today.

The house is a three-bay, two-story, frame structure with rear addition similar to Forkfields in form and the Alexander Farm in plan. It is built on a short foundation and had exposed fireplace backs on the first floor.

In the 1877 Atlas, Third District, the house is assigned to L. Usilton.   K-372

Mansfield-Eliason House

Spring Street, Chestertown
c. 1840

Soon after establishing his mercantile business on the first floor of the Masonic Hall, Thomas W. Eliason purchased parts of Lots No. 42 and 48 along with the *"Club House Lot"* across Club Lane (now Spring Avenue).[1] Eleven years earlier, James Mansfield had acquired the same, for which he paid $300—not enough to have represented a substantial dwelling at the time.[2] The purchase price of $1510 paid by Eliason, however, probably reflects either a newly constructed or greatly improved building on the property at the time of that transaction.

The house which Mr. Eliason purchased consisted of a three-bay, two-story frame section with an addition out the rear. The plan was typical of the period with central stairhall, two flanking rooms and a two-story, two-room wing in the back. There were most likely entry and rear porches attached to the house in its original configuration. On both the 1860 map and in the 1877 Atlas, T. W. Eliason is listed as owner. In the latter, the plan appears to be more of a *T* plan than the *L* which exists today. In the back yard there was a brick meat house with steeply pitched *A* roof, which had a batten door with an overall wrought nail pattern.

Sometime after the death of T. W. Eliason in 1893, the house was moved, remodeled and enlarged by its new owner. The enlargement details and especially the semi-octagonal dormer above the new projected entrance resemble closely the design of the dormer of the residence of Walter T. Pippin, a well known Chestertown designer/contractor. At one time the house was the home of Dr. Benge Simmonds, a homeopathic doctor who photographically recorded Chestertown and its surrounding areas in the early twentieth century.

The original brick meat house remains on the Eliason lot and is numbered K-74 in the survey of Kent County.   K-351

Mansfield-Eliason House, Chestertown. The original three-bay structure was a plain vernacular building that stood on the adjoining lot, adjacent an old brick smokehouse. Michael Bourne photograph, 1997.

Mansfield-Eliason smokehouse, Spring Street, Chestertown is one of several such buildings in Kent. Its original door has a uniform nailing pattern, approximately 2½" on center. Michael C. Wootton photograph, 1996.

1. Land Records, Lib. JNG 12, fol 436.
2. Land Records, Lib. JNG 5, fol. 512.

Jewell Farm

Near Stillpond
c. 1840

ACROSS THE ROAD FROM SHEPHERD'S DELIGHT, STOOD A derelict frame house which had belonged to the Hebron family in the mid-nineteenth century. An account of the property appears in the Orphans Court Records of 1847 where the farm is described for four of the orphaned Hebron sons:

"There is a new frame dwelling house part two stories 20 x 30 feet and part one story 18 by 25 including kitchen; the two story part has a cellar and the whole is lathed and plastered; Granary 12 x 18 feet with shed stabling on each side of the same dimensions; cornhouse log 9 by 10 feet with a 12 foot shed on each side; poultry house 10 by 12 feet all in good repair; a brick meat house 11 feet square in bad condition ... ."[1]

Apparently the farm was sold, since it appears under the name of Reverend J. B. Ayers on the 1860 Martenet Map, and in 1877, under the name of J. R. Stavely. It was during the Stavely ownership at the turn of the century, that the photograph was taken with numerous members of the Stavely family standing in the front yard.   K-225

1. Guardian Bonds Accounts, Lib. JFB 2, fol. 380.

Primary School No. 3

Near Kennedyville
c. 1840

IN THE NINETEENTH CENTURY, TRUSTEES WERE ELECTED FOR EACH school district in Kent County. Their appointment gave them complete authority over their districts. It was with that authority that, in 1840, Francis Wallis, Benjamin Parott and Daniel Jones purchased 0.88 acres from William Maxwell, whereupon School No. 3 was built that year.[1]

The building which was constructed was five bays long and faced north. Its walls were laid in common bond with plain jack arches over the openings. There was a three-course corbeled cornice. The interior was divided into a central passage and two rooms, with chimneys located in the center partitions. In form and plan, the building appeared residential, but in that respect the location of the chimneys would have been uncommon for the day. Their placement however, could perhaps be seen as a forerunner of post Civil War residential styles.

Apparently the building served the needs of the community for a relatively short period of time. In 1868, according to the provision in the original deed of 1840, it reverted back to the Maxwell family, as it was no longer being used a a school.[2] It remained part of the original Maxwell farm until 1970, after which time it was rehabilitated into a residence.[3]

It is a rare survival and example of a mid-nineteenth century school. The only other school of the early nineteenth century to survive in the county is the old Millington Academy.   K-214

1. Land Records, Lib. JNG 7, fol. 175.
2. Land Records, Lib. JKH 8, fol. 147.
3. Land Records, Lib. EHP 34, fol. 245.

Neglect

Crumpton
c. 1840

Neglect is a somewhat misleading name for the farm west of the Comegys Farm near Crumpton. The name refers to a 45 acre vacancy surveyed for Jervis Spencer in 1719. The name is encountered in the 1783 will of Isaac Spencer, son of Jervis, when he wrote his first bequest:

"... Principally and first of all I give and bequeath unto my loving son William Spencer begotten of my wife before marriage my plantation and mill on prickle pare branch in Kent County called Darby, Smally, Billy's Lott and Neglect."[1]

It appears again in both William Spencer's will and the tax assessment, of the same year (1822). William Spencer bequeathed all of his real estate (713 acres in total) to his brother Isaac, who resided at the Hynson-Ringgold House in Chestertown, for the benefit of Isaac's children. He also stated that his niece, Charlotte Ringgold Knight (Kitty Knight's sister-in-law) could live on the plantation for her lifetime.

Contrary to his wishes, the farm was sold out of the family in 1850 to Thomas Slaughter.[2] Twenty three years later, Slaughter lost his farm to the Sheriff who sold it in 1873 to two gentlemen from Dover: John D.

Burton and William Wallace.[3] Wallace later sold his half to Burton in 1884. It remained in the Burton family until 1969, the whole time being farmed and lived on by tenants. In 1977, the present owner purchased not only Neglect, but also two other farms that had previously been owned by Col. William Spencer, reuniting much of the tract again.

The house called Neglect was constructed during the second quarter of the nineteenth century, or possibly as late as 1850, after the land had been purchased by Thomas Slaughter. The four bay long, two-story brick residence is unique in its use of exposed wooden lintels, similar to the Logan House and the Moffett House in Millington, but lacking ornamentation. It possesses a four course corbeled cornice and a lower two-bay, two-story brick kitchen wing. Its original plan was similar to Grantham, i. e. two nearly equal size rooms, two bays each. A recent remodeling has altered, for the best, both plan and detail.   K-199

Neglect, near Crumpton, possesses features common to the second quarter nineteenth century: corbeled brick cornice and wood lintels. Marsha L. Fritz photograph, 1980.

1. Wills, Lib. 7, fol. 109.
2. Two other Slaughters with roots in Delaware purchased farms along the Chester River at this period. Jonathan purchased Travilla Farm and Henry purchased Buck Hill and Billy's Lott next door. Land Records, Lib. JKH 2, fol. 434.
3. Land Records, Lib. JKH 12, fol. 125.

Mitchell Home Farm

Shrewsbury Neck
c. 1840

WHILE THE HOUSE AT MITCHELL HOME FARM STANDS ON the west side of the road to Kentmore Park, the barns which serviced the farm are located across the road to the east. The house itself is a nineteenth century brick structure built in two parts.

Originally part of Shrewsbury Farm, the eighteenth century plantation of General John Cadwalader, this part passed first through the hands of Samuel Wethered of Baltimore before being sold to Robert and Margaret Polk of New Castle County, Delaware in 1842. Detailing in the house points to a construction date in the the second quarter of the nineteenth century; however, it has not been determined if it was the product of the Wethered or Polk ownership.

The form of the house is one common in Kent County; two sections, each two stories, but one being taller than the other. Its plan is actually similar to another tenant house constructed on Shrewsbury Farm, with parlor and stairhall in the main section and a dining room and kitchen in the wing. The number of windows differs between first and second story suggesting that there were porches on both sides, as was the case at Little Neck near Rock Hall.

The house suffered a fire in the 1960s and has been vacant ever since. While it was severely damaged, it is not beyond repair and could, if rehabilitated, serve its original purpose as a dwelling house. K-145

Mitchell Home Farm of Shrewsbury Neck, was built on the old Cadwalader farm, "Bennett's Regulation," in the second quarter of the nineteenth century. Michael C. Wootton photograph, 1996.

White Plains, near Massey, was the home farm of William Cacy, a prosperous farmer during the second and third quarters of the nineteenth century. It was probably built by Cacy c. 1840. Marge Q. Fallaw photograph, 1986.

White Plains

Near Massey
c. 1840

THE FARMHOUSE KNOWN AS WHITE PLAINS IS a five-bay, two-and-a-half story frame structure with *A* roof. The kitchen wing on its south gable is also two stories, but has a unique shed roof. The house is one of several in the Massey vicinity having the same plan and detail, constructed around the 1840s.

A two-story porch, later enclosed, and the two dormers on either side of the *A* roof are later additions to the central hall house. The details are late-Federal in design. The doors possess panels with applied moldings.

On both the 1860 Map of Kent County and the 1877 Atlas, this farm is shown as owned by William Cacy, who also owned Timberwick and the Donahoe Farm, north of Massey. When he wrote his will in the 1880s, he was living at White Plains. K-637

Myers House

Hanesville
c. 1840

BUILT C. 1840, THE MYERS HOUSE WAS LOCATED ON A TRI-angular parcel bounded on two sides by the Hanesville Road and Route 298. Originally part of a larger triangular tract known in the eighteenth century as Hill Top Farm, the first mention of this section is in a deed in 1845 when it was sold from Thomas Blackiston to John N. Mensch.

"Except 2 acres which was sold ... to Turbutt Betton, lying near Worton Heights and on which said excepted piece a small house has been erected ... ."[1]

Apparently the deed to Betton was not recorded, as the next record of transfer is from Mensch to William Lowe in 1845 [2], who later sold it to John A. Miller in 1848.[3] In 1850 Miller purchased fourteen additional acres and built a house which stood on the hill.[4] In 1858, Miller sold a parcel measuring *"3 roods, 13 perch-es"* to Daniel Hanes [5] who had established a store and post office on the west side of the road by the time the Martenet Map was published in 1860. (Hanes' farm was on the east side of the road.) After Daniel Hanes died, his properties were left to his nephew E. A. Vannort, whose heirs later sold three-quarters of an acre to Christian Myers in 1889.[6] Twenty years earlier Mrs. Myers had purchased the adjoining one-and-a-half acres.[7]

The little plank building was constructed on a gradual slope of ground and was composed of a rectangular plank hall-parlor plan house with a leanto kitchen on the west gable. Its south facade had a central door, two windows and a dormer on the *A* roof. The exterior was covered with wide weatherboard. One window had a single board and batten shutter with strap hinges. Its east gable had two small casements looking as though they should have flanked a chimney, but none remained. The only chimney was located off the west gable, within the leanto.

Inside, the building was plank and had exposed beams. There was a back-to-back fireplace serving both the dirt-floor leanto kitchen and the hall, which was about two steps higher. Headroom was very low throughout. A small enclosed stair in the northwest corner of the hall ascended to the attic. The house stood until the late 1960s.

K-120

1. Land Records, Lib. JNG 9, fol. 546-550.
2. Land Records, Lib. JNG 10, fol. 155.
3. Land Records, Lib. JNG 12, fol. 1.
4. Land Records, Lib. JR 1, fol. 348.
5. Land Records, Lib. JKH 1, fol. 222.
6. Land Records, Lib. SB 12, fol. 466.
7. Land Records, Lib. JKH 9, fol. 55.

Lawrence House

High Street, Chestertown
c. 1840

THE LAWRENCE HOUSE IS SO NAMED FOR THE OWNER WHO appears on Martenet's 1860 Map of Chestertown, as well as in a deed to the adjoining house with reference to its boundary.[1] This house, as well as the neighboring Laybourn House, were both initially constructed as modest residences. However, both have had their first floors converted into commercial spaces in the early twentieth century.

Originally, the building appears to have been a two-bay, two-story, frame dwelling. In the second quarter of the nineteenth century, two dormers were installed on the front slope of the roof. These dormers are actually the earliest features to survive on the street facade. The existing asymmetrical roof appears to be a result of an extension to a one-bay-deep building.

Soon after the construction of the main block, the building was lengthened one

Myers House, Hanesville, was probably built by Turbutt Betton around 1840. It was a plank building and was owned by Mr. and Mrs. Christian Myers and family from the late 1860s until it was demolished about one-hundred years later. Maryland State Archives, courtesy of the Myers Family.

Lawrence House, Chestertown, was initially a modest second quarter nineteenth century dwelling. It was converted to commercial space around the turn of the twentieth century. Michael Bourne photograph, 1996.

John Russell House, Chestertown, was built after 1841 by either John Russell or his mother, Ann Russell Rollins. It had the same form it has at present but with individual dormers instead of the twentieth century shed dormers. Tyler Campbell photograph, 1996.

bay toward the river. Its rear roof slope followed that established by the original block, mentioned above. Behind this one-bay extension, there was a leanto of one story.

In the early twentieth century, a long, two-story wing was constructed out the rear using the same type windows which were used on the remodeled facade. They are two-part, two-pane-wide casements which appear on the second story only. There the original fenestration was replaced by a wide bay window with three casements in the first section and a single casement in the second.

On the first floor both sections contained entrances and plate glass store windows with paneling above and below. Around the time the first story was converted to commercial use, an enclosed entry/stair was added on the westernmost gable for access to the second story apartment(s). Since the early twentieth century, there have been several remodelings which have obliterated any early materials. The commercial facade has remained.   K-55

1. Land Records, Lib. JNG 11, fol. 111.
2. Apparently John Russell received 518 High Street a second time in a foreclosure.
3. Land Records, Lib. JKH 1, fol. 578.

John Russell House

High Street, Chestertown
1841

T HE HOUSE AT 512 HIGH STREET, ADJACENT THE OLD Catholic Church, is situated on part of Lot No. 61. The house appears to have been constructed on part of the lot after it was purchased by Ann Russell Rollins in 1841. An 1846 deed for the adjoining property, 518 High Street, mentions this house indirectly *" ... palings between the Brick House part and the new frame house*

part ... ." referring incidentally to the one-and-a-half-story building.[1]

The house was built as a one-and-a-half-story, three-bay, frame structure with a leanto kitchen off the northeast half of the rear facade. It consisted of a basic hall-parlor plan with entry into the hall. The house possesses the slightest hint of the Greek Revival style in the use of a wide frieze board below the cornice. Otherwise, it is a simple representation of the period, similar to the Cochran House in Galena and the Davis Tenement on Mill Street.

John Russell kept the property in trust for his children while either residing there or holding it as a rental property. He sold the lot in several parcels in 1859, including 518 High Street, a store house with eave overhanging the latter, and 512 High Street.[2] The latter was sold to Simon and Joseph Lehmeyer of Baltimore, in whose family it remained until 1895.[3]

In the early twentieth century, the original stair was removed from the east corner of the hall and a new one was installed in the parlor, ascending between the two second floor bedrooms. Large shed dormers were built on both sides of the roof at the same time, creating enough space for a bedroom and bath over the old hall.

The rear leanto had been lengthened to create another room behind the parlor in the late nineteenth century. A second leanto was added to the former, creating an unusually long line on the gable. All of the additions were evident when the building was remodeled in 1975.   K-62

1. Land Records, Lib. JNG 11, fol. 111.
2. Apparently John Russell received 518 High Street a second time in a foreclosure.
3. Land Records, Lib. JKH 1, fol. 578.

Olivet Methodist Church

Galena
1842

In 1802, Cornelius Comegys sold one acre of property for £12, to Robert Moody and other trustees of the Methodist Episcopal Church. At this time the deed refers to the property as *"with the meeting house erected thereon."*[1] In 1808, Moody and other trustees transferred the same one acre parcel to the Trustees of Olivet Chapel.[2] Like most other churches in Kent County, the first structure was a modest frame structure which stood until being replaced in 1842 with a brick building.

When the 1842 church was built, it was a plain, vernacular, meeting house. Its plainness would make it different from that of the many Methodist chapels which would be built only a decade later in the widely popular Greek Revival style. It was most like the third building which was erected at nearby Shrewsbury Episcopal Church. It had a gable facade which was laid in uniform Flemish bond brick with thin white mortar joints, clearly a carry over of the late Federal style which had persisted in Kent County into the 1840s. The church was three bays wide and three bays deep, but the sides and back were laid with irregular brick in common bond. The windows were rectangular and there was no covering over the central entrance.

In 1887, Olivet Chapel was transformed into a country Gothic church with the addition of a bell tower/vestibule, a major reworking of the windows, removal of the gallery, etc. After this time, many of the windows were stained glass memorials to the guiding elders of the congregation.   K-585

1. Land Records, Lib. TW 2, fol. 83.
2. Land Records, Lib. BC 5, fol. 234.

Olivet Methodist Church, Galena, was built in 1842 as a plain meeting house, similar to Shrewsbury Church. It was remodeled into a Gothic Church in 1887. .

Olivet Methodist Church, Galena. The difference between the original 1842 building and the 1887 tower is easily discernible in the brick work. Michael C. Wootton photographs, 1996.

Alfalfa Dell Farm

Near Chestertown
c. 1845

Located a short distance west of Chestertown, this frame Italianate farmhouse has been considerably altered by the installation of aluminum siding and *wrought iron* porch posts and balustrades. The elements which make the building recognizable to architectural historians as Italianate are still visible. The boxy two-story building has a low-pitched hip roof and bracketed cornice. Originally it was nearly identical to a structure on the adjoining farm built for Francis Cann in the 1840s or 50s and which Henry Ward Carvill incorporated into his larger Italianate house now known as Brampton. The two front windows had jib doors beneath the sash for easy access to a front porch which no longer exists. The service wing appears to have been only one room long.

In the 1877 Atlas, the farm appears to have belonged to Josiah Ringgold, Jr., whose father had owned the adjoining farm, part of Killy Langford. It was called Mount Pleasant or the Worrell Farm and adjoined the Alms House Farm.   K-478

Alfafa Dell Farm, near Chestertown, was built in the late 1840s or early 1850s by Josiah Ringgold. It was nearly identical to the house which Francis Cann built at the adjoining farm, Fairy Hill.

The Bonwill Farm, near Stillpond, was built in the middle of the nineteenth century, a vernacular structure with brackets and arched fretwork being the only elements of style. Marsh L. Fritz photographs, 1980.

The Bonwill Farm Site

Near Still Pond
c. 1845

Like several other nineteenth century Kent County farmhouses, Bonwill House was torn down in the 1980s. Although it was not an outstanding example of mid-nineteenth century architecture, it nevertheless exhibited some features of interest to an architectural history. The front portion of the two-story, frame house was five bays long and stood on a tall stone basement. The brackets of the cornice were somewhat small and differed from the gables which had an arch motif. Its plan had a typical central hall, but the stair ascended to a landing at the back of the house and then there was one step on either side to the two sides of the hall. Both first story rooms had marbleized slate mantels with Latrobe stoves.

Opening from the hall and north room was a five-bay-deep wing which contained the kitchen and other service rooms. Behind the house there were three interesting outbuildings, including a dairy, smokehouse and storage shed, all of which opened into a fenced kitchen yard.

In the 1877 Atlas, the farm is owned by George Krebs.   K-449

Sunnyside Farm

Near Kennedyville
c. 1845

ARTHUR J. WALLIS IS LISTED ON THE 1860 MARTENET MAP as owner of Sunnyside Farm. Interestingly, the map also shows a road between this farm and the farm owned by Hugh Wallis which ran from there to the landing at Travilla Farm. Today that road exists only as a farm lane from Route 290 to Travilla.

Sunnyside was built about twenty years before the Martinet Map was printed and had some molding details similar to Edick Farm near Chesterville. In form it was more like Fairview near Lambson's Station, but the details were catalog millwork items as opposed to the handmade millwork of the two buildings mentioned above. Although the windows of the first floor were longer than those of the second, both were larger than the windows at Fairview. Both houses had two dormers on each side of the roof. Those at Fairview however were more architectural in design.

As can be ascertained from the exterior, the interior of the house was composed of the typical central hall plan with two room service wing. The newels of the stair were neatly turned with a plain balustrade. The mantels were very simple and the doors had four panels with applied panel molding.

In many ways, the simplicity of the building was similar to the Wickes House located on Broad Neck. It was an exceedingly plain house, made plainer when the shutters and original porch were removed. The house survived until 1994, when it was burned by the fire department.   K-191

Sunnyside Farm, near Morgnec, was a plain mid-nineteenth century farmhouse similar to Fairview, Lambson's Station. It was demolished in 1994.
Marsha L. Fritz photograph, 1980.

Cochran House Site

Galena
c. 1846

THE COCHRAN HOUSE HAD SUFFICIENT EVIDENCE OF ANTIQuity to be included in the first years of photographic documentation by the Historic American Building Survey in the 1930s. At the time, there were at least three similar buildings in Galena, but only one (the Orlando Sutton House) remains, and it has been altered considerably in the last sixty years.

An early deed (1846) described the property as a one acre part of Mount Airey. In this deed from Mary Turner to William A. Miller, the one acre parcel was transferred for a consideration of $100.00.[1] The purchase price is too little to indicate the existence of a dwelling on the property at the time. Miller owned the property for the next fifty years.

Probably soon after 1846 the house was built. Facing the street, it was a one-and-a-half-story dwelling. It stood on brick piers, later filled in with boards, and contained two gable-end chimneys with fireplace backs exposed. A third chimney was located on the back of the leanto kitchen. In form and plan (hall-parlor), it was nearly identical to the John Russell House in Chestertown, but was devoid of any suggestion of style. It was a vernacular structure in the true sense of the word. On the 1877 Atlas, the house is shown with an *L* plan, suggesting the leanto extended only behind the eastern half of the structure.

Cochran House, Galena, stood on the north side of the Chestertown Road when this photograph was taken for the Historic American Buildings Survey in the 1930s. It had been built around 1846, perhaps by William A. Miller.

In 1896, the property was offered for sale at the door of the Hotel of Jeremiah Peacock, but there were no bidders.[2] In 1901, it was sold for $225.00 to William Steele,[3] who turned it over immediately for $100 profit.[4]

Between 1901 and 1919, the property was owned by Verna Nickerson who married John Bottomly. At the time that HABS recorded the house, Keith and Nellie Cochran owned the house (1919–1939).[5] Since that time there have been five owners of the property. The house was removed from the property in 1969.

K-533

1. Land Records, Lib. JNG 11, fol. 240.
2. Land Records, Lib. JTD 5, fol. 250.
3. Land Records, Lib. JTD 5, fol. 249.
4. Land Records, Lib. JTD 5, fol. 250.
5. Land Records, Lib. APR 5, fol. 167, 168.

Orlando Sutton House

Galena
c. 1846

THE ORLANDO SUTTON HOUSE IS THE LAST ONE-AND-A-HALF story house surviving from Galena's early nineteenth century past. Although it has been enlarged, altered and remodeled through the years, its form is still in evidence.

John Medders, a blacksmith, purchased two ten acre parcels of Mount Airy from George William Wilson in 1811 and 1818 respectively.[1] In the 1822 Tax Assessment he was listed with the following properties:

Geo Tn Rds–½ acres–$125 yrly rent

Mount Airy– 12½ acres–$60 Assessment

Chance–9 acres–$118 Assessment

In 1846, John and Rebecca Medders sold one acre to Orlando Sutton for $150.00, hardly enough to cover the cost of constructing a six room frame house.[2] Sutton was probably responsible for erecting the house soon after he purchased the lot. Certainly the existing millwork is evidence of this period.

Orlando Sutton House, Galena, was built about 1846, a late vernacular structure which originally had individual dormers. It is similar to the John Russell House in Chestertown. This photo was taken before the chimneys were removed. Michael Bourne photograph, 1969.

In 1873 the one acre parcel was in his estate and it was sold to Alice R. Nowland for $880.00, a considerable jump over Sutton's purchase price. In that deed, Shrewsbury Academy is mentioned as bordering on the south and James Wilson on the north.[3]

The house that Sutton built was like the Stephens House on the Chestertown Road. It consisted of a hall-parlor plan with kitchen attached to the parlor end and the entire structure covered by a continuous *A* roof. Original trim remains at the front door and around the interior doors—all of which have corner blocks. The front door, composed of raised panels with applied moldings, is original, as is the parlor mantel. The latter is nearly identical to the one in Fairview Farm at Lambson's Station.

Many changes have occurred in the house, but the basic form and foot print remain the same.   K-150

1. Land Records, Lib. WS 2, fol. 161.
2. Land Records, Lib. JNG 11, fol. 26.
3. Land Records, Lib. JKH 12, fol. 496.

Colechester

Near Georgetown
1846

IN 1668, A 1000 ACRE TRACT ON THE SASSAFRAS RIVER CALLED Colechester was first patented to William Smith.[1] Later in the seventeenth century, it was acquired by William Pearce (who resided down river at Marshy Point) who gave the plantation to his son Gideon in 1713. Gideon established a ferry operation there which provided passage across the Sassafras. *"Ferry Point"* was mentioned as the location for George Town when it was formally established in the Legislative Act of 1736. That same year, Gideon Pearce was named as the grantor of the original 100 lots surveyed. In 1742 Pearce had his plantation resurveyed. *"Colechester Resurveyed"* included 1051 acres.[2] After his death in 1751, Colechester descended to Pearce's son James who in turn had George Town resurveyed in 1787, which increased the boundaries and the number of lots.

James Pearce (d. 1802) served in the Lower House from Kent County after the Revolution. He was also a vestryman of Shrewsbury Parish and Commissioner of Tax as well. Beside his farm, he owned a grist mill and was actively involved in the buying and selling of real estate, primarily in Kent and Cecil Counties. When Pearce died, his personal estate was valued at £2796, a large fortune for the period.

While there are remnants of a basement and west wall dating from the eighteenth century upon which the present house was constructed, too little remains to conjecture its original appearance. What exists today was constructed under the ownership of Jacob Malsberger who purchased the farm in 1845.

The house is a late Federal style frame building composed of a five bay, two-and-a-half-story frame section with a three bay, two story lower service wing. Both parts are one room deep—the typical arrangement in Kent County. The plan was similar to many farmhouses with central stairhall. A third section which once stood on the west end was demolished many years ago. Between the two parts of the house there is a brick gable reputed to belong to the eithteenth century Pearce farmhouse.

In the basement, the western half is indeed early and it possesses some unexplained recesses in its north wall. The eastern half of the basement is contemporary with the rest of the structure above. In that portion there is a six foot deep storage pit which measures 6' x 8' across.

On both the 1860 map and the 1877 Atlas, two houses appear on the farm. The latter labels it *"Capt. A. Woodall Res."* His name also appears at the bottom of the hill in Georgetown, where he was to live later, adjacent his warehouse. Woodall purchased Colechester in 1875. To this day it remains in the possession of his descendants.   K-149

1. Patents, Lib. 10, fol. 25.
2. Patents, Lib. EI 6, fol. 675.

Colechester, near Georgetown, is the tract from which Georgetown was laid out in 1736. The farmhouse was built in 1846 for Jacob Malsberger. Its main section is similar to Fairview, especially the curved roof dormers.

Colechester, near Georgetown, has a brick gable between sections. Part of the basement is earlier than 1846. Marge Q. Fallaw photographs, 1985.

The Alms House

*Broad Neck
1847*

WHEN THE TRUSTEES OF THE POOR HOUSE PURCHASED 293 acres of the Josiah Ringgold, Sr. plantation in 1847, there was no dwelling standing thereon, only the buildings for running the farm operation. The deed for the property was executed the very same day as it was advertised for sale. In the advertisement in the Kent News the description of the property reads:

"About 306 Acres ... the dwelling house has been destroyed by fire but the outbuildings a large barn with sheds, stable, corn house and meat house all in good order. The land is distant about three miles from Chestertown and adjoins the lands of Samuel Ringgold and the heirs of William Perkins ... ."[1]

Since the accommodations which the Trustees of the Poor leased had recently burned, it was necessary for them to begin immediately with their construction project. The first building to house the poor consisted of a brick structure looking remarkably like a typical residence of the period, at least from the front.

The taller section of the building was three bays long with central double doors (board and batten). The rear, however, was quite different, with the first floor central bay occupied by three doors, the center one at ground level leading to the basement. The brick used in the construction of the first part is darker and less uniform than the later two story wing on its north gable.

The first part was built with a steeply pitched *A* roof and had chimneys protruding from the apex at both gables. The lower wing was only two bays long and two stories tall with a shallower roof pitch, leaving enough space on the tall gable for two windows flanking the chimney. Across the entire west facade there was a leanto porch, the same type of arrangement as at Little Neck built earlier in the century. The north gable had a window on each level, but no chimney.

Although the layout of the building was similar to residences of the period, it differed considerably in that

The Alms House, near Langford, was constructed by the Trustees of the Poor after acquiring the property in 1847. Its wing was built later at which time a porch extended across the entire facade. Historical Society of Kent County Collection.

Donahoe Farm

Massey
c. 1850

In 1822, the tract on which the Dona-hoe House was built was owned by Stephen Boyer. William E. Cacy purchased the land from the Boyer estate in 1845.[1] Later, Cacy's son and daughter-in-law occupied the house which had probably been built by his father.

Built in the Italianate style, the house had many exterior features typical of the period. The entrance with double doors, side lights and transom, occupies the central bay of the three bay facade. On the second story there is a three-part window which balances the entry below. The present porch replaces an earlier one which was nearly three times larger and onto which the entry and jib-doored windows opened.

Like many of the farmhouses of the late eighteenth and nineteenth centuries in Kent County, the Donahoe House has an *L* out the back of the one room deep main part. It is much plainer and slightly shorter than the main block, both in length and height. Its interior trim retains some elements of the Greek Revival style which co-existed with the Italianate.   K-629

1. Land Records, Lib. JNG 10, fol. 183.

there was no stairhall, only a tiny entry with door on each side. Opposite the door, the stair ascended in one straight flight between two plastered partitions. There was a landing at the top of the stair, with two steps going to opposite doors. There was no interior access from the main house to the wing. Instead, inhabitants had to go outside along the porch and reenter the building from another exterior door. The single room in the wing appears to have been heated from a stove with pipe into the adjoining chimney. There was an enclosed stair to the second floor where there were three small rooms.

The second building to be erected on the farm was the manager's residence, a large frame house that was much more typical of the second half of the nineteenth century. It was a two-and-a-half-story, five bay, L-plan building with front and side porches that had a good jig-saw balustrade and brackets. Otherwise, it was devoid of ornamentation.

A dormitory building constructed around 1900 stood to the south of the manager's residence. It consisted of a common room and cells. Another, built in 1927, burned the same year.

When the welfare system was implemented after World War II, the Alms House Farm became redundant and was sold from the steps of the Courthouse in October 1951. Walker and Susie V. Lamb purchased the farm and it remained in their family until 1990.[2]   K-95

1. Kent County News, August 7, 1847.
2. Lamb, Francis, "Notes on Mount Pleasant Plantation."

The Donahoe Farm, north of Massey, was built by William Cacy for his son and daughter-in-law around 1850-60. The form of the house was like several mid-century Italianate houses. Marge Q. Fallaw photograph, 1986.

Windy Curve Farm

Near Galena
c. 1850

STANDING ON THE SOUTH SIDE OF THE OLD GALENA-Massey road, Windy Curve is an unusual Greek Revival Style frame structure probably constructed in the mid-nineteenth century. It appears to have been constructed on part of an early tract called *Free Gift*.

This is the only house in Kent County to use three-part windows on its entire facade. In Howard County, Folly Quarter, a great Greek Revival building uses the same device. Windy Curve Farm, however, is a modest vernacular version of the same.

When constructed, the 38' x 32' house had a service wing on the back and a Greek Revival porch on the front, both of which have since been removed. It retains pilasters on the front corners of the house and the central entrances with typical Greek Revival architrave, sidelights and transom.

There are many unexplained details in the house, such as the asymmetrical room plan and the position of the stair. Only one original mantel remains in a second story bedroom. Equally puzzling is the fact that no house is shown on this site in the 1877 Atlas, whereas it appears in the ownership of William Armstrong on the 1860 map.   K-631

Windy Curve Farm, near Galena, was built on part of Free Gift, a tract owned in the eighteenth century by George Forrester, the rector of Shrewsbury Church. This mid-nineteenth century house is the only one in Kent to use three-part windows throughout its facade. They are normally confined to the central bay.
Marge Q. Fallaw photograph, 1986.

Forkfields

Near Galena
c. 1850

AT THE HEADWATERS OF ISLAND CREEK, THIS SMALL FRAME farmhouse was probably built in the mid-nineteenth century for a tenant family. It is a very plain three-bay, two-story building with two rooms separated by an enclosed stair, similar in plan to the County Alms House and Marsh Point after its nineteenth century remodeling. Its original kitchen was replaced in the early twentieth century with a true one-and-a-half story wing.

In 1819, Forkfields was part of the estate of Isaac Freeman III who lived at the northern end of Shallcross Neck. Later in the century, in the 1877 Atlas, the owner is James W. Hurtt, who owned and lived on the adjacent Woodland Hall Farm. It remained in the family of James Hurtt until recently. The house has been updated and remodeled by new owners.   K-572

Forkfields, near Locust Grove, was probably built by James Woodland as a tenant farm in the middle nineteenth century. It was similar to the Andelot tenant house until its recent remodeling. Marge Q. Fallaw photograph, 1985.

Simpkins Farm

Near Rock Hall
c. 1850

A VERNACULAR BUILDING IN THE TRUE SENSE, THE OLD HOUSE on the Simpkins Farm illustrates what happens to a traditional building when it is trimmed out in later period woodwork. The plan is a modified hall-parlor with attached kitchen wing. The main house is brick and has a gable roof. The lower kitchen wing is frame and has

Simpkins Farm, near Reeses Corner, is one of the latest hall-parlor plan houses in the survey of Kent's historic buildings. It possesses a few interior elements reminiscent of the Greek Revival style. Marsha L. Fritz photograph, 1981.

Bloomfield Farm, near Kennedyville, may have been built of the old bricks from St. Peters Parish Church at I. U. which Benjamin Howard purchased from the vestry. The house was built for his daughter Mary Ellen Haman. Marsha L. Fritz photograph, 1980.

a steeper roof. All of these characteristics are seen in buildings dating from the late eighteenth and early nineteenth centuries. Here, however, the window and door details, the brick type, the roof pitch, and related proportioning of the house are mildly Greek Revival, which makes this a significant example of rural building practices in Kent County in the fourth or fifth decade of the nineteenth century.

D. Smith appears to be the owner in the 1877 Atlas.   K-489

Bloomfield Farm

Near Kennedyville
c. 1850

THE OLD BRICK HOUSE WHICH STOOD ON THE BLOOMFIELD Farm until the early 1980s was a unique residence of the mid-nineteenth century. Its three-bay facade was on the narrower side of the rectangular three-story building, with the entrance door closest to the four-bay, two-story brick wing. One chimney was placed between the two remaining windows of the facade while the other was opposite it on the back wall. The three-bay northeast wall was the longer one and, with the

placement of the chimneys, appeared more like the principal facade than did the entry facade. A porch which once extended across the entry must have helped to define the entrance.

The plan of the house consisted of a side hall with double parlors and two rooms in the wing. The unique placement of the chimneys is better understood when the plan is seen because the two parlors had large double doors between them, resulting in the fireplaces facing one another when the doors were open.

As would be expected, the kitchen chimney was on its gable end, but the dining room chimney was located adjacent the hall and rose to the height of the other

main chimneys. This odd placement of chimneys can also be seen at Moreton Hall.

The house was constructed in the mid-nineteenth century by Benjamin Howard who resided at Suffolk and built Green Forest. In his will dated 1865, he left Suffolk to his daughter, Mary Ellen Haman, who was living on Bloomfield and Bloomfield to his son, George Howard.[1] George is listed as owner in the 1877 Atlas. K-422

1. Lib. JF 1, fol. 286.

Kennard House

Near Still Pond
c. 1850

According to local tradition, the existing structure replaces a large house which once stood on this property and burned to the ground. If indeed an earlier house stood in this same spot, it's hard to imagine one to be any larger than the present one which appears to have been built in the mid-nineteenth century.

In the 1877 Atlas, this property is listed as owned by Dr. Thomas C. Kennard (b. 1809, d. 1883), whose headstone is located in a private graveyard behind the house. Another stone with the inscription *"Dr. Kennard B-1834 D-1879"* may mark the grave of his son.

This brick house is composed of two, two-story sections, one five bays long, the other four bays long and both two rooms deep. Like many houses of the mid-nineteenth century, the south walls are constructed of very uniform brick with narrow mortar joints. The others are stuccoed.

The outstanding features of the Kennard House are the entry porches which have bracketed cornices, round Doric columns and wooden balustrades of elongated lozenge patterns. The central entrances, both front and back, have double doors with sidelights and transoms. The central window above also has sidelights and all of the windows have large wooden lintels. At the juncture of the low-pitched roof with the walls is a plain Greek Revival cornice with brackets and frieze that matches the porches. In all likelihood, the roof had a deck with balustrade to match those of the porches. K-361

Kennard House, near Stillpond, is perhaps the largest of the antebellum houses of Kent County, with a four room service wing. Built for Dr. Thomas Kennard, its form and detail is Greek Revival.

Kennard House, has the most graceful of Kent's mid-nineteenth century stairs with a continuous rise around its first landing. Like Radcliffe Cross, it has curly maple balusters and mahogany newel and handrail. It is the only house to have the same front and back entrance with double doors, sidelight and transom. C. Engstrom photographs, 1977.

Stephney Farm

Broad Neck
1850

THE NAME STEPHNEY IS A CORRUPTION/SIMPLIFICATION OF the original name of the 1000 acre tract patented in 1659—Mannour of Stephen Heath.[1] It is not the first such corruption. In the tax records of 1783, the land is called *"Stephen Heath Manor"* and in 1852 it is called *"Stepney Heaths Manor."*[2]

The Greek Revival house standing on a part of the manor possesses a brick with the inscription *"Beck 1850."* In the 1852 Tax Assessment, Benjamin F. Beck is listed as owning 386 acres referred to as *"pt. Stepney Heaths Manor & Berwick."* In the assessor's description, the mentioning of a *"New Brick House & other Buildings in good repair"* confirms the date of construction shown on the brick.[3]

Beck is also listed as owning the adjoining *"Middle Plantation, Crows Chance and Addition, called Trap Farm with an Old House in Bad Repair. Formerly to John Claypoole."*[4] Within the decade, he built another brick house for his son, Benjamin, Jr. which is called

Stephney Farm, Broad Neck. Benjamin Beck built his new house in 1850 in form and detail like the Greek Revival building at Washington College. Tyler Campbell photograph, 1996.

Middle Plantation. In 1865, Benjamin F. Beck purchased the mill and farm now called Brice Mill and operated the grist mill until 1882, when it was sold to John Brice.[5]

Benjamin Beck's residence is probably the best example of the Greek Revival style used for farmhouses in Kent County. The main difference between other farmhouses and Mr. Beck's is the use of the short third floor that is treated as a frieze for the cornice, the stepped parapet gables and relatively shallow-pitched roof. The porches add a considerable amount of classical detail to the otherwise plain brick box of the plan. In the central bay there is a small Ionic portico with pressed tin wreaths on the wall similar to the dormers of Beck's Landing. A larger Doric porch runs across the entire four-bay facade of the low two-story wing. Its lozenge balustrade is similar to those on the Kennard House near Still Pond.

The plan of Stephney Farm is well developed and contains one more first-story room than most others of the antebellum period. The main block has a central stairhall with two flanking parlors. Continuing in a straight line are two additional rooms and behind the last is the original kitchen and a frame addition.

K-253

1. Patents, Lib. 4, fol. 528.
2. 1852 Tax Assessment, First District.
3. Ibid.
4. Ibid.
5. Land Records, Lib. JKH 4, fol. 611.

Spear Farm

Near Millington
c. 1850

The first district of Kent County has many homes built between the 1820s and 1860, due primarily to the fact that the owners improved their farming methods producing results that would enable them to build anew. Many of the houses of this area which date from the late eighteenth century were log, so it is also feasible that they were by this time at the end of their useful lives.

During this period, many of the farmers owned several farms which enabled them to build of brick, like the Massey houses and the Cacy holdings. James Spear was another of the successful farmers of the first district who acquired several farms—all of which totaled 1114 acres.

The house which James Spear built was similar in plan to Timber Wick and the house built for William Cacy's son, now called the *"Donohoe Farm."* It was built of brick and was the usual five bays in length with a rear extension of two two-bay sections. The Spear house, unlike the houses compared to it immediately above, was only two stories tall. It had a very low pitch hip roof with end chimneys. Its facades were severely plain with the exception of the cornice which was made of corbeled brick with one course of brick set on the diagonal to create dentils or *mouse teeth.*

The back wings, brick and frame respectively, have the same roof line, though obviously the frame wing lacks the corbeled cornice. The interior trim is nearly identical to the trim at the Donohoe Farm, with slightly arched crossetted door and window heads, typical of the Greek Revival style. Indeed, with the lack of brackets and porches usually associated with this form of house, it falls clearly into the Greek Revival style. Another feature of the house that is unusual for the form, is the use of relatively low ceilings and a stair with winder at the top—features normally associated with smaller vernacular dwellings.

Spear Farm, near Millington, is now the center of a nursery operation, with the residence remodeled into offices. Michael C. Wootton photograph, 1996.

Spear Farm, near Millington, is the only Kent farmhouse to have a corbeled cornice with mouse tooth course (projecting corners). It is otherwise a standard Greek Revival farmhouse of the mid-nineteenth century. Marge Q. Fallaw photograph, 1985.

When James Spear died in 1874, he left six children. Each child inherited a farm. *"The tract of land on which I now reside ... "* he left to his daughter Georgianna[1] who remained there at least until the Atlas was printed three years later (1877). The farm remained in the Spear family for another hundred years, gradually falling into disrepair. It was thought that there was no hope for the future of this house, but in the late 1980s the farm was purchased and the house was restored as an office for the nursery operation.   K-167

1. Wills, Lib. EC 1, fol. 98.

Wilson Point

Near Galena
c. 1850

Throughout the eighteenth century the land on which Shorewood would later be built was owned by Simon Wilmer II (d. 1737), Simon Wilmer III (d. 1768), and John Lambert Wilmer.[1] It was Simon Wilmer III who actually left Chestertown for the upper reaches of the County and established his *"dwelling plantation … between Swan Creek and Herring Creek and Sassafras River down the county … ."*[2] At the time

of his death in 1768, he left nearly everything to two of his four children—John Lambert Wilmer, mentioned above, and his daughter, Mary Wilmer Geddes, who had recently married the Customs Collector at Chestertown. His will also mentioned John's son, Simon, who later became a physician and also lived on the family plantation. By 1822, the heirs of Simon Wilmer were taxed on 853 acres consisting of parts of the Adventure, Cock of the Game, Cockstail, Hen Roost, Linkhorn and Browning's Addition.[3]

The farm stayed in the Wilmer family until it was acquired by Alexander Wilson in 1859.[4] In his will which was probated in 1875, Wilson referred to himself as a farmer. By the time his will was written, Wilson had married a second time and had two daughters to

Wilson Point (Shorewood), near Galena, replaced the eighteenth century house of the Wilmer family. Alexander Wilson acquired the farm in 1859 and built his mansion in the popular Italianate style, using cast iron ornamentation on the extensive porches.

Wilson Point (Shorewood), has a handsome stair with mahogany handrail and octagonal newel. C. Engstrom photographs, 1977.

Wilson Point (Shore-wood). The living room mantel is a handsome colonial revival piece that blends well with the bolection trim.
C. Engstrom
photograph, 1977.

whom he bequeathed his home place *"known as Wilmer's Point."*[5] Annia, daughter by his first marriage had married Walter J. Griffith and had lived at Moreton Hall, a farm adjoining on the east. Griffith and Wilson must have talked about the designs for their homes, as many of the details are similar.

Around 1860 Alexander Wilson and his wife built one of the most impressive Italianate style frame dwellings in the county. Typical of the style, it was three stories in height, had a bracketed cornice and a lantern on a low-pitched hip roof. It was, however, deeper than usual. Nearly square, its three porches were embellished with cast iron supports and balustrades similar to Moreton Hall and the Dreka House nearby.

The five-bay facade had a double door with sidelights and transom. The central stairhall affords a view straight out the back door to the Sassafras River. Mahogany was used for the large octagonal newel post and handrail of the stair which ascends to the third floor without intermediate newels. Two boldly turned balusters per step were used throughout. Door and window trim were wide and bold, similar to the bolection work at Moreton Hall.

Twentieth century alterations to the house include a fine Georgian Revival style mantel with bolection moldings in the east parlor and a one and a half story kitchen wing on the west. On the river side, the second and third story paired windows had a third window added to each, creating a window wall in each of the rooms facing the River.

The property was purchased in the 1930s by Guiseppe M. Bellanca, a pioneer in American aviation. He was responsible for the superb formal Italian garden laid out east of the house. Shorewood is one of the best Antebellum houses of Kent and possesses a dramatic site on the upper reaches of the Sassafras River.   K-155

1. Wills, Lib. 4, fol. 361.
2. Ibid.
3. 1822 Tax Assessment.
4. Land Records, Lib. JKH 1, fol. 579.
5. Wills, Lib. EC 1, fol. 98.

Moreton Hall

Near Sassafras
c. 1850

MORETON HALL DERIVES ITS NAME FROM THE 600 ACRE patent, Moreton, granted to Richard Lake in 1670. At the time of the patent, the land was considered part of Baltimore County. After 1674, however, it became part of Cecil County. Finally, in 1707, this area became part of Kent County.

The tract remained undivided throughout the seventeenth century and was not resurveyed for almost 75 years. The certificate of survey prepared for Joshua George of Cecil County, in 1746, enumerates several buildings:

> *"squared log barn 40 x 20*
> *squared log quarter 20 x 20*
> *squared log corn house*
> *and very old dwelling house propt up have 2*
> *very old brick chimneys much crackt*
> *one very old clapboard house ... ."*[1]

None of these has survived into the twentieth century.

When George's daughter, Mary, married James Loutit, she came in possession of *"George's Part of Moreton."* She and her husband, however, lived at Mount Harmon, Cecil County. They sold Moreton in the 1750s and 60s to Alexander Baird, a prosperous planter living in Kent County.[2] Baird built his home not on Moreton, but on the adjoining tract called the Adventure. Moreton remained in the Baird family until it was sold in 1844 to Joseph Griffith, the builder of Moreton Hall.[3]

Griffith's house was composed of the house which remains today, plus a one-and-a-half-story addition on the south gable. Typical of the antebellum period, it had a standard *L* plan composed of a central stairhall with two parlors in the front, a dining room and back stair in the middle wing and two other service rooms in a final frame wing.

Its five-bay facade included a two-story verandah with cast iron ornamentation on both levels. The verandahs, as well as the main body of the house, were included beneath a single hip roof. Moreton's cast iron treatment was a feature it had in common with several houses of the area. The Dreka House in Sassafras, Shorewood on the adjoining farm and Ward's Knowledge in Cecil County all had similar ornamentation. Moreton's treatment, however, remains the most elaborate of the local collection of antebellum houses. The house was further embellished with a belvedere in the center of the roof.

Both parlors opened onto the verandah by means of tall windows. The center window of the second story was similar. Inside, the stair occupied most of the entry due to the very tall ceiling. Its newel and balusters were turned and octagonal, a bold treatment with continuous handrail from the newel to the second floor bedroom wall. All openings on the first floor were finished with wide bolection-molded trim. The doors and other elements were grained in imitation of finer wood. Its parlors were most likely finished with marbleized slate mantels with coal stove inserts. In the east parlor a cabinet was built next to the fireplace and from its south wall a door opened into the brick wing's dining room.

The dining room was finished in a plainer fashion with corner block trim around the doors and windows. Adjacent the fireplace on the north wall was another built-in cabinet. The back stair had a plainer balustrade than the front, with turned newel and plain tapered dowel like balusters of maple. The east door with transom opened onto a flat roofed porch with large square columns supporting a plain classical frieze. Three walls of the two-and-a-half-story two-bay wing were built of orange-red brick laid in common bond. The fourth butted up to the main house and possessed only a brick chimney.

The existing two-story, two-bay kitchen wing was two steps lower than the rest of the house and both it and the dining room wing were built over full basements. In the southwest corner of the kitchen was an enclosed stair with mid-eighteenth century raised panel doors. Its framing members were hewn, and may predate the rest of the house, which was built with sawn members. From the second story interior of the kitchen stair, the outline of a doorway to a now non-existing wing is visible. It was one-and-a-half-stories tall.

One of the other extraordinary features of the farm was the huge brick bank barn that survived up until the 1980s, when it collapsed and was subsequently bulldozed. It was built on a stone foundation let into a bank. Its lower floor was for the livestock, above which was the hay floor with enclosed area in the center for the storage of grain and other materials. A third level was used for bringing in the wagons from which the

Moreton Hall barn was the largest of Kent's mid-century bank barns, with a bridge to the upper loft having corn cribs on each side. A granary was located in the central story with flanking bay storage to the roof. Cattle were housed in the lower level, which opened at the lower grade. C. Engstrom photograph, 1977.

Moreton Hall. Detail of cast iron porches, cornice, and lantern. Gene Johnstone photograph, 1997.

Thomas B. Hynson's Store

High Street, Chestertown
c. 1850

IN 1848, THOMAS B. HYNSON PURCHASED THE PART OF Lot No. 11 upon which he would build his store. Its similarity in detail to the Greek Revival buildings both at Washington College and Middle Plantation, point to the store's construction shortly after Hynsons' purchase of the property.

The original configuration of doors and windows leaves little doubt that the building was indeed intended for commercial use from its beginning. Two bays of the four-bay facade are store windows with the bay between allowing access to the store rooms themselves. The fourth bay and current entrance was originally intended as the entrance to the living quarters of the store keeper. This arrangement was prevalent from the eighteenth century into the middle of the twentieth century and can be seen across the street at the Buck-Bacchus Store as a result of its remodeling in 1824.

In 1883, the Hynson Store and adjoining duplex were purchased by Alexander J. Cahall and thereafter known as the Cahall Store. It is currently the private Chestertown Library.   K-36

Thomas B. Hynson's Store, Chestertown, originally contained a store with central entrance beside the second entrance to the residence above. The plan may have been derived from the Buck-Bacchus store across the street which had been so converted in 1824. Michael C. Wootton photograph, 1996

hay and straw were unloaded. This was accessible from the west side by a dirt ramp. Between the ramp and barn was a covered bridge-like structure with corn cribs on either side. In many ways the barn was similar to the frame one on the Rich Hill Farm (the Adventure) built by either Griffith's father, Joseph, or brother, Robert.

Moreton Hall remained in the Griffith family until 1884 when Stephen Boyer purchased it.[4] For the next twenty years Moreton Hall was in the Boyer estate. Between 1904 and 1927 it was owned by Andrew Woodall and his wife Josephine.[5] Frances W. Welch bought it in 1927,[6] and later sold to the Craddock family.[7] While the Craddock family retains ownership of the bulk of the farm, the house and a small amount of acreage has been sold. Plans have been made for the restoration of Moreton Hall, a good antebellum house which has been left without care for many years.

K-126

1. Unpatented Certificate No. 143, Hall of Records, 2 April 1746.
2. Rent Rolls, Lib. 5, fol. 164.
3. Land Records, Lib. JNG 10, fol. 53.
4. Land Records, Lib. SB 5, fol. 206.
5. Land Records, Lib. JTD 10, fol. 191.
6. Land Records, Lib. RRA 10, fol. 192.
7. Land Records, Lib. RAS 37, fol. 222.

George Vickers House Site

Mill Street, Chestertown
c. 1850

NEARLY A HALF CENTURY BEFORE THE CONSTRUCTION OF the old grammar school on the lot bounded by High, Mill and Calvert Streets, the home of the Honorable and Mrs. George Vickers stood as one of the most formidable examples of the Italianate style in Chestertown.

Vickers, educated at Washington College, entered the office of the Clerk of the Court after graduating. While there, he studied law and was admitted to the Bar in 1832. In 1836 he became a state senator, but eventually returned to the practice of law and was quite successful in that respect for several years. He was re-elected to the State Senate in 1868, just four years after having been appointed Major General of the Militia of the Eastern Shore. And in 1868, he was elected to the United States Senate. Locally, Vickers donated three acres for the formation of Chester Cemetery at the edge of town and was also president of the Kent County Railroad which was built before he died in the 1870s. Vickers' name is indeed one which is frequently encountered in the study of mid-nineteenth century documents of the area.[1]

George Vickers House Chestertown, was built in the 1850s while he was a State Senator. In 1868 he was elected to serve in the United States Senate. His home was one of Chestertown's most gracious, containing one-half of an acre fronting on Mill Street. It was replaced in 1903 by the Chestertown Elementary School. Maryland State Archives, Jane Brooks Sprinkle Collection.

Miller Farm was owned before 1860 by Thomas Walker, one of Kent County's significant merchants and agriculturalists. He is probably responsible for building the house for his tenant. Marge Q. Fallaw photograph, 1986.

Vickers had married Mary Mansfield in 1828. It was from Miss Mansfield's parents that they acquired the lot on which they built their home sometime before 1860.[2] The house was similar to the Captain Taylor House built a few years earlier on the river front, but the Vickers House was a full three stories tall. The view over Chestertown from the observatory must have been impressive, as it was the highest residential rooftop in town at that time.

The house designer employed many of the stock millwork items available through catalogues of the period. There were corner pilasters, window cornices, and brackets. The low-pitch hip roof was topped with a covered belvedere. It appears that the High Street yard was the pleasure garden or yard and the Calvert Street yard was a service area. It was the most ambitious antebellum residence to be built in Chestertown.

In 1880, after the death of Senator Vickers, his widow sold the house and lot to Amanda M. Hurtt,[3] whose daughters sold it to the School Commissioners in 1900[4]. In 1903, the house was replaced with the Grammar School. **K-514**

1. Biographical Cyclopedia of Representative Men of Maryland, 1876.
2. Land Records, Lib. JNG 4, fol. 380.
3. Land Records, Lib. SB 1, fol. 92.
4. Land Records, Lib. JTD 3, fol. 473.

Miller Farm

Near Chesterville
c. 1850

THE MILLER FARMHOUSE IS LOCATED EAST OF MILL BRANCH on the Chesterville/Millington Road. It is a very plain two-part, frame house, with hall-parlor plan in the main, two-story section, and two rooms in the service wing. It is believed that the one-and-one-half story frame wing predated the remainder of the house, but it all seems to have been built very close to the middle of the nineteenth century. Like Grantham and Forest Farm, across the road, the two rooms each have their own enclosed corner stair. The second story is divided into three rooms, similar to the second story of Big Fairlee

Ellwood Farm was built for Richard and Elizabeth Betterton Turner in 1851, a curious non-traditional building that differed from the Greek Revival and Italianate styles that were so popular in Kent during the 1850s and 60s. The Turners were to develop Betterton into a summer resort that was popular in the late nineteenth and early twentieth centuries. Michael C. Wootton photograph, 1996.

on the Bay. There were originally board and batten doors between the rooms, trimmed with a beaded board without a backband. The service wing was plainly finished on the first story and unfinished on the second. There is access from the wing to a half basement under the east side of the main section.

On Martenet's Map of Kent County (1860), the farm was in the ownership of the heirs of Thomas Walker. Walker had been a very successful merchant of Millington and Chestertown and was active in the formation of the Agricultural Society earlier in the century. It is likely that he built the house for a tenant farmer. On the 1877 Atlas, the farm is listed under the name of T. Price. K-634

Ellwood Farm

Betterton
1851

Ellwood Farm stands on the south edge of Betterton. Built for Richard and Elizabeth Betterton Turner in 1851, it is a frame two-and-a-half-story, three-bay building with a two-story, two-bay service wing. The house is late Georgian in style and vernacular in form, resembling farmhouses that were built a hundred years earlier. Pilasters located at the corners of the main section, columns on the front porch, and the entrance itself were all executed in the Greek Revival style. Most often these are found in Kent County in combination with Italianate elements in houses dating from the same antebellum era. Ellwood is the only house in

Kent County to have a gallery or deck running from chimney to chimney. It resembles Garden of Eden in Dorchester County in that respect. The plan of the house is composed of a central stairhall with two flanking rooms. The service wing contains pantry and kitchen. The house was built on a basement of granite that was shipped from Port Deposit, a short distance by water.

Richard T. Turner was a lumber merchant and developer of the town of Betterton, named for his wife's family. They were Quakers and attended meeting at Cecil Meeting near Lynch, where the births of their children were recorded.[1] The Turner family owned Ellwood until 1897, when it was sold out of the family to Harvey Brice.[2] It was afterword the home of Senator Arthur Brice.   K-221

1. Carroll, Kenneth, Quakerism on the Eastern Shore, p. 273.
2. A history of Ellwood and the family was published by H. Chandlee Forman in his book entitled The Rolling Years, 1985.

Spry Home Farm

Near Chesterville
c. 1852

William T. Spry purchased the 253 acre farm from the estate of Lancelot Moffett in 1852 and built his house soon thereafter.[1] Like the other antebellum houses of Kent County, the form of the Spry Home Farm is that of a main block with wing set perpendicularly out the back so as to emphasize the symmetry of the front facade. There are numerous examples of such form in the County: Maple Grove, Thomas' Purchase, Mt. Airy, Brampton and Stepney—all similar in form, their differences lay mainly in their details.

William T. Spry owned this as well as another farm south of Chesterville. This farm, however, as the name implies, was his residence where he and his wife, Mary Ann raised their ten children. Their oldest daughter, Vermadilla, married Robert B. M. Massey, who owned and occupied Godomar, north of Massey and their youngest daughter, Eliza Jane, married Samuel Ford and lived at Fair View near Lambson's Station. Other daughters married into the Hurlock, Jarman, and Ireland families.[2]

In 1872, the farm was rented to William E. Jarrell, a young energetic farmer from Queen Annes County. When Spry's estate was being settled after his death in 1874, Jarrell purchased the farm and resided there with his wife and son, Frank. He was to be very successful not only in farming, but in the sale of farm machinery and phosphates for the land. By the time of his death he owned 1500 acres.[3]

The farm was later acquired by Albert and Julia Jervis in whose family it remains. The house burned in the 1970s.   K-185

1. Land Records, Lib. JR 2, fol. 365.
2. Wills, Lib. EC 1, fol. 118.
3. Portraits and Biographical Record, Chapman Publishing Co., NY 1898.

bly in the year of his immigration, as well as in 1641–42. Appointed Surveyor General in the latter year, Langford served in that capacity until 1648.

Langford's Neck, as the tract was called, is one of the earliest grants in Kent County.[1] Greys Inn Creek, on its south side bears the name of Langford's alma mater in England, while the large creek to the north shares his surname. Langford probably died in England after 1666, the year in which the land was sold.[2]

Belle View's origins begin with the purchase of 68 acres at the head of Spring Cove by Augusta Browne, wife of James Browne.[3] By 1852, the Browns had built the present house, for in the Tax Assessment of that year the buildings were referred to as *"new Frame House & other Buildings in good repair, formerly to John Hynson and E. Curry."*[4]

When new, the house was a very late example of Federal architecture. At a time when other dwellings were being decorated with corner pilasters, brackets and other Greek Revival and Italianate details, Belle View was devoid of ornamentation. Its plan was similar to Melfield or Plaindealing in the Second District, with side hall and double parlors in the tall, two-story section and two rooms adjoining the hall in a one-and-a-half-story wing.

The farm remained in the possession of Augusta Browne until her death in 1876. She left it to her niece, Charlotte Augusta Strong (nee Wickes).[5] The following year it was shown in the Atlas as the property of Strong's husband, T. R. Strong.

Belle View

Near Rock Hall
c. 1852

BELLE VIEW IS A CLOSELY DATED, MID-nineteenth century, frame, vernacular farmhouse. Its twentieth century remodeling, however, has greatly diminished what architectural significance it may have had. Perhaps of greater interest is the history of the land on which it stands.

The farm occupies a small section of the 1658 grant of 1500 acres to John Langford, one of the closest allies of Cecilius Calvert. Having immigrated originally to Kent Island from Kent, England in 1637, Langford was most likely granted this tract as a reward for his support of the Calverts evidenced in a pamphlet he authored (1655) in their defense against their Puritan critics. Earlier he had served in the Assem-

Belle View, a plain mid-nineteenth century vernacular farmhouse occupies a prominent site overlooking the confluence of Langford Bay with the Chester River. It was built by Augusta and James Browne on part of Langford's Neck, now part of Piney Neck. Michael Bourne photograph, 1996.

In 1918, the Strong heirs sold Belle View to Herman Copeland of Alleghany County.[6] During the long ownership of the Brownes and Strongs the property grew in acreage from 68 to 176½. From 1918 to 1995 there have been six owners.

K-268

1. Patents, Lib. Q, fol. 328, 1658.
2. Papenfuse, p. 516.
3. Land Records, Lib. JFG 11, fol. 753.
4. Kent County Tax Assessment, 1st District, 1852.
5. Wills, Lib. EC 1, fol. 214.
6. Land Records, Lib. APR 3, fol. 492.

Wesley Chapel

Near Rock Hall
1852

THE FIRST ORGANIZATION of Methodists in this part of Kent County occurred on September 19, 1829, at which meeting the members subscribed to the construction of a meeting house. The meeting house, called Weslyan Chapel, was a frame building measuring 24 feet by 14 feet, and was built by Thomas Bryan for the sum of $220.00. The building served the needs of the community until 1839, when there was a poll among members about constructing a new church. A new church, however, was not to be built until fourteen years later. In the May 1, 1852 issue of the Kent News there appears a solicitation for *"carpenters work"* which spells out the specifications for the Church:

Sealed Proposals
"Will be received by the building committee of Wesley Chapel near Rock Hall, Kent County, Maryland, for the carpenters work of a brick church to be built during the present year, on or near the site of Wesley Chapel. Said Church to be fifty feet in length and thirty seven feet in breadth, to have three windows on each side with double box frames so arranged that both upper and lower sash shall be hung upon weights, to slide; also a window over the pulpit and a window over the door in the gallery, both to have the same kind of frames and fixtures as the side windows. The side windows shall be made with twelve lights of glass to each sash—ten by sixteen inches—and the window over the pulpit shall have six lights of the same size glass to each sash; and the window over the door shall have six lights of the same size with side lights of four lights each of glass of the same size as the windows. The floors to be laid with mill-dressed yellow pine flooring; to have a gallery ten feet deep on one end. There shall also be a vestibule, five feet deep on the same end as the gallery, an entrance with two doors opposite the isles covered with baize or cloth. The interior of the church shall be filled with seats with scrolls on the ends and backs of walnut, cherry or other hard wood, at the option of the committee; also a suitable plain pulpit shall be erected, the roof shall be framed with six pairs of principle rafters, with a king post to each pair and a straight jack and a perloin and raising plate to each rafter; and all the necessary intermediate rafters to be thrown in, sheathed and shingled with cypress or juniper shingles; a stairway to the vestibule leading to the gallery shall

Wesley Chapel, near Rock Hall. The congregation was founded in 1829, the same year a small frame chapel was built. It was replaced in 1852 by the brick church which still serves the community.
Michael Bourne photograph, 1996.

"the ceremonies of laying this corner-stone were conducted by the Rev. J. J. Murray, who delivered an appropriate, eloquent and very impressive address on the occasion, in the grove which surrounds this consecrated spot, to a large and attentive audience." Michael Bourne photograph, 1996.

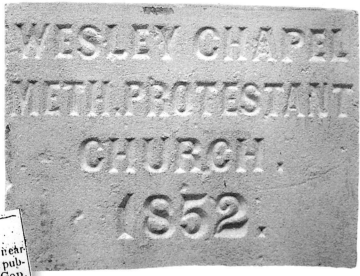

DEDICATION.

The New Wesley Chapel, near Rock Hall, Kent County, will be publicly dedicated to the worship of God, on Sunday morning, the Second of January, 1853.

Rev. E. Y. Reese, D. D., and other clergymen from abroad are expected to officiate on the occasion.

Service to commence at 10½ o'clock. A collection will be taken up to aid in extinguishing the debt. The public are respectfully invited to attend.

Jno. J. Murray,
Wm. S. Hammond.
Chestertown, December 25, 1852.

On July 31, 1852, the cornerstone for the church was laid with orations both before and after the act of laying the stone. The ladies of the congregation *"prepared an elegant and plentiful dinner, the proceeds of which, with those of various kinds of confectionary sold upon the ground by the young ladies, is to be appropriated towards defraying the expenses incurred in the erection of this temple of the living God."*[1]

The only discrepancy between the specifications and the actual building as constructed appears to have been a wooden cornice on both sides of the building in place of a brick cornice mentioned in the solicitation for bids.

In the Christmas issue of the Kent News, Dec. 25, 1852, there is an announcement of the dedication of the Church to take place on January 2, 1853, which by this time was called Wesley Chapel. Reverends E. Y. Reese, D. D. and J. S. Reese officiated at the dedication.

The first major alteration to the building occurred in the 1880s, when the tower was constructed in the center of the gable facade. This structure was built with three levels beside the actual belfry, each level having Romanesque arched openings with projecting brick at the outer edge of the arch, like Emmanuel Church, Chestertown (1883) built in the same period. The window sash have single panes surrounded by small panes of colored glass, a style of sash used at Lauretum Place (1881), the home of Harrison Vickers, near Chestertown.

The next alterations occurred in 1905 when the single window behind the pulpit was replaced by a large gothic arch window with *"art glass,"* the same type as used in the side windows. At the same time the gallery was removed and a *"metal ceiling of paneled design, decorated with a galaxy of soft rich mellow shades of happily blended colors"* covered the old cracked plaster ceiling. In 1913, a new half ton McShane bell was installed in the belfry. Many other alterations and additions have been carried out over the years since the brick church was constructed. In most cases, the costs have been defrayed through the efforts of the congregation, in the same spirit that was evident when the ladies prepared dinner at the laying of the cornerstone and at the dedication of the church, which nearly paid off the debt of the new church in 1852 and 1853.[2]   K-536

also be included. The church is to be finished outside with a heavy wooded cornice on the front end, returning and meeting the brick cornice on the side; also a similiar cornice forming the barge board on the other end being plain. All the work to be executed in a workmanlike manner, agreeable to the plan and drawings kept at the office of George Vickers, Esp., Chestertown for inspection.

The front doors shall be folding doors of three panels each, as represented in said drawings; and finishing pieces are to be set in the Greek columns as shown in the drawings. The committee will receive proposals for the space of two weeks; the materials will all be furnished by the building committee.

Proposals will also be received for the bricklayers work of said church, rated at a price per thousand, for laying the brick, which will be common red brick, no pressed or front bricks to be laid.

They will also receive proposals for the plastering, at a certain price per square yard, the plastering to be finished with three coats—one brown and one white coat, to be troweled down hard and smooth; the committee furnishing the materials for the bricklayers and plasterers, also.

The whole of the carpenters work to be finished, fitted and hung. Each and every part to be completed. Carpenters in making their estimates must estimate to do the entire carpenters' work of the church, agreeably to the drawings and not excepted in these specifications.

Signed on behalf of the committee,
Hiram Jones, Chairman"
May 1, '52

1. A Heritage of Faith, Wesley Chapel United Methodist Church. Rock Hall, MD, Economy Printing, Easton, 1978, p. 5.
2. Ibid, the majority of the above was gleaned from the history of Wesley Chapel.

which they heard the preachings of itinerant ministers as they traveled through Kent County.[2]

Handy's Chapel served the new St. James congregation for twenty years before it was replaced with a new church in 1853. That church was a simple Greek Revival brick structure that resembles Salem Church in Fairlee. From the old photograph of the church the building appears to have been a three-bay-wide, three-bay-deep, brick structure which had corner pilasters and a moderately pitched roof. Between the windows, crude brick buttresses are visible which were installed to keep the walls from bulging. Over the central entrance, there is the date plaque with the inscription *"St. James Methodist Protestant Church 1853."*

In the 1904 history of the church, the recollections of Samuel Vannort mentions that *"During his last year (Rev. E. C. Makoskey 1898-1904) the church was remodeled and made nearly a new church, with gothic roof, tower vestibule and windows (all memorial), metal ceiling, walls painted inside and out, new pews, pulpit and carpet, at a cost of $4,560.00; and now we have one of the prettiest churches in the district."*[3] The key word in his description is *nearly* for it points to the remnants of the old church that are now only partially discernible.

On the 1904 church, the crude brick buttresses are still visible and the original date plaque can be seen as having been relocated in the lower right corner of the front pilaster. St. James has a building chronology that is similar to several other churches in Kent County—Wesley Chapel, Kennedyville, and Olivet Church, Galena. These all began as simple meeting houses in the mid-nineteenth century and each received a tower or was completely remodeled around the turn of the century.   K-234

St. James Church

Hanesville
1853

THE EARLY HISTORY OF ST. JAMES IS, CURIOUSLY ENOUGH, tied to the history of St. Peter's Episcopal Church, I. U. By 1825, St. Peter's had fallen into such a state of disrepair that it had to be abandoned. The closest Episcopal church was located in Chestertown which meant the parishioners residing in the Third District had quite a distance to travel. As a result, the Reverend D. H. Handy, an Episcopal priest, purchased a parcel of land near the head waters of Mill Creek in the same year and built a small chapel there, one which the locals called *"Handy's Chapel."*[1] It was not as successful as Rev. Handy had hoped and in 1832 it was sold to the newly formed Methodist congregation of St. James, a group which had actually used the chapel previously in

St. James Church, Hanesville, was nearly identical to Salem Methodist Church, Fairlee, when it was built in 1853. In 1904, the church was remodeled into the gothic design it retains today. Michael Bourne photograph, 1996.

St. James Church, Hanesville. The buttresses were added in the 1904 remodeling to counteract the steeper roof structure. Michael Bourne photograph, 1996.

1. Land Records, Lib. TW 4, fol. 683.
2. Land Records, Lib. JNG 2, fol. 695.
3. "A Tower of Strength, 1825-1975, St. James United Methodist Church," page 270, Printed by St. James Church, Hanesville, MD.

Still Pond Methodist Church

Still Pond
1853

AT THE WEST END OF STILL POND STANDS THE ONLY BRICK-building in the village, the Methodist Church. By tradition, the congregation at Still Pond traces its roots to the first visit of Bishop Asbury to a farm about a mile west of town belonging to John Randel. By the year 1788 a small wooden chapel had been built for meetings. That chapel was replaced in 1820 by a brick chapel. This building in turn was replaced in 1853 by a larger building, perhaps built on the lines of the original St. James or Wesley Chapel. From the exterior of the present building the 1853 structure cannot be traced because the remodeling of 1882 was so thorough as to conceal any of that building from view.

The present church is a country Gothic structure, similar to St. James, Kennedyville and Olivet Churches, once they too were remodeled. The gable facade and tower are laid in cut brick with narrow mortar joints. The basement level windows have standard residential size sash, whereas the windows of the main body of the church and the tower have tall lancet arches with the sash fit with geometric patterned stained glass. The tower is the most architectural part of the building, with buttresses at the outer corners, a large lancet arched entry with double doors and large transom above and round windows with star of David muntin pattern on three sides. At the top of the brick, which terminates at the roof, is a series of brick corbels, a stylistic reference to medieval castles. The belfry and steeple are built entirely of wood and possess some finely crafted details of the period. The interior of the church is plain, with an arched ceiling, plaster walls and a gothic arch defining the altar area.

The earliest grave stones date from the 1830s and are contemporary with the first brick church that was built on this site.   K-434

Salem Methodist Church

Fairlee
1853

THE FIRST LAND TRANSACTION for the specific use of a Methodist meeting house in Bel Air was recorded in the year 1853 for a parcel west of the present church. On that land was built a frame chapel by the Trustees named in the deed. It remained in use for a number of years until the present parcel was purchased in 1868. The old frame church was moved to the new site and encased in brick in the Greek Revival style. From the old photograph of St. James and the verbal description of Waters Chapel in Kennedyville, Salem Church looked nearly identical to them, even to the placement of a date plaque in the gable above the central entrance. The original four-bay long structure has pilasters at the corners and large rectangular windows. The sash are fit with colored glass with a lancet arch motif and probably post-date the 1868 date. The small frame vestibule is a twentieth century addition. Salem Church is the only one of the Greek Revival Methodist churches to retain its original mid-nineteenth century form.   K-428

Salem Methodist Church, Fairlee. The old frame church was encased in brick in the Greek Revival style.

Still Pond Methodist Church owes its present appearance to a major remodeling undertaken in 1882. It reputedly retains the 1853 church within its walls. Michael C. Wootton photograph, 1996.

Mount Airy

Fairlee Neck
c. 1854

Mount Airy (Fairfield) c. 1900, during the occupancy of the Harry Stavely family. From the collection of the late Frances Stavely.

Mount Airy, Fairlee Neck. A plat prepared after the death of John B. Anderson, when the farm was sold to William and Elizabeth Overend. Chancery, Lib. JKH 3, fol. 122.

THE FRISBY FAMILY IS ASSOCIATED with this farm on Great Oak Manor from the early eighteenth century until 1872. Upon his death in 1779, William Frisby bequeathed it to his wife, Elizabeth, for her lifetime, after which time it was to go to one of his three children (Joseph, James or Martha).[1] When Elizabeth died 20 years later, she named her son James as her sole heir.[2] Local folklore tells of this house, as well as its neighbor, Handy Point, being destroyed by the British in 1814. Recent research, however, confirms that this story refers to another Frisby house which was located south of Fairlee Creek.

After the death of James Frisby (1830s), John B. Anderson began acquiring the farm in 1839 from the three heirs. Since he had married Elizabeth Frisby, he had only two thirds to acquire. The first part was from William and Ellen Frisby who had moved to Peoria, Illinois.[3] In 1852 he acquired the last third from his sister-in-law Susan R. Frisby.[4] In this last deed, the property was referred to as that *"on which Anderson resides."*[5]

In the 1852 Tax Assessment, there is mention of a *"frame house & other buildings in good repair,"* on Anderson's farm. Sometime between this tax assessment and the printing of the Martenet Map in 1860, Anderson constructed a new house typical of the antebellum period.

Although similar to Brampton and Stepney in style, Mount Airy differed from the other buildings in that it was built all at one time. The entire structure was built of brick atop a stone foundation in a simplified Greek Revival form with Italianate details. The front section of the two part building is three stories with the third story being shorter than the first two. Beside the bracketed cornice and window shutters, the chief decorative feature of the facade was the entry porch. It was only as wide as the central bay and had bracketed cornice, pierced brackets at the tops of the square posts and a pierced splat balustrade. Typical of the period and style, the low pitched roof was topped with a small monitor centered between the two chimneys. The entry had double doors with transom and sidelights, but no external architrave. The second floor central bay had a three-part window to balance the entry below.

A two story back wing continued on the plane of the southwest side. Like the facade, it was five bays long. On the northeast side, a porch extended from the back door of the main hall to the end of the wing.

The plan of the house consisted of central stairhall with two large parlors in the front section and a narrow central stairhall with kitchen and dining room in the wing. In the front, all windows and doors were trimmed with simple Greek Revival architraves. The fireplaces were trimmed and fitted with marbleized wood mantels with arched openings. The main stair had a huge turned mahogany newel post and two turned balusters per step with wide handrail rising to

Mount Airy (Fairfield) in 1954 during the occupancy of the John Plummer family. John Plummer Collection.

Mount Airy (Fairfield). The L plan building was built in the 1850s by John B. Anderson. It incorporated some materials from the previous house. Michael Bourne photograph, 1982.

the third floor. Plaster medallions were installed in the ceilings of the two front parlors and stairhall. The remainder of the house was trimmed with plain beaded trim with corner blocks. Only the mantels in four of the other rooms were similar to the architectural trim of the principal rooms. The rear stair had a turned newel, plain rectangular balusters and a round handrail.

The biggest difference between the first and second floor plans was the addition of a narrow corridor connecting the main stair landing with the back hall and two rooms above the kitchen (one of which is a bathroom). At one time the western most room of those two had been divided into two rooms with its original access from the kitchen being a ladder-stair. This room was intended for use by servants. On the third floor the ceilings were slightly over six feet and there were two rooms flanking the central stair.

The Andersons raised six children at Mount Airy (the name used during their ownership) and died in the 1860s. As a result of an equity case in 1865, George Vickers was appointed to sell the property for the benefit of the children, which he did on May 3rd, to William Overend of Ohio.[6]

William and Elizabeth Overend owned the farm from 1865 until they returned to Cincinnati in 1881. They,

like the Andersons, had six children to fill the house. The children apparently enjoyed living on the farm for their youngest child, Lizzie Overend Hart wrote the following to a niece, Cecil Overend on December 15, 1930 about her visit after many years absence:

" ... *Although there were many new roads and very bad ones at that, we got there all right and found the dear old home still standing and well preserved for the 50 years that I had not seen it. I recognized it from the roadside, but the land was very much changed, and very much impaired, nothing like it was when we lived there. Stables and grannerys moved up around the house. Oh, but that made me feel sick, but the dear old home was there and when I got inside I was full of old memories and had a good cry. There was an old Jew and his wife there, that knew Father, Charlie, Ed, Sam, Rob and Sherrie and me, as a little girl, but I could not place him. They let me go in all the rooms even up in the third story, and you don't know, or could you imagine, how I felt—so alone, and no one of the family to tell of the many changes that had taken place."*

"We too stopped in Chestertown and I thought I would know just how to get to the old home, but there were so many new roads, I gave up, but I said I would know when we got to the cross roads near Buckneck, but some people we inquired of never heard of that place, so then I said it was somewhere between Worton and Fairlee, so when we got to the oil station Will got out and asked them and he told him just where it was. When Will got back in the machine he told to me to "keep your eyes open," and I did, but did not know we were so near. They had changed the entrance to the place. No front gate, no peach orchard, nothing but corn fields as far as the eye could reach, but when we got to the opening I spied the house and I cried "there it is," it didn't take so long to get there, but oh the change in the ground around the house. Horses and cows running all over the lawn. It made me feel awfully bad, and the old oak tree that it got its name from—gone. The real old land mark "Great Oak Manor."[7]

The Overends may have called the place by its oldest name—Great Oak Manor Farm—as that is the name which appears in the 1877 Atlas.

For seven months in 1881 the farm was owned by Samuel W. Thomas, a Methodist minister living in Philadelphia with roots in Kent County.[8] He owned several other properties in and around Chestertown at this period.

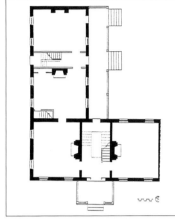

Mount Airy (Fairfield). The stair ascended to the third floor with only one newel post on the first floor. It has oak balusters and mahogany railing. Michael Bourne photograph, 1980.

Mount Airy, c. 1854. First floor plan. Michael Bourne, 1997.

In October of 1881 he sold the farm to Lucas Alrich of New Castle County, Delaware[9] who mortgaged it to Samuel Dunn in 1892. Dunn's attorney foreclosed on Alrich in 1897, after which time it was sold to Benjamin Ferris.[10] Ferris sold the farm to George L. Bowers and Harry Stavely in 1900, but Bowers sold his share to Stavely in 1902.[11]

In need of financing the construction of a new barn, Harry and Florence Stavely sold the farm to Rufus Parks,[12] a Chestertown lawyer, but remained as tenants. Frances Stavely (1900-1996), Harry and Florence's daughter was born in the house and shared the same fondness for the place as Lizzie Overend. She frequently visited the farm and told stories of how things used to be. The old photograph was taken while her father lived on the farm.

After the deaths of Mr. and Mrs. Parks, the farm was sold by their heirs to Alice and Bramwell Geddes in 1944.[13] It was at this period that the farm became known as Fairfield. The Geddes had also purchased Handy Point earlier and had established their residence there as well as an important stock farm. Buying the adjoining farm enabled them to increase their operation considerably. They improved the old residence which had been allowed to disintegrate and installed the farm manager and his family therein. The John Plummer family lived there until 1979, thirteen years after the Geddes heirs had sold the farm to Louisa Copeland and her brother, Gerret.[14] The Copelands placed the farms in scenic and agricultural easement which will serve to protect it from uncontrolled development in perpetuity.

In 1982, Michael (this book's author) and Ann Bourne purchased the house and five acres after having rented it for two years. During their occupancy the kitchen was fitted with cupboards made of old pine and an additional bath was installed on the second floor of the rear wing. The Bourne children, Mark and Sarah, were born during these years and spent their early childhood at Fairfield. Like Lizzie Overend and Frances Stavely, they remember Fairfield and its surroundings with fondness.

The house and five acres were sold again in 1987 and drastically and insensitively remodeled. Once again, the house was the subject of a foreclosure in the 1990s. It was bought again by Gerret Copeland who has undertaken its revitalization.   K-240

1. Land Records, Lib. EF 6, fol. 61.

2. Wills, Lib. 7, fol. 21. (For more information about the Carvills, see Carvill Hall).

3. Inventories, Lib. 8, fol. 188.

4. Wills, Lib. 7, fol. 469.

5. Inventories, Lib. 10, fol. 302.

6. Inventories, Lib. 11, fol. 447.

7. Wills, Lib. 11, fol. 180.

8. Inventories, Lib. 20, fol. 409.

9. Land Records, Lib. JNG 3, fol. 484.

10. Land Records, Lib. JNG 10, fol. 134.

11. Land Records, Lib. JKH 6, fol. 578.

12. Land Records, Lib. SB 11, fol. 598.

13. Wills, Lib. JRC 1, fol. 294.

14. Land Records, Lib. RAS 32, fol. 25.

Dreka Mill Site

Sassafras
c. 1854

The village of Sassafras is defined by the main branch of the Sassafras River on the north and a small branch on the south, both of which were dammed in the eighteenth century for the establishment of grist mills. The mill on the north was located in Cecil County and the one to the south in Kent. The southerly mill was owned by various members of the Wilmer and Boyer families until 1853, when it was purchased by August Dreka. The deed of that year describes the property as including *"the mill & mill seat & parcel of land."* It was sold from the estate of Mary Ann Boyer by her trustee, James B. Ricaud.[1] Five years later, Dreka purchased an additional 1.5 acres with *"… the dwelling House and improvements thereon erected … ."*[2]

Whether the mill and house depicted in the photograph collection of the Historical Society of Kent County were standing at the time of the deed is not known,

but they are certainly representative of building types of the mid-nineteenth century.

The mill was a substantial frame two-and-a-half-story building constructed on a stone foundation. To its right in the photograph the wooden sluice to the water wheel is visible.

The house appears to have had a partial basement below the five-bay, hip-roof, frame structure. It possessed decorative cast iron porch supports, a feature it had in common with three other Sassafras River dwellings.   K-296

1. Land Records, Lib. JFG 2, fol. 324.
2. Land Records, Lib. JKF 1, fol. 423.

Dreka Mill House, was probably standing when August Dreka acquired the property in 1858. It is one of three Kent County houses on the upper Sassafras River with cast iron porch. Historical Society of Kent County Collection.

Dreka Mill, Sassafras, was located on the south side of the village. It was established in the eighteenth century and owned by the Wilmer and Boyer families until 1853, when it was acquired by August Dreka. He was responsible for the mill that appears in the photograph. Historical Society of Kent County Collection.

Worthmore Farm

Near Stillpond
1854

Hedgewood Farm, as it is called today, was part of the large seventeenth century grant called Camelsworthmore. Owned by Sewell Hepbron, it adjoins Shepherd's Delight, another part of the same tract which was first acquired in 1824 by his father, Thomas Hepbron, Jr.

In an account book of Sewell Hepbron, the costs involved in constructing his brick house are recorded for the years 1854 and 1856. They show that much of the lumber and millwork were obtained from Port Deposit and Baltimore, with some minor materials coming from Chestertown. The names of some of the workers are also mentioned: Reynor Stavely for digging the cellar; Jim Turner and James Crew. It took 80,000 bricks (cost—$400.00) to construct the dwelling, kitchen and probably the foundations of the carriage house, shop and hen house.

The house was a three-bay, two-story, central hall dwelling with a lower, two-story kitchen wing. Both sections were built of brick laid in common bond. The only unusual masonry features were stone door sills and corbeled brick cornices. On the south facade there was a semi-octagonal porch.

The interior plan was a typical Kent County farmhouse, but on a small scale. It consisted of a central stair and two flanking rooms and a kitchen. The central entrance with its narrow sidelights and transom, and the balustrade of the stair are typical of manufactured millwork available to the public in mid-nineteenth century Maryland. An unusual feature is the somewhat naive Greek Revival mantel with its elongated diamonds in the legs and frieze and the heavy dentils employed beneath the shelf. It was a plainly finished house, which with the paling-in of the front yard, cost Mr. Hepbron under $1,700.00 to construct.

Although the house is a simple brick farmhouse, it was built well and remains one of the few buildings in the county which has documentation concerning its date and cost of construction.   K-226

Worthmore Farm (Hedgewood Farm) near Stillpond, was built by Sewell Hepbron, Sr. in 1854–56, whose accounts for construction still exist. An original semi-octagonal porch was built on the front of the house.

Worthmore Farm. The naively executed dining room mantel could have been built on the site.

Worthmore Farm was very simply finished with lumber and millwork purchased from Baltimore, Port Deposit, and Chestertown. C. Engstrom photographs, 1977.

Davis Duplex

*Mill Street, Chestertown
c. 1854*

THE HOUSE LOCATED AT 105-107 SOUTH MILL STREET IS INtimately connected with the histories of its neighbors, 101 and 103 South Mill Street as they are all located on the southwest half of Lot No. 84 in Chestertown.

In the chain of title and tax assessment for this property there appears to have been only one residence from the first transaction to 1854 when Thomas Lorrain McClean sold it to Charles Davis.[1] McClean inherited it after the death of Anna Maria McClean who had owned the property in 1841.[2] In the assessment of that year the one house on Anna's part of Lot No. 84 was occupied by the Reverend G. Heritage. It was appraised at the time for $600, the same amount paid for it in 1823.

By the time Charles Davis wrote his will in 1866, he had acquired two lots with houses on High Street, one of which was occupied by his son Charles. He had also built 105-107 South Mill Street. To his daughter Mary Anna Davis, he bequeathed *"that part of my new*

Davis Duplex, Chestertown, was built on part of Lot No. 84. It was called Sterling Castle by Charles Davis after acquiring the property in 1854. The one-and-a-half-story house is similar in form to houses built 150 years earlier. Tyler Campbell photograph, 1996.

house with lands now rented to P. T. McN Thomas" (107 South Mill). It appears that he had lived in the other half of the new house (105 South Mill) and bequeathed it to his daughter Sally. His son John lived in the old house (103 South Mill) adjoining.[3]

Charles Davis' double house was built on a brick foundation with four bays on the facade, the inner two of which have doors with transoms. Three dormer windows with 6/6 sash and a beveled cornice, returning slightly in the front, complete the facade. In style, the dormers are very similar to those on the back of the Baker House at 119 High Street which was built in 1876.

Behind the one-and-a-half-story dwelling there was a two-bay, one-story wing set at right angles on the northeastern side. Behind the other half there was a two-bay leanto. All four chimneys had their fireplace backs exposed.

The interior spaces were originally divided unevenly, with one front room and one back room in each. In the back corner of each front room there was an enclosed stair to a vestibule and two small chambers. In 105 South Mill Street there was a third space in the *A* roof of the back section, accessible from a ladder adjoining the fireplace. One curious feature of the back room of 107 South Mill Street is the presence of weatherboard on the inner wall, suggesting there was a period of time before that room was constructed.

Prior to her death in 1916, Sally Davis acquired her sister's half interest in the property. Before that, Sally and/or her sister Mary Anna had built the duplex on the corner of Mill and Cannon Streets in the space remaining on their part of Lot No. 84. In Sally's will of 1916, the house located at 105-107 South Mill Street is described as *"now occupied by Mr. E. G. Nickerson and Mr. James E. Everett, who rent from me as tenants."* The newer duplex at 109-111 South Mill Street is described as *"occupied by Miss Nettie Russell and … Mr. John L. Hudson."* These two houses were bequeathed to her nieces and great nieces respectively.[4]

Between 1916 and 1959, the house at 105-107 South Mill Street remained a tenement and gradually deteriorated. Maynard P. White, Jr. and Kathleen Bracket purchased the house prior to their wedding in 1959 and began the work of restoring and rehabilitating the house into a single family dwelling.[5] K-72

1. Land Records, Lib. JFG 2, fol. 26.
2. Wills, Lib. JFB 1, fol. 43.
3. Wills, Lib. JF 1, fol. 376.
4. Wills, Lib. JRC 1, fol. 338.
5. A mantel from "Angels Rest" was installed during the rehabilitation.

Middle Plantation

Broad Neck
1856

Benjamin F. Beck, Sr. purchased Middle Plantation[1] from John Claypoole in 1846.[2] He is assessed for it in the 1852 tax records. Local tradition states that the house was built for Benjamin F. Beck, Jr., by his father upon his marriage. Like the father's house, there is a date brick with initials and the date 1856. B. F. Beck is listed on both the 1860 Martenet Map and in the 1877 Lake, Griffing, Stevenson Atlas.

While only three bays long, it is similar to the Davis or Kennard House (five bays) in form. It does, however, have several unusual features. The house is two rooms deep and covered with a low pitched hip roof with chimneys on the side walls and has a windowless monitor on the roof (like Cahall's Store, Chestertown). Normally the modillion cornice would be deeper on a Greek Revival house, but the late 1850s was a transitional period into the Italianate style and the cornice here is representative of that change.

Inside, the house has the plan of a central passage flanked by (originally) double parlors on the east, and a dining room with secondary passage (behind the pantry and stair) to the kitchen on the west. The kitchen is located in a back brick wing. The use of the rooms was totally changed after 1956 when the last owner purchased the property. Since then, the property has been well maintained. K-252

> 1. Middle Plantation was patented to Joseph Wickes in 1678 (350 acres) Patents, Lib. 20, fol. 23.

Plaindealing

Near Chestertown
c. 1857

In 1857, John B. Walmsley purchased 127 acres consisting of parts of Plaindealing, Wyatt's Chance and Wyatt's Addition from Christopher Deering and his wife, Julia Ann.[1] In subsequent transactions the farm is simply referred to as Plaindealing.

Walmsley built the house that has survived to this day close to the road leading from Chestertown to Millington. Its basic form was a popular one for the period, a rectangular two-story structure with low-pitched

hip roof. However, unlike the majority of others of this period, the plan consisted of a side hall with double parlors and the service rooms were contained in an attached one-and-a-half-story wing on the other side of the hall.

Stylistically, the house's form and Italianate detail closely resemble the Lusby House located at the corner of High and Mill Streets in Chestertown. In contrast, however, here there was no attempt to emphasize the entry bay. The second story porch did have jib doors which led to a former deck. The present porch appears to date from the turn of the century with its almost Colonial Revival simplicity. The latter feature was probably installed by William F. Melvin who purchased the property in 1899.[2] It remained essentially unchanged until the third generation, present owner, built a small brick wing on the west side in the late 1970s. K-382

Middle Plantation, Broad Neck, bears a brick with the date 1856 and the initials of Benjamin F. Beck. Built in the Greek Revival style, it retains its monitor on the low-pitched roof. Maryland Historical Trust Collection, c. 1981.

Plaindealing (Melfield) near Morgnec is a three-bay version of the popular antebellum house form that is seen elsewhere in Kent County at the Lusby House, Spry Landing and Doe Neck. This house was probably built soon after 1857 when the farm was purchased by John B. Walmsley. Marsha L. Fritz photograph, 1980.

> 1. Land Records, Lib. JFG 4, fol. 446.
> 2. Land Records, Lib. JTD 3, fol. 89.

Capt. James F. Taylor House

*Water Street, Chestertown
c. 1857*

CAPTAIN JAMES FRISBY TAYLOR IS CREDITED WITH THE CONstruction of this Italianate house located on the corner of Front and Cannon Streets, sometime after his purchase of Lot No. 22 in 1857.[1] Captain Taylor also built a wharf in front of his residence and leased it to the Chester River Steamboat Company of which he was general agent.

Captain James F. Taylor House, Chestertown, stands on Water Lot No. 22, the same site previously occupied by the town residence of Richard Tilghman IV. Captain Taylor's Italianate style house boasts a belvedere on the roof from which the busy river traffic could be observed. Tyler Campbell photograph, 1996.

Captain James F. Taylor House from the river side. Original kitchen and service rooms were located in the ground level. William Creager Collection.

Being in a position of observing what was currently being built around the bay and particularly in Baltimore, it is not surprising that he chose to build a very *"modern"* dwelling in the latest Italianate style. The large rectangular frame structure was built over a full basement which originally housed the kitchen and other service rooms. Its low-pitched roof, over two stories, is adorned with an open cupola or belvedere in the center. The lyre pattern balustrade, bracketed cornice and square columns of the cupola are repeated on the front and rear porches of the house. At the corners of the house there are tall paneled pilasters. Both fa-

cades are five bays long with bold double doors having sidelights and transom. Each of the windows has a bracketed cornice with fretwork in the frieze, like those at Brampton and Pentridge.

The floor plan consists of a central stair passage with two rooms on the southwest side and one large room on the northeast. The latter, although one room, is divided by a wide arch and has a fireplace in either section—representative of the nineteenth century desire for larger spaces in which to entertain. There are plaster cornices in all of the first story rooms. The fireplaces have marbleized black slate mantels. The fine stair with its massive turned walnut newel post decorated with applied fretwork, walnut railing and oak balusters is representative of the finest quality millwork which could be purchased from companies in the major cities of the time.

Since Taylor's construction and ownership, the house has passed through the hands of nine subsequent owner/occupants. It was known locally for many years as the Whitsitt House in honor of Dr. and Mrs. Anderson Whitsitt who resided there from 1948–1971.[2] After Dr. Whitsitt's death, the house was sold to Dr. and Mrs. Neil Brayton.[3] Interestingly, shortly after their purchase in the 1970s, the ownership of the house was exchanged with that of Rye Hall in Queen Annes County, the property of Judge and Mrs. Stephen Collins who then occupied the house in Chestertown.[4]   K-7

1. Land Records, Lib. JNG 4, fol. 433.
2. Land Records, Lib. WHG 7, fol. 630.
3. Land Records, Lib. EHP 58, fol. 346.
4. Land Records, Lib. EHP 64, fol. 433.

Old Methodist Protestant Church

Cross & Cannon Streets, Chestertown 1858

No SOONER HAD THE CHAPEL BEEN CONSTRUCTED ON THE Town Square than differences in the Methodist Church as a whole resulted in a breakdown of its unity. In 1827, at the Baltimore Conference, the differences were perceived as so great that one group decided to leave the Church and form its own. The plan was to hold services initially in private homes, just as the forefathers of Methodism in America had done in their early days. The effects of this dissension were felt even in the rural outreaches of the Church. In 1830, the corner part of Lot No. 93 in Chestertown was sold to the *"Trustees of the Associated Methodist Church."*

When the present building was begun in 1858, there is reference to the demolition of a previous meeting house. The new church was dedicated on January 30, 1859. It was one story with a classical Greek Revival form and Italianate details. The three-bay facade had a central entrance with tripartite window above, both fitted with bracketed architrave. At the corners of the buildings and between the four-bay sides, pilasters were built which extended to the cornice. The interior was fitted with a gallery, but that configuration has since been lost. As with most Methodist churches built in the county in the mid-nineteenth century, a small protrusion was built in the sanctuary to cast light onto the communion table. This new building was featured on the Martenet Map of Kent County (1860). It is depicted as possessing tall windows on the Cannon Street side which matched the existing windows of the facade.

The church was used for only thirty years before another structure was begun on High Street in 1887. Thereafter, the old church was sold and has since been used for commercial purposes. The interior was divided into two stories with several spaces. The windows on the sides were converted into two tiers of smaller windows which continue to reflect the changes made inside. K-347

Rehobeth Methodist Protestant Church

Sassafras 1859

AT THE EAST CORNER OF THE INTERSECTION OF CALDWELL Corner Road and Route 290, in the village of Sassafras, stood a deteriorating Greek revival style frame chapel. The Methodists, who were living in the area around the village, constructed this building in 1859.

In the eighteenth and nineteenth centuries *"Head of Sassafras,"* as it was called before the Post Office shortened the name, was one of two points of crossing on the Sassafras River. The first was at Georgetown where the river could be crossed by ferry and the second was at Head of Sassafras where crossing was accomplished via a road over two mill dams. Located on the main route north, Head of Sassafras had one hotel, four stores, two churches, a mill, restaurant and ten houses in 1860. All of these helped to support the local agrarian economy, as well as travelers.

Although certainly not the most impressive Methodist church of the style in Kent County, Rehobeth M. P. Church was one of the few buildings to have a distinctive style in the village, (The Rock Hall M. E. Church was far more sophisticated with its full temple portico). In many ways, Rehobeth was like dozens of Eastern Shore methodist chapels built in the nineteenth century. It differed, however, in the treatment of its facade with corner pilasters, full pediment and double entrances. These are unique in Kent. Like many of the chapels of the period there was a small chancel projection on the opposite gable, where the table would have been located, lighted on both sides by a tall narrow window. The interior of the church possessed two aisles and three rows of pews, wainscoting and a balcony supported on two exaggerated columns. Most of the woodwork had been grained in imitation of oak.

Rehobeth Church was last used in 1976 for a homecoming festival.   K-128

Old Methodist Protestant Church, Chestertown, 1858, now Kent Printing. It was converted to commercial use long before the term "adaptive re-use" was coined. The front windows have remained untouched, but the side windows show current spacial requirements. Tyler Campbell photograph, 1996.

Rehobeth Methodist Protestant Church, Sassafras. It was built in 1859 and remained until 1997 when in a state of collapse, it was burned. The Greek Revival style of the church was the most popular of Methodist Churches in the 1850s. Maryland Historical Trust, c. 1986.

Andrew Woodall House Site

Georgetown
c. 1860

Andrew Woodall House, Georgetown, stood on Lot No. 7 before its demolition around 1970. It was similar to Spry's Landing and Doe Neck in that it was a three bay long, three-story structure with nearly flat hip roof. All three were built prior to the Civil War. Maryland State Archives, Mr. and Mrs. James Woodall Collection, c. 1950

Coleman-Thompson Farm, near Millington, has the same form and fenestration as many antebellum farmhouses in Kent County, but many original features have been removed or covered to the detriment of the style. Marge Q. Fallaw photograph, 1986.

THE ANDREW WOODALL HOUSE IS OF SIGNIFICANCE TO THE study of architecture as it is the location of the only Italianate style house to have been built in Georgetown. Its historical significance is enhanced by the fact that its builder was a man of great energy and enterprise. Captain Andrew Woodall was the most successful mid-nineteenth century shipper of Georgetown, having had a greater impact than anyone else on the port of Georgetown since it was burned by the British in 1813.

It is unclear from the records when Andrew Woodall acquired Lot No. 7, but Lots Nos. 14 and 15 were acquired by his father, Simon, from Catherine Pearce, in 1849.[1] Woodall purchased adjoining lots from the Tax Collector in 1852 on which he built his warehouses.[2] With the profit he made on shipping merchandise to market, he invested in other properties, sometimes holding the mortgages for others. In some instances, when the mortgagees were unable to meet their commitment, the property was foreclosed. By the time of Woodall's death, he owned about a dozen farms in Cecil

and Kent Counties, some of which remain in the ownership of his descendants.

On the 1860 map, Andrew Woodall is shown residing in the house on Lot No. 7. The townhouse remained in the family until the 1960s when it was sold to the Georgetown Yacht Basin Company. It was demolished soon thereafter.   K-527

1. Patents: Lib. Y & S No. 8, fol. 50.
2. Land Records, Lib. WHG 74, fol. 420.

Coleman-Thompson Farm

Near Millington
c. 1860

SIMILAR IN FORM TO WINDY CURVE FARM and Shipyard Farm, the Coleman-Thompson farmhouse is a five-bay, two-story, rectangular, frame structure with low-pitched hip roof which probably had a balustrade around a central deck. It, like the other houses above, is two rooms deep. Constructed around 1860 in the popular Italianate style, the Coleman-Thompson Farm lies on part of a tract called Partnership which was originally patented to Daniel Toaos in 1684.[1]

The front porch and bracketed cornice which gave it the distinctive Italianate flavor, have been removed and replaced with aluminum and/or vinyl. Inside, its four room plan with central stairhall retains many original features, even the graining on some of the mantels and doors. Much of the interior trim is actually more Greek Revival than Italianate. A three-centered arch divides the hall into front and main stairhalls. The appearance of the arch is similar to the double parlor separator in the Taylor House in Chestertown.

At one time there was a two-story kitchen wing out the back of the house, but it was demolished and the kitchen is now located in the northeast room. This room has had a distinct purpose from the beginning since it had a winder stair to the space above, thought to be chambers for the kitchen/farm help.

In the 1877 Atlas, the farm is owned by Biggs & Ely, who apparently lived in Wilmington and kept the farm tenanted. In 1944, the father of the present owners purchased the farm from a Mr. Biggs.[2]   K-626

1. Land Records, Lib. JNG 12, fol. 392.
2. Land Records, Lib. JFG 4, fol. 435.

Maple Grove

Near Langford
c. 1860

The site of Maple Grove is one of the most dramatic in the County. Without landscaping or trees, the house is perched on a ridge of ground and can be seen for miles in several directions. Located on the sev-enteenth century tract Pentridge, the site slopes primarily to the south. It is likely that the house was constructed in the late 1850s by Laurence M. Strong to replace a pre-vious dwelling in the same location. An earlier house is mentioned in the 1852 Tax Assessment where Strong was taxed on 304 acres of *"Scott's Farm"* with an *"Old House in bad repair."*[1]

The house which Strong built was not only tall and well-situated, but also built using some of the best cat-alogue millwork available in the mid-nineteenth centu-ry. Like Henry Ward Carvill and several other neighbors, Strong chose the popular Italianate style. The usual features of this style are in evidence in the main part of the house which faces north toward the Langford Road and its lane.

Paneled pilasters are found on each of the four cor-ners of the main block which is three stories tall. At the low-pitched roof there are well-executed brackets. There are also bracketed cornices over each of the win-dows of the five-bay facade and two-bay ends. Origi-nally there was a balustraded deck atop the roof which

afforded extensive vistas in every direction. Like Brampton, there were porches on the front and sides of the house. A two-part *L* wing out the south side origi-nally contained a dining room, kitchen and pantry with quarters above.

The main house had a central stair plan. Both first floor rooms had jib doors which opened onto the front porch and standard doors to the side porches. The wal-nut stair ascended to the third floor in a graceful man-ner so typical of this period.

In the 1877 Atlas, the property is occupied by *"J. Rasin."*[2] It was purchased in the 1880s by Thomas W. Eliason, in whose family it remained for 100 years. Most sadly, it has recently been left vacant and open to the elements and is now in derelict condition. Its surround-ing farmland is slated for development. If Maple Grove is eventually destroyed the County will suffer a true archi-tectural loss.   K-467

1. 1852 Tax Assessment.
2. 1877 Atlas.

Shipyard Landing, near Rock Hall, was shown on Martenet's Map of Kent County in the ownership of Captain J. Hadaway, who may have been responsible for its construction. It was similar to Captain James Taylor's house in Chestertown. Marsha L. Fritz photograph, 1981.

Skirven Farm, near Fairlee, was a plain stuccoed vernacular structure with corbeled cornice. It may have included an earlier house under the stucco. It was demolished in the 1980s. Marge Q. Fallaw photograph, 1981.

Shipyard Farm

Near Rock Hall
c. 1860

SHIPYARD FARM IS COMPOSED OF PARTS OF several early tracts including Standaway, Broadnox, Timely Discovery and Childers. John P. Smith appears as the owner in the 1852 Tax Assessment and is assessed on 377 acres with *"a Frame and a Brick Dwelling in good repair."*[1]

The brick dwelling may be the house called Bennington today. Whether or not the frame house mentioned in the assessment is our subject is not certain. The Italianate style, form, and detail is typical of the mid-nineteenth century. Many details are similar to the Taylor House in Chestertown which was built in 1857.

Its plan has a central stairhall with four flanking rooms. The important interior architectural elements are largely intact, but the exterior has lost much of its decorative trim. The front and rear porches have been en-

closed and the cupola or lantern has been replaced.

Local tradition holds that the house was constructed by Captain Columbus Leary who purchased the farm from Richard Hynson.[2] Hynson acquired it from George B. Westcott who foreclosed on a mortgage from James Hadaway (John Smith's son-in-law).[3] Hadaway appears as the owner in the 1877 Atlas. The current owners purchased the farm from the Leary heirs in 1947.[4]   K-491

1. 1852 Tax Assessment.
2. Land Records, Lib. SB 3, fol. 178.
3. Land Records, Lib. SB 3, fol. 178.
4. Land Records, Lib. WHG 2, fol. 392.

Skirven Farm Site

Near Fairlee
c. 1860

ALTHOUGH BUILT A YEAR PAST THE PLANned parameters of this architectural history, the Skirven Farmhouse is so akin to the earlier vernacular forms and plans that it is included herewith to illustrate the persistence of the vernacular tradition in Kent County.

The Skirven Farmhouse stood on the south side of Route 20 between Fairlee and McCleans Corner until the mid-1980s. It was a two-story, stucco-covered, brick house, four bays long with central chimney and had a shallow-pitched roof above a corbeled cornice. There was a one-and-a-half-story frame wing on the south gable. Its plan was hall-parlor in the main section with back-to-back fireplaces and a straight-run stair along the east side of the building. The wing had a plan nearly identical to the kitchen at Greys Inn Point Farm with kitchen at the end and pantry and corridor adjacent the main house. There were two stairs in the wing to separate quarters originally; one in the corner of the kitchen and the other opening from the corridor.

The trim throughout was typical of the mid-nineteenth century millwork, but many details were obviously handmade and reminiscent of vernacular Federal work of the area. There were porches, but no photographic evidence has survived.

In the 1877 Atlas, the house was owned by Thomas W. Skirven.   K-484

Stephens Farm

Melitota
c. 1860

THIS HANDSOME ITALIANATE FARMHOUSE SITS ATOP THE long slope southeast of the Melitota crossroads. Probably built about 1860 for William Stephens and his second wife Margaret, the farm had been inherited by his first wife, Jane Gamble from her grandfather, Darius Gamble.[1] In the 1852 Tax Assessment, William W. Stephens is listed as owner of 278 acres of *"Coney Warren"* with *"Frame House in good repair formerly Jane Gamble."*[2] Jane bequeathed the farm in trust to her children, but William and Margaret purchased it from the trust in 1860 and replaced the house listed on the assessment.[3] The Stephens apparently went overboard on their dreamhouse and lost it in 1881 to the creditor.[4] Between 1896 and 1941, the farm was owned by Jennie and Arthur Rivers.[5] In 1941, it was purchased by Carroll and Hazel Dulin,[6] in whose family it remained for three generations before being sold to the present owners.

The central hall plan house is five bays wide, two bays deep and two stories tall. Its roof is a shallow hip that terminates in a tall roofed belvedere, like 201 Front Street in Chestertown. Behind the house there was a period wing which had been larger but was modified by the Dulins after 1941. The present owner has installed a new wing in its place. The centrality of the facade is emphasized by the three-part door and second story window as well as the placement of the columns on the belvedere. During the Dulin occupancy, the porch had been reduced to the central bay. It has recently been restored to its original full length.   K-401

1. Land Records, Lib. JKH 2, fol. 21.
2. 1852 Tax Assessment.
3. Ibid No. 1.
4. Land Records, Lib. SB 2, fol. 202.
5. Land Records, Lib. JTD 5, fol. 234.
6. Land Records, Lib. RAS 28, fol. 32.

Stephens Farm, Melitota. It is similar to the James F. Taylor House in Chestertown except that it is only one room deep. The original service wing was replaced with a new one in the 1980s. J. Tyler Campbell photograph, 1996.

scribed as a vernacular farmhouse with some Italianate details. Its facade has only sidelights and transom around the entry to suggest the mid-nineteenth century date. All windows are uniform, including the three dormers in the steeply pitched *A* roof. The other two Italianate elements are a bracketed cornice and a plain, three-bay porch. Otherwise, it resembles many other Kent County farmhouses of the late nineteenth century in its straight forward simplicity.

Its plan is a central stairhall with flanking rooms. There is a service wing of two rooms to the rear of the westernmost room. Details are quite plain, with Greek Revival style mantels. The stair has a 'catalogue' balustrade with huge newel and balusters.

In the 1877 Atlas, the name J. Wickes accompanies the dot on the map. It probably stands on part of the seventeenth century tract called Mannour of Stephen Heath which has been corrupted to Stepney (not to be confused with the Simon Wickes property on which Chestertown was laid out in 1706). It may have been constructed by Benjamin F. Beck who appears to have owned the farm in 1852.   K-474

J. Wickes Farm, Broadneck. This farm appears to have been owned or occupied in 1860 by Isaac Gale. Maryland Historical Trust photograph, c. 1981.

J. Wickes Farm

Broad Neck
c. 1860

OVERLOOKING SINAI COVE, OFF THE west branch of Langford Bay, this five-bay, two-and-a-half story, mid-nineteenth century, frame dwelling can best be de-

Kennedyville Methodist Church

Kennedyville
1860

A BRICK CHURCH WAS AUTHORIZED TO BE BUILT AT Kennedyville by resolution of the quarterly conference of the Methodist Protestant church in May of 1860. By August, the building was under contract and the deed to the property was recorded. When completed, it was called Waters Chapel, in honor of the Reverend Frances Waters, D. D., who served the dual role of President of the Maryland Conference and President of Washington College in Chestertown.

The Kennedyville congregation was in close contact with St. James, Hanesville and the two churches are reputed to have been built by the same contractor. Certainly the two churches resemble one another as they exist today, and most likely, Kennedyville had a parallel building history to St. James. It would have resembled the squarish form of the Greek Revival style which still exists at Salem and Rehobeth Churches. Around the turn of the century, a major remodeling included the rebuilding of all of the windows with lancet arches, the raising of the roof, and the addition of the bell tower, transforming it into the Gothic Revival church it is today.   K-371

Kennedyville Methodist Church was originally called Waters Chapel and like St. James, from which it was established, had the same physical development: a typical mid-nineteenth century Greek Revival chapel, later remodeled into the Gothic style church of today. Michael C. Wootton photograph, 1996.

Lusby House

High Street, Chestertown
1860

O N THE SOUTH CORNER OF HIGH AND MILL STREETS THIS frame, three-bay, two-story house is essentially Italianate in design. Built in 1860, it is composed of a high front section and a lower rear wing and possesses a side-hall plan with two parlors in the front and two rooms and stair in the rear. Prior to a devastating fire in the 1970s, there was also a rear porch and semi-detached summer kitchen. Some of the decorative features which set it in a category of its own include the front entrance which is glazed with etched sidelights and transom, cornices over the door and windows which have brackets and applied fretwork. The cornice of the main house has ogee brackets with rosettes on their outer faces and fretwork applied to the sides to emphasize the shape of the brackets. At each corner there are turned drop finials.

The interior was well-finished, with fine mahogany stair railing and newel post and marbleized slate mantels in the double parlors. Like other houses of the period and houses that were updated in and around Chestertown at that time, there are tall double doors between the parlors. The rear wing was devoid of ornamentation, both inside and out.

The house was constructed on part of Lot No. 84, and according to Usilton's History of Chestertown, it replaced a one-and-a-half-story structure that was used for the rectory of Emmanuel P. E. Church between 1817–1856.[1] Because of its use, the building did not appear on the Tax Assessment of 1841. Its pre-1817 history is closely related to that of the adjoining property.

The buildings' construction is well documented in the deed recorded in 1861 which reads as follows:

" … Whereas, on or about the thirty first day of December in the year eighteen hundred and fifty-nine the said Samuel Frazier contracted and agreed to sell to the said William O. Smith, part of the said lot of land so as aforesaid purchased of the said Richard S. Thomas, being 32' front by 132' back and hereinafter particularly described at and for the sum of $320. And whereas the said William O. Smith has erected a Dwelling house and back building, on that part of the said lot of land so as aforesaid purchased by him of the said Samuel Frazier, and hath agreed to sell the same with that part of the said lot of land so as aforesaid purchased by him, to the said Richard Smyth at and for the sum of $24,000 … ."[2]

Since the initial deed had not been recorded, Martenet's Map of 1860 indicates that the house was owned by Richard S. Thomas. He and the two afore-

Lusby House, Chestertown, A complex chain of events recorded in the deed to the property in 1861, tells of the house being constructed by William O. Smith and sold to Richard Smyth. Tyler Campbell photograph, 1996.

Lusby House smoke house. This 1860 building is framed and covered with vertical board and batten, but they continued to use wrought strap hinges. Tyler Campbell photograph, 1996.

Lusby owned Fancy Farm as well, but resided in town. The town house was passed to his son and grandson and remained in the family until 1965.[6] Since that time the house has been converted into apartments, along with the office and studio of J. Tyler Campbell, photographer.   K-314

Lusby Farm

Near Kennedyville
c. 1860

Robert J. Lusby's name appears on Martenet's Map of Kent County (1860) in this location and it is probable that the house was built for him close to that time. Actually built on the foundation of an earlier house, the construction of this house resulted in one of the most classical Greek Revival style dwellings in Kent County. A distinct separation in texture was employed between the attic story with its ship lap siding and the lower stories which were sheathed with lapped weatherboard. The use of heavy brackets around the cornice is a testament to the influence of the Italianate style. Its combination with Greek Revival details became a common practice in Kent County during this time.

The Lusby Farmhouse was composed of a principal three-story section, five bays long, with a wing built behind, so as to avoid asymmetry in the principal facade. There was a one-story porch along the front which covered the classical architrave (most likely purchased from a millwork shop in either Baltimore or Philadelphia).   K-209

Lusby Farm, near Kennedyville, has short third floor windows with clear differentiation of siding, similar to Stephney Farm, 1850, and Middle Hall, 1844. It was probably built by Robert J. Lusby whose name appears on both the 1860 and 1877 maps. Marge Q. Fallaw photograph, 1985.

mentioned gentlemen joined together in a deed, January, 1861, to Richard Smyth, above.

Purchased in 1870 by Richard S. Usilton,[3] the house was sold four years later to Mrs. Harrison Vickers.[4] During the Vickers occupancy the small office was built between it and the house next door. Mr. Vickers' father, Senator George Vickers, lived diagonally across the street in a very large Italianate house which stood where the school was later built in 1903. Mr. and Mrs. Vickers sold the house four years after they built their country estate, Lauretum, near Whaland's Mill (1881).

Josiah Lusby purchased the house in 1885, including a nine foot alley which Mrs. Vickers had purchased from a neighbor in 1877.[5]

1. Usilton, Fred, A History of Chestertown, 1898, p. 67.
2. Land Records, Lib. JKH 2, fol. 408.
3. Land Records, Lib. JKH 8, fol. 602.
4. Land Records, Lib. JKH 12, fol. 361.
5. Land Records, Lib. SB 6, fol. 280.
6. Land Records, Lib. EHP 8, fol. 69.

Fellowship Farm

Near Millington
c. 1860

Fellowship Farm, was created out of sections of Partnership and Henberry which extended to the River. In 1854 James R. Jones purchased the 255 acre farm from Jonathan and Hannah Jones, who had lived on the adjoining farm to the east.[1] This was one of the most successful times for agriculture in Kent County and James Jones displayed his prosperity by building an Italianate three story brick house on the property in 1860. That same year, Henry Carvill built Brampton, near Chestertown, in the same style.

Like Fairfield on Great Oak Manor, the entire house was constructed at the same time and was composed of a five-bay long (46' x 21') three-story front section with a five-bay long two-story back wing (41' x 20'), all built of brick. Its facade was laid in very uniform brick with thin mortar joint while the remainder was laid in a less uniform brick with flush mortar joint. The builder had a date stone installed on the blank east wall: 1860.

Across the entire north facade there was a porch from which there was access to the central door with classical architrave. A door on the second floor once led to the second level of the porch, like the Hollingsworth House in Church Hill. Another porch was built across the east facade of the rear wing, in the same manor as at Fairfield.

Fellowship Farm, near Millington. It consisted of parts of two tracts, Partnership and Henberry when purchased by James R. Jones in 1854. Like Brampton, the three story house used wood lintels over the windows, but lacked the cornices of Brampton. It was built with access to the roof of the porch.

Andover Farm, near Millington, appears on the 1860 map and 1877 atlas in the ownership of Edward Turner, the probable builder. It is similar to the Coleman-Thompson farm northwest of Millington. Marge Q. Fallaw photographs, 1986.

The floor plan of Fellowship Farm was similar to that at Fairfield with a few minor variations—the chief difference being that the second floor plan was reversed.

Twentieth century alterations have caused the house to lose some of its distinctive features. The front porch was removed and replaced by a stoop and part of the back porch was enclosed for a kitchen. The house nevertheless retains its observatory in the center of the roof.   K-177

1. Land Records, Lib. LFG 2, fol. 50.

Andover Farm

Near Millington
c. 1860

In its heyday, Andover Farm was the best house east of Millington. Built in the Italianate style around 1860, the house was similar to the Thompson Farm to the north of town. On both the 1860 Map and the 1877 Atlas, Edward Turner appears to be the owner. He was undoubtedly the builder as well.

When completed, the house was a square two story frame structure with low hipped roof with observatory in the center. A wing with hyphen was connected on the southwest side of the house. Brackets with drop finials were installed in the deep frieze around the house and all of the windows were fitted with louvered blinds. Like most of the houses of the era and style, the front entrance had a classical architrave (naively executed) and a front veranda.

Unfortunately, the house has had most of its period detail removed or covered with enameled aluminum. Only the form, architrave and brackets remain.

Andover Farm borders a former mill on the Andover Branch. The mill is mentioned on both of the previously mentioned maps.   K-176

Christ Church I.U.

Near Worton
1860

THE PRESENT CHURCH AT I. U. IS THE SECOND church TO stand on the site The original structure had been contracted for in 1766 as a result of the General Assembly passing an Act for the erection of Chester Parish out of parts of the original two parishes.

When Kent County received its final boundaries in 1707, the established Church had two parishes: St. Paul's and South Sassafras (Shrewsbury). A chapel of ease for St. Paul's Parish at Chestertown was the first to be built in the two parishes because Chestertown was the County Seat and was the first planned town to develop adequately to warrant a Chapel of Ease. A steady increase of population in Kent County over the next half century created a need to establish a third parish out of parts of the other two. Thus, in 1765, after petition by parishioners of both Shrewsbury and St. Paul's Parishes, the General Assembly authorized an *"Act for erecting a new Parish in Kent County called*

Conjectural drawing of
St. Peter's Church, the
Parish Church of
Chester Parish as it
may have appeared in
1767. Margaret Wright
Ingersoll, 1994,

Original Pew Plan from
the Vestry Minutes of
Chester Parish,
Aug. 11, 1767.

Chester Parish and for Building a Parish Church and enlarging a Chapel of Ease within the said New Parish."[1]

The boundaries were established in the same Act but it appears they were to be altered after the death of the incumbent rector of Shrewsbury, George William Forrester, which occurred nine years later. As written in the Act, the boundaries were to extend from Great Oak Manor on the bay to Muddy Creek (the Country Club pond) on the Chester River and From Turner's Creek on the Sassafras River to Perkins Mill and finally to the Chester River, including all of the land between that

and one half wide by Nine feet with Double Sashes, four on each side, two at one End and three at the other, The Walls to be Sixteen feet Between the Floor and the plate, and the Foundation to be Let Sufficiently Deep in the Ground and the Sleepers to be a Proper height from the Ground. The said Walls to be four Colums or pillars in each, carried up in the Bricks, half a brick thick from the outside and of a Proper breadth thereto. To have a Neat well Framed Square Roof of good and Sufficient Scantling, and Arched within, Covered with good Eighteen Inch Cypress shingles well Dressed. The said church to have all Door Frames, Window Frames, Sashes, Doors and Window Shutters Neatly made. The Frames all of good Old White Oak clear of Sap. To have also a Sufficient Gallery at one End, with Stair Case and open Seats across, a Good Pulpit, Reading Desk and Communion, all Neatly Finished. The Roof to be well lathed, Plaistered and White washed. The walls well Plaistered and white washed, and the Windows well glazed with good glafs, a Good lock to one Door and bolt to the other, and the whole Church to be compleatly finished in a good Workmanlike Manner ... ."[2]

Christ Church, I. U. built around 1858, it was consecrated in 1861 by Bishop Whittingham. It was the first of Kents country churches to use the Gothic style, the same style used twenty years earlier at the Chapel of Ease of St. Michael's Parish, Talbot County. Michael C. Wootton photograph, 1996.

Rev. Sewell S. Hepburn, (1845–1932) at I. U. Church. Rev. Hepburn was Rector of I. U. Church from 1874-1881 and again from 1911-1926. His home was Shepherd's Delight. Rebecca Hepburn photograph, 1932. Jane Brooks Sprinkle Collection

One of the large oak trees that once surrounded I. U. Church. This one probably was here when the first Church was built. Michael C. Wootton photograph, 1996.

had been parts of St. Paul's and Shrewsbury parishes. In 1766, after appointing vestrymen and wardens, the new vestry met to discuss building a new parish church. By May of that year, an agreement had been prepared and signed by the Vestry and Charles Tilden " *... to build and erect and compleatly finish a good Neat and Sufficient Brick Church near I. U., the County aforesaid to be the Parish Church of the said Parish, of very well burnt good Bricks and good Materials of all kinds ... That the said Church shall be Sixty feet long and forty feet wide, the Walls to be three Bricks thick from the Foundation to the Water Table and two bricks and an half from thence to the plate in the sides, and two Bricks thick from the Water Table On the Ends, to have two Doors, one in each side and thirteen good Arched Windows five feet*

In September, 1767, the vestry ordered Mr. Charles Tilden to meet with them as " *... The frame of the Church is not done according to agreement ... ."[3]*, an indication that the roof trusses were inadequately structured. The minutes go in great length to describe the method of making the trusses *"sufficient"* and appointed Mr. George Wickers as the inspector for the Vestry. In August of 1767 the vestry drew up the pew plan, calling for fifty pews on the ground floor. A list of the owners of the pews followed.

Apparently the Church, which was called St. Peter's, was finished in a timely manner for the records of the Parish show that Tilden was paid £300 in May, and £902 in October of 1767. The minutes relate the fact that the church wall was raised from sixteen feet to eighteen feet between the floor and plate and for that extra work £26 was paid.

With the expansion of Chestertown and the new chapel of ease that the Chestertown parishioners finished by 1772, the emphasis gradually shifted from I. U. to Chestertown. By the end of the eighteenth century, the Parish Church was in very poor condition and after the first decade of the nineteenth century, it was unusable. Finally, in 1830, the bricks from the walls were sold to Benjamin Howard, who lived at Suffolk near Turner's Creek. He dismantled the old building and used the bricks to build a house on one of his farms.

For those Episcopalians still residing in the northern part of Middle Parish in the nineteenth century, attending Church was a hardship. Rev. D. H. Handy built a small chapel at Worton Heights (later Hanesville) after the parish church had been demolished, which was used for both Episcopal and Methodist services. It was later sold to the Methodists who formed St. James.

In 1855, the Vestry of Chester Parish appointed a committee to look into the possibility of building a new church on the old site of the original parish church at I. U. Apparently the committee recommended that a new church would better serve the needs of the parish, especially those who resided in the northwestern section of the county. As a result, the present building was built in 1860 and consecrated the following year by Bishop Whittingham. Within two years, the church had petitioned for and was granted the status as a new parish.

The church building was constructed in the increasingly popular Gothic Style, with lancet arch windows and doors. The contemporary wooden cornice is an Italianate feature which is frequently encountered in residences of the period. In form, the church is composed of a tall, rectangular, four-bay structure, which contains a vestibule and nave, and a shorter, narrower sanctuary. Each of the four bays is distinguished by a brick pilaster which terminates at the cornice line. The east end pilasters wrap around the corners, giving definition to the three-bay entry facade. Its door is further defined by being set back from the face of the gable, which creates a shadow-like effect.

Within, there is a vestibule or narthex with stair to the gallery above. The nave, which is three of the four bays, has a tall-pitched roof composed of three major rafters with purlins, brackets and trefoil designs. Between the nave and the sanctuary there is a large lancet arch opening with trim that corresponds to the windows and doors. All of the interior woodwork is grained and finished with several coats of varnish.

With the exception of the church furnishings, which have accumulated over the years, virtually everything is intact. The church is a product of the antebellum period and remains the best example of Gothic Revival church architecture from that period in Kent County.   K-133

Christ Church, I. U. The interior is essentially unchanged from the time it was consecrated in 1861. Michael C. Wootton photograph, 1996.

1. The contract for erecting the original church is quoted in Chapter 3 of this work, where a conjectural drawing of its appearance can also be found.
2. Pilasters were also used in the original church in order to strengthen the walls and support the roof trusses. St. Lukes, Church Hill and Old Wye, Wye Mills were other churches that were built with pilasters.

Darby Site

Near Chestertown
c. 1860

THE EARLY HISTORY OF THE CLEMENTS FARM IS INTIMATELY connected with the history of the Spencer family. In the eighteenth century, a mill was established on the farm on the banks of Prickle Pear Branch. It was one of two mills on the branch, both operated at one time or another by the Spencer and Comegys families. In 1730, Jervis Spencer acquired two parcels, Smally and Darby, both located on the east side of Prickle Pear Mill Pond.[1] It is the latter tract that remained in the family until it was sold in the mid-nineteenth century. Darby was mentioned in the will of Jervis Spencer, although he and his legatee, Isaac, lived at Marrowbone.[2] Isaac's son, William, apparently did not marry and lived at Darby where he carried on a successful farming operation. In 1822, the year of his death, he was taxed on 1169 acres consisting of the following parcels: Darby and Smally, Buck Hill, Neglect, Mount Hope, Smith's Discovery, John's Addition, Killingsworthmore, and two parts of Prickle Pear.[3]

William Spencer's nephew and namesake, then living in Annapolis, sold the farm to David Clements in the 1850s. Clements' name appears on both the Martenet Map of 1860 and the 1877 Atlas. Around 1860, Clements built a large frame Italianate house on Darby which survived for slightly over a hundred years. The form of the house is not difficult to make out from the aerial photograph. While the details are less discernible, the overall impression is that of a somewhat plain structure.

The building was an *L* shaped, three-story structure which appears to have had the same basic floor plan as Mt. Airy, a con-

temporary house on the Bay. That plan consisted of a central entrance/stairhall with two flanking rooms and a wing to the rear. Here the wing is behind the eastern room and probably included a kitchen, dining room and back stair. Looking carefully at the photograph, a one-room deep, two-story addition is noticeable behind the western room. There was a deck at the apex of its hip roof, similar to the Spry Home Farm nearby.

One contemporary outbuilding survived the houses's destruction in the 1960s. It is a brick dairy with steeply pitched pyramidal roof. The actual structure occupied slightly more than one quarter of the space covered by the roof. It is similar to other dairies remaining around the Wye River.   K-368

1. Patents, Lib. PL 7, fol. 470, Lib. PL 8, fol. 606.
2. Wills, Lib. 4, fol. 128, Lib. 7, fol. 109, Lib. 10, fol. 263, Lib. 11, fol. 259.
3. 1822 Tax Assessment.

Columbia Farm

Near Melitota
c. 1860

JOHN WILSON Corey came from Dublin, New Hampshire in 1850 and purchased this farm which is part of Coney Warren. In the 1852 Tax Assessment, two houses are listed on his farm—one brick, the other frame. There is also reference to the former owner John G. Black

Soon after getting reestablished in Maryland, Mr. Corey set about building a good house for his family. The old frame one-and-a-half story house that was here when he came was sawn in two and one part was used for the kitchen. The other part was pulled out into the field where it was used by the help for many years.

Onto this kitchen wing a new two-story, back wing was added which housed the dining room, pantry, enclosed back stair and a more formal stairhall. In front of that was the typical center hall section with two flanking parlors set at right angles to the back wing. Like many other houses built during this period, the symmetry of the facade is heightened by the three-part en-

Darby Site, near Crumpton, was owned in the eighteenth century by the Jervis Spencer family. The mid-nineteenth century house was constructed by David Clements. Maryland State Archives, Alday Clements collection.

In recent years, the pantry has been converted into a kitchen and the whole house has had a facelift as well as some structural replacement. It is one of the finest third quarter nineteenth century houses of its form in Kent County.

Behind the early nineteenth century kitchen is an early plank smokehouse, doubled in size by the addition of a frame wing.   K-407

Suydam House

Near Pomona
c. 1860

JOSEPH S. TREW ACQUIRED THIS part of Thomas's PURCHASE after Thomas W. Trew's (his father's) estate was settled in 1859.[1] Upon his inheritance he built a fine three-bay, three-story frame, Italianate house with back wings. It was very similar to the house built on the adjoining farm called Maple Grove, except that Maple Grove had five bays across the facade. Joseph sited his house near the center of the farm.

From the brackets used on the wide cornice and the porch to the interior stair balustrade, the house contains many of the millwork details which were readily available through catalogues of the day. Like Pentridge and the Spry Home Farm, Trew's house had a deck on the roof with balustrade all around. From this deck he could view all parts of his farm.

In 1962, the house was moved nearer the east branch of Langford Creek and restored. In the process the old back wing was demolished and in its place a two-bay, two-story wing was built in good proportion to the old section. During the restoration the owners found the inscription *"J. Trew, May 1869"* on a third floor window.   K-250

Columbia Farm, near Melitota. It was purchased by John Wilson Corey of Dublin, New Hampshire in 1850. At the time of his purchase there stood a one-and-a-half story frame house, of which half remains at the east end of the house. He later built the remainder of the house over a full basement, using the vernacular form of farmhouses popular one-hundred years earlier. Tyler Campbell photograph, 1996.

Suydam House, Quacker Neck, was built for Joseph S. Trew on part of "Thomas's Purchase" after he inherited it from his father in 1859. "J. Trew, May 1869" etched on a third floor window may record the date of construction. It was built in the same Italianate style as neighboring Maple Grove. Tyler Campbell photograph, 1996.

Opposite: Columbia Farm Smokehouse and quarter. The plank smoke house received two additions, reputedly for slaves quarters. In recent times it was used for chickens. Marsha L. Fritz photograph, 1980.

try door and window above. Undercut brackets were used in the cornice and overhanging eaves. Unlike many of the same period, Columbia Farm has an *A* roof with two chimneys flanking the center hall and three equal size dormers.

It is said by the present owner (fourth generation) that the porches were installed after the Civil War, including not only the one-story verandah on the south and west sides, but the two-story porch on the back wing and the leanto off the kitchen as well. The latter is separated from the main porches by a screen of lattice—a device that was used frequently to separate the work area from the rest of the living area.

The interior is well appointed with marbleized slate mantels, bold walnut balustrade and fine ceiling medallions.

1. Land Records, Lib. JFG 5, fol. 120.

Brampton

Near Chestertown
1860

Brampton, near Chester-
town, was built around
1860 for Henry Ward
Carvill on land called
Fairy Hill. It is one of the
great ante-bellum houses
of Kent County. It is now
run as Brampton Bed
and Breakfast.

Brampton. The living
room has walnut doors,
sash and baseboard. The
mantel is marbleized
slate and was originally
fit with a coal stove.
Tyler Campbell
photographs, 1995.

HENRY WARD CARVILL WAS THE YOUNGEST SON OF John Carvill IV and was probably raised on the family farm, Carvill Hall on Fairlee Creek. When he came of age, after his father's death, he inherited part of the original farm including the house. He ran the farm for many years but finally sold it and purchased Fairy Hill near Chestertown in 1860. A year after purchasing Fairy Hill, he married Anna Whaland, a young woman who was about forty years his junior. He served on the vestry of St. Paul's Parish where his body was buried in the 1890s.

The house standing on the property in 1860 was a three-bay two-story hip roof frame Italianate style house almost identical to Alfalfa Dell, the farm immediately to the west of Fairy Hill. Carvill was not satisfied with the relatively modest house so began building a new residence in its place. Since the existing house was relatively new, he moved it to form the back wing of the brick house that he built facing the main road.

The brick section of the house is one of the most impressive of the antebellum dwellings of Kent County. It is a five-bay wide three-story building with moderately pitched metal roof having a cross gable above the central bay. Paired brackets enrich the cornice on all sides. In many details it is similar to the Kent County Courthouse that was built in 1860. As built, there was a porch around three sides of the structure. Three bays of the original seven bays remain. When it was completed, there was also a lantern on the roof enclosed with windows. Bracketed cornices decorate the second story windows. Unlike most houses of this period, and specifically unlike the earlier house, three part windows were not used in the central bay. The entrance is, however, composed of double doors with sidelights and transom and have crossetted trim around the assemblage. Since there was a porch on three sides, the first story windows extended nearly to the floor. Beside the older house being used for the wing, there was also a

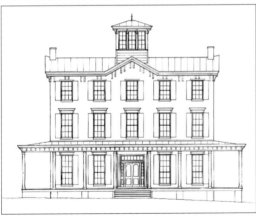

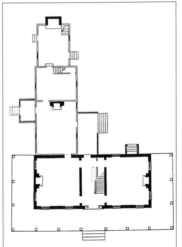

a small room at the head of the third story. An enclosed stair continues up to the bottom of the former lantern.

Judging from the arrangement of other contemporary houses and the position of the chimney in the relocated house, the older house was probably turned into a dining room and pantry, with the old central entrance opening into the dining room. The old stair was removed and a new enclosed stair was installed in the southwest corner of the pantry, next to the kitchen door. The kitchen level was two steps lower than the main two parts of the house. It too had an enclosed stair in its southwest corner, part of which ascended over the fireplace.

For many years Carvill grew peaches on his farm, but toward the end of his life, a blight killed the trees and the income they had produced. When he died in the 1890s, his great house and land were sold to settle the estate. Harrison W. Vickers, who lived at Lauretum on the adjoining farm, purchased the property in 1896. During the Vickers ownership the house was tenanted. It was not sold from his widow's estate until 1934, when Dr. & Mrs. Frank Hines acquired the farm.

Brampton. The stair hall contains the finest walnut balustrade in the county, with acanthus leaf and rope carvings and flutes. Tyler Campbell photograph, 1995.

Brampton. Detail of the balustrade ascending gracefully to the third floor. Note the plaster medallion on the second story ceiling. Tyler Campbell photograph, 1995.

Brampton. Conjectural north elevation based upon evidence in the brickwork and the roof as well as the Baxter family who lived here in the early 1930s. Michael Bourne, 1994.

Brampton First floor plan, at the time of its completion by Henry W. Carvill drawn by Michael Bourne, 1994

two-bay two-story frame kitchen, which has recently been reconstructed.

The interior of the house was even more impressive than the exterior. The plan of the front section is standard for the period, consisting of a central stair hall with two flanking rooms. The balustrade of the stair is not the usual mahogany structure, but rather is made with a turned and carved newel post of walnut with acanthus leaves, rope molding and flutes on an octagonal base. The remainder of the balustrade which extends to the third floor is also made of walnut. The doors, sash and baseboards are likewise made of walnut, the only such use of the fine wood in the county. The two flanking rooms have somewhat standard marbleized slate mantels which were originally fit with integral arched coal stoves. In the center of the ceilings of the two large rooms as well as the first and second story halls are plaster medallions. The second and third stories are also arranged in the same manner, except for

By that time, the house had been neglected and was in need of repair. It was during the ownership of the Hines that the porch was reduced to the existing three bays, and the lantern was removed from the top of the roof. The Hines also detached the old kitchen and moved it to the west side of the yard where it was enlarged for use as a tenant house. The old name, which had been lost to memory, was changed to Brampton in honor of Mrs. Hines' ancestral home in England. The house remained basically the same until the present owners converted it into a bed and breakfast, after which time the old kitchen was reconstructed in its former location. Plans are under way to reconstruct the remainder of the porch and to reinstall the lantern on the roof. It was entered on the National Register in 1983.   K-465

The Church was the social center of the black community prior to the Civil War. It remains so today. Constance Stuart Larrabee photograph.

Chapter 6
The Black Community in Early Kent County

Davy Henderson McCall

Future research may confirm the hypotheses that many of the black settlements in Chestertown and in the county were initially begun by free blacks before 1860.

Very few buildings of any sort remain from the earliest period of Kent County's settlement by English colonists. We know from the records that slaves began to be imported at an early period, late in the seventeenth century. Simon Wilmer's "man James" supplied the county courthouse with horsehair for the plaster in 1696. Mrs. Wilmer (d. 1724) wrote in her will that James was to be free after operating the mill (Radcliffe Mill) for two years after her death for the benefit of her brother and son who owned the mill in common.

Where did James live during and after his servitude? Simply answered, nobody knows ... yet. Did he live in the Wilmer's house, in a quarter on the plantation, in the loft of the mill, or in a shed somewhere? These are all places that may have been the dwellings of slaves in the eighteenth century. Some fragments of information are available from Orphans Court records that commence in the year 1779, but they are spotty. The Tax Assessment of 1783 is equally sketchy, with ten *"quarters"* listed in the Morgan Creek and South Sassafras Hundreds, and five in Chester and Worton Hundreds, one belonging to the Town's Relief plantation of Kevin Wroth, Jr. A *"Steward's House"* belonged to a Ringgold plantation. There are many other buildings mentioned in the tax assessment that probably doubled as habitations as well. They include such entries as shops, stores, old or very bad houses, loom or spinning houses, and obviously main houses of all descriptions. The survey of historic sites has revealed that one log *"quarter"* exists at Fair Hope Farm on Quaker Neck, but it was encased in brick in the twentieth century. The old log building at Napley Green may have been a *"quarter,"* but this type one or two room log structure was inhabited by white families as well as black. A third such building is a frame addition built onto a log smokehouse at Columbia Farm that by tradition was inhabited by slaves prior to the acquisition of the farm by an antislavery New Englander in 1850.

From the study of Kent County dwelling houses belonging to whites, we can glean the fact that there are hierarchical spaces, meaning that ground floor rooms are better the farther away they are from the kitchen. Similarly, second floor spaces follow the same rule of thumb, usually without communication between rooms at some juncture. For example, at Godlington Manor, prior to rehabilitation in the 1970s, the kitchen wing comprised the kitchen, a servant's room and pantry on the ground floor. The space above was divided into at least three separate spaces, two of which were accessible by means of a ladder from the kitchen, the other by a ladder from the servant's room. This is the most common arrangement of spaces for the period which is covered in this book. At Big Fairlee on the Bay, the space over the kitchen and pantry was divided into four tiny spaces, separated by rough board partitions.

At Knock's Folly on Turner's Creek the kitchen wing was one-and-a-half stories tall with space above the ceiling of the second story. That space, only large enough to crawl in, was floored. The underside of the roof, rafters, nailers and shingles were whitewashed, an obvious indication that the space had been used as a resting place for its less fortunate inhabitants. This type of finish is not only found in accommodation for black inhabitants, but was found in many instances as the first stage for white houses as well, many of which existed well into the twentieth century.

A better accommodation within the house was found to have existed at River House and the Tilghman House, both in Chestertown and both probably built after the Revolution. From advertisements in early newspapers, we find that their kitchen basements included two servants rooms, which may have been inhabited by either slave or servant, either black or white. This reference to the use of basement space in which there was a kitchen gives rise to the question about such houses as Redmore's Supply, Nicholson House, Geddes-Piper

Godlington Manor, kitchen ladder/stair to the servants room above.

Godlington Manor, kitchen chamber before restoration. This room was accessible only from the ladder/stair. The other side of the board partition was plastered, including the door. Historic American Buildings Survey photographs.

House and many of the houses along Water Street, Chestertown, all of which had basement kitchens.

Few buildings identified as occupied principally by blacks remain from the eighteenth century in Kent County. Since slaves made up nearly 90% of the county's black population in the 1790 census and there are so few buildings designated as *"quarters"* in the 1783 Tax Assessment, we can only guess that their habitations sometimes were in less than regular housing. If the small frame addition to the smokehouse at Columbia Farm is any indication of the crude dwellings built for blacks, we can only guess that their dwellings were so poorly constructed as to be not worth mentioning in the 1783 Tax Assessment. An example from the 1783 Tax Assessment is the entry *"Old Brick House,"* coupled with the fact that there were no *whites* living on the upper part of Thornton, points to the possible conclusion that the house was inhabited by blacks, a house that would have been built by a white owner. By tradition, it has been said that when the owner of a plantation built a new house for the family, the old one was frequently given to the servants, free or slave, to inhabit as their own. Traveling around the Eastern Shore it is possible to see old houses that have obviously been moved

from their original sites and are now in black communities. It was told by his granddaughter that as recently as 1905, when Mr. John Parr Nicholson built a new dwelling on Poplar Hill Farm, he gave the old one-and-a-half-story frame house to a black family who moved it to Georgetown, near Fairlee. As recently as the second quarter of the twentieth century, servants were living in a granary on the Queen Anne's County farm of Mrs. Cora Green Bash.

After the eighteenth century, it became more common for slave owners to free their slaves. This phenomenon occurred because of the influence of Quakers in the upper part of the county, whose religious beliefs were contrary to slavery, the efforts of Methodist preachers who traveled the length and breadth of the Delmarva Peninsula and the general trend that slavery was an inhumane institution. With each successive census, the number of free blacks increased until the Emancipation Proclamation was signed into law, in 1862.

The growth of free blacks and the quality of their lives has been studied more in Chestertown than in the rest of the county. In the first half of the nineteenth century, two black leaders bought small parcels of land on which there were existing houses, then sub-divided the lots and sold to other free blacks. Thomas Cuff bought several lots in Scott's Point, beginning in 1820, then sold parcels to members of Bethel Church, after its founding in the following decade. James Jones bought land on upper Cannon Street and proceeded to sell to other free blacks. In both instances, the initial grantors of the property were important white men who were concerned about the welfare and future of free blacks.

Future research may confirm the hypothesis that many of the black settlements in Chestertown and in the county were initially begun by free blacks before 1860. These communities continued to grow. By the time the Martenet map was published in 1860, it showed the location of five African-American churches. They were: Big Woods (Fountain Methodist M H), Galena (next to Olivet Church), near Golts (Wesley Henry Church), near Chesterville (Asbury Church), and north of Edesville (Hynson's Chapel), the latter three simply referred to as *"African M H."* Several other Methodist Chapels are not mentioned on the map, but had been formed prior to the map's publication. The two churches that existed in Chestertown at that time are not shown on the inset map.

Four houses which were owned by free blacks in the early nineteenth century are located on Lot No. 5 in Chestertown and may have been those mentioned in the 1767 will of Dr. William Murray. The house referred to as the Levi Rogers House was one of the four Murray houses. The other three, the Thomas Cuff House, Maria Bracker House, and the Boyer House have details which indicate a later eighteenth century date, however, this may have been caused by renovation or alteration. Free blacks purchased and resided in existing buildings on Lot No. 5 that may include parts of the aforementioned Murray houses.

DAVY HENDERSON MCCALL, PH.D., Harvard University, is professor of economics at Washington College. He resides in Chestertown and is active in historic restoration and preservation.

Thomas Cuff House

Cannon Street, Chestertown
c. 1780

THOMAS CUFF PURCHASED PART OF LOT NO. 5 IN 1820 from Dr. Peregrine Wroth. He purchased additional lots or parts of lots in succeeding years including much of Scott's Point. He was a founding member of Bethel Church in 1828, which was located on Princess Street, just around the corner from his home. A year before the founding of the church he advertised in the Telegraph that he had lost a pig and offered a reward, an unusual occurrence for a free black. An archeological dig undertaken in 1987–88 unearthed many artifacts from the third quarter of the eighteenth century as well as during Cuff's occupancy. University of Delaware archeologists concluded that the refuse was on par with that of a lower middle class white family.

The house which was standing when Cuff purchased the lot was a two-bay, two-story frame dwelling with central door and brick chimney, serving back-to-back fireplaces in the two first and second story rooms. The windows had 6/6 sash, and there were similar size windows in each gable. Behind the northerly room was an addition of unknown size and form, probably the kitchen, with a brick patio or work space adjacent. The interior was very simply finished, with the stair located in the northerly room. Vertical beaded board walls separated the low-ceiling rooms on both floors. The corner posts of the house frame were exposed and beaded in the outer corners of the house. Restoration of the house in 1989 revealed the fact that the house had stood on stone piers until being filled in with brick at a later date.

K-545

Thomas Cuff House was owned and occupied by a free black man and his family from 1820 until his death in 1858. The form of the house appears to date sometime after the 1760s. Michael Bourne photograph, 1996.

The Isaac Boyer House

Front Street, Chestertown
c.1780

THE BOYER HOUSE ON FRONT STREET, NOW CALLED WATER Street, was owned by Thomas Cuff before he sold it to Isaac Boyer in 1849. It is very similar to the Cuff House in that it has a central chimney and is two stories

Maria Bracker was the daughter of Thomas Cuff. During the 1840s and 50s she operated an ice cream parlor from her home. It was later converted into a duplex. Michael Bourne photograph, 1996.

Zion Methodist Church stood on Queen Street before it was replaced by a new structure in 1866. In the early twentieth century it was moved to Calvert Street where it was converted to a residence. Michael Bourne photograph, 1996.

Maria Bracker House

Cannon Street, Chestertown
c. 1780

MARIA BRACKER WAS THE DAUGHTER OF THOMAS Cuff, who had purchased this part of Lot No. 5 in 1820. It became Maria's property upon the death of her father in 1858. In the 1840s and 50s Maria apparently lived here and advertised in the Kent County News: *"Maria Bracker is now prepared to accommodate ladies and gentlemen with ice cream, cake, and lemonade, prepared every day from 11 am until 10 pm. Her saloon is on Cannon Sts., between Queen and Water. Families can be supplied by the quart or gallon, or molds, pound or sponge cake by the pound."* She sold the property in 1866 to William Cotton, whose daughter Mary married Jonas Haughton in 1888. The property is still in the ownership of their descendants.

The Bracker House had not been maintained in years and is in danger of being lost. Its present facade consists of two entrances on the outer sides of the facade with two windows between. There are only two windows on the second floor. Fragments of old woodwork remain within and it is assumed that the house had a central chimney, like the two aforementioned dwellings. The house may have begun life as a single family dwelling before being converted into a duplex.   K-543

Zion Methodist Church

Calvert Street, Chestertown
c.1830

THE ZION CHURCH (NOW JANES UNITED METHODIST Church) congregation was organized in 1831 by some of the black leaders of the community and soon thereafter purchased a building on Princess Street in which to hold services. That building was a three-bay two-story frame building, possibly an original dwelling. Like the aforementioned buildings, there have been

tall. The three bay facade is asymmetrical between the first and second story openings, indicating that the house either began as a one-and-a-half-story dwelling or was remodeled in the nineteenth century with new window placement. Some early beaded board walls remain in the house along with ovolo molded window and door trim.

Boyer was a co-founder with Thomas Cuff of Bethel Church in 1828 and was an associate for the remainder of Cuff's life. Boyer died in 1869 and the inventory taken after his death revealed that the two room addition on the back of the house was standing by that time. His inventory included *"old bay horse, one old work wagon, one cart, and an old carriage,"* undoubtedly an indication of his trade.   K-544

considerable alterations to this structure. The building served the needs of the community until being replaced in 1866 by a new church near the present railroad track. The old church building became the parsonage and part was used as an annex to the school on Cross street, before being moved to its present location on Calvert Street in the early twentieth century.   K-546

James A. Jones House

Kent and Cannon Streets, Chestertown
unknown date

WHEN THIS HOUSE WAS UNDERGOING A NEW SIDING JOB several years ago, the building appeared to date from the eighteenth century, at least the first story, where evidence of a log structure was found. It is currently a two-bay, two-and-a-half-story frame building facing Kent Street, with a two-bay two-story addition to the rear, plus a leanto kitchen. There is nothing currently that would indicate that the house is as early as it appeared before the application of siding.

In the middle nineteenth century the house was owned by James A. Jones, a prominent member of Chestertown's African-American community. Jones was a grocer and butcher along with being involved with the development of several lots along upper Cannon Street and the owner of a tavern in the 300 block of High Street. He was the most successful of contemporary blacks in Chestertown. Jones was also a money lender, mortgaging property for William Perkins, a restauranteur on Bridge Street. He was a founding member of Zion Methodist Church in 1831 and was active in the church for the remainder of his life. He was a delegate to the 1852 Baltimore Convention on the movement to establish colonies for free blacks in Africa, which he favored. Before the 1870 election, Jones actively organized the community to vote for Republican candidates and later sold one foot square lots to eleven African-Americans in an effort to enfranchise more of his contemporaries.   K-547

William Perkins Restaurant Site

Maple Avenue, Chestertown
c.1855

THE *"RISING SUN,"* ONE OF CHESTERTOWN'S BEST RESTAUrants in the 1850s and 1860s was established by William Perkins, a free black, in 1855 when he purchased part of Lot No. 38, which he mortgaged to

James A. Jones. He advertised his business in the Kent News in 1860 as a *"Summer Resort! The East Room is reserved for ladies and no gentleman is allowed except with ladies."* There was an Oyster Salon for men. Perkins advertised that he would *"serve ladies and gentlemen with all the choice articles of confectionery. Cake, and ice cream, lemonades in the French style, mineral*

waters from celebrated fountains, oysters pickled secendum antem, diamondback terrapins, soft crabs, hard crabs, and deviled crabs."

Perkins was a political as well as economic leader of the local African American community. He represented Chestertown at the first political convention held by and for blacks in Maryland in 1852, the convention at which James A. Jones was also a representative. He was a member of Zion Church and one of the organizers of a rally in Chestertown to celebrate the ratification of the Fifteenth Amendment. He and George Westcott, president of the major Chestertown bank and president of the local insurance company, generated enough additional support among the newly enfranchised black community to elect a straight Republican ticket for local offices. In the 1870 Census, William Perkins was one of the wealthiest black men of Kent County.

The site of Perkins establishment is now occupied by the Chestertown Fire Department, but is a highly significant site in the pre-emancipation rise of African-Americans out of slavery. A house on North Queen Street, which has recently been gutted, and was moved to the site in the twentieth century, may have been Perkins House.   K-548

The house on the west corner of Kent and Cannon Streets was owned by James A. Jones in mid-nineteenth century. Jones was one of the most successful free black men of his day in Chestertown. Michael Bourne photograph, 1996.

Appendix A
Map of Kent County, 1877.

Martinet Map, 1860
First District

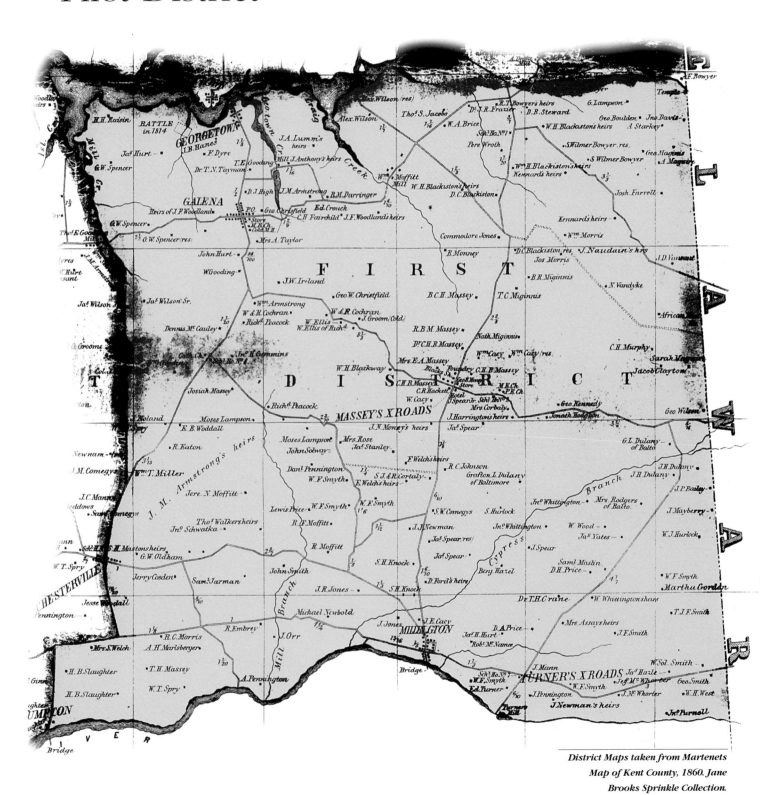

District Maps taken from Martenets
Map of Kent County, 1860. Jane
Brooks Sprinkle Collection.

Martinet Map, 1860
Second District

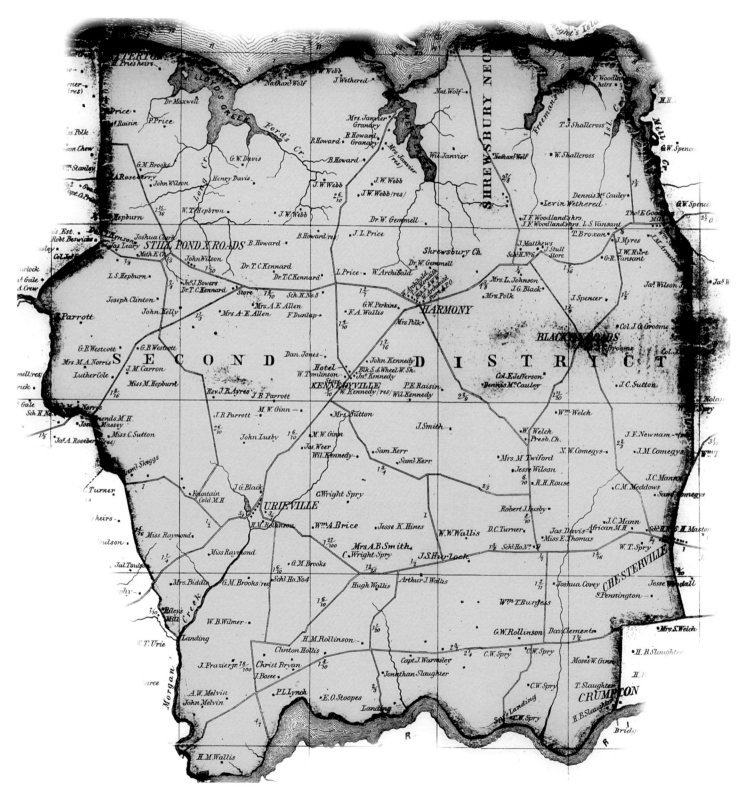

Martinet Map, 1860
Third District

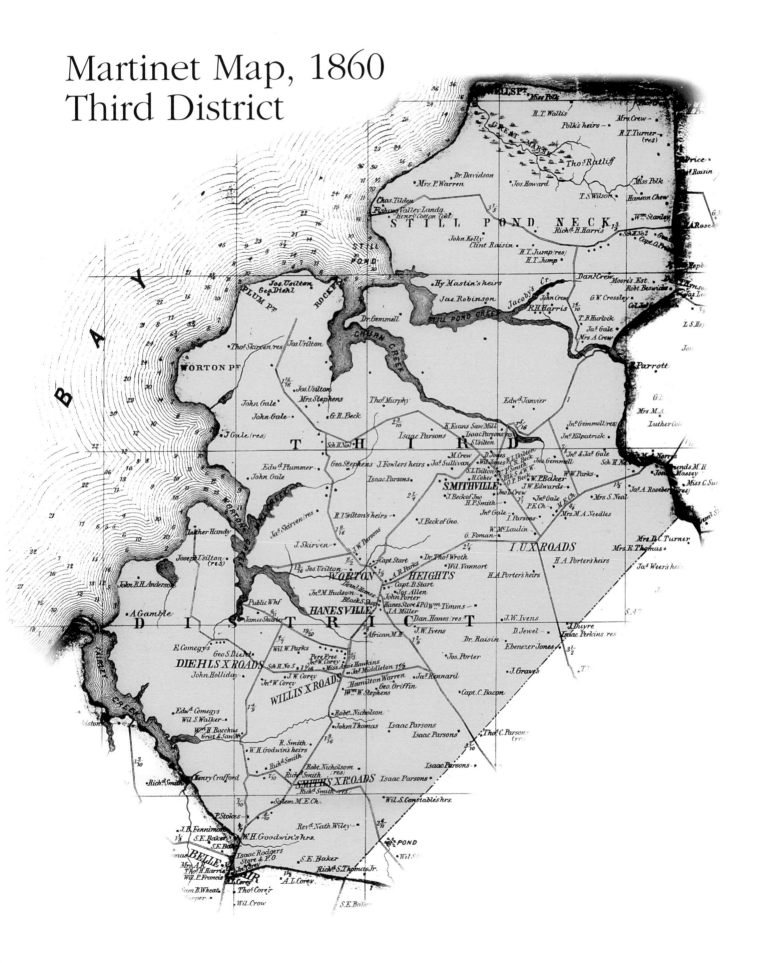

Martinet Map, 1860
Fourth District

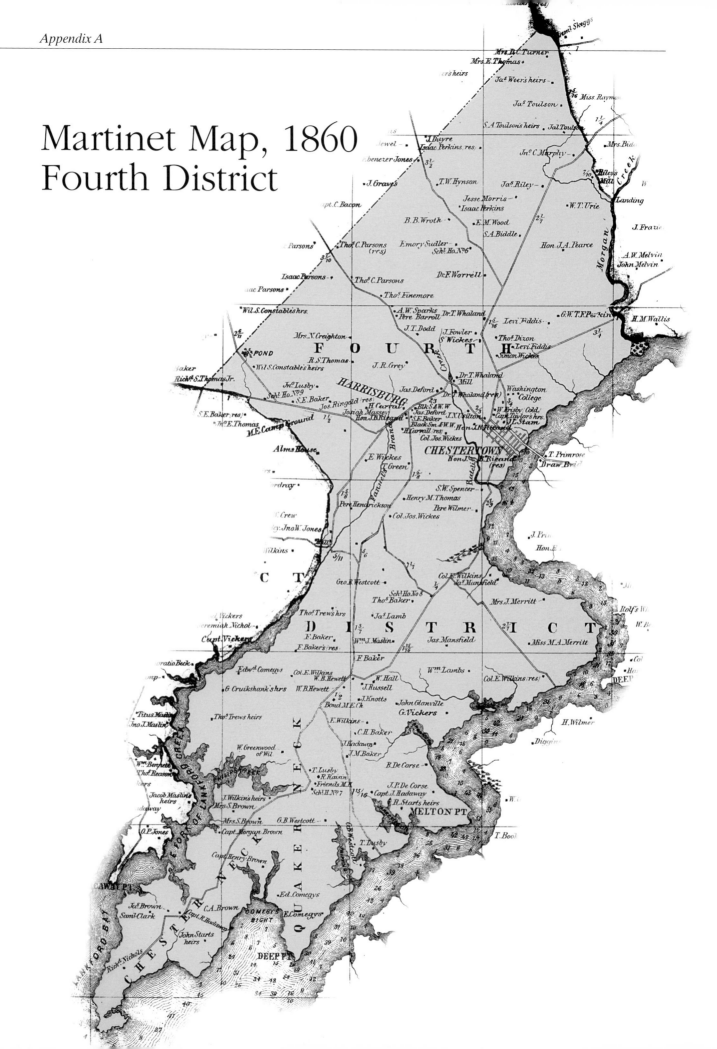

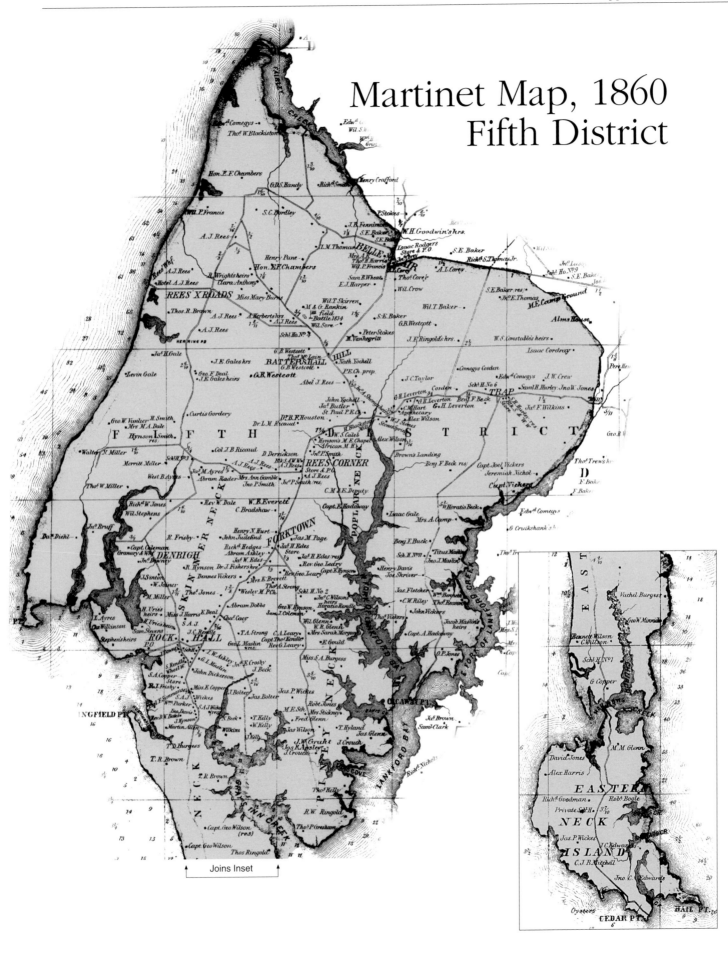

Martinet Map, 1860
Fifth District

Joins Inset

Appendix B
Historic Inventory: 1659–1860

The following is a list of historic sites that have been included in this book. These sites have been broken down into the five districts which correspond with the preceding Martenet Map of 1860.

When each Kent County site was surveyed for the Maryland Historical Trust, it was assigned an inventory number, for example, K-9 is for The Custom House in Chestertown. This number is for record purposes only

and numbered by the date of the survey. It has been placed at the end of each site presented in the text.

The original copy of the Maryland Inventory of Historic Properties has been accessioned into the Trust's library and is available for public use. A copy of the county sites has been placed at the Kent County Public Library. Chestertown inventory forms are on file at the town office.

K-571	Glencoe	468
K-572	Forkfields	483
K-598	Timber Level Site	468

District III

K-106	Handy Point	326
K-110	Trulock	346
K-120	Myers House Site	475
K-132	Sandy Hill	392
K-133	Christ Church I. U.	515
K-134	I.U. Sexton House	343
K-218	Camp Tockwogh	439
K-219	Lavenham	399
K-220	Stanley's Hope	143
K-221	Ellwood	493
K-228	Muddy Branch Farm	250
K-230	Friendship	305
K-231	Hopeful Unity	227
K-232	Big Meadows	322
K-234	St. James Church	497
K-237	Whichcote Castle	157
K-238	King's Grant Cottage	359
K-239	Hosier Farm	387
K-240	Mount Airy	499
K-241	Carvill Hall	39
K-263	Buck Neck Site	158
K-279	Part of Kent Land	404
K-372	Andelot Tenant House	470
K-401	Stephens Farm	511
K-407	Columbia Farm	518
K-414	Drayton Manor	220
K-428	Salem Methodist Church	498
K-518	Essex Site	384

District IV

K-1	Washington College*	297
K-6	Levi Rogers House*	126
K-7	Capt. James Taylor House*	506
K-8	Hynson-Ringgold House*	138
K-9	Custom House*	144
K-10	Widehall*	206
K-11	Anderson-Aldridge House*	370
K-12	River House*	306
K-13	Esau Watkins House*	121
K-14	McHard House*	229
K-17	Simon Wickes House*	256
K-19	Smith Ringgold House*	166
K-20	Bolton-Anderson House*	258
K-21	Bolton House*	170
K-22	Dunn House*	331
K-23	Houston House*	238
K-24	Geddes-Piper House*	317
K-26	Chambers House*	350
K-27	Buck-Chambers House*	112
K-28	Bedingfield Hands House*	153
K-29	Wallis-Wickes House*	213
K-30	Page-Hines House*	382
K-31	Dougherty-Barroll House*	135
K-33	Harris House*	401
K-36	Thomas B. Hynson's Store*	491
K-48	Masonic Building*	450
K-49	White Swan Tavern*	107

K-50	Kent County Courthouse*	83
K-51	Emmanuel Episcopal Church*	201
K-52	Methodist Meeting House*	395
K-53	Hackett House*	410
K-55	Lawrence House*	475
K-56	Ferguson House*	341
K-60	Rebecca Lloyd Anderson House*	106
K-61	Bordley-Usilton House*	230
K-62	John Russell House*	476
K-63	Robert Reid House*	302
K-64	John Reid House*	253
K-65	The Palmer House*	303
K-66	The Hopkins House*	254
K-71	James Anderson House*	105
K-72	Davis Duplex*	504
K-73	Sterling Castle*	160
K-74	Eliason Smoke House*	471
K-78	Wilmer's Mill House	103
K-80	Cedar Hill	150
K-81	Killy Langford	259
K-84	Providence Plantation	275
K-85	Stepney Manor	33
K-86	Radcliffe Cross	234
K-88	Godlington Manor	122
K-89	Fair Hope Farm	438
K-90	The Reward	130
K-91	Comegy's Bight	204
K-92	Clark's Conveniency	152
K-94	Airy Hill	365
K-95	The Alms House	481
K-96	Brice's Mill Farm	192
K-107	Dunkan's Folly	191
K-108	Worth's Folly	259
K-119	Rose Hill	172
K-121	Blackhal's Hermitage Site	393
K-204	Fairy Meadow Site	220
K-205	Hopewell	91
K-229	Charles Joiner's Stone Dairy	452
K-233	Brick House Farm	434
K-236	Fancy Farm	266
K-242	Piney Grove	242
K-243	Kentfields Site	399
K-244	Tulley's Fancy	446
K-246	Grieb Log Smokehouse	387
K-249	Moffet House	398
K-250	Suydam House	519
K-251	Thomas's Hill	228
K-282	Kinsale Site	159
K-283	Stratford Manor	430
K-310	Capt. John Nicholson House*	339
K-314	Lusby House*	512
K-331	Buck-Bacchus Store*	116
K-343	Lorain House*	199
K-347	Old Methodist Church*	507
K-351	Mansfield-Eliason House*	471
K-360	Overbeck House	430
K-380	Massey Farm	429
K-395	Parson Farm Smokehouse	385
K-403	Town's Relief	218
K-465	Brampton	520
K-473	Piner's Grove Site	127
K-478	Alfalfa Dell Farm	478
K-487	Lyons Hall	273
K-488	Melton Point	469

K-501	Jessup Farm Site	453
K-503	Redue House Site*	115
K-504	Tilghman House Site*	362
K-514	George Vickers House Site*	492
K-515	Worrell's Tavern Site*	164
K-534	Banning House*	325
K-543	Maria Bracker House*	526
K-544	Issac Boyer House*	525
K-545	Thomas Cuff House *	525
K-546	Zion Methodist Church*	526
K-547	James A. Jones House*	527
K-548	William Perkins Restaurant Site*	527

District V

K-82	Kentland	454
K-83	The Plains	200
K-93	Caulk's Field	133
K-97	The Violet Farm	195
K-98	Broadnox	151
K-99	Springfield Farm	231
K-100	Hinchingham Farm	329
K-101	Hinchingham on the Bay	248
K-102	Hodge's Bar Farm	344
K-103	Boxley	165
K-104	Bungay Hill	161
K-105	Fairlee Manor	442
K-123	St. Paul's Church	88
K-124	St. Paul's Vestry House	88
K-125	King's Prevention	437
K-252	Middle Plantation	505
K-253	Stephney Farm	486
K-254	Beck's Landing	433
K-255	Maslin's Possession	229
K-256	Cacaway Farm	398
K-257	Reese's Corner House	432
K-259	Rosedale	386
K-260	William's Venture	252
K-261	Miller's Purchase	360
K-262	Tavern Creek House	400
K-264	Little Neck	448
K-267	Kimbolton	265
K-268	Belle View	494
K-269	Huntingfield Site	95
K-271	Trumpington	270
K-272	Ingleside Site	377
K-273	Hynson's Division Site	101
K-274	Wickcliffe Site	36
K-275	Napley Green	386
K-276	Mitchell House	443
K-277	Big Fairlee	405
K-467	Maple Grove	509
K-474	J. Wickes Farm	511
K-479	Poplar Hill Site	454
K-484	Skirvin Farm Site	510
K-489	Simpkins Farm	483
K-490	Wesley Manor Site	394
K-491	Shipyard Farm	510
K-492	Standaway	363
K-507	Alton Site	469
K-509	Cedar Point Farm Site	37
K-510	Boyer-Williams House	385
K-536	Wesley Chapel	495
K-537	Greys Inn Point Farm	363

*In Chestertown

Appendix C
River House

Designer Showcase
May 30—June 30, 1992

T HE HISTORICAL SOCIETY OF KENT COUNTY WISHES TO extend its appreciation to the following individuals and firms for their generous contributions in the form of talent, financial support, and services.

IN APPRECIATION

The Maryland Historical Trust: Owner of River House: 1967–1993

COMMITTEE

Honorary Chairmen: Mrs. Robert W. Duemling and Mrs. Horace Havemeyer, Jr.
Chairman: Mrs. Allan D. Housley.
Vice-Chairmen: Mr. Michael Bourne and Mr. Eugene H. Johnstone.
Design Consultants: Janet Richardson, ASID President, Maryland Chapter of ASID and Gail Winkler, ASID, Historic Preservation Officer Pennsylvania East Chapter ASID.

COMMITTEE CHAIRMEN

Catalogue and Printing: Mr. Eugene H. Johnstone and Mr. Jeffery S. Davis.

Preview Party: Mrs. George Fenimore Johnson and Mrs. Frederick O. Dutton III.

Publicity: Mrs. John E. Nunn III and Mrs. John Eliason.

Advertising: Mrs. Harrison Bristoll, Jr. and Mrs. Richard B. Goodall, Jr.

Parking: Mr. Donald Rypka.

Photography: Mr. Tyler Campbell.

House Repairs: Mr. Michael Bourne.

House Operations: Mr. G. Robert Tyson and Mr. Robert T. Hollett.

Docents: Miss Anne Elizabeth Burris and Mrs. Laurens H. Fritz.

Treasurer: Mr. William B. Seitzer and Mr. Roger D. Brown.

Designer Sales: Mrs. G. Robert Tyson.

Grounds: Mrs. Frank P Dwyer, Jr. and Mrs. Robert T. Hollett.

DESIGNERS

Winterthur Design Group, Winterthur, Delaware
Sarah Boyer Jenkins & Associates, Inc., Chevy Chase, Maryland
Rhodes, Chestertown, Maryland
C. Dudley Brown & Associates, Inc., Washington, D.C.
TM Designs, Great Falls, Virginia
Interior Consultant Services, Annapolis, Maryland
Maureen A. Daly & Associates, Inc., Bethesda, Maryland
Beverly Brown Interiors, Alexandria, Virginia
Kristin Parsons Interiors, Dover, Delaware
Katherine Lee Interiors, Clayton, Delaware
DCA Landscape Architects, Inc., Washington, D.C.
Linda Daly, ASID, Ivyland, Pennsylvania
Decorating Den, Delmarva Region, Cambridge, Maryland

SPECIAL RECOGNITION

All Seasons Garden Club, Anthony's Flowers, Atlantic Security, Benchmark Enterprises, Dan Brittingham Paint & Paper, Brunschwig & Fils, Chesapeake Home Center, Chesapeake Land Company, Chester River Contracting, Chestertown Garden Club, Robbin Clark, Deep Landing Workshop, Duron Paints, Edad Astra, Elburn's Florist, Everett Painting, The Great Atlantic & Pacific Tea Company, Hoon and Barroll, Wilbur Ross Hubbard, Magnolia Caterers, Maryland Historical Society, Masten Home Centers, National Trust for Historic Preservation, Park Rugs and Dry Cleaners, Pip's Liquors, The Sherwin-Williams Company, Jack R. Schroeder, Sutton's Towne Stationers, Brice B. Sutton, Tyler Campbell, Washington College, Westwind Construction Company, Terry Wolf, Gunter Zierfuss & Sons Company.

Bibliography

Andrews, Matthew Page. History of Maryland, Hatboro, Pennsylvania: Tradition Press, 1965.

Barringer, Brandon & Barroll, L. Wethered. The Wethered Book, Peterborough, New Hampshire: Richard R. Smith Publishers, 1969.

Barroll, Hope H. Barroll in Great Britain and America, 1554-1910, Baltimore: John H. Saumernig & Co., 1910.

Beckerdite, Luke. "William Buckland and William Bernard Sears: The Designer and the Carver" and "William Buckland Reconsidered: Architectural Carving in Chesapeake Maryland, 1771–1774," The Journal of Early Southern Decorative Arts, Vol. 8, No. 1, Winston-Salem, North Carolina: MESDA, November, 1982.

Brooks, Neal & Rockel. A History of Baltimore County, Towson, Maryland: Towson Library, 1979.

Browne, William Hand, ed. *Archives of Maryland,* various volumes, Baltimore: Maryland Historical Society.

Carson, Cary, Barka, Norman F., Kelso, William M. Stone, Garry Wheeler, and Upton, Dell, "Impermanent Architecture in the Southern American Colonies," Winterthur Portfolio, Vol. 16, #2/3, Chicago: University of Chicago Press, 1981, p. 135–196.

Chester Parish Vestry Records, Maryland State Archives and Emmanuel Episcopal Church, Chestertown, Maryland.

Daniels, Christine. "Alternative Workers In A Slave Economy: Kent County, Maryland: 1675–1810," M A thesis, The Johns Hopkins University, 1989.

DeProspo, Katherine Myrick. A History of Shrewsbury Parish Church, Wye Mills, Maryland: Chesapeake College Press, 1988.

Dumschott, Fred W., Emmanuel Episcopal Church, Chestertown, Maryland: privately printed, 1972.

Duvall, Elizabeth S. Three Centuries of American Life: The Hynson-Ringgold House of Chestertown, Chestertown, Maryland: Washington College, 1988.

Earle, Swepson. The Chesapeake Bay Country, New York: Weathervane Books, undated reprint, (originally, 1923).

Emory, Frederic. Queen Anne's County, Maryland, Baltimore: Maryland Historical Society, 1950.

Everett, Wilson W. Plantation Life at Rose Hill: The Diaries of Martha Ogle Forman, 1814–1845, Wilmington, Delaware: Historical Society of Delaware, 1976.

Forman, H. Chandlee. The Rolling Year, Privately printed, 1985.

Forman, H. Chandlee. Early Manor and Plantation Houses of Maryland, Privately printed, 1934.

Forman, H. Chandlee. Tidewater Maryland Architecture and Gardens, New York: Architectural Book Publishing Co., 1956.

Forman, H. Chandlee. Old Buildings Gardens and Furniture of Tidewater Maryland, Cambridge, Maryland: Tidewater Publishers, 1967.

Hanson, George A. Old Kent, The Eastern Shore of Maryland, Chestertown, Maryland: R. H. Collins & Sons, 1936.

Kent County Court Records, various volumes, Maryland State Archives, Annapolis.

Kent County Land Records, Kent County Courthouse, Chestertown, Maryland, and Maryland State Archives, Annapolis.

Kent County Patents and Rent Rolls, Maryland State Archives, Annapolis.

Kent County Probate Records, Kent County Courthouse, Chestertown, Maryland and Maryland State Archives, Annapolis.

Kent County Tax Records, Kent County Courthouse, Chestertown, Maryland and Maryland State Archives, Annapolis.

Lake, Griffing, Stevenson, Atlas of Kent County, Maryland, Baltimore: 1877.

Martenet, S. J. Martenet's Map of Kent County, Maryland, Baltimore: 1860.

Maryland Gazette, Annapolis. Maryland: various issues, Maryland State Archives.

Maganzin, Louis, Economic Depression In Maryland And Virginia, 1783–1787, Ann Arbor, Michigan: University Microfilms, Inc., 1967.

Middleton, Canon Arthur Pierce. Ph.D., Anglican Maryland, 1692–1792, Virginia Beach, Virginia: The Donning Co., 1992.

Morrison, Hugh. Early American Architecture, New York: Oxford University Press, 1952, 4th printing, 1969.

Neill, Robert, Bourne, Michael, White, Kathleen B. Chestertown, Maryland, An Inventory of Historic Sites, published by the Town of Chestertown, 1980.

Papenfuse, Edward C. Biographical Dictionary of the Maryland Legislature, 1635–1789, 2 vols., Baltimore: The Johns Hopkins University Press, 1979 and 1985.

Radoff, Morris L. The Old Line State, A History of Maryland, Annapolis, Maryland: Hall of Records Commission, 1971.

Reps, John W. Tidewater Towns, Charlottesville, Virginia: University of Virginia Press, 1972.

Rock Hall Historical Collection, privately printed by Rock Hall Commemoration, Inc., 1957.

St. Paul's Church Vestry Records, Maryland State Archives, Annapolis.

Scharf, Thomas. History of Maryland, Vol. I., Hatboro, Pennsylvania: Tradition Press, 1967.

Swain, Robert L., Jr. "Creeks and Manors of Old Kent," The Enterprise, Chestertown, Maryland, April 6–May 11, 1938.

Tate, Thad W., Ammerman, David L. The Chesapeake in the Seventeenth Century, New York: W. W. Norton & Co., 1979.

The Telegraph, Kent County News, Kent News; Chestertown Maryland: various issues on microfilm, Washington College Library.

Usilton, Fred G. The History of Chestertown, Gem City on the Chester, Chestertown, Maryland: privately printed, 1898.

Usilton, Fred F. History of Kent County, Maryland, Chestertown, Maryland: privately printed, 1916.

White, Maynard P. "An Account of the First College Edifice of Washington College, Chestertown, Maryland, 1783–1827," Masters Thesis, University of Delaware , 1966.

Williams, William H. The Garden of American Methodism, published for the peninsula Conference of the United Methodist Church, 1984.

Wroth, Peregrine. "Memoirs," original manuscript, Washington College, Chestertown, Maryland.

Index

Compiled by Marian Fry

In some cases, Roman numerals following a name have been added for identification purposes. Multiple spellings for the same persons and properties may be listed in the text.

J.L.Stam
Res.

A V E

C-O-L-L-E-G-E

C A L V E R T   S T.   S

S T.

Cath. Ch.

W.B.Usilton

Mrs.Bowers

Heirs of T.S.Dodd

Hon. Geo. Vickers

Meth.E.Ch.

HIG

KENT

J. P. Howard

Dr. B.F.Houston Res.

MILL

H.Vickers

C A N N O N

J.M.Vandyke Res.

KENT   COUNTY

J.N.Usilton